This Volume Was Reproduced
From An 1859 Edition
In The Library Of
The Rhode Island Historical Society
Providence, Rhode Island

An Introduction

To The Author

Samuel Greene Arnold, historian and United States Senator, was born in Providence, Rhode Island, April 12, 1821.

Son of a prominent Rhode Island mercantile family, Arnold was educated in private schools in Providence; and, at the age of fifteen, he entered Brown University. Due to ill health, he left school and visited Europe. On returning, he resumed his university studies and was graduated in 1841.

Following a short period clerking in a counting room, and after a brief trip to Russia, he entered Harvard Law School. He was graduated in 1845 with the degree of LL.B. and was admitted to the Rhode Island bar.

A gentleman of wealth and leisure, he spent much time in travels abroad. In England and France he examined and copied records and state papers dealing with American colonial history, having already planned while in law school, to write the history of Rhode Island. This work, entitled *History of the State of Rhode Island and Providence Plantations*, was published in 1859-60.

Arnold's services to his state and country included three terms as lieutenant governor of Rhode Island and service as a United States Senator from December 1, 1862, until March 3, 1863. He served throughout the Civil War as aide-de-camp to Governor William Sprague with the rank of colonel.

In 1868 he was elected president of the Rhode Island Historical Society and he filled that position until his death February 13, 1880 in Providence.

This reprint edition of Arnold's *History* is part of a larger program, being carried forward by The Reprint Company, specializing in reprints of basic titles pertaining to the Colonial and Revolutionary War periods of history in the thirteen original colonies.

The Reprint Company
March 1970

HISTORY

OF THE

STATE OF RHODE ISLAND

AND

PROVIDENCE PLANTATIONS.

BY

SAMUEL GREENE ARNOLD.

VOL. I.

1636—1700.

NEW YORK:

D. APPLETON & COMPANY, 346 & 348 BROADWAY.
LONDON: 16 LITTLE BRITAIN.
1859.

Rhode Island Heritage Series No. 2

The Reprint Company
154 West Cleveland Park Drive
Spartanburg, South Carolina 29303

Reprinted: 1970

ISBN 0-87152-057-5
Library of Congress Catalog Card Number 79-120136
Printed in the U.S.A. on Long-life Paper

TO THE

PEOPLE OF RHODE-ISLAND

𝔗𝔥𝔦𝔰 𝔥𝔦𝔰𝔱𝔬𝔯𝔶

OF THE TRIALS AND THE TRIUMPHS OF THEIR ANCESTORS

IS INSCRIBED

BY THEIR FELLOW-CITIZEN,

SAMUEL GREENE ARNOLD.

PREFACE.

THE work, of which the first volume is now presented, is the result of many years' labor. To trace the rise and progress of a State, the offspring of ideas that were novel and startling even amid the philosophical speculations of the seventeenth century; whose birth was a protest against, whose infancy was a struggle with, and whose maturity was a triumph over, the retrograde tendency of established Puritanism; a State that was the second-born of persecution, whose founders had been doubly tried in the purifying fire; a State which, more than any other, has exerted, by the weight of its example, an influence to shape the political ideas of the present day, whose moral power has been in the inverse ratio with its material importance, and of which an eminent historian of the United States has said that, had its territory " corresponded to the importance and singularity of the principles of its early existence, the world would have been filled with wonder at the phenomena of its history," is a task not to be lightly attempted or hastily performed.

The materials for Rhode Island history are more abundant than many have supposed. They are widely scattered and difficult to collect or arrange, and hence the opinion has seemed to prevail that too much was lost to render the preservation of the remainder an object of interest. But some persons have thought otherwise, and three attempts, prior to this, have been made to write the history of the State. The first was by Governor Stephen Hopkins, one of the signers of the Declaration of Independence, who, in 1765, commenced to publish "An historical account of Providence," since reprinted in the second series of.

Massachusetts Historical Collections, volume ix. Only one chapter was completed when the struggle for independence interrupted the work, which was never resumed. The second was by Hon. Theodore Foster, a Senator in Congress from Rhode Island, who collected a large number of original papers and made copies of nearly the whole of the colony records. But one chapter of this work was ever written. His death prevented its completion. The third attempt, by the late Henry Bull of Newport, was more successful. He published in the Rhode Island Republican, 1832-6, a series of articles entitled "Memoirs of Rhode Island," embracing the principal events of each year from the settlement of the State down to 1799. The care taken in the preparation of these articles leads us to regret that Mr. Bull did not extend his labors still further, and embody them in a more permanent form. These, with the five volumes of the Rhode Island Historical Collections, with the valuable notes of the editors and authors of each, the more than thirty volumes of the Massachusetts Historical Collections, the lately published Colonial Records of Connecticut, of Massachusetts, and now those of this State in the course of publication under the admirable supervision of the Secretary of State, the later editions of early Massachusetts authors, Morton, Prince, and others, but particularly the Journal of Winthrop with the copious notes of its liberal and learned editor, Hon. James Savage, the life of the founder of Rhode Island by Professor Knowles, a perfect magazine of important facts,—these are some of the principal printed authorities most accessible to the general reader. There are also a great number of books in the libraries of Harvard and Brown Universities, and more than all in the unrivalled collection of works on American history in the possession of Mr. John Carter Brown, of this city, which shed much light upon the annals of Rhode Island. Besides these there are several religious discourses, following the plan of Callender, also historical addresses, and some local narratives, that contain interesting facts bearing upon the general history of the State.

The unpublished materials are the records of the several towns, those of this and the neighboring States that have not been included in the printed volumes, the private collections of Hutchinson, Trumbull, Hinckley, Prince and others, in possession of the Massachusetts Historical Society, of Foster and Backus in the Rhode Island Historical Society, and yet more important, the hitherto undeveloped resources in the British archives, at London, which clear up many points never before explained. These are the chief sources of information that have been consulted in preparing this work, and will be found referred to in the notes.

Several months were spent abroad in 1846–7, in the examination of government archives, chiefly in England and France, in search of materials not to be found in America. The kindness of gentlemen in official station, particularly in Her Britannic Majesty's Government, in securing permission to examine their records, and of those in the State Paper Offices at London, Paris and the Hague, in facilitating his labors, should receive the grateful acknowledgments of the writer.

Copies of the English documents herein referred to are now in Mr. Brown's library, he having given orders, previous to the author's visit to England, to have every thing pertaining to Rhode Island, and much more besides, copied for his private collection; which was done under the supervision of Henry Stevens, Esq., a gentleman whose experience eminently qualified him for the task.

Many of these authorities extend beyond the limits of this volume, and with a large number of new ones, both local and general, will be used in the later portions of the work.

The thanks of the writer are due to many friends who have rendered assistance in various ways to lighten his labors: to Mr. John Carter Brown, to Hon. William R. Staples, late Chief Justice of the State, the editor of Gorton, and author of the Annals of Providence, to Judge George A. Brayton of the Supreme Court, to Dr. David King and Rev. Henry Jackson, D. D. of Newport, to Hon. John R. Bartlett, Secretary of State, to William J. Harris, Esq., and others, all deeply interested in whatever pertains to the history of their State, who have given efficient aid by the loan of books and manuscripts.

The first object attempted in this work has been to make it reliable both as to facts and dates; that it should be a standard authority upon the subject and period of which it treats. To accomplish this design no pains have been spared, and it has been kept steadily in view even at the risk of making the book less readable than it might have been. Many subjects are mentioned that, to the general reader, can have little or no interest, the value of which can only be understood by those who consult history for a specific purpose. For the benefit of this latter and more limited class of readers, the reference notes are made more numerous than they would otherwise have been. The most important dates have been verified by a tedious mathematical process, unnecessary here to describe, but which is essential to accuracy in many cases, owing to a strange diversity that existed in the mode of dating under the Julian calendar before the adoption of the Gregorian or New Style in 1751. The Julian year began on the 25th of March. February was the 12th month and March the 1st month of the year. Many papers between the first and twenty-fifth of March, bear date as of the coming year, while others are dated correctly, according to the Julian system, as of the expiring year. This diversity of course throws a doubt upon the true date of all correlative documents throughout the year, and has led many writers into error. That the reader need not be misled on this point the double date of the year, between January 1st and March 25, is given in the margin. If it is desired to reduce the day of the month to New Style, eleven days are to be added to the marginal date.

That, notwithstanding the labor and care bestowed upon these pages, they contain some errors of fact or date, perhaps important ones, it would be presumptuous to deny. The more one explores the labyrinth of historical investigation, the less positive will he become of the entire accuracy of his conclusions. A conscientious desire to arrive at the truth, is all that the author dares to claim in submitting this work to the judgment of his peers. That it will grate harshly upon the ears of some, whose views upon the questions of politics and theology involved in the settlement of this State, differ from those of its founders, he is well aware. That some may assail it upon these grounds is not improbable, and for such he is prepared; while at the same time he courts a generous criticism that may aid his future labors.

So far as was compatible with the above mentioned object, he has endeavored to make the work interesting to those who read simply for the sake of reading; but he can claim nothing upon this score. The minutiæ of local or of State history, demand an attention to details which broader fields do not require, and limit, in the same proportion, the power of the pen. To make a State history both authentic and popular, where the ground has not already been occupied, would require it to be too voluminous. To enlarge upon the philosophy of the fundamental principles involved in the settlement of Rhode Island, would afford a pleasing relief from the labor of critical research; but this can be better done by the reflecting reader, or it may furnish a theme for some future historian, more fitted for the task than the writer feels himself to be, who will reap the laurels that he must forego.

PROVIDENCE, May 17, 1858.

ABBREVIATIONS.

R. I. H. C.—Rhode Island Historical Collections, in 5 vols.

R. I. Col. Rec.—Rhode Island Colonial Records, 3 vols. now published, 1636–1706.

Conn. Col. Rec.—Connecticut Colonial Records, 2 vols. now published, 1636–1677.

M. C. R.—Massachusetts Colonial Records, 6 vols. now published, 1628–1686.

M. H. C.—Massachusetts Historical Collections, in series of 10 vols. each, of which 3 series are completed, and 4 vols. of the fourth. The figure before the letters denotes the series.

Br. S. P. O.—British State Paper Office.

CONTENTS.

———•••———

THE

HISTORY OF RHODE ISLAND.

CHAPTER I.

INTRODUCTION—FROM THE SETTLEMENT OF NEW ENGLAND
TO THE BANISHMENT OF ROGER WILLIAMS.

1620—1636.

THE direct causes which led to the settlement of New England, had been in active operation for nearly seventy years before that event transpired. The more remote influences that led to this result date back to the commencement of the English Reformation. The spirit of resistance to clerical authority and papal aggression, was first inculcated in Great Britain by John Wickliffe, Professor of Divinity in the University of Oxford. It soon spread to the continent of Europe, where the teachings of Huss and Jerome, in opposition to the claims of the hierarchy, roused the vengeance of the Council of Constance, and led to their martyrdom.

A period of quiet succeeded the Bohemian struggle, until the laxity of the pontifical court, under Leo X., gave rise to the Reformation of Luther. From that time

CHAP.
I.

the history of Europe presented a continuous scene of action and reaction upon the fundamental principles of religion and politics. The inquisitive mind of Germany was occupied in speculations which were to open a new and brighter era to humanity. England, already in some degree prepared for the mighty movement, soon asserted her sovereignty by severing her allegiance to the church of Rome. The spell of the Papacy was broken; the first great result of the Reformation was achieved. A spirit of inquiry was awakened, which could neither be quelled by the fire of persecution, nor controlled by the decrees of princes or parliaments. During the reign of Edward VI., the English Liturgy was completed and promulgated as the ecclesiastical law of the land. The priestly vestments were retained in the service, although strenuously opposed by many of the reformed clergy. The more resolute Protestants resisted at the outset all attempts to fasten upon them the livery of a church from whose communion they had withdrawn. Uniformity was the rock upon which the early Reformers split. The first demonstration of nonconformity occurred at Frankfort. The virulent persecution of the Protestants, which commenced upon the accession of Queen Mary, caused great numbers of them to seek refuge on the continent. A small church was gathered at Frankfort, who objected to the use of some portions of King Edward's service book. These were supplanted the next year by a party of their countrymen under Dr. Cox, who restored the English forms in full as prescribed by King Edward, and were hence called "Conformists." Most of the others went to Geneva, where they were kindly received by Calvin, were there organized, and adopted a liturgy agreeable to that of the French churches. The coronation of Queen Elizabeth was the signal for the return of the exiles, and the permanent though gradual establishment of the Protestant Faith. The reign of Elizabeth was emphatically the age of prerog-

1554.

ative in England. Never did the authority of the crown
maintain itself so absolutely. Although some of the Stuarts
afterwards attempted to exercise arbitrary power in repeated instances, yet none of them wielded so uncontrolled
a sceptre, or conducted with the firmness or the success
that characterized the last of the Tudors. Mary had been
a bigot in religion ; Elizabeth became a tyrant in prerogative ; and because theology was the prevailing topic of
the times, she seized upon that as the most convenient
medium for confirming and manifesting her authority.
The earliest enactments of her first parliament were to
this end. The act of uniformity, prescribing the regulations of church service, preceded by a single day the act
of supremacy, which vested in the queen the right of
ecclesiastical control. Immediately upon the passage of
these acts two parties arose in the Protestant Church, one
favoring the royal prerogative, the other, somewhat more
true to the spirit of the Reformation, maintaining that in
things indifferent, liberty should be allowed. Both were
at this time pretty nearly agreed in points of doctrine,
in the necessity of uniformity in public worship, and in
the right of the civil power to enforce it. The prerogative
party, or Conformists, held that the will of the queen was
the only guide in church affairs ; the Puritans, that councils or synods were the proper tribunals. The idea of
freedom of conscience as applied to the individual was unknown, or unrecognized, by either party. It was reserved
for another age and a distant land to develop in its full
significance the grand result of the Reformation.

The passion of Elizabeth for pageantry of every kind,
together with her inordinate love of power, were the chief
causes which distracted her reign. The one inclined her
to retain as far as possible the gorgeous ceremonial of the
church of Rome, the other led her to punish those who
desired a simpler ritual and plainer robes. The severity
of her measures against the Puritans at length resulted in

CHAP.
I.

1559.

the separation, which commenced in 1566. The press had already been closed against them by a decree of the Star Chamber. The opposition of a large portion of the people to the Romish vestments, and to certain ceremonies, of trifling import in themselves, which could easily have been assuaged by temperate policy, was increased by the exercise of arbitrary power. Accordingly, after solemn deliberation, a number of the deprived ministers, with their friends, determined to withdraw from the communion of the established church, and laying aside the English Liturgy, they adopted the Geneva forms. Henceforward there was to be no longer a cordial union of Protestants against Popery, but rather a union of the prerogative and papal parties against the Puritans. This was less apparent during Elizabeth's reign than in that of her successor. But the Reformation in England, so far as the government was concerned, had attained its culminating point. The breach thus commenced rapidly widened. The doctrinal articles of the church, some of which, in the opinion of many learned and pious men, were too strongly tinctured with Erastian principles, began to be questioned. Other sects arose, distinct in many respects from the Puritan church, and carrying the principles of the separation to a greater extent, but all who were zealous for the Reformation, were indiscriminately branded with the same invidious epithet. In vain did the Puritans seek to appease the resentment of their enemies by disowning the sectaries. Papists, Familists, Baptists and Brownists, were denounced by the Puritans with equal zeal as by the Prelatists, and alike held up as worthy of persecution ;[1] but the attempt thus made to ingratiate themselves with their rulers was without success. In proportion as the ranks of non-conformity were augmented, the severity of government increased, and exile, or death, for crimes of

[1] Neal, 312.

conscience, became more frequent as the long reign of
Elizabeth drew to its close.[1]

The union of the crowns of Scotland and England, in the person of James I., inspired the Puritans with a new but delusive hope. This fickle prince, whose consummate vanity as a man, was the source of his weakness as a monarch, very soon forgot the precepts of the Scottish church, which he had sworn to support, and became the tool of ambitious prelates and designing courtiers. Six months after he came to the throne, occurred the celebrated conference at Hampton Court, between the bishops and the Puritans, at which the king himself presided, and made his first public display of that combination of pedantry with tyranny which has made his character, when viewed in the light of history, the object of mingled aversion and contempt. The result of that conference crushed the hopes of the Puritans. The triumphant bishops, no longer doubtful of their position, at once proceeded to urge severe measures against the whole body of Protestant non-conformists, and secretly to court the favor of the papal party. At the death of Archbishop Whitgift, Bancroft, bishop of London, was raised to the See of Canterbury. This haughty prelate revived the persecution of the Puritans, and conducted it with unparalleled rigor, excommunicating many who would not receive a set of canons prepared by himself and passed by an obsequious convocation, although not confirmed by parliament. He it was who first asserted in England the divine right of the order of bishops, and prepared the church for the usurpations of Laud, which afterwards involved the United Kingdom in civil war.

To bring the kirk of Scotland under the dominion of the English hierarchy was a favorite project of James, and was actively promoted by the intrigues of Bancroft. This was a bold design, against which the armorial bearings and

---

[1] For the last three years of her life she became more tolerant.

CHAP.
I.
1559.

motto of Scotland might have furnished a significant warning. It was an index of that aggressive and intolerant
spirit which drove a large number of the English non-
conformists into voluntary exile. Holland became a refuge
for those whom persecution deprived of their native home.
The larger portion of the refugees were rigid Separatists,
whose views, crude as they might appear at the present
time, were very much in advance of those held by the
mass of non-conformists in respect to the essential objects
of the Reformation. These were the men who, with their
descendants a few years later, made the first permanent
settlement of New England. The Puritans for the most
part remained in England, still clinging to the slender
chance of some favorable current of affairs. The succession of Archbishop Abbot to the high position vacated by
the death of Bancroft, gave them renewed hope. He is
described as a thorough Calvinist, a sound Protestant,
and as being suspected of Puritanism. But his views, although they served for awhile to mitigate the asperities
of the times, failed to effect permanent relief. The
worthy primate soon became unpopular at court, and fell
into disgrace. The pretensions of King James to arbitrary power increased, and all who opposed the prerogative, although friends of the established church, were denounced as Puritans, as well as those who were Calvinists
in theology, or reformers in church government and worship. The former were called State Puritans, the latter
Doctrinal Puritans. The two, when united, comprised
a majority of the nation. The Arminian party, of whom
most of the newly appointed bishops, with Laud at their
head, were the leaders, allied with the Papal faction in
supporting the king. Such was the condition of affairs at
the close of the reign of James I.

Meanwhile, a portion of the refugees in Holland, after
twelve years' residence in that country, resolved to emigrate to America. Protracted negotiations with the

Virginia Company to secure a patent to lands, and with
merchants in London to provide the necessaries for emigration, together with earnest consultations with their
friends in England, now occupied the attention of the
Pilgrims. After their departure from Holland, further
delays awaited them at the English ports. Twice were
they compelled by the insufficiency of their transports to
return, and on the second occasion their smaller vessel,
the Speedwell, of sixty tons, in which they had first embarked at Delft Haven, was abandoned as unseaworthy.
At length, on the 6th of September, 1620, the Mayflower
finally set sail from Plymouth, with her precious freight
of one hundred souls,[1] to seek a better land beyond the
seas.

Whether we contemplate this act in its intrinsic
character, or regard it in the magnificence of its results, it
assumes a degree of importance scarcely equalled in the
history of our race. The stern devotion to principle which
impelled them to encounter the severest hardships, when
a simple act of submission to a creed would ensure them
peace and plenty in their English homes—the lofty courage
which inspired even women and children gladly to brave
the perils of the deep—and, above all, their unwavering
faith in the promises of an Omnipotent Deity, present a
picture whose moral sublimity is not enhanced even by
the success which has crowned their enterprise. After a
stormy passage of sixty-five days, they dropped anchor on
the dreary coast of Cape Cod. At the end of another
tedious month, consumed in exploring the vicinity, and
in preparations for landing, the Pilgrims stood at last on
Plymouth rock.

About this time a company of merchants and others
which had been formed in the West of England, with Sir
Ferdinand Gorges, governor of Plymouth, at their head,

---

[1] 100, not 101.—Young's Pilgrims, 122, note 1, and p. 100, notes 2, 5.

CHAP.
I.
1620.

encouraged by the reports of the celebrated Captain John Smith, and supported by the influence of some of the most powerful noblemen in the kingdom, obtained a charter of incorporation, with the exclusive right of planting and governing New England. This company, known as the council of Plymouth, were thereby invested with unlimited jurisdiction over a region of almost boundless extent, embracing the entire breadth of the continent from sea to sea, between the fortieth and forty-eighth parallels of north latitude. But the apparent compass of their power was the real measure of their weakness. So violent was the opposition to this monstrous monopoly, that not even the proclamation of King James, enforcing the terms of the grant, and sustained by the utmost stretch of the prerogative, could preserve inviolate the charter of the company. The spirit of English liberty, nourished by the Puritans in proportion as the encroachment of the crown increased, spurned the authority of an instrument which fettered both sea and land. Extensive fishing expeditions were fitted out for the coast of New England, and conducted without regard to the claims of the council. In vain did the company send out officers to maintain their authority in New England, or appeal to the king to sustain their pretensions. The parliament stood firmly on the rights of the subject, until the company, exhausted by fruitless efforts to secure their monopoly, at length resorted to the sale of charters as their sole source of revenue. In the course of a few years they disposed, in various grants, of all the lands in New England, some of them twice over ; nothing of value remained to them ;

1635.
June
7.

many of the original patentees had already abandoned their interests, and the council itself finally surrendered its charter and became extinct.[1]

From this company the purchase of a large grant of

[1] Report of Board of Trade on Duke of Hamilton's claim to Narraganset. —*British State Paper Office, New England Papers*, vol. xxxvi. p. 222.

lands in Massachusetts was made, and a party of emi- CHAP.
grants, under the direction of John Endicott, came over the I.
same year, and established themselves at Salem, where 1628.
Roger Conant, from New Plymouth, had already made a March
settlement. That enterprise, originating in a commercial 19.
speculation, and proving unfortunate, had been abandoned
by all but Conant and a few associates, who, inspired by
the zeal of friends in England, had remained to found
another home where the exiles for religion might find rest.
A few of Endicott's followers settled at Charlestown.
The next year a royal charter was with much difficulty
obtained, and the Massachusetts company became legally 1629.
a distinct trading corporation. This was followed by an March
emigration of about two hundred persons under the pastoral 4.
care of Rev. John Higginson. These settled at Salem and
Charlestown. The powers and privileges which the Massachusetts charter conferred differed in no essential particulars from those of similar companies already existing.
That it was soon to be virtually erected into a basis of
civil government became apparent, when, at a meeting of
the company in London, it was resolved to transfer the
charter to the freemen of the company inhabiting the
colony. By this act a powerful stimulus was given to the
scheme of colonization. Large numbers prepared to cross
the sea. A meeting of the company was held to transfer Oct.
the government to America, by appointing an entire board 20.
of officers who would agree to emigrate. John Winthrop
was chosen governor. In the month of March following,
the great expedition, consisting of about eight hundred 1630.
souls, embarked in eleven ships at Yarmouth, and reached
their destination in June and July. Nearly as many more
followed in the course of the year. The settlement of
Boston and the final establishment of the colony of Massachusetts Bay date from this period.

Although the terms of the patent, and the royal
intent in granting it, point only to a commercial ad-

venture, yet the circumstances which determined the emigration, the documentary proofs in relation to it, and the character and subsequent conduct of the men, furnish sufficient evidence that a large portion of them were actuated by other motives than pecuniary gain. What were these motives? Certainly not those assigned to them by Charles I., " the freedom of liberty of conscience ;" for scarcely had the royal charter been obtained, and the church under Higginson established itself in Salem, while the government had not yet been transferred to America, or the settlement of Boston commenced, before the permanent policy of the Puritans was developed in active hostility to dissenters. Two men named Browne, occupying influential positions in the colony, were foremost in opposition to the new church organization, and strenuously demanded that the English liturgy should not be abandoned. Thus the enemy from which they had fled appeared at once among them. Episcopacy asserted its rights in the stronghold of the Puritans. But should the exultant hierarchy, which had driven them across the sea, be allowed to dictate to them in their new-found homes, and perhaps in time expel them from their " New English Canaan?" The colonists thought not, and availing themselves of a clause in the form[1] of government prescribed by the company under their charter, which permitted the expulsion of "incorrigible persons," the two Brownes were summarily sent back to England, by order of Endicott, in the very ships which had brought them over. Thus early was dissent rebuked, and theological contumacy punished, before the Puritan church itself was fairly established in Massachusetts. "The freedom of liberty of conscience" then formed no part of the Puritan polity in its inception, nor yet, as we shall presently see, in its completion. The Puritans fled from England because they could not conform to the usages of the estab-

[1] 1629, April 30.—Young's Chrons. Mass., 196.

lished church, because they desired a still further extension of the principles of the Reformation, because they
would not assent to those forms of church service attempted
to be enforced by the celebrated act of uniformity. Differing widely on these points from the government creed,
they looked for a home in the new world, where they might
erect an establishment in accordance with their peculiar
theological views. "They sought a faith's pure shrine,"
based on what they held to be a purer system of worship,
and a discipline more in unison with their notions of a
church. For this they crossed the Atlantic and obtained
a home, where the Pilgrims had preceded them, on the
dreary coast of New England. Here they proceeded to
organize a State, whose civil code followed close on the
track of the Mosaic law, and whose ecclesiastical polity,
like that of the Jews, and of all those then existing, was
identified with the civil power. They thus secured what
was denied them in England, the right to pursue their
own form of religion without molestation, and in this the
object of their exile was attained. The hardships of the
infant colony are evinced in the fearful havoc which death
and desertion made in their ranks. More than one hundred, discouraged at the prospect which pestilence and
famine presented, abandoned the enterprise, and returned
immediately to England, while of those who remained,
double that number, before the close of the year, had
fallen victims to disease. So great was the decrease from
these causes, and so disheartening the effect produced in
England by the report of those who returned, that the
accessions by emigration for the next two years were not
sufficient to make up the losses. A similar series of disasters had occurred to the Pilgrims in commencing their
settlement. Sickness and starvation had reduced their
numbers one-half within a few months, and the additions
were at no time so considerable as those which the sister
colony afterwards received. Ten years of hardship and

CHAP.
I.
—
1630.

suffering elapsed before the great emigration of the Puritans, and at that time the Plymouth colony contained only three hundred persons. Such were some of the difficulties encountered by the early settlers of New England.

1620.
Nov.
11.

The government of Plymouth was for many years a pure democracy. In the cabin of the Mayflower the first solemn compact in the history of America, creating a body politic by voluntary act of the signers, was subscribed. Upon this brief but comprehensive constitution rests the whole fabric of American republicanism.[1] The right to frame laws, and the duty of obeying them, were here simultaneously declared by the free act of the whole people. As the Pilgrims were more liberal towards those who differed from them in points of religious doctrine than the Puritans, so were they more free in their political constitution. There were good reasons for this difference. In the first place, the principles of the early Separatists, although falling far short of the full idea of liberty of conscience, were much more liberal than were those of either of the two parties into which the Puritans were divided in the reign of James I. They were upon the right line of action, without having yet attained the ultimate result of their movement, or having traced back to its source, in the philosophy of mind, the secret impulse

---

[1] In the name of God, Amen. We, whose names are underwritten, the loyal subjects of our dread sovereign lord, King James, &c., having undertaken, for the glory of God, and advancement of the Christian faith and honor of our King and country, a voyage to plant the first colony in the northern parts of Virginia, do, by these presents, solemnly and mutually, in the presence of God and of one another, covenant and combine ourselves together into a civil body politic, for our better ordering and preservation, and furtherance of the ends aforesaid; and by virtue hereof to enact, constitute, and frame such just and equal laws, ordinances, acts, constitutions, and offices, from time to time, as shall be thought most meet and convenient for the general good of the colony; unto which we promise all due submission and obedience. In witness whereof, &c.—*Bradford's & Winslow's Journal, Mourt's Relation. Young's Chrons. of Pilgrims,* p. 121.

which urged them onward. Their conceptions of the
great truth which they were unconsciously developing were
but vague and uncertain, but their course seems to have
been guided in no small degree by its dawning light.
Their venerable teacher, Robinson, in his final sermon,
before their departure from Leyden, had given them a
solemn charge, which seemed to foreshadow the new revelation that was to spring from the oracles of God. " I
charge you, before God and his blessed angels, that you
follow me no farther than you have seen me follow the
Lord Jesus Christ. If God reveal any thing to you, by
any other instrument of his, be as ready to receive it as
ever you were to receive any truth by my ministry ; for I
am verily persuaded, I am very confident, that the Lord
has more truth yet to break forth out of his holy word." [1]
The contrast to the bigotry of England which this liberal
and Christian advice presents, is a proof, how far in advance of his age was this learned and pious pastor of the
Pilgrims. Had Robinson been able to accompany the
emigrants to America, the future apostle of religious freedom would have found in him a sympathizing friend. The
result of his teaching is seen in the milder treatment of
those who differed from them, which the records of Plymouth present when compared with those of Massachusetts. The spirit of Robinson appeared to watch over his
feeble flock on the coast of New England, long after his
body was mouldering beneath the cathedral church at Leyden. Again, their twelve years' residence in Holland had
brought the Pilgrims in contact with other sects of Christians, and given them a more catholic spirit than pertained to those whose stay in England had been embittered
by the strife of contending factions in the established
church. Whether these reasons fully account for the
superior liberality of the Plymouth Colonists, or not, the
records show, that as they were distinct from the Puritans

[1] Morton's Memorial, p. 29, note.

CHAP.
I.

1620.

in England, and had been long separated from them in Holland, so did they preserve that distinction in some measure in America. The Pilgrims of Plymouth were more liberal in feeling, and more tolerant in practice, than the Puritans of Massachusetts Bay. The simple forms of democratic government were maintained in Plymouth for eighteen years, until the growth of the colony compelled the introduction of the representative system. The laws were enacted by the entire people, and their execution intrusted to a governor, and council of five assistants, afterwards increased to seven.

1629.
April
30.

1630.

Aug.
23.

The government of Massachusetts was much more restrictive, and the circumstances of the colony compelled more frequent changes in its forms than was the case with Plymouth. The royal charter, with the plan of government adopted under it, by the company in which John Endicott was named as governor, had formed the fundamental law, until the corporation itself emigrated the next year to America, with Winthrop at its head. A new organization under the king's patent now took place. By this patent, a governor, deputy-governor, and eighteen assistants were to be elected annually by a majority of the freemen of the company.[1] Soon after the arrival of Winthrop, the first Court of Assistants was held at Charlestown. The proceedings of that court were singularly indicative of the future policy of the colony. The first measure proposed was "how the ministers shall be maintained."[2] This question, so honorable to the colonists, who, amid the hardships of an infant settlement, made the support of the clergy their earliest care, would prove, if other evidence were wanting, that the religious sentiment was the most active cause of Puritan emigration ; and it might further serve as a premonition to all those whose creed was heterodox, or whose conduct was at

---

[1] 1 Holmes's Annals, 195.　　　　[2] 1 Prince, 246.

variance with the spirit of the times, that the Massachusetts colony was no home for them. And, as if to confirm the latter position beyond mistake, the second measure of the court was to order, " that Morton of Mt. Wollaston be sent for presently." Thomas Morton was one of a company under Capt. Wollaston, who, some years before, had located in what is now the town of Quincy. Wollaston, on his return to England, left the place in charge of one of his companions, who was displaced by the intrigues of Morton, and the establishment under the new name of Merry Mount, became a scene of riot and dissipation, to the infinite annoyance of the neighboring settlements.   The colonists had once equipped Miles Standish with an armed force to abate this nuisance, and having captured Morton, sent him to England as a prisoner, with charges against him to be disposed of as the company there might see fit. He found means to return the next year, and renewed the orgies of Merry Mount, until the summary proceedings of the Court of Assistants broke up this resort of idlers.[1] This was a step for which no one can censure the court. The dissolute character of Morton and his crew rendered their expulsion necessary for the welfare of the colony, while the fact of their supplying the Indians with firearms merited the severest punishment. But it is the promptness of the government in taking action upon the case, which is chiefly worthy of note. Scarcely had they landed in New England, before they provide, first for the support of the ministry, and second for the purification of society. The only other measure of the court at this session related to the price of labor. However much we may approve of their action in the two preceding

1625.

1628.

1629.

1630.

---

[1] Morton's house was burnt by order of the Court at their next session, Sept. 7 (1 Prince, 248), and himself imprisoned until sent for the second time to England, whence he again returned in 1643, and finally died at Piscataqua. For particulars concerning this notorious " old roysterer," see Morton's New England's Memorial, 135–142, with the Editor's note ; also 1 Mass. Hist. Coll. iii. 61–64. His own account of himself in his book entitled New English

CHAP.
I.
1630.

matters, this certainly was ill-advised, and as the event proved, injurious. Mechanics' wages were fixed at two shillings a day, and a fine of ten shillings was decreed against giver and taker for any excess above this rate. The experiment of arbitrary values, whether placed upon labor, or affixed to things intrinsically worthless, has been often tried with ruinous results, and the attempt in this case displayed a disposition to excessive legislation, incompatible with the real interests of society.[1]

Oct.
19.

The first General Court, composed of all the freemen of the colony, was held in the autumn. The spirit of this assembly was liberal and yielding. Over one hundred persons were admitted freemen of the company, many of whom were not connected with any of the churches.[2] Among the applicants for freedom was William Blackstone, the earliest settler of Boston, having resided there four or five years previous to the arrival of Winthrop, and the same who afterwards removed to what is now the town of Cumberland, being unable to brook " the tyranny of the Lord's brethren " at the Bay.[3] The influence of the governor and assistants and the disposition of the people to repose confidence in their authority, led the Court to order that for the future the freemen should choose the assistants only, and that these should select the governor and deputy from among themselves, and should also make laws and appoint officers.[4]

Canaan, by Thos. Morton, Amsterdam, 1637, 4to., 191 pp., a copy of which I have read in the British Museum, does not display his character much more favorably than does the indignant secretary of the court of N. Plymouth in the pages above referred to.

[1] These absurd regulations were several times repealed and re-enacted, and were the occasion of much trouble in Massachusetts, frequently requiring the interposition of the courts to adjust variations in the price of labor between different towns.—1 Savage's Winthrop, 31, note. This was not the only subject upon which the rulers of the Bay abused their legislative prerogative.

[2] 1 Hutchinson's Mass., 26.

[3] 1 Savage's Winthrop, 53, note (1853). He was admitted at the next Court, May 18, 1631.

[4] Prince's Annals (1826), 320.

This was a wide departure from the terms of the charter, and a concession of power which, however safely reposed in this case, furnished a dangerous precedent for the future. At the next General Court, being the first court of election in Massachusetts, this power was wisely restricted by the people, who reassumed the right to choose their own officers, and although they did not at this time expressly limit the term of office to one year, they established their right to make such annual changes in the board as the majority might wish. Thus they partially rescinded the act of the previous Court by which they had yielded too much. It would have been well if they had stopped at this point, and not made the legislation of the two Courts present a still further contrast, by an order which entirely reversed the liberality of the former in admitting freemen without a religious test. This measure, which was to be the exciting cause of future troubles, and the means of calling into existence a new State based upon principles as yet untried, was considered essential to the preservation of purity in the community. " To the end the body of the commons may be preserved of honest and good men, it was ordered and agreed, that for the time to come, no man shall be admitted to the freedom of this body politic, but such as are members of some of the churches within the limits of the same."[1] This extraordinary law continued in force until the dissolution of the government,[2] and the spirit of intolerance which it necessarily, if not intentionally fostered, survived in the hearts of the people, and was displayed in the conduct of the rulers, long after the odious enactment was expunged from the statute book. The apologists of this

---

[1] Prince's Annals (1826), 354.

[2] It was nominally repealed in 1665 (1 Holmes's Annals, 210, note), but its features were essentially retained, by substituting for church membership a minister's certificate that the candidate for freedom was of orthodox principles. and of good life and conversation. 1 Hutchinson's Mass., 26, and note, p. 231.

law have excused its existence on the ground of dangers, which were feared from the hostility of the prelatical party in England, requiring a strong bond of union, and the incitement of religious zeal in those to whom was intrusted the exercise of political power. They overlook or conceal the facts that the requisites for church membership in Massachusetts were far more strict than in England, and that it was a greater grievance to be deprived of civil liberties for this cause in New England than in Old ; and again, the direct effect of such a law must be to inculcate hypocrisy, since no rectitude of conduct could procure the immunities,which were the reward of profession only, so that if any one did not feel himself to be at heart a Christian, and could thus conscientiously unite with a church, he must submit either to dissemble or be disfranchised.   At this day it appears strange that men, who in so many respects showed that they were wise and good, should not have seen and shunned the consequences of such a law. It would seem as if they believed that the act of legislation was omnipotent, having in itself an efficacy to change the heart of man, and to reverse the principles of human nature. How, otherwise, could they sanction a statute which placed a premium upon deception, and which required a spiritual change, such as they held could only be effected by divine grace, as a prelude to the exercise of civil rights, while, as the evidence of this change, they could require only the assurance of the applicant, accompanied by such proofs, in outward conduct, of his sincerity as might suffice to satisfy public opinion ?   The external conditions of citizenship were too easy, and its advantages too great, to be overlooked by those whose lives were governed by any other motives than those of conscience. The terms of the law are such as to defeat its avowed object. To preserve men " honest and good," we should avoid the occasion of evil, and not offer an inducement to practise it under the cloak of sanctity.   The spirit of this law is one which would blot out from the great canon of petition, "lead us not into temptation," to substitute for the teachings of Infinite Wisdom the devices of man's invention, which would expose frail humanity to a powerful allurement under the name of a sanctifying trial, and expect it to emerge unscathed, or even strengthened, from the dangerous ordeal. The operation of the law could not fail to introduce into the body politic elements the very opposite to what was intended, and to assimilate the institutions of the State to those from which they had fled, by making still more close, in Massachusetts than ever it had been in England, the union of civil with ecclesiastical power. To establish a tyranny of the church, to cherish a feeling of intolerance, and to foster a spirit of dissimulation, were the inevitable results of this baleful statute. To infuse discontent into the minds of many, and thus to involve the State in continual difficulty, was its legitimate and immediate effect. It was the first direct legislative exposition of the feeling of the colonists towards those who differed from them in religious opinions, however blameless might be their lives. It foreshadowed a similar fate to others, under the sanction of law, which had already been visited upon the Brownes, by order of Endicott, under a construction of the charter. Nor was it many years before the emigration of some prominent citizens, and the open opposition of others, displayed the light in which independent men viewed the infringement upon freedom of thought and action of which this statute was the harbinger.

A few weeks previous to the meeting of this General Court, the ship Lyon arrived at Nantasket, with twenty passengers and a large store of provisions. Her arrival was most timely, for the colonists were reduced to the last exigencies of famine. Many had already died of want, and many more were rescued from imminent peril by this providential occurrence. A public fast had been appointed for the day succeeding that on which the ship reached Boston. It was changed to a general thanksgiv-ing. There was another incident connected with the arri-val of this ship, which made it an era, not only in the affairs of Massachusetts, but in the history of America. She brought to the shores of New England the founder of a new State, the exponent of a new philosophy, the intel-lect that was to harmonize religious differences, and soothe the sectarian asperities of the New World; a man whose clearness of mind enabled him to deduce, from the mass of crude speculations which abounded in the 17th century, a proposition so comprehensive, that it is difficult to say whether its application has produced the most beneficial influence upon religion, or morals, or politics. This man was Roger Williams, then about thirty-two years of age.[1] He was a scholar, well versed in the ancient and some of the modern tongues, an earnest inquirer after truth, and an ardent friend of popular liberty as well for the mind as for the body. As "a godly minister," he was welcomed to the society of the Puritans, and soon invited by the church in Salem to supply the place of the lamented Hig-ginson, as an assistant to their pastor Samuel Skelton. The invitation was accepted, but the term of his ministry was destined to be brief. The authorities at Boston re-monstrated with those at Salem against the reception of Williams. The Court at its next session addressed a letter to Mr. Endicott to this effect: " That whereas Mr. Williams had refused to join with the congregation at

April
12.

[1] See Appendix A for research into his early life. A Rhode Islander may be permitted to notice the coincidence of a general thanksgiving day " by or-der from the Governor and Council, directed to all the plantations," to cele-brate the arrival of the ship which brought the founder of his State to the shores of the New World. With the exception of the thanksgiving held July 8, upon the arrival of " the great emigration " by the emigrants themselves, this was the first instance of what has long since become, by universal cus-tom, one of the " institutions " of these United States. And happily for the country, the principles which emanated from the cabin of the Lyon have been no less widely diffused than has the custom to which her arrival gave occa-sion.

Boston, because they would not make a public declaration of their repentance for having communion with the churches of England, while they lived there ; and, besides, had declared his opinion that the magistrate might not punish the breach of the Sabbath, nor any other offence, as it was a breach of the first table ; therefore, they marvelled they would choose him without advising with the council, and withal desiring him, that they would forbear to proceed till they had conferred about it."[1]

This attempt of the magistrates of Boston to control the election of a church officer at Salem, met with the rebuke it so richly merited. The people were not ignorant of the hostility their invitation had excited ; yet on the very day the remonstrance was written, they settled Williams as their minister.[2] The ostensible reasons for this hostility are set forth in the letter above cited. That they were to a great extent the real ones cannot be questioned. The ecclesiastical polity of the Puritans sanctioned this interference. Their church platform approved it.[3] Positive statute would seem to require it. Nevertheless, we cannot but think that, underlying. all this, there was a secret stimulus of ambition on the part of the Boston Court to strengthen its authority over the prosperous and, in some respects, rival colony of Salem. Salem was the oldest town in what was then Massachusetts, and had been the seat of power under Gov. Endicott until the corporation emigrated to America, supplanting his authority by that of Gov. Winthrop, and making Boston the capital of New England. But the advantages of Salem were considerable, and the feeling of independence resulting from these circumstances was apparent. The expediency of reducing the people of Salem to more complete subjection to the central power, could not have been

---

[1] Winthrop, i. 63.   [2] Bentley's Hist. of Salem, 1, M. H. C. vi. 246.
[3] Mather's Magnalia, B. v. ch. 17, § 9.

overlooked by the Court, and accordingly we find them speedily embracing the earliest opportunity to assert that power—gently, at first, expressing wonder and requesting delay on certain theological grounds, but more harshly afterward as we shall presently see. As a political measure this interference failed of its object. The people resented so great a stretch of authority, and the church disregarded the remonstrance. The reasons assigned by the Court, we do not propose here to discuss. The first involved a point in which Williams was not alone. The "great John Cotton" himself withdrew from communion with the churches of England, and persuaded other eminent divines to adopt the same course."[1] The second reason redounds to the everlasting honor of Williams as "the great, *earliest* assertor of religious freedom."[2] What could not as yet be accomplished by direct intervention of the Court was effected in a surer manner. The fearlessness of Williams in denouncing the errors of the times, and especially the doctrine of the magistrate's power in religion, gave rise to a system of persecution which, before the close of the summer, obliged him to seek refuge beyond the jurisdiction of Massachusetts in the more liberal colony of the Pilgrims.[3]

Aug.

At Plymouth "he was well accepted as an assistant in the ministry to Mr. Ralph Smith, then pastor of the church there."[4] The principal men of the colony treated him with marked attention. Gov. Bradford, in his Journal, speaks well of him,[5] and Gov. Winthrop, who had uniformly opposed him, mentions having partaken of the Holy Sacrament with him, in company with Mr. Wilson, pastor of the Boston church, when on a visit at Plymouth. Williams remained for two years at Plymouth.[6] The

---

[1] Magnalia, B. iii. ch. 1, § 10–18.   [2] Mr. Savage in note 2, Winthrop, i. 41.
[3] Bentley's Salem, 1, M. H. C. vi. 246.   [4] Morton's Memorial, 151.
[5] Prince, 377.
[6] The weight of authority assigns this limit to R. W.'s residence at Plymouth. See citations in Knowles, p. 55, note.

opportunities there presented for cultivating an intimate acquaintance with the chief Sachems of the neighboring tribes were well improved, and exerted an important influence, not only in creating the State of which he was to be the founder, but also in protecting all New England amid the horrors of savage warfare.

Ousamequin, or Massasoit, as he is usually called, was the Sachem of the Wampanoags, called also the Pokanoket tribe, inhabiting the Plymouth territory. His seat was at Mount Hope, in what is now the town of Bristol, R. I. With this chief, the early and steadfast friend of the English, Williams established a friendship which proved of the greatest service at the time of his exile.

West of the Pokanoket country, embracing the islands in and around Narragansett bay, the eastern end of Long Island, with nearly the whole mainland as far as Pawcatuck river, was the powerful tribe of the Narragansetts, including several subordinate tribes, all owning the sway of the sagacious and venerable Canonicus, with his brave and generous nephew, Miantinomo, as their chief Sachems. Tradition speaks of this tribe as a fierce and warlike race, extending their conquests from the main, over all the adjacent islands, and it still points to the spot on the island of Rhode Island, where in a great battle, anterior to the arrival of the English, the former proprietors of these beautiful shores were vanquished by the valor of their assailants. There is a clause in the Indian deed of Aquidneck to Wm. Coddington, which appeaⅰs to confirm this tradition. It is, however, certain that at this time the schemes of the Narragansetts for territorial aggrandizement had ceased, and their attention had become directed in some measure to the arts of civilization. They coined money in their rude way from sea-shells, and were skilled in various branches of Indian manufacture. With these Indians, as with Massasoit, Williams sought friendship, and by kindness and attention, making them pres-

CHAP.
I.
1632.

ents and visiting them, as his letters describe, "in their filthy smoky holes to gain their tongue," he overcame the shyness of the old Canonicus and won the esteem of the high-spirited Miantinomo. It proved well for himself and for New England that this intercourse was maintained.

The generous spirit of the Pilgrims preserved Roger Williams in a great measure from the annoyance which had caused his removal from Salem, and protected him from the offensive interference of the civil authorities. Still his own views were too liberal for the times in which he lived ; he was misunderstood by the enlightened, and misrepresented by the bigoted who sympathized with their brethren of the Bay. His attachment appears never to have been withdrawn from the people of Salem, who reciprocated the warmth of his regard and invited his return.[1] So great was the respect and love entertained

Aug.
1633.

for him at Plymouth, that it was not without difficulty he obtained his dismissal from the church, through the influence of Brewster, the ruling elder, who was one of those who dreaded the effect of his opinions. It illustrates the singular power which, through his whole life, Roger Williams exerted on the minds of his companions, whether savage or civilized, that several members of the Plymouth church, unwilling to be separated from him, desired their dismission at the same time and followed him to Salem.[2] Here he again assisted Mr. Skelton, whose health was rapidly failing.

Now, within the jurisdiction of the Bay, was resumed a conflict between the despotic spirit of theocracy and the genius of intellectual liberty, which was to result in the temporary triumph of arbitrary power over abstract right ; which was to call into existence an independent State, and finally to achieve the emancipation of the human soul from the thraldom of priestly oppression. It should be borne in mind that in most of the points of dispute which

---

[1] Backus, i. 56.   [2] Morton's Memorial, 151.

now arose Williams was not alone or even foremost in the discussion, while in respect to some of the most important encroachments of the Court upon the rights of the people all the inhabitants of Salem were with him. His detractors have delighted to represent him as if he were the only thorn in the side of the authorities, the sole disturber of fraternal harmony in the otherwise happy family of the Puritans. To fasten upon Roger Williams the stigma of factious opposition to government, as has often been attempted, is to belie history by an effort to vindicate bigotry and tyranny at the expense of truth. It is a memorable fact, which a careful examination of the evidence presented by the Puritan writers themselves will establish, that of the many singular and bitter controversies which raged at this time, in most of which Roger Williams bore a conspicuous part, and for all of which his enemies have endeavored to make him solely responsible, only one was initiated by him, save that which has become his crowning glory. The contentious spirit with which he has been charged was characteristic of the age in which he lived, and eminently so of the society in which he moved. Transition periods are necessarily eras of agitation, more or less prolonged according to the importance of the principles to be evolved. In this case the Protestant reformation had opened a discussion, in the 16th century, involving the dearest rights of humanity, which had already convulsed all Europe, and was about to subvert the ancient monarchy of England. To establish the inherent right of private judgment, the free agency of the mind in spiritual matters,—this was the grand result towards which a hundred years of toil and strife, in camp and court, in school and closet, were slowly tending. In the controversy which directly led to this result, Williams had many ardent friends among his Puritan compeers, the more perhaps from his bearing only a secondary part in the subordinate agitations which first occurred.

CHAP.
I.

1633.

A meeting of the ministers, held at each other's houses, to debate "questions of moment," inspired the cautious mind of Skelton with fear lest[1] " it might grow in time to a presbytery, or superintendency, to the prejudice of the church's liberties." In this feeling Williams shared, but remained passive, while Skelton openly denounced the frequent meetings of the clergy."[2] They had both seen enough of priestly arrogance in England to dread its appearance in America. Already had the interference of the Court at Boston, at the instigation of the ministers, given warning of the actual usurpation from which the church at Salem was shortly to suffer. Liberty is rarely subverted at a single blow. Its foundations are sapped by gradual and regular approaches under the guise of lawful authority, and often in the very name of freedom itself. These manifestations could not escape the vigilance of the Salem pastors, or fail to fill their minds with anxious forebodings. The event justified the anxiety of these watchful guardians of public liberty, notwithstanding the remark of the amiable Winthrop, who was soon to feel in his own person the fickleness of popular favor, withdrawn at the dictation of the clergy, that " this fear was without cause."

The custom of women wearing veils in public formed a theme of pulpit discussion at that time, which has unjustly been charged upon Williams. The earnestness of Endicott and the eloquence of Cotton upon this topic are recorded by contemporary writers. It has remained for the ignorance or the ill-will of more recent times, to cast upon Roger Williams the absurdity of a controversy which began before his arrival,[3] and in which there is no reliable evidence to prove that he took a prominent part.[4]

---

[1] Winthrop, i. 117.   [2] Bentley's Salem, 248.   [3] Bentley, 245.

[4] Hubbard is the earliest Puritan writer who connects the name of Williams with this ridiculous controversy. His tirade upon Roger Williams. chap. 30, General History of New England, is the source whence most of the abuse of the Founder of Rhode Island is derived, wherein he is closely fol-

More serious difficulties soon arose.   During Williams' residence at Plymouth, he had written a treatise upon the royal patent, under which the Massachusetts colony held their lands, wherein he maintained that the planters could have no just title except what they derived from the Indians.   The Court, as usual, took advice of the ministers, "who much condemned Mr. Williams' error and presumption, and were greatly offended at these three passages : " 1. For that he chargeth King James to have told a solemn public lie, because in his patent he blesses God that he was the first Christian prince that had discovered this land : 2. For that he chargeth him and others with blasphemy for calling Europe Christendom, or the Christian world : 3. For that he did personally apply to our present King, Charles, these three places in the Revelation, viz."[1]   As to the first point, we are at loss to discover any very strong grounds for clerical indignation. If it was "presumption" in Williams to deny to the reigning family the honor of discovery, it certainly was not an error.   To the Tudors, and not to the Stuarts, that honor belongs.   It was under the auspices of Henry VII., more than a century before James I. ascended the throne, that New England was discovered.[2]   Politically Williams

---

lowed by Cotton Mather a few years later.   Other portions of his history are equally unreliable ; in fact, nowhere is he to be trusted as an original authority.   His prejudices color his whole narrative.   His plagiarisms and his carelessness are sufficiently exposed by the diligent editor of Winthrop, in an ample note on p. 296, vol. i., to which the reader is referred.

[1] Mr. Savage's note at this place should be cited : " Perhaps the same expressions, by another, would have given less offence.   From Williams they were not at first received in the mildest, or even the most natural sense ; though further reflection satisfied the magistrates, that his were not dangerous.   The passages from the Apocalypse were probably not *applied* to the honor of the King, and I regret, therefore, that Winthrop did not preserve them."—*Winthrop*, i. 102.   In his 2d edition, p. 145, Mr. S. adds : " No complaint of such indiscretion would have been expressed ten years later, when the mother country far outran the colony in these perversions of Scripture."

[2] The author does not propose to discuss the question of the Ante-Columbian discovery of America.   If the claim of the Danish writers for their

CHAP.
I.
1 6 3 3. may have been presumptuous ; historically he was correct in this first charge.   That the second point should have given offence, displays more earnestness to preserve the royal favor than zeal in the cause which they considered to be the only true one.   Men who had repeatedly denied the Christianity of Europe, need not so suddenly have become indignant that one of their number should write what all of them spoke and believed.   This spasmodic loyalty may be attributed to a fear lest the influence of Laud, Archbishop of Canterbury, should so far prevail with the Crown as to lead to a repeal of the New England patent.   The solicitude for the honor of the king, manifested in the third stated ground of offence, furnishes an amusing contrast to the conduct of the same reverend legislators a few years later. The arbitrary action of the Court, in calling for a paper Dec.
27. written beyond the jurisdiction of Massachusetts, " for the private satisfaction of the Governor of Plymouth," and which had never been published, would have been properly resented by refusing to obey the summons.   None of his persecutors in those days, or of his detractors in later times, ever displayed a more Christian, or less " contentious spirit," than did Williams on this occasion.   He " offered the book, or any part of it, to be burnt, and gave satisfaction of his intention and loyalty."   On a further examina- 1633-4.
Jan.
24. tion of the offensive passages by the council, " they found the matters not to be so evil as at first they seemed."   Thus the subject rested for a few months until it was found convenient again to call it up.

Upon the death of Mr. Skelton, the church ordained Roger Williams as their pastor, although the Court a sec-

northern progenitors were fully established, identifying New England, and especially Rhode Island, with the Vineland of Icelandic explorers, it would have no bearing upon the New England of our day ; while in the present state of the subject it is more a matter for archæological investigation than of historical research.   For a view of this point see R. I. Hist. Coll's, iv. Ap. 2, and for the whole subject, Prof. Rafin's Antiquitates Americanæ.

ond time interfered to prevent it. We shall presently see how severely their contumacy was punished.

In the autumn Williams was again summoned to appear at Court, for promulgating his views concerning the patent. When we remember that the practice of the Puritans accorded precisely with the theory of Williams, in respect to the Indian titles—that all the land they occupied, except what they found deserted, owing to the pestilence which preceded the arrival of the Pilgrims, had been purchased by them of the original proprietors—we cannot discover in the ostensible reasons for this second arrest, any sufficient cause for such treatment. That he took what we should consider a needless exception to the language of the patent is apparent. Perhaps he thought that words are sometimes things. The sense of justice which formed so striking a feature of his character, compelled him to deny the royal claim to possession by right of discovery. Yet this language was in itself harmless so long as it remained merely a form of kingly phraseology. We are forced to the conclusion that the real reasons for pursuing this matter are not upon the record, and that the repeated refusal of the Salem church to permit the interference of the Court in their choice of a teacher was the principal cause. This opinion is strengthened by the fact that after this time we hear nothing further of the controversy about the patent ; more tangible and serious causes of complaint being found by the Court.

One other subordinate point remains to be noticed before we arrive at the immediate causes of the banishment of Roger Williams. The conduct of Endicott in cutting out the cross from the national colors, for which singular action he was suspended from office for one year by order of the Court, has been ascribed to the influence of Williams, who has been made, as in the dispute about veils, the convenient author of most of the erratic deeds and notions of the times. The opposition to Popery and all its

CHAP.
I.

1635.

symbols, which formed so deep a feeling in the Puritan mind, was the real cause of this unwarrantable act of the Salem magistrate. That Williams countenanced the act is nowhere asserted, unless such a construction be given to the language of Hubbard.[1] Even Mather, who cannot be suspected of any bias in favor of Williams, says of this proceeding, " that he was but obliquely and remotely concerned in it." [2] How far he may be considered as morally responsible for this application of an abstract opinion which he entertained in common with his fellows, is rather a question of ethics than of history. The clearness with which he discerned the dividing line between civil and spiritual concerns, in an age when these subjects had scarcely begun to attract public attention, forbids the idea that he advised the mutilation of the ensigns. The subject afterwards assumed a much greater prominence ; the Court, at first divided in opinion as to the lawfulness of the cross, at length ordered the ensigns to be laid aside entirely, two months before Endicott, from motives of policy, was disgraced for defacing them ; and when a year later, at the request of certain shipmasters, these colors were hoisted upon the castle, it was done " with the protestation, that we held the cross in the ensign idolatrous, and therefore might not set it up in our own ensigns." [3] This was subsequent to the banishment of Williams, and furnishes fair presumptive evidence to acquit him of responsibility for this singular transaction.

March
4.

May
6.

A more serious occasion for complaint was found in the views entertained by Williams on the nature of judicial oaths. He was cited before the council for teaching "that a magistrate ought not to tender an oath to an unregenerate man." It appears that he considered taking an oath to be in itself an act of worship, recognizing as it does the existence and power of a Supreme Being, and

April
30.

---

[1] Hubbard, ch. 30, p. 205, in which he is followed by Hutchinson, 1, 38.
[2] Magnalia, B. 7, ch. 2, § 8.   [3] June 16, 1636, Winthrop, ii. 344.

hence, as a direct result of his views in respect to liberty
of conscience, he denied the right of any one to enforce it.
There was nothing in this proposition to excite alarm, so
long as it did not come in conflict with the tenets of the
ministers or the designs of the magistrates.

Passages in his writings indicate that he had long entertained, and in some cases had suffered losses in chan-
cery on account of his views on this subject, which in
some respects resemble those held by the Society of
Friends, and for which, to this day, they are liable to pecuniary damage by the laws of England. Very soon,
however, the action of the Court, in requiring a new oath
to be taken by all the citizens, brought Williams' abstract
notions into practical opposition. Alarmed at the rumors
of "some Episcopal and malignant practices against the
country," the Court decreed that an oath of fidelity to
the laws of the colony should be taken by all freemen. It
will be remembered that "the freeman's oath" had already
been taken by all who were admitted freemen of the colony.
The terms in which it was expressed, requiring obedience
to laws which should be "lawfully" made by the Court,
acknowledged the charter as the fundamental law, and the
source whence it was derived as the sovereign power. But
this new oath of fidelity ignored the charter, and bound
the citizens to obey the acts of the Legislature without
reference to their compatibility with the laws of England.
What right had the magistrates, with their ever present
counsellors, the clergy, to adopt this new law? There
were more reasons for Williams' earnest hostility to the
measure than his enemies saw fit to assign. The charter,
although general in its terms, was yet a safe guide in the
broad principles of legislation. No laws repugnant to those
of England could be enacted under it. It shielded the
colonists from the possible tyranny of the king, and protected them from the more probable despotism of their own
local magistrates. A friend of popular liberty might well

be alarmed at a movement designed to destroy the only
guarantee of freedom, and whatever his abstract opinions
in regard to oaths may have been, the illegality of the
measure was enough to ensure the opposition of Williams.
It appears that he was not alone in this opposition. So
many were found to resist the unlawful attempt, that for
a time "the Court was forced to desist from that proceeding." It was not until the spirit of free inquiry was more
effectually checked, and submission compelled by the coer-
cive policy of the Court, that the act was finally passed,
and the oath enforced, under severe penalties, upon every
man over sixteen years of age.

While the authorities, and especially the ministers,
were thus diligent in establishing their power over the
colonists, seeking to punish as seditious persons all those
who ventured to exercise their freedom by calling in question the acts of the Legislature, they were aiming to accomplish a virtual independence of the mother country.
At the very time they were arraigning Williams as an
enemy to the patent, for his too faithful defence of the
rights of the Indians, and disgracing Endicott for mutilat-
ing ensigns which they had already laid aside as idolatrous, they were nullifying their charter by decreeing an
oath of fidelity to themselves, and were preparing for
more overt acts of treason, should circumstances render
it expedient. The council, alarmed by the evidence of
serious designs against the colony, fomented by the high
church party in England, convened the clergy to consider "what ought to be done if a general governor
should be sent out of England." Four months prior to
this, unusual activity was displayed in completing the
fortifications, when these designs were first detected, and
the idea of resistance to the home government was freely
canvassed by the General Court. Thus early was the
spirit of colonial independence entertained by the fathers
of Massachusetts, while as yet they were ignorant of the

leading principles of national freedom, and were pursuing
a policy fatal to the existence of popular liberty. That
they should conceive the idea of eventual separation from
the mother-country as an act of necessity, was natural
and commendable under the circumstances in which they
were placed; but that they should at the same time ar-
raign Williams for a constructive hostility to the patent
they were designing to supplant, and degrade Endicott
for violating colors which they had already disowned, was
inconsistent in itself, and accords with the real motive
which animated the dominant class—to make independence of England the means of establishing a theo-
cratic despotism at home. The republican feeling with
which the name of independence is associated in our
minds was unknown to the authorities of Massachusetts. At this time there was no sympathy with the
spirit of progress in the stern assemblies of the Puritans. The all-pervading element of religious controversy had withered every generous sentiment and dried
up the fountain of Christian benevolence. No respect
was felt for individual opinions, and no regard was
shown for private rights, that conflicted in any degree
with the rules of a coldly intellectual system of theology.
The sanctity of domestic life was disturbed by the sur-
veillance of the State. Even parents were known to report to the magistrates incautious remarks made by their
children in the familiar intercourse of home. Cotton,
whose influence was paramount in the colony, preached
publicly " that a magistrate ought not to be turned into
the condition of a private man without just cause," a doctrine calculated to perpetuate power in the hands of men
over whom the clergy already exercised unbounded control. The strong common sense of the Puritan masses rejected the dangerous dogma, but was not sufficient, as yet,
to withstand the organized efforts of the magistrates and
clergy. Every thing in the polity of Massachusetts was

CHAP.
I.

1635.

made subservient to the interests of the State, and that State was virtually and exclusively the Puritan church. No wonder that religious toleration and political freedom were alike abhorrent to its rulers, or that the conscience which could not accept an oath designed to perpetuate despotism was treated as an enemy to the State.

The punishment inflicted upon the people of Salem for the alleged contempt of installing Roger Williams, contrary to the repeated remonstrance of the Court, was characteristic, and illustrates the incongruous mingling of temporal and spiritual affairs which must exist with a church and state establishment. The authorities of Salem petitioned the General Court for some adjacent land which they considered as belonging to their town. The petition was refused, "because they had chosen Mr. Williams as their teacher." This was certainly an extraordinary reason to assign for denying an act of justice. The Salem people so considered it, and Williams may be pardoned for having united with the whole body of his parishioners in an earnest protest against what they considered to be a flagrant wrong. The church at Salem addressed letters to the other churches desiring them to remonstrate with the magistrates and deputies who were their members on account of this injustice, and warning them of the danger to which their liberties were exposed. This appeal to the people brought no relief. Popular sentiment was not so keenly alive to a sense of violated right, or so vigilant in guarding the outposts of freedom, as it is in our day. At the next General Court the deputies from Salem were refused their seats until their constituents " should give satisfaction about the letter."[1] Subsequently Mr. Endicott protested against the action of the Court, and

May
6.

July
8.

Sept.
1.

[1] Winthrop, i. 164. Mr. Savage here justly remarks, in a note: "This denial, or perversion of justice, by postponement of a hearing, on a question of temporal right, for some spiritual deficiency in the church or pastor, will not permit us to think that the judges of Williams were free from all blame in producing his schism."

justified the Salem letter; for which exercise of his rights
as a citizen he was committed by order of the government
until he acknowledged his fault.   By such arbitrary measures, the authorities were shortly to subdue the manly opposition of the people of Salem, and to rule without restraint over their submissive subjects.

At the same Court which disfranchised the Salem
deputies, Roger Williams was summoned to answer
"for divers dangerous opinions, viz. :—1, that the magistrate ought not to punish the breach of the first
table otherwise than in such cases as did disturb the
civil peace; 2, that he ought not to tender an oath
to an unregenerate man; 3, that a man ought not
to pray with such, though wife, child, &c.; 4, that a
man ought not to give thanks after the sacrament nor
after meat."   To what has already been said upon the
first two points, it is only necessary to add, that the concluding clause of the first charge proves that Williams'
views were not opposed to civil magistracy, as has been
represented, but only to the extension of authority over
subjects for which man is alone amenable to his Maker.
With respect to the third charge, there is nothing in Williams' writings to show that he entertained the views
therein expressed.   It should be borne in mind that the
only reports we have of his opinions, during the ordeal
through which he was made to pass while a minister at
Salem, are given by his opponents, of whom Winthrop is
the earliest writer, and the only one who was superior to
the influence of prejudice.   And we know that inferences
from his abstract notions, drawn by those less skilful in logical deduction than himself, have been recorded as his
real opinions, and that, with equal recklessness, he has
been charged with acts which he never committed, but
which were supposed by his enemies to be the legitimate
results of views which they could not comprehend.[1]   Wheth-

[1] Morton, Hubbard, Mather, and other nearly cotemporary writers, have
erred in this way ; e. g. Morton's Memorial, 153, says, " he would not pray

CHAP.
I.
1635.

er in this case he entertained the precise views alleged against him or not, is of little importance. If he did, it may be attributed to the effect of the prevailing idea of English worship, where all present are supposed fervently to unite in the prescribed forms of prayer, however inconsistent may be their lives. An undue prejudice may have biased his judgment in this particular. The fourth allegation is immaterial otherwise than as evidence of his wisdom and zeal in opposing the attempt to establish by law "a uniform order of discipline in the churches." Uniformity, the rock upon which, a century before, the reformed church of England had well-nigh been wrecked, and which ever since had been the principal occasion of difficulty, which had led to the expatriation of the Pilgrims, and to the emancipation of the Puritans, was about to be attempted in Massachusetts. The Court had already taken measures to accomplish this object, and, if, as probable, these minor observances were to form a part of the religious system, we can well understand why Williams should oppose them.

But these errors of doctrine appear to have had less weight in determining the action of the Court than did the "contempt of authority," by the Salem church, of which he was both the instrument and the victim. Church and pastor were each warned to expect sentence at the next General Court, unless satisfaction should meanwhile be given. For two years this harassing treatment had continued with little intermission. Williams' health failed under the accumulated burden of pastoral duties and legal vexations. While in this condition, "being sick and not able to speak, he wrote to his church a pro-

Aug.
16.

nor give thanks at meals with his own wife," &c. Hubbard copies him verbatim. A more open slander Mather in his History has exposed, although with no good intent to Williams, in Magnalia, B. 7 ch. 2, § 6, which is cited by Knowles, 69, who significantly adds : "We may wonder, nevertheless, that Mr. Williams has not been accused of starving his children, to the horror of succeeding generations !"

testation, that he could not communicate with the churches ~CHAP.~ I. in the Bay; neither would he communicate with them, except they would refuse communion with the rest." The ~1635.~ cup of his anguish was full when he penned this last epistle, the only one upon the record of this protracted controversy of which even his enemies could say that "it was written in wrath;" nor can we know that the apparent bitterness of his rebuke did not spring from a spirit more in sorrow than in anger.

The period of his sufferings was shortly to terminate. The letter of the Salem church was an unpardonable sin, which he, as its author, was to expiate, while that addressed to his parishioners was considered an equally proper subject of judicial condemnation. For the fifth and last time he was summoned by the authorities to appear at the next General Court, where these two letters were ~Oct.~ presented as the sole charges against him. He justified their contents, and remained unmoved by the arguments of Hooker, who was appointed to dispute with him. The result was a decree of banishment in these words: ~Nov.~ "Whereas Mr. Roger Williams, one of the elders of the ~3.~ church of Salem, hath broached and divulged divers new and dangerous opinions, against the authority of magistrates; as also writ letters of defamation, both of the magistrates and churches here, and that before any conviction, and yet maintaineth the same without any retractation; it is therefore ordered, that the said Mr. Williams shall depart out of this jurisdiction within six weeks now next ensuing, which, if he neglect to perform, it shall be lawful for the governor and two of the magistrates to send him to some place out of this jurisdiction, not to return any more without license from the Court."[1] It is a

---

[1] Winthrop says the sentence was passed "the next morning" after the examination by the General Court, which met in Oct., but the colonial records, which we adopt as being documentary evidence, fix the date Nov. 3d. An explanation of the discrepancy may perhaps be found in the fact recorded

CHAP. singular fact, that in this Court, composed of magistrates
  I. and clergy, while some of the laymen opposed the decree,
1635. every minister, save one, approved it. A practical com-
mentary is thus afforded on the danger of uniting the
civil and ecclesiastical administrations. It suggests the
reflection that, of all characters, the most dangerous and
the most despicable is the political priest.

Liberty to remain until spring was afterward granted
him, accompanied by the injunction that he should refrain
from disseminating his opinions, a restriction not easy to be
borne by an earnest mind, conscious of possessing important
truths and actively employed in diffusing them. To continue his connection with the Salem church was incompatible with his present position. The church, subdued by the
severity of the Court, surrendered at discretion, and apologized for the offensive letter. The lands for which they had
petitioned and been refused, were soon afterwards granted
to them. The stern exercise of power, although it accomplished its purpose in breaking the spirit of the people, could
not alienate their affections from one who had been their
fearless champion and devoted pastor. Great was the grief
in Salem when the sentence of banishment was pronounced,
1635-6. and many prepared to follow him into exile. The per-
Jan. mission to remain until spring was suddenly withdrawn at
a meeting of the council, and his immediate departure for
England, in a ship then ready to sail, was resolved upon.
The reason of this harsh treatment was that he had promulgated his views among those friends who visited him
at his own house, and was planning a settlement in Narraganset Bay, which was considered as being too near for

by Winthrop, that "a month's respite" was offered him to prepare for the
disputation, but "he chose to dispute presently." When the dispute with
Hooker was ended, the Court doubtless agreed upon the sentence, as Winthrop
states, but still indulged him with the month's respite before entering up the
judgment, which seems to have been formally done at a meeting of the Court
of Assistants, Nov. 3d, as appears by the record, which is therefore the proper
date to assign for this important event in the life of Williams.

the safety of Puritan institutions. An order was sent for him to come to Boston, which he declined to do. A boat was then despatched to take him by force and place him on board the ship. Warned by the previous order, he had already escaped three days before, no one knew whither. Leaving his wife and two infant children, he set out alone in midwinter to perform that arduous journey of which, thirty-five years later, he wrote, " I was sorely tossed for one fourteen weeks, in a bitter winter season, not knowing what bed or bread did mean." Happily for the world, and most fortunately, as the event soon proved, for the people of New England, he eluded the vigilance of his pursuers. Had their designs succeeded, the grasp of intellect and the energy of purpose which had evolved the grand idea of religious toleration, and was about to establish it as the primary article in the government of a State, would have been transferred to another field of action, and generations might have passed away, in the stormy period of English history then commencing, before the man and the opportunity again arose to test the great experiment ; while the removal of the only man in New England who could control the elements of Indian warfare, might have given another and fatal termination to the desperate struggle which Pequot cruelty was preparing.

Driven from the society of civilized man, and debarred the consolations of Christian sympathy, Williams turned his steps southward, to find among heathen savages the boon of charity which was refused at home. The now venerable Ousamequin, who sixteen years before had first welcomed the weary Pilgrims to his shores, and with whom Williams, during his residence at Plymouth, had contracted a friendship, received with open arms the lonely and twice-exiled Puritan. From him Williams obtained a grant of land near what is now called Cove Mills, on the eastern bank of Seekonk river, where he built a house, and commenced planting with the view of permanent residence. But this

was not to be his home.   In the quaint scriptural language of the day, "he had tarried on this side Jordan, while
the promised land lay still beyond."   He was soon advised
by his friend Gov. Winslow that, as his plantation was
within the limits of Plymouth colony, who "were loath to
displease the Bay, he should remove to the other side of
the water."   This he resolved to do, and in company with
five others, who appear to have followed him from Salem,
he embarked in his canoe to find at length a resting-place
on the free hills of Providence.   Tradition has preserved
the shout of welcome, "What cheer, netop,"[1] which
greeted his landing at "Slate Rock;" poetry has em-
balmed it in enduring verse; good taste affixed the name,
"what cheer" to the adjacent farm, and even the spirit
of enterprise and the growth of population, which have
thrown these broad lands into the market of a proud and
prosperous city, have respected the consecrated spot, and
reserved "What Cheer Square," with its primeval rock,
forever to mark the place where the weary feet of Roger
Williams first pressed the soil of Providence.[2]   Pursuing
their course from Slate Rock around the headland of Tock-
wotten, passing what are now called India and Fox points,
they entered the Moshasuck river, and sailing up what was
then a broad and beautiful sheet of water, skirted by a
dense forest, their attention was attracted by a spring close
on the margin of the stream, where they landed, and commenced a settlement, to which, in gratitude to his supreme
June. deliverer, Williams gave the name of Providence.

There is a singular confusion among the writers as to

---

[1] How are you, friend ?   "What cheer, *netop*, is the general salutation of
all English toward them (the Indians).   *Netop* is friend."—*R. W.'s Key to the
Indian Language*, ch. 1.

[2] The writer hopes that the Rhode Island of the twentieth century will
not have occasion to question the accuracy of his narrative, by finding that
the aforesaid square has never been laid out, unless upon some then long-lost
plat, and that Slate Rock exists only in the pages of history.   At present
there seems a likelihood of this.

the period at which this memorable event occurred, arising rather from ignorance or carelessness than from the absence of authentic data. The precise day of Williams arrival at Seekonk, or at Providence, cannot be determined, but both events may be established with sufficient accuracy for historical purposes. The Massachusetts records fix the date of his banishment, and also the proximate time of his flight, early in January, from which time the " fourteen weeks," that he describes as the period of his wandering, would establish his settlement at Seekonk about the middle of April, near the usual planting time of this region. The warning letter from Gov. Winslow, after he had " begun to build and plant at Seekonk," makes it certain that he was there after March, 1636, at which time Mr. Winslow became governor of Plymouth, and the only year between 1633 and 1644 in which he held that office. A letter to Gov. Vane of Massachusetts from Mr. Williams is dated from Providence, July 26, proving that he had already been some time in his new plantation ; so that in placing the foundation of Providence in June, 1636, we feel assured of a tolerable degree of accuracy.

In reviewing the measures which led to the banishment of Roger Williams, we find that they all proceeded from the firmness with which, upon every occasion, he maintained the doctrine that the civil power has no control over the religious opinions of men. To adapt this new theory to practical life was to effect a revolution in the existing systems of government ; to sever the chain, which, since the days of Constantine, had linked theology to the throne ; to restore to the free mind the distinctive, but long-fettered gift of Deity—free agency ; and, in fine, to embody in civil polity that principle, but dimly understood by the Reformers, which, from Wittenberg to Rome, in the cloister and the camp, had aroused the spirit of all Europe—the right of private judgment.

The entire separation of Church and State had already

been advocated by a small portion of English dissenters, consisting of Baptists and Independents, but the great majority of Puritans, as we have seen, still maintained the prerogative of the crown to interpose in matters of faith. Their chief objections to the English Church related to forms and ceremonies, and these they sought to alter. Persecution failed to make them liberal or tolerant to the scruples of others.

The right of every man to worship God according to his own conscience, untrammelled by written articles of faith, and unawed by the civil power, implies a degree of advancement in moral science and political philosophy, utterly at variance with the tone of feeling in that age. If to this assertion of natural right we add the denial of any power in civil government to enquire even whether a citizen believes in the existence of God, we have a proposition far more bold than many which had already led a host of martyrs to the gibbet and the stake. Yet this was the sentiment which, in those days of political darkness, Roger Williams had the clearness to discover, and the courage to defend. He dared assert the freedom of the soul. Thus was introduced a new principle in political science, by eradicating an old element of civil polity. The church was no longer to be a portion of the state, and the state must undergo a thorough re-organization, when deprived of its powerful auxiliary. Roger Williams saw that government could be more efficient in its object and more just to its citizens, if independent of the church ; and he knew that the church could best sustain its spiritual nature when freed from the clogs of state. Religion, ethics, and politics, as now received, are alike indebted to him for their fundamental principle.

Yet plain and immutable as these truths appear to us, they were but dimly comprehended by the wisest statesmen two centuries ago. Their exponent was driven to found a new state, which should illustrate the great principles for which he contended. From England he had fled to Massachusetts, seeking sympathy among those who had suffered with him in a common cause. But affliction, which should serve to soften the heart to the sufferings of others, seemed only to increase the acerbity of the Puritans. Even among the ministers of Christ, from whom he might expect forbearance, if not kindness, he met his most virulent enemies. By their influence he was banished, and escaping to the headwaters of the Narragansett, he found a spot in the pathless wilderness, where he could rear a temple of liberty, consecrated to the Lord of the whole earth, before whose ample shrine Jew and Gentile, bond and free, might each worship God according to the dictates of his own conscience.

Although the conduct of the Puritans in this transaction cannot be justified, it may admit of palliation. It is a source of regret to be compelled, from the nature of the subject, to treat chiefly of the dark side of characters who possessed so much true piety and essential greatness of soul—to apologize for their errors and expose their obliquities.

We observe in the Fathers of Massachusetts a degree of virtue and intelligence, and a supreme regard for the dictates of religion, and for the preservation of a sound morality, such as has never fallen to the lot of any other country in its early history. The germs of a powerful state, competent to give laws to the world, and to transmit the heritage of a wise example to future generations, are seen in the feeble band of Pilgrims, planted on Plymouth rock, and in the throng of earnest Puritans gathered along the shores and headlands of Massachusetts Bay. But while we recognize these noble attributes in the men who persecuted Roger Williams for opinion's sake, justice requires that we should relate facts as they occurred without abatement or reservation. We may regret the conduct of our ancestors, but we are not entitled

to defend, or to extenuate, their errors. We may account
for them from the circumstances of the case, and may show
that they originated in an honest misapprehension of
principles, thereby proving that the actors, though mistaken, were consistent, and that their sins were rather of
the head than of the heart. This view we adopt in our
judgment of the Puritans.

In estimating their characters, we are too apt to judge
them by the light of the present day. Two centuries of
progress have wrought so great a change in opinions and
views, by increasing so largely our fund of knowledge,
that what was expedient or proper, or even right in those
times, would be justly regarded as absurd or erroneous in
this age. We might as well revile our ancestors for the
use of the handloom, since modern science has introduced
self-moving machinery, as to denounce them for not acting
upon principles, which, in their day, were unrecognized in
civil polity. They founded a colony for their own faith
without any idea of tolerating others. For doing this,
they have been charged with bigotry, fanaticism and folly.
Every epithet has been applied to them that can be employed to express detestation of the conduct of men acting
under a sober conviction of truth. Regarding their conduct from the standpoint of the nineteenth century, all
this may be just. The like proceedings in this age would
deserve the severest sentence of condemnation. But not
so two hundred years ago. The bigotry of the Puritans
was the bigotry of their times. In every act they illustrated the spirit of the age. They committed some wrongs,
for which, even with all this allowance, we are at a loss to
account, which seem to us unpardonable, and to these we
shall have occasion to refer ; but intolerance is not one of
them. Toleration was a word conveying to their minds
an image of terror. It was so held in England and
throughout Europe. The principle was regarded with
the same heartfelt abhorrence that conservative statesmen

now express for the feculent emanations of the Jacobin clubs of France; for, to their minds, it was attended with the like fatal results. The simple cobbler of Agawam informs us that "he who is willing to tolerate any religion, or discrepant way of religion, besides his own, unless it be in matters merely indifferent, either doubts of his own, or is not sincere in it." To the same end, and about the same time, the illustrious Bossuet was employing his almost superhuman eloquence to obtain the royal interference in enforcing the supremacy of the Papal church. The churches of Scotland and England were alike zealous in effecting uniformity. Edwards, an eminent divine of that period, says, "Toleration will make the kingdom a chaos, is the grand work of the devil, is a most transcendental Catholic and fundamental evil." This was the policy of Massachusetts Bay, and with this state of public opinion among themselves, and these high authorities to countenance them abroad, we cannot in fairness condemn them for desiring to free the colonies of all dissenters. The abuse of their principles arose mainly from the tenacity with which they maintained them, and the trying situation in which they were placed. Had their own views been more liberal, we may well doubt whether the home government, actuated by the same spirit of intolerance, would have allowed the dissemination of free opinion in so large and prominent a colony. It was not till some years after, when a convulsion had shaken the institutions of England to their foundation, and the public mind was too intent on the fearful crisis at home to regard the affairs of distant provinces, that a free charter was obtained for the then obscure plantations in Rhode Island. Again, the Puritans looked on every departure from the established creed as being, what in fact it was, an infringement of the civil code; for in their constitution government was merely secondary, and the church was the primary function. Hence they regarded every dissent

CHAP.
I.

1636.

from their religious polity as revolutionary, as subversive of social order, and treated it as a crime. We, therefore, find them summoning Roger Williams before their highest tribunal, to answer for the crime of holding to certain opinions of a purely religious nature ; and with these views we are not inclined to wonder so much at their expulsion of Williams, as to condemn their subsequent conduct towards him and his colony, and their horrible treatment of the Quakers and Gortonists, which form the darkest chapters in Puritan history.

It is pleasing to find in the personal kindness of many eminent men towards Roger Williams at this time, a strong contrast to the severity of the magistrates and elders. The mild and amiable Winthrop, who was the ablest as well as the most liberal man of his age and place, appears to have regarded Williams with great affection and respect. He had ceased to direct the public councils some months before Williams' ordination at Salem, and the bigoted Dudley had succeeded to the chief magistracy as the leader of the most restrictive party in Massachusetts. The persecution of Williams is to be attributed to a policy of which Dudley and his successor Haynes were the exponents. The latter, who was governor when Williams was banished, openly censured Winthrop for the mildness of his administration. The faithful friendship of Endicott, who afterwards became governor, has been recorded, and Williams' letters bear testimony to the kindness of Gov. Winslow and others of the prominent men of Plymouth.

There was nothing personal in the hostility of his enemies, the bitterest of whom were among the clergy, who sought to establish a political theocracy, and dreaded the promulgation of principles which they could not comprehend. A yet greater obstacle to their scheme of uniformity had already appeared among themselves, and after distracting for two more years the councils of church and state, was destined in like manner to be violently expelled, and to result in the settlement of the island of Rhode-Island.

Roger Williams had scarcely established himself at Providence, before the Antinomian controversy burst forth in Massachusetts.

———•••———

APPENDIX A.

EARLY LIFE OF ROGER WILLIAMS.

THE early career of Roger Williams has been the subject of frequent and labored investigation, but, until very recently, with little result. Gradually, however, facts have been presented which throw some light on his history prior to his embarkation for America, Dec. 1, 1630. The discovery of the Sadleir letters, a correspondence between Roger Williams and Mrs. Anne Sadleir, daughter of Sir Edward Coke, has shed light upon the important point of his education, and established the fact of his being a protege of Lord Coke. The original MSS. are in the library of Trinity College, Cambridge. Hon. George Bancroft, while Minister at the Court of St. James, procured copies, and presented them to the R. I. Hist. Society. They are also published in Dr. Elton's life of Roger Williams, ch. xiii. By these papers, it appears that his illustrious patron, on account of his ability displayed in taking notes of proceedings in the Star Chamber, placed him at Sutton's Hospital, now the Charter House, the records of which institution show that he was elected a scholar, June 25, 1621, and that he obtained one exhibition, July 9, 1624. (Elton's Roger Williams, ch. ii.)

The writer regrets that he cannot adopt the other particulars relating to the birth-place and university education of Williams, contained in this interesting chapter. The learned author is undoubtedly correct in assigning

Wales as the country of Roger Williams. The name is
eminently Welsh, and abounds even more remarkably in
Anglesea and the northern counties than at the south.
Still it is not unlikely that Maestroiddyn was the birth-
place of our Roger Williams. The testimony of the aged
Nestor of Cayo is conclusive of the fact, that *a* Roger
Williams, of sufficient celebrity to be known, at least
among the natives of his mountain hamlet and the inher-
itors of his blood, by the epithet "the great," was born
there. But two points of difficulty occur in identifying
him with the founder of R. I. and the graduate of Oxford.
The records of Jesus College, cited by Dr. Elton, give the
name as "Rodericus" in the Latin style of the University,
which we submit should be "Rogerus" to meet this case.
Or, admitting that the two names were used inter-
changeably, which is barely probable, we are met with
a fact which has added greatly to the perplexity and labor of this research, that there were two other persons of
the same name, filling somewhat conspicuous positions at
about the same time. One of these was a distinguished
soldier in the wars of Holland, and either of them would
seem as likely as the founder of R. I. to be the "Rodericus" of Conwyl Cayo. But, Roderick and Roger are
distinct names, and it seems an unnecessary violence to
assimilate them, when a more natural, and in other respects also, a more obvious explanation of the difficulty
may be found. Mr. Collen, the obliging Portcullis of the
Herald's College, London, has made the genealogy of the
founder of R. I. the subject of diligent research in the
archives of that institution, at the instance of a wealthy
family in Paris, who are lineal descendants of Roger Williams. At his suggestion, the writer, assisted by Mr.
Romilly, the venerable registrar of the University, examined the records of Cambridge, the alma mater of Lord
Coke, and where, from the connection between them, the
probability is that Williams would complete his education

in preference to Oxford. In the admission book of Pem-
broke College is an entry "——— Williams, 29 Jan.,
1623." For the better understanding of these facts it
may be stated that the students in the English Universities are classed in three grades, according to their social
position. At Cambridge the first are called Fellow Com-
moners. This grade is composed of the nobility and the
wealthy. The second are called Pensioners, from their
boarding at the College, and this is the most numerous
grade. The third, called Sizars, consists of the indigent
students. When a student enters the University, his
name is enrolled on the admission book of the particular
College he joins, and is often very loosely entered, as in
this case—no Christian name or particulars being given.
The matriculation, which occurs after an interval of several months, and often, as in this case, of a year or two,
is the registering the name on the books of the *University*. This is done by the registrar, with the student's
name in full, the date, and a list of degrees taken, each
in its appropriate column. By this book it appears that
Roger Williams was matriculated a pensioner of Pem-
broke College, July 7, 1625, and took the degree of Bach-
elor of Arts in Jan., 1626-7. He took no other degree.
A more decisive evidence, in its bearing upon the present
discussion, is contained in what is called the "subscrip-
tion book." This was introduced in 1613 by James I.,
who required every student to subscribe to the thirty-nine
articles. In the first volume of this book, under date of
1626, the time he took his degree, is the autograph signature of ROGERUS WILLIAMS. A copy of this signature,
carefully compared with the known autograph of the
founder of Rhode Island, leaves little doubt of their iden-
tity of origin.

Again, the testimony of Williams in one of his letters dated July, 1679 (Backus, Hist. of the Baptists, i.
421), that he was then "near to fourscore years of age,"

is strongly corroborative of the received opinion that he
was born in 1599, and not seven years later, as was Rodericus Williams, the Oxonian.   In that case he would
have been only in his 73d year when writing the letter,
and would hardly have described himself as "near 80."
For these reasons the writer is reluctantly compelled to
dissent from the conclusions of his early instructor and
friend, the learned Doctor Elton, on the point of the
University education of Roger Williams, and hence likewise as to his being identical with the Roderic Williams
of Conwyl Cayo.

The difficulty of this research in England, occasioned
by there being three persons of the same name there, is
further continued in this country by the presence of two
Roger Williams's at the same time in New England,
which has led the accurate Prince, and all subsequent
writers, into error with regard to the admission of *the*
Roger Williams as a freeman of Massachusetts, until the
mistake was corrected by the diligence of Mr. Savage,
the editor of Winthrop's Journal, and late President of
the Massachusetts Historical Society, than whom no more
thorough or more liberal historian ever lived.   In the
Massachusetts Colonial Records, i. 79, is a list of "the
names of such as desire to be made freemen," among
whom is Roger Williams.   This is under date of October
19th, 1630, nearly four months before the founder of
Rhode Island arrived.   Most of these, including Roger
Williams, with many others, took the freemen's oath at
the next General Court, 18th May, 1631, at which time
our Roger Williams had been three months in the country, but never applied for admission.   The freeman was a
resident of Dorchester at that time, and afterwards removed to Connecticut.

CHAPTER II.

THE ANTINOMIAN CONTROVERSY.

1636—1638.

WHILE the colonists were legislating for the preservation of sound morals, by enacting sumptuary and other
laws to regulate their domestic economy, there arrived a
large accession of emigrants with news confirming the reports of the contemplated encroachments upon their liberties by the English hierarchy, which led to the adoption
of prompt measures, on the part of the General Court, to
place the country in a posture of defence. Among these
new comers was one who was destined to cause greater
disturbance to the Puritan settlements than any that they
were to receive from the prevalence of "immodest fashions"
at home, or from the designs of ambitious prelates abroad.
A woman of great intellectual endowments and of mascu-
line energy, to whom even her enemies ascribed unusual
mental powers, styling her "the master-piece of woman's
wit,"[1] and describing her as "a gentlewoman of an
haughty carriage, busy spirit, competent wit, and a volu-
ble tongue,"[2] who by a remarkable union of charity, devotion and ability, soon became the leader, not only of her
own sex, but of a powerful party in the state and church,
so that her opponents have termed her, by a species of ana-

CHAP.
II.

1634

Sept.

---

[1] Johnson. Wonder-working Providence, B. i, ch. 42.
[2] Magnalia, B. vii. ch. 3 § 7, 8.

grammatic wit, " The Nonsuch," was Mrs. Ann Hutchinson, the founder and champion of the Antinomian " heresy." Acting upon the principle that " the elder women were to teach the younger," [1] she established a weekly meeting at her own house, where she promulgated her views in the form of comments upon the sermons of Mr. Cotton. These meetings soon became largely attended, and to them was traced directly the origin of many opinions which were denounced by the authorities as heretical and seditious.

We have seen that the Puritans had already changed their position in becoming the founders of a State, and were disposed to mete out to all dissenters the same measure of persecution which had led to their own emigration. The system that they had established was one of rigid formalism, exacting a great regard to externals, and enforcing strict conformity in matters of abstract belief. This was a position in accordance with the spirit of the existing age, but contrary to that which was about to commence, of which the premonitions had already appeared in Massachusetts as well as in England. The new comers, who formed a large proportion of the inhabitants of Boston, had little sympathy with the established order of the state, and were prompt to embrace the novel tenets that were started at variance with the prevailing creed. These opinions related primarily to the doctrine of free grace, or justification by faith alone, which was stoutly asserted by Mrs. Hutchinson, and maintained by her brother-in-law, Wheelwright, minister at Braintree, who had recently arrived. Although this cardinal article of the Reformation was equally upheld by the Puritans, they did not overlook the external evidence of sanctification, or forget the apostles' injunction that " faith without works is dead." Mrs. Hutchinson artfully contrived, by giving undue prominence to the scriptural idea of free grace, to make it

[1] Titus, ch. 2, vs. 3–5.

appear that her opponents denied the sovereign efficacy of CHAP. II.
faith, and grounded their hopes of salvation upon their
good works, and she denounced them as being "under a 1636.
covenant of works," while she claimed for herself to be
living "under a covenant of grace." The starting point
of disagreement between the two parties related to the
evidence of justification. The followers of Mrs. Hutchinson contended for an inward light as the only sure witness of divine grace, and without which no degree of moral rectitude could give assurance of a saving faith, while
the legalists held that obedience to the moral law, being
an evidence of sanctification, was thus far a proof of our acceptance with Christ. So long as the difference was confined to this, it made no disturbance. The new views
were embraced by a majority of the Boston church, including Mr. Cotton himself, and were warmly espoused by the
governor, afterwards Sir Henry Vane. The prime doctrines of the Reformation, justification by faith, and the
right of private judgment, were too nearly allied to
these views to admit of their being disputed. The
message sent to England by Cotton, who favored the
new opinions, and by Wilson, who opposed them, contains the substance of the controversy up to this point :
"That all the strife here was about magnifying the
grace of God ; the one person seeking to advance the
grace of God *within* us as to sanctification, and another
person seeking to advance the grace of God *toward* us as
to justification," to which Mr. Wilson added, "That he
knew none who did not seek to advance the grace of God
in both."[1] Soon however the breach widened. The Hutchinson party, who claimed, theologically speaking, to be
living "under a covenant of grace," not only denied the
intrinsic efficacy of good works for the salvation of man,
but carried this scriptural doctrine so far as to pervert
its obvious meaning, by rejecting all external proofs of a

---

[1] Magnalia, B. vii., c. 3, § 1.

CHAP.   change of heart, as being indications that the convert was
  II.   living under a " covenant of works."
1636.   The idea of inward revelation was no novelty in the
history of theology.   It is one which in all time has been
effectively employed by the zealot or the impostor for the
accomplishment of purposes requiring the incitement of
religious fervor.   It appeals to the imagination of men, and
in this case, it thoroughly aroused the latent enthusiasm
of the Puritans.   The " opinionists," as they were at first
called, soon received another name, and from the disregard
of the divine law, both as an evidence and a means of
grace, with which they were charged by their opponents,
were termed Antinomians.   The controversy increased until it reached an alarming height, interfering with the efficient prosecution of the Pequot war, dividing families, and
threatening a dissolution of society.   The more enthusiastic people, a large proportion of the new comers, among
whom was the governor, and those who cherished a secret
feeling of dislike at the preponderating influence of the
clergy in secular affairs, espoused the Antinomian cause,
while those who were attached to the old order of things
in church and state, with all the ministers except Wheelwright and Cotton, formed the party of the legalists.   With
these popular elements on one side, based upon a free system
of theological enquiry, and conducted by ardent and ta-
lented leaders, it was a natural result that new and often
startling opinions were promulgated, and the whole community involved in a giddy maze of abstruse speculation.
Questions pertaining to " our personal union with the
Spirit of God," " the insignificancy of sanctification to be
any evidence of our good estate," " the setting up of immediate revelation about future events, to be believed as
equally infallible with the Scriptures," with similar recon-
dite or fanciful themes, were everywhere discussed with
more than scholastic zeal, and with " the exquisite rancor
of theological hatred."

The first evidence that public attention was directed to CHAP.
the new opinions appeared in a visit made by the other min- II.
isters of the Bay, while the General Court was in session at 1636.
Boston, to ascertain the truth of the rumors, intending, if
need were, to write to the Boston church, warning them of Oct.
the dangers of heresy. Cotton and Wheelwright both attended at this conference and satisfied them all, that on the
point of sanctification as an evidence of justification, there
was no difference of opinion, while on the question of the
indwelling of the person of the Holy Ghost there appeared
no material disagreement, many of the clergy holding to
that doctrine in a limited degree, but not to a personal
union of the believer with the Holy Spirit, which was the
tenet of Mrs. Hutchinson. Some of her followers, who
were members of the Boston church now sought to have
Mr. Wheelwright appointed over it as one of the teachers.
This was opposed by Ex-Governor Winthrop on the 30.
ground that the church was already furnished with able
ministers, and that Wheelwright was known to advocate
certain doctrines at variance with the received opinions, as
" that a believer was more than a creature," and " that
the person of the Holy Ghost and a believer were united."[1]
A discussion ensued, in which Deputy Governor Winthrop,
Cotton, Wheelwright, and Governor Vane, took part, resulting in the success of the former, so that the church gave
way that Mr. Wheelright might be called to a new church
about to be established at Braintree. The defeated members felt aggrieved at this attack upon their candidate, 31.
whereupon the next day Winthrop apologized for his
offence, stating that Wheelwright had since denied holding
the opinions charged against him ; and then, not satisfied
with this recantation, most unwisely proceeded to argue
from the doctrines which Wheelwright admitted, that he
must necessarily hold to these objectionable dogmas also.
It was a question of metaphysical distinction too nice to
be debated in a mixed assembly, and it would have been

[1] Winthrop 1, 202.

well had Winthrop been satisfied with the explana-
tions of his Christian brother. A similar instance of the
dangerous display of logical acumen had occurred a year
before at the trial of Roger Williams where the dialectics of Hooker convinced the court that Williams did
maintain opinions which he expressly denied. The habit
of deducing from the premises of enthusiastic theologians
conclusions not admitted by themselves, and then charging upon them not only errors of doctrine, but of conduct as the legitimate result of these conclusions, was
one to which the Puritans were addicted, that caused
them infinite trouble, and was the occasion of great injustice to the dissenting parties. In the discussion concerning the settlement of Wheelwright, the first public exposition of the new opinions was made. Heretofore they had
been confined to Mrs. Hutchinson's private assembly, or
made the subject of anxious deliberation by the ministers
alone. The rupture resulting from Winthrop's impru-
dence on this occasion, revealed how deeply the heterodox
notions had taken root. Cotton and Vane, with many
others, had adopted them, while Wilson and Winthrop
resisted the heretical novelties. A disputation concerning the nature of the Holy Ghost was held in writing,
that the peace of the church need not be disturbed thereby. The prudent conclusion was agreed to, that as neither the Scriptures nor the primitive Fathers made mention of the "person" of the Holy Ghost, that term
should not be used.

At this juncture, an unfortunate incident occurred to
give a political aspect to existing differences, and added
the bitterness of partisan feeling to the asperity of religious
controversy. Governor Vane convened the Court of Deputies to tender his resignation, alleging, in the first place,
that his private affairs required his immediate return to
England, and then assigning as his reason, the prevalent
dissensions, which he said were, by some, falsely attributed

Dec.

to him. The court silently consented to his departure, and decreed a new election. In the interval, some members of the church represented to the court that the governor's reasons were not conclusive ; whereupon Vane, acting upon this demonstration " as an obedient child to the church," declared that " without leave of the church he durst not go away " although the court had assented. The result was that a great portion of the people declared in favor of his continuance in office, and the Court of Election was adjourned to meet at its usual time, the following May. The vacillating conduct of Vane in this affair has greatly prejudiced his reputation. He has been freely charged with dissimulation in attempting to extort an expression of popular opinion in his favor, by a course more becoming a demagogue than a Christian statesman. The sequel gives the color of plausibility to this severe condemnation. Happy had it been for Vane and for the country if he had embraced the opportunity, given at his own solicitation by the court, to withdraw from New England. His career in Massachusetts had thus far been unique and brilliant. No other man had ever received such honors at her hands, or been more warmly admired by the people. Six months after his arrival at Boston he was chosen governor, when only twenty-four years of age. His high connections and popular qualities, notwithstanding his extreme youth, and inexperience in public affairs, combined to place him at once at the head of the State—an injudicious choice, as it proved in a few brief months.

At this court an attempt was made to reconcile the differences in the churches, and the ministers were convoked to give their advice. The governor took a prominent part, and by some unseasonable remarks drew upon himself a rebuke from the fiery Hugh Peter, who openly charged him with destroying the peace of the churches. The session assumed a polemic character, and closed with a debate upon the nature of sanctification. The peace of

CHAP.
II.

1636.

May
25.

Dec.

the churches, as might have been foreseen, was more disturbed than promoted by this attempt at judicial interference.   A speech made at this court by Mr. Wilson,
pastor of the Boston church,[1] gave offence to some of the
members, who demanded a public explanation.   To this
Wilson acceded, and the opportunity was embraced by the
Governor, and others of his congregation, to assail him with
bitter reproaches.   The excited laity were only restrained
from passing a direct censure upon their pastor, by the
firmness of Cotton, who, in lieu of it, " gave him a grave
exhortation."   The people seemed beside themselves with
indignation during this earnest dispute upon nice points
of polemic theology, which, probably, very few of them
could understand.[2]   The effect of these public discussions
was to spread the Antinomian doctrines.   Those heretofore
enumerated were now avowed by nearly the whole Boston
church, while still wider departures from the orthodox creed
were secretly entertained, and awaited only the stimulus
of opposition to be openly declared.   The defection of Cot-

[1] The organization of the Puritan churches differed from those of the
present day.   Beside the pastor, there were ruling elders and teaching elders,
the latter of whose duties did not vary materially from those of the pastor,
while the ruling elders seem to have had equal jurisdiction with him in the
government of the church.   Wilson was the pastor, Cotton a teacher of the
Boston church, beside whom were other teachers at various times, the number of these seeming to be decided by the size of the church.   Beside these
two classes of elders, there were deacons also, who assisted the elders.   Our
modern deacons approach to the character of ruling elders, while assistant
pastors, as in some large churches now, occupy somewhat the position of the
teaching elders.   There were two ruling elders of the Boston church at this
time, Oliver and Leverett, both Antinomian in their feelings, as indeed were
the entire church a little later, excepting Wilson, the pastor, Winthrop, and
some two or three others.—1 *Win.* 212.

[2] The hair-splitting distinctions, enunciated with all the energy of an oracle, by the disputants on either side of this controversy, remind one of the
Scotchman's definition of metaphysics—" When twa persons be talkin' t'gither,
an' t'ane dinna understan' t'ither, an' t'ither dinna understan' hi'self," while
the violence with which the factions supported their respective leaders, illustrates the intensity of what an eminent writer has termed " the exquisite
rancor of theological hatred."

ton was a sore trial to the clergy, who drafted a list of sixteen points of supposed disagreement, upon which they
desired his opinion.   His answers were published, and also
the ministers' reply to them.   The dissensions at home,
together with the distractions and 'disasters occurring at
this period throughout the Christian world, were the occasion of a general fast in Massachusetts.   The unhappy
dispute now assumed a more general character, extending
beyond the limits of Boston, and disturbing the quiet of
other churches.   The baleful distinction of men under " a
covenant of works," or under a "covenant of grace," divided
the whole community.   It was at this crisis that the message, before recited, was sent to England by Cotton and
Wilson, which, however truly it might describe the controversy in its earlier stages, gave no idea of the party
virulence that had since prevailed.

The ensuing session of the General Court presented
more the character of an ecclesiastical council than of a
legislative or judicial body.   The majority were legalists.
The proceedings against Wilson, arising out of his speech
at the preceding court, were investigated, but as it was
impossible to identify those who had prejudiced him, no
action was taken, except to pass a vote approving of the
speech.   The clergy were consulted as to the authority
of the court over the churches, and gave the opinion that
the court might proceed independently in cases of heresy
dangerous to the State.   This advice they immediately
followed, by summoning Wheelwright to answer for a sermon preached by him on the recent fast day, wherein as
they alleged, he had fanned the flame of dissension, instead
of quenching it, thus perverting the object of the fast, and
adding contempt of court to the crime of seditious preaching.   The sermon was produced by his accusers, and
defended by its author.   After much debate Wheelwright
was pronounced guilty of sedition and contempt, but sentence was deferred until the next court.   The governor and

CHAP.
II.

1637.

Jan.
20.

Feb.
3.

March
9.

some of his party protested against the judgment, but without effect. The Boston church petitioned in his behalf and justified his sermon. This act was declared to be presumptuous ; the petition was pronounced to be " a seditious libel," and was indignantly rejected. It subsequently furnished the pretence for unwarrantable severity. So great was the excitement, that it was decided to hold the next session of the court at Newtown,[1] a motion which itself produced a violent struggle between the two parties. The dispute had now become so warm that the leaders of the Boston church, Wilson of course excepted, even refused to sanction by their presence the ordination of ministers of the opposing faction.

Such was the temper of the people when the Court of Elections was held at Newtown. Party tactics were applied to defer the election as long as possible. It was the last struggle of political power on the part of Vane and his friends. The zeal of Wilson, who climbed a tree to harangue the assembled multitude; decided the fortunes of the day. The people clamored loudly for immediate election, and the governor was overborne by the tumult. Fierce denunciations on either side had already given place to acts of violence, when this timely exertion of the Boston pastor no doubt prevented actual bloodshed. The legalists triumphed at every point. Winthrop, who for the past year had been only deputy governor, was restored to his former office of governor, and Vane, with his assistants, Coddington and Dummer, were no longer magistrates. Boston had deferred the election of deputies until the result of the general election was known. The next day Vane and Coddington, with another of the same party, were returned as deputies from Boston. The court refused to receive them on the plea of informality, but on the following day, the same deputies were again chosen, and the court was compelled to admit them. Wheelwright appeared to receive

[1] Now Cambridge.

his sentence, but was again respited, the triumphant party
wishing to give an example of leniency by thus affording
him further time for retraction. The prisoner remained
firm, inviting sentence of death, but threatening an appeal
to the king in case the court should proceed. This conduct was fatal to the Antinomian cause. Thus far, the
popular feeling, especially in Boston, had been with the
liberal party, in opposition to the clergy, and to the old
order of magistrates. The threat of appeal changed the
political aspect of the case, and created a revulsion of public feeling. The new comers, equally with the old settlers, dreaded the interference of England, where the prelatical party was now in the ascendant. This feeling was
more potent than any domestic difference. The right of
appeal admitted the English claim to regulate the internal affairs of the province, so that the question now appeared like one of independence against subjection, in
which the legalists supported the popular side. This
event hastened the downfall of their opponents, and stimulated the dominant party to those acts of injustice which
were now to be consummated. An order of court was
passed, imposing a penalty upon all persons who should
harbor any emigrant for more than three weeks without
leave of the magistrates. This combination of an alien
law with a passport system was aimed directly at the
Antinomians, who were expecting accessions from England, and occasioned a great outcry. Social visiting was
interrupted, and personal insults were of frequent occur- July.
rence. The arrival of a brother of Mrs. Hutchinson, with
others of the same party, afforded opportunity for a practical application of the new law, and thus increased the
rancor of faction.

A pamphlet controversy, respecting Wheelwright's ob- Aug.
noxious sermon, occupied both parties until the all-en- 30.
grossing synod assembled at Newtown, which was to heal
every difference, and to settle the creed of New England.

CHAP.
II.

1637.

A list of eighty-two "erroneous opinions" and nine "unsavory speeches," supposed to embrace the whole catalogue of prevalent heresies, was presented and condemned.[1] Only five points of difference remained between Cotton and Wheelwright on one side, and the rest of the ministers on the other.[2] An earnest and protracted effort at reconciliation upon these metaphysical niceties, at length, through the medium of ambiguous expressions, wrought the desired end in the case of Cotton, who, with more perhaps of prudence than good faith, "explained, distinguished, and prepared to yield."[3] Wheelwright maintained his ground, and calmly awaited the penalty of contumacy.

Sept.
22.

Oct.
12.

The synod, after twenty-four days' labor, dissolved, with the gratifying result that Cotton, heretofore the great leader and theological dictator of the Puritans, after having suffered a temporary eclipse, "recovered all his former splendor among the other stars."[4] A day of thanksgiving was appointed for the success of the synod, and for the recent defeat of the Pequots. A little later it was discovered that, in respect to the former, the result had not been decisive. Although the pliant Cotton had

---

[1] These are duly set forth in T. Welde's pamphlet entitled "A short story of the Rise, Reign and Ruin of the Antinomians, Familists and Libertines that infested the Churches of New England," a very scarce and curious specimen of our early polemic literature. The copy which I have read is the London edition, 1644. It contains, besides an elaborate preface, 66 quarto pages, 20 of which contain the catalogue of errors, with their confutation, by the synod; 24 embrace the proceedings of the General Court of Nov. 2d, (erroneously printed Oct. 2d in the book,) 1637, which punished the Antinomian leaders, and the remainder are occupied with the trial of Wheelwright in the preceding March, with an account of Mrs. Hutchinson's excommunication. The whole is a bitter and bigoted ex parte statement by an actor in the scenes described, and will only repay a reading by the antiquary or the curious theologian. A remarkable instance of "bibliographical disingenuity" in relation to this book is exposed by Mr. Savage in a lengthy note in 1 Winthrop, 298–300.

[2] They are enumerated in 1 Winthrop, 285.

[3] The expression is Hildreth's. Hist. of U. S., i. 247.

[4] Magnalia, B. vii. c. 3, § 5.

deserted to the stronger party, Wheelwright and his friends were none the less active in disseminating their views.

At the next General Court a summary course was adopted, based upon the petition or remonstrance that the Boston church had presented, the preceding March, in behalf of Wheelwright, and which had then been branded as a "seditious libel" upon the court.[1] Wm. Aspinwall and John Coggeshall, both deacons of Boston church, and deputies from that town, were dismissed from the court ; the one for having signed, and the other for defending the remonstrance. One of the two deputies elected to fill the vacancies thus created, was immediately dismissed for the same cause, and the town properly refused to elect another in his place. William Coddington, the third deputy from Boston, acting under instructions, then moved a reversal of the censure against Wheelwright, and a repeal of the alien law. This demonstration of the firmness of Wheelwright's friends caused the court to summon him the same day to receive sentence, which, since his conviction in March, had been from time to time deferred. He was sentenced to banishment, and required to leave the jurisdiction within fourteen days, upon penalty of imprisonment. John Coggeshall, who a few days before had been expelled from his seat, was then summoned, and narrowly escaped the same punishment, but was released upon being disfranchised, and admonished to keep the peace on pain of banishment.[2] William Aspinwall was next called to trial for the same offence, and sentenced to be disfranchised and

---

[1] This petition is preserved in Welde's "Rise, Reign and Ruin," p. 23–25, and is copied by Mr. Savage in 1 Winthrop, App. E., where the reader will find it difficult to detect sedition or presumption in its earnest but respectful language. It was drawn up by Wm. Aspinwall, afterwards the first Secretary of R. I. Colony, and signed by about sixty of the principal men in Boston, some of whom, banished at this court, soon after settled the island of Rhode Island.

[2] He was soon after exiled, and became the first President of R. I. Colony.

banished, but was allowed to remain until spring.   Several
other signers of the petition and chiefs of the Antinomian
party, were in turn brought before the court, and punished by disfranchisement and fines, among whom were
William Balstone [1] and Captain Underhill, who thus received the reward of his distinguished services in the Pequot war.   The male leaders being thus summarily disposed
of, the author of all this commotion, Mrs. Hutchinson
herself, was brought into court.   Her trial occupied two
days.   It was opened in the form of questions between
the court and the accused, the object of which was to
deduce from her own admissions the evidence of her guilt.
Even the report given by Welde, one of her prosecutors
and judges, leaves her, at the end of the first day, unscathed by the dialectics of the court.   The next morning, however, she undertook a defence in a lengthy speech,
wherein she broached the doctrine of inward revelations,
enforcing her views by scriptural quotations, and claiming
in a manner to be herself inspired ; in evidence of which,
she enumerated sundry revelations that she had received,
and among them that she should go to New England and
be persecuted, of which revelation she asserted her present
trial to be a fulfilment.   " The court saw now an inevitable necessity to rid her away ;" [2] sentence of banishment
was pronounced, and she was handed over to the marshal
to await its execution.

A most remarkable act, unparalleled in the subsequent history of the American States, concluded the proceedings of this memorable court.   The principal men
of the proscribed party in all the towns were ordered to
deliver up their arms and ammunition before the 30th
of the month, unless they would " acknowledge their sin
in subscribing the seditious libell," before two magistrates. [3]

---

[1] He was one of the four assistants chosen in 1641 in the island of R. I.
[2] Welde, p. 41. For this and all the foregoing cases tried at the Nov.
court, 1637, see Welde's Rise, Reign and Ruin, pp. 23–42.
[3] Winthrop, i. 296, note.

Seventy-five names are enumerated as the objects of this
astonishing order, which naturally enough, as the finale to
so much tyranny, aroused a strong feeling of indignation.
The governor took an early occasion to justify the conduct
of the court to the excited congregation with whom he
was a worshipper.

The secular arm having been so efficiently exercised to
purge the state, the ecclesiastical authority was next exerted to purify the church.   Many of the signers of the notorious petition were proceeded with "in a church way"
by admonition, and when this failed to convince them of
their sin, excommunication was pronounced against them.
The more serious errors before alluded to, as being secretly
entertained by the followers of Mrs. Hutchinson, were now
openly avowed, and gave occasion for earnest consultations between the magistrates and elders.   A few of the
most intelligible of these notions were : "That the law
is no rule of life to a Christian," that "union to Christ is
not by faith," that "there is no such thing as inherent
righteousness," that "the Sabbath is but as other days,"
that "there is no resurrection of the body," and many
other dogmas, which, however harmless they might appear
when explained by their propounders, were fraught with
danger when adopted in their literal significance by the
multitude, unskilled in ethical subtleties.[1]   Mrs. Hutchinson was examined before the church upon these latter
charges, and gravely admonished by the teacher, Cotton.
A vain hope was felt that she might recant, for which
end she was permitted to reside for a few days at Cotton's
house ; but when the examination was renewed her ob-
duracy was manifest, and "the church with one consent
cast her out."   The virus of Antinomianism had become

---

[1] A list of twenty-nine theses, from which the above five examples are selected, was presented at the examination of Mrs. Hutchinson before the
church, 15 March, 1638, all of which she defended.   They may be found in
Welde's book, pp. 59–61.

neutralized by its own excess. A warrant to execute the sentence of banishment was immediately issued, and the arch heretic departed into exile, to meet ere long a dreadful death.[1] Wheelwright with his family removed to the head waters of the Piscataqua, where he commenced the settlement of Exeter.[2] The larger portion of the exiles, among whom was the husband of Mrs. Hutchinson, had already gone forth to seek a refuge in the wilderness.

Thus ended the Antinomian controversy in Massachusetts—the most bitter strife that has ever agitated New England, adding the severity of political conflict to the fierceness of doctrinal contention. Now that two centuries have passed away, and the names of Legalist and Antimonian are known only to the student of history, we may calmly review the causes and trace the results of this stormy episode in Puritan annals.

The different phases presented in the progress of the dispute are accounted for by the changing elements which at various periods it involved. Originally it was purely of a theological character. Matters of abstract belief, upon which all were agreed in their practical application, were discussed in their metaphysical bearing. Terms not used in the Scriptures were employed to express shades of thought in relation to the sublimest mysteries of the inspired volume. The specific purpose for which this "barbarous terminology" was first applied, was soon overlooked, and the fact that such expressions were merely "of human invention" was forgotten in the heat of discussion. Thus they came to assume a reality in the minds of the dis-

---

[1] Her subsequent history is soon told. She went first to Providence, and thence to Aquedneck, which had just been purchased by the fugitives of her party, and where her husband died in 1642. Soon after this bereavement she removed with her family to a spot near Hurl Gate, within the Dutch jurisdiction, where in a short time she, and, with the exception of one child, all her household, sixteen in number, were murdered by the Indians in 1643—a tragedy which the bigoted Welde narrates, as a special providence upon this "American Jezebel."

[2] Belknap's New Hampshire, i. 37.

putants, and gave to the argument a material instead of an abstract significance. The people who listened received the subtile theses of the debaters as the words of an oracle, while fanaticism readily embraced the doctrine of inward revelation, which was first cautiously insinuated and then boldly announced. The spread of dangerous heresies was stimulated by the rigid discipline of the Puritan churches. The desire for uniformity in creed and ceremonial produced a stringency of regulation that precluded, even in non-essentials, that latitude which a sound discretion would allow. This strictness, however congenial to those who ordained it, was offensive to subsequent settlers, whose feelings were thus enlisted, from the moment of their arrival, in any movement that promised relaxation. Furthermore, the principles of the Reformation, with which the new-comers were strongly imbued, but which had lost some portion of their hold upon the Puritan mind, when the possession of power had diverted their application, favored a degree of liberality and tolerance distasteful to the rulers of Massachusetts. The right of private judgment was merged in the authority of corporate decrees. The doctrine of justification by faith alone, which in the hands of Luther and Calvin, had shivered the gorgeous ritual of Rome, seemed, to the Antinomians, to be lost in the scrupulous attention paid to formal and protracted worship. On the other hand, " Calvinism run to seed " was an expression used by the Legalists to describe the position of their opponents. The antagonist elements of human character were here developed on the arena of religious strife. In its theological aspect, the Antinomian controversy was the system of Geneva, logically pursued, in conflict with the practice of Massachusetts—a struggle for freedom of thought and action against the spirit of formalism.

Politically considered, it presents a phenomenon not unusual in the history of the world, but singular enough in

CHAP.   a community so entirely controlled, through moral means,
II.   by the clerical profession.   It was a demonstration by the
1638. masses against spiritual domination—a protest of the people in opposition to the clergy.   The colony was still a
close corporation in which but a small number of residents
were admitted to the privileges of freemen.   The test
act [1] was now working its legitimate effect in arousing
a spirit of hostility to existing institutions, which was
specially directed against those who were supposed to be
its authors and most strenuous advocates.   A sense of injustice was preparing the minds of the people for overt
resistance to the supremacy of the clergy.   The shrewd
and cautious Cotton maintained their cause until the reaction, caused by the indiscretion of Wheelwright, was
apparent, and the political leader of the faction was disgraced at the general election.   When the powerful influence of Vane was thus withdrawn, Cotton made good his
reconciliation with his offended colleagues, and still appeared as the devoted servant of the people.   Up to this
period the political phase of the controversy was as distinctly marked as its theological character.

There is one other point, somewhat akin to this,
which should not be overlooked, as it helps to explain the
position of parties in this obstinate strife.   Viewed in its
social aspect, this was a contest between the new-comers
and the old settlers.   Nearly three thousand passengers
arrived the same year with Henry Vane, and only one
hundred and forty-five freemen were added to the colony.[2]
This disparity, together with what has before been written, will account for the feeling which disturbed even the
proprieties of social life.

From these various causes the Antinomian party were,
at one time, far the most numerous in Boston, recruiting
its ranks from the most accomplished as well as the most
liberal of her citizens ; while in other towns it was rapidly

[1] Passed May 18, 1631.   [2] Holmes's Annals, 229.

augmenting its forces, and preparing to imbue the exclusive spirit of the Puritans with more of liberality in feeling and practice.

Thus much for the causes of this celebrated dispute.
Its results upon the Puritans were exhibited in a gradual
relaxation from the severity of their political system, demanded by the growing jealousy of the people at the
power of their ministers and magistrates. This was slow
but certain in its operation, so that the union of church
and state became much less oppressive in the next generation. Its farther results, upon the victims of its fury
who were driven to establish their principles in an independent colony, soon afterwards united by parliamentary
patent with the Providence Plantations, the progress of
this history will develop.

By Clark's narrative it appears that during the preceding autumn many of the Antinomians, for the sake of
peace, and to enjoy freedom of conscience, had determined
to remove. The suffocating heat of the past summer induced them to seek a place at the north, but the severity
of the ensuing winter compelled them in the spring to
move farther south. With John Clark and William
Coddington as their leaders, the exiles designed to establish themselves on Long Island or near Delaware Bay,
and while their vessel was doubling Cape Cod they went
by land to Providence. Narraganset Bay, which seemed
the destined refuge for outcasts of every faith, attracted
the wanderers by its fertile shores and genial climate.
Roger Williams recommended them to settle at Sowams,
now called Phebe's Neck, in Barrington, on the main
land, or on the island of Aquedneck, now Rhode Island.
He accompanied the exploring party, consisting of Clark
and two others, to Plymouth, to inquire about Sowams,
when finding that this was claimed to be within Plymouth patent, they selected the large and beautiful island

of Aquedneck.[1]   Upon their return to Providence a number of the principal people formed themselves into a body politic by voluntary agreement, as the inhabitants of Providence had already done, and chose William Coddington to be their judge or chief-magistrate.

Through the powerful influence of Roger Williams, who in his account of the affair, modestly divides the honor with Sir Henry Vane, negotiations were shortly concluded with Canonicus and Miantinomi for the purchase of the island.   As soon as the deed was obtained

---

[1] This name is spelled in several ways, a common thing with all the Indian names, as Aquetnet, Aquiday, Aquetneck, Aquidneck, Acquettinck, &c., but the writer preserves the orthography used in the original Indian deed of the island. He also, to avoid confusion, will apply to the island colony its original name down to the time of the second charter, 1663, when the official designation in the first patent, 1643, of " The incorporation of the Providence Plantations in Narraganset bay in New England," gave place to the title which has ever since been preserved of " Rhode Island and Providence Plantations," now abbreviated in common use to the name Rhode Island. It was not till 1644 that the colonists changed the Indian name to " Rhode Island," or the " Isle of Rhodes." The derivation of this name has given rise to much discussion. By what strange fancy this island was ever supposed to resemble that of Rhodes, on the coast of Asia Minor, is difficult to imagine, and it is equally strange that the tradition that it was named from such resemblance should be transmitted or be believed, unless, indeed, because it is easier to adopt a geographical absurdity than to investigate an historical point.

Verrazano, a Florentine navigator in the service of Francis I. of France, explored the American coast, and spent more than two weeks in the spring of 1524 in the spacious harbor upon which Newport now stands. The passage in his narrative that has been cited as authority by the advocates of this prevalent mistake, refers to Block Island, which with much more geographical accuracy than in the case of Rhode Island, may be thought to resemble the Mediterranean island.

The celebrated Dutch navigator Adrian Block, gave his own name, still preserved with the omission of the Christian name, to that island which Verrazano had before noticed as resembling the Isle of Rhodes. The name in full is found on the Dutch charts of that day. Afterward, like his Italian predecessor, he sailed into Narraganset Bay, where he commemorated the fiery aspect of the place, caused by the red clay in some portions of its shores, by giving it the name of Roodt Eylandt—the Red Island, and by easy transposition, Rhode Island ; and Verrazano's casual notice of the neighboring island has been inadvertently transferred to this.

they commenced a settlement called Pocasset, at the cove on the northeast part of the island, in the town of Portsmouth. The colony increased rapidly during the summer, so that, in the following spring, a portion of their number moved to the southwest part of the island, and began the settlement of Newport.

CHAP.
II.

1638.
March
24.

1639.

CHAPTER III.

THE ABORIGINES OF RHODE ISLAND—PEQUOT WAR.

WE have now traced the causes which led to the settlement of Providence and Aquedneck. Before speaking of the later settlements within what is now the State
of Rhode Island, let us glance at the condition of the
country at the time when Wm. Blackstone first broke
the stillness of the primeval forest with the axe of the
English pioneer, on the banks of the stream that now
bears his name; when Roger Williams with his little
band first crossed the Seekonk, to found a State upon
principles as novel to his own race as to the swarthy
Indians with whom he sought a home; when John Clark
and his brave companions peaceably purchased " the Eden
of America " from its aboriginal lords, and founded a
Christian colony in the midst of heathen barbarism.

A fertile soil yielded an ample return for the simple
agriculture of the Indians. Numerous streams, frequented
by the trout and the salmon, discharged themselves into
a broad and beautiful bay, whose full extent was yet unknown to the sails of commerce, but which was dotted
with emerald islands, and on its shores were found the delicious shellfish that furnished the favorite food and the
only money to the rude natives. Forests, the undisturbed
growth of centuries, overspread the land and sheltered

alike the bear, the panther, the wolf, the red deer and the fox, with their natural master the aboriginal Man. Dense swamps furnished a lurking-place for the serpent, and a safe retreat for the feeble in time of war. Hills and rocks, sloping valleys, and verdant plains diversified the scene, spread out with all the wildness of nature, and over all the Indian roamed, unmindful, as yet, of that other race which was so soon to supplant his own.

The principal tribes of southern New England were the Massachusetts on the east, the Pokanokets inhabiting the Plymouth region, and including among their subordinate tribes the Wampanoags, who dwelt around Mount Hope Bay ; the Narragansets, who inhabited nearly all of the present State of Rhode Island, including the islands in the bay, Block Island, and the east end of Long Island ; and the Pequots, who with the Mohegans, with whom they soon became blended, occupied the whole of Connecticut. Westward of these in New York were the savage tribes of Mohawks, part of the Six Nations, who were accused of being cannibals, and were every where dreaded for their cruelty. The great tribes were ruled by one or more chiefs or sachems, and were divided into many subordinate tribes, each with its own petty sachem or sagamore. The Narragansets were at one time the most numerous and powerful of all the New England tribes. Shortly before the landing of the Pilgrims a pestilence, by some supposed to have been the small-pox, and by others the yellow fever, had swept over the seaboard of New England and nearly depopulated some of the tribes.[1] Prior to this the Narragansets had extended their conquests over all the eastern tribes, and at that time their dominion spread from the Pawcatuck River to the Merrimack. The Massachusetts and the Pokanokets paid them tribute, as did the Montauk Indians of Long Island. Wonumetonomy, Sachem of Aquedneck, confessed the

---

[1] Gookin's Indians of N. England, chap. 2.

sovereignty of the Narragansets. The Niantics around Pawcatuck River, whose sachem was Ninnigret, a portion of the wandering Nipmucks to the north and west, and the tribes of Pumham and Soconoco, inhabiting what is now Kent County, were all subsidiary to and formed a portion of the great Narraganset tribe, whose chief sachems were the sage and peaceful Canonicus and his high-souled nephew Miantinomi. How long the empire of the Narragansets had been established over the other subject tribes is unknown. At the time of the arrival of the English it had reached its culminating point. That they were a proud and martial race is proved by the extent of their conquests. These were savage virtues in which at one time certainly the Narragansets held preeminence. The empire which the valor of his predecessors had acquired, was preserved by the wisdom of Canonicus, until the English emigration gave opportunity to the Pokanokets gradually to withdraw their allegiance, and seek the dangerous friendship of the colonists. The policy of Canonicus was peace, and was pursued so far as the warlike spirit of his neighbors would permit. Under it the Narragansets became the most commercial and civilized of any of the natives, and on this account they were taunted by the hostile Pequots. At one time the Narragansets could bring over five thousand warriors into the field,[1] and one would meet a dozen of their towns in the course of twenty miles travel.[2] Their weapons were the bow and arrow and club. It was not till intercourse with Europeans had made them acquainted with the use of metals that hatchets were used, which being placed on the end of their clubs formed the dreaded tomahawk that has since become the adopted emblem of Indian warfare.

1622.　Two years after the English landed at Plymouth the Narragansets sent to them, by way of challenge, a bundle

---

[1] Gookin's Indians of New England, chap. 2.
[2] Key to the Indian language, chap. 1.

of arrows tied with a snake skin.[1] The tomahawk was of later date, and the horrible custom among the Indians of scalping their prisoners was taught them by the French, before which time the heads of their victims were taken as trophies.[2]

The natives are described, by one who knew them well, as being of two sorts. The better class were sober and grave, yet cheerful, and as ready to begin as to return a salute upon meeting the English, while the lower class, of whom the more obscure had no names, were more rude and clownish and rarely saluted first, "but upon salutation re-salute lovingly."[3] Their mode of doing obeisance to an offended sachem was by stroking him upon both his shoulders, and using a word which signified " I pray your favor."[3] Hospitality and a grateful remembrance of kindness, proportionate to their vindictive resentment for injuries received, were marked traits of Indian character. They freely shared their scanty meals with the passing stranger, and extended to him the protection of their wigwams, often, with a delicacy that finds no parallel in civilized life, sleeping out of doors themselves to allay the fears or promote the comfort of their temporary guests. Their domestic feelings were very strong. So dearly did they hold the tie of brotherhood that it was usual for the survivor to pay the debts of a deceased brother, and the brother of an escaped murderer was executed in his stead as full atonement for the crime. Their fondness for their children was carried to an excess that made them unruly and disobedient. Orphans were always provided for, and beggary was unknown among them. Marriage was publicly solemnized by consent of the parents. Fornication was not considered criminal in single persons, but adultery was severely condemned. The injured party might claim a

---

[1] Winslow, in Prince, p. 200.

[2] Niles' Hist. of French and Indian Wars, p. 174 in 3 M. H. C. v. 6. The French learned it from the Huns. [3] Key to the Indian language, chap. i.

divorce, and if the woman was false, the husband, in presence of witnesses, might beat the offender without resistance on his part, and if death resulted from the punishment it was not revenged. Polygamy was toler- ated, but among the Narragansets monogamy prevailed. Dower was given by the husband to the parents of the maid, or if he were poor his friends contributed for him. Divorce was permitted, as among the Jews, for other causes than adultery. The Indians were very prolific, and as usual among savage nations where the women till the ground and perform the severest manual labor, the pains of childbirth were very light. The proportion of deaths in infancy was larger than among the English, from the want of proper treatment and ignorance of medicine. In sickness they used such simple remedies as experience had taught them, and which their Powwaws, or priests, or medicine men, dispensed, accompanied with hideous singing and howling, in which the rest of the people joined, until the patient either recovered or expired. The Powwaws extorted large sums for these services, often to the ruin of their patients. The principal treatment in use among them was the sweat bath, which was taken in this manner. A small cave made in the side of a hill near some brook, was heated with wood placed over a heap of stones in the middle ; when the fire was removed the stones still retained great heat. Small parties of Indians then stripped themselves and entered the cave, sitting around the hot stones for an hour or more, smoking and talk- ing, while a profuse perspiration opened every pore, cleans- ing the skin and often removing the sources of disease. Emerging from the cave in this condition they would plunge into the brook, whether in summer or winter, and receive no harm from this sudden and violent transition.[1] When one was taken ill the women of the family black-

---

[1] Among the Tartar tribes of Siberia and in Lapland the same severe treatment is in common use, particularly for fevers.

ened their faces with soot, and when death ensued all the men of the neighborhood adopted the same peculiar style of mourning, smearing their faces thick with soot, which was continued for several weeks, or if the deceased was a distinguished person, for a whole year. Their visits of condolence were not less remarkable than the mode and length of their lamentations. They were frequently made, and were always accompanied by patting the cheek and head of the afflicted parties, and bidding them "be of good cheer." Their burial service was still more singular. The corpse was wrapt in mats or coats, answering to our winding sheets. This was a sacred duty not to be performed by a common person, but devolving upon some one who was held in high esteem. The body was then laid beside the grave and all sat down to bewail their loss for some time. The corpse was then placed in the grave, and sometimes some of the personal effects of the deceased were buried with him. A second lamentation was then held over the grave, and upon it was spread the mat upon which the person had died and the dish from which he ate. Often too his coat of skin was hung upon a tree nearest the grave, and there left to decay, as a sacred thing which it would be sacrilege to touch. In the case of the death of a prince the ceremonies were yet more striking. Canonicus, after the burial of his son, burned his own residence with all its contents, of great value, in solemn remembrance of the dead, and as a kind of humble expiation to the gods who had thus bereaved him. The Indians carefully avoided mentioning the name of a deceased person, but employed some circumlocution when referring to the dead. If a stranger accidentally spoke the name of such he was checked, and whoever wilfully named him was fined. If any man bore the name of the dead he immediately changed his name, and so far was this idea carried, that between different tribes the naming of their departed Sachems was held as a just cause of war.

CHAP.
III.
1622.

In religion it is difficult to say whether the Indians were Polytheists or Pantheists. They imagined a God in every locality and connected with every phenomenon of nature. Roger Williams obtained the names of thirty-seven of their deities, to all of which they prayed in their solemn worship. Their great God Cowtantowit lived in the southwest, the region of balmy airs. From him came their grain and fruits, and to his home sped the souls of their virtuous dead to enjoy an eternity of sensual bliss, while the spirits of the wicked wandered without rest. Here we find the doctrine of the Immortality of the Soul entertained by a barbarous race who affirmed that they received it from their ancestors, and whose connection with civilized nations had not then been sufficient to account for its existence in that way. They were ignorant of Revelation, yet here was Plato's great problem solved in the American wilderness, and believed by all the aborigines of the West.

What connection subsisted between Cowtantowit and their many other Gods does not appear. It is probable that their religious system was too vague and undefined to admit, even in their own minds, of any fixed relationship among their deities. But Cowtantowit certainly held the place of a Supreme Being, clothed with all the attributes of Deity, while the existence and nature of their many other Gods argues a species of pantheism which minds so clear and thoughtful, unaided by higher knowledge, yet capable of evolving the idea of the soul's immortality, might readily adopt. They acknowledged the power and agency of their Deity in all things whether good or ill. If a child died their God was angry, and was entreated to withhold his chastening hand from the surviving offspring. If an accident occurred, the wrath of God occasioned it ; and so in case of good fortune they returned thanks to God for the blessing. In the time of disaster, and after a plentiful harvest or successful hunt,

or on the occasion of peace or war, they held a great feast
or dance. The Powwaws commenced with an invocation
to the Gods, in which the people joined with violent dan-
cing and shouting. Always once a year, in the winter,
they held a great public feast, or thanksgiving, to Cowtantowit, for the fruits of the harvest. Private feasts
upon particular occasions were frequent, where besides
feasting the whole company, a great amount of money
and goods was distributed among the guests, a small sum
to each one, who as soon as he received the gift went out
and shouted three times for the health and happiness of
the donor.

The Indians were fond of sports and addicted to gam-
bling, using a kind of dice made of plum stones. Public games were often held in houses from one to two hundred feet long, erected for the purpose, where many thousands would meet to dance. Towns would often meet to
play against other towns with dice, on which occasions
an arbor or play-house was built of long poles sixteen or
twenty feet high, from which large amounts of their money, staked on the game, were suspended, and two men
were chosen out of the rest, in course, to play amid the
shouting of their abettors. Individuals would often stake
every thing, their money, houses, clothes, and even themselves, like the ancient Germans, described by Tacitus, in
this absorbing vice. Football was a favorite summer di-
version, when they would meet, town against town, to
contend on some smooth plain or sandy shore, and stake
large sums on the result.

Hunting, fowling and fishing were the chief occupations of the men, in which they often displayed great
skill and powers of endurance. They often met in large
parties to drive the woods for deer. In the autumn they
took them in traps, of which they had many kinds. In
fowling they were expert, being excellent marksmen with
the bow or gun, and skilled in laying snares for the ducks,

geese, turkeys and other fowl that abounded on the sea and shore. Cormorants which frequented the rocks off the coast they would take in great quantities at night while these birds were asleep. Blackbirds caused the Indians great annoyance by their countless numbers. For protection against them the seed was planted quite deep, lodges were built in the middle of the cornfields, where they staid at sprouting time to frighten away the birds, and hawks were tamed and kept about their houses as a still greater security from the depredation of the smaller birds. Crows, although doing some harm, were held in veneration by the Indians, and were rarely killed. They had a tradition that a crow first brought to them a grain of corn in one ear, and a bean in the other, from the fields of their great God Cowtantowit in the south-west, and from that seed came all their corn and beans. They were very fond of fishing, and would endure much hardship in its pursuit. They chiefly used nets made of hemp, setting weirs across the rivers and killing the bass with their arrows as they became entangled in the meshes. The head of the bass was considered a great luxury. The sturgeon they caught with a kind of harpoon of their own invention, going out in their canoes to attack it, and so highly was its flesh esteemed by them that they would rarely sell it to the English.

Their canoes were made from the trunk of the pine, oak, or chestnut tree, burnt out and hewn into shape. Ten or twelve days were required to complete one. They were of all sizes, carrying from two to forty men, and were worked with paddles, or when the wind was fair a blanket raised upon a pole was used as a sail. In these canoes they would push boldly out on the open sea, sometimes in fleets of thirty or forty, and if they met an enemy a regular sea fight would ensue. They were such expert swimmers that if overset two or three miles from land they would reach the shore unharmed.

The Narragansets were skilled in the manufacture of bracelets, stone pipes and earthen vessels, and were the principal coiners of wampumpeage, the established currency of the country, and which continued to be so long after the European settlement. This was of two sorts, the white called wampum, made from the stem or stock of the periwinkle shell, and valued at six for an English penny, and the black, made from the shell of the quahawg or round clam,[1] and of twice the value of the white, or three for a penny. The dark part or eye of this shell was ground to a smooth round surface, polished and drilled, ready to be strung,[2] and thus worn as a necklace or bracelet, or sewed to bits of cloth and used as a girdle, or carried as a scarf about the shoulders. The name wampum or peage was applied to both sorts. The regalia of their Princes was made of these beads, with the different colors handsomely blended and curiously wrought in figures. The people living on the seashore generally made peage, and no license from the Sachem was required to do so. A string of three hundred and sixty white beads made a fathom, and its ordinary value was five shillings sterling. A fathom of black was worth two of white. Before the extent of the fur trade had reduced the value of beaver in England the fathom of wampum was worth ten shillings, and the Indians could not understand why their money, in consequence, would bring only half as much as formerly. This currency was used by the Indians for six hundred miles in the interior, in trading among themselves, and also with the English, French and Dutch, who made it legal tender. This money was often counterfeited, but the Indians were quick to detect the real value, requiring an allowance for defective pieces and rejecting the spurious article. Their trade consisted chiefly in furs, provisions and their rude manufactures, wherein the principle of division of labor was well understood,

---

[1] Venus Mercatoria. Linneus.   [2] Morton's Memorial, Ap. p. 388.

some making only bows, some arrows, some dishes, while
some hunted and others fished, and those on the seashore
made wampum, collecting the shells in summer to coin
them in winter.   They were shrewd at a bargain and
would try all markets, taking their wares forty or fifty
miles or more to secure a good price, and being ever suspicious of attempts to deceive them it required great prudence and integrity in dealing with them.   They eagerly
sought European trinkets, mirrors, knives, tools and fire-
arms.   The latter it was forbidden by law to sell to them,
but through the French and Dutch, and from unprincipled English they obtained them.[1] The habit of beg-
ging, which in their primitive state was unknown among
them, they soon contracted after the English came, and
were very troublesome in that way.   True to the maxim
that "flatterers always want something," they would preface their petition with some adulation of the wealth, the
wisdom, or the valor of the English.   They were fond of
running in debt, and those who trusted them usually lost
both their goods and their customer.   These habits, together with drunkenness and gluttony, to none of which
were they previously addicted, were acquired by contact
with Europeans.   Still there were many fair and honorable traders among them who scorned alike to beg or to
deceive.

Among their primitive virtues punctuality was prominent.   The exactness with which they kept a promise involving attention to time was remarkable, and they were
slow to receive excuses from any who failed in this respect.   They measured time accurately by the sun by
day and by the moon or stars by night, and divided their
year into thirteen lunar months.   They had an intuitive
sense of justice, were prompt to award it, and quick to
retaliate where it was withheld.   If a robbery occurred
between different tribes the offended party demanded jus-

[1] This was one of the chief complaints against Morton of Mt. Wollaston.

tice, and if recompense were refused resort to reprisals
was had, yet care was taken not to seize more than a just
compensation for the loss sustained. A strict regard to
public opinion controlled the action of their sachems,
whose authority, although hereditary and absolute, was
rarely exerted, in important affairs, in opposition to the
popular will. Punishments, whether capital or only
corporal, were usually inflicted by the sachem, although
sometimes, when a public execution might endanger the
peace of the tribe, the sachem would send one of his
chief warriors secretly to behead an obnoxious person.

Their love of news amounted to a passion. Their
civilized successors do not peruse the teeming columns of
the daily press with more avidity than the red man welcomed to the council fire or the wigwam the bearer of
some novel intelligence. Upon these occasions they
would all sit round in a circle, two or three deep, each
man with his pipe, while amid profound silence the news
was told, or a consultation was held, the orator speaking
for an hour or more with earnest language and impas-
sioned gesture. Eloquence was a native gift with these
rude sons of the forest, and exerted as powerful an influence upon their deliberations as ever it did on the Gre-
cian stage, or in the Roman forum. Their mode of collecting an audience, especially when the news was of
great importance, such as a declaration of war, was to
send swift messengers to rouse the country, and at every
town to which the runner came a fresh messenger was
sent to the next town, until the last, coming near the
royal residence, shouted often, every man who heard it
taking up the shout, and all assembled quickly at the
council place. The speed of these runners was extraordinary, owing to constant training at races, and having
their limbs anointed from infancy. They have been
known to run from eighty to a hundred miles in a summer day, and back again in two days. The farm labor

and domestic drudgery was performed entirely by the women, except on the breaking up of new ground, when the
whole neighborhood, men and women, would unite in the
task.   The women planted, tilled and harvested the crops
with little or no aid from the men, dried the corn, beat it
and prepared it for food.   They made all the domestic
utensils of earthenware, and would carry incredible bur-
dens of provisions, mats, and a child besides, on their
backs.   The tobacco plant alone was cultivated by the
men.   This they used for the toothache, to which they
were very subject, and as a stimulant, prizing it as highly
as do their civilized successors.

Their staple article of food was Indian corn pounded
to meal and parched, which they mixed with a little water.   A spoonful of this preparation, with an equal quantity of water, would suffice for a meal.   A small basket
of it would support a man for many days.   It was easily
taken on long journeys, slung to the back or carried in a
leathern girdle about the loins.   Of the unparched meal
they made a pottage called "nassaump," whence the English name "samp," the same which in New England is
now called hasty pudding or mush.   Chestnuts they dried
and preserved the year round as a luxury.   Acorns also
were used when there was a scarcity of corn, or for a variety.   They extracted the oil from walnuts and used it
in cooking and also for anointing their persons.   Straw-
berries were very abundant, and during the season they
lived almost wholly upon a delicious bread made by bruis-
ing them in a mortar and mixing them with meal.
Whortleberries and currants were dried and kept the
year round ; beaten to powder and mixed with their
parched meal they made a favorite kind of cake.   Summer or bush squashes, of which the Indian name was
askuta-squash, and beans, which next to corn was their
principal dependence, were much used.   The sea and the
forest supplied them with an abundance of animal food.

Their venison and other meats were dried in the sun and CHAP.
III.
smoked for winter use, as were some varieties of fish.
But of all their different sorts of food none were more 1622.
highly esteemed than clams. In all seasons of the year,
at low tide, the women dug for them on the sea-shore.
The natural juices of this shellfish served them in place
of salt as a seasoning for their broth, their nassaump and
their bread, while the tenderness and delicacy of the flesh
have preserved its popularity to this day, amid all the
culinary devices of an advanced civilization. Whales,
sometimes sixty feet in length, were often cast up on the
shores, and being cut in pieces were sent far and near as
a most palatable present.

Their wigwams were made with long poles, usually
set in a circle and drawn nearly together at the upper
end, leaving a hole at the top to serve the double purpose of a window and chimney. This part was the work
of the men. The covering and lining was done by the
women. The summer houses were covered with birch or
chestnut bark finely dressed ; the winter ones with thick
mats woven by the women. The interior was lined with
mats fancifully embroidered. A house of sixteen feet
diameter would accommodate two families. Some of the
houses were oblong, and were designated by the number
of fires that could be made in them. The entrance was
closed by a hanging mat, although sometimes a door was
made of bark. They rarely fastened their wigwams, except when about to leave the town, in which case the last
one secured it on the inside by a cord and got out at the
chimney. It was a universal custom, which all the Indians strictly observed, to have small detached houses
where the women dwelt secluded during the term of their
monthly sickness, and no male ever entered these wigwams.[1] Their household furniture consisted of large

[1] It is very remarkable that, of all other nations of whom we have any
knowledge, the Jews alone held to this singular custom.

CHAP.
III.

1622.

hemp sacks, baskets, mats and earthenware, the products of female industry. They often removed their houses, in summer and winter, and for convenience in hunting, or for their agricultural labors, and always when a death occurred among them. The mats were easily transported, so that setting new poles was the only labor attending a removal, and a few hours sufficed to accomplish the whole. Of their houses erected for public purposes we have already written. They were larger and often more loosely constructed than their wigwams. The great council house of the Narragansets was fifty feet in diameter.

In personal appearance the Indians were very erect, with firm, compact bodies, high cheek bones, hazel eyes, straight black hair and light copper-colored complexion. They painted their faces, chiefly with a red pigment prepared from clay or the bark of the pine tree, the women for ornament, and the men, in war, to appear more terrible to their enemies. During the period of mourning, as before related, they besmeared their faces with soot or lampblack, and refrained from painting for decoration.

The Indian languages were remarkably rich and copious, regular in their inflections, and susceptible of combinations beyond almost any other known tongue. The native languages of North America have been reduced to four classes : 1, the Karalit, of the Esquimaux ; 2, the Delaware, of the East ; 3, the Iroquois, of the West, and 4, the Floridian, of the Gulf regions. They were divided into numerous dialects, of which those of New England were considered as varieties of the Delaware. The language of the Narragansets, to which Roger Williams' Key is devoted, was spoken, with more or less of idiomatic variation, over a region of country extending north and south from Rhode Island about six hundred miles.

Such was the condition of the aborigines of Rhode Island when a new and discordant element was engrafted

on their social and political system by the advent of the
English. Massasoit was the first to recognize the importance of this new element, and by formal treaty, to
enlist the English upon his side, in throwing off the yoke
of the Narragansets ; a treaty which his tribe preserved
inviolate for more than half a century, and was only
ruptured when the fiery spirit of Philip of Pokanoket, the
younger son of Massasoit, could no longer brook the wrong
and outrage heaped upon him by the whites. The Narragansets viewed with a jealous eye this dangerous alliance, and threatened the English with hostilities ; but
the bold attitude of the colonists averted the danger.

The Pequots, the ancient enemies of the Narragansets,
perhaps emboldened by the partial defection of the eastern Indians, and by the fact that Miantinomi, the younger
sachem of the Narragansets, was in his minority, embraced every opportunity to make war against them.
Block Island and Montauk fell into their hands, and
the Pequot conquest was extended ten miles east of
Pawcatuck river. But a fatal disaster was soon to overwhelm the Pequot tribe and to efface their name from off
the earth. A number of murders had been committed
in which it was proved that they had participated, either
directly or by affording shelter to the perpetrators. One
Captain Stone and his entire crew of ten men, in a ship
from Virginia, trading on the Connecticut river, were
murdered while asleep, and during a few months succeeding the death of Oldham some twenty more were
tortured and killed on Connecticut river. The murder
of John Oldham was the immediate cause of the Pequot
war. He was a daring trader with the Indians, and was
perhaps the first Englishman who contemplated settling
in Rhode Island. So highly was he esteemed by the Indians that Chibacuwese, afterwards sold to Gov. Winthrop and Roger Williams and called Prudence Island,
was freely offered to him as an inducement to establish

CHAP.
III.

1621.
March
22.

1622.
Jan.

1632.

1633.

1636.
July.

himself among them. Oldham, with two English boys and two Narraganset Indians, had been upon a trading voyage to the Connecticut river ; on his return, touching at Block Island, he was murdered and his companions carried off. John Gallup, who was also returning from the river in a small vessel, seeing Oldham's boat full of Indians near the island, bore up for it. The Indians made sail for the main land, but Gallup gallantly pursued them and, after a sharp contest, boarded the craft, driving most of the enemy into the sea. The mangled corpse of Oldham was found on board. His companions and most of the goods had already been taken away.

July
20.

26.

30.

Aug.
8.
13.
The news of this outrage reaching Boston caused great excitement. In a few days a deputation, including the two Indians who were with Oldham, arrived from Canonicus with a letter from Roger Williams to Gov. Vane, concerning the tragedy, and soon afterwards the two boys were safely returned to their homes, with another letter from Mr. Williams, stating that Miantinomi had sent an expedition to Block Island to recover the boys and the property, and to avenge the murder of Oldham. An embassy accompanied by Catshamekin, sachem of the Massachusetts, as interpreter, was sent to Canonicus to treat with him on the subject of the murder. Upon their return they reported " good success in their business," and that " they observed in the sachem much state, great command over his men, and marvellous wisdom in his answers and in the carriage of the whole treaty, clearing himself and his neighbors of the murder, and offering assistance for revenge of it, yet upon very safe and wary conditions." It was proved that some of the Narraganset sachems had been in the plot, but that their chiefs, Canonicus and Miantinomi, were not concerned in it.

An expedition, consisting of ninety volunteers, under command of John Endicott, was forthwith equipped to demand satisfaction of the Indians. They embarked in

three pinnaces, with orders to take Block Island, and
thence to proceed to the Pequot country to secure the
murderers of Captain Stone, to obtain indemnity for the
crime, and hostages for the future good conduct of the
Pequots. After a short skirmish they landed on the isl-
and, where they remained two days, and having burnt
the wigwams and staved the canoes, they left for the
Connecticut river. At Saybrook they received a reinforcement of twenty men and sailed for the Pequot harbor, at the mouth of Thames river. Sassacus, the chief
sachem, was absent at Long Island. A skirmish ensued,
in which some of the Indians were killed, their town was
burned, and the next day the wigwams on the opposite
side of the river were destroyed, and the canoes broken
up, after which the expedition returned in safety to Boston without the loss of a man. By this affair the Pequots
had fourteen killed and forty wounded, and were greatly
exasperated. The policy of this hostile expedition has
been severely condemned by Lieut. Gardiner, commander
of Fort Saybrook, in his history of the war. Had the
instructions to Endicott limited his powers to the Oldham
matter, the settlers of Connecticut might not have suffered so much from the fury of the Indians. The governor of Plymouth remonstrated with the Massachusetts
authorities for having needlessly provoked a war.

But the mischief was already done. The Pequots
were thoroughly roused, and wreaked their vengeance, in
the ensuing winter, upon the defenceless inhabitants of
Connecticut. They also sent ambassadors to the Narragansets, with whom they had been in perpetual enmity,
offering to bury the hatchet, and proposing a league with
them and the Mohegans to effect the utter destruction of
the English, and thereby to avert the calamity which
they foresaw must soon annihilate the Indian race. It
was a perilous hour for New England when the envoys of
Sassacus opened their negotiations with the assembled

CHAP.
III.
1636.

Oct.

court of their ancient foe, the wary and thoughtful Canonicus. Right was on the side of the Pequots—the right to the lordship of the soil, in which the rapid encroachment of the whites must soon restrict them. National existence depended upon a prompt and united effort to extirpate the race whose moral superiority was already asserted in reducing the aboriginal princes of the eastern tribes to a state of vassalage. Life, liberty, and the pursuit of happiness, the same considerations which in the next century were urged as the inalienable rights of man, in the struggle with the mother country, were as clearly understood by the Indians, and were no less dear to them than to their enemies, while to these arguments there was the added bitterness of a conflict of races. Every inducement that could be brought to bear upon the case was skilfully employed by the Pequot emissaries to attain their end. The decision was one that involved results equally momentous to the Indians and the English, and already the truthful eloquence of the Pequots seemed about to prevail in the wavering council of the Narragansets.

At this imminent crisis Roger Williams appeared among them. He was the only man in New England who could avert the impending evil. His own life, and that of the few who were with him, was secure in the love of the Narragansets. Still, though smarting under the injuries of recent oppression, he threw himself between his own persecutors and their relentless foes. At the risk of his life, from the Pequot tomahawks and the perils of the way, he sought the wigwam of Canonicus, and accomplished, what a high authority has pronounced " the most intrepid and most successful achievement of the whole war ; an action as perilous in its execution as it was fortunate in its issue."[1] At the earnest request of the Boston magistrates, now seriously alarmed at the

---

[1] 1 Bancroft, 398.

aspect of affairs, Williams undertook this dangerous mission.   His own words can best describe the nature and result of his labors :—

"Upon letters received from the Governor and Council at Boston, requesting me to use my utmost and speediest endeavors to break and hinder the league labored for by the Pequots and Mohegans against the English, (excusing the not sending of company and supplies by the haste of the business,) the Lord helped me immediately to put my life into my hand, and scarce acquainting my wife, to ship myself alone, in a poor canoe, and to cut through a stormy wind, with great seas, every minute in hazard of life, to the sachem's house.   Three days and nights my business forced me to lodge and mix with the bloody Pequot ambassadors, whose hands and arms, methought, reeked with the blood of my countrymen, murdered and massacred by them on Connecticut river, and from whom I could not but nightly look for their bloody knives at my own throat also.   God wondrously preserved me, and helped me to break to pieces the Pequots' negotiation and design ; and to make and finish, by many travels and charges, the English league with the Narragansets and Mohegans against the Pequots."[1]

[1] Letter to Maj. Mason.   It is a singular fact that Winthrop alone, of all the old writers upon this war, makes any mention of the part performed by Roger Williams in averting a fatal catastrophe.   Had not the well-laid plan of the Pequots been frustrated by the influence of Williams, the result of this earliest American war of extermination would, according to all human calculation, have been reversed.   Yet none of the Massachusetts historians, before the present day, have had the candor to admit the fact.   We can excuse the military writers, Mason, Underhill, Vincent and Gardiner, for the omission, as they aim chiefly to describe the active hostilities in which themselves bore a part ; but that Morton, Hubbard, Johnson, Mather, Hutchinson, and others, who give a more or less detailed account of the negotiations connected with the war, should omit all mention of the debt of gratitude they owed to the founder of Rhode Island upon that occasion, is somewhat remarkable.   Even the liberal Prince in his preface to Mason's history simply says, "An agency from the Massachusetts colony to the Narragansets happily preserved their staggering friendship ;" leaving us to apply the remark either to the deputation sent on

CHAP.
III.
1 6 3 6.
Oct.
21.

22.

1 6 3 7.
April
1.

April
23.

Upon the conclusion of this all-important negotiation, Miantinomi, being sent for by Gov. Vane, went to Boston, together with two sons of Canonicus, another sachem, and nearly twenty attendants. He was received with military honors, and the preliminaries of a treaty being at once agreed upon, it was formally concluded the next day, when the Indians were dismissed in the same manner. It was a treaty of amity, and of alliance, offensive and defensive against the Pequots ; and, because the Indians could not perfectly comprehend all the articles, it was agreed that a copy should be sent to Mr. Williams, who could best interpret it. This management was honorable alike to Mr. Williams and to the government of Massachusetts. It showed the confidence which both the contracting parties placed in the good faith of their interpreter, and it attests the integrity of the Puritans that they should submit an instrument of such importance to the scrutiny of so strenuous an advocate of Indian rights.

The Pequots, foiled in their attempt, both with the Narragansets and the Mohegans, rashly resolved to prosecute the war unaided. The garrison of Fort Saybrook was constantly alarmed by their menaces. Capt. Underhill, with twenty men, was sent to the relief. The massacre at Weathersfield, where six were killed and seven taken prisoners and tortured, followed by another slaugh-

the 8th August, (which Johnson, one of the above-named writers, seems to have accompanied, and Williams did not,) or to the later and more dangerous mission in October, undertaken by Williams alone, whose name, in either case, is not even mentioned. There is a maxim of Rochefoucault, which is verified in this instance ; " Il n'est pas si dangereuse de faire du mal a la plupart des hommes, que de leur faire trop de bien." Gov. Winthrop and some of his council, in view of the signal services rendered by Mr. Williams throughout the war, moved in the General Court, that he be recalled from banishment and honored by some high mark of favor. The silence of the court records upon the question is *significant*. But ample, though tardy, justice has since been rendered to the memory of Williams by a son of Massachusetts. The elegant historian of the United States has more than atoned for the want of magnanimity in his literary predecessors, by the generous spirit displayed in the ninth chapter of his eloquent work.

ter of nine persons, and the capture of two young girls,
decided the infant colony of Connecticut to declare war
without delay. Three small towns, Hartford, Windsor
and Weathersfield, which had been organized scarcely a
year, and contained in all much less than two hundred
men, formed the whole colony of Connecticut. The Pequots could muster nearly a thousand warriors, and had
two fortified villages, one on the Mystic river, near the
sea, and the other but a few miles distant, where Sassacus, the chief sachem, dwelt. A force of ninety men,
under Capt. John Mason, was immediately despatched to
the scene of conflict, accompanied by Uncas, sachem of
the Mohegans, with about sixty of his warriors. All
doubts of the fidelity of these savage allies, who preceded
the main body to Fort Saybrook, were speedily dispelled.
The Mohegans vanquished a party of Pequots near the
fort, and brought in the scalps of the slain as trophies of
their prowess. From Saybrook, Mason, being reinforced
by Capt. Underhill, sent home twenty of his troops, while
the main body sailed for Narraganset bay, designing to
surprise the Pequots in the rear. The forces reached a
harbor near Wickford on Saturday, passed the Sabbath
in religious exercises, were detained two days more on
board their vessels by a northwest gale, and then after
two days of severe march across the country, and being
joined by a strong force of the Narragansets, they encamped on Thursday night near Fort Mystic.
　　The Pequots spent their last night in carousal, exulting over the English, who they supposed, from seeing the
vessels sail by some days before, had abandoned the attack. Their songs were distinctly heard at the English
outposts until midnight. At daybreak the English, in
two divisions, assaulted the fort. The Indian allies, except Uncas and one other, remained behind through fear of
their redoubtable foe. The Pequots were buried in profound slumber. The crash of musketry roused them to

inevitable doom, as the English, bursting through the palisade of sticks and brushwood, rushed upon them sword in hand. It was the intention to put the garrison to the sword and to save the plunder, but this plan was changed. The Indians, as fast as they awoke either crept under the beds or fled, when Mason gave the terrible order, " WE MUST BURN THEM," and seizing a firebrand from one of the wigwams applied it to the matted roof. A northeast wind was blowing at the time. The fire spread with great rapidity, soon involving the whole village in conflagration. Some of the Pequots, climbing the palisades to escape, were shot down by the English ; others rushed wildly into the flames and perished by fire ; a few boldly charged upon the enemy and fell by the sword. The allied Indians were stationed in a circle at a distance and killed with their arrows the few, who, fleeing unscathed from their fiery furnace, had escaped the triple peril of shot and flame and steel. The massacre was complete. One short hour had done the work, and when the sun arose, a heap of smouldering ruins, over the mangled and crisping corpses of nearly seven hundred Indians, was all that remained of this stronghold of the Pequots. Men, women, and children fell alike in this indiscriminate and wholesale slaughter. Of the hundreds who an hour before were slumbering in fancied security, seven only were taken captive and but seven escaped. The loss of the English was but two killed and twenty wounded.

As they were leaving the ground a party of three hundred Indians from the other fort advanced to the attack, ignorant of the fate of their comrades. Upon reaching the spot they gave way to the wildest demonstrations of grief, and then rushing down the hill, charged upon the retiring English whose ammunition was nearly exhausted. A few skirmishers sufficed to keep them at bay, while the English reached the harbor just as their vessels, coming round from Narraganset, had entered it. There they met

Capt. Patric with forty Massachusetts troops. Underhill placed the wounded on board a vessel and sailed for Connecticut river. The remaining troops marched across the country, and were "nobly entertained by Lieut. Gardner with many great guns," upon reaching Fort Saybrook the next evening. A day of thanksgiving for this signal victory was held in all the churches.

CHAP.
III.

1637.
May
27.

June
15.

About a month after the battle of Mystic Capt. Staughton with one hundred and twenty men arrived in Pequot river to continue the war, and was joined by Mason with forty men from Connecticut. The remnant of the Pequot tribe concealed themselves in swamps or fled to the westward. One of their hiding-places was broken up and one hundred Indians taken. The men were killed, the women and children distributed among the Narragansets, and sent to Boston as slaves. The troops pursued the main body of the fugitives to a swamp near New Haven. Surrounding the swamp they held a parley with the Indians, resulting in the surrender of the old men, women and children, not belonging to the Pequot tribe, to the number of two hundred. The warriors resolved to fight it out, and some sixty of them succeeded during the night in breaking through the English lines, after an obstinate struggle, and effected their escape. One hundred and eighty were taken prisoners. In this fight it is said that a few of the Indians had fire-arms, which is the first account we have of their use by the natives.

July
13.

This encounter virtually closed the war. Sassacus, the great sachem, whose name but a few months before had been a terror to both whites and Indians in New England, was murdered, with twenty of his men, by the Mohegans, to whom he fled for shelter, and a part of his skin with a lock of his hair was sent as a welcome present to Boston. The Massachusetts troops returned home with only the loss of one man. The Pequots now became a prey to their savage foes and were hunted down like wolves, the

Aug
26.

CHAP.
III.

1637.
Oct.
12.

1638.
Sept.
21.
allied Indians daily bringing in their heads or hands to the
English. A general thanksgiving was observed throughout New England for the successful termination of the
war. The miserable remnant of the tribe delivered themselves up at Hartford on condition that their lives should
be spared. More than eight hundred had been slain in the
war, and less than two hundred remained to share the
fate of captives. These were distributed among the Narragansets and Mohegans, with the pledge that they
should no more be called Pequots, nor inhabit their native country again.[1] To make the annihilation of the race
yet more complete, their very name was extinguished in
Connecticut by legislative act. Pequot river was called
the Thames, Pequot town was named New London.

Thus perished the race and name of the Pequots.
The first aboriginal tribe who defied the English power,
had fallen in the desperate struggle for liberty and life.
In their fate they were but the precursors of a long line
of Indian races who were, one after another, to disappear
as the gathering tide of European civilization swept onward to the west. In quick succession from the Atlantic
to the Alleghanies, and thence to the Mississippi, the
native tribes have melted away ; and westward still, from
the river to the Rocky Mountains, the fatal tide flows
swiftly on, driving before it the few whom it does not
slay. Already it breaks in narrow streams through those
mountain passes, until the far west is no longer the undisturbed home of the red man. A few years more will
see the fate of the Pequots repeated on our western
shores ; the great tragedy of New England will be re-
acted on the hills of Oregon ; the "notes of the last
aboriginal death song shall mingle with the murmur of
the Pacific."

---

[1] Trumbull's Hist. of Connecticut, vi. pp. 92, 93, Book 1, ch. v.

CHAPTER IV.

HISTORY OF PROVIDENCE FROM ITS SETTLEMENT, 1636, TO THE
ORGANIZATION OF THE GOVERNMENT UNDER THE PARLIA-
MENTARY CHARTER, MAY, 1647.

THE original companions of Roger Williams, by his own account, were four in number, William Harris, John Smith, Francis Wickes, and a lad whom tradition asserts to be Thomas Angel. [1] By a letter from Joshua Verin, on the town records, it appears that he also accompanied the above named persons to Providence, as he speaks of "we six which came first." This apparent discrepancy is readily explained. The four persons named by Williams probably joined him in his first planting at Seekonk, while Verin came later but in season to remove with them across the river, and thus to become one of the six original settlers of Providence.

That it was not the intention of Roger Williams, in seeking a refuge in the wilderness, to become the founder of a State, his own declaration proves. Driven from the society of civilized men, who showed little sympathy with the enlightened and progressive views that placed him so

CHAP.
IV.

1636.

---

[1] " My soul's desire was to do the natives good, and to that end to have their language, (which I afterwards printed,) and therefore desired not to be troubled with English company, yet out of pity I gave leave to William Harris, then poor and destitute, to come along in my company. I consented to John Smith, miller at Dorchester, (banished, also,) to go with me, and at John Smith's desire, to a poor young fellow, Francis Wickes, as also to a lad of Richard Waterman's. These are all I remember."—*R. Williams' Answer to W. Harris before the Court of Commissioners, 17th Nov., 1677.*

far in advance of his age, his earnest, toiling spirit, sought among the savages a field of action, and their debased condition presented a fitting object for his philanthropy. Had his only motive been to escape from the vexations of a discordant community he would have refused, even against the plea of pity, all English companionship, and, like Blackstone, [1] who at the quiet retreat of Study Hill, had preceded him to Rhode Island, would have found, in communion with nature in her solitude, that rest which human fellowship denied. But the Supreme Ruler of events had ordered otherwise. The missionary spirit which led Williams to devote his energies to the good of the Indians, gave him that hold upon their affection and esteem which enabled him to dwell securely among them, and to acquire that ascendency in their councils which afterwards made him the averter of war, and the virtual protector of New England. The humanity of his disposi-

[1] There is a mystery in the life of Wm. Blackstone which probably can never be explained. When and how he came to America is unknown. The first planters of Massachusetts Bay found him already established, the earliest English settler on the peninsula of Shawmut, now Boston, where he planted an orchard, the first in Massachusetts. He was a clergyman of the church of England, and no doubt left his native country on account of nonconformity, the same reason that led him soon after to seek a home for the second time in the wilderness, when he used this memorable expression : " I left England to get from under the power of the lord bishops, but in America I am fallen under the power of the lord brethren." At his suggestion the larger portion of the colonists of 1630, who had settled at Charlestown, removed to Boston. In 1634 he sold out his title to Shawmut, each inhabitant paying him sixpence, and some of them more, and, purchasing cattle, removed soon after to a spot named by him " Study Hill," within what is known as " the Attleboro' Gore," in Plymouth patent, now in the south part of the town of Cumberland, R. I., near the banks of the Pawtucket river. He thus became the first settler of Rhode Island, if we except the three English referred to in Winthrop's Journal, (1, 72) as occupying a house at Sowamset, now Warren, which was attacked by Indians in April, 1632, and as this seems to have been but a temporary trading post, such as were frequently set up in the Indian country, and not a permanent settlement, such as Blackstone's was, no other reference being anywhere made to it, the honor here claimed properly belongs to the proprietor of Study Hill. At the time of his removal he is supposed to have resided at Shawmut about ten years. Lechford says,

tion prompted him so far to vary his exclusive design in favor of the Indians, out of pity to those who had likewise suffered persecution in Massachusetts, that, contrary to his own desire, he brought with him a small but resolute band of immigrants and thereby formed the nucleus of a State. These were soon joined by others, but at what precise time or in what numbers it is now impossible to know. Many of the records were lost, probably in the burning of the town during Philip's war, and those which are still preserved were but imperfectly kept.

The earliest deed upon record is in the form of a memorandum dated the twenty-fourth of March in the second year of the plantation. It refers to a sale made two years previous, of the lands upon Mooshausick and Wanasquatucket rivers, by Canonicus and Miantinomi to Roger Williams, confirming the same, and by its terms extending the grant on either side so as to include

---

" One Master Blackstone, a minister, went from Boston, having lived there nine or ten years, because he would not join with the church ; he lives near Master Williams, but is far from his opinions," p. 42—*Plaine Dealing, London,* 1641. He lived peacefully at his new plantation the remainder of his days. Here he planted an apple orchard, the first that ever bore fruit in Rhode Island. " He had the first of that sort called yellow sweetings that were ever in the world perhaps, the richest and most delicious apple of the whole kind." (2 M. H. C. ix. 174.) Many of his trees planted one hundred and thirty years before were still in bearing when Gov. Hopkins wrote in 1765, and Mr. Newman in his Discourse on 4th July, 1855, before the Blackstone Monument Association, says that as late as 1830 three of these trees were living, and two of them bore apples. They were then nearly two centuries old! He frequently came to Providence to preach the Gospel, " and to encourage his younger hearers gave them the first apples they ever saw." When no longer able to travel on foot he rode on a bull that he had broken to the saddle. His wife, Mrs. Sarah Blackstone, died in June, 1673. His own death occurred May 26th, 1675, at an advanced age, having resided probably more than fifty years in New England. He was spared from witnessing the desolation of his place, and the burning of his house and library by the Indians in Philip's war, which broke out a few days after his decease. He left but one child, John, for whom guardians were appointed by Plymouth government in 1675. His family is now extinct. An inventory of his estate, taken ten days after his death, is contained in 2 M. H. C. x. 172. The name was originally spelt Blaxton.

all the land between Pawtucket and Pawtuxet rivers, with the grass and meadows upon the latter stream. This extended grant is made "in consideration of the many kindnesses and services he hath continually done for us," and the instrument is signed by the original grantors. A memorandum appended the following year states that this was all again confirmed by Miantinomi, "up the streams of Pawtucket and Pawtuxet without limits we might have for the use of our cattle." By this document it appears that the sole title to all the lands vested in Roger Williams. When years afterwards a bitter dispute arose among the settlers, in which the opponents of Williams denied his exclusive original title to the lands, he wrote, "they were mine own as truly as any man's coat upon his back." Nor was it true, as alleged, that the purchase was made by him as agent of the company. The sources of his ability to treat with the Indians, and the reasons of his having any companions at all in his settlement, as above recited, are sufficient proof, apart from his own positive statements, that his assertion upon these points is correct. But it was not his intention to secure to himself the exclusive advantage which his position afforded him. Soon after the purchase he executed a deed giving an equal share with himself to twelve of his companions "and such others as the major part of us shall admit into the same fellowship of vote with us." It was a simple memorandum, like the first Indian deed, without date, and known as the "initial deed," from its containing simply the initials of the grantees. These were Stukely Westcott, William Arnold, Thomas James, Robert Cole, John Greene, John Throckmorton, William Harris, William Carpenter, Thomas Olney, Francis Weston, Richard Waterman, Ezekiel Holyman, who, with Roger Williams, the grantor, form the thirteen original proprietors of Providence.

This remained for more than twenty years the only

evidence of title possessed by the town, until Dec., 1661, when Mr. Williams executed a more formal conveyance by request of the citizens, and five years later he executed still another deed, being an exact transcript of the " initial deed," except that the names of the grantees were given in full, and the instrument was dated the 8th of 8th month, 1638, to conform as nearly as possible with the time the original was given.   The sole object of this instrument appears to be to explain the first one as to date and names.[1]   It will be observed that only two of the original settlers appear as proprietors by this deed. Of the remaining four, two at least were minors, one, Verin, had already abandoned the settlement and returned to Massachusetts, while the non-appearance of John Smith, the miller, as a copartner in the deed, is not easily explained.   Some of the grantees it is known did not leave Massachusetts until 1638.   But all of them, the six settlers and thirteen proprietors, being seventeen persons, had lots assigned them, together with many others, fifty-four in all, in the first division of land which took place soon after the " initial deed " was accepted.   The proprietors divided the lands into two parts, one called " the grand purchase of Providence," the other " the Pawtuxet purchase."   In the first of these divisions fifty-four names appear as the owners of " home lots," as they were called, extending from " the town street," now North and South Main streets, eastward to Hope street, beside which each person had a six acre lot assigned to him in other parts of the purchase, some on the banks of the Seekonk, where Roger Williams' out lot was located, at Whatcheer, the farthest north of all, and some on the Wanasquatucket river.[2]   The division known as the " Pawtuxet purchase," which from the beauty of its meadow

---

[1] See Staple's Annals of Providence, pp. 26, 28, 30, 33, for these deeds.

[2] The grantees were prohibited from selling to any but an inhabitant without consent of the town, and a penalty was imposed upon such as did not improve their grounds.

lands soon began to be settled,[1] was the source of long and angry contention in the subsequent history of the colony, as will hereafter appear.[2]

The government established by these primitive settlers of Providence was an anomaly in the history of the world. At the outset it was a pure democracy, which for the first time guarded jealously the rights of conscience by ignoring any power in the body politic to interfere with those matters that alone concern man and his Maker. The inhabitants, " masters of families," incorporated themselves into a town and made an order that no man should be molested for his conscience. As yet there was no delegated power. The little community had not swelled to the dimensions that required a division of labor in the conduct of public affairs. The people met monthly in town meeting, and chose a clerk and treasurer at each meeting. It is much to be regretted that the records of the town were so loosely kept.[2] An experiment like this, which had no precedent to furnish in doubtful cases a criterion of action, must have often presented questions of the deepest importance to the colonists, in the decision of which there could be no other guide than their own clear minds. Principle, not precedent, formed their only stand-

[1] The first settlers of Pawtuxet were Wm. Arnold, Wm. Carpenter, Zechariah Rhodes and Wm. Harris, who removed from Providence in 1638.

[2] The details of the various divisions of land in the town and vicinity, and the localities assigned to individual proprietors, so far as they can now be ascertained, are given in Judge Staple's Annals of Providence, and are not repeated here because they belong more properly to a local history of the town, which has already been most diligently prepared in the aforenamed book, than to a general history of the State.

[3] The only officer whose election is recorded is Thomas Olney, Treasurer. The earliest record is dated 16th of 4th mo., (June,) but without year. It provides for a fine upon all persons who may be more than fifteen minutes late at town-meeting, and but three other entries are made under that year, the last of which, dated 3d of 10th month, is but a repetition of the first memorandum. The next page is headed " Agreements and Orders of the 2d year of the Plantation," under which but seven entries are made, all relating to grants of land and preservation of timber, and but three have a date affixed.

ard of judgment. Could the record of their proceedings
have been preserved, with what interest should we now
peruse the debates of this earliest of modern democracies !
The first written compact that has come down to us is as
follows : " We whose names are hereunder, desirous to
inhabit in the town of Providence, do promise to subject
ourselves in active or passive obedience to all such orders
or agreements as shall be made for public good of the
body, in an orderly way, by the major assent of the present inhabitants, masters of families, incorporated together
into a town fellowship, and such others whom they shall
admit unto them, only in civil things."   It is signed by
thirteen persons—Richard Scott, William × Reynolds,
John × Field, Chad. Brown, John Warner, George Rick-
ard, Edward Cope, Thomas × Angell, Thomas × Harris,
Francis × Wickes, Benedict Arnold, Joshua Winsor,
William Wickenden.   The five with the mark × affixed,
signed by their mark, but whether through inability to
write their names, or from some other cause, may be questioned, as we know that at that period instruments having
more than one signature were often thus signed by some
of the parties who knew how to write.   This agreement
is without date on the original record.   It refers in terms
to an agreement between the first settlers and to their incorporation into a town fellowship, and is therefore presumed to be the agreement of the " second comers "—a
view strengthened by the fact that it is signed by T. Angell and F. Wickes, who came with R. Williams, but being, according to tradition, minors, were not named in
Mr. Williams' deed, and now, having attained their majority, they take this occasion to sign the compact of citizenship.   The parties bind themselves " only in civil
things," thus securing the rights of conscience inviolate
as their predecessors had done.   The different and often
conflicting views of the members of this infant State upon
the exciting topics which caused their exile, and the un-

tried principles upon which their settlement was made, would afford a curious example of diversity of thought and action converging to the same great end. Unfortunately our only authorities upon these subjects are the scattered and often biassed statements from the chronicles of Massachusetts. The fairest of these annalists has preserved a fragment of discussion, so curious as an illustration of the nature of the difficulties which must have been constantly arising in the colony, and of the shrewd, practical character of the people in their solution of knotty questions, that we transcribe it. "At Providence, also, the devil was not idle. For whereas at their first coming thither, Mr. Williams and the rest did make an order that no man should be molested for his conscience, now men's wives, and children, and servants, claiming liberty hereby to go to all religious meetings, though never so often, or though private, upon the week days ; and because one Verin refused to let his wife go to Mr. Williams' so often as she was called for, they required to have him censured. But there stood up one Arnold, a witty man of their own company, and withstood it, telling them that, when he consented to that order, he never intended it should extend to the breach of any ordinance of God, such as the subjection of wives to their husbands, etc., and gave divers solid reasons against it. Then one Greene replied that if they should restrain their wives, etc., all the women in the country would cry out of them, etc. Arnold answered him thus : Did you pretend to leave the Massachusetts because you would not offend God to please men, and would you now break an ordinance and commandment of God to please women ? Some were of opinion that if Verin would not suffer his wife to have her liberty, the church should dispose her to some other man who would use her better. Arnold told them that it was not the woman's desire to go so oft from home, but only Mr. Williams' and others. In conclusion, when they would have censured Verin, Arnold told them that it was against their own order, for Verin did that he did out of conscience ; and their order was that no man should be censured for his conscience." This then is the earliest record we have of the struggle between liberty and law, the rival elements which Rhode Island was to reconcile in the novel experiment of a self-governed State. The only entry referring to it upon the town books is in these words : "It was agreed that Joshua Verin, upon the breach of a covenant for restraining of the libertie of conscience, shall be withheld from the libertie of voting till he shall declare the contrarie." Here was a case involving the cardinal principle of the Rhode Island settlers with the most delicate subject of family regulation. One of greater difficulty could not well be imagined. On the supposition that Mrs. Verin felt bound in conscience to attend the meetings, and did so without detriment to her domestic duties, the restraint imposed by her husband was a violation of the Rhode Island principle, and as such the punishment was correctly administered, although the report, as given by Winthrop, doubtless derived from Verin himself, naturally gives the best of the argument to the latter.

About this time Mr. Williams, jointly with Gov. Winthrop, purchased of Canonicus the island of Chibachuweset, which had formerly been offered by the Indians to John Oldham, on condition that he would settle there for purposes of trade, which he failed to do. This he named Prudence, and two smaller islands adjacent, which he soon after purchased, he called Patience and Hope. These lands, with other property, he afterwards sold to meet his expenses in England when on service for the colony. Gov. Winthrop retained his half of Prudence island, and left it in his will to his son Stephen.[1]

CHAP.
I.

1637.

May
21.

Nov.
10.

---

[1] 3 M. H C. i. 165. Knowles' R. W. 124. The deed of Prudence island is dated 10th Nov. R. I. H. C. iii. 29. Williams' letter to Gov. Winthrop on the subject is dated Oct. 28th.

The annals of crime have rarely contained a more atrocious murder than was committed near Providence, upon the person of an Indian, by four English from Plymouth in the following summer. The murderers were taken at Aquidneck, and Mr. Williams, writing to Gov. Winthrop for advice as to where they should be tried, gives the particulars of the tragedy.[1] One escaped. The remaining three were sent to Plymouth, tried and executed. The chief interest of the affair at this day relates to the question of jurisdiction, and to the diverse reasons assigned for having the trial at Plymouth. Williams thought they should be tried at Aquidneck, where they were taken, and if not they should be sent to Plymouth, where they belonged. The Aquidneck settlers desired to send them to Providence, where the crime was committed, and this certainly was the correct view. Gov. Winthrop advised that they be delivered to Plymouth if sent for, otherwise that the ringleader be given up to the Indians, and the other three be detained till further consideration, and gives as his reasons that there was no English jurisdiction where the crime was committed, and no government at the island where the criminals were arrested.[2] Plymouth also applied to Massachusetts for advice, and the Secretary assigns opposite reasons from those given by Gov. Winthrop himself for his advice, and very different ones from any that could have influenced the Aquidneck people in surrendering the prisoners. He says the Massachusetts refused to try them because the crime was committed within the jurisdiction of Plymouth, and that the Rhode Island men having taken them, delivered them to Plymouth " on the same grounds."[3]

The birth of Mr. Williams' eldest son, said to be the first male child born of English parents in Rhode Island, took place in the autumn of this year. He was named

[1] 3 M. H. C. iii. 170–3.   [2] Winthrop's Journal, i. 267.
[3] Morton's Memorial, p. 208.

Providence. The first English child born in the colony was a female, in the same year, but a few months previous to the birth of Providence Williams.

The period had now arrived when a church was to be organized in the new plantations. That religious services had not previously been neglected in their exile, we may fairly infer from the character of the people and the earnest nature of their leader, himself an ordained preacher of the Gospel, as also was Thomas James, another of the original proprietors. And we know too that Mr. Blackstone, also a regular minister, residing within six miles of Providence, was in the habit of visiting the settlement for this purpose. As the views entertained by the Providence colonists differed so widely from those of their Puritan brethren in other respects, a similar variance may be looked for in their religious belief; and as they had instituted a civil government on principles entirely novel in that age, so were they about to establish an ecclesiastical system, approaching, more nearly, as they considered, to that of the primitive church, than any then existing in the new world. Gov. Winthrop says : " Many of Boston and others, who were of Mrs. Hutchinson's judgment and party, removed to the isle of Aquiday ; and others, who were of the rigid separation, and savored anabaptism, removed to Providence, so as those parts began to be well peopled." Some time between this date and the following spring, when the account of the baptism of Williams, Holliman and ten others, is recorded by Winthrop, the event then related occurred, which places the formation of the first Baptist church in America probably in the autumn of 1638, and certainly prior to the 16th of March, 1639.[2]

CHAP. IV.

1638.

Aug. 3.

1638-9. March 16.

---

[1] These twelve were Roger Williams, Ezekiel Holliman, William Arnold, William Harris, Stukely Westcott, John Green, Richard Waterman, Thomas James, Robert Cole, William Carpenter, Francis Weston and Thomas Olney. —*Benedict's History of Baptists*, i. 473.

[2] An interesting discussion occurred a few years since between the First

CHAP.
IV.

1640.

July
27.

The growth of the colony soon rendered a purely democratic government impracticable. Too onerous for the individual and too feeble for the purposes of the State, it was reluctantly and cautiously abandoned. The jealousy of delegated power is conspicuous in the instrument that authorized it, as well as in the frequent elections by which it provided for a choice of the " disposers." The necessity of some change was apparent, and a committee was appointed by the inhabitants of Providence to consider certain difficulties that had arisen in regard to a division of the lands, to adjust the same, and to report a form of future government for the action of the town. This report, consisting of twelve articles of agreement, was accepted by the people, thirty-nine of whose signatures are attached to the only copy in existence, certified by the town clerk twenty-two years later.[1] It was but a slight departure from the primitive democracy, still it

Baptist Churches of Providence and Newport, the latter claiming seniority, contrary to received opinions and the records of the Warren Association. A report to the Association was made in 1849, stating the grounds of the Newport claim. This report was ably refuted by the Rev. Drs. Granger and Caswell and Prof. Gammell, a committee in behalf of the Providence church, and their review presented to the Warren Association at its next annual meeting, Sept. 12th, 1850, and printed in pamphlet form soon after. In November of the same year, Rev. S. Adlam, pastor of the Newport church, published a pamphlet entitled, " The First Baptist Church in Providence Not the oldest of the Baptists in America." This is a very ingenious attempt to show, 1st, That the present First Baptist Church is not the original church referred to in the text, but a seceder from an older church. 2d, That this older church disappeared about 1718, and 3d, That the Newport church is older than either of them. The last proposition, at least, proves too much, for Winthrop settles the fact of the formation of a Baptist church at Providence prior to 16th March, 1639, while the town of Newport was not founded till May 1st, six weeks afterward. Many of the facts relied on to sustain these positions will be found to be already answered in the committee's Review, and the additional statements are well weighed by Rev. Henry Jackson, D. D., in " Churches in Rhode Island," pp. 15–22, 79–85, 95 and 122, 23. Mr. Adlam's pamphlet is a fine specimen of historical reasoning, requiring an intimate knowledge of the times and subject, and some experience in critical analysis, to detect the errors in its premises and the consequent fallacy of its conclusions.

[1] Staple's Annals, p. 40–3.

forms an era in our colonial history, and for several years constituted the town government.

The first article fixes the bounds between Pawtuxet proprietors and those of Providence. The second prescribes that five men be appointed by the town to dispose of the common lands, and to do the general business of the town, but in receiving freemen they are first to notify the inhabitants, lest any objections should exist against the applicant. If any one felt aggrieved by the action of the " disposers," he could appeal to the town meeting. A town clerk was to be chosen in addition to these five selectmen, and the guaranty of liberty of conscience is again expressly given. The next two articles provide for the settlement of all private difficulties by arbitration, and empowered the five disposers to appoint arbitrators when either of the disputants refuses to do so. The fifth requires all the inhabitants to unite in pursuit of any delinquent. The sixth enables any party, aggrieved by the acts of any one of the " disposers," to call a town meeting, in case of an emergency. By the seventh article all land conveyances from the town were to be made by the five selectmen. The next two articles provide for monthly meetings of the selectmen or " disposers," and quarterly meetings of the town, at which the former were to render their accounts and a new election to be had. The fees of the clerk and his term of office, to be one year, are the subjects of the tenth article. The eleventh quiets all prior land titles. The last article levies a tax of thirty shillings upon all inhabitants of the town.

The provisions for elections, and for a revision of the acts of the " disposers" at quarterly town meetings, and for extra town meetings in the brief intervals, to redress any private grievance inflicted by the selectmen, or any one of them, are remarkable proofs of the tenacity with which the founders of Providence held in their own hands the reins of delegated power. The largest liberty of the

citizen, civil as well as religious, consistent with the existence of society, was their cherished object, and one which
they protected with the jealousy of men escaped from the
tyranny of a church and state combination.   But the
element of strength which it was sought to embody in the
new system was not there.   The passions of men were
not restrained, and the crude ideas of many who sought
the new colony as a refuge from oppression, were not definitely shaped by this new agreement.   Latitude of opinion upon fundamental points of civil government still
existed.   Theories subversive of all legal restraint were
broached, and although the angry discussions which they
produced resulted in the triumph of social order, they
gave occasion for the calumny that " at Providence they
denied all magistracy and churches."   The doctrine that
conscience was to be the sole guide of the individual, in
civil as well as in religious matters, was held by some who
did not see clearly the distinction as it existed in the
mind of Roger Williams.   In the neighboring colonies
these perversions of the idea of soul liberty were magni-
fied, and the disorder that threatened during the discussions, which finally ended in the united triumph of religious liberty, and social law, was misrepresented as the result of the established system in the State.   Any attempt
to enforce the laws was attended with danger to the existence of the settlement, so much so, that on several occasions aid from abroad was solicited to sustain the decisions of arbitrators legally appointed, in accordance with
the new form of government.   The earliest instance of
this impolitic action is found in a letter from thirteen of
the colonists addressed to the Massachusetts, complaining
of the conduct of Gorton and his partisans, one of whom,
Francis Weston, had refused to submit to the " arbitration of eight men orderly chosen."   To enforce their decree a levy was made on Weston's cattle.   A riot ensued,
in which some blood was spilt and a rescue effected by his

friends, who then openly declared that a similar result should follow any attempt to attach any property of theirs. The writers urge the necessity of the case as the reason for their asking assistance and advice. In reply the government of Massachusetts declined to send aid, because they " could not levy any war without a general Court ; " and " for counsel, that except they did submit themselves to some jurisdiction, either Plymouth, or ours, we had no calling or warrant to interpose in their contentions, but if they were once subject to any, then they had a calling to protect them." How such a submission by any inhabitants of Rhode Island could operate to extend the Massachusetts charter beyond its prescribed limits, or, if it could do so, how any of the people could invite such a usurpation we cannot understand.

A few months after this affair four of the principal inhabitants, then resident at Pawtuxet, dissatisfied with the conduct of Gorton and his company, who had moved to their neighborhood, offered themselves and their lands to the government and protection of Massachusetts, and were received by the General Court. These were William Arnold, Robert Cole, William Carpenter and Benedict Arnold. The first three were among the original purchasers. The last was the son of the first-named. They were appointed by the General Court as justices of the peace.[1] Thus a foreign jurisdiction was set up in the very midst of the infant colony, which greatly increased the difficulties of its existence, and continued for sixteen years to harass the inhabitants of Providence, and threaten the peace of Rhode Island long after the Parliamentary charter had secured to the people the right of self-government.[2] The motives of the Court in this act are

---

[1] Mass. Col. Rec. 2, 27.

[2] It was not till 1658 that this unnatural condition of things was terminated upon the petition of Wm. Arnold and Wm. Carpenter in behalf of themselves and all the inhabitants of Pawtuxet, asking for a full discharge of their

CHAP.
IV.

1642.

stated by the Governor to be " partly to secure these men from unjust violence, and partly to draw in the rest in those parts, either under ourselves or Plymouth, who now lived under no government, but grew very offensive, and the place was likely to be of use to us, especially if we should have occasion of sending out against any Indians of Narraganset, and likewise for an outlet into the Narraganset Bay, and seeing it came without our seeking, and would be no charge to us, we thought it not wisdom to let it slip." In a few weeks a letter was addressed by Massachusetts " to our neighbors of Providence," informing them of this submission of the Pawtuxet men, notifying them that the Courts were open for the trial of any complaints against these men, and accompanied with the assurance that equal justice should there be rendered, and with the threat that if violence were resorted to against them it would be repelled in like manner.[1] This official demonstration of the grasping policy of Massachusetts alarmed the colonists, who naturally preferred their own system of arbitration to the decision of Courts in another, and as they had good reason to consider, a hostile jurisdiction. Gorton and his companions, who, as the parties specially complained of, deemed this letter to be aimed directly at them, shortly removed beyond the limits of Providence, and purchasing from the Indians lands at Shawomet, south of Pawtuxet, commenced the settlement of Warwick. But the rest which they sought was denied them in their last retreat. The persecution of their enemies followed them to the homes which the heathen, in pity for their sufferings, had bestowed. A dark contrast between the kindness of the savages and the cruelty of their civilized brethren, is presented in the early history of the Warwick settlement.

Oct.
28.

1642-3.
Jan.
12.

submission to the Massachusetts jurisdiction, which was granted at the May session. M. C. R., v. 4, Part i., p. 333.

[1] The letter is published in 2 R. I. H. Col., p. 53, and in Staple's Annals of Prov., p. 47.

The three colonies now existing in Rhode Island were independent of each other. They felt the necessity of union in case of an Indian war which constantly threatened, and perhaps a still greater need of an authorized government, which should cause their rights to be respected by their neighbors. As yet each settlement depended solely upon the consent of its inhabitants for the efficiency of its government, and this basis was not recognized by the Puritan colonies as valid. The only ties that bound them together were those of a common danger from the Indians, the memory of sufferings endured in a common cause, and the peril to their existence as a State, which threatened all alike from the ambitious policy of the surrounding colonies. To strengthen their position at home, to fortify themselves against encroachments from abroad, and above all to secure the enjoyment of that liberty of conscience for which they had suffered so much and were destined to endure still more, they sought from the British Parliament a charter which should recognize their acts of self-government as legal, and invest with the sanction of authority the novel experiment they had commenced. The movement was made by the colony at Acquedneck. Providence united in it, and Roger Williams was selected as the agent. Early in the following summer he embarked at New York in a Dutch ship for England, being compelled to this course by the refusal of Massachusetts to permit him to pass through their limits, or to take passage in one of their vessels. He arrived in the midst of the civil war. The King had already fled, and the Long Parliament ruled the realm of England. The administration of the colonies was intrusted to a committee, of which the Earl of Warwick was chairman, with the office and title of " Governor-in-Chief and Lord High Admiral of the Colonies." His efforts with this committee resulted in obtaining a charter uniting the three Rhode Island colonies, as " The Incorporation of

CHAP.
IV.

1642.

Sept.
19.

1643.

Nov.
2.
1643-4
March
14.

CHAP.
IV.

1644.

Sept.
17.

Providence Plantations in the Narraganset Bay in New England."[1] The arrival of Mr. Williams with this all-important document was the occasion of general rejoicing. By virtue of an official letter to the Massachusetts, which he brought with him,[2] he landed in Boston, and was allowed to proceed unmolested to his home. This letter however failed, in its chief object, to produce a relaxation of the stern policy of the Bay towards the founder of the "heretical colony." Hubbard, in his History of New England, says : " Upon the receipt of the said letter the Governor and Magistrates of the Massachusetts found, upon examination of their hearts, they saw no reason to condemn themselves for any former proceedings against Mr. Williams ; but for any offices of Christian love and duties of humanity, they were very willing to maintain a mutual correspondency with him. But as to his dangerous principles of separation, unless he can be brought to lay them down, they see no reason why to concede to him, or any so persuaded, free liberty of ingress and egress, lest any of their people should be drawn away with his erroneous opinions."

He passed quietly through the unfriendly territory, whose people he had already once preserved, and from

---

[1] With respect to the exact date of this charter there is some difference of opinion, evidently caused by the carelessness of transcribers. It is published in the 2d and 4th vols. of R. I. H. Col., dated 17th March. The 3d R. I. H. Col., Hazard's State Papers, and 2 M. H. C. vol. 9, print it with the date of 14th March. Various writers have followed each of these authorities. The latter, however, is the correct date, as ably argued by the learned and accurate editor of Winthrop's Journal in a note, vol. ii., p. 236, edit. 1853. The fact that the 17th March 1643–4 fell on Sunday, not a legal day of date, is of itself conclusive against that date. The writer, in the course of his investigations in the British State Paper Office at London, examined the official MS. charter there preserved. It bears date 14th March. This positive evidence, aside from the negative proof adduced by Mr. Savage, appears to settle the question. The charter was signed on Thursday, 14th March, 1643–4.

[2] The letter is given in Winthrop, 2, 193 (236.)

whom he was destined shortly, for the second time, to avert the horrors of Indian war, and reached Providence by the same route that eight years before he had pursued, a homeless wanderer, dependent on the kindness of the red man. His entry was like a triumphal march. Fourteen canoes, filled with the exulting population of Providence, met him at Seekonk, and escorted him across the river, while the air was rent with shouts of welcome. How the contrast which a few short years had wrought in all around him must have pressed upon his mind, and more than all the feeling that the five companions of his exile, and those who had followed them, were now raised, by the charter he had brought, from the condition of despised and persecuted outcasts to the rank of an independent State !

During the absence of Mr. Williams an event of great importance in its effect on the welfare of the colonists occurred. This was the murder of Miantinomi, the faithful ally of the English and the steadfast friend of Rhode Island. A union for mutual assistance, to which we shall refer more fully in the succeeding chapter, was formed by the other New England colonies, and from which the Rhode Island settlements were excluded, upon grounds that reflect no credit upon the Puritan confederates. The prospect of Indian war was the most urgent cause for this union, and the exclusion of Rhode Island was a virtual abandonment of her inhabitants to the chances of savage warfare. A war broke out between Uncas, sachem of the Mohegans, and Sequasson, a sachem on the Connecticut river, who was an ally of Miantinomi. Both parties appealed to the English, who declared their intention to remain neutral. Miantinomi espoused the cause of his ally against Uncas, his hereditary foe, and applied to the Governor of Massachusetts, " to know if he would be offended if he made war upon Uncas ? " The Governor replied, " If Uncas had done him or his friends

CHAP
IV.

1644.

1643.

May
19.

July

CHAP.
IV.

1643.

wrong and would not give satisfaction, we should leave him to take his own course." That the high spirited sachem of the Narragansets should have thus asked leave, as it were, to exercise the right of a sovereign Prince against his enemies, is explained by the existence of a treaty formed six years before, when he aided the English to crush the Pequots. The whole career of this haughty chieftain, in his intercourse with the English, displays the nicest sentiment of honor, blended with a proper regard for his own dignity and absolute sovereignty. He regarded every article of the treaty he had made as binding to the last hour of his life, not only in its terms but in its spirit, and expected, though unfortunately, and as it proved fatally to himself, to receive from his civilized allies an equally honorable conduct. He had been repeatedly the guest of the authorities at Boston, and his deportment on those occasions, as well as in his own dominions, when receiving embassies from the English, was such as to win the confidence and command the admiration of

1642.
Aug.

those with whom he negotiated. But of late suspicions had been excited in the mind of the General Court, by intelligence from Connecticut, spread, as it appears, by the intrigues of the Mohegans.[1] At a summons from the

Sept.

Court Miantinomi promptly attended, and vindicated his innocence, demanding to be confronted with his accusers, and charging Uncas as the author of the calumny. The Court were satisfied and Miantinomi was honorably dismissed. A fatal act of kindness soon afterward performed by him, in selling Shawomet to the arch heretic Gorton, seems to have inclined the Massachusetts more readily to entertain suspicions of their high-souled ally, and to have had no little weight in causing his death. However this

1643.
July.

may be, the leading events are well known. Uncas attacked Sequasson. Miantinomi took the field with one thousand warriors, and was defeated in a bloody action.

[1] An account of this plot is given in 3 M. H. C., 3, 161–4.

By the treachery of two of his captains he was delivered up to Uncas. An effort to obtain his ransom was made by his subjects, and also by Gorton. Upon this Uncas carried him to Hartford, where at his own entreaty he was left as a prisoner in the hands of the English, till the Commissioners of the United Colonies met at Boston.

By them his fate was decided. They "were all of opinion that it would not be safe to set him at liberty, neither had we sufficient ground for us to put him to death. In this difficulty we called in five of the most judicious elders, and propounding the case to them, they all agreed that he ought to be put to death ; and we agreed that, upon the return of the commissioners to Hartford, they should send for Uncas and tell him our determination, that Miantinomi should be delivered to him again, and he should put him to death so soon as he came within his own jurisdiction, and that two English should go along with him to see the execution, and that if any Indians should invade him for it, we would send men to defend him." The sentence was executed in its *spirit* and letter by the savage Uncas.[1] Thus fell the most powerful of the native princes, and the most faithful and honorable ally with whom the English had ever dealt. Unskilled in theological subtleties, he received all alike, with a noble charity which might be called Christian, did it not contrast so strangely with the cruelty towards their brethren, of those who claimed the name and asserted the prerogative of the " Saints." Perhaps it was the igno-

---

[1] The particulars of this atrocious sacrifice are given by Trumbull, Hist. of Conn., i. 135. A justly severe criticism on the authors of the outrage is penned by Mr. Savage in a note on pp. 158–161, vol. ii., edit. 1853, of Winthrop's Journal. The scathing remarks of the editor, honorable alike to himself and to humanity, come with a better grace from a Massachusetts man than any comments from a son of Rhode Island could do—who will find enough beside to denounce in the conduct of the Puritans towards his State, although nothing more needlessly cruel than the clerico-judicial murder here recorded.

CHAP.
IV.

1643.

Dec.
10.

rance of this barbarian upon points of abstract belief that made him so liberal a protector of "heresy." To him and to his uncle, the sage Canonicus, who survived him four years, Rhode Island owes more than to all others, Christian or heathen, for the preservation of the lives of her founders. The immediate executioner of this remorseless edict was rewarded for his fidelity. His abettors had reason afterwards to deplore their impolitic haste.

While these events were taking place in the colonies, a yet more dangerous influence was at work in England to foil the efforts of Williams at obtaining the charter that was to establish the independence of Rhode Island. The Massachusetts government were attempting to annex, by a similar patent, the whole soil of Rhode Island to their jurisdiction, and thereby to legalize their acts of usurpation. The effort was so far successful that a charter was actually obtained from the Colonial Committee, adding to the patent of Massachusetts the whole of what is now the State of Rhode Island, and expressly including the Narraganset country, three months before the Rhode Island charter was granted. The reasons assigned for this act in the body of the instrument are the excessive charges to which the Massachusetts planters had been subjected in founding their colony, its rapid growth, requiring an expansion of its territory, and the desire to Christianize the natives. By what means this patent was obtained, or how, so soon afterwards, the same territory was erected into an independent government, and no reference made to the previous grant to Massachusetts, although the boundaries are described in precisely the same language in the two documents, or yet why no allusion is made to it on the records of Massachusetts, for more than twenty months after it was granted, are points which cannot now be determined. It is worthy of remark that the Narraganset patent, as it was termed, provides a reservation of

all lands previously granted, " and in present possession
held and enjoyed by any of His Majesty's Protestant subjects," while the Providence charter, dated three months
later, contains no such proviso. In the Narraganset patent this proviso, so far as relates to lands " heretofore
lawfully granted," is mere surplusage, no grants ever having been made within the described territory by the British government, unless intended to secure the grantees
under the original Plymouth company, who, as before
stated, when about to throw up their charter, had made
extensive sales within what they claimed as their propriety, among which was one to the Marquis of Hamilton, of the tract from Narraganset Bay to Connecticut
river, including all the Narraganset country. But if this
was the intention of the proviso, why was it not also embodied in the Providence charter ? The reservation has
an important bearing, however, in its relation to those in
actual possession, and could we disconnect the two portions of this clause of the proviso, it would explain much
that now appears difficult ; for it would show that it was
not the intention of the Colonial Committee to extend
the Massachusetts authority over those who were actual residents prior to the tenth of December, but only
that the natural increase of the Massachusetts population,
spreading into the granted territory, might carry with
them the protection of their own laws. The omission of
the proviso in the Providence charter strengthens this
view. Mr. Williams had no doubt represented the actual
relations between the Rhode Island settlers and their
neighbors, and his charter, being absolute and without
reserve, intentionally cancelled that of December previous.
The protracted silence of the Massachusetts government
seems likewise to favor this view. The first notice that
appears of the existence of this document, is found in a
letter addressed to Mr. Williams at Providence, by order
of the council, informing him that they had " lately " re-

ceived this charter from England, warning him and others not to exercise jurisdiction there, or, otherwise, to ex-
hibit their authority for so doing at the General Court,
and temporarily remitting, for that specific purpose, the
decree of banishment.[1] It is not the least of the misfor-
tunes resulting from the destruction of the Providence
records in Philip's war, that we are ignorant what reply
was made to this arrogant missive.

Although the purchase of Providence from the Narraganset sachems was considered by the contracting parties
as complete, the settlers were careful to conciliate the
good-will of the Indians residing within their limits, or
who claimed any sort of interest in the lands. Those
who had built wigwams or tilled the soil, received gratuities in addition to what had been paid to the sachems,
and even the claim to sovereignty over a part of the land,
asserted by Massasoit, sachem of the Wampanoags, a tribe
subordinate to the Narragansets, several years after the
purchase, although unfounded, was virtually admitted,
and compensation made to him by the colonists. The
claim embraced portions of what is now Smithfield, but
it is doubtful whether the rights of the Wampanoags
ever extended west of the Seekonk river. A committee,
of which Roger Williams was the head, visited the sachem to treat for this pretended claim. The report of
their negotiation presents a curious picture of Indian
shrewdness and importunity. Many years elapsed before
the last Indian titles were extinguished. Confirmatory
deeds from the successors of the first grantors were taken,
every new deed requiring some further gratuity.

In their sales to each other the colonists pursued a
plan which, however ill-adapted it might be to our present modes of doing business, had the advantages of brevity
and publicity in a striking degree, and perhaps better pre-

---

[1] The letter is printed in R. I. Col. Rec., i., 133, and in Mass. Col. Rec.,
iii., 49.

cluded the possibility of fraud than any methods that have
since been adopted. The records for many years contain
simply the date of the transfer, the names of the grantor
and grantee, and the location and bounds of the land. A
dozen lines suffice to contain the whole transaction. No
consideration is named, and no verbose reiteration of conveyance amplify the deed to the tedious length of modern
instruments. These transfers were made, or acknowledged, in open town meeting, and if the town approved
the sale they voted to record the deed, which made the
conveyance valid, but if they disapproved the whole was
void.

The population of the colony rapidly increased; a
natural effect of the broad system of religious freedom established by its founder, which made it the refuge of
many who differed from the state creed of its neighbors.
President Styles, in his diary, says that at this time there
were in Providence and its vicinity one hundred and one
men fit to bear arms. This corresponds precisely to the
whole number of proprietors of house lots, in the last
division of the lands made seventy-three years later. But
besides the original purchasers, and those who were admitted by them to an equal share in the franchise, many
were received as townsmen who had no interest in the
lands, and others were admitted as twenty-five acre or
quarter-right purchasers, who in all subdivisions of land
received one-quarter as much as a full proprietor. The
terms of admission to the propriety varied very much at
different times. The latest agreement upon the records
is signed by twenty-eight quarter-right proprietors, who,
having received a free grant of twenty-five acres each and
a proportionate right of common, promise to obey the
laws, and not to claim any right to the purchase, nor any
privilege of vote, until they shall be received as freemen
of the town.[1]

[1] Staple's Annals, 60.

CHAP.   With so thrifty a growth and with a similar increase
 IV   in the other settlements, it is difficult to understand why
1646.   a united government was not organized immediately upon
receipt of the charter from England.   Yet more than two
and a half years elapsed before this event occurred.   The
patent prescribed no form of government, nor any mode
of organization.   All was left to the people, with the full-
est powers to adopt and act under it as they pleased.   It
was a task as delicate and difficult as it was imperative
to consolidate the towns.   A spirit of compromise and
mutual concession was requisite for the work.   Although
the same causes had led to these settlements, they were
independent of each other in every respect, managing
their affairs in their own town meetings, and conducting
for themselves, as best they could, their disputes with the
Puritan colonies.   This very independence must have
presented obstacles, which local or personal jealousies
would enhance.   The distracted condition of the mother
country extended in some measure to the colonies, where
parties for the King and for the Parliament existed, although with less violence than in England, and both parties would fear the effect upon their charter liberties, in
case of the victory of either.   These reasons may account
for the delay which otherwise would appear inexplicable.
The news of the Narraganset patent doubtless had an
immediate influence in hastening the consolidation so essential to their preservation and to the maintenance of
1647.   their cherished principles.   At length all obstacles were
so far removed that the four towns, Providence, Portsmouth, Newport and Warwick appointed committees to
meet at Portsmouth on the eighteenth of May.[1]   A town
meeting was held in Providence, at which Roger Williams
May   presided, and a committee of ten men were chosen for
16.   this purpose.[2]   The committee received full power to act

---

[1] It appears by the records that the Assembly was held on the 19th, 20th
and 21st.

[2] These were Gregory Dexter, William Wickenden, Thomas Olney, Rob-

for the town in arranging the General Court, in choosing general officers, and, in case the Court should consist of less than ten from each town, to select from themselves this lesser number, to whom the same powers are given. They were instructed to obtain a copy of the charter, to signify their submission to the terms of the charter, and to such laws as might be adopted under it, to secure for the town the right to manage its own affairs, trials of causes and executions, except such as might be reserved for general trials, and to elect its own officers, and to see that the powers of general and local officers were clearly defined, to provide for appeals of causes to the General Court, and, in case charters of incorporation were given to the towns for the conduct of their local business, to procure one for Providence suited to promote the general peace or union of the colony, and securing the equal rights of the town in general affairs. The instructions close by wishing them "a comfortable voyage, a happy success and a safe return." Thus commissioned, the committee, accompanied probably by a large proportion of the population of the town, embarked in canoes on their perilous "voyage." The result of their labors opens a new chapter in our work, and commences the history of "The Incorporation of Providence Plantations in Narraganset Bay in New England."

ert Williams, Richard Waterman, Roger Williams, William Field, John Green, John Smith and John Lippitt.

CHAPTER V.

HISTORY OF AQUEDNECK FROM ITS SETTLEMENT, MARCH, 1638,
TO THE ORGANIZATION OF THE GOVERNMENT UNDER THE
FIRST CHARTER, MAY, 1647.

CHAP.
V.

1637-8.
March
7.

THE civil compact formed at Providence and signed by nineteen [1] of the Aquedneck settlers was as follows : " The 7th day of the first month, 1638. We whose names are underwritten do here solemnly, in the presence of Jehovah, incorporate ourselves into a Bodie Politick, and as he shall help, will submit our persons, lives and estates unto our Lord Jesus Christ, the King of Kings and Lord of Lords, and to all those perfect and most absolute laws of his given us in his holy word of truth, to be guided and judged thereby.—Exod. xxiv., 3, 4 ; 2 Chron. xi., 3 ; 2 Kings xi., 17."

24.

The account of the purchase of the island, through the joint influence of Roger Williams and Sir Henry Vane, with the Narraganset sachems, has already been given. The Indian name of the place where the settlement was commenced, on the northeast part of the island,

---

[1] These were Wm. Coddington, John Clarke, Wm. Hutchinson, John Coggeshall, Wm. Aspinwall, Samuel Wilbore, John Porter, John Sanford, Ed. Hutchinson, jr., Thomas Savage, Wm. Dyre, Wm. Freeborne, Philip Shearman, John Walker, Richard Carder, Wm. Baulstone, Ed. Hutchinson, sen., Henry Bull, ——— Randall Holden. Holden's name is separated from the others by a line. He is believed to be the one not concerned in the purchase, as his name and that of Roger Williams are signed as witnesses to the deed. There were eighteen original proprietors and nineteen signers of the compact. See Bull's Memoirs of Rhode Island in R. I. Republican, 1832, April 17.

was Pocasset, and was retained for some time by the settlers, until changed to Portsmouth. This name was equally applied by the Indians to the opposite shore on the main land, and probably was the name of the narrow strait between them, across which a ferry, now known as Howland's ferry, was soon after established. The consideration paid for the fee of Aquedneck, and for the grass on the other islands, was forty fathoms of white peage, besides which ten coats and twenty hoes were given to the resident Indians to vacate the lands, and five fathoms of wampum to the local sachem. The purchasers adopted the same policy as those of Providence towards the Indians, giving gratuities to all who claimed any interest in the lands. Some of the purchasers expressing dissatisfaction that the title stood in the name of William Coddington, in 1652 he executed a joint deed to them, as Mr. Williams had done for the same reason in Providence.

Callender says that the Aquedneck settlers " were Puritans of the highest form," and we know that their opponents in Massachusetts called the Antinomian doctrines " Calvinism run to seed." The peculiar phraseology of their civil compact verifies the remark of Callender. So prominent indeed is the religious character of this instrument that it has by some been considered, although erroneously, as being itself " a church covenant, which also embodied a civil compact.¹" Their plans were more matured at the outset than those of the Providence settlers. To establish a colony independent of every other was their avowed intention, and the organization of a regular government was their initial step. That their object was to lay the foundation of a Christian State, where all who bore the name might worship God according to the dictates of conscience, untrammelled by written articles of faith, and unawed by the civil power, is proved by their declarations and by their subsequent conduct. The dif-

¹ Minutes of the Warren Baptist Association, 1849.

ference between the Aquedneck settlers and the followers of Roger Williams upon this point was, that the latter did not confine his principles of toleration to men professing Christianity, but allowed room for those of every faith, Jew or Gentile, Christian or Pagan. The views of Clarke and Coddington were very far in advance of the age, too far for the peace of the colony in its intercourse with the neighboring provinces. The doctrine of " soul liberty," as established by Williams, went still farther, carrying his premises to their logical conclusion, and has come to be the recognized doctrine of the present age on this continent. The distinction between the two, although having no practical effect at that time, is important to be borne in mind, for it will explain some points in the later history of the State which might otherwise appear inconsistent. The Aquedneck settlements for many years increasd more rapidly than those on the main land. The accessions appear to have been, for the most part, from a superior class in point of education and social standing, which for more than a century secured to them a controlling influence in the colony. Many of the leading men were more imbued with the Puritan spirit, acquired by their longer residence in Massachusetts, which sympathized somewhat more with the law than with the liberty element in the embryo State.[1] The evidence of this is frequent, and its existence was very early displayed. It is foreshadowed in the language of the compact, and in a few years was realized in action. It had its advantages, however, and the chief of these were that it enabled the people at once to organize a government, and strengthened them to preserve it better than those of Providence, while it also was a means of securing and extending their influence over the other settlements, who looked up to them in many things, and received from them their first code

[1] Judge Durfee's discourse before the R. I. Hist. Soc., January, 1847, pp. 15, 16.

of laws. But we are anticipating events in commenting upon principles.

Of the nineteen signers of the compact, William Hutchinson died on the island, the other two Hutchinsons, Savage and Aspinwall, afterward returned to Massachusetts, were well received and promoted to office there. All of them, except Coddington and Holden, had been disarmed in the famous act of November previous, but the shafts of party malice still followed them in their retreat, and five days after the compact was signed Wm. Coddington and ten of his companions, with their families, were formally banished by the General Court.[1] This event had no influence on their plans. Their government was already organized at a full meeting of the signers, at which Wm. Aspinwall was chosen Secretary, and Wm. Coddington was elected, and took his engagement as Judge, or chief magistrate, and Wm. Dyre was elected Clerk. This meeting was held in Providence. A few days afterward the purchase of the island was completed, and the settlement very shortly commenced. Town meetings were frequent. The records are full and pretty well preserved, so that we are enabled to know more concerning their early movements than we can of those at Providence. But a small number of acts were passed at each meeting, relating to matters of immediate concern.

At the first meeting the earliest recorded act passed in Rhode Island related to the admission of freemen, that none should be admitted as such but by consent of the Body, and who submit to the established government. The other acts fix the location of the town, to be "builded at the spring;" order that every inhabitant should be fully equipped with certain arms; establish a site for the meeting house; and make a temporary apportionment of

CHAP.
V.
1637-8.

March
12.

7.

24.

1638.

May.
13.

---

[1] Their names were Wm. Coddington, John Coggeshall, Wm. Baulstone, Ed. Hutchinson, Samuel Wilbore, John Porter, Henry Bull, Philip Shearman, Wm. Freeborne and Richard Carder.—M. C. R., i., 223.

land to each inhabitant, of an acre of meadow for every beast and sheep, and an acre and a half for a horse, which latter act was afterward repealed, and a more definite division made. The town was built around the head of the pond, or cove, from which there was formerly an outlet to the bay deep enough for small vessels to enter. The remains of this first settlement may still be traced. Somewhat later a new town was laid out more to the south and east, called Newtown, to distinguish it from the old, which name that part of Portsmouth still retains. The following week the town was laid out, six-acre lots were assigned to the proprietors, and provision made for recording land titles. An inn, brewery and general grocery "to sell wines and strong waters and such necessary provisions as may be useful," was also established, to be in charge of Wm. Baulston. This was doubtless the first tavern in the State. A military organization was the next object of attention. At their third meeting officers for the train bands were chosen.[1] Already the colony had received accessions to its numbers. Land on the island had been taken up, for which the new-comers were required to pay into the town treasury two shillings an acre, which price was fixed for all future inhabitants. Two treasurers, William Hutchinson and John Coggeshall, were chosen for one year. The highways were ordered to be repaired, and a fine of one shilling was laid upon all who should be fifteen minutes late at town meeting, or should leave it without permission before adjournment. The first admission of freemen occurred in August,[2] and at the same time "a pair of stockes [3] and a whipping

May
20.

June
27.

Aug.
20.

[1] Wm. Baulston and Ed. Hutchinson, sergeants; Samuel Wilbore, clerk; Randal Holden and Henry Bull, corporals.

[2] There were four admitted, viz., Richard Dummer, Nicholas Easton, Wm. Brenton and Robert Harding.

[3] This was a pet punishment with the landed aristocracy of the old country, and early transplanted to the new. The condition of English society which tolerated the stocks, is graphically described by Sir E. Bulwer Lytton

post [1]" were ordered to be made. Three days afterward a prison, twelve feet by ten, was ordered to be built, thus completing the preparations for the vindication of violated law, and Randal Holden was appointed Marshal of the colony for one year. They were very soon required, for in a few days eight men having committed " a riot of drunkenness," were brought before the town meeting by warrant, and variously fined, and three of them sentenced to the stocks. Viewers of corn and other produce were chosen, whose duty was to examine the crops, and report any damage that might be done to them by cattle running at large. The object of this law was to enable those whose crops might suffer in that way to recover damages before the court from the owners of the cattle. The military having before been organized, as stated, a general training was appointed, at which all men between the ages of sixteen and fifty years were warned to attend on the following Monday. This no doubt was the first militia muster ever held in Rhode Island.

The growth of the town now required greater prudence in the apportionment of land. The size of house lots was fixed at three acres, being one-half the quantity held by each of the original inhabitants. A baker was appointed for the plantation, from whom the town was to

CHAP.
V.

1638.
Aug.
23.

Sept.
13.

15.

Nov.

5.

12.

Nov.
5.

in " My Novel," where the reader will find in the first three books some scenes related such as this island may have witnessed two centuries ago ; always excepting the one in book third, chapter ix., where the inimitable Riccabocca pays the forfeit of benevolent curiosity, by being caught in the stocks, himself, and is thus found by his friends, quietly meditating under his red umbrella. There may have been some Lenny Fairchilds in Rhode Island, but no counterpart to the fatherly and philosophical Italian. I am sure the reader will pardon this note if it leads him to peruse the admirable sketch of English life here referred to, and if he is already familiar with it the recollection will serve to relieve his mind from the dry record of actual history.

[1] This punishment nominally existed until a recent period in this State. The last public infliction of it was on the Court House parade in Providence, July 14th, 1837, for horse stealing. It had long been in disuse until this recurrence of it aroused public attention to its legal existence, when it was soon after struck from the statute book. It still exists in many of the States.

CHAP.
V.

1638.
Nov.
16.

purchase the bread used at the meeting of the courts. A few days after we find that a water-mill was projected by Mr. Nicholas Esson,[1] for the use of the plantation, and a grant of land and timber made to him for this purpose. The earliest case of an absconding debtor in the colony occurred at this time. John Luther, a carpenter, fled from the island, leaving sundry debts unpaid. His property was duly appraised and sold for the benefit of his creditors. The disposition to regulate trade by establishing prices at which articles should be bought and sold, which had already given much trouble in Massachusetts, and continued to do so until the repeal of the statute left such matters to regulate themselves, showed itself early among the Portsmouth settlers. Four "truckmasters," as they were called, were appointed for the venison trade with the Indians, and the prices fixed upon this staple article of food were limited to a penny ha'penny a pound to be paid for it, and two pence a pound as the selling price. One farthing a pound, being one-half the profit thus secured to the dealers, was to be paid into the treasury.[2]

1638-9.
Jan.
2.

Up to this time the government had been a pure democracy. All acts had been passed in public meetings of the whole body. The Judge and Clerk had acted only as chairman and secretary of the assembled townsmen, by whom all laws had been passed, and all proceedings, whether legislative, judicial, or executive, conducted. A change now took place by appointing three Elders to as-

---

[1] The name was also spelt Eason and Easton in the records. This was the same who with his two sons, Peter and John, built the first house in Newport, six months later.

[2] A net profit of about seventeen per cent. on the capital invested, is here allowed, and is a better margin than is usually left to the dealer under restricted laws of trade. It also compares well with average results of modern traffic. In this case the capital was all that was required. Deer and Indians were both abundant, so that but little labor and no skill were needed on the part of the "truckmasters."

sist the Judge in his judicial duties, to frame laws, to have the entire charge of the public interests, and with the Judge to govern the colony. These officers were to render an account of their proceedings at quarterly meetings of the town, where their acts were subject to revision, or repeal, if disapproved. A jealousy of delegated power is here apparent, like that which existed in the Providence plantation, and which presents a marked contrast to the feeling then prevalent in the community which they had so lately left. Sealed ballots were used at this election. Nicholas Easton, John Coggeshall and William Brenton were chosen Elders, and their election was duly ratified. At the next meeting the town united with the Judge and Elders to choose a Constable and town Sergeant, and to define their duties. Samuel Wilbore was elected for the former office, whose duties were to see that peace be kept, and to inform of any breaches thereof, with power to command aid for that purpose if needed. Henry Bull was elected Sergeant, to execute orders of the Court, to serve warrants and to keep the prison, with similar power to demand aid from any persons in the discharge of his office. The business of the town for the ensuing three months was transacted by the Judge and Elders. By their act new comers were admitted as inhabitants, and complaints for exaction in trade were redressed. A singular proceeding was taken in regard to William Aspinwall, upon whom suspicions of sedition against the State rested. Neither the grounds of suspicion nor the nature of the sedition is stated, but an order was issued forbidding further work upon a boat that he was having built. This kind of security for good conduct seems to have been usual, for one Osamund Doutch, who at the same Court was admitted an inhabitant, was likewise complained of for some wrong-doing, and his shallop pledged in a bond of indemnity that he was required to give. Probably boats were considered the most

CHAP.
V.

1639.
April
6.

available and desirable property in an island settlement.[1] Swine were considered a nuisance, and their removal or confinement was early provided for. They were ordered to be sent six miles distant from the town, or to some adjacent island, or else were to be shut up so as to be inoffensive, and subsequently the act was enforced by a fine of two pence for each hog that was found in the town after four days. A cattle pound was also provided. To guard against invasions from the Indians, and likewise to secure the peace of the settlement from the chances of riot, an alarm was established. The firing of three muskets, with the cry of " Alarum," was the signal upon which all the inhabitants were to repair to the house of the Judge.

28.

The colony had now so greatly increased that a division was deemed expedient. A meeting was held, at which the following agreement was entered into by the signers, by whom the settlement of Newport was commenced on the south-west side of the island.

"POCASSET. On the 28th of the 2d, 1639.

" It is agreed by us whose hands are underwritten, to propagate a Plantation in the midst of the Island or elsewhere ; And doe engage ourselves to bear equall charges, answerable to our strength and estates in common ; and that our determinations shall be by major voice of judge and elders ; the Judge to have a double voice.

" PRESENT :

WM. CODDINGTON, *Judge.*

NICHOLAS EASTON,
JOHN COGGESHALL,
WILLIAM BRENTON,
JOHN CLARKE,   } *Elders.*
JEREMY CLERKE,
THOMAS HAZARD,
HENRY BULL,

WILLIAM DYRE, *Clerk.*"

[1] As we hear no more of the charge of sedition, we may infer that it was

All the members of the Pocasset government, it will be observed, are among the emigrants.   They carried with them their records up to this date.   Why they did this does not appear, for although they were the most prominent men, and their settlement soon became the leading one in the State, yet by far the largest number then residing at Pocasset remained.   Thus deprived at once of their government and their records, a new organization was necessary, and two days afterward they formed a new compact as follows : " We whose names are under[written do acknowledge] ourselves the legal subjects of [His Majesty] King Charles, and in his name [do hereby bind] ourselves into a civill body politicke and [do submit] unto his lawes according to matters of justice.[1]"   Thirty-one names are signed to this document,[2] following which, of

CHAP.
V.
1 6 3 9.

April.
30.

unsustained, and that the boat was allowed to be finished, for about three months later, 28th April, it was attached for debt, which is the only complaint ever afterward brought against Aspinwall.   He occupied many positions of trust in the colony.   Early in 1642, probably in April, he returned to Massachusetts, and "upon his petition and certificate of good carriage was restored again to his former liberty of freedom."   M. C. R., ii. 3.

[1] The record is much mutilated and defaced.   The words in brackets are interpolated to preserve the sense.   These interpolations are all at the end of the lines where the edge of the sheet is torn off.   The remaining words are very legible.

[2] Wm. Hutchinson, Samuel Gorton, Samuel Hutchinson, John Wickes, Richard Maggson, Thomas Spicer, John Roome, John Geoffe, (Sloffe ?) Thomas Beddar, Erasmus Bullocke, Sampson Shotten, Ralph Earle, Robert Potter, Nathanyell Potter, George Potter, Wm. Heavens (W. T. Havens ?) George Shaw (Chare ?) George Lawton, Anthony Paine, Jobe Hawkins, Richard Awarde, John More (Mow ?) Nicholas Browne, Wm. Richardson, John Trippe, Thomas Layton, Robert Stainton, John Brigges, James Davis.   In R. I. C. R. i. 70 but twenty-nine names are given.   The other two on the Record have a pen mark across them as if to expunge them from the list, and probably for this reason are not copied in the printed records.   One of these names is that of Wm. Aspinwall, who, on the same day, was chosen one of the assistants, and continued, for three years, a resident of the colony.   His signature belongs there, and why erased we cannot say unless it was done after his return to Massachusetts in 1642.   We infer the same, although with less positive proof of the other erasure, and hence state the number of signers at thirty-one, two more than the printed records show.

the same date, is their agreement of government. " According to the true intent of the [foregoing, wee] whose names are above perticularly [recorded, do agree] jointly or by the major voice to g[overn ourselves by the] Rulee or Judge amongst us in all [transactions] for the spacr and term of one [year, he] behaving himself according to the t[enor of the same.]" They then proceeded to elect William Hutchinson Judge. The mutilation of the records has destroyed the name, and no clue to it is given in any of the subsequent pages, but Winthrop has fortunately preserved it.[1] Seven assistants were also chosen,

The writer devoted a whole summer to studying and making extracts from the Portsmouth records, a year before they were printed by the State, and may be permitted to follow the results of his own researches, even where they differ somewhat from the version since printed by Authority. In the foregoing list, where the writer's version differs from that of the printed records, the name, as given in the latter, is enclosed in brackets. It will be observed that there are four of these variations, besides the two first explained, which require that the author should state further reasons, besides the evidence of his own eyes, why he prefers the versions here retained. The names of Goffe, Shaw and More occur often on the records, and are perpetuated in a very numerous descent at this day on the island, while the names as printed are nowhere else to be found or traced. W. T. Havens should be Wm. Havens, as afterward appears on the records. Middle names were not in use in that age. The difficulty of deciphering these ancient records is greatly increased by the fact that many of them are written in the German script or old English letter, and unless the student is familiar with that language or character, his only mode of reading such passages is by making an alphabet, somewhat in the way pursued by Champollion in his application of the Rosetta Stone to Egyptian hieroglyphics. The chances of error are much increased by this process.

Lest these remarks should be misapprehended as throwing a doubt on the reliability of the printed records, the writer deems it just and proper to say that the errors therein contained are few and of little practical importance, so far as he has discovered. Some errors have occurred in printing that are readily detected. The completeness and accuracy of the work as a whole, can only be duly appreciated by those who know the many difficulties incident to such a task. Mutilation, erasure, fading ink, blotting, insects, dampness, ever-varying orthography, and often bad chirography, to all which add the frequent use of a foreign character, as above stated, and we have some of the inevitable hindrances that attend the reading of our earliest records.

[1] i. 295, May 11th, 1639. " At Aquiday the people grew very tumultuous, and put out Mr. Coddington and the other three magistrates, and chose

"for the help and ease of conducting public business and affairs, and to lay out lands," viz. : William Balston, John Porter, John ———, William Freeborne, John Wall, Philip Shearman and William Aspinwall. The surname of the third assistant, like that of the Judge, being near the edge of the page, is torn off. These officers were constituted a court for settling any dispute involving less than forty shillings. Provision was also made for a quarterly court of trials with a jury of twelve men.

Two distinct governments, which lasted the remainder of the year, were thus established on the island. That at Pocasset was occupied with business of a local nature, chiefly in apportionments of land and house lots, which were to be forfeited if not built upon within one year. No man was allowed either to sell his lot or to offer it to the

Mr. Wm. Hutchinson only, a man of very mild temper and weak parts, and wholly guided by his wife, who had been the beginner of all the former troubles in the country, and still continued to breed disturbance." The " putting out" here recorded, is evidently a Puritan version of the emigration from Pocasset to Newport a few days previous, which shows how carefully we should regard the statements of the Massachusetts chroniclers, when the most liberal of them all can thus construe the acts of those from whom he differed in opinion. He is in error in using the word "only" in the passage above quoted; the records of Portsmouth showing, as stated in the text, that seven Assistants were chosen at the same time with the Judge. There are also two singular errors, one of omission and one of misstatement, in Judge Eddy's letter to the Editor, quoted in the note appended to this passage.

The first consists in overlooking the fact of the emigration of the Magistrates, and the election of others by those who remained at Pocasset, of which Judge Eddy does not seem to have been aware, and which led him to assert wrongly of Wm. Hutchinson's election as an Assistant in 1640, that "this was the only time he was chosen to office." The diligence of Judge Eddy and his general accuracy is admitted by all who have pursued the same path of research in our State Archives. The two errors here noticed could not have been avoided by one who only examined, however carefully, the State records, and it is evident from this letter that its writer had not, up to that time, consulted the Portsmouth town records.

It is fortunate that Winthrop has thus accidentally enabled us to supply a defect caused by a mutilation of the records. Without this confirmation we should still have conjectured that Hutchinson was the man selected as Judge, for he was one of the eighteen original proprietors, and was perhaps the most important person left at Pocasset after the emigration.

CHAP.
V.

1639.
July
1.

town. The only act of public interest was to change the name of the place to Portsmouth, which was done at the first quarterly meeting under the new organization, and confirmed by the united government the next year.

April
28.

30.

May
1.

The nine men who signed the agreement at Pocasset proceeded at once to make their new settlement. By a manuscript journal kept by Nicholas Easton, it appears that he with his two sons, Peter and John, came by boat to an island where they lodged, and the next morning named it Coasters' Harbor. Thence they came to Newport the same day, where they erected the first English building.[1] The others were not far behind, if they did not accompany the Eastons, for in their first meeting they

16.

speak of "the plantation now begun at this south-west end of the island," naming it Newport, establishing the site of the town "on both sides of the spring, and by the seaside southward," and fixing the line dividing it from Pocasset at a point five miles north and east from the town. The spring referred to was on the west side of Spring street, near the State House, whence a stream ran a north-west course to the harbor. It appears that some doubt existed at first as to the best location for the town. A dense swamp skirted the harbor where Thames street now is. This fact led them to direct their attention to the beach. There they found only an open roadstead unsafe for shipping ; so they returned to the harbor, surveyed it, and wisely decided on the present location. The

---

[1] This fact entitles N. Easton to the honor of being considered the founder of Newport, unless an equal share is claimed for his eight associates, who do not appear to have been as prompt in their arrival or in establishing their settlement by actual building. That he was endowed with the peculiar energy of a pioneer appears by his previous history. The house was on the east side of Farewell street, a little west of the Friends' meeting-house. It was burnt down in 1641 by the carelessness or the malice of some Indians, who kindled a fire in the woods near by. There and in Tanner and Marlborough streets the first houses were built. Gov. Coddington's house was on the north side of the latter street and fronting Duke street.—*Bull's Memoir of Rhode Island.*

swamp has long since given place to crowded thorough- CHAP.
fares, and the finest harbor in America remains to attest   V.
the wisdom of their choice. Provision was made for every 1639.
servant who remained with them to have ten acres of land
as a free gift upon his admission. The business of laying June
out the lands was soon commenced. The opinion of the   5.
body is recorded " that the land might reasonably accommodate fifty families." Four acres were assigned for each
house lot, and six acres were granted to Mr. Coddington
for an orchard.[1] Free trade with the Indians was permitted to all men. Some differences on this subject had
arisen which probably occasioned this decree. The ap-   Sept.
pointment of " truckmasters " had not given satisfaction   2.
at Pocasset, and the Newport settlers profited by their
experience. A justice's court, composed of the Judge   Oct.
and Elders, was appointed to meet the first Tuesday   1.
in every month, to decide such causes as might come
before them. At the quarterly town meetings, called also
courts, a majority was to rule, and the Judge was allowed
two votes. Under this date appears a list of fifty-nine
persons, "who by the general consent of the company were
admitted to be inhabitants of the island, now called
Aquedneck, having submitted themselves to the government that is or shall be established, according to the word
of God, therein," and also a supplemental list of forty-two
" inhabitants admitted at the towne of Niew-Port since
the 20th of the 3d, 1638," (1639,) making one hundred
and one registered inhabitants at that time.[2] Nearly one
half of the first list is composed of names signed to the

---

[1] This is the second orchard known in Rhode Island. The first was planted
by W. Blackstone in 1635.

[2] There is a singular recurrence of this precise number of persons in our
early history. The Pilgrims landing from the Mayflower in 1620 were one
hundred and one. The number of men in Providence fit for military duty in
1645 was one hundred and one. The number of proprietors there at the last
division of lands in 1718, was one hundred and one, and we here see the
number of registered inhabitants of Aquedneck in Oct., 1639, to be one hundred and one.

Pocasset agreement of April 30th, and the greater part of it is made up of those who still resided there, by which we may foresee the union of the governments shortly to take place. None of the proprietors' names are in either list. They were the company by whom, with such as they from time to time admitted, all others were received. The supplemental list contains only the names of such as had come to the island during the summer.

We have before seen that the organization of courts very early occupied the attention of the colonists. The administration of justice was promptly provided for, contrary to the slanders of their neighbors, who from the absence of any law religion at either Providence or Aquedneck, freely charged them with a disregard for both law and religion. A division of labor in judicial matters, it is true, was not immediately provided. Their circumstances did not at once permit the establishment of a variety of courts, with limited and well-defined jurisdictions, as at the present day. The number of the colonists was too small, and the nature of the causes arising among them did not require any extended judicial system. Yet we have seen that something of this had already been undertaken at Pocasset. The Court of Assistants was to have cognizance of small causes, and a quarterly court for jury trials was established. This progress in one year, with the establishment of justices' courts immediately upon their settlement, fully attests their regard for law. The character of the men, with the fact that a majority of them were members of the Boston church before their exile, and many still continued to be so, answers the other portion of the charge. A formal act of the whole people, passed at this time, will set their regard for justice, and their care in providing for its administration, in still clearer light. " By the Body Politicke in the Ile of Aquethnec, Inhabiting this present 25 of 9 month, 1639.

"In the fourteenth yeare of y⁰ Raign of our Soveraign Lord King Charles. It is agreed, That as Natural subjects to our Prince, and subject to his Lawes, all matters that concerne the Peace shall be by those that are officers of the Peace, Transacted ; And all actions of the case, or Debt, shall be in such Courts as by order are here appointed, and by such Judges as are Deputed : Heard and Legally Determined.

"Given at Niew-Port on the Quarter Courte Day which was adjourned till y⁵ Day.

"WILLIAM DYRE, Sec."

Meanwhile their spiritual concerns were not neglected. We have the same reasons that were assigned in the previous chapter for supposing that at Aquedneck, as well as at Providence, religious services were regularly conducted before any positive notice is found of the formation of a church. In Winthrop's Journal we read, "They also gathered a church in a very disordered way ; for they took some excommunicated persons, and others who were members of the church of Boston and not dismissed." The position of this record in reference to what precedes it,[1] seems to indicate that the church was formed at or about the time ·of the Newport settlement, but whether there or at Pocasset, by the emigrants or by those who remained, is not so apparent. The construction of the sentence makes it probable that the latter is intended. No other contemporary record of the formation of such a church remains.[2] Whatever were its doctrines it existed

CHAP. V.

1639.

May 11.

[1] Winthrop, i. 297, under date of May 11th, 1639, and immediately following the statement of the ejection of the magistrates quoted in note 1, p. 134.

[2] It is this church, if any in Rhode Island, that can be claimed to antedate the Baptist church already formed in Providence. Yet the record of Winthrop mentions the formation of that church nearly two months earlier than the one at Aquedneck. The former is distinctly described as Baptist in its ordinances. Of the latter the only clue given to its doctrines is that some of its members were still members of the Boston church, which fact, if it

but a short time in its original form, if we may rely on the authority of Lechford, but gave place in a few years to a flourishing Baptist church, under the pastoral charge of the Rev. John Clarke, who had been Elder of the former church.[1] The same authority states that at Portsmouth there was then no church, "but a meeting of some men who there teach one another and call it Prophecie."[2] That a due regard was felt for religious matters at both the Aquedneck towns, as well as at Providence, we think has now been sufficiently shown on firmer grounds than simple inference. That "at Aquiday they gathered a church in a very disordered way," which they could not

proves nothing else, shows pretty conclusively that they were not Baptists. If some writers whose ability entitles their judgment to respect had not, of late years, expressed a doubt upon the point, the Author would feel little hesitation in expressing what is in his own mind a firm conviction, that the church at Aquedneck was formed some little time prior to May 11th, 1639, and was in its faith and ordinances an Independent Congregational Church, of the Puritan pedobaptist order. Mr. Savage, in a note to the passage quoted in the text, has a just comment on the way the church is there described as being gathered. See note (2) p. 107, ante.

[1] Plaine Dealing or News from N. England, London, 1641. The writer used the copy in the British Museum, and collated the parts relating to Rhode Island, with the re-publication in 3 M. H. C., iii. 96, 7, where the book is dated 1642. Perhaps there were two editions. Lechford says: "At the island called Aquedney are about two hundred families. There was a church where one Master Clarke was elder. The place where the church was is called Newport, but that church I heare is now dissolved." He is quoted as evidence against the existence of the Baptist church at Providence at the time he wrote, but nothing he says on that subject is so direct to that point as the passage here given, bearing upon the other side of the question, and which is quite overlooked in the discussion referred to in the foregoing chapter, note (2) p. 107. The probability is that Lechford's statement is correct, that this earliest Aquedneck church was dissolved, and that in the change of doctrinal opinion so rife in that age, there soon after arose from the materials of the old church, and including its pastor, a Baptist church, founded, as Callender believed (R. I. H. C. iv. 117), "in 1644, by Mr. John Clarke and some others."

[2] The views of "Thomas Lechford, of Clements Inne, in the county of Middlesex, Gent.," as he describes himself on his title-page, the High Churchman, writing confessedly to prove his right to be so considered, may be presumed to differ materially from those of our antinomian progenitors of Aquedneck, upon the controverted question, "What constitutes a church?"

avoid, and that " at Providence things grew still worse," CHAP.
in Puritan opinion, and a Baptist church was the result, V.
will not be held, at this day, to militate against the piety 1639.
or the prudence of our ancestors.

The military organization was very soon completed, Nov. 25.
as at Portsmouth. It was kept distinct from the other
branches of government, but subject, in the choice of officers, to the approval of the Magistrates. Every man capable of bearing arms was enrolled. " The Body of the
people, viz., the Traine Band," were left free to choose
their own officers to exercise and train them, who were to
be approved by the Magistrates. No man was allowed
to go two miles from town, or to attend any public meeting, under penalty of five shillings fine, without carrying
a gun or sword. The danger of Indian hostility occasioned this great precaution.

Negotiations with Pocasset were already in progress
with a view to a united government. A yet more important project was discussed. Mr. Easton and Mr. John
Clarke were desired to write to Sir Henry Vane about the
condition of the island, in order to obtain his influence in
securing a charter from the King. Mr. Thomas Burr-
wood, a brother of Mr. Easton, was also to be written to
on the same subject. The Court adjourned for three
weeks. In the interval two men, having broken the peace Dec.
by drunkenness, were tried by the Magistrate's, or " par- 3.
ticular Court," and fined five shillings each, " according
to the law in that case provided." No respect of persons
was shown in the infant commonwealth, when any violated law required a vindication. At the adjourned meet- 17.
ing of the Quarter Court the first act was to impose a
fine of five shillings upon Mr. Easton, one of the Elders,
or assistants, for attending without his weapon. The
sanitary precautions, noticed at Pocasset, were taken also
at Newport. Hogs were prohibited from running at large
between the middle of April and October. A repeal of

CHAP.
V.

1639.
Dec.
17.

the former order on this subject, which, it may be remembered, required their removal to a distance of six miles from the town, or to some adjacent island, would make it appear that the orders passed the previous year at Pocasset were held to be in force at Newport, a view that is strengthened by the fact of their having carried with them all the records, as before stated. A pair of stocks and a whipping post were now ordered for the town.

1639-40.

Jan.
7.

The earliest export trade of Rhode Island was in lumber. The home prices were regulated by law. In the earliest enactment on this subject these are fixed at eight shillings the hundred for sawed boards, seven shillings for half inch boards, delivered at the mill, and one shilling a foot for clapboards and fencing, to be sound, merchantable stuff. Timber was not to be cut or exported without a license. By a record at Portsmouth, now much defaced, it appears that a ship load of pipe staves and clapboards was obtained there about this time. A few years later [1] ship building was commenced, and has ever since been an important branch of business in the State.

22.

A scarcity of provisions, which, but for the ample supply of fish and game that abounded in the sea and the forests, would have threatened a famine, caused a survey and census to be taken. This showed that there were ninety-six persons inhabiting the town, and only one hundred and eight bushels of corn among them. [2] This was equally divided, and the stock was calculated to last for

[1] In 1646 the New Haven colony built a ship of one hundred and fifty tons at Rhode Island. Trumbull's Conn., i. 161.

[2] The apparent discrepancy between this census of ninety-six *persons* and the registered list of one hundred and one *males* in October, is reconciled by the fact that nearly all of the first list of fifty-nine men resided at Pocasset. The second list of forty-two were new comers on the island and lived at Newport. The apportionment of only thirty-six quarts of corn to each person to last for six weeks, being less than one quart per day, and that too in midwinter, with six months yet to harvest time, shows a fearful scarcity. It was evidently contemplated to obtain supplies from abroad within the six weeks, but where or how does not appear.

six weeks. The next quarterly meeting was held four
days sooner than the regular time, which fell on Sunday.
Provision was made for the annual election of all the officers, to be held on the twelfth day of March, forever after, in a General Assembly of the Freemen, and such as
could not be present were " to send in their votes, sealed
up, to the Judge." At the expiration of the six weeks
from the time the corn was divided, all the sea banks were
declared free for fishing, but whether in consequence of the
scarcity of provisions, or as a simple matter of public
right, is not stated—probably the latter.

At the first General Court of Election ever held in
Newport, very important proceedings were had. William
Hutchinson, Judge, and several of the principal men of
Portsmouth, who had not before applied, were reunited
to the Body, and some who had been registered as inhabitants in October were now admitted as freemen, and a
general act for the admission of freemen was passed by
the united Bodies of both towns, hereafter to constitute
but one government. The style and number of the magistrates were changed. The titles of Judge and Elder
were abolished. The Chief was called Governor, the next
in office Deputy Governor, and the other four Magistrates,
Assistants. An equal number of the general officers were
to be chosen from each town, the Governor and two Assistants from one, and the Deputy Governor and two Assistants from the other. The change of the name of Pocasset to Portsmouth, which had been there made the previous July, was now confirmed. The election resulted in
the choice of William Coddington, Governor, William
Brenton, Deputy Governor, Nicholas Easton, John Coggeshall, William Hutchinson and John Porter, Assistants.
The two latter and Mr. Brenton lived at Portsmouth.
Robert Jeffreys, of Newport, and William Balston, of
Portsmouth, were chosen Treasurers. William Dyre,
Secretary, Jeremy Clark Constable for Newport, and John

CHAP.
V.

1639-40.
Jan.
29.

March
6.

12.

Sandford for Portsmouth, and Henry Bull, Sergeant, all for one year, or till others should be chosen. The Governor and Assistants were made Justices of the Peace. Five men were selected for Portsmouth and three for Newport to lay out lands, and provision was made to record land titles in conformity thereto.

This union of the towns was a most desirable event. Already the evils of a divided jurisdiction had become apparent, while the rights of the proprietors, in whom rested the fee of the whole island, would have occasioned disputes which were thus happily prevented. The idea of a free charter also, which was seriously entertained by the people, doubtless contributed largely to effect a union. The movement was particularly beneficial to Newport, which at that time was much the smaller of the two. It soon became virtually the capital, although the Quarter Courts, or meetings of the General Assembly, and the General Courts of Election were held in both towns at various times. The "particular Courts," consisting of magistrates and jurors, were ordered to be held monthly in each town. These Courts had jurisdiction in all causes not involving "life and limb." From their decision there was a right of appeal to the Quarter Sessions, which were held the first Tuesdays in March, June, September and December. The laws were revised and several of them repealed, among which was the one forfeiting house lots that were not built upon within one year from the grant.

A formal convention or treaty was made by the government with the Narraganset Indians, and duly ratified at the next General Court. It provides that no fire should be kindled by the Indians on the island, but such as should be extinguished on their departure, and if any damage result therefrom it shall be made good on legal trial ; that for a hog that had been killed by an Indian, ten fathoms of wampum should be paid at the next harvest ; that no traps for deer or cattle should be set by Indians on the island ; that if any Indian was unruly, or committed any small crime, he should be punished by a magistrate, according to law ; but if the charge involved a greater sum than ten fathoms of beads, or if the accused party was a sachem, however trivial the charge, then Miantinomi was to be sent for to be present at the trial ; that neither English nor Indians should take the canoes belonging to the other ; that no bargain once made should be revoked, and that no idling about should be allowed.

A militia law, by far more complete than any law upon that subject that had before been passed, and the most copious of any of the existing acts, now appointed that eight times a year the bands of both towns were to be exercised in the field, and that two general musters, one at each town, were to be held every year. The unusual minuteness of this statute, the penalties attached to its violation, and the stringency of its application, including as it did every man who should remain for twenty days on the island, and exempting no one except by commutation, evinces the feeling of insecurity at that time pervading the whole of New England.

It has been said that at one time Rhode Island was behind all other States in providing for the education of her people. However true this might be of other portions of the State it was not so of the island. At this Court, Mr. Robert Lenthal was admitted a freeman. He had been invited to come and conduct public worship, which had previously been done by Mr. Clark, and to teach a school. By a vote of the town of Newport he was " called to keep a public school for the learning of youth, and for his encouragement there was granted to him and his heirs one hundred acres of land, and four more for a house lot ; " it was also voted " that one hundred acres should be laid forth and appropriated for a school, for encouragement of the poorer sort, to train up their youth

CHAP.
V.

1640.
Aug.
6.

20.

in learning, and Mr. Robert Lenthal, while he continues to teach school, is to have the benefit thereof."

The two towns were placed on an equal footing in all respects. They were allowed to draw similar amounts from the public treasury. " Two Parliamentary (or General) Courts" were appointed to be held equally at Portsmouth and Newport, on the Wednesday after the twelfth of March and of October.[1]

The local affairs of each town being left to its own management, we find occasionally some matters initiated there which afterwards became of public interest. Such
is the establishment of a ferry by the town of Portsmouth, probably at or near the spot long afterwards known as Howland's ferry, where " the stone bridge" now is, being the narrowest part of the east passage, and but a short distance from the original settlement of Pocasset. Thos. Gorton was appointed ferryman. The fares were fixed at sixpence a man, or threepence each if more than three were taken at one trip, and fourpence a head for goats and swine.

The Secretary was required to attend the two General and the four Quarter Sessions courts, receiving threepence a day for so doing. The Governor was instructed to write to the Governor of Massachusetts to learn the plans of that colony with regard to the Indians. Winthrop has fortunately given the substance of that letter, which was a joint communication from the Governors of Hartford, New Haven and Aquedneck, "wherein they declared their dislike of such as would have the Indians rooted out, as being of the cursed race of Ham, and their desire of our mutual accord in seeking to gain them by justice and kindness, and withal to watch over them to prevent any

---

[1] The record so reads, but in fact the fall session was held in September, six months after the spring session. The fact and the time both concur in rendering it probable that September was intended, and that October was written by mistake of the Secretary.

danger by them, etc. We returned answer of our consent

with them in all things propounded, only we refused to include those of Aquiday in our answer, or to have any treaty with them." The action of the General Court of Massachusetts on this subject is instructive. It gives an official stamp to that vindictive spirit which was soon to display itself yet more signally in their treatment of Rhode Island. "It is ordered that the letter lately sent to the Governor by Mr. Eaton, Mr. Hopkins, Mr. Haynes, Mr. Coddington and Mr. Brenton, but concerning also the Generall Courte shal bee thus answered by the Governor; that the Courte doth assent to all the propositions layde down in the aforesaid letter; but that the answer shall be directed to Mr. Eaton, Mr. Hopkins, and Mr. Haynes, only excluding Mr. Coddington and Mr. Brenton, as men not to be capitulated withal by us, either for themselves or the people of the island where they inhabit, as their case standeth."[1]

The second General Court of Election was held at

[1] M. C. R., i. 305. Upon this record of the Puritan Legislature Mr. Savage comments with unsparing severity in a note to the above quoted passage in Winthrop. He says: "This is the most exalted triumph of bigotry. Papists, Jews, Musselmen, Idolators, or Atheists, may be good parties to a civil compact, but not erroneous Protestant brethren, of unimpeachable piety, differing from us in explication of unessential, or unintelligible, points of doubtful disputation. It was not enough that the common charities of life were broken off, but our rulers proved the sincerity of their folly by refusing connection in a just and necessary course of policy, which demanded the concurrence of all the plantations on our coast. This conduct also appears little more civil than prudent; for when those of Aquiday were associated by the gentlemen of Connecticut and New Haven in their address, the answer should have been directed to all without scruple." The Governor of Massachusetts at this time was the bigoted Dudley, the man upon whose person there was found, when on his death-bed, this original couplet, which embodies the prevailing sentiment of the age :—

"Let men of God in court and churches watch
O'er such as do a toleration hatch."——

a verse no doubt considered equally creditable to the piety and the poetic genius of the author. We think it was. That such a Governor should adopt such a course might be expected.

Portsmouth and lasted three days. The court roll of
freemen contains sixty names. An engagement to be
taken by all officers of the State was framed as follows :
"To the execution of this office, I judge myself bound
before God to walk faithfully, and this I profess in the
presence of God." The only change in general officers
was in substituting Robert Harding and William Balston
as assistants, in place of Nicholas Easton and William
Hutchinson. The nature of the government was defined
in these remarkable words : "It is ordered and unanimously agreed upon, that the Government which this
Bodie Politick doth attend unto in this Island, and the
Jurisdiction thereof, in favor of our Prince is a DEMOC-
RACIE, or Popular Government ; that is to say, It is in
the Powre of the Body of Freemen, orderly assembled,
or the major part of them, to make or constitute Just
Lawes, by which they will be regulated, and to depute
from among themselves such Ministers as shall see them
faithfully executed between Man and Man." Not less
remarkable is the act establishing forever the tenure of
lands. "It is ordered, Established and Decreed, unani-
mouslie, that all men's Proprieties in their Lands of the
Island, and the Jurisdiction thereof, shall be such, and
soe free, that neyther the State nor any Person or Persons
shall intrude into it, molest him in itt, to deprive him of
anything whatsoever that is, or shall be within that, or
any of the bounds thereof ; and that this Tenure and Propriety of his therein shall be continued to him, or his, or
to whomsoever he shall assign it for Ever." And thus it
continued to be for more than two centuries. The feeling of inviolability which invested real estate in Rhode
Island has ever formed a striking characteristic of the
people. For more than two hundred years the ownership
of land was essential to the privileges of a freeman, and,
by the law of primogeniture, entitled the oldest son to
the same immunities, in right of his father, until altered

by the adoption of the State constitution in 1843. And yet more singular was it that until the revision of the code in January, 1857, nowhere in Rhode Island could real estate be attached for debt except in the absence of the debtor. So long as he remained anywhere within the jurisdiction of the State, his land was secured to him by the operation of this earliest law and its subsequent modifications.

A " State" seal was ordered, to be a sheaf of arrows bound up, with the motto " *Amor vincet omnia*," engraved upon the leash. The word " State" appears for the first time in this decree. The possession of a seal has always been held as one of the insignia of sovereignty, or of exclusive rights. Its adoption by a yet unchartered government was significant. The motto was no less so. From the absence of the all-conquering affection, as displayed in the conduct of their brethren, they had suffered too much not to feel its value. They thus emblazoned their opinions to the world, and at the same time passed an ever-memorable law which illustrates their motto : " It was further ordered, by the authority of this present Courte, that none be accounted a Delinquent for *Doctrine :* Provided, it be not directly repugnant to ye Government or Lawes established." Religious liberty was here set forth in terms not to be mistaken, when it is remembered that no laws existed relating to matters of faith. " The people having recently transferred the judicial power from their own control to the Court and Juries, they enacted this law protecting liberty of conscience, not choosing to trust the Judiciary with the keeping of that sacred principle for which they had transported themselves, first from England and then from Massachusetts. It was the foundation of the future Statutes and Bills of Rights, which distinguished the early laws and character of the State and people of Rhode Island from the other English Colonies in America." [1] At no

---

[1] Bull's Memoir of Rhode Island.

period of the world has religious inquiry been more rife than during the seventeenth century. It was eminently an age of progress in spiritual development, and as a natural result, or cause, as different minds may view it, it was the palmy era of theological controversy. Elsewhere an avowal of independent thought was attended with danger to the liberty, the property, or the life of the earnest thinker. Here it was intended to remove all such obstacles to free discussion, and to leave a fair field for truth to work out its deepest problems. That in this process many opinions, which in our day may appear fanciful, fanatical, or visionary, and which may be regarded as idle vagaries or spiritual absurdities, were warmly expressed and stoutly maintained, is no reproach to the principle that permitted their utterance. In an inquiring age, when the minds of men were agitated by new and startling theories in religion and government; when the progress of liberal sentiments was awakening to fresh life the dormant energies of the old world, and urging its oppressed people to seek an asylum in the new; when education was becoming more diffused, and philosophy was no longer confined to the schools, or the elements of polity to the court; when men had begun to think for themselves, and dared to question kingly prerogative and priestly assumption; when all Europe was embroiled in wars and distracted by revolutionary sentiments, it is not strange that crude, grotesque, and unstable notions should blend with the essential truths which lay at the bottom of all this commotion. Novel ideas were started, new sects were established, secret societies abounded, and those phenomena which ever attend a transition state, and which, in this case, were a continuation of the movement of the preceding century, were everywhere apparent. The law of Rhode Island first sanctioned their existence, and foreshadowed the spirit of a future age. That "heresies" should

abound in such a community was inevitable, and our
Puritan neighbors found delight in recording them with
more fulness of detail than accuracy or propriety of expression.   Again we are indebted to Winthrop's Journal
for facts of which no record is to be found in our own collections ; and we prefer to quote him, because he was the
most liberal man of his age and station, to citing the
more bitter denunciations of Hubbard and Mather, or the
many other writers of that and the succeeding century,
whose Dudleian spirit would perhaps more truly portray
the prevailing temper of the times.   Governor Winthrop
says : " Mrs. Hutchinson and those of Aquiday island,
broached new heresies every year.   Divers of them turned
professed anabaptists, and would not wear any arms, and
denied all magistracy among Christians, and maintained
that there were no churches since those founded by the
apostles and evangelists, nor could any be, nor any pastors ordained, nor seals administered but by such, and
that the church was to want these all the time she continued in the wilderness, as yet she was ; " [1] and again,

CHAP.
V.

1641.
March
16-18.

Aug.

[1] ii. 38, 40.   The terms anabaptist and antinomian were used generally to
designate all dissenters from the established faith, and were not applied, as is
often supposed, specifically to the Baptists and Independents as Christian sects.
In the above enumeration of doctrines ascribed to the former, there is not
one that was, or ever has been held by the Baptists, while the distinctive feature of that denomination is not even mentioned.   Most of the doctrines
named were held by the Seekers, who were afterwards chiefly merged in the
Society of Friends, and by their opponents styled Quakers, until that name,
like that of Christian, has grown from an epithet of contempt to be an honorable appellation.   Many, if not all, of these doctrines, in a modified form,
are held by them at this day.   The term applied by Winthrop is liable to
mislead.   That similarity of name implies concurrence of sentiment, is an
idea as common as it is superficial—a truth well illustrated in the vague use
here made of the word ' anabaptist' by our Puritan journalist, and since so
often repeated by his Prelatical brethren.

The slur upon Mr. Easton in the next passage needs no comment.   If the
reader desires one he will find it in a note to Winthrop, i. 281.   The first
three gentlemen there named were all, at various times, Governors of the
colony.   Some, of whom was Mr. Coddington, became Quakers, and others
Baptists with Mr. Clarke ; which is no doubt the " schism " that broke up the
original Aquedneck church, of which Mr. Clarke was elder.

"Other troubles arose in the island by reason of one Nicholas Easton, a tanner, a man very bold, though ignorant. He using to teach at Newport, where Mr. Coddington their governor lived, maintained that man hath no power or will in himself, but as he is acted by God, and that seeing God filled all things, nothing could be or move but by him, and so he must needs be the author of sin, etc., and that a Christian is united to the essence of God. Being showed what blasphemous consequences would follow hereupon, they professed to abhor the consequences, but still defended the propositions, which discovered their ignorance, not apprehending how God could make a creature as it were in himself, and yet no part of his essence, so we see by familiar instances ; the light is in the air and in every part of it, yet it is not air, but a distinct thing from it. There joined with Nicholas Easton, Mr. Coddington, Mr. Coggeshall, and some others, but their minister Mr. Clark, and Mr. Lenthall, and Mr. Harding, and some others dissented and publicly opposed, whereby it grew to such heat of contention, that it made a schism among them."

An event that greatly alarmed the inhabitants of the island occurred soon after the adjournment of the Court. Some Indians, contrary to the treaty of July previous, kindled a fire on Mr. Easton's land, whereby his house, the first one built at Newport, was destroyed. A misunderstanding ensued that threatened the most serious results. An armed boat was fitted out to ply round the island to prevent any Indians from landing. Two English were wounded and one Indian killed, in a skirmish. Fortunately peace was soon restored.

At the ensuing Court, the law of liberty of conscience was re-enacted. "It is ordered that the law of the last
Court, made concerning Libertie of Conscience in point of Doctrine, is perpetuated." A license to practise surgery was granted to Mr. Robert Jeffreys, the Treasurer of

Newport. This is the earliest record of a licensed sur-
geon, but it was not the only case where such a license
was granted by the Legislature in this State. The price
of corn was fixed at four shillings a bushel. Inspectors
of pork were appointed, to whom all swine killed on the
island were to be shown, under penalty of five pounds.
Earmarks for swine and goats were regulated by the
Court, the right of property in them recognized, and the
marks required to be recorded.

The following spring the same general officers were
chosen, except that Mr. Easton, who had been superseded by Robert Harding at the last election, was re-
elected an assistant, and Mr. Harding dropped. [1] These
gentlemen continued in office until the charter government was organized, five years later. Sentence of disfranchisement was passed upon four freemen, [2] and their
names struck from the roll, and in case they came armed
on the island, they were to be disarmed and put under
bonds for good behavior. Unfortunately the reasons for
this earliest decree of virtual banishment are not given.
Three others were suspended the privilege of voting, two [3]
until they should give satisfaction for their offences, who
were afterward restored, and Mr. Lenthal, the minister,
who had returned to England. Amendments and alterations of laws were constantly made. Only such as were
permanent or of special interest can here be noticed.
The fee list was remodelled. Any arms or ammunition
were forbidden, under heavy fine, to be supplied to the
Indians. Jurors were elected by the freemen in town
meeting. Those who were only inhabitants could serve,

---

[1] In the term " general officers," are here included the Governor, Deputy Governor, the four Assistants and Secretary only. The two Treasurers, two Sergeants and two Constables, one of each for each town, are not specified in the text, as their duties were mostly local, and the repetition of so many names would be tedious.

[2] Richard Carder, Randal Holden, Sampson Shatton and Robert Potter.

[3] George Parker and John Briggs.

as well as freemen, on the jury, by virtue of their freehold estates. The pay of the jurors was fixed at one shilling for every cause brought to trial.

The island abounded in wild animals. Deer were very abundant and were made a source of revenue ; every man who killed one, except on his own land, being, at one time, required to give one half of it into the treasury, or to pay a commutation of two pounds sterling. Hunting parties were sent out to obtain venison for public use at the meetings of the Courts. The Indians were not allowed to kill them, except occasionally by special license, nor were traps permitted to be set for them, under a penalty of five pounds, except by the freeholder on his own land, and at a later period they were protected by game laws. Foxes gave much trouble. A premium of six shillings and eight pence a head was offered for them, to be paid by the treasurer of the town where they were killed. Wolves were numerous, and so destructive to the cattle that men were hired by the day to hunt them, and were paid besides, thirty shillings a head for every one killed, which bounty was soon increased to five pounds, and a special tax levied for this purpose, to be paid by the farmers in proportion to their number of cattle. Roger Williams was commissioned to arrange with Miantinomi for a grand hunt to extirpate them, which, however, was not so thoroughly done but that, for several years, they continued to be a source of annoyance. [1]

The important subject of a charter, which three years before had been discussed, was again considered at this session, and a committee, composed of the general officers, with Mr. Jeffreys, Mr. Harding and Mr. John Clark,

---

[1] Wolves are often mentioned in the records of Aquedneck, as in Jan., 1658, when Portsmouth asked Newport to aid in driving the island—and again on 10th Nov., 1663, when " the island was to be driven the next fair day on account of the destruction of sheep by wolves and other vermin." On the main land they existed much longer, and were repeatedly the subjects of legislation by the Assembly, to the close of the century, and even later.

was appointed with full power to act. Actual residence
on the island was required to entitle any freeman to vote,
but no one could be disfranchised unless the majority of
the entire body was present at the meeting. Only eleven
days before this Court convened, the four Pawtuxet men,
mentioned in the previous chapter, had submitted themselves and their lands to the jurisdiction of Massachusetts.
An act so dangerous to the independence of the colony,
and which might be taken as a precedent by other disaffected persons, could not fail to create much excitement.
The people of Aquedneck promptly took precaution to
avoid such a peril to themselves, by adopting an order
that no person should sell his lands to any other jurisdiction, or person therein not subject to the government of
the island, on pain of forfeiture.

Arrangements were made at this time to establish a
regular trade with the Dutch at Manhattan. It is indicative of the feeling existing towards Rhode Island in the
other colonies that she was driven to this step ; a feeling
of which the most painful evidence was shortly to be given.
The governor and deputy were instructed to " treat with
the governor of the Dutch to supply us with necessaries, and to take of our commodities at such rates as
may be suitable." Had there been a spirit of kindness,
or even of passive indifference, in place of open hostility,
in the neighboring provinces, Rhode Island would not
have been obliged to treat with the foreign and distant
settlement at New York for the supply of her wants.[1]
But the prejudice excited by her different faith, and more
liberal sentiments, was about to be manifested in an act
which few men at this day can contemplate without sur-

[1] Prior to the arrival of the English the West India Company established
a trading-post at Dutch Island in Narraganset Bay. Mr. Broadhead says :
" About the same time (1625) the Indian title to the island of ' Quotenis,'
near the ' Roode Island,' in Narraganset Bay, was secured for the West India
Company, and a trading-post was established there, under the superintendence
of Abraham Pietersen." Broadhead's History of New York, ch. viii. vol. 1, p.
268, and note. Besides this the Dutch had two fortified trading posts on the
south shore of Narraganset, in what is now Charlestown.

CHAP.
V.

1643.

May
19.

prise and indignation. The exposed condition of the country had suggested the idea of a union of all the New England colonies in a league of defence against the Indians. Six years before, just at the close of the Pequot war, when the plantation at Providence was in its infancy and the settlement of Aquedneck had not begun, the subject was first considered. Many difficulties served to retard the consummation, chiefly arising from jealousy in the other colonies of the power or the designs of Massachusetts. These fears had no good foundation, unless on the part of Rhode Island, which was the only one that did not, at some time during the negotiation, display them. We have seen that two years ago she united with Plymouth and the two Connecticut colonies in a joint letter to Massachusetts, upon the subject that formed the basis of the confederacy ; and we have read how those overtures were approved as related to the rest, and repelled with unmanly insult as regarded her. The times now demanded immediate action. Fears were entertained of the Dutch, especially by Connecticut, while the Indians daily threatened a general combination to exterminate the whites. They were becoming supplied with fire-arms and skilled in their use. The peril was imminent. The New England confederacy was formed by Massachusetts, Plymouth, Connecticut and New Haven, with their subordinate settlements, and styled the United Colonies of New England. By express stipulation no other jurisdiction was to be admitted. It was mainly a league for mutual defence, but contained an article for the rendition of fugitive servants and escaped criminals, with some other matters of international comity. From some suddenly conceived jealousy on the part of Massachusetts, Maine, then a propriety of Sir Ferdinando Gorges, which had been included in the preliminary negotiations, was not permitted to join the alliance. [1] Rhode Island was

[1] Hubbard assigns the reason, " because they ran a different course from the rest, both in their ministry and their civil administrations. Nor indeed

perhaps the most exposed of all the colonies, yet although
the confederated States already owed their existence to
the heroism of her founder, (and were shortly again to
receive the benefit of that practical Christianity which
they could not comprehend, in averting for the second
time a general war, by his effective influence in the
wavering councils of the Narragansetts,) neither of the
colonies within her limits was invited to join the league,
and her subsequent application for that object met with a
stern refusal. [1] She was left to stand alone amid dangers
from famine, pestilence and war. Her only strength was
in the valor of her sons and the truth of her principles.
Had the *lex talionis* been her guide, as it has been of
most governments, she would have been justified by the
necessities to which she was reduced, and might have
compelled admission to the league, by withdrawing her
restraining influence from the Indians. It is one of the
brightest spots in her history that in this dark hour the
magnanimity of her founder actuated her councils. Turn-
ing from the ingratitude of the Puritans, she appealed to

were they at that time furnished with inhabitants fit for such a purpose, for
they had lately made Agamenticus (a poor village) a corporation, and had
made a mean person mayor thereof, and had also entertained a contentious
person, and one under offence, for their minister." 2 M. H. C., vi. 467. Yet
the year before Maine was not considered so unworthy. Winthrop's Journal,
ii. 85.

[1] It would be ungrateful not to acknowledge the grace extended by the
General Court to the people of Aquedneck, by a vote of Sept. 7th, 1643.
"They of Aquidneck are granted to buy a barrell of powder, provided Lieut.
Morris give caution that it bee implied for the defence of the iland by the advice of the Governor and Deputy." M. C. R., ii. 44. But even this favor
was denied to the Providence colony, who were forbidden all trade with Boston, even to the purchase of arms and ammunition in this fearful crisis. That,
after such cruel and ungrateful conduct, Roger Williams should again interpose to save the United Colonies, when his own life and those of his friends
were secure in the love of the Narragansetts, who made a treaty of neutrality
with them at this very time, reminds us of Gibbon's comment on the conduct
of Belisarius in a case of domestic infidelity, "the unconquerable patience
and loyalty of Belisarius appears either *below* or *above* the character of a
MAN."

CHAP.
V.
1643.
Sept.

the king. Roger Williams was sent to England to intercede for a charter ; and because the tyranny of Massachusetts Bay would not relax, he was obliged to take
passage at New York. A free charter was obtained.
The despised colonies soon assumed the rank of a united
and independent State, and to the subsequent harshness of
her neighbors, was enabled to oppose the language of bold,
but courteous remonstrance. One of the earliest proceedings of the league was to sanction the dark deed recorded
in the preceding chapter, the murder of Miantinomi, the
too faithful friend of Rhode Island.

Oct.
5.

The frequent alarms led to the establishment of a
night watch in Portsmouth, which seems to have perfected the system of precautions that had so long occupied the attention of the people. The next General
Court changed the name of Aquedneck to the "Isle of
Rhodes or RHODE ISLAND."[1] The last recorded act of
the Aquedneck assembly declared that the majority of
the major part of the body appearing, should have full
power to transact business, and to impose penalties upon
those who did not attend, or who left the meeting without leave.

1643-4.

March
13.

1644.
May
20.

The alarm of Indian war again spread through the
colonies. A letter from Canonicus and Pessicus was received by Gov. Winthrop, announcing their intention to
revenge upon Uncas the death of Miantinomi. Two
messengers were sent at once to the Narragansetts to dissuade them, but without effect. The people of Aquedneck applied to Massachusetts for powder, but were refused, as Plymouth had been, owing, no doubt, to a
scarcity of ammunition ; a refusal which Winthrop records as an error of policy, for " although they were des-
perately erroneous " it would be " a great advantage to
the Indians " if they were cut off, " and a great inconvenience to the English should they be forced to seek pro-

July.

Oct.

[1] See note on the origin of this name at the close of chapter ii.

tection from the Dutch." The commissioners of the CHAP.
United Colonies, at their next meeting, removed the im- V.
mediate danger, having summoned the disputants to 1644.
Hartford, where an armistice was agreed upon till the
next year.

The records of the General Court of Aquedneck now
cease, and no town records of Newport remain to enlighten
us on the current events of the next two years. That
the same general officers, who had already been elected
three successive years, and whose term of office was "for
one whole year, or till a new be chosen," continued to
carry on the government, and that its judicial powers
were exercised by them as far as was necessary, there can
be no doubt. The mutilated pages of Portsmouth aid
somewhat in filling this unwelcome gap, and confirm
the fact that if no General Courts were convened in this
interval, town meetings were held in both the towns, and
their decrees executed by the general officers. The
deputy governor and one assistant were authorized to
appoint all town meetings at Portsmouth. Leave was Aug.
given to Osamequin, or Massasoit, with ten men to kill 29.
ten deer within the limits of the town, which were to be
shown to Mr. Brenton and Mr. Balston, and he was to
quit the island within five days. Several other meetings
are recorded during this year relating solely to local affairs. It was at this time that Plymouth colony sent
a magistrate to Aquedneck to forbid the government Nov.
there from exercising any authority, and claiming the
island to be within their jurisdiction, contrary to their
express admission at the time of the purchase seven years 8.
before.

A copy of the instructions given to Mr. John Brown,
who was commissioned for this purpose, is fortunately
preserved by Winslow, [1] at that time Governor of Plymouth. These are : 1. That a great part of their sup-

[1] Hypocrisie Unmasked, 83.

posed government is within the line of the government of Plymouth. 2. That we assuredly know that this ever to be honored House of Parliament would not, nor will when they shall know it, take from us, the most ancient plantation, any part of the line of our government formerly granted ; it being contrary to their principles. 3. To forbid them and all and every one of them to exercise any authority, or power of government within the limits of our letters patent. 4. To certify them that Coweset is not only within the said limits, but that the Sachem thereof and his sons have taken protection of this, our government. And, therefore, to forbid them to enter upon any part of his or their lands without due order and leave from our government."

A settled purpose was displayed by the Puritan colonies, soon after the charter was received by Rhode Island, to set it aside by every possible plea that could affect its validity. The active measures thus taken by Plymouth were at the same time pursued, yet more vigorously, if indeed they were not directly instigated, by Massachusetts. The more liberal Pilgrims were overborne by the dictatorial spirit of their Puritan neighbors, and were led to press claims which, had they ever existed, were become invalidated by their own acts. Yet this very messenger boldly withstood the pretensions of Massachusetts to other parts of Rhode Island as we shall presently see, and was perhaps the only man whose influence could have sustained the manly position he assumed in behalf of Shawomet. Gov. Winslow says, that Mr. Brown arrived at Aquedneck just as a public meeting was being held to apportion lands, a measure disapproved by Mr. Coddington and Mr. Brenton, who kept aloof from it, and who apprehended danger from the lawlessness of the people. He states also that Gorton, who after his release from prison in Massachusetts, had again settled at Aquedneck, was appointed a magistrate and had accepted the office—

a fact which he adduces as proof that the fears of the above-named gentlemen were well grounded. Mr. Brown's mission was futile. Gorton accuses him of privately seeking to dissuade the people of the island from recognizing the charter. The spirit of his instructions would harmonize with almost any means he might employ to fulfil them. Winslow says, he performed his duty publicly at the meeting. This meeting was probably held in Portsmouth to subdivide the lands there, as was usual at that time. No legible record of it, or of any other meeting for more than a year, remains.

The fact that a new government was about to be formed under the charter, no doubt led to this evident neglect of the old one so soon to expire. That this apathy was increasing is apparent from a vote at Portsmouth, making nine men a quorum at any town meeting, and requiring that the business to be done should be specified in the warning.

Newport had passed an order that no deer should be killed for two months, which Portsmouth concurred in, assigning as the reason that in that way the wolves would more readily come to bate and so be caught. At the same time it was ordered that of the five pounds bounty on each wolf, which had been established some years before, Newport should pay four and Portsmouth one. An act like this could not be valid unless passed by a General Court or concurred in by a town meeting at Newport. A more efficient law for the protection of deer was passed at the same meeting, forbidding their being shot in the summer, from May to November.

The most interesting record of this, the last meeting of the people of Aquedneck under their primitive government, contains the first notice of indentured apprenticeship in Rhode Island. " Memorandum : That whereas, Nicholas Niles, the father-in-law of Abell Potter, hath [bound him] the said Abell Potter with Mr. William

CHAP.
IV.

1644.

1645.

1646.
Nov.
28.

1646-7
Feb.
4.

CHAP.
V.

1647.
May
19.

Balstone for the term of eighteen years, with the consent of the said Abell. For the better securitie off Mr. Balstone, the towne consenteth herein and approveth thereof."

The three months that intervened before the first General Assembly of the now chartered State convened at Portsmouth we may suppose was employed in discussing the all absorbing topic, and in the preparation of that admirable code of laws then to be presented for adoption.

CHAPTER VI.

HISTORY OF WARWICK AND NARRAGANSET DOWN TO THE FORMATION OF THE GOVERNMENT UNDER THE FIRST PATENT, MAY, 1647.

WARWICK was settled some years later than Providence and Aquedneck, and chiefly by emigrants from them; but the same primitive cause, the intolerance of Massachusetts, forced most of its founders into banishment, while their peculiar views, differing from those of the other Rhode Island settlers, influenced them in selecting another spot for their resting place. No man has suffered more in reputation from the calumny of his enemies, or been made to feel more severely the penalty of nonconformity, or the trials of an independent spirit, than Samuel Gorton, the founder of Warwick. "A most prodigious minter of exorbitant novelties," "a proud and pestilent seducer," " a beast," "miscreant" and "arch heretic," are some of the epithets with which he has been branded by the malevolence of his age. It was in vain, in those days, that any dissenter from the established church of Massachusetts strove to deny whatever results the authorities saw fit to ascribe to his views. The fate of Williams and of Clark, was sure to be his. There was no reason why the Gortonists should be treated any better than the Anabaptists or the Antinomians had been, cr than the Quakers were soon to be. The same power that had driven Williams into exile and had disarmed the followers of Mrs. Hutchinson, was ready to vindicate its

CHAP.
VI.

superiority upon the sturdy spirit of Gorton. In 1636, Gorton arrived at Boston from London. But little is known of his earlier history, and that little is of no importance to our present purpose. He soon removed to Plymouth, where "he gave some hopes that he would prove a useful instrument." These hopes were soon dispelled by the wayward and independent spirit which he manifested. Cotton assigns as the reason of his leaving Boston that it was to escape from the claims of a creditor in England. Hubbard and Mather, with their accustomed bitterness, repeat the charge, but more reliable historians are silent upon it, and its truth has been reasonably doubted, from the fact that a removal to Plymouth would not secure him from arrest. It soon appeared that his religious views were widely at variance from those of his associates. The key note of a persecution that was destined to pursue him for many years, even beyond the chartered grasp of civilized man, was early sounded by one Mr. Ralph Smith, who had formerly been a minister at Plymouth, and a part of whose house Gorton had hired for four years. Some of Smith's household were in the habit of attending the morning and evening religious service held by Gorton in his family, which displeased the former. Gorton refused to vacate the premises. The only mode of ejecting him was by an appeal to the popular bigotry through the medium of the Court. Opportunity was not wanting in the case of one so peculiar in his views and so fearless in expressing them. What was the form of the action brought by Smith, or the nature of the charge against Gorton, is not distinctly stated, but the result was that the contract was broken, he was ordered to provide for himself elsewhere within a certain time, and to give bonds for his good behavior in the interval. A more serious breach of order was shortly alleged against him. A female servant in Gorton's family was seen to smile in church. To escape the proceedings which threatened in consequence of this overt act against the peace and dignity of the State, the woman fled to the woods. .Gorton spoke in her behalf, for which he was called to account by the Court, where, conducting himself in a very rude and contemptuous manner, his bonds were forfeited, he was bound over to the next General Court, and required to find new sureties for his conduct till that time. He obtained the sureties but immediately left for Aquedneck. Morton mentions only the difficulty with Smith, and assigns this as the cause of his banishment, which he says was decreed on the fourth of December 1638, to take place within fourteen days. Winslow and Gorton himself, both correct the error of fact, while other circumstances make it equally apparent that there is also an error of date. Six months before the time of his banishment, as given by Morton, Gorton was admitted an inhabitant of Aquedneck, as the records show. It is probable that the date in Morton should be one year earlier, and that the sentence of banishment within fourteen days was passed at a later court than the one in December. The difficulty with the Court, in the case of the servant woman, happened after that with Smith, and is not referred to by Morton. Perhaps the Smith case was tried in December 1637, and the subsequent one at the next March term. Very soon after the latter trial, all accounts agree that he went to Aquedneck, where a settlement had just been commenced by the Antinomian refugees. The Massachusetts writers, while they freely denounce the heresies of Gorton, deny that these were the cause of his banishment. There can be no doubt that the charge brought by Smith, in the first instance, for the purpose of annulling the lease and thus ridding himself of a disagreeable tenant, was that of heresy, and the inference is equally direct that the truth of the allegation had aroused ·popular feeling against the accused. The evidence is equally plain that his conduct, when on trial,

CHAP.
VI.

1637.

1638.
June
20.

was most abusive and his language insulting to the Court, so much so that "divers people being present desired leave of the Governor to speak complaining of his seditious carriage, and requested the Court not to suffer these abuses but to inflict condign punishment." That he was deeply imbued with the principles of "soul liberty" already established by Roger Williams, and indignantly repelled any attempt to fetter the free mind in its communion with the Creator, is so much in his favor, and at this day will go far towards exculpating his conduct at Plymouth.

In fact, it was on this account that he was warmly received at Aquedneck, and ever since, his name has been associated in this State, with those whose first coming hither was caused by Puritan persecution. That he afterwards so severely suffered from this cause has tended to confirm this opinion. But on the other hand, the minute account of his offensive bearing towards the Court is so consistent with the repulsive traits of his character, as afterwards displayed at Portsmouth, and still later at Providence, in a more dangerous degree, causing his banishment from Aquedneck, and his flight to Pawtuxet, that we are forced to believe him not to be so guiltless in his course at Plymouth as his defenders allege. This was indeed one of those common cases where neither party in a contest is altogether right, and in our view of it the plea of persecution cannot cover his errors until a later period of his history. Up to this time there is enough of wrong apparent on both sides to excuse in some measure the conduct of each, according as the sympathies of the writer may incline him to either party.

We might think more favorably of Gorton's course at Plymouth, had not his avowed principles, and his acts in accordance therewith, been so outrageous as not to be borne by the people of Aquedneck ; beside which we know that the Plymouth colony was more liberal in its feeling

than that of the Bay, permitting a greater latitude of in- CHAP.
dividual opinion. Assuming as above that the sentence VI.
of banishment was passed upon him in March, he must 1638.
have reached Aquedneck very soon after the settlement of
Pocasset commenced. His name appears the seventh on
the list of fifty-nine inhabitants in October, with that of
his companion John Wickes, who, Morton says, was one
of his earliest proselytes at Plymouth; and henceforth
their fortunes were closely united. As an evidence of the
distinction in which he was held at that time, it may be
stated that his is one of only four names on the list to
which Mr., used in that day as a special mark of respect,
is affixed. The date appended to these names is that of
their admission as inhabitants, not that of their coming
to the island, which must have occurred somewhat earlier. But the time of his arrival at Aquedneck is a point
of little moment compared with the history of his conduct
while there. That he was whipped and banished from
the island has been doubted,[1] because the State records
contain no notice of the fact. The evidence, however, is
too strong to permit us to doubt it. That it is not found
on the records is simply because judicial proceedings were
not entered there. But few of the court trials of that
day are preserved. Incidental references to them appear
occasionally on the State archives, as in the case of
Wickes, the earliest disciple and constant companion of 1642.
Gorton. The day after the four men,[2] who were after- March
wards among the first settlers of Warwick, were disfran- 16.
chised, it was ordered that if they, with John Wickes,
should come upon the island armed, the constable was to
disarm and take them before a magistrate, "Provided
that this order hinder not the course of law already begun
with J. Wickes;" by which it appears that Wickes had 17.

---

[1] Judge Eddy in Winthrop ii. 58, note, and Staple's Simplicities Defence,
10.

[2] Richard Carder, Randal Holden, Sampson Shatton and Robert Potter.

previously got into trouble and left the island—a virtual
banishment, although no record of any proceedings against
him, and no sentence of disfranchisement is found, any
more than there is against Gorton. It is probable that
both were involved at the same time, and that had the
Court files been preserved, the judicial punishment pronounced against both, of whipping and banishment, would
there be found. Lechford, who resided in New England
" almost for the space of four years," prior to August,
1641, relates the circumstances ; Winthrop and Morton
both refer to them, and Gorton himself not only does not
deny the facts, but, so far as he refers to his sufferings
prior to the settlement of Warwick, corroborates their
truth, speaking of " fines, whippings and banishment out
of all their jurisdiction," as suffered by himself and his
associates. The most positive and detailed evidence in
regard to his conduct and treatment at Aquedneck, is
given by Winslow, in an official form, as agent for Massachusetts, replying to Gorton's Simplicities Defence. [1]
There can be no doubt of the truth of the statements
there officially promulgated, however much we may dissent from the author's inferences. That Winslow and
Gorton were on good terms personally at the time of its
publication, although both were in England engaged in
conflicting business pertaining to the Warwick settlement,
and that Gorton never read but little of it, appears by his
letter to Morton. [2] Had the official documents been false
he would certainly have seen them and denied their truth,
instead of quoting the indefinite remark of a third person "that he would maintain that there were forty lies
printed in that book." The contempt expressed by Gor-

[1] Hypocrisie Unmasked. By Edw. Winslow, London, 1646. 4to., 103
pp. Published by Authority, and Dedicated to Robert, Earl of Warwick. It
is an extremely rare work. The writer examined the copy in the British
Museum, and since then the "sole duplicate" of that copy, which is now in
the splendid library of John Carter Brown, Esq., of Providence.
[2] Hutchinson's Massachusetts, i. 552 Ap. xx.

ton for the government of Aquedneck as being self-constituted, is of itself sufficient explanation of the source
whence his troubles arose, while the charges preferred
against him by the grand-jury of Portsmouth justify the
punishment he received. He says he conducted himself
" obediently to the government of Plimouth, so farre as it
became me at least, for I understood that they had com-
ission wherein authoritie was derived, which authoritie I
reverenced ; but Rhode Island at that time had none,
therefore no authoritie legally derived to deale with me.
Neither had they the choice of the people, but set up
themselves. I know not any more that was present in
their creation but a clergie man who blessed them in their
inauguration, and I thought my selfe as fitt and able to
governe my selfe and family, as any that were then upon
Rhode Island." That he ignored all civil authority at
Aquedneck he here admits, and gives his reasons for it,
thinking himself " as fit and able to govern himself and
family, as any that were then upon Rhode Island."
This spirit could not long exist in harmony with
the views of the settlers anywhere in this State, for
although there was no law religion here, there was an
organized government demanding respect for its officers,
and obedience to its statutes. The views of Gorton, as
above given in his own words, were too much like those
which the Puritan calumniators of Williams and Clarke
charged as being held by their associates, that they " denied all magistracy and churches." The banishment of
Gorton refutes the slander. And yet Gorton did not
deny all magistracy, but only the right of the people to
set up for themselves a form of government. After the
charter was received, his mind was relieved upon this
point. Meanwhile it was the constant source of trouble
to himself, and of annoyance to his neighbors.

The origin of his difficulty at Portsmouth, as stated 1640
by Winslow, was a trespass by a cow belonging to an old

woman, upon some land owned by Gorton. The woman, while driving off her cow, was assaulted by a servant-maid of Gorton's, and complained to the deputy governor, Nicholas Easton, who had the maid brought before the court. Gorton appeared in her behalf, refusing to allow her to come to court. One of the witnesses called for the defence, gave testimony strongly the other way, which enraged Gorton, who commenced abusing her, and had his friend John Wickes brought to the stand. Wickes refused to be sworn. Gorton sustained him in the refusal, and both insulted the court. At length the Governor summed up the case to the jury. While doing this, Gorton was very abusive to the governor and deputy, interrupting the former in his charge, insomuch that "many of the freemen present desired the court not to suffer such insolencies." He was committed, and when the Marshal was ordered to take him to prison, he cried out that Coddington should be taken. Wickes, Holden and others, made so much disturbance, that an armed guard was summoned to clear the way, and Wickes was put into the stocks. After this affair, Gorton was indicted by the grand jury as a nuisance, upon fourteen separate counts. A copy of this remarkable presentment signed by the Secretary of the Colony, is given by Winslow,[1] as follows:

"The sum of the presentment of Samuel Gorton, at Portsmouth, in Rhode Island, by the Grand Jury.

First, that Samuel Gorton, certaine days before his appearance at this Court, said, the Government was such as was not to be subjected unto, forasmuch as it had not a true derivation, because it was altered from what it first was.

2. That Samuel Gorton contumeliously reproached the Magistrates, calling them Just Asses.

3. That the said Gorton reproachfully called the

---

[1] Hypocrisie Unmasked, p. 54–5.

judges, or some of the justices on the Bench, (corrupt judges) in open Court.

4. That the said Gorton questioned the Court for making him to wait on them two days formerly, and that now hee would know whether hee should bee tryed in an hostile way, or by law, or in sobriety.

5. The said Gorton alleged in open court, that he looked at the Magistrates as Lawyers, and called Mr. Easton, Lawyer Easton.

6. The said Gorton charged the Deputy Governor to be an Abetter of a Riot, Assault, or Battery, and professed that he would not touch him, no, not with a pair of tongs : Moreover, he said, I know not whether thou hast any ears or no : as also, I think thou knowest not where thy ears stand, and charged him to be a man unfit to make a warrant.

7. The said Gorton charged the Bench for wresting witnesse, in this expression, I profess you wrest witnesse.

8. The said Gorton called a Freeman in open Court (saucy boy and Jack-an-Apes), and said the woman that was upon her oath, would not speak against her mother, although she was damned where she stood.

9. The said Gorton affirmed that Mr. Easton behaved himself not like a judge, and that himself was charged either basely or falsely.

10. The said Gorton said to the Bench : Ye intrude oathes, and goe about to catch me.

11. The said Gorton being reproved for his miscarriage, held up his hand, and with extremity of speech shooke his hand at them, insomuch that the Freemen present said, He threatens the Court.

12. The said Gorton charged the Court with acting the second part of Plymouth magistrates, who, as he said, condemned him in the chimney corner, ere they heard him speak.

CHAP.
VI.

1640.

13. The said Gorton, in open court did professe to maintaine the quarrell of another, being his maid-servant.

14. The said Gorton being commanded to prison, imperiously resisted the authority, and made open proclamacion, saying, take away Coddington, and carry him to prison ; the Governor said again, all you that owne the King, take away Gorton and carry him to prison ; Gorton replyed, all you that own the King, take away Coddington, and carry him to prison.

William Dyre, Secretary."

March.

Oct.
1.

Gorton was tried, and sentenced to be whipped and banished from the island, upon which he threatened an appeal to King Charles. The sentence was executed forthwith, and Gorton went to Providence. This was when " the weather was very cold," probably in March, as a few months later we find, by a letter from Roger Williams to Gov. Winthrop, that he was " bewitching and bemadding poor Providence." [1] His reckless and

---

[1] This letter fixes the time of Gorton's being in Providence earlier by more than a year than any other known data. It is as follows : " Providence, 8th 1st, 1640. Master Gorton having abused high and low at Aquidnick, is now bewitching and bemadding poor Providence, both with his uncleane and foul censures of all the ministers of this country (for which myself have in Christ's name withstood him), and also denying all visible and externall ordinances in depth of Familisme, against which I have a little disputed and written, and shall (the most High assenting), to death. As Paul said of Asia, I of Providence (almost) all suck in his poyson, as at first they did at Aquidnick. Some few and myself withstand his inhabitation, and town privileges, without confession and reformation of his uncivil and inhuman practises at Portsmouth : Yet the tide is too strong against us, and I feare (if the framer of hearts helpe not) it will force me to little Patience, a little isle next to your Prudence. Jehovah himself be pleased to be a sanctuary to all whose hearts are perfect with him; in him I desire unfeignedly to be, Your worship's true and affectionate Roger Williams."—*Winslow's Hypocrisie Unmasked*, 55, 56.

The trial of Gorton could not have been in 1639, as Hutchinson was that year the Judge at Portsmouth, where the indictment was found. Coddington and Easton, the latter residing at Portsmouth, were chosen Governor and Deputy Governor, on 12th March, 1640, on the union of the two towns.

lawless spirit, opposed as much to magistrates constituted, like those of Rhode Island, by the popular will, as to ministers supported by law, like those of the other colonies, found a fitting arena for its exercise in the feeble and distracted plantation of Providence. A bitter partisan by nature, with talent and energy to consolidate and control discordant elements into a vigorous and relentless opposition, he soon made himself the leader of all who were factious or discontented, and organized a destructive and revolutionary party in the hitherto comparatively peaceful settlement of Williams. The career of Gorton in Rhode Island illustrates how completely the extremes of conservatism and radicalism in civil affairs may unite in a single mind. While on religious matters he maintained with Williams the great doctrine of the underived independence of the soul, in civil concerns he was an absolutist, a stickler for authority, yielding, theoretically at least, entire obedience to chartered power, but ignoring any other, and steadily denying the right of the people of Aquedneck or Providence to govern themselves, and hence refusing to be controlled by them. And because of this defect in the basis of their government he used every effort to weaken or destroy it, assuming for that object the attitude of the veriest leveller recorded in history. His disorderly course in Providence was such as to prevent his being received as an inhabitant. It was required, as a condition of his reception, that he should confess the wrong he had done at Portsmouth and promise reformation, which we presume to mean, that he should admit the error of his theory of government. So great was the contention caused by his presence, that Mr. Williams seriously thought of abandoning his plantation and removing to Patience Island. The next year matters

---

Gorton was in Providence in Oct., 1640, and had been there some time. The weather was cold when he went there, which must therefore have been early in the spring, after the 12th March, or in April, 1640.

grew worse.   The refusal of the first application of Gorton and his associates to be received into town fellowship
did not discourage them.   A second attempt was made,
upon which William Arnold, then one of the five "disposers," to whom such applications were referred, addressed a letter, "To the rest of the five men appointed
to manedge ye affaires of our Town," giving reasons based
upon the weak condition of the town, why this further request should be denied.   These were, that Gorton had
"showed himself an insolent, railing and turbulent person," since, as well as before he came to Providence ; that
some of his company had insulted the disposers ; that
their former request had been refused and no new reasons
advanced why this should be granted ; that they had distracted and divided the town into parties, aiming to drive
away its founders, and had been ringleaders in breaking
the peace ; and finally he denies that any element of persecution is contained in a refusal to admit into a civil society men so turbulent.   He concludes by offering his
house and land for sale to the town, as the law required,
stating that if these men are received he shall sell and
move away.[1]   Not long after this a riot ensued in which

some blood was spilt, and the aid of Massachusetts
was invoked by some of the inhabitants.[2]   Gorton and
his company moved to Pawtuxet soon after this affair,

where their conduct induced four of the principal residents
to submit themselves and their lands to the government
of Massachusetts.[2]   The "warrant," as Gorton terms it,
issued by Massachusetts on this occasion,[3] greatly alarmed

[1] Hypocrisie Unmasked, 59–62.   New England Gen. Register, 216–18.

[2] See ante, chap. iv., pp. 110–111.

[3] "Massachusetts to our neighbors of Providence : Whereas, Wm. Arnold
of Pawtuxet, and Robert Cole and others, have lately put themselves and
their families, lands and estates, under the protection and government of this
jurisdiction, and have since complained to us, that you have since (upon pretence of a late purchase from the Indians), gone about to deprive them of
their lawful interest, confirmed by four years possession, and otherwise to mo-

his party, and drew from them a letter, addressed " To our neighbors of Massachusetts," signed by nearly all of them, which afterwards caused them much trouble. In this letter they justly call the document "an irregular note," "because it went beyond the bounds and jurisdictions limited unto them." They then discuss the submission of the Pawtuxet men, of which the "warrant" was simply a formal notification, denying the claim of Massachusetts to extend her jurisdiction beyond her chartered limits on account of any such act, whether done by English or Indians. The complaints of the submissionists are fully discussed and their conduct harshly reviewed. The invitation to implead them in the courts of Massachusetts is duly considered and declined in terms of unsparing severity. Through the whole protracted epistle there is interwoven a mass of abtruse theology, and a parade of biblical learning, of which the application is often difficult to discover, and the chief object of which is to hurl upon those to whom it is addressed a storm of theological invective. None but a mystical enthusiast could have written it, and he must be a zealous antiquary in these days, who would read it.[1] The bitter rebuke that it contained rankled in the minds of the magistrates, and the heresy they detected in its doctrines soon afforded a pretext for their vengeance. Soon after this letter was written the Gortonists left Pawtuxet, and purchasing of the Indians lands at Shawomet, beyond the limits of Providence,

---

lest them; we thought good therefore to write to you on their behalf, to give you notice that they and their lands, &c., being under our jurisdiction, we are to maintain them in their lawful rights. If, therefore, you have any just title to any thing they possess, you may proceed against them in our court, where you shall have equal justice ; but, if you shall proceed to any violence, you must not blame us if we shall take a like course to right them." Signed, Jo. Winthrop, Governor. Tho. Dudley, Ri. Bellingham, Incr. Nowell. The 28th of the 8th month, 1642. Simp. Defence, 53.

[1] This letter occupies nearly one-fifth of Winslow's book, and twenty-six closely printed pages, 60–86, of Staple's Simp. Defence R. I. H. C., v. 2.

CHAP.
VI.
1642-3.
Jan.
12.

removed to the wilderness, where English charter, or civilized claim, could legally pursue them no longer.

There were twelve purchasers, but eleven of whom are recited in the deed.[1] The tract extended along the bay from Gaspee point to Warwick neck and twenty miles inland, embracing the greater part of the present townships of Warwick and Coventry. The consideration was one hundered and forty-four fathoms of wampum peage.[2] The land was conveyed by Miantinomi, chief Sachem of the Narragansets and hereditary lord of the soil, and the deed was witnessed by Pomham, the local Sachem of Shawomet, with others.

No form of government seems to have been adopted. Their numbers were too small to require an organization. Some mode of adjusting differences was all they needed, and this was provided for by arbitration, which was the essential feature of the government of Providence. This was only a temporary arrangement to continue until a charter could be obtained from England. Had they remained unmolested until the settlement attained greater size, and no charter had been received, it would have been curious to see what method they could devise to secure social order without violating their fundamental principles. But this experiment was not to be tried. Scarcely had the settlement of Warwick begun when a fresh occasion of strife was presented, arising from the dissatisfaction of the natives, fomented, as there is too much reason to believe, by the intrigues of Massachusetts. At the first meeting of the General Court a committee of three, one of whom was William Arnold of Pawtuxet, who had re-

1643.

---

[1] They were Randal Holden, John Greene, John Weeks (or Wickes), Francis Weston, Samuel Gorton, Richard Waterman, John Warner, Richard Carder, Samson Shatton, Robert Potter, William Wuddall, and Nicholas Power. The latter is not named in the deed, but we learn from his letters that he was one of the purchasers, and Gorton mentions that there were twelve.

[2] Equivalent to £72 sterling, if black peage is meant, or half that sum if the payment was to be in white.

cently submitted to Massachusetts, was sent to Warwick
"to understand how things were," and to bring back with
them a certain Indian if possible [1] On the same day the
magistrates and certain deputies were appointed a committee to treat with the Sachems of Warwick and Pawtuxet about their submission, "and to warn any to desist
which shall disturb them." The next month Pomham,
with Soconoco, Sachem of Pawtuxet, submitted themselves
and their lands to the jurisdiction of Massachusetts, denied having assented to the sale of Warwick, or having
received any portion of the payment, and by this act of
submission afforded another pretext, of which their enemies at once availed themselves, to harass the unhappy
Gortonists in this their last retreat. The proceedings that
followed are so extraordinary, that we are led to examine
closely the motives and the means employed by the General Court.

Gorton was beyond the reach of any English jurisdiction. Having left Pawtuxet, he was no longer a tres-
passer on the lands of the protegés of Massachusetts.
Some new pretext must be found to secure their object.
A submission of the Warwick Sachem would furnish it,
claiming, as Massachusetts always did, that an act of
submission to their government by any party extended
their jurisdiction over the lands of such party. Gorton
had purchased Shawomet of its undoubted lord. The attempt of Pomham to deny the sale is, to say the least,
suspicious. The witnesses on this point, at the General
Court, were deeply interested parties. Arnold had bought
land of Soconoco, the Pawtuxet Sachem, a short time before, and the validity of his title depended on establishing
the independence of his grantor. The Pawtuxet men
were bitter against Gorton, and naturally desirous to
please their new and self-imposed rulers. They were prominent, if not the instigators, in the whole matter. The
Narraganset empire was rapidly falling. Massasoit had

[1] M. C. R., ii. 35.

CHAP.
VI.
1643.

Sept.
7.

12.

availed himself of an English alliance to sever his allegiance to the Narragansets, and the petty Sachems of Pawtuxet and Shawomet wished to follow his example. English ambition assisted their design. Miantinomi was shorn of his vassals by the act of the General Court in receiving their submission, as a few months later he was deprived of his life by a like interested tribunal. The motive in all this is barely concealed. At the time of the submission of the Pawtuxet men, Winthrop honestly gave as one reason for accepting it, that it would furnish them "an outlet into the Narraganset bay;" an object which Massachusetts kept steadily in view, and which furnishes a key to this dark intrigue. One other motive animated the actors in the coming drama. The heretics yet lived, and the sting of their last impolitic, although truthful, letter could only be assuaged by their blood. Territorial ambition, religious bigotry, and wounded pride, all united to demand their persecution, and for the time, blinded their assailants to the illegality, the injustice, and the dishonesty of the means employed to accomplish their end. At the next General Court active measures were taken to follow up this scheme to its consummation. The Comissioners of the United Colonies were in session, the same day, at Boston. The case of Gorton was referred to them and their assent obtained, in advance, to whatever course Massachusetts might see fit to adopt.[1] A letter, or warrant as Gorton again terms it, similar to the one sent on the submission of the Pawtuxet men, was written to the purchasers of Shawomet, informing them of the submission and the complaints of the Sachems, requiring them to appear at once before the court, where the plaintiffs were then present, and granting them a safe conduct for that purpose. A verbal reply by the messenger was returned to the court denying their jurisdiction, and rightly asserting that they were amenable only to the

[1] Hypocrisie Unmasked, p. 79, where the Act of the Commissioners is published.

government of Old England from which they expected
" in due season to receive direction for their well ordering
in all civil respects." A lengthy letter was also sent, addressed " To the great idol General now set up in Massachusetts," signed by R. Holden, if possible more bitter from
a sense of accumulated wrong, than that of November
previous. In this letter they denounce the conduct of
Pumham and forbid his return to Shawomet ; they complain of outrages committed by the Indians under the
shield of Massachusetts, and refer to two rumored threats,
uttered by subjects of that government, which foreshadow
the crimes that were to follow—one, that Miantinomi
should die because he had sold Shawomet to Gorton, the
other that the Gortonists should be subdued or driven off
even at the cost of blood. The proposal to attend the
court, and the offer of safe conduct for that purpose, are
rejected with scorn. An array of charges are next brought
against the two sachems, and a demand is made that the
Massachusetts should come to Warwick and answer them.
A postscript refers to their treatment of Mrs. Hutchinson,
news of whose massacre had lately been received, and for
which they are held morally responsible. The letter, as
usual, is full of scriptural allusions disparaging those to
whom it is addressed. The General Court could have
expected no other reply than one that would increase the
rancor engendered by the former letter. These two letters were furnished to Winslow, and form the chief evidence against Gorton, published in his official reply to
Simplicities Defence. They give occasion for " certaine
observations collected by a godly and reverend divine,"
classed under three heads :

1. Their reproachful and reviling speeches of the government and magistrates of Massachusetts.

2. Their reviling language against magistracy itself
and all civil power.

3. Their blasphemous speeches against the holy things of God.

Gorton says they "framed out of them twenty-six particulars, or thereabouts, which they said were blasphemous, changing of phrases, altering in words or sense ; not in any one of them taking the true intent of our writings ;" and it is certain, by Winthrop's account of the trial, that whatever may have been the real cause of hostility towards Gorton, his heresy was the ostensible reason of their severity.

The court immediately dispatched another letter, acceding to the demand of the Warwick men that Massachusetts should send to them, and informing them that they should shortly send commissioners to obtain satisfaction ; adding, that an armed guard would attend the commission, and closing with the assurance " that if you will make good your own offer to us of doing us right, our people shall return and leave you in peace, otherwise we must right ourselves and our people by force of arms." The following week Capt. Cooke, Lieut. Atherton, and Edward Johnson with forty soldiers were sent to Warwick. On their way to Providence they received a third letter from the " owners and inhabitants of Shawomet," informing them that their offer to Massachusetts was a peaceable and not a warlike one, and warning them upon their peril not to invade Warwick. To this the commissioners replied that they desired to speak with the men of Warwick, to lead them, if possible, to see their misdeeds and repent, but if they failed in that they should " look upon them as men prepared for slaughter," and would proceed accordingly. This outrageous missive spread terror in the humble settlement of Shawomet. The women and children fled for their lives, some to the woods and others in boats to gain the neighboring plantations. The men fortified a house and there awaited their assailants. A number of Providence men accompanied the troops to see what would be done, and to aid in effecting a peaceable adjustment of the difficulty. A parley was proposed. Four Providence men were selected as witnesses thereto. The commissioners briefly stated their case ; that the Gortonists had wronged some of the Massachusetts subjects, and that they held certain blasphemous errors of which they must repent or be carried to Boston for trial, or otherwise be put to the sword, and their goods seized to defray the charges of the expedition. From this proposition the owners of Shawomet dissented, on the ground that their adversaries would thus become their judges, but offered to appeal to England, which was refused. The Gortonists then proposed to refer the dispute to arbitration, offering their persons and property as security that they would abide by the decision of impartial men mutually chosen for the purpose. This seemed so reasonable that a truce was agreed upon until a messenger could be sent to Massachusetts to learn the views of the magistrates. The Gortonists charge the troops with many outrages during this truce, which are stoutly denied by Winslow. The four Providence witnesses [1] sent a letter to Gov. Winthrop giving an account of the parley, and entreating him to accept the proposal of arbitration. " Oh, how grievous would it be (we hope to you) if one man should be slain, considering the greatest monarch in the world cannot make a man ; especially grievous seeing they offer terms of peace," is the earnest language they employ. The commissioners also wrote a letter. A committee of the General Court happened to be convened, upon news of the murder of Miantinomi, when these letters were received. The elders, as usual, were consulted. The result was what we might anticipate from such a tribunal. It was " agreed that it was neither seasonable or reasonable, neither safe nor honorable, for

CHAP.
VI.

1643.
Sept.
28.

Oct.
2.

---

[1] They were Chad. Brown, Thomas Olney, William Field, William Wickenden. Simp. Defence, 108.

us to accept of such a proposition. 1. Because they would never offer us any terms of peace before we had sent our soldiers. 2. Because the ground of it was false, for we were not parties in the case between the Indians and them, but the proper judges, they being all within our jurisdiction by the Indians and English their own grant. 3. They were no State, but a few fugitives living without law or government, and so not honorable for us to join with them in such a course. 4. The parties whom they would refer it unto were such as were rejected by us, and all the governments in the country, and besides, not men likely to be equal to us, or able to judge of the cause. 5. Their blasphemous and reviling writings, etc., were not matters fit to be compounded by arbitrament, but to be purged away only by repentance and public satisfaction, or else by public punishment. And lastly, the commission and instructions being given them by the General Court, it was not in our power to alter them." [1]

Gov. Winthrop replied to the Providence letter, declining
3.   arbitration. The commissioners were directed to proceed at once. They notified the besieged that the truce had expired. A final effort was made to speak with the commissioners, but failed. The Providence men were warned to have no more intercourse with those of Shawomet. All hope of accommodation was at an end. The cattle were first seized and then the assault commenced. The Warwick men hung out the English flag in token of their allegiance to Old England. It was immediately riddled by the shot of their assailants. The troops had entrenched themselves and opened a regular system of approaches, so that the siege lasted some days. During all this time the Gortonists acted solely on the defensive, not firing a shot, although prepared to do so in case the house should be set on fire, or a forcible entry be at-

[1] Winthrop, ii. 139, 40. How far these reasons justify Gorton's suspicions of the impartiality of his adversaries, the reader can judge.

tempted. On Sunday morning the works of the besiegers CHAP.
were advanced so near the house that an effort was made VI.
to set it on fire, which failed. The commissioners sent 1643.
to Massachusetts for more soldiers. The affair had reached Oct.
a crisis. The Gortonists must surrender, or a fearful 8.
slaughter on both sides, with certain death, under form
of law, to those of the besieged who might survive the
conflict, would result. They submitted to superior force,
and were carried in triumph as prisoners to Boston,[1] where 13.
they were committed to jail to await their trial. The
next Sabbath morning the prisoners refused to attend 15.
church. The magistrates determined to compel them.
They agreed to do so if they might have liberty to speak,
should occasion require, after the sermon. This was conceded, so accordingly they came in the afternoon. Mr.
Cotton preached at them about Demetrius and the shrines
of Ephesus, after which, Gorton, leave being granted, replied, somewhat varying the application of the text, to
the great scandal of his hearers.[2]

[1] Gorton says this was a violation of the articles of surrender, by which
they were to "go along with them as freemen and neighbors," and not as
captives; and also that they took eighty head of cattle, besides swine and
goats which were divided among themselves and their subjects, and broke
open the houses, robbing the corn and other supplies. A part of these allegations are rather feebly denied by Winslow, while other parts are admitted
by Winthrop. Gorton in a note on page 119, Staples' Simplicities Defence,
taunts his captors with the extent of their triumph, "a whole country to
carry away eleven men," and says that one had died, Sampson Shatton, before, of his hardships, and but ten handled arms in this memorable siege.
Winthrop, p. 140, says three escaped, and that nine were brought in as prisoners, p. 142, but the Court records show that ten were put on trial.

[2] This was not the last time that our over-zealous neighbors found, to use
an expressive phrase, that they had "caught a Tartar." The author of the
Ecclesiastical History of Massachusetts, in a note to 1 M. H. C., ix. 38, relates a
pertinent anecdote as having come under his own observation in Boston. "A
man from the State of Rhode Island was accused of blasphemy, and brought
before a Court of Justices. He was said to be a *Deist,* an *Atheist,* blasphemer
of the Bible, &c. He denied it all. Witnesses were produced who had heard
him say that the Bible was *not* the *word of God.* He acknowledged that he
said it, and that every Christian would say the same; that he was no Atheist

CHAP.
VI.

1643.
Oct.
17.

20.

Gorton and his company were brought before the court upon the following charge of heresy and sedition : "Upon much examination and serious consideration of your writings, with your answers about them, wee do charge you to bee a blasphemous enemy of the true religion of our Lord Jesus Christ and his holy ordinances, and also of all civil authority among the people of God, and perticularly in this jurisdiction." It is worthy of notice that nothing is here said about Pumham. The ostensible cause of the first summons by Massachusetts is no longer regarded now that the heretics are in their power. Upon this absurd accusation, containing no fact that admitted of any possible reply, the captives were put on trial for their lives. A warrant was also issued for the arrest of Waterman, Power, and John Greene and son, who had fled during the siege. The two former appeared ; the latter escaped entirely. The prisoners' exceptions to the jurisdiction were overruled on the ground that Plymouth claimed them, and had yielded its power, in this

or Deist, but loved his Redeemer, and venerated his Bible. Being asked how he could be consistent, he answered, ' That his Bible told him that Christ was the *Word* of God, and the Bible a *record* of the *divine will*. This was all he meant by saying the Bible was not the *Word of God*.' He was dismissed, and he laughed heartily at his accusers. This man had been a Quaker preacher ; became a preacher of the Universalists, and had a small congregation in the county of Berkshire, in 1794 ; but has never been permitted to preach in the other churches of Universalists, his notions being very peculiar, and such his manner of expressing himself as people of all persuasions must dislike. Yet he possesses that acuteness of reasoning, and recollective memory for quoting Scripture, which would have been fully equal to Gorton, had he met with the same opposition. But the spirit of persecution has flown from this State, to the mortification of many who wish to be of consequence, and would fain raise its ghost, for the sake of complaining of the present magistrates and clergy, but cannot find even the shadow on the wall."

The writer of this history desires here to express his concurrence in the truth and the spirit of the concluding sentence above quoted, because thus far in the progress of this work the hostility between the two colonies was so constant that a casual reader might infer that the feeling, for which there was so much occasion two centuries ago, still lingered, at least in the mind of the author. This he expressly disavows, and only regrets that the nature of his

case, to the Bay ; and that, if·they were under no jurisdiction, then Massachusetts had no redress for her wrongs,
and must either right herself by force of arms, or submit
to their injuries and revilings. This was but a weak defence in a desperate cause ; nor is it strengthened by the
special pleading of Winslow, who says, on this important
point, " And if any ask by what authority they went out
of their own government to do such an act, know that his
former seditious and turbulent carriage in all parts where
he came, as Plymouth, Rhode Island, a place of greatest
liberty, Providence, that place which relieved him in that
his so great extremity, and his so desperate close with so
dangerous and potent enemies, and at such a time of conspiracy by the same Indians, together with the wrongs
done to the English and Indians under the protection of
that government of the Massachusetts, who complained
and desired relief ; together with his notorious contempt
of all civil government, as well as that particular, and
his blasphemies against God, needlessly manifested in his
proud letters to them. All these considered you shall see
hereby cause enough why they proceeded against him as
a common enemy of the country." If these general
charges were the real cause of their proceedings, why are
they not all specifically alleged in the indictment, since,

theme requires him, while speaking of the Puritans, to dwell almost wholly
upon the dark side of characters that possessed so much real piety and essential
greatness of soul. The Massachusetts writers of recent date have well atoned
for the injustice committed by their forefathers, displaying the liberality of
feeling which ever accompanies elegant scholarship. Bancroft, Dean, Elliott,
Felt, Hildreth, Savage, Sparks, Upham, Young, and since this work was commenced, Mr. Barry's stirring and truthful volumes, have all illustrated the triumph of truth over prejudice, and shown how a scholar may rise superior to
the biases that misled his ancestors. The times have changed, and the seventeenth century was the period of transition. The Puritans exemplified the
spirit of the past ; the founders of Rhode Island foreshadowed that of the future ; and we of the present may render justice and do honor to both, by
placing ourselves, so far as practicable, in the position of those whose acts
we record. The Puritans we should view in the light of bygone centuries ;
their opponents in that of the present age, which has adopted their principles.

if true, they might easily be proved?—instead of which the latter only is brought out at the trial, and the whole attention of the Court engaged in proving it.

Their letters were produced as evidence against them. These they were required to retract or explain, which they refused to do. "The Court and the elders spent nearly a whole day in discovery of Gorton's deep mysteries, which he had boasted of in his letters, and to bring him to conviction, but all was in vain." He denied the consequences imputed to them by the elders, and shrouding his opinions beneath an impenetrable veil of mysticism, maintained them to the last. A series of questions were propounded by the Court, upon which he was to answer for his life. These were—

1. Whether the Fathers, who died before Christ was born of the Virgin Mary, were justified and saved only by the blood which he shed, and the death which he suffered after his incarnation!

2. Whether the only price of our redemption, were not the death of Christ upon the cross, with the rest of his sufferings and obediences in the time of his life here, after he was born of the Virgin Mary!

3. Who is that God whom he thinks we serve?

4. What he means, when he saith, We worship the star of our god Remphan, Chion, Moloch? Written replies, signed by himself, were given to the Court. They appeared so reasonable that even the governor said he could agree with them in their answers though not in their writings,[1] to which concession the bigoted Dudley objected, while the more liberal Bradstreet, at Gorton's desire, requested that no further questions should be put to him.

It was a peculiarity of the mystical philosophy of the age, that ideas were couched in language of which the apparent meaning would lead to every excess, and which

[1] Simps. Defence, 132. Hutch. Hist. of Mass., i. 121. Eccles. Hist. of Mass., 37.

were too transcendental to be otherwise understood by the greater part. Such ideas were announced and defended by Gorton and the Antinomian school, all of which, as explained by the promulgators, were harmless enough ; but their danger consisted in the possible and probable abuse of them by the masses, while their opponents, as in the present trial, imputed to them results which the authors denied. Heresy was the only charge against the Gortonists, and the sole object to which the attention of the Court was directed. The crime being sufficiently proved, the punishment was the next consideration.

Upon this " the Court was much divided." The case of Gorton was the most difficult. All the magistrates, but three, condemned the great heresiarch to death, but a majority of the deputies refused to sanction the diabolical sentence. In the end he, with six others, were sentenced to be confined in irons, during the pleasure of the Court, to be set to work, and should they break jail, or in any way proclaim heresy or reproach the church or State, then, upon conviction thereof they should suffer death. They were sent to different towns, Gorton to Charlestown, Wicks to Ipswich, Holden to Salem, Potter to Rowley, Carder to Roxbury, Weston to Dorchester, and Warner to Boston. The other three were more mildly treated. Waddell was allowed to remain at large in Watertown ; Waterman, giving bonds to appear at the next Court, was dismissed [1] with a fine, and Power, denying having signed the first letter, a year previous, was dismissed with an admonition. A warrant was forthwith directed to the constables of the several towns to be ready within one week to receive the prisoners. Their cattle were appraised and sold to defray the cost of the seizure and trial.[2] The

---

[1] At the Court on the 29th May following, being " found erroneous, heretical and obstinate," he was remanded to prison till the September Court, unless five magistrates should meanwhile see cause to send him away, in which case he was banished on pain of death. M. C. R., ii. 73.

[2] The justice of this piece of judicial robbery can only be defended on

prisoners were allowed to name two of the five appraisers selected for this purpose, which they properly declined to do.[1] The convicts, secured in chains, were sent off to the several towns named in their sentence, not however till they had been paraded in a body before the congregation at Mr. Cotton's lecture, with their irons upon them, as an instructive spectacle. In this condition they were confined the whole winter, in the course of which Gorton accused Cotton of having advised, in a sermon, that he

1643-4.
Jan.
12.

should be starved to death. This charge could scarcely be credited had not the elders and magistrates, at the trial, doomed him to die. This led Gorton to write a letter to the ruling elder of the Charlestown church, which is preserved in his book. But public opinion did not sustain such severe proceedings, and what was more to be dreaded by these zealots, the prisoners corrupted the people with their heresies. Now this offence, by the terms of the sentence passed upon them in November, was to be punished with death ; but a mightier power demanded their release. At the next General Court they were set

March
7.

at liberty, and banished from all places claimed to be within the jurisdiction of Massachusetts, including Providence, and the lands of the subject Indians ; and if found anywhere within those limits after fourteen days, they were to suffer death.[2] But even this brief period was not allowed them, for three days after, while Gorton and a

10.

some such ground as that taken by the " cannie Scot," in the anecdote quoted by Judge Staples, in a note to Simplicities Defence, p. 136, as having occurred several years since in the island of Jamaica. " A Scotch officer, with several others of his corps, engaged in a billiard match with some Jews. The children of Israel, it seems, were much too expert at that game for the Caledonian and his companions. The latter, after having lost some money, mustered their whole joint stock, and staked it against the sons of circumcision ; the game was played ; the Scot lost ; but he swept the stakes into his hat, drew his sword, and protected by his friends, retired, calling out, ' D—n yere sauls, ye scoundrels, yere a' enemies to the Lord Jesus Christ.'"

[1] See M. C. R. ii. 51–4 for official proof of the foregoing facts.
[2] M. C. R., ii. 57.

few others were awaiting the arrival of their comrades at
Boston, a warrant from the Governor was served on them,
ordering them to leave the town within two hours. They
departed for Aquedneck, lodging one night in their own
houses at Shawomet, whence they wrote a letter to Gov.
Winthrop to inquire if their own purchased territory was
included in the sentence of banishment. To this the
Governor replied that it was, and ordered them to leave
on peril of their lives. They did so, and once more sought
refuge at Aquedneck. Thus ended these atrocious proceedings, which form one of the darkest pages in the history of Massachusetts.[1]

CHAP.
VI.

1644.
March
26.
April
1.

The controversy was about to be transferred to England.
The settlement of Warwick was for a time suspended.
Its persecuted owners were kindly received at Aquedneck,
whence they had been driven in disgrace a few years before. The cause for which they had since suffered, and
the measure of cruelty they had lately received, were
enough to ensure them an earnest welcome. Here they
hired houses and lands, and remained till after the reception of the charter had deprived their enemies of the last
semblance of claim to intermeddle with the affairs of
Rhode Island.

It produced a curious effect on the minds of the Indians, that, after such harsh treatment, and so many
threats from their opponents, the Gortonists had returned

[1] The details of this memorable trial reminds us of the application of a
nursery rhyme as made by the late Archbishop of Dublin :—

> "Old Father Long-legs wouldn't say his prayers :
> Take him by the right leg—
> Take him by the left leg—
> Take him fast by both legs—
> And throw him down stairs! "

"There," said his Grace, " in that nursery verse you may see an epitome
of the history of all religious persecution. Father Long-legs refusing to say
the prayers that were dictated and ordered by his little tyrants, is regarded as
a heretic, and suffers martyrdom." Who shall say hereafter that there is no
moral conveyed in Mother Goose's Melodies ?

CHAP.
VI.

1644.
April
1.

alive. They imagined that two distinct races inhabited Old England, one the English, whom they called Watta-conoges,[1] and the rival race they now termed Gortonoges. The civil war, of which they had heard, confirmed this idea, and the release of the Gortonists they naturally enough attributed to the preponderance of the Gortonoges at home, which alarmed the English lest they should come over to America, and revenge the injuries that their feebler compatriots here had sustained.

Soon after the return of Gorton the Narragansets sent messengers, asking him and his friends to come over and speak with Canonicus. The venerable savage, with Pessicus, the brother and successor of Miantinomi, received them with a courtesy to which they had long been strangers. A council of the tribe was assembled. Their own situation, impoverished by the heavy ransom paid in vain for the life of their murdered prince, and the condition of their guests, robbed by the same remorseless power, formed the subject of their conference. The result was most important. This powerful tribe, upon whose fidelity, in former years, had hung the destiny of New England, voluntarily submitted, in a body, " unto the government and protection of that honorable State of Old England." In

19.

a written instrument they declared their allegiance to King Charles, " upon condition of His Majesty's royal protection ; " and the signers, as having been successively from time immemorial, sovereign princes of the country, say that they cannot yield "unto any that are subjects themselves in any case." They appointed Gorton, Wicks, Holden and Warner their agents to carry their submission to England ; soon after which Gorton and Holden embarked at New York with the instrument.[2] The

---

[1] Signifying coatmen, or those who wear clothes. R. W'ms Key R. I. H. C., i. 60.

[2] The exact time of Gorton's departure is unknown. Staples and Mackie say it was " in 1644, probably in the summer; " but by Gov. Winslow's account in his answer to Gorton's Simplicities Defence, it appears that in No-

other two remained at home.   John Greene, of Warwick, CHAP. VI.
also accompanied Gorton.   Besides their Indian agency,
their business was to enter a complaint with the Com- 1644.
missioners of Foreign Plantations against Massachusetts,
in behalf of the people of Shawomet, to obtain for them Sept.
the restoration of their property.   Notwithstanding the 17.
arrival of Mr. Williams with the free charter of Providence, Massachusetts strove, though vainly, to continue
her usurpation over the lands of Shawomet.   A notice
was issued warning any persons from settling there without leave from the General Court.   The following year a 1645.
yet bolder step was taken by the General Court.   A pe- Oct.
tition, signed by thirty-two persons, of whom twenty were 1.
freemen, asking for the lands of Pumham, was granted.
Ten thousand acres were given them.   They had power
to admit or keep out others as they pleased.   Benedict
Arnold was appointed to negotiate with the sachem for
his right in any improved ground.   The houses of the
Gortonists were placed at the disposal of the petitioners,
provided only that they should pay to the owners what
the Court should appoint, " if they see cause so to do,"
and that ten families should take possession within one
year.[1]   No settlement upon this grant was made.   Mr.
John Brown, a magistrate of Plymouth, and then one of
the Commissioners of the United Colonies, prohibited the
settlement, claiming the lands as within Plymouth jurisdiction, and saying it should be restored to the rightful
owners, Gorton and his associates.   This bold stand, so
creditable to Brown, although partially disowned by his
government, deterred the settlers,[2] and before the dispute

---

vember of that year he was still at Aquedneck, and was a magistrate there
when Mr. John Brown was sent to assert the Plymouth claim to the island.
Winslow was Governor of Plymouth that year, and signed Brown's commission Nov. 8, 1644.   On 14th January, 1645-6, Gorton dates his book at London.   I infer that he left during the winter of 1644-5.   Perhaps Brown's
visit at Aquedneck hastened his departure.

[1] M. C. R., ii. 128.   [2] Winthrop, ii. 252.

that arose on the question between Massachusetts and Plymouth was decided by the Commissioners in favor of the former, the Parliament had already ordered its restoration to the lawful purchasers. Similar annoyances continued for many years, summons being often issued to require the attendance of parties at the Massachusetts Courts, upon the suit of her subjects resident in Rhode Island.

The efforts of Massachusetts to extend her jurisdiction in this direction seemed to receive a fresh impetus by the arrival of that charter which was designed as a shield to the feeble colonists of Rhode Island against her all-grasping ambition. The coveted shores of the Narraganset assumed a new importance in her eyes when the action of Parliament placed them beyond her reach. Every effort was made to attach to herself any residents of Rhode Island who were dissatisfied with the existing order of things, and thus to sow the seeds of discontent more widely in the heretical plantations. The insane idea was cherished by her rulers and inculcated upon the other colonies, that in this way the people of Rhode Island might be led to question the validity of their charter, and be discouraged from organizing their distracted settlements into one corporate body under its provisions. Plymouth, we have already seen, was led to claim the eastern shore and the island, and Connecticut was ere long to assert her right to the Narraganset country, while Providence and Warwick were apportioned to the fomenters of this tripartite division. As we examine the progress of this deep-laid scheme, and observe the steadiness with which it was pursued through a long series of years, we cannot but admire the firmness of our ancestors in foiling it at every turn, nor can we fail to recognize the hand of a Superior Power in preserving a colony whose peculiar principles at first made it an object of aversion, and finally were adopted as the cardinal doctrines of a whole nation.

The result of Gorton's mission, so far as falls within CHAP.
the limits of our present chapter, was briefly this. The $\underset{\sim}{\text{VI.}}$
Commissioners issued an order requiring Massachusetts to 1646.
reinstate the proscribed parties, and forbidding any at- $\underset{15.}{\text{May}}$
tempt to exercise jurisdiction over them. It was brought
over by Holden in a ship to Boston. With some difficulty Sept.
he was allowed to land. Many wished to commit him to $^{13.}$
jail, but better counsel prevailed, and he was permitted
to pass quietly through to Rhode Island, by virtue of the
protection given him by Parliament. Upon receipt of Nov.
this order the General Court seriously debated how far $^{4.}$
they owed allegiance to England, but wisely concluded,
on advice of the elders, that they were not yet independent.[1] They decided to send Mr. Edward Winslow to
England as their agent. An answer to Gorton's memorial, a copy of which had been enclosed in the aforemen-
tioned order, was prepared, which Winslow, being duly Dec.
commissioned, carried, together with two sets of instruc- $^{4.}$
tions, one public, in accordance with his commission, the
other secret, concerning the course he was to adopt and
the answers he was to make to the objections against the
conduct and government of Massachusetts, contained in
the Commissioners' order.[2] The controversy in regard to
the lands of Warwick, so named by Gorton in compliment
to the Earl through whose influence his mission was successful, was prolonged for thirty-five years. It soon became involved in the greater dispute relating to the adjacent territory of Narraganset, which will be considered in
future chapters. The first decision, above given, was final

[1] This rather remarkable discussion is given at length by Winthrop, ii.
278–284. It shows the temper of the times, and demonstrates more clearly
than any other proceedings since those of 1635, when a general governor was
expected from England, (Winth. Jour, i. 154, and ante chap. i. pp. 32–3,)
the feeling with which the Puritans viewed any act of the home government
that threatened to abridge their virtual independence.
[2] Copies of all these papers are given in Winthrop, ii. 295–301, and of the
most important ones in R. I. Col. Rec's. i. 367–373.

CHAP. in its effect, although, after hearing Mr. Winslow, the
VI.   committee wrote to Massachusetts that if the Shawomet
1647. lands were in their patent, or in that of Plymouth, the
May   case would be altered ; but they soon afterwards wrote
25.   to all the colonies that the Warwick men should be as-
July   sisted and not molested during the examination of the
22.   question at issue.[1] The purchasers of Shawomet returned
to their homes, and successfully withstood the pertinacious
efforts of Massachusetts to retain her unlawful dominion
over them.

The Warwick men were strict constructionists of the
most rigid school. They neither recognized the existing
governments of Providence and Aquedneck, as we have
seen, nor did they establish any of their own ; not, as
their enemies represented, because they were opposed to
all magistracy, but because, as English subjects, they
could not lawfully create or submit to any government
that was not authorized by patent from the Crown or
Parliament of England. Hence we have no record of
May.   their proceedings until after the organization of the colonial government. They were few in number, so that the
mode of settling difficulties, by arbitration, adopted by
them before their expulsion, was probably continued till
their scruples were removed by the adoption of the charter. After this took place their rigid adherence to all the
forms of law, as well as to its spirit, was no less remarkable than had been their previous neglect. The charter
supplied their theoretical wants, and devotion to its letter
and spirit marked all their subsequent conduct.[2]

[1] Both these letters are in Staples' Gorton. R. I. H. C. ii. 203–6.
[2] One or two examples of this may here be mentioned. For many years
their numbers were few, and some of the requirements of the common law
bore heavily upon them, especially that requiring twelve men to constitute a
jury. Accordingly we find them altering that provision to conform, in the
language of the charter, "to the nature and constitution of the place," in
these words : "Whereas the townsmen of Warwick having taken into consideration that it cannot stand with the constitution of the place to continue

The act of submission arrayed the Narragansets in CHAP.
hostility to the pretensions of Massachusetts, and virtu- VI.
ally annexed their country to the State of Rhode Island, 1644.
of which, thereafter, it formed an important part. Three 1641.
years prior to this Richard Smith had purchased land and
erected a trading house, in what is now North Kingston,[1]
in the midst of the Indian country, which was the only
settlement south of Warwick until after the charter went
into operation, when Roger Williams set up a similar establishment for a few years and sold out to Smith, upon
his second appointment as agent to England.[2]

Both English and Indians were now the acknowledged 1644.
subjects of Great Britain, and the haughty spirit of the

twelve men for the tryal of causes, It is therefore ordered that there be established six jurors for the trial of causes, and to have six pence a man for each
cause, and for counsellor's fees three shillings and four pence, and this to be
of force notwithstanding any law formerly to the contrary." Warwick Records of Feb. 5, 1656,7. This change might appear as a violation of law instead of a real conformity to its spirit, if the preamble were not recited and
their circumstances were not considered.

But still later we have a more striking instance of their attachment to
"law and order." At a town meeting, Oct. 12, 1663, we find it "Ordered in
regard that there is a writing directed to the warden or deputy warden of the
town of Warwick, bearing date the 23 September, 1663, and subscribed
James (I. R.) Rodgers, and not the title of any office annexed thereto; the
Town do therefore protest against it as being *contrary to law and order*, and
that report be made hereof to the next Court of Commissioners. It is further ordered that the town being sensible of matters that do depend, which
concern our agent, Mr. John Clarke, do therefore conclude to choose commissioners to attend the Court notwithstanding illegality of the sayd writing,
and that justice may proceed notwithstanding the sayd neglect do likewise
order to choose jurymen to attend the Court of Trials." See Warwick Records of that date. Rogers was General Sergeant of the colony, and should
have affixed the title of his office to his name in an official communication.

[1] On the site of the present (1835) Updike house, which is said to be
built, partly, of the materials of Smith's. Potter's Early Hist. of Narraganset, R. I. H. C. iii. 32.

[2] M. H. C. i. 211. The precedence of Smith was denied by Howlden and
Greene in their sketch of Narraganset, in 1680. They say Warwick was settled first, and that Williams preceded Smith, but the evidence is all the other
way, and their error perhaps arose from there being two Richard Smiths, father
and son, in the concern. Br. S. P. O. New England Papers, vol. iii. p. 81.

CHAP.
VI.

1644.
May
24.

May
29.

July
15.

Sept.
1644-5.
Feb.

native chiefs refused to account for their conduct to any but their common Master. A summons was received from Massachusetts for them to attend at the next Court. They declined to do so, and informed the government of their submission to King Charles, and of their intention to make war on Uncas. This letter, with one of like purport from Gorton, gave great anxiety to the General Court. Two messengers were sent to the Narragansets to counteract the influence of Gorton, and to dissuade them from their purpose. They were coldly received and failed in their mission. Pumham and Soconoco, dreading the anger of the Narragansets, applied to Massachusetts for a guard. An officer was sent with ten soldiers to build a fort, and to remain for their protection till the danger was passed. Although the Commissioners of the United Colonies prevented immediate war between the hostile tribes, they could only avert it for a while. In a few months the Narragansets sent messengers to Boston, declaring that unless Uncas should pay a hundred and sixty fathoms of wampum, or come to a new hearing of the case within six weeks, they would make war upon him.[1]

1645.

June
18.

July
28.

In the spring the long restrained wrath of the Narragansets vented itself upon the Mohegans. One thousand men, some of whom were armed with guns, attacked Uncas and defeated him with considerable slaughter. Connecticut and New Haven sent troops to protect Uncas. The General Court despatched a letter to the Narragansets requiring them to desist from war, and soon after sent Benedict Arnold as a messenger to them. The Indians afterward stated that he had misrepresented their answer, and sent for Roger Williams to assist them in their troubles. A special meeting of the New England Commissioners was held in this emergency, and messengers [2] were

---

[1] Hubbard's New England, ch. li.

[2] Sergeant John Davis, Benedict Arnold and Francis Smyth.

sent a second time to require both the hostile tribes to send
deputies to Boston, who should explain the cause of the war,
receive satisfaction, and make peace.   This attempt failed.
The embassy was haughtily treated by the Narragansets,
who were resolved to have the head of Uncas.   On their
return they brought a letter from Mr. Williams, stating
that terms of neutrality had been made by the Indians
with the colonies of Rhode Island, and that war was inevitable.[1]   The United Colonies at once declared war
against the Narragansets, and a force of three hundred
men, under command of Major Edward Gibbons, was
raised.[2]   Forty mounted men were impressed by Massachusetts within three days, and sent on in advance under
Lieut. Atherton.   Messengers [3] were also sent to carry
back a present that the Indians had lately sent as a peace
offering to the English.   The Narragansets, alarmed at
these active demonstrations, sued for peace.   Through the
mediation of Williams, to whose influence, now for the
second time within eight years, New England owed her
peace and safety, Pessicus, with two other principal sachems, and a large train of attendants, came to Boston.
A treaty was concluded which bore heavily upon the Narragansets.   They were to pay two thousand fathoms of
wampum in four equal instalments, the last at the end of
two years.   Captives and canoes were to be mutually restored by them and the Mohegans, and the disputes between them were to be settled by the Commissioners.
They were to give up all right to the Pequot country,

CHAP.
VI.

1645.

Aug.
19.

27.

[1] Hubbard's New England, ch. li. and Trumbull's Connecticut, i. 150–4.

[2] The declaration of war contains a summary of previous occurrences
with the Indians, signed by John Winthrop, President, and is given at length
by Hubbard, ch. li. and in 2 M. H. C. vi. 454–62.

[3] Capt. Harding, Mr. Wilbore and Benedict Arnold—the latter as interpreter, but he could not be found in Providence, and dared no longer to venture among the Indians, who charged him with misrepresenting their reply
two months previous.   Roger Williams, whose influence was paramount with
the Indians, acted as interpreter on this occasion at the solicitation of the
messengers. (Knowles, 204.)

CHAP.
VI.
1645.
which they had aided the English in conquering. Other hard terms were enforced, and hostages were required of them. Sadly they signed this compulsory and oppressive treaty, and sullenly they retired to their native fastnesses to brood over the wrongs thus newly inflicted. The severe exaction almost ruined them. The following spring they failed to send the tribute, and when a small part only was sent the Commissioners refused to receive it unless they could have the whole that was due.

1646.
June

The remainder of this painful story, although it carries us beyond the limit assigned to this chapter, is better told here. The next year an extra meeting of the New England Commissioners was called on account of the failure of the Narragansets to fulfil the treaty, and of their alleged attempts to allure the Mohawks to unite in a war against the English. A threatening letter was sent to Pessicus requiring his appearance at Boston. He excused his attendance on the plea of sickness, declared that he had been forced by fear to accept the treaty, and promised to send Ninigret, sachem of the subordinate tribe of Nianticks, to Boston, and to abide by any agreement he should make. When Ninigret came before the Commissioners he denied all knowledge of the treaty, or of any reason why the Narragansets should pay tribute to the English, to whom they owed nothing. The case being explained to him, he desired ten days to send home for the wampum, while he remained as a hostage. His messenger brought back but two hundred fathoms, which Ninigret attributed to his absence. It was finally agreed that he should pay a thousand fathoms within twenty days, and the rest by the next spring, upon which condition he was dismissed.

1647.

Aug.
3.

The wampum was not paid. Why should it be? When we consider the foul death of their almost idolized chieftain, to avenge which—not upon the English, its real authors, but upon Uncas, their ruthless tool—they had

begun a war after due notice given, as agreed, to the
English, who at first gave their consent ; and that then the
English had marched an army against them, and by ter- 1647.
ror had forced them to a treaty of which the avowed object was to disable them, we cannot blame Pessicus for
disavowing, or Ninigret for ignoring it, or either for neg-
lecting to comply with its provisions. Again messengers
were sent to the Narragansets without effect. Rumors of 1648.
an Indian alliance continued to alarm the colonists, who
persisted in identifying the cause of Uncas with their
own, and in considering any attempt of the Narragansets 1649.
to avenge their wrongs upon the Mohegans as a conspiracy
against themselves. An abortive attempt was made to
assassinate Uncas. Another special meeting of the United July
Colonies was called upon this occasion, and Ninigret again 23.
appeared to excuse his breach of faith, and to defend the
recent attack upon the mortal foe of his tribe. The patience of the English was exhausted in this last fruitless
effort to obtain the tribute. The next year the Commissioners sent Capt. Atherton with twenty men to collect 1650.
it. Pessicus tried in vain to avoid an interview while he
assembled his warriors. Seeing this, Atherton forced his Sept.
way, pistol in hand, into the wigwam, and seizing the sa- 5.
chem by the hair, dragged him from the midst of his attendants, threatening instant death if any resistance was
offered. This summary conduct, which reflects more
credit on the courage of the Captain, than on the justice
or the policy of his government, produced the desired result. The debt was paid. The troopers departed, leaving behind them, in Indian memory, one more act of
wrong and insult to rankle till the day of retribution.
From the murder of Miantinomi, down to the savage expedition of Atherton, the whole seven years is filled with
acts of aggression and of unjust interference on one side,
and with the haughty protests of an injured, a high-spirited, and a feebler race of Indians on the other.

CHAPTER VII.

1647—1651.

HISTORY OF THE INCORPORATION OF PROVIDENCE PLANTA-
TIONS FROM THE ADOPTION OF THE PARLIAMENTARY CHAR-
TER, MAY, 1647, TO THE USURPATION OF CODDINGTON, AU-
GUST, 1651.

CHAP.
VII.

1647.

" THE Incorporation of Providence Plantations in the
Narraganset Bay in New England," was the legal title
under which the several settlements in Rhode Island were
united by the terms of the patent. The origin of this
charter we have already noticed. Its peculiar character
deserves attention. It was very general in its provisions,
and conferred absolute independence on the colony. The
single proviso with which it was fettered, to wit that " the
laws, constitutions and punishments, for the civil government of the said plantation, be conformable to the laws
of England," was practically annulled in the same sentence by the subjoined words, " so far as the nature and
constitution of that place will admit." Thus the people
were left free to enact their own laws, for this qualifying
clause in effect defeated the proviso. No charter had ever
been granted up to that time which conferred so ample
powers upon a community, and but one as free has ever
emanated since from the throne of a monarch.

The other remarkable feature in this instrument consists, not in what it specified, but in what it omitted.
The use of the word " civil," everywhere prefixed to the

terms "government" or "laws," wherever they occur in CHAP
the patent, served to restrict the operation of the charter VII.
to purely political concerns. In this apparent restriction 1647.
there lay concealed a boon of freedom, such as man had
never known before. A grant so great no language could
convey, for the very use of words would imply the power
to grant, and hence the co-ordinate power to refuse.
Here was the essence of the Rhode Island doctrine. They
held themselves accountable to God alone for their religious creed, and no earthly power could bestow on them a
right they held from Heaven. Hence the expressive silence of the charter on the subject of religious freedom.
At their own request their powers were limited to civil
matters. Beyond this a silence more significant than
language proclaimed the triumph of soul-liberty.

More than three years had elapsed since the patent
was obtained, and for thirty-two months, since its reception, it had served only as an apology for the self-constituted governments of the several towns. The higher object for which it was designed could no longer be kept in
abeyance. The necessity of union was daily becoming
more apparent. So long as distinct organizations were
maintained, a color of plausibility was given to the constant efforts of the neighboring colonies to impair its validity. The difficulties in the way of consolidation were
at length overcome. A General Assembly of the people
was held at Portsmouth. Providence sent ten delegates May
to act for her. The records of Portsmouth and Newport 19-21.
do not show that any were chosen from those towns, although it is probable that this was done. Warwick was
not named in the charter, and her records do not begin
till after this Assembly, but she was admitted to the same
privileges with the rest at the opening of the session.

This first General Assembly was in fact a meeting of
the Corporators formally to adopt the charter, and then
to organize a government under it. It was not simply a

convention of delegates but of the whole people. A majority being present their acts were binding upon the whole, as is expressed in the opening of the Assembly, when, having first chosen Mr. John Coggeshall, Moderator, " It was voted and found, that the major part of the colony were present at this Assembly, whereby was full power to transact." The next step was to provide against the withdrawal of so great a number as to defeat the object of the meeting by putting a stop to legislation. For this purpose the number of forty was agreed upon, who, in case the rest should depart, were required to remain " and act as if the whole were present, and be of as full authority." In the establishment of this compulsory quorum we see the germ of the representative system, which the increasing number of the colonists now rendered necessary. The Assembly being thus organized, and the initiatory steps taken to secure its permanence and authority, " It was agreed that all should set their hands to an engagement to the charter." The engagement is embodied in the preamble to the code of laws adopted at this time, and hence has no signatures. This was a safer course to pursue, as the other might imply that those only were bound by the charter who had given in their written consent. The Assembly then adopted the representative system, by ordering that " a week before any General Court, notice should be given to every town by the head officer, that they choose a committee for the transaction of the affairs there," and they also provide for a proxy vote in the words " and such as go not may send their votes sealed." After unanimously adopting a code of laws, which had been prepared previous to the meeting, for the government of the colony, they proceeded to elect by ballot the general officers, to continue for one year, or till new be chosen.

John Coggeshall was chosen President of the Province or Colony, with one Assistant from each town, viz. : Roger

Williams of Providence, John Sandford of Portsmouth,
William Coddington of Newport, and Randal Holden of
Warwick.   William Dyer was chosen General Recorder,
and Jeremy Clarke, Treasurer.

The mode of passing general laws was then prescribed,
and deserves attention for the care with which it provides
for obtaining a free expression of the opinions of the whole
people.   All laws were to be first discussed in the towns.
The town first proposing it was to agitate the question in
town meeting and conclude by vote.   The town clerk was
to send a copy of what was agreed on to the other three
towns, who were likewise to discuss it and take a vote in
town meeting.   They then handed it over to a committee of six men from each town, freely chosen, which committees constituted " the General Court," who were to
assemble at a call for the purpose, and, if they found the
majority of the colony concurred in the case, it was to
stand as a law " till the next General Assembly of all the
people," who were finally to decide whether it should continue as law or not.   Thus the laws emanated directly
from the people.   The General Court had no power of revision over cases already presented, but simply the duty
of promulgating the laws with which the towns had intrusted them.   The right to originate legislation was,
however, vested in them to be carried out in this way.
When the Court had disposed of the matters for which
it was called, should any case be presented upon which
the public good seemed to require their action, they were
to debate and decide upon it.   Then each committee, on
returning to their town, was to report the decision, which
was to be debated and voted upon in each town ; the
votes to be sealed and sent by each town clerk to the
General Recorder, who, in presence of the President, was
to count the votes.   If a majority were found to have
adopted the law, it was to stand as such till the next
General Assembly should confirm or repeal it.   The jeal-

CHAP.
VII.
1647.
May
19-21.
ousy with which the people maintained their rights, and the checks thus put upon themselves in the exercise of the law-making power, as displayed in this preliminary act, present most forcibly the union of the two elements of liberty and law in the Rhode Island mind.

The " Court of Election " was appointed for " the first Tuesday after the fifteenth of May, annually, if wind and weather hinder not ; then the General Court of trials immediately to succeed." The manner and time of organizing monthly and quarterly Courts, was left to the town councils of Newport and Portsmouth to arrange within thirty days. From them had emanated the code of laws, and to them it was intrusted to perfect the means of enforcing that code. Acts were passed regulating the powers of the towns in specific cases, and requiring that six men, to compose a town council, should be chosen by each town at its next meeting. " The sea laws, otherwise called Laws of Oleron," were adopted " for the benefit of seamen upon the island," and two water bailies [1] were chosen for the colony. An anchor was adopted as the seal of the Province. Reciprocal duties with foreign nations, upon all imported goods, except beaver, were established, and they were prohibited from trade with the Indians. A military system, very like the one adopted seven years before at Aquedneck, was ordered.[2] No arms or ammunition were to be sold to the Indians under a heavy penalty. The remoter settlements were apportioned among the towns. Newport was to have the trading posts in the Narraganset country ; Portsmouth, the island of Prudence, and the people of Pawtuxet were allowed their choice to belong to Providence, Portsmouth or Newport. A letter was ordered to be sent to them to make their selection, and another to Massachusetts respecting her claim to jurisdiction over them.[3] A form of engagement for the

[1] John Cooke and Thomas Brownell.   [2] Ante, chap. v. p. 145.
[3] These letters cannot be found on the records of Massachusetts or Rhode Island.

officers was adopted, and what in our day seems curious,
but is not the less just, a form for " The reciprocal engagement of the State to the officers" was agreed upon
as follows :—

" We the inhabitants of the Province of Providence
Plantations, being here orderly met, and having, by free
vote chosen you ——— to public office, as officers for the
due administration of justice and the execution thereof,
throughout the whole Colony, do hereby engage ourselves,
to the utmost of our power, to support and uphold you in
your faithful performance thereof." The clerk of the Assembly represented the State in giving and receiving these
engagements.

A tax of one hundred pounds was levied, as a free gift
to Mr. Roger Williams, for his labor in obtaining the charter. Of this Newport was to pay one-half, Portsmouth
thirty, and Providence twenty pounds. By this apportionment it appears that Newport had rapidly advanced
in wealth. Although the latest settled, she was already
equal to the two older towns, and the island embraced
four-fifths of the strength of the Province. Warwick was
too weak as yet to bear any part of the burden.

The preamble and bill of rights, prefixed to the code
of civil and criminal law adopted at this time, is a remarkable production. Brief, simple and comprehensive,
the preamble asserts in a few words the two cardinal doctrines of the founders of Rhode Island. It declares "that
the form of government established in Providence Plantations is Democratical, that is to say, a government held
by the free and voluntary consent of all, or the greater
part, of the free inhabitants." This position was no less
novel and startling to the statesmen of that day, than
was the idea of religious freedom, which, in the next enacting clause, it carefully guards. Both of these principles
were exclusively Rhode Island doctrines, and to her belongs the credit of them both. This first General Assem-

bly aimed to adopt a code that should secure each of these objects, and thus be " suitable to the nature and constitution of the place." They succeeded ; and we hazard little in saying that the digest of 1647, for simplicity of diction, unencumbered as it is by the superfluous verbiage that clothes our modern statutes in learned obscurity ; for breadth of comprehension, embracing as it does the foundation of the whole body of law, on every subject, which has since been adopted ; and for vigor and originality of thought, and boldness of expression, as well as for the vast significance and the brilliant triumph of the principles it embodies, presents a model of legislation which has never been surpassed.

The bill of rights embraces in concise terms, under four distinct heads, the fundamental principles of all our subsequent legislation. In the first it re-enacts a clause of Magna Charta guaranteeing the liberty and property of the person, and guards against constructive felonies, which at that time were sapping the foundations of English liberty, by restricting criminal suits to violations of the letter of the law. In the second it prevents the assumption or the abuse of delegated power, by forbidding any to hold office who are not lawfully called to it, and requiring those who are, to perform neither more nor less than their proper duties. These two heads secure the rights of individuals against the government. The third protects the right of minorities against the majority, by restricting the legislative power of the Assembly to laws " founded upon the charter, and rightly derived from the General Assembly, lawfully met and orderly managed." The last section requires that adequate compensation be paid to all officers, that every man should serve when elected or submit to a fine, and that " in case of imminent danger no man shall refuse." In conclusion they proceed to adopt generally the common law of England, with the reiterated restriction that they enact only " such of them

and so far, as the nature and constitution of our place
will admit." Upon this all-important saving clause in
the charter they laid great stress. It was their guarantee
and shield of independence. Under their patent they
claimed that they could do as they pleased, so long as
they did not violate any law of England, and they acted
accordingly. Practically they declared that " their government derived all its just powers from the consent of the
governed," and expressly they established, for the first
time in the history of the modern world, a " Democratical
form of government." To secure this and their cherished
idea of religious freedom, were the two objects aimed at
throughout the digest of laws then adopted. For these
high purposes they sacrificed their early predilections for
English laws wherever they conflicted with them. They
commenced their career as an independent State, by virtue of a charter that made them such, and which they
knew, although it might be forfeited by abuse, could not
be revoked at pleasure. Their statutes were so framed
as to be within both its letter and its spirit, and so long
as this was the case they felt secure in their liberties.

The code, in its divisions of the law, is not remarkable for precision, and the definitions of crime are not such
as we should find at this day in a work on criminal juris-
prudence ; but the meaning is clear and unmistakable.
Each offence is separately defined, and its penalty distinctly stated. A feeling of humanity pervades the whole,
as if the object were to repress crime rather than to punish it. In this point it presents a striking contrast to the
vindictive spirit of cotemporary codes ; sometimes indeed
erring, it may be, on the side of mercy, and ever displaying a marked respect for the rights of conscience. An
instance of the former peculiarity is found in the statute
against burglary, of which the penalty was death, save
where the convict was under fourteen years of age, or was
a poor person impelled by hunger to commit the crime ;

in which case it was declared to be larceny. The preamble to the law against perjury well illustrates the regard
felt for private scruples. "Forasmuch as the consciences
of sundry men, truly conscionable, may scruple the giving
or the taking of an oath, and it would be nowise suitable
to the nature and constitution of our place, who profess
ourselves to be men of different consciences and not one
willing to force another, to debar such as cannot do so,
either from bearing office among us or from giving in testimony in a case depending ; be it enacted by the authority
of this present Assembly, that a solemn profession or testimony in a court of record, or before a judge of record,
shall be accounted, throughout the whole colony, of as
full force as an oath ;" and then it proceeds to decree the
penalty of perjury against any who should falsify such
testimony. This deference to conscientious motives is the
more remarkable as at that time the Friends did not yet
exist as a distinct society, holding to the unlawfulness of
oaths. It is a practical and legal exposition of the Rhode
Island doctrine upon one of the very subjects for which
the Founder of the State had suffered twelve years before.[1] The law for the recovery of debts contains a provision in behalf of the honest debtor, which later codes
might well embody—" but he shall not be sent to prison,
there to lie languishing to no man's advantage, unless he
refuse to appear or to stand to their order."

Marriage was held as a civil contract throughout New
England. The statute required the banns to be published
at two town meetings, and confirmed before the chief officer of the town. It was then to be entered on the town
records, thus providing, in that early day, a registry of
marriage, such as recent legislation has attempted to re-
vive. The statute regulating the probate of wills contains a singular provision in the case of intestates, or of

[1] On 30th April, 1635, Roger Williams was called before the Council for
his views on the matter of oaths. Chap. i. p. 30, ante.

executors declining to act. The town council were to CHAP.
have an inventory taken, and then to distribute the estate <u>VII.</u>
among the heirs at law, appointing an executor for that 1647.
purpose ; in other words, they were to make a will for 19-21.
him. This was a common thing, and many such quasi
testaments remain upon the town records, in some of
which a largely discretionary power appears to have been
exercised by the councils.[1] It was not unusual to prove
a will in the presence of the testator, before his death.
The instrument being executed, and witnesses examined,
it was returned to the testator duly certified, and after
his decease testamentary letters were issued to the executor. The advantage of this course where questions of
sanity or fraud are involved is obvious.

There are very many points in this digest that make
it an interesting study, illustrative of the progressive
views of our ancestors, and of the dangers that surrounded
them. We can allude to but one other statute, bearing
upon the latter point. So important was the subject of
archery considered, in view of the menaces to which they
were exposed from warlike tribes, whose weapon was the
bow, and of their own liability to be deprived of the use
of their fire-arms from want of ammunition, that it was
not left, like the other laws relating to military defence,
to be established in the acts and orders of Assembly, but
was embodied in the code itself. Every man between the
ages of seventeen and seventy was required to keep a bow
and four arrows, and to exercise with them ; and every
father was to furnish each son, from seven to seventeen
years old, with a bow, two arrows and shafts, and to bring

---

[1] Judge Staples says upon this subject : " They were not simply a division
and distribution of the estate of the deceased among his heirs at law, but in
one instance now in existence in the city clerk's office in Providence, they disposed of part of the real and personal estate to the widow, part for life and
part in fee, and divided the residue among the children as tenants in fee tail
general, with cross remainders. This is believed to be peculiar to this colony." Code of 1647, p. 50, note.

them up to shooting. Violation of this statute was punished by a fine which the father was to pay for the son,
the master for the servant, and to deduct it from his
wages.

At the close of the criminal and other general statutes
of the code occur these remarkable words :—

" These are the laws that concern all men, and these
are the penalties for the transgression thereof, which, by
common consent, are ratified and established throughout
the whole colony ; and, otherwise than thus what is herein
forbidden, all men may walk as their consciences persuade
them, every one in the name of his God ; and let the
saints of the Most High walk in this colony without molestation, in the name of Jehovah their God, forever and
ever."

Thus they deny the existence of any crime not specified in the code, and expressly permit any act not therein
forbidden. The famous statutes of 2d Elizabeth, concerning uniformity and ecclesiastical supremacy were not
" conformable to the nature and constitution of the place."
The code preserves as significant a silence on this subject
as does the charter upon which it is based, while the last
clause of this appended sentence proves that it was by no
oversight that the aforenamed acts of intolerance were
not recognized in Rhode Island.

The concluding sections of the code, " Touching the
public administration of justice," relate to the appointment of officers, very fully defining the duties of each,
and regulate the proceedings in Courts. By these it appears that the President and Assistants had no part in
legislation. That power was reserved to the General Assembly of all the people, and to the Courts of Commissioners, six from each town, appointed at this time. Thus
it remained until altered by the royal charter. They
composed the General Court of Trials, having cognizance
of weighty offences, and were also a Court of Appeal in

cases that were too difficult for the town Courts to decide. Causes between different towns, or between citizens and strangers were also tried by them. This Court met in May and October. The town Courts had original jurisdiction in suits among their own citizens. The President was conservator of the Peace over the colony, and the Assistants in their respective towns, where they also acted as Coroners. Besides these officers there were a General Recorder, a Public Treasurer, and a General Sergeant ; afterwards [1] a General Attorney and a General Solicitor were added.[2]

Such were the proceedings of the first General Assembly of Rhode Island. From them we may gather the spirit of all her subsequent legislation, and with a knowledge of the condition of affairs in England, and in the neighboring colonies at this period, we may almost foresee the leading events of her history. The young Commonwealth was now fairly started on its career of progress, with no precedents to guide its earnest statesmen in their perplexities ; nothing but their own clear minds and strong hearts could aid them in solving the two grandest problems in civil government. Well has the philosophical historian of the United States said of Rhode Island : " Had the territory of the State corresponded to the importance and singularity of the principles of its early existence, the world would have been filled with wonder at the phenomena of its history.[3] "

The death of Canonicus, the earliest and firmest friend of Rhode Island, took place at this time. The venerable sachem of the Narragansets, who was an old man when the first plantation was made at Providence, just lived to

---

[1] In May, 1650.

[2] The similarity between the New England Confederacy of 1643 and the National Confederation of 1783 has been often remarked ; but there is yet a stronger resemblance in the relative position of the four towns of Rhode Island in 1647, and the States of the Federal Union under the constitution of 1787.

[3] Bancroft's Hist. of U. S., i. 380.

see the scattered and feeble settlements of the English united into one Province. He died at a critical period in the history of his nation, when they were striving by vain delays to evade the ruinous treaty imposed on them by the New England confederates. As he passed in review the events of his long and chequered life, it is no wonder that his declining years were clouded by gloomy forebodings. Under the guidance of his warlike ancestor, Tashtassuck,[1] the tribe had become a nation, and successive conquests had swelled the nation into an empire. Long before the Pilgrims landed at Plymouth Rock, Canonicus had inherited the sceptre of a wide-spread dominion, by far the most powerful of any that were found by the English. He was " a wise and peaceable Prince," aiming to advance his race in the arts of civilized life, even before any contact with the English had made them acquainted with the means and appliances of civilization. When conquest had secured his kingdom war was laid aside ; commerce and manufactures, limited and rude to be sure, were encouraged, and the Narragansets became rich as well as strong, spreading the knowledge of their language and the customs of their trade over a region of more than six hundred miles in extent.[2] But the spell of their power was broken when the Pilgrims received the proposal of Ousamequin, or Massasoit, to form a friendly alliance. The defection of the Pokanokets carried with them all their subordinate tribes, and since that time one after another of the native chiefs had deserted their proper prince, to seek the dangerous protection of the English. In all his intercourse with the English, from the time of

---

[1] The Indian tradition is that he was greater than any prince in the country, and having two children, a son and daughter, whom he could not match in dignity, he married them to each other. Their issue was four sons, of whom Canonicus was the eldest. Hutchinson's Mass., i. 458, note. The Peruvian Incas have a similar tradition respecting the origin of the founder of their dynasty.

[2] Roger Williams' Key, p. 18.

his first treaty to the day of his death, they could never charge him with violated faith. Yet he could name ten different instances in which their solemn pledge to him and his tribe had been broken. " I have never suffered any wrong to be offered to the English since they landed, nor never will ;—if the Englishman speak true, if he mean truly, then shall I go to my grave in peace, and hope that the English and my posterity shall live in love and peace together." These were the truthful and half-desponding words once spoken by him to the Founder of Rhode Island, " in a solemn Assembly." There were reasons, and he recounted ten, for the doubting spirit that oppressed him, and which imparted to his language the saddening force of an omen. With the settlers of Rhode Island, whom he had received in their weakness, he ever maintained the most intimate and friendly relations ; and it should be said in justice to our ancestors that, from them, he never had cause to repent or to withhold his kindness. That he suffered from the jealousy of the other colonies, who were hostile alike to him and to them, is no fault of theirs ; while the fact that his unwavering fidelity to the founders of Rhode Island was the principal cause of his disasters, affords ample reason why their descendants should revere his virtues and embalm his memory.

The union of the towns under one government did not serve to heal the disputes with which each one was more or less disturbed. Their distinct powers were in no degree abridged by the compact they had formed. Their local affairs were as much under their own control as before, and we shall soon see that even the burden of a general union, so essential to their strength, was more than they could bear. Between Newport and Portsmouth a difficulty arose as to their relative positions under the new government. For the past seven years they had, for the most part, acted together as one colony. Whether to

CHAP. VII.

1647. July

6.

Aug. 26.

1647-8. Jan. 27.

Dec.

continue thus, or to act as separate towns, which was the reasonable construction of the charter, appears to have been the question. The loss of the Newport records of this period leaves us only the fragmentary notices of meetings at Portsmouth, from which to conjecture the real nature and extent of this difference. By these it appears that certain messengers, sent by Newport to Portsmouth, were informed " that if they will joyn with us to act according to the General Corte order for this year we are redie thereto, if not we must go bye ourselff by the corte order." It also appears that forty-one votes were given in Newport to act jointly, and twenty-four to act alone. It was proposed to call a special meeting of the General Assembly, but the grounds for so doing were deemed insufficient. A few months later it was " voted unanimously by the freemen of Portsmouth that they would act apart by themselves, and not jointly with Newport, and be as free in their transactions as anie of the other towns in the colonie." Providence was more distracted than either of the others by domestic difficulties, and many were the expedients proposed by her citizens to secure tranquillity. But they were too general in their nature, not bearing directly upon the specific causes of contention, to effect their object. One of these agreements adopted at Providence is transcribed by Judge Staples,[1] who justly says that little good could come of such instruments, since those who signed them did not need them, and those who required them would not agree to them, and that every one was left as before to decide whether his own or other's acts were in accordance with their letter or spirit, and hence they would afford new causes of dispute, thereby endangering the peace they were intended to promote. The democratic element was too strongly infused, and the conservative principles that underlie it were as yet too little understood by a portion of the peo-

[1] Annals of Providence, p. 70.

ple, to admit of that perfect harmony in civil concerns CHAP. which the successful application of the same doctrine of VII. individual responsibility had already produced among 1647. them in religious matters. It is an easier thing to apply Dec. the principle of personal liberty in religion than in politics, in the affairs that relate solely to man and his Maker, than in those that pertain to human intercourse. Both applications of the great idea were equally novel. The one had already met with triumphant success, for eleven years of trial among men of various and earnest faith, had established its practicability, while the other was still an experiment of which the result as yet appeared doubtful.

Gorton still remained in England, where his presence was required to counteract the designs of the Massachusetts agent. Winslow attempted to justify the conduct of his government towards the men of Shawomet, by denouncing their heresies, but could not satisfy the Admiralty that the Massachusetts had any jurisdiction beyond the bounds of their patent, although he pleaded that, " 1st, they were within the jurisdiction of Plymouth or Connecticut, and so the order of the Commissioners of the United Colonies had left them to those of the Massachusetts ; and 2d, the Indians, upon whose land they dwelt, had subjected themselves and their land to their government." [1] Upon this the committee of Parliament again wrote to Massachusetts, referring to their letter of the May previous year, and declaring that " we intended not there- 25. by to encourage any appeals from your justice, nor to restrain the bounds of your jurisdiction to a narrower compass than is held forth by your Letters Patent, but to leave you with all that freedom and latitude that may, in any respect, be duly claimed by you," and adding that if it proves, as claimed, that Narraganset Bay falls within the limits of Plymouth patent, it " will much alter the state of the question." Soon afterwards the committee

[1] Hubbard's New England, 507. Winthrop ii. 317.

wrote another letter, saying that they could not decide whether Shawomet was covered by any of the New England patents, without an examination on the spot, but if it should so prove they " commend it to the government, within whose jurisdiction they shall appear to be, not only not to remove them from their plantations, but also to encourage them with protection and assistance, in all fit ways ; provided that they demean themselves peaceably, &c." Letters to the same effect were sent to the other New England governments.[1]

It is difficult to see what encouragement could be drawn from these letters, by the parties to whom they are addressed, yet the Puritan chroniclers are jubilant over the prospect of having their illegal and outrageous proceedings sanctioned by Parliament, and their agent at once " proceeded to have the charter, which they had lately granted to those of Rhode Island and Providence, to be called in, as lying within the patent of Plymouth or Connecticut." In this we know he signally failed.

The town of Warwick being received into the corporation on equal terms with those mentioned in the charter, conformed to the orders of Assembly by electing a town council, and commenced keeping records. They made a compact, instigated by their position in regard to Massachusetts, and by the troubles resulting at Pawtuxet from the same source, binding themselves not to convey their property by sale, gift, or otherwise to any but those who should sign this agreement, and prohibiting such conveyance to any other jurisdiction on pain of disfranchisement and of forfeiture of the whole estate to the town. This article formed the fundamental law of the town. Every inhabitant was required to sign his name to it. It was confirmed a few months later,[2] and was always known as " the grand law."

---

[1] Both of these letters are given in Winthrop, ii. 318–20, and are copied by Hubbard, chap. lv.

[2] 23d January, 1648. See Warwick records.

But the Massachusetts were careful not to lose their
hold upon Warwick through any lapse of watchfulness.
Some of their subjects had settled there, and the Indians
of Shawomet were under their protection. Complaints
were made by both of these of injuries received from intruders. The corn of the natives had been destroyed, and
an English house had been forcibly entered and its occu-
pant threatened. The General Court sent three messengers to warn off the depredators, and to compel restitution. In case they did not obtain satisfaction at Warwick, they were to proceed to Aquedneck and Providence,
and demand of the authorities there whether they sanctioned these acts.[1]

Gorton, no doubt satisfied that Winslow could effect
nothing, returned to America in the spring. As in the
case of Holden, the Court, upon his arrival at Boston, ordered his arrest. A letter which he brought from the
Earl of Warwick saved him from imprisonment, although
so many favored violent proceedings, that the most urgent
considerations of State policy alone prevented the Earle's
request from being disregarded ; and Gorton was allowed
to pass safely to his home only by the casting vote of the
Governor.

The General Assembly was then in session at Providence. Two messengers[2] were sent to Boston with a letter " concerning the Warwick business," but on reaching
Dedham they heard that the General Court was adjourned,
and one of them, Barton, a resident of Warwick, wrote
to Gov. Winthrop to ascertain how he would be received
by him if he continued his journey. What reply, if any,
was made to this letter, does not appear. The terms in
which it is expressed are almost servile in their extreme
courtesy. The narrow escape that Gorton had just had,
although protected by the powerful Earl of Warwick,

---

[1] Their instructions are found in M. C. R., ii. 228.
[2] Captain Clarke and Rufus Barton.

might well teach caution to the humble envoy of Rhode
Island, and the more so as he was one of the outlawed
company, perhaps himself involved in the recent complaints. His letter would not here be noticed but for the
use made of it by Hubbard, the absurdity of which is too
palpable to be passed over. He says : " By the style of
this letter it appears how this company were crest-fallen,
who but a little before had a mouth speaking great things
and blasphemies ; but thanks be unto God, they had not
power to continue very long ; for being now reduced to a
little more sobriety in their language and behavior, they
were permitted quietly to enjoy their possessions at Shawomet. This was the issue of the address made by these
Gortonists to the Commissioners, who after the great
clamor and noise they had made could make nothing appear of that which they had affirmed." That the man-
date of the Lord High Admiral of England, and of the
Commissioners of Plantations should depend for its fulfilment upon the courtly expressions of a letter from an
humble inhabitant of Warwick to the magnates of Massachusetts, will excite a smile. That after this the Gortonists "were permitted quietly to enjoy their possessions," should have caused them to feel ever grateful to
their courteous messenger, who had so softened the hearts
of their magnanimous oppressors.[1] Notwithstanding the
concluding assertion of the Ipswich divine, the event
proved that they made enough to appear not only to prevent the Parliament from revoking their first decision in

[1] Taking Hubbard's absurd comment as correct, no more palpable instance
can be found in history of the truth of the maxim that "nothing is lost by
civility." Winthrop inserts Barton's letter, addressed to himself, but does not
say what he did about it, nor does he make any comments upon it. The
bigotry of Hubbard must have been of the most Pharisaical and self-satisfy-
ing kind to enable him to draw, from a private letter of the Warwick messenger, any solace for the wound inflicted upon ecclesiastical pretension by
triumphant heresy. To attribute, as he does, to the accidental phraseology
of such a letter the subsequent compulsory forbearance of the Puritans, is
simply ridiculous.

favor of the Gortonists, but also to have it confirmed, a CHAP.
few years later, by Royal charter, to the final discomfiture <u>VII.</u>
of their implacable enemies.

1648.
May.

An amendment of the law organizing the General
Court was now made. This Court, composed of six men
chosen from each town, soon came to be in fact the General Assembly, although if any others chose to remain,
those whose help was desired were allowed to do so. In
case any town refused to elect members, the Court, by
this amendment, was required to choose for them. The
General Court, as now constituted, was often called the
Court of Commissioners, or the "Committee"—a name
still preserved in styling the two branches of Assembly,
when united for the choice of officers, "the Grand Committee." The act making this body a General Court of
trials was continued. In their judicial capacity they were
to hear causes in the place where the action arose or the
criminal was arrested, and at such times as were appointed
by law. Hence, we presume, arose the custom, existing
until a recent date, of the General Assembly's meeting in
the different chief towns of the State.

The first business of the Assembly, or "General Court
of Election," as it was termed, when opened for the
choice of general officers, was to go into the election. A
Moderator and Clerk were chosen ; the State officers were
then elected. The Clerk of Assembly was required to
send a copy of the proceedings to each town.

The changes made at this time were remarkable, when
we consider that it was the first election since the government was organized. They indicate already the existence of opposing parties. William Coddington was elected President, Roger Williams of Providence, William
Balston of Portsmouth, John Smith of Warwick, and
Jeremy Clarke of Newport, Assistants. The latter was
also continued in his office of Treasurer. Philip Sherman was chosen General Recorder, and Alexander Par-

tridge, General Sergeant.   By the list of the twenty-four members of this Assembly, it appears that one might be a member from any town, and at the same time a general officer.   The towns were ordered to meet within ten days to choose their town officers.   The " Act made and agreed upon for the well-ordering of this Assembly," corresponding to our modern " Rules and Orders," is worthy of attention for the conciseness and simplicity with which it regulates the business and decorum of the legislative body.

" It is ordered, That yᵉ Moderator shall cause yᵉ Clark of yᵉ Assembly to call over the names of the Assembly.

" That the Moderator shall appoint every man to take his place.

" That all matters presented to the Assembly's consideration, shall be presented in writing by bill.

" That each bill be fairly discust, and if by yᵉ major vote of the Assembly it shall be putt to a committee to draw up an order, which being concluded by yᵉ vote, shall stand for an order threwout yᵉ whole colony.

" That the Moderator shall putt all matters to vote.

" That every man shall have liberty to speak freely to any matter propounded yett but once, unless it be by lease from yᵉ Moderator.

" That he that stands up first uncovered, shall speake first to the cause.

" That the Moderator by yᵉ vote of yᵉ Assembly shall rejourne or dissolve yᵉ Court, and not without, at his great perile.

" That he that shall returne not to his place at yᵉ time appointed, shall forfeitt sixpence.

" That they that whisper or disturb yᵉ Court, or useth nipping terms, shall forfeitt sixpence for every fault.[1]

" WM. DYRE, Clerk of the Assembly."

---

[1] Were the latter rule, especially the last clause of it, now in force, it would aid the revenue of the State; although it might be difficult to define with the precision of a statute what should be held as " nipping terms."

Complaints were made at this Assembly against the President elect. He was not present at the election, nor did he appear to repel the charges, whatever they were. That he was chosen to that high office under such circumstances seems strange. As he continued to absent himself Jeremy Clark, Assistant, of Newport, was chosen to fill his place temporarily, with the title of President Regent; and provision was made that in case of vacancy by the death, or absence from the colony, of the President, then the Assistant of that town from which the President was chosen should supply his place.

The dissensions on the Island were not healed by this Assembly. Just before it met, the Town Clerk of Portsmouth was ordered to inform Newport of their decision to act separately The proceedings of the Assembly seem to have widened the breach. It appears that even "the legality of the Corte and orders thereof" was questioned by Portsmouth. There was evidently some serious trouble on the Island, threatening the existence of the colony.[1] Portsmouth was disaffected, and the conduct of Coddington favored the alienation. His subsequent acts may furnish a clue to his motives at this time. Roger Williams, who appears as a peacemaker in all the troubles of the colony, wrote a letter to the town of Providence, wherein he represents the State as distracted by two parties, Portsmouth and its partisans being one, and the remaining three towns the other, and suggested a plan of reference by which the dispute might be settled, viz., that Portsmouth and its friends should select three men, and the other towns three, one from each, whose decision

CHAP.
VII.

1648.
May.

May 9.

July 10.

Aug.

---

[1] It is probable that this difference between Portsmouth and Newport referred to the Courts of trials which up to this time had been held jointly by the two towns, but were now appointed by the General Assembly to be held separately in each town. This view is strengthened by the passage of an act at the first meeting of the Assembly after the reunion, giving these towns leave to hold their Courts jointly or apart as they pleased. See Act No. 13, Sept. session, 1654.

should be final. Unfortunately Mr. Williams does not mention the causes of disagreement. That affairs in England, now approaching a crisis, had some influence in these contentions is more than probable. Coddington was a royalist, and was about attempting to withdraw the island from the other towns and unite it to Plymouth. Clarke and Easton were republicans, and leaders of the dominant party on the island.

The hostile attitude of the Indians, occasioned by the determination of the United Colonies to protect Uncas at every hazard, from the punishment due to his crime at the hand of the Narragansets, caused more serious alarm than ever before. The dissensions prevailing among them, those of Shawomet and Pawtuxet owning allegiance to Massachusetts, and viewing as enemies all Englishmen whom she denounced, while the Niantics and Nipmucks remained true to their proper princes, made the situation of Rhode Island, surrounded as she was by these distracted and exasperated tribes, extremely perilous. The inhabitants of Warwick suffered severely from this cause. A letter written by Mr. John Smith, Assistant, in behalf of the town, was carried by Randal Holden and John Warner to Plymouth, where the New England Commis-
sioners were convened. They complained that the Indians had killed their cattle, abused their servants, entered their houses by force, maltreating the occupants, and stealing their goods ; and desired advice on the subject. This was a proper course to adopt, since those Indians were under their protection. But the island of Rhode Island went still further. Mr. Coddington, who had been chosen President of the colony, but had never taken his engagement, with Captain Partridge, the General Sergeant, presented, at the same time, a written request, signed by themselves in behalf of Rhode Island, " That wee the Ilanders of Roode Iland may be received into combination with all the united colonyes of New

England in a prime and perpetuall league of friendship
and amity : of ofence and defence, Mutuall advice and
succor upon all just occasions for our mutuall safety and
wellfaire, and for preserving of peace amongst ourselves,
and preventing as much as may bee all occasions of warr
and Diference, and to this our motion we have the consent
of the major part of our Iland." [1]

This appears almost like an act of treason against the
colony ; much more so than those acts which a few years
later gave rise to the famous trials for that crime.   But
the imminent danger to which they were exposed might
excuse a greater sacrifice than they proposed, while it
makes the refusal they received appear absolutely inhuman.   That the islanders intended nothing more than a
defensive alliance which would not compromise their position as members of the colony under the charter, may be
inferred from their refusal of the offered terms of safety.
It is unfortunate that any expression occurs in the petition
that could be construed as an allusion to their internal
difficulties, for it strengthens the evidence that Coddington, and many whom he represented, inclined to accede to
the terms imposed.   The Commissioners, in their reply,
commiserate the petitioners upon their domestic strifes,
and the dangers of their position, but, claiming the island
to be within Plymouth patent, they refuse the request unless this claim should be recognized.   This answer might
have been expected from the treatment Rhode Island had
before received.[2]   It is said that Coddington and the town
of Portsmouth were willing to accept the condition, but
were prevented by the other towns.   Had they submitted
the charter would have been virtually annulled by the act
of its holders, and the schemes of the surrounding colonies to appropriate the rest of the State might have

CHAP.
VII.

1648.
Sept.
7.

---

[1] Hazard's State Papers, ii. 99.
[2] In Oct., 1640, when a league was first proposed, and in May, 164?.
when it was formed.

CHAP.
VII.
1648.
Sept.
10.

12.

Oct.
7.

proved successful.[1] Rhode Island would soon have been absorbed by Massachusetts and Connecticut.

The notice taken of the Warwick complaint was rather remarkable. The Commissioners wrote a letter to the sachems, advising them to abstain from such conduct in future, and telling them that, if they received any injury from the English, satisfaction should be given them, as the like would be expected from them.[2] The mildness of this rebuke to their offending subjects, contrasts with the severity of the terms dictated to the islanders. Scarcely had this missive been sent when letters were received from Roger Williams and others, warning the United Colonies of preparations making by the Narragansets to renew the war on Uncas. Messengers were sent to Pessacus requiring him to desist, and demanding anew the arrears of tribute. Acts of violence were becoming daily more frequent. The United Colonies, as they were in no small degree the cause of these outrages, were looked to for redress by the sufferers. Henry Bull, of Newport, soon afterward complained that he had been beaten by some Narraganset Indians, and asked aid in obtaining satisfaction. He was referred to Rhode Island for relief, and further referred to the advice lately given to the islanders how they might secure protection. A copy of the letter to the sachems, that was given to the Warwick men, was also furnished to him, " for his future security." This paper, in the opinion of the Commissioners, possessed the virtue of a passport.

[1] Hutchinson, i. p. 150, note, says : " Plymouth would soon have been swallowed up in Rhode Island from the great superiority of the latter. Besides, the principles of the people of the two colonies were so different that a junction must have rendered both miserable." But as Plymouth was herself annexed to Massachusetts in 1692, when the provincial government was formed under Sir William Phipps, the whole of Rhode Island, under this supposition, except the King's province, claimed by Connecticut, would then have belonged to Massachusetts.

[2] Hazard, ii. 100-1.

Coddington, having failed in his attempt to detach the island from the other towns, soon after sailed for England to procure for it a separate charter. His design was not known at the time. His daughter accompanied him, and Captain Partridge was left to manage his affairs, including, no doubt, his political interests.

The discovery of what was supposed to be gold and silver ore upon the island, caused great excitement in the colony. A special meeting of the General Assembly was held at Warwick. No record of it remains, but by the letter of Roger Williams, and from other sources, we are informed of its proceedings. The distracted state of the towns, and the importance attached to this discovery of precious metals, probably led to the meeting. The violence of party spirit had so compromised many of the leading men in the colony that, to the sagacious mind of Williams, the only mode of escape from increasing danger was by the passage of a general " act of oblivion." At his suggestion such an act was passed. Mr. Williams was not present at that session, but was elected Deputy President of the Colony, probably owing to his constant efforts to promote peace. He declined the honor, and in a letter to Mr. John Winthrop [1] says, " I hope they have chosen a better," but they did not, and Mr. Williams acted as President till the election in May.

[1] The son of Gov. Winthrop of Massachusetts, himself afterwards Governor of Connecticut. The father died at this time, March, 1649, so that we have no longer his reliable journal, the last entry in which is on Jan. 11th, as a guide. This book, with its full and admirable notes by the editor, Hon. James Savage, is worth all the other authorities on this period of New England history put together. The lines of Milton, quoted by the translator of the Decameron, will apply with greater force to Savage's Winthrop's Journal:—

> " Hither, as to their fountains, other stars
> Repairing, in their golden urns draw light."

In fact they all draw from him, while Hubbard, whose General History of New England was more esteemed when it was less known, in the only reliable portions of his work, copies *verbatim* from the MS. of Winthrop, which was not then (1680) printed, and carefully conceals the source of his information.

CHAP.
VII.
1649.
March.

The Assembly passed an act taking possession of the mines in the name of the State of England, and forbade all persons from interfering with the ore.   The Clerk published the proclamation, and the arms of England and of the Earl of Warwick were set up at the mine.   Closer examination dispelled the illusion.   A more certain and less demoralizing source of wealth has, within a few years, been developed in the discovery of coal mines on the island, now in profitable operation.[1]

14.

Special charters of incorporation were granted at this session to the several towns.   That of Providence, granted on petition of the town, is given by Judge Staples, and follows closely the terms of the colonial charter.   Warwick had one of the same date.   The Portsmouth records of their next town meeting held for the election of officers,[2] refer to " the particular charter granted unto them for choosing their town officers."   A similar one must have been given to Newport at the same time.

May
2.

The intolerance of the General Court of Massachusetts was again shown towards Randal Holden, who petitioned that his sentence of banishment might be revoked, to enable him to give his personal attention to some business that required his presence in Boston.   The favor was refused, and he was informed that his affairs could be as well conducted by an attorney as by himself.[3]

22.

The regular session of the Court of Commissioners was held at Warwick and lasted four days.   John Smith of Warwick was chosen President ; Thomas Olney of Providence, John Sandford of Portsmouth, John Clarke

---

[1] An account of these mines with the causes of their failure when first opened, and the reasons for their subsequent success, is given by Dr. Jackson in his Report on the Geological Survey of Rhode Island, made in 1840, p. 95–104.   Since the date of this Report the business has been revived, and is now conducted with profitable results.

[2] On first Monday of June, 1649.

[3] M. C. R., ii. 275.

of Newport, and Samuel Gorton of Warwick, Assistants ; CHAP.
John Clarke Treasurer, and Richard Knight, Sergeant. VII.

Already had fraudulent voting, the bane of all free 1649.
governments, appeared in the colony. The system of May 22.
proxies afforded facilities for this, which it was attempted
to prevent by requiring that no one should bring any
votes that he did not receive from the voters' own hands,
and that all votes should be filed by the Recorder in presence of the Assembly. The fall in the price of beaver in
England, and the increased manufacture of peage by the
Indians, had reduced the value of that currency nearly
one-half. The depreciation was not so great in Rhode
Island, where this medium continued to be used much
longer than in the other colonies, but a law was passed
lowering the standard of black peage, which was double
the value of the white, one-third. Four, instead of three,
for a penny was now made the legal rate. Prisons were
ordered to be built in each town ; meanwhile the one at
Newport was used for the whole colony, and the General
Sergeant was appointed to keep it. The organization of
the Court of Trials, heretofore composed of the members
of Assembly alone, was amended by adding to it the magistrates of the town where the Court might be held. The
sale of ardent spirits to the natives was forbidden, except
that Mr. Williams was allowed to dispense it, in cases of
sickness, at his discretion. This law displays a commendable regard for the welfare of the Indians, and an honorable confidence in the Founder of the State.

There was a strong feeling in Rhode Island in favor of
Mr. John Winthrop, son of the late Governor of Massachusetts, who before the Pequot war had made a purchase
near Thames river, which the government of Connecticut
had recently refused to recognize. It was thought that
he might move further east, perhaps to Pawcatuck, in
which case many desired to make him President of the
colony, and his name was used for that purpose in this

election. He had been suggested as one of the referees in the difficulty with Portsmouth the previous summer. The liberality of the Winthrops, often displayed by the father in his trying position as Governor of Massachusetts, and inherited by the son, their close friendship with the Founder of Rhode Island, and the sympathy they manifested with the struggling colony on more than one occasion, all go to account for this partiality.

The desire for public service was so little felt by our ancestors, that heavy fines were imposed upon any who should refuse to accept an office. Any one elected President, and declining to act, was to be fined ten pounds ; or an Assistant five pounds, and his place was to be filled by the person having the next highest number of votes. A similar law was enacted in the towns to compel the acceptance of town offices. In Portsmouth, whoever was chosen to be a magistrate and refused was fined six pounds, and for an inferior office the fine was fifty shillings. The reciprocal engagement of the State and its officers was also administered to the town councils in the following form : " You, A. B., being called and chosen by the free vote of the inhabitants of Portsmouth unto the office of a town magistrate, in his Majesty's name, do in this present assembly engage yourself faithfully to execute the office of a justice of the peace, in the due execution of justice in this town, according to the laws established unto us by our particular charter, according to the best of your understanding. The town reciprocally engage themselves in his Majesty's name, to maintain you in the just execution of your office, according to the best of their understanding." The use of the words " in his Majesty's name," in a formula adopted just at this time is peculiar. The King was beheaded on the 30th of January. News of his death had reached the colony either while the Assembly was in session, or shortly before it met, yet no notice was taken of it by that body—possibly because it yet

needed confirmation. And this might be the reason why the freemen of Portsmouth, as a matter of precaution, retained the old form of expression ; or perhaps that they did so was owing to the fact of the predominance of the royalist or Coddington party in that town. The news was confirmed by an arrival from England the following week.

The Warwick men again wrote to the Commissioners of the United Colonies, sitting at Boston, to complain of the Indians, and to remind them of the order of Parliament that they should be protected.[1] The Commissioners, in their reply, deny having received any such command, or that the petitioners could reasonably expect aid in their position, but say they are ready to obey the order requiring them to ascertain under what patent the lands of Warwick are included.[2]

The next General Court of election was held at Newport at the same time with that at Boston. At both business of great importance, affecting the relations of the two colonies, was transacted. That there was some difficulty in this election is evident from the record of a vote that it should " be authentic notwithstanding all obstructions against it."

Nicholas Easton was chosen President ; William Field of Providence, John Porter of Portsmouth, John Clarke of Newport, and John Wicks of Warwick, Assistants ; Philip Sherman, Recorder ; Richard Knight, Sergeant, and John Clarke, Treasurer. An Attorney General and Solicitor General were also appointed, for the first time, and their duties defined. William Dyre was chosen to the first-named office, and Hugh Bewett to the latter. The committee of each town, which should consist of six men, were empowered to fill any vacancy in their number. It was also ordered that in case any member, upon complaint and trial, should prove to be unfit to hold his seat, the Assembly might suspend him, and

CHAP.
VII.

1649.
June
11.

July
26.

31.

1650.

May
22.

---

[1] In the letter of July 22, 1647, ante.   [2] Hazard, ii. 135.

CHAP.
VII.
1650.
May
22.

choose another in his place.   Heretofore the Assembly had been usually styled " the Court of Commissioners," the term General Assembly applying only to a meeting of all the people ; but we have seen that gradually the legislative power had centred in this Court, and they now, for the first time, style themselves the General Assembly, and fix their salaries at two and sixpence a day.

The order apportioning the amount of military stores to be kept by each town, gives an idea of their relative strength at this period.   Providence and Warwick were each to have one barrel of powder, five hundred pounds of lead, six pikes and six muskets in their magazines, fit for service.   Portsmouth was to have twice this amount, or as much as both of these towns, and Newport was to have three barrels of powder, a thousand pounds of lead, twelve pikes and twenty-four muskets.   Each town was to regulate its own militia.

By an order of the previous Assembly letters had been sent to the Pawtuxet men, respecting their allegiance to the colony, and a summons issued to the sachems of Pawtuxet and Shawomet to attend upon the Court.   This procedure led the parties to petition the General Court of Massachusetts, complaining, as usual, of injuries received, and asking redress.   Upon this the General Court addressed a letter to Rhode Island, advising all whom it

30.

concerned, not to prosecute any suits against the subjects of Massachusetts, nor to do them any harm till they should hear again from the Court, which would not be long.

June
1.

A committee was appointed to treat with Plymouth about the title to the land of Shawomet and Pawtuxet, and protection to the English and Indian subjects of Massachusetts at those places.   The Court adjourned for a few days to await the issue of the negotiation.   The General Court of Plymouth was then in session.   By a formal instrument they resigned all claim to the territory in question, yielding in every thing to the proposals of Massachu-

setts, but with one proviso, that does honor to their sense
of justice, and to their clearness of perception, viz., that
the lands of Providence should not be included in the relin-
quishment, but should remain as before to be freely enjoyed
by the inhabitants. That Providence should be named
at all in the deed of cession, since it was not referred to
in the instructions of the Committee, is proof that Plymouth suspected, and not without reason, that the design
of Massachusetts embraced more than she professed, and
by making this exception she declared her own opinion of
the rights of the people in Providence, and barred any
claim that Massachusetts might afterward set up to that
territory, based upon the action of Plymouth in this case.[1]
The Court having reassembled at Boston, received the report of their committee, and proceeded to annex their
newly-acquired possessions to the county of Suffolk.
They also, in gratitude to Captain Atherton, for his services in this and in the brutal affair with Pessacus,[2] voted
him a farm of five hundred acres. The officers of the
County Court were authorized to treat with any of the
Warwick associates who might appear to complain of this
outside disposition of themselves and their property.

There is one question that the high contracting parties to this remarkable transfer of land and power, to
which neither had any right, quite overlooked. Admitting that the claim of either one of them under their patents was valid, how could that one lawfully divest itself
of, or invest another government with, a portion of its
power ; or how could the recipient, simply on the ground
that the cession was voluntary, enlarge the limits of its
own patent ? The illegality on both sides is apparent.
The injustice to the rightful owners need not be considered after the outrages they had suffered seven years before.

These acts called for decisive action on the part of

[1] M. C. R., iv. Part I. 14–20.   [2] Close of chap. vi., ante.

CHAP.
VII.

1650.
July
20.

Sept.
13.
Oct.
16.

18.

26.

Rhode Island.   The President of the colony called a convention, composed of a special committee of three from each town, to meet at Portsmouth, to deliberate on the conduct of Massachusetts in the premises.   No report of their proceedings can be found.   But these convenient interchanges of jurisdiction were not yet ended.   The Commissioners of the United Colonies advised, for many cogent reasons, that Warwick and Pawtuxet should be restored to Plymouth.[1]   The General Court yielded the point, and re-assigned the territory to Plymouth.[2]   President Easton had written to Massachusetts that Rhode Island and Warwick now formed one colony, and would defend her rights.   Letters were sent to Rhode Island, forbidding her to exercise jurisdiction over Shawomet, to the Pawtuxet men to transfer their allegiance to Plymouth, and to Gov. Bradford that he should protect them and the subject Indians.

The General Assembly met at Portsmouth.   The order prescribing the mode of passing general laws was repealed and a new one made.   The Assembly, or " Representative Committee," as it is here termed, having enacted any laws, these were to be sent to the towns within six days after the adjournment, and then, within three days, to be read in town meeting.   Any freeman who disliked the laws or any one of them, was to send his vote, with his name upon it, within ten days after the reading, to the General Recorder.   If a majority were found to oppose it the Recorder should signify the fact to the President, and the President to the towns, that such law was annulled.   Silence as to the rest was considered assent. Banishment, as a punishment, was abolished.   Divorce was prohibited except, at the suit of the party aggrieved, for adultery.

Roger Williams was urged once more to go to England.   The active measures taken by the other colonies

---

[1] Hazard ii. 153–'4.   [2] M. C. R. iii. 216.

in regard to Warwick and Pawtuxet, required that Rhode Island should be represented before the Committee of Plantations.   The sum of one hundred pounds voted three years before, in remuneration of his services in obtaining the charter, had never been paid, although attempts had been made to raise the money by taxation. The Assembly now voted to pay the arrears, and one hundred pounds more, if he would go a second time, but if he would not, Mr. Balston, John Clarke and John Warner were named, any two of them to go.

This was the last session of the General Assembly, as at first constituted, under the charter.   A more serious calamity than any that the malice or the ambition of her neighbors could inflict, was about to overwhelm the State, and for a time to palsy the arm of the sons of Rhode Island.

In the following spring there was no meeting of the Assembly. News of Coddington's design had been received, although his success was not yet known. Consternation pervaded the colony. Within and without, at home and abroad, enemies to the peace and liberty of the State appeared on every side. The Pawtuxet men complained to Massachusetts that Providence had assessed them to the amount of twelve pounds ten shillings, and on their refusal to pay the tax had threatened them with distraint. Upon this the General Court sent a letter to Roger Williams, warning him that if this levy was made they would seek satisfaction " in such manner as God shall put into their hands."[1] Amid these complicated

---

[1] M. C. R. iii. 228, and iv. part. i. 46. There could be no mistaking the meaning of this. The Puritans in their dealings with their weaker neighbors, English or Indians, evidently believed with the Great Frederick, that " Providence favors the strong battalions." Their reliance upon Divine aid in all their forays, attempted or threatened, into Rhode Island, was of that commendably precautionary character displayed by Cromwell in the order to his troops at " the crowning mercy of Worcester," which was fought on a rainy day—" Trust in God but keep your powder dry ! "

difficulties, an outrage was committed upon some of the best men of Rhode Island, which is without a parallel save in the treatment of the Gortonists. Rev. John Clarke, pastor of the first Baptist church in Newport, Obadiah Holmes, who shortly before had aided to establish a church of that order in Seekonk, and, being presented for it by the grand jury at the General Court of Plymouth, had fled to Newport,[1] and John Crandall, a member of the same church, were deputed by the church to visit an aged member, residing near Lynn, who had requested an interview with some of his brethren. Arriving at the place on Saturday, Mr. Clarke preached the next day to those who were in the house. While thus engaged two constables served on them a warrant for the arrest of the "erroneous persons, being strangers." In the afternoon they were carried to church by the officer, where, after service, Clarke addressed the congregation till silenced by a magistrate. Next day, although being under arrest, he administered the communion to the aged member of his church and to two others. The party were examined and ordered to be sent to Boston, where they were imprisoned to await their trial the following week. At the trial Gov. Endicott charged them with being anabaptists. Clarke denied that he was either an anabaptist, a pedobaptist, or a catabaptist, and affirmed, that although he had baptized many he had never re-baptized any, for that infant baptism was a nullity. The others agreed in this, and the Court sentenced them upon their own declarations, "without producing either accuser, witness, jury, law of God, or man." Clarke was fined twenty pounds, Holmes thirty pounds, and Crandall five pounds, and in default of payment each was "to be well whipped." They refused to pay the fine, as that would be to admit their guilt when they felt they were innocent, and were

July
16.

19.

20.

22.

25.

31.

---

[1] After the death of Dr. Clarke he succeeded him as pastor of the Newport church. Knowles', 239, note.

committed to prison. On the following day Clarke, by a letter to the Court, challenged the members to a discussion of the doctrinal views for which he had been condemned. The magistrates appointed a time for the debate. Clarke prepared the heads of discussion, but before the day arrived an order of Court was sent to the jail for his discharge, the fine having been paid by some one without his knowledge. Anxious to hold the debate, and seeing how this ill-timed kindness might be represented as being caused by his desire to avoid it, Clarke, on the same day, renewed the challenge, offering to come to Boston at any time they might name. In their reply the Court seemed to accept the invitation, but fixed no time. Cotton was to be the chosen champion of Puritan theology—the man of all others, as the leader of their church, with whom Clarke most desired to meet, and to discuss the two great principles of Baptist faith, voluntary baptism and individual responsibility. These were the two grand points upon which Church and State in Massachusetts were antagonist to the sentiment of Rhode Island. But although Mr. Clarke a third time notified the Court of his readiness, they failed to appoint a day, so that the debate was never held. Crandall was allowed to go home on bail, the jailer being his surety. Holmes was so cruelly whipped, receiving thirty lashes with a three-corded whip from the public executioner, that for many days he could take no rest except by supporting himself on his elbows and knees. Two of the spectators, one an old man named Hazel, who had come from Seekonk, fifty miles, to visit him in prison, were arrested for shaking hands with him after the punishment was over, and were sentenced to pay a fine or to be whipped. The fine was paid by their friends, but Hazel died before reaching home.[1]

CHAP.
VII.

1651
Aug.
1.

11.

14.

Sept.
5.

[1] See Ill Newes from New England, by John Clarke, London, 1652, 4to., 76 pp. The writer consulted the copy in the British Museum. This very scarce work by one of the ablest men of the seventeenth century, and a

Thus severely was the savage law of 1644, against the anabaptists, carried out by magistrates and ministers, who shunned a discussion of the doctrines which they ignorantly denounced.

founder of Rhode Island, has lately been reprinted by the Mass. Hist. Soc., in the 2d vol. of the 4th series of their Collections.

CHAPTER VIII.

1651—1663.

FROM THE USURPATION OF CODDINGTON, AUGUST, 1651, TO THE
ADOPTION OF THE ROYAL CHARTER, NOVEMBER, 1663.

WHEN Coddington arrived in England the King was
already beheaded, the House of Lords 'had been voted
useless, the Commonwealth was declared, and the supreme
power vested in the hands of forty persons as a Council of State. A revolution as complete had taken place
in ecclesiastical affairs. Episcopacy had been abolished
three years before ; the Directory had supplanted the
Liturgy ; a greater part of the livings were distributed
among the Presbyterian clergy, and finally Presbyterian-
ism was established by act of Parliament as the national
faith. The new church were as tenacious of their " divine right," as ever the old one had been. The rights of
conscience were as little understood or respected by Pres-
byterians as by Prelatists. Toleration was denied to the
Independents by both alike. Humanity gained nothing
by the change till the master-spirit of Cromwell curbed
the persecuting will of these Protestant Papists. For
two years the efforts of Coddington were without result.
More momentous concerns than any that related to distant
plantations employed the Council. At length he obtained
a hearing. By what representations, or through what in-

CHAP.
VIII.

1649.

1646.

1649

1651.

CHAP.
VIII.
1651.
April
3.

Aug.

Sept.
1.

fluence he succeeded in virtually undoing the acts of the Long Parliament in favor of Rhode Island, we can never know. He obtained from the Council of State a commission, signed by John Bradshaw, to govern the islands of Rhode Island and Connanicut during his life, with a council of six men, to be named by the people and approved by himself. With this authoritative document he returned home to sever the islands from the main land towns, and to be in effect the autocrat of the fairest and wealthiest portion of the State. Great was the alarm felt throughout the colony, more especially by the large party in the now subjected islands who, being opposed to Coddington, found themselves, as they thought, at the mercy of a dictator. This party at once prepared to send John Clarke to England, to obtain a revocation of Coddington's powers. Providence and Warwick recognized the peril to which their charter was exposed, and hastened the departure of Roger Williams to secure to them again the rights he had first obtained. William Arnold, one of the Massachusetts subjects at Pawtuxet, wrote to the Commissioners of the United Colonies to inform them of this movement, that Warwick had already raised one hundred pounds, and men in Providence were giving ten or twenty pounds apiece to speed the object of Williams' mission. John Greene, in behalf of Warwick, the same day officially notified the Commissioners, that as the United Colonies had failed to conform to the order of Parliament to protect them, but as they "were bought and sold from one patent and jurisdiction to another," had been threatened with expulsion since the above order was received, summoned to attend Courts in Massachusetts, deprived of trade, and exposed to violence from both English and Indians, therefore they should send a messenger to England to obtain redress, and the United Colonies might instruct their agents accordingly to prepare their answers. This official notice was a gratuitous act of courtesy on the part of Warwick that was not appreciated by the Commissioners.

The United Colonies coldly recognized the commission of Coddington, and addressed him a letter inquiring what course he would pursue as to fugitives from justice; whether he would return them on legal demand, or bring them to trial on the island. The Warwick letter caused much discussion. The Massachusetts members of the Commission presented a declaration on the subject, to which those of Plymouth replied, disowning the cession made to Massachusetts the previous year, and protesting against the seizures she had made at Shawomet and Pawtuxet. The other members, on the ground that Plymouth had refused to accept the transfer made by Massachusetts, recognized the claim of the latter, and concluded that trespasses committed by the Warwick men should be punished by force if necessary, " but with as much moderation as may be." [1]

A General Assembly of the two remaining towns was called, at which Samuel Gorton was chosen President. Roger Williams was urged, by every consideration that could move him in such a crisis, to leave home to advocate the cause of the colony in England. On the island forty-one of the inhabitants of Portsmouth, and sixty-five, being nearly all of the freemen, in Newport, joined to persuade Dr. Clarke to go out and obtain a repeal of Coddington's commission. They both consented to go. Mr. Williams was obliged to sell his trading-house in Narraganset, to sustain his family during his absence. The objects of their missions were distinct. Clarke was the agent of the island towns, to procure a repeal of Coddington's commission. Williams was the agent of the main land towns, to obtain a confirmation of their charter. In effect the same result was aimed at and secured—a return to their former mode of government by

CHAP.
VIII.

1 6 5 1.
Sept.
13.

16.

Oct.

[1] Hazard's State Papers, ii. 198–203.

a reunion under the charter. The two agents sailed together, with some difficulty securing leave to embark from Boston.

The Court of Commissioners, the relic of the colonial Assembly, being the committees of Providence and Warwick, met at Providence to consult on the state of the colony. They resolved to continue under the charter, making laws and choosing officers as before. They re-enacted several laws, modified to meet their present condition, and also passed an act forbidding the purchase of land from the Indians, without consent of the State.

Williams and Clarke presented a joint petition to the Council of State, which was referred to the committee on foreign affairs. The island meanwhile quietly submitted to the rule of Coddington. The main land towns held their regular Court of Election in the spring. John Smith was chosen President of the colony; Thomas Olney of Providence, Samuel Gorton of Warwick, General Assistants; John Greene, jr., Recorder; Randall Holden, Treasurer; and Hugh Bewett, Sergeant.

At this session the famous law against slavery was passed, believed to be, with one exception,[1] the first legislative enactment in the history of this continent, if not of the world, for the suppression of involuntary servitude. This law was designed to prevent both negro and white slavery, each of which was in use at that time. By it no man could be held to service more than ten years from the time of his coming into the colony, at the end of which time he was to be set free. Whoever refused to let him go free, or sold him elsewhere for a longer period of slavery, was subject to a penalty of forty pounds.

Between Rhode Island and the Dutch at Manhattan, there existed quiet an active trade, and occasional intermarriages resulted from the intercourse thus maintained. A serious disturbance occurred at this time in Warwick.

[1] The Act of Massachusetts, 4th Nov., 1646, in 2 M. C. R., 168.

The crew of a small Dutch vessel which had arrived there in January, on a trading voyage, boarded for some two months with John Warner, who was this year the Assistant, or second magistrate of the town, and had stored their goods in his house for sale. One of these men, named Geraerd, was a brother-in-law of Warner, both having married into the family of Ezekiel Holliman. Upon settling their accounts a dispute arose, which it was vainly attempted to adjust by arbitration, and the Dutchmen appealed to the Court. At their request a special session was held. Warner refused to answer to the case, and judgment was entered against him by default, and execution granted for the damages assessed by a jury. Warner's wife was also indicted upon suspicion of felony, and the case carried up to the General Court of trials for the colony. The conduct of Warner before and at this trial was so bad that he was degraded from his office as Assistant and disfranchised. A copy of the declaration was sent to Providence, and also to Massachusetts, and the whole proceedings upon the case were afterwards forwarded to Roger Williams in England. A few weeks later, "upon suspicion of insufferable treachery against the town," which is conveyed in the seventh item of the declaration, his house and lands were attached. For want of proof the property was shortly released, but not without a formal protest being entered upon the records by the leading men of the town. The proceedings are so remarkable, and the form of the declaration, resembling somewhat the indictment against Gorton,[1] is so curious that they should be preserved.[2]

The war between England and Holland having commenced, the Dutch were forbidden to trade with the Indians in the colony, and the President was instructed to notify the Governor of Manhattan[3] of this prohibition.

CHAP. VIII.

1652.

April

24.

June 7.

22.

July 5.

May 19.

---

[1] Ante, chap. vi. p. 120.   [2] See Appendix B.
[3] Peter Stuyvesant. This prohibition was repealed in May, 1657.

Letters from Roger Williams caused a town meeting to be held in Providence, at which a letter was directed to be sent to Warwick, proposing a meeting of Commissioners to prepare suitable replies. The town of Warwick agreed to the proposal, and further suggested a conference with the island towns, with a view to their all uniting to obtain a renewal of the charter, as such united action would remove some obstacles then existing, by reason of the separate duties of the two agents, and would also help to secure to the colony the Narraganset country, which the Greenwich men were striving to obtain. A meeting was accordingly held, but no record of it remains.

29.

Aug.
2.

Another letter from Mr. Williams, saying that the Council had granted leave to the colony to go on under the charter until the controversy was decided, gave great satisfaction. A few days later an order of Council was issued vacating the commission of Coddington, and directing the towns again to unite under the charter. The mission was successful at every point. The agents remained in England on their private business, and also to sustain the rights of the colony, while William Dyre, who had probably gone out with them, returned home with the joyful news.

Sept.
8.

Oct.
2.

The General Assembly met at Providence, and passed two important acts, an alien and a libel law. By the former no foreigner was to be received as a freeman in any town, or to have any trade with the Indians, but by consent of the Assembly. The latter made disparaging language, spoken in malice, actionable in every town. They also wrote to Roger Williams a letter of thanks for his services, the successful result of which was not yet known to them, and proposed that he should get himself appointed Governor of the colony for one year, as it would give weight to the government. This proposal affords the strongest proof of the respect and confidence felt in the colony towards its illustrious Founder. But Williams

28.

had little desire for power. Such a course would have established a dangerous precedent, and might appear to take from the colony a portion of its liberty in the selection of officers. They also wrote a letter to the town of Warwick, where doubts had been expressed as to the legality of the Assembly, protesting against such expressions as tending to discredit the authority of the Assembly, thereby weakening the government, and likewise affirming both the validity of the committee chosen from Warwick, and the legality of the Court. The occasion for such a letter displays the lamentable distraction that pervaded the colony at this time.

A more serious cause of dissension led to a special meeting of the Court of Commissioners at Warwick. The President of the colony and the Warwick Assistant, upon an examination before the Court of Trials, charged Hugh Bewett, one of the committee from Providence, with high treason. The trial lasted four days, and resulted in the acquittal of the prisoner, thus reversing the decision of the Court of Trials, and thereby increasing the divisions in the colony. The grounds of the indictment cannot now be ascertained.

Upon the arrival of William Dyre from England, with the repeal of Coddington's power, he wrote letters to Warwick and to Providence, naming a day when he would meet all the freemen who chose to appear at Portsmouth, to communicate the orders of the Council of State. A town meeting was held in Providence, at which, in accordance with a request from Warwick,[1] a meeting of the Commissioners of the two towns was agreed upon. It was held at Pawtuxet the following week. This Assembly drafted a reply to a letter from the island, relating to a reunion of the colony, and appointed two of the members from each town to carry it, and to consult with those of the island concerning the peace and welfare of the

CHAP VIII.

1 6 5 2. Oct.

Dec. 20.

1652-3. Feb. 18.

20.

25.

[1] Warwick records of 22d February, 1652.

State. Their labor was fruitless. The point of difficulty
was this. The mainland towns contended that they were
the Providence Plantations, their charter never having
been vacated, and their government having continued uninterrupted by the defection of the island, and therefore
the General Assembly to hear the orders of Council,
should be held with them. The island towns claimed
that as they formed the greater part of the colony, and
hence had a larger interest in the matter, the Assembly
should meet there. The original letters from the Council
of State were deposited by Dyre with the town clerk of
Newport, from whom certified copies were obtained, after
some trouble, by the other towns. Neither party was disposed to yield. On the following Monday an Assembly
of the colony, as it was called, met at Portsmouth, " to
hear and receive the orders from y⁰ right Honorable y³
Council of State." The officers who had been displaced
by Coddington's commission were reinstated until the
next election, which was appointed for the usual time.
Proposals for reunion, and for the government of the colony till the ensuing election, were sent to Providence by
the town of Newport. The mainland towns replied that
they were ready to meet by Commissioners, and desired
the island to appoint the time, to arrange all matters.
They did not accept the terms proposed by Newport, nor
was any meeting of Commissioners appointed by the
island. The division therefore continued for another year,
to the imminent peril of the liberties of the colony and of
its internal peace.

Two distinct Assemblies convened for a general election at the same time. That of the mainland towns met
at Providence, the other at Newport, each sitting for two
days. By the former a letter was sent to the island, giving as a reason why they did not meet with them, that
the island had not given any notice of agreement to meet
them by Commissioners, and hence they must proceed

with their own election as before. They chose Gregory Dexter, President ; Stukely Westcott, General Assistant for Warwick ; John Sayles, General Assistant for Providence, and Treasurer ; John Greene, Recorder, and Hugh Bewitt, Sergeant. The Council of State having directed the colony to annoy the Dutch, with whom war had been declared, it was ordered that no provisions should be sent to the Dutch ; that each plantation should prepare for its defence ; and that no seizures of Dutch property should be made in the name of the colony without a commission from the General Court. All legal process was to issue in the name of the Commonwealth of England, and in Providence and Warwick an engagement in these words was subscribed upon their records :—" I do declare and promise that I will be true and faithful to the Commonwealth of England, as it is now established, without a Kinge or House of Lords." [1]

The enemies of Rhode Island afterwards sought to injure her position with the King on account of this engagement, but did not succeed. The only policy that Rhode Island could adopt was that which is pursued at this day by the United States in its intercourse with foreign countries, to acknowledge the government *de facto.* To that government, whether royalist, republican, or protectorate, she was always loyal, and her success from that cause rankled in the breasts of her Puritan opponents, whose professions of loyalty to the Kings were equally loud and much less sincere.

The Assembly at Newport elected John Sandford, sen., President ; Nicholas Easton of Newport, and Robert Borden of Portsmouth, Assistants ; William Lytherland, Recorder ; Richard Knight, Sergeant ; John Coggeshall, Treasurer, and John Easton, Attorney General. They re-established the code of 1647, and gave liberty to the mainland towns to choose their own General Assistants,

CHAP.
VIII.

1653.
May
16-17.

17-18.

[1] Warwick records, 8th March, 1652-3.

in case they decided to unite with the island. The next day some freemen from Providence and Warwick came to the Assembly, and an election for Assistants of those towns was made. Thomas Olney was chosen for Providence, and Randal Holden for Warwick, thus making two sets of Assistants for the mainland towns, and raising a question of conflicting powers to render the difficulties yet more complicated.

Mr. Coddington, upon demand of the Assembly to surrender the statute book and records, declined to do so without advice from his Council, having received no order from England to resign his commission, or any proof, as he said, that it had been annulled. A more inextricable series of entanglements than now existed in the colony could not well be imagined.

Active measures were taken against the Dutch. Cannon and smaller arms, and twenty volunteers were voted for the aid of the English on Long Island. Commissions to act against the enemy were granted to Capt. John Underhill, William Dyre and Edward Hull, and a Court of Admiralty for the trial of prizes was appointed, consisting of the general officers and three jurors from each town. The island was more energetic than the mainland in these measures, assuming at once offensive ground, while the latter acted chiefly on the defensive. Both did more than the United Colonies, who, although they had received similar orders from the Council of State, were more prudent, if not lukewarm, in their conduct. This military proclivity in Rhode Island was early shown. Their exposed position made it necessary on account of the Indians in the first instance, and long habit cultivated the martial spirit of the people till it became a second nature. Their maritime advantages favored commercial enterprise, and the two combined prepared them for those naval exploits which in after years shed so much glory on the State. That the bold proceedings of the Island Assembly were considered rash by the rest of the colony, appears from a remonstrance made by the Court of Commissioners, assembled at Providence for this purpose. The acceptance of commissions to fight against the Dutch was a direct violation of their act in May, and as they claimed to be the lawful Assembly under the charter, they at once disfranchised those who owned the validity of those commissions, until they should give satisfaction to Providence and Warwick. The remonstrance recited the attempts made at re-union, as before given, and denounced the conduct of the Island Assembly in granting commissions of reprisal, not only as rash in the feeble condition of the colony, but as subversive of all government, in that they assumed to do it by authority of the whole colony. In conclusion an appeal to England was threatened in case the island should attempt to engage the mainland towns in the said commissions, or to molest them on that account. The Court adjourned to meet at the call of either of the General Assistants. This was not long delayed.

The Pawtuxet men again, as two years before, petitioned Massachusetts on the subject of taxes levied by the Providence Plantations. The General Court sent a letter protesting against such exaction, or the exercise of any sort of jurisdiction over its subjects, and granting leave to them to arrest and sue in the county Courts any person of another government that should usurp over them, whenever such person or his property should be found within the jurisdiction of Massachusetts.[1] To reply to this protest a special session of the Commissioners was held at Warwick. No copy of the reply remains.

The decided conduct of the island in the Dutch war increased the dissensions of the State, and involved her in further controversies with her neighbors. Capt. Hull, under his commission, captured a French ship in a mode

CHAP.
VIII.

1653.
June
3-4.

Aug.
13.

[1] M. C. R. iv. Part 1, 149.

1653.

Sept.
5.

April
19.

Sept.
12.

20.

13.

alleged by Massachusetts, in a letter to Rhode Island, to be unlawful. Among the reasons for this allegation, the dissolution of the Parliament was mentioned. This was seized upon by Gorton as a ground of accusation against Massachusetts in England, whither the original letter, signed by the magistrates, was to be sent as evidence, with other charges, against them. William Arnold, of Pawtuxet, wrote to the General Court, informing them of this design.[1] Great anxiety was felt by the United Colonies lest the Indians should ally with the Dutch. The Council of Massachusetts had sent two messengers in the spring to question Pessicus, Ninigret and Mexham, the son of Canonicus, being the three chief sachems of the Narragansets, upon this subject. They all denied any such intention, but their denial did not satisfy the Confederates,[2] who, at their next meeting, hearing of an assault made by the Narragansets upon the Long Island Indians, again sent messengers to them, demanding an account of their conduct. The explanation not being satisfactory war was declared against the Narragansets, but Massachusetts deeming the cause insufficient, refused to raise her quota of troops, so the expedition was abandoned.[3] The energy of the Rhode Island privateers had alarmed the United Colonies in the spring. Another seizure, of one of their own vessels, by Capt. Baxter, under a commission from this colony, caused them to send a special messenger with a letter to Rhode Island, remonstrating against the act. The Desire, of Barnstable, belonging to Samuel Mayo, was seized in Hempstead harbor, an English settlement within the Dutch limits, having stores on board, which the owner affirmed were intended for a plantation of English at Oyster Bay. Lieut.

[1] Hazard's State Papers, i. 582.

[2] The queries, eleven in number, with the answers of each sachem, are given in full in Hazard, ii. 205–9.

[3] Hazard ii. 283–5, 288–93.

Hudson was instructed to learn by what authority Rhode
Island issued letters of marque, and also to demand satisfaction for Mayo.   President Easton replied that the
colony was authorized to act against the enemies of England, and had sent to the supreme authority an account
of Baxter's proceedings, which they disowned so far as he
had exceeded his commission.   No satisfaction was given
to Mayo.   Upon Hudson's return the Commissioners advised Connecticut to bring the Desire to trial if found in
her harbors, the owner agreeing to pay damages, if it
should prove true that she had been justly seized by Baxter.
Baxter also captured a Dutch vessel near New York,
and was pursued to Fairfield harbor by two armed Dutch
ships.   The New England Commissioners thereupon prohibited Dutch vessels from entering any English port.
This was a very mild course to adopt towards a belliger-
ent foe, and contrasts with the vigorous conduct of Rhode
Island.

The report of dissensions in Rhode Island had reached
England, and grieved the advocates of liberal principles
in that country.   Among these none were more earnest
than Sir Henry Vane, whose sympathies, when Governor
of Massachusetts, were with the party of progress, and
who at home opposed in turn the despotism of the Stuarts and the ultimate designs of Cromwell.   Vane always
manifested a deep interest in the welfare of Rhode Island,
and a cordial appreciation of the principles of its founder,
who for a considerable time during this visit to England
became his guest.   He wrote to the people of Rhode Isl-
and a most kind and imploring letter, urging them to
reconcile their feuds for the honor of God and the good
of their fellow-men.   "Are there no wise men among
you?   No public self-denying spirits," he asks, "who can
find some way of union before you become a prey to your
enemies?"   This letter no doubt had some effect in com-

CHAP.
VIII.
pleting a reconciliation which, before it was received, had already begun.

1654.
May.
16-18.
The next spring but one General Assembly was held, although the union was not yet perfected. A majority in the mainland towns seem to have agreed to the course pursued by the island, as these towns held no separate Court of Commissioners. A large minority still held out. There was no cordiality between the parties. A committee of eight persons, two from each town, was appointed to prepare some mode of healing the division. Nicholas Easton was chosen President of the colony. Randall Holden had the next highest number of votes. Thomas Olney was elected Assistant for Providence, Richard Borden for Portsmouth, Edward Smith for Newport, and Randall Holden for Warwick ; Joseph Torrey, Recorder ; John Coggeshall, Treasurer ; Richard Knight, Sergeant, and John Cranston, Attorney General. Some men were examined on a charge of illegal trading with the Dutch, and another commission of reprisal was granted against the enemy. Fugitives from labor, belonging in other colonies, were to be returned on proper proof, at the expense of the master.

Mr. Williams had so often succeeded in calming the ruffled spirits of the colonists, that he felt his presence might be useful in the existing crisis. Leaving Mr. Clarke to protect the rights of the colony in England, he returned home early in the summer, bringing with him the above-mentioned letter of Sir Henry Vane, and also an order from the Lord Protector to the government of Massachusetts, to permit him in future to pass unmolested through that territory. Soon after his return he wrote to his friend Winthrop an account of his occupations while abroad, from which we learn of his teaching the Hebrew, Greek, Latin, French and Dutch languages, thus making his many accomplishments a means of subsistence, and also of his intimacy with Milton, then

July
12.

Secretary of the Council of State, to whom he taught
Dutch in exchange for other languages.[1] That he should
be obliged to teach for his support while employed on
public business, is a proof of the poverty of the colony
at this time. He also addressed a most earnest and conciliatory letter to the town of Providence, concerning the
dissensions in the colony, wherein he thanks God "for
his wonderful PROVIDENCES, by which alone the town and
colony and that grand cause of TRUTH AND FREEDOM OF
CONSCIENCE, hath been upheld to this day," and suggests
a mode of settling the unhappy quarrel. He was appointed to reply to the letter from Sir Henry Vane, which
he did in behalf of the town. From that letter we are
confirmed in the opinion that the usurpation of Coddington, and the difficulties arising from the granting of commissions of reprisal against the Dutch, were the chief
causes of discontent in the colony.

At length a reunion was effected. A full Court of
Commissioners, six from each town, assembled at Warwick. Articles of agreement, settling the terms of reunion, were signed by the whole Court. It was agreed that
all acts of the separate Assemblies from the time of the
division should remain to the account of the towns, and
of the persons taking part in those acts ; that the colony
should proceed under authority of the charter ; and that
the General Assembly for all public affairs, except elections, should be composed of six members from each town.
Thus ended this most dangerous period of disunion, that
had lasted for three years, of which the first half was
owing to the ambition of Coddington, and the last to the
local jealousies of the towns, and to the refractory spirit
of individuals. After this happy consummation the Court
continued in session two days. They re-established the
code of 1647, forbade the sale of liquor to the Indians,
and prohibited the French and Dutch from trading with

[1] This extremely interesting letter is given in Knowles, 261–4.

CHAP. VIII.

1654. Sept. 1.

them. The care of the colony to avoid all legislation that could in any way affect the rights of conscience, is conspicuous in the action taken upon " several complaints exhibited to this Assembly against y* incivilitie of persons exercised upon y* first day of y* weeke, which is offensive to divers amongst us." They passed no Sunday laws, such as existed all around them, but, judging rightly that such disturbances arose from the want of any regular season for recreation, they referred it to the towns to appoint days for their " servants and children to recreate themselves," and thus to prevent similar annoyances in future.

12.

The General Court of election met at Warwick. Roger Williams was chosen President ; Thomas Harris Assistant for Providence, John Roome for Portsmouth, Benedict Arnold for Newport, and Randall Holden for Warwick ; Wm. Lytherland Recorder, Richard Knight Sergeant, Richard Burden Treasurer, and John Cranston Attorney General. These were to hold office until the

13.

spring election. The next day the Court of Commissioners fixed the first Tuesday in May for the election of members by the towns, and the Tuesday after the fifteenth of May for that of general officers. Legal process was to issue " in y* name of His Higness y* Lord Protector of y* Commonwealth of England, Scotland, and Ireland, and y* dominions thereto belonging." The President and Gregory Dexter, then town clerk of Providence, were desired to " send letters of humble thanksgiving to His Highness the Lord Protector, and Sir Henry Vane, Mr. Holland, and to Mr. John Clarke, in y* name of y* colonie." The two island towns were authorized to hold their court of trials together, if they pleased, or apart as they had previously done, and the same liberty was given to the two mainland towns. This act seems intended to remove what was apparently the first source of alienation in the colony, soon after the organization of the charter government.[1]

---

[1] Ante chap. vii. p. 214, 221.

War had again broken out between the Narragansets CHAP.
and the Long Island Indians. The United Colonies were VIII.
much alarmed, and sent messengers to inquire of Ninigret 1654.
the cause, and to demand his presence at Hartford. Nin- Sept.
igret replied that the enemy had slain a sachem's son and 13.
sixty of his people. The haughty spirit of the chieftain 18.
appears in his answer : " If your governor's son were
slain, and several other men, would you ask counsel of
another nation how and when to right yourselves ? " He
refused to go to Hartford, and desired only that the English would let him alone. President Williams wrote to
the government of Massachusetts a long letter in defence Oct.
of the Indians,[1] maintaining that the Narragansets had 5.
always been true to the English, and that the present war
on Long Island was an act of self-defence. A force was
sent against Ninigret under Major Willard. The In- 9.
dians took refuge in a swamp. The troops returned un- 24.
successful, to the great chagrin of the Commissioners at
Hartford. But Massachusetts, from humane motives, opposed the war, and the other colonies were obliged to
submit.[2]

Military affairs always received great attention in
Rhode Island, but were not always a matter of record.
This year the first mention is made of an election of offi- Nov.
cers in Providence. All were required to do military duty ; 6.
only one man could be left at home on each farm, one mile
from town, on parade days.

An entry in the Portsmouth records shows that mem- 13.
bers were elected from that town to attend a meeting of
the General Assembly to be held the next day at New- 14.
port. No record of any such session exists, nor is any
other reference made to it elsewhere.

When Aquidneck was purchased, only the grass upon

---

[1] The letter in full is given in R. I. Col. Records, i. 291, and Knowles, 272-8.

[2] Hazard's State Papers, ii. 308, 318, 324-5, 340, etc.

the other islands was conveyed in the deed.   The fee still vested in the native owners.   A movement was now made in town meeting at Portsmouth to join with Newport in the purchase of Conanicut and Dutch islands, and a committee was appointed to treat with Newport on the subject.   These islands were afterwards bought, the former by Coddington and Benedict Arnold, Jr.,[1] the latter, together with Goat and Coasters Harbor islands, by Arnold and others.[2]

Although harmony was for the most part restored to the colony, there still remained many who were restive under restraint, some advocating an unlawful liberty, and others, royalists in feeling, refusing to obey the government. This winter was one of unusual turbulence in Providence. Under pretence of a voluntary training a tumult occurred in which some of the principal people were implicated.[3] A paper was sent to the town asserting the dangerous doctrine " that it was blood-guiltiness, and against the rule of the gospel, to execute judgment upon transgressors against the private or public weal."   This dogma was subversive of all civil society.   If allowed it would pervert one of the two distinctive principles of Rhode Island liberty to the destruction of the other and the consequent annihilation of them both.   It was then that Roger Williams wrote to the town that masterly letter which will endure so long as the principles it so admirably defines shall be cherished among men.

" There goes many a ship to sea, with many hundred souls in one ship, whose weal and woe is common, and is a true picture of a commonwealth, or a human combination, or society.   It hath fallen out sometimes that both Papists and Protestants, Jews and Turks, may be embarked in one ship ; upon which supposal I affirm, that all the lib-

_____

[1] April 17, 1657.   [2] May 22, 1658.
[3] Thomas Olney, Robert Williams, John Field, William Harris and others. Staples' Annals, 113.

erty of conscience, that ever I pleaded for, turns upon these two hinges : that none of the Papists, Protestants, Jews, or Turks, be forced to come to the ship's prayers or worship, nor compelled from their own particular prayers or worship, if they practise any. I further add, that I never denied, that notwithstanding this liberty, the commander of this ship ought to command the ship's course, yea, and also command that justice, peace, and sobriety, be kept and practised, both among the seamen and all the passengers. If any of the seamen refuse to perform their service, or passengers to pay their freight ; if any refuse to help, in person or purse, towards the common charges or defence ; if any refuse to obey the common laws and orders of the ship, concerning their common peace or preservation ; if any shall mutiny and rise up against their commanders and officers ; if any should preach or write that there ought to be no commanders or officers, because all are equal in Christ, therefore no masters nor officers, no laws nor orders, no corrections nor punishments ; I say, I never denied, but in such cases, whatever is pretended, the commander or commanders may judge, resist, compel, and punish such transgressors, according to their deserts and merits." [1]

Nowhere have the limits of civil and religious freedom been more aptly illustrated than in this letter of the christian statesman who first reduced them to harmonious union.

Complaints made to Cromwell of the divisions in the colony, drew from him a brief letter confirming the charter and promising to adjust the difficulties.

At the regular annual election held in Providence the same general officers were chosen as in September, except Harris, who gave place to Thomas Olney as Assistant for Providence, Knight who was defeated by George Parker for Sergeant, and Burden who was displaced by John Sand-

[1] Knowles, 279-80.

ford, as Treasurer. John Greene, Jr., was chosen Solicitor General, an office not filled at the former election. The court roll of freemen at this time numbered two hundred and forty-seven persons, of whom Providence had forty-two, Warwick thirty-eight, Portsmouth seventy-one, and Newport ninety-six. More than two thirds of the strength of the colony was on the island. Newport had already by far the largest portion and was rapidly increasing. The difference between an inhabitant and a freeman should be borne in mind. Not every resident was a legal inhabitant. Some time elapsed after one's arrival in the colony before he could be received as an inhabitant, participating thereby in certain rights to the common lands, doing jury duty, and being eligible to some of the lesser town offices. If his conduct while thus situated gave satisfaction he might be propounded at town meeting to become a freeman, and if no valid objection was brought against him, at the next meeting he was admitted to all the rights of the freemen, or close corporators of the colony.

In the earlier years an admission as freeman sometimes brought with it a joint ownership in the land purchased, but soon it came to convey only the elective franchise, and even this was not always confined to freemen, for afterwards by a town law in Providence[1] any inhabitant was liable to be elected to office and finable for not serving. Two years later all who held lands in the town were declared to be freemen.[2] This latter feature remained, with some modifications, till the adoption of the State Constitution.

At this session the general Court of trials was appointed to sit once a year in each town. All persons were required to sign a submission to the Lord Protector and the Parliament. Those who refused were deprived of the benefit of the colony laws till they did so. Prisons were ordered to be built at Newport and Warwick. Providence and

---

[1] Passed at town meeting, June 1656. Annals of Prov., 118.
[2]   do.   do.   May 1658.   do.   do.   124.

Portsmouth were each to build a cage and to furnish it with a pair of stocks. Very full laws were passed regulating the sale of liquors. This subject received the attention of nearly every Assembly and has been the most fruitful theme of legislation for more than two hundred years. Two taverns were licensed in each town, and leave was granted to the towns to add one more if they saw fit. The armed opposition to authority by Olney and others, in the winter, was discussed and a committee appointed to inform him of the Assembly's view of the matter. That the disturbance was not very serious may be inferred from the choice of Olney as an assistant and from his taking the engagement after conferring with the committee. At the next town meeting it was wisely concluded "that for the colony's sake, who have since chosen Thomas Olney an assistant, and for the public union and peace's sake, it should be passed by and no more mentioned."

The reception of the letter from Cromwell caused a special session of the Assembly at Portsmouth. Letters of thanks were voted to the colony agent and to the Lord President of the Council, requesting the latter to present their submission to His Highness the Lord Protector. A law was passed requiring that any who might be convicted by the Assembly as leaders of faction should be sent as prisoners to England at their own expense, there to be tried and punished.

That strict decorum was not always preserved, although its necessity was appreciated, appears by the last act of this session ; " that in case any man shall strike another person in yᵉ Court, he shall either be fined ten pounds, or be whipt, accordinge as yᵉ Court shall see meete."

The shortness of the sessions, and the early hour at which the Assemblies met, are worthy of remark. Three or four days were then found to be sufficient for the most important business, and the daily adjournments were usually until six o'clock, or till half an hour or one hour after

CHAP.
VIII.

1655.
May.

June.

28.

29.

30.

sunrise the next morning. A fine of one shilling was imposed for absence from roll call.

The Warwick dispute remained unadjusted. An action
for damages in the sum of two thousand pounds was brought
by the Gortonists against Massachusetts, before the Council of State. The Indians subject to Massachusetts there
and at Pawtuxet continued their depredations. The English subjects at the latter place, now consisting of but four
families[1] only two of whom still held out against Rhode
Island, were a source of obstruction to the authority of the
colony. The law prohibiting the sale of powder and arms
to citizens of Rhode Island was still in force in Massachusetts. Upon these four points, of vital importance to the
prosperity of the State, President Williams wrote to the
Government of Massachusetts, urging them so to alter their
policy as to prevent complaints against them from being
sent to England, in ships then ready to sail.[2] Although
the General Court was then in session no immediate notice
was taken of this communication.

The people of Providence, alarmed by hostile demonstrations of the Indians, decided to erect a fort on Stamper's Hill.[3] At the same meeting they established a justice's Court for the trial of cases not exceeding forty shil-

---

[1] Stephen Arnold, Zachary Rhodes, William Arnold and William Carpenter. Of these the first-named desired to unite with Rhode Island, as did the
second also, for, being a Baptist, he was virtually banished by the law of 13th
Nov. 1644. The last two alone held out, under pretence of fearing to offend
Massachusetts by withdrawing their allegiance. This they did, however,
three years later, Oct. 22, 1658, by consent of the General Court.

[2] The letter is found in R. I. Col. Rec. i. 322–5, and Hazard's State Papers, i. 610–11.

[3] The tradition, preserved by Judge Staples, in Annals of Providence, p.
117, gives a curious derivation for this name, and illustrates the constant dangers to which the early settlers were exposed. " Soon after the settlement of
Providence a body of Indians approached the town in a hostile manner.
Some of the townsmen, by running and stamping on this hill, induced them
to believe that there was a large number of men stationed there to oppose
them, upon which they relinquished their design and retired. From this circumstance the hill was always called Stamper's Hill."

lings in amount. Roger Williams, Thomas Olney, and
Thomas Harris, were chosen judges of this Court. The
former was then President of the colony, Olney was the
General Assistant for Providence, and Harris was a member
of the Assembly. That the smallest tribunal in a town
should be composed of such members speaks well for the
public spirit of the leading men, and for the care taken in
the administration of justice.

At the general Court of trials held at Warwick, Mr.
Coddington appeared as one of the newly elected commissioners from Newport. His election caused so much dissatisfaction that an investigation was had by the Assembly,
the jury meanwhile being dismissed. The result was a
formal submission to the authority of the colony in these
words :

" I William Coddington, doe hereby submit to yᵉ
authoritie of His Highness in this Colonie as it is now
united, and that with all my heart."

The Assembly then adjourned, while the Court of trials
proceeded, after which it again convened at the same
place. The committee of investigation reported favorably on Coddington's right to a seat, but advised that a
letter be sent to the Agent in England, giving their
reasons for receiving him, and asking for a discharge of
the complaints entered against him before the Council of
State. He had incurred a fine for withholding the colony
records from the last Assembly, and this fine it was voted
not to remit. Guns, similar to some he had brought over
from England, were found in possession of the Indians.
He was therefore required to account for the disposal of
his. Certain proceedings prejudicial to Coddington during
the time of his usurpation, were cut out from the records
and given to him—a mutilation much to be regretted, as
it deprives us of all information concerning his administration. The presentments against him and some of his
partisans on the Island records were annulled.

CHAP.
VIII.
1655-6.
March.

The custom of referring particular items of business to sub-committees, which gave rise to the modern system of standing committees, was early introduced into our Assembly. There is scarcely a session, since the reunion, at which one or more sub-committees were not appointed. Prior to that time, all business was done by deliberation of the whole body. A warrant was issued to bring Pumham before the Court to answer complaints from the town of Warwick, and a committee was appointed to treat with him, and to report at the next session. Marriages were ordered to be published at town meetings, or on training days at the head of the company, or by writing posted in some public place, signed by a magistrate. If the banns were forbidden, the case was to be heard by two magistrates ; should they allow it, the parties might marry ; but if not, the general Court of trials were to decide it. Tavern bars were to be closed at nine o'clock at night. The age of majority was fixed at twenty-one years. No magistrate, during the trial of a case, was permitted to leave the bench without permission from the Court, under a heavy penalty, as such an act might bias the jury, and thus imperil a just cause.

1656.

May
12.

17.

The letter to the General Court, at their November session, having received no reply, Williams, in the spring, wrote to Governor Endicott, who invited him to come to Boston. A second official letter was sent to the Court, of the same tenor as the former one ; and a few days after, Mr. Williams, then in Boston, wrote to the Court, expressing his gratification at the progress of affairs with Pumham, which, it would seem, were intrusted to his management.[1]

[1] An amusing entry in the Warwick records of 15th May of this year shows the provision made by that town for this journey of the President. " Ordered that forty shillings be sent out of the treasury unto Mr. Roger Williams, and a pair of Indian Breeches for his Indian, at seven shillings sixpence at 6 pr penny, as also a horse for his journey unto Boston and back again."

At the general election held in Portsmouth, Roger CHAP.
VIII. Williams was again chosen President. The Assistants were Thomas Olney for Providence, William Balston for 1656. Portsmouth, John Coggeshall for Newport, and John May 20. Weeks for Warwick, he having the next highest vote to Randall Holden, who, being elected, declined to serve, and whose fine of five pounds for refusing was offset by his services previously rendered. John Sandford was made Recorder and Treasurer ; George Parker, Sergeant ; John Easton, Attorney-General ; and Richard Bulgar, Solicitor. The Assembly, as usual, met the next day, and sat three days.

It was agreed that the controversy with the Pawtuxet 21-23. men should be closed by arbitration, after which they were to be received as freemen of the colony. Whoever should deface or destroy any instrument of justice was to make reparation for the injury, and to be confined for six hours in the stocks. Leave was granted to William Blackstone to enter the titles of his land in the records of land evidence in the colony. This was doubtless for the sake of convenience, he living near Providence, although at that time in the Plimouth jurisdiction, as appears from letters of administration granted by that colony at his decease. At the autumn session, held like- Oct. wise at Portsmouth, provision was made for supplying 10. any vacancy caused by the death of a general officer. Whoever had the next highest number of votes was to fill the place till the ensuing May election, or in case the choice had been unanimous, the town where the vacancy occurred was to elect a successor. This action was caused by the death of the Sergeant, George Parker, the first general officer who died in place. He was succeeded by Richard Knight, who had been his competitor at the spring election.

One of the most serious differences that ever disturbed the colony commenced about this time. The free princi-

ples of the State were constantly liable to abuse by those
whom they attracted hither. The distinction between license and legal liberty was not yet so clearly drawn but
that some strong intellects failed to see it as it existed in
the mind of Roger Williams, or as set forth in his remarkable letter before given. The paper which produced that
letter expressed a most dangerous idea, but one that found
an earnest and able champion in William Harris, between
whom and Williams an inveterate hostility arose. The
sources of this enmity appear to have been their different
views of the nature of liberty, and the proceedings resulting from this difference. It was carried to a degree of
personal invective that mars the exalted character of Williams and detracts from the dignity and worth of his opponent. It was never forgotten by the one or forgiven by
the other. Both were men of ardent feelings and of great
address, whose mental activity was never at rest. Harris,
unfortunately, was almost constantly employed in business
that was inimical to the interests of Rhode Island, and
from this time forward assumed the position that the Ar-
nolds of Pawtuxet had before held, either as a leader of
faction within the State or the agent and representative
of adverse interests abroad. This is the more to be regretted because he brought to whatever he undertook the
resources of a great mind and, to all appearance, the honest convictions of an earnest soul. On this account he
was a more dangerous opponent and required stringent
measures to suppress the errors of his political creed. So
far only as this controversy had a public character we shall
follow its development through a long series of years.
Let the more repulsive features of personal rancor be consigned to oblivion! Harris had published "that he that
can say it is his conscience ought not to yield subjection
to any human order amongst men;" and had attempted to
sustain the subversive doctrine by abundant perversions
of scriptural quotation. It was much such an announce-

ment as had aroused the pen of Williams two years before. He now adopted severer means to crush the reiterated fallacy.   As President of the colony he issued a warrant for the arrest of Harris on the charge of high treason against the Commonwealth of England.[1]

At the next election held in Newport, Williams was not a candidate.   Benedict Arnold was chosen President ; Arthur Fenner of Providence, William Balston of Portsmouth, Richard Tew of Newport, and Randall Holden of Warwick, Assistants, John Greene Jr., Attorney General, and James Rogers, Solicitor.   The other three general offices remained as before.   The trial of Harris could not proceed on account of the absence of his accuser.   Both parties were warned to appear at an adjourned session in Warwick.   At this special session Harris was required to

CHAP.
VIII.

1656-7.
March
12.

1657.
May
19.

July
4.

[1] Two copies of this warrant are still preserved among the papers of William Harris, now in the possession of Wm. J. Harris, Esq., of Providence, whose kindness in placing these valuable MSS. in the hands of the writer he here begs leave to acknowledge.   The warrant reads as follows : " Whereas, William Harris of Providence, published to all the towns in the colony dangerous writings containing his notorious defiance to the authority of his hightness the Lord Protector, &c., and the high Court of Parliament of England, as also his notorious attempts to draw all the English subjects of this colony into a traitorous renouncing of their allegiance and subjection, and whereas the said William Harris now openly in the face of the Court, declareth himself resolved to maintain the said writings with his blood ; These are therefore in the name of His Highness the Lord Protector, strictly to will and require you to apprehend the said William Harris, and to keep him in safe custody until his appearance before the General Assembly of the colony in May next ensuing at Newport, before which Assembly he is to be convicted and sent for England, or acquitted according to law of the colony established amongst us.   And you are also hereby authorized to take all due care that his land and estate be faithfully secured to the use of his highness, the Lord Protector, in case of the conviction of the said William Harris in the General Assembly of the colony as aforesaid ; for the due performance of all which premises, all his Highness' officers in this colony, both civil and military, and all his Highness' subjects in this colony are hereby straightly required to be aiding and assisting, as they will answer to the contrary at their peril.
                                          " ROGER WILLIAMS, President.
" To Mr. RICHARD KNIGHT, General Sergeant."
This warrant is dated " Newport, 12th of the 1st mo., 1656 and 1657, so called."

read a copy of his book upon which the impeachment was based while Williams read the original. Williams then read to the Court his letter containing the accusation, also a copy of his charge, and his reply to Harris' book. It was referred to a committee to report what further proceedings were desirable. They advised that the papers be sent to England for examination and that Harris should give bonds for good behavior till the result was known. A committee was thereupon appointed to write to John Clarke a suitable letter to accompany these papers, and Harris and his son Andrew were placed under bonds of five hundred pounds.

The English settled in the Pequot country were ever thwarting the efforts of the Narragansets to avenge their wrongs upon Uncas. The Mohawks were in league with the Narragansets against the Mohegans, and were advancing in force to attack them. The Narragansets applied to the General Assembly to remonstrate with the English on their conduct in always giving warning, through their scouts, to Uncas of the approach of an enemy, lest the Mohawks, being enraged thereby, should attack the English themselves. The Assembly wrote a letter to Capt. Denison and others in accordance with this request, that for peace sake they should allow the Indians to fight out their own quarrels—a grain of advice which, if followed, would have done more than any thing else to secure the good-will of those powerful tribes.

The year 1656 will be darkly memorable in the annals of New England for the arrival of the Quakers and the commencement of their persecution at Boston. The appearance of this " cursed sect of heretics "[1] so alarmed the Puritans that a day of public humiliation was appointed[2] to be held in all the churches mainly on their account. A stringent law was enacted for their suppression[3] and

[1] Preamble to law of Oct. 14th, 1656, M. C. R., iii. 415.
[2] May 14th, 1656, to be held June 11th.
[3] Oct. 14th, 1656.

two years later their tenets were made a capital offence.[1] CHAP.
Fines, imprisonment, whipping, banishment, mutilation, VIII.
and death, were denounced and inflicted upon them. The 1657.
wildest fanaticism on their part was met by a frenzied
bigotry on the other. Acts that made the perpetrators
amenable to the statute against nuisances were visited
with the penalties provided against heresies. The strait-
jacket or temporary confinement would have been the
proper treatment in many cases that were consigned to
the scourge or the scaffold. The vagaries of morbid minds,
not morally accountable for the indecencies they committed,
were visited with the same penalties that awaited the rob-
ber or the assassin.[2] Nor was severity confined to cases
like these, but people of blameless conduct alike suffered,
on the same ground, for heretical opinions. For five years
this persecution continued, until stayed by an order from
Charles II.[3] requiring that capital and corporal punishments of the Quakers should cease, and that such as were
obnoxious should be sent to England.[4] That Rhode Island
became a city of refuge for those who fled from this fiery

[1] Oct. 19th, 1658.

[2] "At Boston one George Wilson, and at Cambridge Elizabeth Horton
went crying through the streets that the Lord was coming with fire and sword
to plead with them. Thomas Newhouse went into the meeting house at Boston with a couple of glass bottles, and broke them before the congregation,
and threatened 'Thus will the Lord break you in pieces.' Another time M.
Brewster came in with her face smeared and as black as a coal. Deborah
Wilson went through the streets of Salem naked as she came into the world,
for which she was well whipped. One of the sect apologizing for this behavior said, 'If the Lord did stir up any of his daughters to be a sign of
the nakedness of others, he believed it to be a great cross to a modest woman's
spirit, but the Lord must be obeyed.'" Hutch. Mass., i. 203-4. A display
of prurient piety like this last occurred also in one of the churches. New
England Judged, Part ii. p. 69.

[3] 9th Sept., 1661.

[4] See Hutchinson's Mass., i. 196-204 ; Bishop's New England Judged,
Part 1st, 4to., 176 pp. London, 1661, and Part 2d, 4to., 147 pp., 1667. New
England Ensign, London, 1659, 4to., 121 pp. Several Rhode Island people
were victims of this persecution, whose sufferings will be noticed in the proper
place. Mary, wife of Wm. Dyre, Secretary of Rhode Island colony, was put
to death, and Thomas Harris and others were severely maltreated.

CHAP.
VIII.

1657.
Sept.
2.

Oct.
13.

1657-8.
March
13.

ordeal vexed the United Colonies. The Commissioners, assembled at Boston, wrote a letter urging Rhode Island to banish the Quakers already there and to prohibit any more from coming to the State.[1]   To this request the President and Assistants, met at the Court of trials in Providence, replied, that there was no law by which men could be punished in Rhode Island for their opinions, and that the Quakers being unmolested, were becoming disgusted at their want of success ; but that in case of any extravagancies, like those referred to, being committed, the next General Assembly would provide a corrective.   That body met at Portsmouth and addressed another letter to the Massachusetts on the same subject.   In this letter they say that freedom of conscience was the ground of their charter and shall be maintained ; that if the Quakers violate the laws or refuse to conform thereto in any respect, complaint against them will be made in England and the more readily as these people are there tolerated.[2]

On the same day a letter was sent to Plymouth denying the claim set up by that colony to Hog island, which was purchased by Richard Smith from Wamsutta, sachem of the Wampanoags.   The question was left to the President and Thomas Willett to be settled, by whom it was advised to adjust the matter by arbitration, which after much delay was done, and the right of Rhode Island to the land in dispute ultimately sustained.   Hope island had been given to Roger Williams by Miantinomi many years before but was still occupied by Indians.   The Court ordered that the Sachems should remove their subjects to leave Mr. Williams in possession.   Gould island had been purchased of the Indians a year before[3] by Thomas Gould, and about the same time[4] the great Pettiquamscut pur-

---

[1] Hazard, ii. 370-1.

[2] Both these letters and also that to which they are the replies, are given in R. I. Col. Rec., i. 374–380.

[3] March 28th, 1657.   [4] January 20th, 1657.

chase, in what is now South Kingston, was commenced. Repeated additions were made to this tract, and difficulties with adjoining purchasers arose when the claims of Massachusetts to the Narraganset country came to be urged.[1] These frequent purchases caused so much trouble that the Assembly soon afterwards prohibited any further purchases of land or islands from the Indians within the colony without express permission from that body, on pain of forfeiture of the land, and a fine of twenty pounds besides.

At the general election, held in Warwick, the only changes made were in the Assistants for Providence and Newport ; William Field being chosen for the former and Joseph Clarke for the latter. All the other offices remained as before. Upon the conclusion of peace between England and Holland the law prohibiting trade with the Dutch was repealed, but there were still some lawless persons, who, pretending commissions from Rhode Island, annoyed the Dutch commerce by seizing their goods and vessels. To prevent their recurrence these outrages were denounced as felony. The order to build prisons and cages not having been obeyed, it was repealed, and the prison built at Newport was directed to be for the colony use, the other towns contributing towards its cost.

The long pending difficulties with the Pawtuxet men were now terminated by their withdrawal from the jurisdiction of Massachusetts, and acknowledging allegiance to Rhode Island. William Arnold and William Carpenter, for themselves and their friends, petitioned the General Court for a full discharge of their persons and estates from subjection to Massachusetts. This was granted provided they rendered an account of their proceedings against the Warwick men under the commission of Massachusetts fif-

CHAP.
VIII.

1658.

Nov.
2.

May
18.

26.

---

[1] The details and subsequent history of this purchase are given by Mr. Potter, in R. I. H. C., iii. 275–99. The original proprietors were Samuel Wilbor, John Hull of Boston, John Porter, Samuel Wilson, Thomas Mumford. At a later period William Brenton and Benedict Arnold were admitted.

teen years before, and that the Greenes and others should have liberty to prosecute them in any of the Massachusetts Courts[1] for injuries received thereby. This happy result was effected by the mediation of Roger Williams. At the next General Court in October the sentence of banishment against the Warwick men was so far relaxed that leave was granted to John Greene, sen., to visit his friends for one month. The bond required from Arnold to answer any suit brought by the Greenes was limited to one year, at the expiration of which period he petitioned the Court for certain amounts of damage sustained by him in executing the commission against the Gortonists. The account was referred and ultimately extended, and in part allowed, but the committee's report was better calculated to satisfy the Greenes than the petitioner.[2]

Sept.
23.
Oct.
19.
The Commissioners of the United Colonies wrote to all the General Courts urging severer measures against the Quakers. Massachusetts acted at once on the suggestion, and passed a law punishing with death any Quakers who should return after sentence of banishment. Rhode Island again was urged to join in the fierce oppression. Threats of exclusion from all intercourse or trade with the rest of New England were made to force her from her fidelity to the cause of religious freedom, but in vain. The result was an appeal to Cromwell by the General Assembly that

Nov.
5.
" they may not be compelled to exercise any civil power over men's consciences, so long as human orders, in point of civility, are not corrupted or violated." A letter was sent to John Clarke to be presented to His Highness, which contains this request, and clearly distinguishes between the rights of conscience and the duties of the citizen.[3]

[1] M. C. R. iv. Part i. p. 333.
[2] The petition was Oct. 18th, 1659. The report was made Nov. 12th. See M. C. R., iv. Part i. 411, and R. I. H. C., ii. 206–12. He afterwards, 1663, presented an extended account, which was settled by compromise, Oct 21st, 1663. M. C. R., iv. Part ii. p. 78, 93.
[3] This letter is in R. I. Col. Rec., i. 396–9.

While Rhode Island was thus defending her liberal sentiments, her citizens without distinction of sex ·or age were suffering from Puritan persecutions. A Mrs. Gardner of Newport, the mother of several children, and a woman of good report, having become a Quaker, went to Weymouth, with an infant at her breast, taking with her a nurse, Mary Stanton, to attend the child. There they were arrested and taken before Governor Endicot by whom they were sent to prison, flogged with ten stripes each, and closely confined for two weeks.[1] Thomas Harris of Barbadoes, who had settled in Rhode Island, went to Boston with two others of the same sect, where, after service at church, he gave great offence by haranguing the congregation, an indiscretion which may have deserved some punishment but not the severity he received. He was flogged, imprisoned for eleven days, during five of which he was not allowed food or water, because he refused to work at the jailer's bidding, severely whipped by the jailer, and again publicly with several others, receiving fifteen stripes.[2]

Catharine, wife of Richard Scot of Providence, and sister of the celebrated Ann Hutchinson, met with a similar fate. She went to Boston to witness the mutilation of three of her brethren, whose right ears were cut off by the hangman in execution of the law against Quakers. For remonstrating upon this cruelty she was imprisoned for two weeks and then publicly flogged.[3] She was advanced in life, had been married twenty years, and was the mother of several children, two of whom suffered in the same cause. The severity of these proceedings and the increasing rigor of the statutes passed at every session of the General Court against the Quakers, caused many of them to seek a home in Rhode Island. But the spirit of fanaticism was not yet appeased. From fine and imprisonment it proceeded

CHAP.
VIII.

1658.
May
11.

June
17.

22.

Sept.
16.

Oct.
2.

---

[1] New England Ensign, 72-3. Bishop's New England Judged, 47.

[2] July 19th. New England Ensign, 73-5.

[3] New England Judged, 75.

CHAP.   to apply whipping and mutilation, then banishment, and
VIII.   finally death to the unfortunate Quakers. This last out-
1658.   rage upon humanity was opposed by the deputies and by
Oct.
19.   the great mass of the people, who were always ahead of
their rulers in liberal feeling and in their sense of justice
and of right. The magistrates and clergy[1] were zealous
in its favor. The deputies yielded by a majority of one,
and thus placed another blot on the annals of Massachusetts to the eternal disgrace of Puritan legislation. The
next year was to witness the execution of this cruel statute
in the case of a Rhode Island victim.

Nov.   To prevent further trouble like that which had just
2.   been so fortunately ended with Pawtuxet, the Assembly,
convened at Warwick, decreed that no one should hereafter submit his lands to any other jurisdiction, or attempt
to bring in any foreign government within the colony on
pain of confiscation. No law was to be in force until
twenty days after the adjournment of the Assembly. This
was to allow ten days for the recorder to furnish each town
clerk with a copy of the acts of the session, and ten more
for the towns to consider them, and if they disapproved to
notify the President and thus to annul the statute. The
Assembly decided to have but one annual session, to be
held at the May election, but this was rarely found to suffice. They also reduced the sittings of the Court of trials
to two, in March and October. The President and General
Council might call extra meetings of the Assembly. This
council was composed of the President, Assistants, and
Oct.   town Magistrates. No law creating it can be found, and
14.   but three meetings appear on the records—one at Warwick, just prior to this session, at which no business of importance was transacted, and the other two at Providence
in the following spring. At the first of these, warrants

[1] " In hæreticos gladio vindicandum est," was a motto of Calvin, as well
as of Rome, and too faithfully followed by his stern disciples in Massachusetts.

were issued to arrest Pumham for insurrection in causing
a riot to rescue a felon in Warwick, and some other Indians
for robbery committed upon William Arnold at Pawtuxet.
Two days afterward the council met for the last time to
publish the proclamation of Richard, Lord Protector, who
had succeeded to the supreme authority on the death of
his father in September. It was ordered to be read at
town meeting, and at the head of every military company
in the colony on the following Tuesday.

At the general election held in Providence the same
officers were retained throughout, except Knight, Sergeant,
who was displaced by James Rogers. The dispute with
Plymouth about Hog island not having been settled, the
Assembly again appointed four Commissioners to meet
the same number from Plymouth to adjust this matter, and
also the general boundary of the two colonies, and notified
Plymouth accordingly. Four men, one from each town,
were also appointed to mark out the western bounds of the
colony, but nothing was done about it for the present.
The Indians gave much trouble by stealing the goods and
cattle of the colonists. A severe law was passed to prevent
it. If the damage exceeded twenty shillings, the convict
might be sold as a slave to any English plantation abroad,
unless he made restitution, and if less than that sum he
should restore twofold, or be whipped not more than fifteen stripes. The Assembly addressed a letter to Richard
Cromwell asking a confirmation of their charter. It was
never presented, as the Protector had resigned his power
before it reached England. A tax of fifty pounds was laid
to pay for ammunition, and to meet the expenses of the
agent in London. Providence and Warwick were each to
pay nine pounds, Portsmouth fourteeen, and Newport
eighteen pounds. Providence was allowed to buy out and
remove the Indians within its limits, and to enlarge its
bounds by further purchase. Leave was also granted to
purchase certain other lands, and a committee appointed

CHAP.
VIII.

1659.
June
7.

July
4.

Aug.
23.

for that purpose. Fox island and an adjoining tract on the main near Wickford, were bought by Holden and Gorton, and soon afterwards Humphrey Atherton, John Winthrop and others, not citizens of Rhode Island, bought two large tracts on the bay, one called Quidnesett, south of Wickford, and the other, called Namcook, now Boston neck, north of it. This purchase was in violation of an express law of Rhode Island. Its validity depended on the decision of the question of jurisdiction over the Narraganset country, claimed by Rhode Island and disputed by Connecticut and Massachusetts. Roger Williams warned Atherton upon this point, and refused the offers of land made to induce him to aid as interpreter in the purchase. It became a fruitful source of difficulty for many years. The Assembly met at Portsmouth, and appointed a committee of two from each town to write to the Commissioners of the United Colonies, to Massachusetts, and to Atherton, respecting these purchases. During the Debate on this question the Assembly sat with closed doors. They prepared to prosecute the claims of Rhode Island before Parliament, and empowered the committee to call together the Assembly when they saw fit.

Potowomut was ordered to be purchased for the colony from the Indians. Hog island continued to be a source of trouble. Richard Smith claiming it adversely to the colony, and threatening any who should molest him in his possession, the Assembly resolved to bear them harmless. Smith sought to place the island under the jurisdiction of Plymouth. Robert Westcott, a member from Warwick, was tried for a similar offence and suspended, and John Weeks was chosen by the Assembly to fill his place. A further tax of fifty pounds was laid, of which Newport was to pay twenty, Providence eleven, Portsmouth ten, and Warwick nine pounds. Newport it appears had doubled in wealth over Portsmouth, and Providence for the first time seems to have gained upon the other two towns.

Letters from John Clarke informed the colony of the Pro- CHAP.
tector's resignation, and that the Parliament was the sole VIII.
authority, as before the accession of Cromwell. All legal 1 6 5 9.
process was therefore ordered to issue "in the name of the
supreme authority of the Commonwealth of England."
The first instance of the appointment of a deputy sergeant
occurred at this session. James Rogers, Sergeant General,
was allowed to appoint a deputy to serve writs and executions, he being responsible for the acts of such deputy.

The zeal of Puritan persecution was inflamed by the
rancor of the magistrates and clergy. Among those who
had already suffered imprisonment for their adhesion to
the novel and "cursed heresy," was Mary, wife of William
Dyre, the first secretary of Aquedneck. Returning from
England, whither she had probably accompanied her husband when he went over with Williams and Clarke, but
had remained behind and there had embraced the new
tenets, with no knowledge of what had been done in Massachusetts, she was arrested and thrown into prison. With
difficulty she was released by her husband giving bonds
to take her immediately away, and not to suffer her to
speak to any one on the journey homeward. Afterwards
in company with other friends, Hope Clifton, and Mary, Oct.
daughter of Catherine Scot, whose sister Patience, a girl of 8.
only eleven years, was then in prison for the same offence,
she ventured again into Massachusetts to visit some friends
confined in Boston as Quakers. Her two companions were
only imprisoned, but Mary Dyre, having been before banished under pain of death, was tried, together with William Robinson and Marmaduke Stevenson, and condemned
to death. The sentence was executed upon the two men. 19.
Mary was reprieved while on the gallows, after her two 27.
fellow-sufferers had been swung off.[1] With singular infatuation she returned in the following spring, for the third 1 6 6 0.
time, while the General Court was in session, was arrested May
30.

[1] New England Judged, 38, 97, 109.

1 6 6 0.
June
1.
May
22.

and hung.[1] There were other instances of this revolting cruelty practised upon persons not resident in Rhode Island, and which continued till Charles II. peremptorily forbade any further murders to be perpetrated, in the name of God, by these infuriated zealots.

The next general election was held at Portsmouth. William Brenton was chosen President, William Field of Providence, William Baulston of Portsmouth, Benedict Arnold, late President, of Newport, and John Greene of Warwick, Assistants, John Sanford, Recorder and Treasurer, James Rogers, Sergeant, John Easton, Attorney General, and Richard Bulgar, Solicitor General. An important modification of the statute regulating the mode of annulling laws was made. In place of ten days, three months was allowed for the towns to return their votes upon any new law, after its presentation, and instead of a majority of freemen in each town being necessary to annul a law, a majority of those in the Colony was now sufficient, even although any one town made no returns against it. This was a great step towards consolidation, and tended to strengthen the Colonial Government.

29.

A great change was in progress at this time in English affairs. Charles II. landed in England, and amid the joyful shouts of his subjects, entered London in triumph. The restoration was complete, not only in form but in substance. The great mass of the people received their monarch with delight, for they desired relief from the turmoil of civil strife. The religious parties united in the ovations that welcomed his return, and each vied with the other in demonstrations of loyalty. The Episcopalians hated Cromwell because he had crushed them, the Puritans disliked him for curbing their persecuting zeal, while the Roman Catholics hailed the return of the Stuarts as being a family of their own faith.

Oct.
18.

The news of the restoration of Charles II. occasioned a special meeting of the Assembly at Warwick. His

[1] M. C. R. iv. Part i. 419.

Majesty's letter to Parliament, his declaration and pro-clamation were read and entered upon the records. The King was formally proclaimed at eight o'clock the next morning, in presence of the Assembly, with military honors, and the following Wednesday was appointed for his public proclamation throughout the colony, and was made a general holiday. All legal process was to issue in His Majesty's name. A commission was sent to John Clarke confirming his position as agent for the colony, and desiring him to obtain a confirmation of the charter from the crown.

A committee was also appointed to treat with Ather-ton and his company about their purchase in Narraganset, and to arrange the terms upon which they might come into the colony, or if they refused to treat, then to forbid them from entering on their lands. They reported but partial progress at the next session, and were continued.

Meanwhile a great wrong was committed upon the Narraganset Indians by the commissioners of the United Colonies, who, for alleged injuries inflicted upon the Mohegans, which were denied by the Narraganset Sa-chems, levied a heavy fine upon them, and compelled them, by an armed force, to mortgage their whole country for the payment of a sum, amounting to five hundred and ninety-five fathoms of peage within four months. In a month from this time the Sachems mortgaged to the Atherton company all the unsold lands in Narraganset, on condition that they would pay the fine to the United Colonies, and further bound themselves to sell no more lands without consent of the mortgagees. Six months was allowed for redemption. Atherton paid the fine; the land was not redeemed, and afterwards, in the spring of 1662, the Sachems delivered formal possession to the mortgagees. Upon so slight a transaction, founded in force, and followed up in that spirit of acquisition which aimed at the possession of the whole of Rhode Island,

CHAP.
VIII.

1 6 6 0.
Oct.
21.

May
21.

Sept.
29

Oct.
30.

CHAP.
VIII.

1 6 6 1.
May
21.

22.

Aug.
27.

June
4.

rested the claims of a company that was destined to give so much trouble to the colony.

The same President, Assistants, Attorney-General and Sergeant were re-elected at Newport. Joseph Torrey was chosen Recorder, Caleb Carr, Treasurer, and Peter Tallman, Solicitor-General. The assembly passed a lengthy act acknowledging their submission to the King, proposing to send a special agent to England to present it in a humble address to His Majesty, and voting a tax of two hundred pounds for that purpose. The plan was given up on receipt of letters from John Clarke, which were read at the next meeting of the court of commissioners at Portsmouth. A letter of thanks to Mr. Clarke was voted, and the commission, prepared in October, was ordered to be sent to him. The tax was apportioned, eighty-five pounds to Newport, forty pounds each to Providence and Portsmouth, and thirty-five pounds to Warwick. It was to be raised by voluntary contribution for the use of the agent.

An extensive purchase, made the previous year, by some Newport men, in the south-west part of the Narraganset country, called Misquamicock, now Westerly, began to be settled, and gave rise to further difficulties of propriety and jurisdiction.[1] At this session the purchasers petitioned for the approval and assistance of the colony in making a settlement there, which was granted. The commissioners of the United Colonies took up the dispute in behalf of Massachusetts, and wrote to Rhode Island re-

[1] This tract was given to Socho, a brave captain of the Narragansets, by Canonicus and Miantinomî, for services rendered about 1635, in driving off a party of Pequots who had settled there prior to the war between the Pequots and English in 1637. It was deeded by Socho, Jan. 29th, 1660, to William Vaughan, Robert Stanton, John Fairfield, Hugh Mosher, James Longbottom and others of Newport, and the original deed to Socho was confirmed by Pessicus, 24th June, 1661, at which time Ninigret claimed the tract, but his nephew Pessicus denied his right thereto. The documents relating to this subject and the records of the Westerly proprietors are given by Mr. Potter in Early Hist. of Nar't. R. I. H. C., iii. 241-75.

specting this and the Pettiquamscot purchase, protesting against the conduct of Rhode Island in permitting them to be made. Massachusetts, by whom the Pequot country was claimed by right of conquest, had erected the tract on each side of the Pawcatuck river into a township called Southertown, and attached it to the county of Suffolk. Complaints from this town were now made to the General Court, of the intrusion of some thirty-six settlers from Rhode Island into that part of the town east of Pawcatuck river, being the Westerly purchase, claiming it as their own. Upon this a warrant was issued by the council of Massachusetts to the constable of Southertown to arrest the trespassers. Tobias Saunders, Robert Burdett, and Joseph Clarke were seized. Clarke was released, and the others were taken to Boston as prisoners, and committed for want of bail. The magistrates sent a letter to Rhode Island, inquiring if the conduct of these trespassers was sanctioned by that government, and saying if it were so, Massachusetts would prepare to defend her people in their just rights. Receiving no reply, another letter was soon after sent, by special messengers, asserting her claim to all Rhode Island, "from Pequot river to Plymouth line," under the Narraganset patent,[1] and avowing her determination to make it good. At the next session of the General Court the two prisoners were brought to trial. They were sentenced to pay a fine of forty pounds, and to be imprisoned till it was paid, and also to give sureties for one hundred pounds to keep the peace.[2] A third letter was then written, informing Rhode Island of the trial of these men, and requiring her to cause the settlers at Pettiquamscot and Southertown to vacate their lands before the end of June, or they should be treated as Saunders and Burdett had been. But Rhode Island was not to be intimidated by the threats of her powerful neigh-

CHAP. VIII.

1661. Sept. 13.

Oct. 25.

Nov. 14.

Dec. 3.

1662. March 8.

May 7.

10.

---

[1] Obtained Dec. 10th, 1643, ante ch. iv.
[2] M. C. R. iv. Part 2d, p. 44.

CHAP.
VIII.
1 6 6 2.
May.

20.

22.

bor, whose efforts against her peace and existence had so
often been thwarted by her firmness, sanctioned by the
subsequent approval of her conduct by the Supreme Government in England. Relying, as she ever had done, on
the justice of her cause, and looking to her right of appeal
to the King and Parliament, through the medium of her
able and faithful agent, John Clarke, she maintained her
position. The Court of Commissioners, met at Warwick,
sent to Daniel Gookin and others, subjects of Massachusetts, who had intruded at Westerly, prohibiting them
from planting or building there until the order of the
King on that matter could be known.[1] A letter in reply
to Massachusetts was prepared, defending the conduct of
Saunders and Burdett, and denying that the Pequot region ever extended east of Pawcatuck river, or that Massachusetts had any claim to the Narraganset country. The
terms of the letter were as courteous as the subject would
permit. Two messengers were appointed to carry it to
Boston.[2]

At this general election Benedict Arnold was chosen
President, over William Brenton ; Richard Tew, Assistant for Newport, John Sandford, Treasurer, and Richard
Bulgar, Solicitor. The other officers continued as before, but the Attorney General declining to serve, John
Sandford was chosen to that place in June. These officers were re-elected the following year, and served until
the adoption of the Royal Charter.

Wampum-peage up to this time had been the principal circulating medium in Rhode Island. The other colo-

[1] This prohibition does not appear on the records of the May session,
which began on the 22d, while this document is dated the 20th. There was
perhaps a special meeting of the Court prior to the general election two days
later. It is found in the files of the General Court of Massachusetts, and is
printed in R. I. Col. Rec., i. 463, with the three letters from Massachusetts
above referred to, and other papers on the same subject.

[2] These were John Green and John Sandford. The letter is in R. I. Col.
Rec., i. 469-73.

nies had long since abandoned it. It had now fallen so
much in value that it was declared to be no longer legal
tender, and all taxes and costs of court were required to be
paid "in current pay," that is, in Sterling or in New England coin.[1] The confusion of land titles had become so
great, that a law was passed vesting the fee in whoever,
having possession, should record his claim within thirteen
months, if on the spot ; and this record, if undisputed
within that time, should perfect the title even against the
real owner. To those living in other colonies one year
more was given, and to those living beyond the sea two
years longer were allowed to establish their right. The
President or any Assistant was empowered to appoint constables at any of the new settlements in Narraganset to
keep the peace. This act evinced the fixed determination
of Rhode Island to maintain her rights in the disputed
territory. The Court adjourned till the next month, to
await the return of the messengers sent to Massachusetts.
They did not reach Boston till the General Court had adjourned. To prevent the mischief that might result from
the contents of their letter not being generally known,
leave was granted for any person to send copies of it, and
of the prohibition, to their friends in Massachusetts.
Liberty to buy land of the Indians was also given to several parties. These purchases soon became too frequent
to be specially noticed.

Letters were constantly passing between the colony
and its agent. Measures of vital importance to the welfare of Rhode Island were in progress. The position she
occupied was anomalous, and required great tact and
ability to sustain. The charter, by which she existed,
was obtained from an authority inimical to the king,

---

[1] Massachusetts had begun to coin silver in 1652. Shillings and six-
pences, all of which bear the same date, although the coinage was continued
throughout several years, are still extant. Thirty shillings of New England
silver was equal to twenty-two shillings sixpence sterling.

and which had afterwards.dethroned and beheaded his royal father. The principles she avowed were totally unrecognized among men. No form of civil government then existing could tolerate her democracy, and even Christian charity denied her faith. To obtain a renewal of privileges so remarkable, to secure the regard of a sovereign whose arbitrary will was an inheritance, to obtain his sanction to a system which, initiated as an experiment by a republican parliament, had come to be no longer a philosophical problem but an established fact, and which, if extended, must inevitably in time overthrow the fabric of monarchical power—these were the difficult and perhaps dangerous duties that now devolved on the agent of Rhode Island. Well did he conduct his delicate mission, and triumphant was the success that crowned his labors. Two petitions or addresses were presented to Charles II. by John Clarke, in behalf of the people of Rhode Island, wherein he recites briefly the origin of the colony, and states clearly the grounds of their first and second removal for the cause of religious liberty, asserting that they "have it much on their hearts, if they may be permitted, to hold forth a lively experiment, that a flourishing civil state may stand, yea, and best be maintained, and that among English spirits, with a full liberty in religious concernments," and finally surrendering their lands and charter to the crown, and craving "a more absolute, ample, and free charter of civil incorporation." [1]

While the existence of the colony hung on the yet doubtful success of its agent at the English court, affairs at home were scarcely more propitious to its safety or independence. The subjects of Massachusetts in Narraganset

[1] The precise date of these two addresses is unknown. They were found among the archives in the British State Paper Office in London, and belong no doubt to the year 1662. Copies were made for the splendid library of Mr. John Carter Brown, which contains probably the richest collection of MSS. and of rare and valuable works on American history to be found. These two papers are printed in Mr. Secretary Bartlett's R. I. Col. Rec., i. 485–91.

complained to the commissioners of the United Colonies of the conduct of Rhode Island, in maintaining her chartered rights over that country. The appointment of constables by the last General Assembly had filled the cup of New England indignation. The commissioners now wrote to Rhode Island, claiming Narraganset for Connecticut, under the new charter to that colony which had just been received, as the previous year they had claimed it for Massachusetts under the old Narraganset patent. The letter concludes with the usual threat in case of non-compliance with their demands.[1] Connecticut, upon the proclamation of her charter, [2] ordered the inhabitants of Mystic and Pawcatuck not to exercise authority under commissions from any other colony.[3] This order was aimed equally at Rhode Island and Massachusetts, and was justified by the terms of the new charter, which embraced the whole Narraganset country. At the meeting of the Court of Commissioners in Warwick, another letter was ordered to be sent to Massachusetts about the lands of Pawcatuck, in reply to the one from the United Colonies. This letter was more severe than was usual in the official communications of Rhode Island, justly charging the Massachusetts with habitual injury to Rhode Island by wrongful accusations and unchristian acts, and asserting that the Connecticut charter, so far as it conveyed jurisdiction over the Narraganset country, was procured by " underhand dealing," and that it would be revoked. The letter further demanded the release of Saunders and Burdett, who still remained in prison, and also claimed damages for the wrongs inflicted upon them. In conclusion, it offered equal justice in the courts of Rhode Island, to all parties aggrieved by any illegal acts of the Westerly settlers.[4]

CHAP.
VIII.

1662.

Oct.
9.

27.

[1] Hazard, ii. 462-9. R. I. Col. Rec., i. 499.
[2] Dated 23d April, 1662, and received in September.
[3] Conn't Col. Rec., i. 389.
[4] See R. I. Col. Rec., i. 493-5.

CHAP.
VIII.

1663.
May
9.

That the subject of education received early attention in Rhode Island we have already shown in the chapter on Aquedneck. An ample foundation for its support was also made in Providence, by the reservation of one hundred acres of upland and six acres of meadow for the maintenance of a school, which was voted in town meeting at this time.

22.

No changes were made in the general officers at the next election. The session, held in Providence, was very short.

June.

The continued imprisonment of the two Rhode Island men in Massachusetts exasperated the settlers at Westerly, and led to a system of reprisals, and to acts of violence, seriously disturbing the border towns. A house that had been built on the east side of Pawcatuck river by residents of Southertown, being within the asserted jurisdiction of Rhode Island, was torn down. William Marble, a deputy of the Marshal of Suffolk, bearing a letter to the Westerly men upon this subject, was arrested, sent to Newport, and confined in prison for eleven months. Soon after his release he petitioned the General Court of Massachusetts [1] for redress. The petition is on the files of the Court, but no action upon it is recorded.

April
7.

July
3.

10.

By the third article of an agreement made between Clarke and Winthrop, the Atherton Company were to choose whether they would be under the jurisdiction of Rhode Island or of Connecticut. This agreement was immediately sent over to America. The action of the company was prompt and decided. They preferred the government of Connecticut, and so declared in a formal meeting, every one subscribing a paper to that effect, which was sent to Hartford. The Governor and Council immediately accepted the jurisdiction, as being included in the limits of their charter, named the plantation Wickford, and appointed Richard Smith, sen., Edward Hutchinson,

[1] August 3d, 1664.

and Joshua Hewes, Selectmen, and Richard Smith, jun., Constable. Mr. Smith's trading-house was the place designated for the transaction of public business.

The hopes of Rhode Island received a further blow in a letter from the king to the United Colonies, commending to their care the interests of the Atherton purchasers against the vexatious proceedings of Providence colony.[1] How that letter was obtained will appear in the succeeding chapter. But steps had already been taken by Clarke which prevented the injury that the State would otherwise have sustained from these causes. The Assembly met at Portsmouth soon after the receipt of this letter, to expedite measures for the support of their agent.

Oct.
14-19.

The General Court of Massachusetts sent special agents to Rhode Island, to inform the government of their views of her acts against the peace of that colony in regard to Southertown, and to propose a reference of the matters in dispute, until which time further molestation should cease.[2] Soon afterwards warrants were issued to all the towns by the President, requiring the freemen to accompany their commissioners, with their arms, to solemnize the reception of the charter, as advised by the colony's agent. The President also wrote to Massachusetts, enclosing a letter from the king in behalf of Rhode Island, and received a reply that the council should be called at once to deliberate on the subject. They met at Boston, and proposed by letter to President Arnold that all subjects in dispute between the two colonies be referred to arbitrators, to meet at Plymouth at such time as Rhode Island might select, and naming Governor Prince and Josias Winslow as referees on the part of Massachusetts.

21.

Nov.
16.

18.

21.

24.

Once more, and for the last time under the parliamentary patent, the general Court of Commissioners convened at Newport on the appointed day, to receive at the hands

[1] Hazard ii. 498.   R. I. Col. Rec., i. 466.
[2] M. C. R., iv. Part 2d, p. 95.

of Captain George Baxter, lately arrived from England, the rich result of the labors of John Clarke—the Royal Charter of Charles II.

"At a very great meeting and assembly of the freemen of the colony of Providence Plantations, at Newport, in Rhode Island, in New England, November the 24th, 1663. The abovesayed Assembly being legally called and orderly mett for the sollome reception of his Majestyes gratious letters pattent unto them sent, and having in order thereto chosen the President, Benedict Arnold, Moderator of the Assembly," it was, "Voted : That the box in which the King's gratious letters were enclosed be opened, and the letters with the broad seale thereto affixed be taken forth and read by Captayne George Baxter in the audience and view of all the people ; which was accordingly done, and the sayd letters with his Majesty's Royall Stampe, and the broad seal, with much becoming gravity held up on hygh, and presented to the perfect view of the people, and then returned into the box and locked up by the Governor, in order to the safe keeping of it."

The humble thanks of the colony were voted to His Majesty and to the earl of Clarendon, and also a gratuity of one hundred pounds to John Clarke and one of twenty-five pounds to Captain Baxter. The next day the commissioners again assembled, and having passed such acts as were necessary to prevent the failure of justice, "dissolved and resigned up" to the government appointed by the charter.

On the following day the Governor and council named in the charter, held a meeting to receive again the submission of the sachems to the crown of England, and to order the government of the colony, by receiving anew the engagements of all the existing officers to hold their places until the session of the General Assembly, which was appointed for the first Tuesday of the ensuing March.

The government of the colony under the parliamentary

patent was ended. "The incorporation of Providence
Plantations," as a legal title, had ceased to exist. Henceforth the colony was to assume another name, and to be governed under a royal charter, not less free than that which
it supplanted, and better adapted to the exigencies of the
State. The patent of 1644 had accomplished the chief
end for which it was sought. It had gathered the scattered settlements of fugitives from persecution into one
corporate body, and compelled their recognition as a body
politic by their ambitious and vindictive neighbors. But
it was too feeble to answer the full purposes of a charter.
The very freedom of its provisions, which in later days
would give it strength, was in those primitive times a
source of weakness. It was more a patent for the towns
than for the people, legalizing, in effect, so many independent corporations, rather than constructing one sovereign
power resting upon the popular will. It produced a confederacy, and not a union. Its defects are seen in the fa-
cility with which Coddington, contrary to the wishes of the
people at Aquedneck, severed that island from the rest of
the colony, and usurped a power almost dictatorial. Under
its operation, in every town and hamlet were spread the
seeds of discontent and disunion, and nothing but the pres-
sure from without, and the supreme law of self-preserva-
tion, kept the discordant settlements from utter destruction,
and from being absorbed by the adjoining governments.
Its reception had been hailed with extravagant joy by a
despised and persecuted people. Its expiration was attended with no regret, for twenty years had wrought that
change in the feeble colony which the same period works
from infancy to manhood. As a basis of civil polity it had
" outlived its usefulness," and was suffered to depart without a murmur.

Thus closed the second epoch of Rhode Island history.
The first presents a view of scattered cabins reared in the
primeval wilderness, till they become a little village on the

river bank.   One after another these feeble hamlets struggle into life, remote from each other, amid virgin forests
and on the ocean shore.   The hardy settlers, twice exiled
for opinion's sake, have become the pioneers of principles
immortal as truth itself.   What, though wild beasts disturb their rest at night, and the Indian warwhoop rings
around their dwellings !   They have won the savage by
acts of kindness and of justice, and have less to fear from
his untamed but generous spirit than from the brethren
they have left.   Here, each village, by itself, they must
frame their own laws, and submit to their own enactments, till, by force of habit and of necessity, each vil-
lager becomes, unconsciously, a statesman.   The school
of practice precedes the school of theory, and thus four independent governments are formed, self-constituted, in the
wilderness.   But one common sentiment pervades the
whole.   The spirit of liberty animates every heart.   Soul
liberty and civil freedom is their aim, and with one accord
each separate village declares that " all men may walk as
their consciences persuade them, every one in the name of
his God."   Thus in obscurity these outcast men indeed
proclaimed " freedom to the world," and from their secluded settlements sent forth a law which was to redeem the
human soul from spiritual thraldom, and in time to free
a nation, perhaps all nations at some future day, from civil
tyranny, by teaching the doctrine of self-government.

But the villages have grown to be towns, " heresy and
treason " are rampant in the plantations, and Puritan zeal
for Church and State seeks to extirpate the source of so
dangerous an example.   Roused to a sense of impending
danger, and conscious of the vast significance of their
common principles, the towns obtain a patent which re-
cognizes their corporate existence, yet leaves them freely
to enjoy their cherished sentiments.   With this patent of
incorporation the second epoch of their history begins.
Through the last two chapters we have traced this second

period of doubt and change, of conflict and disunion, of CHAP. VIII. threatened anarchy within, and of aggression and insult from without. We have seen how, amid all the troubles 1663. that environed them, the townsmen kept steadily in view the fundamental principles of their organization, and triumphantly sustained their peculiar notions against the arguments and the menaces of the rest of New England; and how the material prosperity of the people kept pace with their fidelity to the truth, until the arrival of a new, "more absolute, ample, and free charter of civil incorporation," ushered in the third epoch of our history—the period of colonial maturity.

APPENDIX B.

PROCEEDINGS IN THE CASE OF JOHN WARNER.

FROM THE WARWICK RECORDS.

"The twentie-fourth of Aprill, 1652.   APP.
                                          B.
"At a town meeting or law making assembly ordered that

"John Warner for his misdemeanures under annexed is degraded by the unanimos consent of the town from bearing any office in the town, and that he is hereby disenabled for ever after bearing any office in the Town untill he gives the town satisfaction.

"It is further ordered that the abovesayed John Warner is put out from having any vote in the town concerning its affairs.

"The charges against John Warner are these, first

"Item—for calling the officers of the town rogues and theives with respect to their office.

"Item—for calling the whole town rogues and thieves.

"Item—for threatning the lives of men.

"Item—for threatning to kill all the mares in town.

"Item—for his contempt in not appearing before the town now met, being lawfully (assembled?) by a summons from the officer with two magistrats hands to it.

"Item—for threatning an officer of the colony in open Court that

if he had him elsewhere he would beate out his braynes, as also calling him rogue.

"Item—for his employing an agent to write to the Massachusetts,
thereby going about to inthrall the liberties of the town, contrary to
the privileges of the town, and to the great indignity of the Honorable
State of England who granted the sayd privaledges to us.

"It is ordered that another be immediately chose for Assistant to
supply John Warner's place while (until?) the next choice."

Mr. John Smith was chosen Assistant in place of Warner. At
the annual town meeting on 7th June it was

"Ordered, that the answer read by Mr. S. Gorton in the town
meeting, to the motions of the Town of Providence with respect to
John Warner, be forthwith drawn forth and signed by the Clarke and
sent to the Town of Providence forthwith.

"Ordered, that the declaration that hath been drawn up in the
town concerning John Warner and the Dutchmen, which hath been
sent to the Bay, as also to Providence, that a copy of it be drawn forth
and signed by the Clarke and sent to Mr. Roger Williams, and ordered that Mr. Samuel Gorton is to write a letter to Mr. Roger Williams in the Town's behalf, to give him information concerning the
town and Colonies proceedings with John Warner and his wife."

The only notice taken of the case by the General Assembly was
on the 19th May, when the matter was left to the decision of the
Court of Trials in these words, "It is agreed that the case of Priscilla
Warner, now depending in the General Court of Trialls, shall there be
issued."

At a town meeting on the 22d June it was ordered,

"That the house and land of John Warner situate and being in
the sayd town be attached forthwith upon suspicion of unsufferable
treacherie against the town, to the forfeiture of the sayd house and
land, and that notice may be given him of the attachment thereof that
so hee by himself or aturney may answer at the next court of Trials
to be held in Warwick the 3d Tuesday in August next ensuing the
date hereof. It is also ordered that all persons are hereby prohibited
from laying any claim or title unto it, or any part thereof by bargain
and sale or otherwise untill he hath answered the law and be cleered
by order of the Court held as aforesayd, but remains in the hand and
custody of the town in the mean time.

"Ordered, that the Sergeant shall have a copie of this order and
set it up upon the door of the house.

"Ordered, that if hereafter John Warner or any for him shall sell
that house and land abovesayd, any part or parcel of it, to any but
such as shall subscribe to our order it shall as before be wholly forfeit
to the town."

On the 5th of July the property was released, under protest, as follows:—

"Ordered by the town of Warwick that the house and land of John Warner, situated in the sayd Town of Warwick, being of late atached upon suspicion of the breach of the grand law of the Town, be resigned up to the said John Warner again.

"We whose names are here underwritten being unsatisfied with the above voate upon the resigning of the abovesayed house of John Warner which was atached upon suspicion of the breach of the grand law of the Town, do hereby enter our protest against the act, as witness our hands.

Randal Houlden,   John Wickes,

John Greene, Jun.,   Samuel Gorton,

Robert Potter."

Thirty-one years later, June 26th, 1683, he was divorced from his wife upon her petition, on the ground of infidelity, and of personal violence towards her, and at the same session was expelled from the General Assembly as he had before been from town offices, in terms as follows:—

"Voted: Whereas, Mr. John Warner was by the town of Warwick chosen to be a Deputy in this Assembly, and being from time to time called, and not in Courte appearing, and there haveing been presented to this Assembly such complaints against him, that the Assembly doe judge, and are well satisfied, he is an unfitt person to serve as a Deputy; and therefore see cause to expel him from acting in this present Assembly as a Deputy."

CHAPTER IX.

1663—1675.

FROM THE ADOPTION OF THE ROYAL CHARTER, NOVEMBER, 1663, TO THE COMMENCEMENT OF KING PHILIP'S WAR, JUNE, 1675.

CHAP.
IX.

THE restoration of the Stuarts, annulling the acts of the Long Parliament, compelled Rhode Island to seek a renewal of her privileges by another charter. It was at an auspicious moment, when Charles II. was yet but recently seated upon his throne, that the talent and energy of Dr. Clarke obtained this instrument. It confirmed every thing that the previous patent had given, and vested even greater powers in the people. Under it the State was an absolute sovereignty with powers to make its own laws, religious freedom was guaranteed, and no oath of allegiance was required. Rhode Island became in fact, and almost in name, an independent State from that day.

There are three points in this charter deserving of special attention, which distinguish it from all other royal patents that have ever been granted. To mention these in the order in which they occur, the first is the acknowledgment of the Indian titles to the soil. Among the reasons assigned for granting the charter is this, that the petitioners "are seized and possessed by purchase and consent of the said natives to their full content, of such lands, islands," &c., and farther on, in the enumeration

of powers granted, the inhabitants are permitted "to direct, rule, order and dispose of all other matters and
things, and particularly that which relates to the making
of purchases of the native Indians." These paragraphs
would appear unimportant, if they did not concede a principle for which the founders of Rhode Island had contended from the beginning, and which was not incorporated in any other charter. Possession by right of discovery was a European doctrine coeval with the days of
Columbus and de Gama. First exercised by the Supreme Pontiff, who claimed the exclusive right, as God's
Vicegerent, to the temporal control of all newly-discov-
ered countries, it was soon adopted by the maritime powers as a part of the royal prerogative. Overlooking that
principle of justice which establishes propriety in the
original possessor, the sovereigns of Europe did not hesitate to assert their claim over both Americas. The rights
of the aborigines, heathens and barbarians as they were,
presented no obstacles to these enlightened and Christian
legislators. Their heathenism was handed over to the
tender mercies of the church, their barbarism to the civ-
ilizing agency of gunpowder and steel. Although the
method of administration was more summary in the Span-
ish and Portuguese possessions, the principle, in its broad-
est extent, was recognized by the British crown, though
rarely acted upon by the English colonists. Against the
abstract right, as well as the positive abuse of these pretensions, the settlement of Rhode Island was the first
solemn protest. Mercy and justice combined to raise the
voice of indignant rebuke against the wholesale assumption of territorial rights, urged by the Council of Plymouth under their patent from King James. For the
bold denunciation of those words of the patent in which
the King, as the "Sovereign Lord" of this continent,
grants by his "special grace, mere motion and certain
knowledge," a large portion of America, reaching from

CHAP.
IX.

the Atlantic to the Pacific, to the Council of Plymouth, Roger Williams was twice subjected to the censure of the authorities of Massachusetts. This principle was the only one, save that of "soul liberty," which Roger Williams initiated in Massachusetts, of the many factious proceedings that later writers, following Hubbard, have laid to his charge. Upon this point, the exclusive right of the aborigines to their native soil, Mr. Williams was decided, and his views were maintained by those who followed him to Rhode Island. They were set forth by Dr. Clarke in his addresses to the King, and thus became embodied in the Royal charter. The operation of the thing was the reverse in this State from what it was elsewhere. The other colonies claimed the soil by virtue of grants from the King, and confirmed their titles by purchase from the Indians, or by conquest. Here the paramount title was held to be in the aborigines, and the right, first obtained from them by purchase, was only confirmed by patent from the crown.

The second remarkable point in this charter is the ample protection which it extends to the rights of conscience. So full and absolute is this guarantee, and so different from the prevailing spirit of the age, that the principle it embodies has come to be considered, not only as the peculiar honor of Rhode Island, but as being the sole distinguishing feature of her history. It declares "that noe person within the sayd colonye, at any tyme hereafter, shall bee any wise molested, punished, disquieted, or called in question, for any difference in opinione in matters of religion which doe not actually disturb the civill peace of our sayd colonye ; but that all and everye person and persons may, from tyme to tyme, and at all tymes hereafter, freelye and fullye have and enjoye his and theire owne judgments and consciences, in matters of religious concernments, throughout the tract of lande hereafter mentioned ; they behaving themselves peaceablie and quietlie, and not using this libertie to lycentiousnesse and profanenesse, nor to the civil injurye or outward disturbance of others." It should be remembered that the laws of England rigidly required uniformity in religious belief. Church and State were essential portions of each other. This grant therefore repealed the laws of England, so far as Rhode Island was concerned, by excepting her from their operation, and left the people of this colony precisely where the parliamentary patent, by its significant silence on this subject, had left them. It was a signal triumph for what is now recognized as the fundamental principle in ethics, in religion, and in politics.[1]

The remaining point to be noticed as distinguishing this charter from all others that have emanated from the throne of a monarch, is its purely republican character. When the colony was organized under the previous patent, the Assembly declared " that the form of government established in Providence Plantations is Democratical, that is to say, a government held by the free and voluntary consent of all, or the greater part of the free inhabitants." This was a novel doctrine, at least in the history of the modern world, and although it was sanctioned by the charter of a republican parliament, it could hardly be expected to pass the seals of a Royal Council. Yet it did so pass, and in almost the same terms in which it had before been secured. After conferring power to elect their own officers and to make their own laws, " as to them shall seem meet for the good and welfare of the said Company," it requires only that such laws " bee not contrarie and repugnant unto, but as near as may bee, agreeable to

---

[1] It is worthy of notice that Charles II., in his famous letter to the Commons, known as the " Declaration," from Breda, April 4-14, 1660, promises religious freedom to his subjects, in the event of his restoration, in precisely the language used in the charter of Rhode Island, " that no man shall be *disquieted or called in question for differences of opinion in matters of religion which do not disturb the peace of the kingdom.*" Echard's Hist. of England, ii. 897 ; Rapin book, 22d vol. xi. p. 180, where the declaration is cited in full.

the laws of this our Realme of England," and adds the same qualifying and practically annulling words, " considering the nature and constitution of the place and people there." The extent of the powers conferred by this charter is indeed surprising. The military arm, always relied upon as the distinctive barrier of the throne, is formally and fully surrendered to the people, in this instrument, even to the extreme point of declaring martial law —a grant which, in repeated cases, the government of Rhode Island successfully defended, in later years, against the threats and the arguments of the royal governors of New England.

Thus it was that Rhode Island continued, as she had begun, an independent State, through all the vicissitudes of the Mother country, and was unaffected, save at one brief interval, by the changes that swept over the neighboring colonies. With this charter, serving as the basis of government rather than prescribing its form, the State led the way in the final struggle for national independence.

Under it Rhode Island, as being no less truly than professedly republican, adopted the Constitution of the United States and was received into the American Union. So far as this charter was concerned, a single provision, fixing the apportionment of representatives for the several towns, which time had rendered unjust in its operation, and which, it was contended, could not be remedied otherwise than by an alteration of the organic law, led to its abrogation in 1843, at which time this venerable instrument was the oldest constitutional charter in the world. For one hundred and eighty years it had been regarded as the shield of popular freedom against Royal prerogative or Federal encroachment. It was the last remaining beacon planted by the Republicans of the seventeenth century, and so firmly that the war of the Revolution had not changed its position, for they both rested upon the same CHAP. IX. foundation—the inherent right of self-government.

The Government was vested in a Governor, Deputy Governor, and ten Assistants, named in the charter, with a House of Deputies, six from Newport, four each from Providence, Portsmouth and Warwick, and two from every other town. The former were to be chosen annually at Newport on the first Wednesday of May, the latter by their respective towns. The whole legislative body was called the General Assembly, and was to meet twice a year, in May and October, but they could alter the time and place of meeting at will. Benedict Arnold was appointed the first Governor, and William Brenton, Deputy Governor.[1]

In view no doubt of the acts of non-intercourse existing against Rhode Island in the neighboring colonies, the charter specially required that the people of this colony should be permitted to pass unmolested through the adjacent provinces, and an appeal to the King was guaranteed in case of further disputes. In all cases the charter was to be construed most favorably for the benefit of the grantees. The boundary lines were minutely defined. They are those which, after more than a century of contest with the adjoining colonies, were finally established in accordance with the charter, and exist at this day.

The western boundary was the source of immediate and violent dispute, prolonging instead of quieting the difficulties already commenced. The charter of Connecticut bore date fifteen months anterior to that of Rhode Island, and bounded that colony on Narraganset Bay. The people of Rhode Island, upon the first notice of this legalized robbery of so large a portion of their territory, charged those of Connecticut with underhand dealing in the

[1] The Assistants were William Balston, John Porter, Roger Williams, Thomas Olney, John Smith, John Greene, John Coggeshall, James Barker, William Ffeild, and Joseph Clarke.

means employed to obtain that result, and maintained
that upon a proper representation of the facts the obnoxious portions would be revoked—and so indeed it proved.
The Rhode Island charter, referring in terms to that of
Connecticut, and expressly limiting the territory therein
conveyed in accordance with the claims of Rhode Island,
designated the Pawcatuck river as her western boundary,
" any graunt, or clause in a late graunt, to the Governor
and Company of Connecticut Colony, in America, to the
contrary thereof in any wise notwithstanding; the aforesayd Pawcatuck river haveing byn yeilded, after much debate, for the fixed and certain boundes between these our
sayd Colonies, by the agents thereof; who have alsoe
agreed, that the sayd Pawcatuck river shall bee alsoe called alias Narraganset river; and, to prevent other disputes,
that otherwise might arise thereby, forever hereafter shall
be construed, deemed and taken to bee the Narraganset
river in our late graunt to Connecticut Colony mentioned
as the easterly bounds of that Collony." Nothing could
be more explicit than this recital, yet it did not suffice to
settle the difficulty. The agreement made by the two
agents, Gov. Winthrop and Dr. Clarke on the part of their
respective colonies, was disowned by Connecticut, on the
ground that their agent had no longer any authority to act
for the colony, his commission having expired, as they
said, upon the completion of his labors in obtaining the
charter.[1] Even if this were so, we do not see how that objection could set aside a Royal grant. It could only affect
the force of a statement in the charter which is simply
explanatory and altogether secondary to the main question
at issue. Of the fact of the agreement there is no denial.
Of its binding effect upon the two colonies there might be
a question if the plenary powers of the Connecticut agent
had ceased, as was asserted, when his charter passed the

[1] See Report of the Royal Commissioners, October, 1683, in 1 M. H. C., v.
238.

seals. But the validity of the grant itself is untouched by the error or the accuracy of one of the reasons therein assigned for making it.

This agreement was the result of arbitration. The points of difference being submitted to five referees were decided by them in four articles. The first fixed Pawcatuck river as the boundary and named it Narraganset. The second gave the Quinnebaug tract to Connecticut. The third allowed the inhabitants around Smith's trading house, being the Atherton company, to choose to which of the two colonies they would submit ; and the fourth declared that the rights of property should be maintained through the colonies. To these four proposals the two agents assented, as a final issue of their differences. The second and fourth are unimportant, the other two include the whole real matter in dispute.[1] We cannot understand how any such agreement could of itself bind either colony. If Winthrop exceeded his powers, as charged by Connecticut, in giving up territory, Clarke equally exceeded his in yielding jurisdiction over a purchase made in violation of the laws of Rhode Island ; for the desire of the Atherton men to submit to Connecticut was well known, and the giving them this choice was nothing less than abandoning all control over their lands. It was in fact admitting a foreign colony into the heart of the State ; an evil from which Rhode Island had already suffered too much in the case of Pawtuxet. But Rhode Island did not set up the plea that her agent had exceeded his powers. She stood on the terms of her charter in the question of boundary, and in that of jurisdiction she adopted conciliatory measures towards the people of Narraganset.

We have already seen abundant reasons why the New England league should sympathize with Connecticut in

[1] The agreement is printed in 1 M. H. C., v. 248, where it is dated 17th April, and in R. I. Col. Rec., i. 518, with the correct date, 7th April, following the copy preserved in the British State Paper Office. New England papers, vol. 3, p. 90.

this new occasion of dispute. The fact that their writers have steadily endeavored to defend the claim of Connecticut against the rights of Rhode Island, confirmed by the King, and to uphold the conduct of Winthrop at the expense of Dr. Clarke, while Rhode Island has to this day silently submitted to the imputations cast upon her agent, conscious of his rectitude, yet careless to preserve his name unsullied, has wrought great injustice to one whose character and whose talents appear more exalted the more closely they are examined. That foreign historians, seeking to give an impartial account of this transaction, should have been misled by the only authorities within their reach, and thus unwittingly have attached an unmerited stigma to the name of John Clarke, is natural and perhaps inevitable.[1] But that New England authors should attempt to honor Winthrop by disgracing Clarke does wrong to both, and is alike ungenerous and unjust. Between these two great men there appears to have existed a cordial friendship, which was not broken even by the delicate position into which they were thrown by the singular conduct of Connecticut colony. It is true that Winthrop in his letters complained that Clarke had not obtained his charter sooner, and that he had done him wrong in opposing the Connecticut charter after its confirmation, thereby hindering his return ; and in the same letter he sends a kind message to his Rhode Island friends, declaring that he had no intent to injure them, but only " to render a service to their old charter," as well as to the people of Narraganset.[2] The geography of New England was but little understood, in the minutiæ of courses and distances, even by its inhabitants, at that time, and the reply to that letter, written by the people of Narraganset, as the Atherton settlers were

[1] For a refutation of the charges brought by Grahame and endorsed by Quincy against Clarke, and for an examination into the reliability of Chalmers, see Appendix C.

[2] This letter is No. 47 of the 22d vol. of the Trumbull MSS. in the archives of the Mass. Hist. Soc. See Appendix D., No. II.

now called, shows a singular misconception on this point
either in their minds or in that of Winthrop. It would
seem as if Winthrop had first, in obedience to instructions
from Connecticut, bounded that colony on Narraganset
bay ; that, upon being convinced by Clarke of the injustice
thereby done to Rhode Island, he agreed to the adjustment
mentioned in the Rhode Island charter, and that thus,
while trying to discharge his duty as the agent of one and
the friend of the other, he deeply offended both, through
want of exact knowledge of the position and limits of the
disputed territory.[1] To retort upon Winthrop the charges
that his defenders have made against Clarke, would be to
pervert the truth of history, as has been steadily done by
those who, anxious to shield their own infamy, or ignorant
of the secret history of this transaction, have sought to cast
upon Clarke the stigma of "underhand dealing" that attaches to themselves, or have blindly copied the falsehoods
of his enemies. Where this disgrace properly belongs, and
how, and why it was shifted upon the shoulders of Clarke,
will now be shown. The Atherton company who, it will
be remembered, had bought lands in Narraganset contrary
to the law of Rhode Island, and who had constantly refused every overture made by the Assembly for their legal
and proper settlement in the State, being composed of residents of the other colonies, and of whom Winthrop himself was one, were earnest in their desire to be placed
under the jurisdiction of Connecticut. They maintained
a constant correspondence with Winthrop during his
mission at London ; the burden of which was that he
should so establish the boundary of Connecticut as to
accomplish their purpose. They also had a special agent
of their own in London, one John Scot, whose incautious
pen has furnished the evidence of his own infamy, and of
that of his employers, while it pays a tacit tribute to the

[1] The reasons that lead to this conclusion would be tedious to embody in
the text, and will best appear by perusing the letters inserted in Appendix D.

CHAP.
IX.

1663.
June
21.

July
8.

April
29.

purity of Winthrop. It was he who obtained the famous letter from the King to the United Colonies, committing to them the protection of the Atherton Company against the claims of Rhode Island,[1] after Winthrop had embarked for America, and only seventeen days before the final passage of the Rhode Island charter which effectually repeals the powers conferred in that letter. It seemed unaccountable that so soon after an agreement had been made by which the controversy was supposed to be settled, and one of the agents had embarked for home, a royal letter should appear, virtually repealing the substance of the agreement, and that in less than three weeks from the date of the letter a royal act of the most solemn nature, an absolute charter, should issue, making special mention of the said agreement, and practically annulling the royal letter. There was a confusion of dates, a confounding of powers, and a manifest contradiction of purposes about all this, which indicated underhand dealing somewhere. Winthrop had left England almost immediately after signing the agreement. He, then, was clear of suspicion. Clarke remained. That circumstance aided the plan of the conspirators to divert suspicion from themselves to him. The letter of June was triumphantly exhibited as proof of the real intentions of the King, and the fact that its tenor was contradicted by the charter of July was held up as proof of baseness on the part of the agent of Rhode Island.

We can now show which was the true document, and which was obtained by fraud. An obscure manuscript heretofore unnoticed, perhaps from the insignificance of its author, fastens upon himself the charge of underhand dealing, describes the manner in which his object was effected, and names the bribe that he gave to obtain it. John Scot, the special agent of the Atherton company, wrote the letter, now for the first time printed,[2] which after the lapse

---

[1] Ante, chap. 8, p. 283. The letter is dated June 21, 1663.

[2] See Appendix E for this remarkable letter, with more copious comments thereupon than are given in the text.

of two hundred years, exposes the baseness of the enemies CHAP.
of Clarke, shows for itself why they so freely charged IX.
him with dishonesty, and subjects its author and his abet- 1663-4.
tors to the double shame of corruption to obtain their ends,
and of meanness in seeking to hide their conduct by de-
faming the character of an honest man. To the honor of
Winthrop it should be mentioned here that seven years
later, while Governor of Connecticut, he refused to exercise
jurisdiction east of Pawcatuck river, alleging as a reason
his agreement with Clarke, which although ignored by
Connecticut, he at least deemed to be both legally and
morally binding upon that colony. The questions of
boundary and of jurisdiction were virtually one, and are so
treated in Governor Winthrop's message to the General
Assembly at Hartford.

A great amount of business, as varied in kind as it was March
complicated in its nature, devolved upon the new Legisla- 1.
ture. The Assistants were now, for the first time, invested
with legislative power by the charter, and acted conjointly
with the deputies. The Courts required to be remodelled
in accordance with the charter. Many laws were to be repealed as being " inconsistent with the present government," and others enacted in conformity thereto. Difficulties of a most serious nature within and without the
colony demanded attention. The new territory of Block
Island was embraced in the charter, and must be provided
for. Magistrates were to be apportioned among the towns,
and the usual amount of private business was to be transacted.

Notice being given to all the people to draw near, the
charter was read, together with Mr. Clarke's letter accompanying it, and Mr. Roger Williams was requested to
transcribe it. A committee was appointed to draw up a
prologue to the proceedings of the Court, which prefaces
the records, and contains a formal acknowledgment of gratitude to the king for his favor. The Assembly then en-

tered upon the business of legislation by prescribing the mode of calling courts, and the times and manner of holding them.   Two General Courts of trials in each year were established, to be held at Newport in May and October, and were to consist of the Governor, deputy Governor, or either of them, with at least six Assistants.   Two other Courts of trials were appointed to be held annually, one at Providence in September, and one at Warwick in March, at which at least three Assistants, and a jury of twelve men selected equally from each town, should be present. An appeal could be taken from these to the General Courts.   Special Courts might also be called, at the request and expense of any person, with the sanction of the Governor or deputy Governor.   In the apportionment of grand and petty jurors, Newport was to furnish five of each, Portsmouth three, Providence and Warwick two each ; but in that of State magistrates, the two Executives and ten Assistants, five were to be inhabitants of Newport, three of Providence, and two each, of Portsmouth and Warwick ; and the precedency of the towns was settled in this latter order, it being that in which they were named in the charter.   The Assistant " nearest the place occation shall present " was to act as Coroner.

A question arose whether by the charter it was provided that the State magistrates, or Council, should be elected by the freemen in town meeting, or by the General Assembly.   It was decided that, unless otherwise explained by advices from England, the right of electing these officers should vest in the freemen.

An act was passed taking cognizance of the intrusions and attempted usurpations of the Atherton company, and a summons was issued requiring them to appear at the next session of Assembly, to answer for their conduct ; and similar attempts to settle in the colony, without leave first obtained from the Assembly, were forbidden under pain of fine and imprisonment.   A committee was named to treat with Massachusetts upon the pending difficulties between the two colonies. Pumham, who, at the instigation of Massachusetts, had subjected himself and his lands to her jurisdiction, and retained possession of part of the tract purchased by the Warwick men, was notified, upon their complaint, that he was within the government of Rhode Island, and must adjust his differences with the complainants or submit to legal process. A remonstrance to Connecticut colony upon the riotous conduct of the men of Southertown, and a notice of intention shortly to run the westerly line of Rhode Island, were ordered to be sent.

A curious act is recorded at this session in favor of Capt. John Cranston, who, for skill in his profession, was licensed "to administer phisicke and practice chirurgery." We have before mentioned instances of physicians being licensed by the Legislature, but in this case the act went further, and we have now to record, for the first time, the formal conferring of the degree of M. D. upon Capt. Cranston in these words : "and is by this Court styled and recorded Doctor of phissick and chirrurgery, by the authority of this the General Assembly of this Collony."

Notice was sent to Block Island that the people should appear at the May Court to be received into the colony, and James Sands, already a freeman, was appointed Constable. This island, the earliest authentic history of which dates from the Pequot war, and has already been noticed in that connection, remained subject to Massachusetts until it was annexed to Rhode Island by the royal charter. It was granted, as a reward for public services, to Gov. Endicott and three others,[1] who sold it two years later for five hundred pounds to Simon Ray and eight associates. The following year they commenced a settlement, liquidated the Indian title, subject to a res-

---

[1] 19th Oct., 1658.   See M. C. R., iv.   Part I., p. 356.

ervation in favor of the natives, and set apart one-six-teenth of the lands for the support of a minister forever. Soon afterwards James Sands, who had followed Ann Hutchinson in her exile to the banks of the Hudson, returned and settled on the island. About two years had elapsed since the settlement was commenced, when the jurisdiction was transferred to Rhode Island. The remoteness of the island rendered it almost independent of the colony, and produced a different system of internal regulation from that which prevailed in the other towns. Its exposed situation rendered it peculiarly liable to suffer, not only from the native Indians, but also from the attacks of piratical vessels, by which it was constantly threatened. The local history of Block Island, truthfully written, would present an interesting study. The traditionary history of the aborigines is full of the romance of war ; their authentic history in connection with the whites, abounds in stirring incidents ; the peculiarities of the English settlers and their posterity, their customs, laws and domestic institutions, are among the most singular and interesting developments of civilized life ; while the martial deeds of a people, within and around whose island there has been more hard fighting than on any territory of equal extent, perhaps, in America, and where the horrors of savage and of civilized warfare have alternately prevailed, almost without cessation, from the earliest traditionary period down to a recent date, would, altogether, furnish materials for a thrilling history that might rival the pages of romance.

10.   A friendly letter was sent to Connecticut, in conformity to the vote of the Assembly, reciting a recent outrage at Westerly, asking that such acts be prevented in future, and requesting the concurrence of Connecticut in running the line between the two colonies at an early date.
The conflict of jurisdictions placed the Narraganset men in a difficult position. They wrote to Connecticut for

advice, saying that Richard Smith, jr., was under bonds
to answer to Rhode Island, and that a constable appointed
by Rhode Island might soon be expected at Wickford.[1]
The Council at Hartford erected a court at Wickford,
and conferred on the inhabitants power to choose their
officers, recommended them to obtain " an able orthodox
minister," and appointed Capt. Hutchinson to exercise
all males between the ages of sixteen and sixty in the
use of arms, six times a year. Wickford was now a fully
organized settlement, with control over " the places adjoining within the colony of Connecticut." Fortunately,
at this crisis, a measure was adopted in the King's Council, that prevented a fatal collision between the determined and excited disputants. A commission was issued
to Col. Richard Nichols, Sir Robert Carr, George Cartwright, and Samuel Maverick, to reduce the Dutch provinces in America to subjection, and to determine all
questions of appeal and of jurisdiction, and all boundary
disputes arising in the New England colonies.[2]

At the same time a new and formidable claimant appeared for the contested territory of Narraganset. The
Duke of Hamilton petitioned the King for confirmation of
his rights in all that country, and much more, against all
persons who had intruded upon the grant made to his
father, the late Marquis, by the council of Plymouth.[3] The
deed held by the Marquis of Hamilton was given by the
Plymouth company when on the point of surrendering
their charter, and was of little intrinsic value.[4] It however served, in the hands of a powerful nobleman, still
further to complicate this intricate question. It was a

[1] MS. records of Connecticut in R. I. Hist. Soc.

[2] S. P. O. New England papers, vol. i. p. 194, and Mr. Brown's MS. Collection, vol. i. 39.

[3] S. P. O. New England papers, vol. i. p. 200, and Mr. Brown's MS. Collection, vol. i. 40.

[4] Ante, chap. i. p. 8. The deed was dated April 22d, 1635, less than
seven weeks before the surrender.

deed of feofment, and conveyed a tract extending from Connecticut river to Narraganset bay, "about sixty miles" up the west side of the bay to the head thereof, and thence north-west sixty miles, where the line turned in a south-west course to a point sixty miles up north-west from the mouth of Connecticut river, and including all islands within five leagues of these limits. The name given to this magnificent grant was "the county of Cambridge."[1]

The session in March had been held chiefly for organization and for the preparation of business. The first regular Assembly, as established by the charter, met at Newport in May. Benedict Arnold was chosen Governor, William Brenton, deputy Governor, Joseph Torrey, Recorder, James Rogers, Sergeant, John Coggeshall, Treasurer, John Easton, Attorney, and Laurence Turner, Solicitor. The latter officer declined to serve and was excused. Ten Assistants were also elected, and these seventeen, with eighteen deputies chosen by the towns, composed the General Assembly. As full lists of the seventeen general officers, chosen annually by the Assembly are given under each year in the printed Colonial Records, we shall hereafter, to avoid a tedious catalogue of names, mention only the two executive officers. For the same reasons we have not heretofore recorded the lists of commissioners, or deputies under the first patent. They were eighteen in number at this session, and increased two with the addition of every new town. The deputies were chosen for each session of the Assembly, always twice a year, and frequently oftener.

The name of "Rhode Island and Providence Plantations," with the word "Hope" above the anchor, was adopted, or rather continued, as the seal of the colony.

The affairs of Block Island were definitely settled at this session. Three messengers appeared[2] from the island

[1] S. P. O. New England, vol. i. 8, and Mr. Brown's MSS., vol. i. No. 10; also see Report of Board of Trade on this claim, 10th May, 1697, in Mr. Brown's MSS., vol. 7, No. 21.

[2] James Sands, Thomas Terry and Joseph Kent.

to signify their obedience to his Majesty's will.   A petition
in behalf of sundry householders on the island, that they
be received as freemen, was granted.   The government of
the town was vested in the hands of three selectmen, who
might call town meetings, hear causes of less amount than
forty shillings, grant appeals to the General Court of
trials where a larger sum was involved, and issue warrants
in criminal cases.   Liberty to send two deputies to the
Assembly was given to the town ; a copy of the laws was
to be furnished them, and their attention was specially directed to that clause of the charter declaring freedom of
conscience.

Massachusetts having appointed two agents to treat
with Rhode Island in regard to Block Island and the Pequot country, John Greene and Joseph Torrey were commissioned to meet them at Rehoboth on the last day of
the month.   Richard Smith, jr., and Thomas Gould of
Narraganset, were bound over in the sum of four hundred
pounds each, and two Newport men in one-half that sum,
to appear when called for, upon the charge of seeking to
bring in a foreign jurisdiction within the limits of the colony.   These bonds were afterwards released.   A warrant
for the same offence was issued against John Greene, sen.,
who appeared and confessed his fault.   Upon petition he
was pardoned, and received again under protection as a
freeman of the colony.   Richard Smith, sen., was written
to, to appear before the Court on a similar charge.   He
made no reply to the letter, but enclosed it to Capt. Hutchinson, desiring him to inform Connecticut of the affair,
which he did.[1]

An active correspondence now ensued between Rhode
Island and the rival claimants for her soil.   The meeting
at Rehoboth with the Massachusetts agents had no important results.   Block Island had become private property before the transfer, and its owners had since cheerfully

---

[1] These three letters are in R. I. Col. Rec., ii. 45–9.

CHAP.
IX.

1664.
June

8.

July
8.

12.

20.

adopted the provisions of the charter annexing it to Rhode
Island.   The Pequot country, still claimed by Massachusetts in right of conquest, was by the Connecticut charter
entirely within her jurisdiction, while the claim of Rhode
Island for that portion of it east of the river, under her
more recent charter, still left Massachusetts out of the
question ; besides which, the royal commissioners had
power to arrange all such disputes, so that further discussion was useless.   The report of the agents was accepted
by the General Court.[1]   Plymouth now entered the field,
complaining in a letter to Rhode Island of intrusions upon
her limits.   But the most serious dispute in progress was
that with Connecticut.   No direct reply having been received to the letter written in March, but only an intimation from Governor Winthrop, that its contents would be
considered by the Assembly at Hartford, another letter
was sent, by a special messenger, referring to the former
one, and stating what had since been done by Rhode
Island with regard to the Connecticut officers in Narraganset, whose commissions, it was urged, should be revoked.   These officers, Richard Smith and William Hudson, with Edward Hutchinson then residing at Boston, also
wrote to Connecticut about some resistance offered to the
administrator of Capt. Atherton's estate, who, in behalf of
the heir, had endeavored to take possession of the property,
but was resisted by the tenant who claimed allegiance to
Rhode Island, although he was one of those who had subscribed the submission to Connecticut two years before.
Indeed, several of the Narraganset settlers had already
changed their views, and were inclined to Rhode Island,
while the original purchasers, many of whom resided in
Boston, remained firm in their preference for Connecticut.
Connecticut replied to both of the Rhode Island letters,
proposing a joint commission to meet in October to settle
all disputes, but asserting her claim to jurisdiction, defend-

[1] 19th Oct., M. C. R., Vol. iv. Part ii. p. 140.

ing the acts of her officers, and desiring Rhode Island to forbear further interference with them.

On the arrival of the English commissioners at Boston, Gov. Endicot assembled the Council, to receive the royal letter and the instructions that required them to raise a force to act against the Dutch, if it should be necessary. A special session of the General Court was held, and two hundred men were voted for the service, to be ready by the twentieth of the month. But their services were not required, for upon the appearance of the fleet off the port, New Amsterdam, now New York, surrendered to the British crown. Arania, now Albany, soon followed, and afterwards Delaware castle, and other forts held by the Dutch and Swedes, likewise surrendered to Sir Robert Carr. The whole conquered territory was placed under the government of Col. Nichols.

The Commissioners of the United Colonies, sitting at Hartford, of course took ground against Rhode Island, and addressed to her a letter full of warning and advice, based upon the royal letter of the previous year, wherein the Narraganset purchasers were placed under their protection.[1] Probably they did not know by what means that letter had been obtained. Rhode Island took no notice of this missive, but acknowledged receipt of the one from Connecticut, and referred it to the General Assembly for a more full reply.

The royal Commissioners, having nearly completed the subjugation of the Dutch provinces, had their head-quarters on board the English fleet now being in the harbor of New York. A delegation consisting of John Clarke, who had lately returned home, Capt. John Cranston and William Dyre, was sent on with a letter from the authorities of Rhode Island, expressing the gratitude of the colony to his Majesty for the charter, and congratulating the Commissioners. It appears by this letter that a previous one, of

CHAP. IX.

1 6 6 4.
July
23.
26.

Aug.
3.

27.
Sept.
11.

9.

20.

7.

---

[1] Hazard's State Papers, ii. 499.

like purport, had been sent by the hands of Capt. Baxter, but at that time it was not known where the Commissioners could be found. The messengers were kindly received, and a gracious answer was sent back on their return. The courtesy was acknowledged by deputy Governor Brenton, in another letter, inviting the Commissioners, upon their visiting Rhode Island, to make their home at his house.[1]

The Connecticut Assembly, at their next meeting, appointed a committee to arrange the boundary questions pending between that colony and both Rhode Island and Massachusetts, but ordered that they should not give up any portion of their charter limits.[2] This, so far as concerned Rhode Island, was equivalent to making no appointment.

At the meeting of the General Assembly the name of John Clarke appears at the head of the list of deputies. He had returned in June, after an absence of twelve years, spent in the faithful service of the colony, in England, and again resumed a place in the public councils, where, under the first patent, he had been so useful. The joy of the Assembly in having him once more among them, is evinced in a singular and emphatic manner in the preamble to the first public law passed at this session, establishing proxy voting ; "and this present Assembly (now by God's gracious providence enjoying the helpfull presance of our much honoured and beloved Mr. John Clarke,) doth declare and ordayne, &c."

It was ordered that at every meeting of the Assembly, whether regular or adjourned, the charter should be read. The inconvenience to the freemen of the remote towns, occasioned by having to vote in person at Newport, had attracted the attention of the Assembly at its May session, and been referred to this Assembly to devise some legal

---

[1] The original letters are both in S. P. O. New England papers, vol. i. pp. 206–9.

[2] Col. Rec. of Connecticut, ii. 435.

mode of voting by proxy. They enacted that all who did not come in person to Newport might give their votes, sealed up and subscribed with their own names on the outside, into the hands of a magistrate at any regular town meeting, to be delivered to the Executive at the Court or election in Newport, there to be opened and counted. If the voter was prevented from attending town meeting, the magistrate might yet receive his vote in the same manner.

Edmund Calverly, a deputy from Warwick, had made serious charges against the Governor, in respect to his official conduct, which were discussed, and the complainant required to prefer his charges in writing. He did so, but failing to sustain them, in the opinion of the court, he was suspended from voting until he should give satisfaction for his offence.[1]

A committee was appointed to revise the laws, to see if any were left unrepealed that were inconsistent with the present charter, and to codify them for more convenient reference. At the head of this committee was John Clarke, and the second member was Roger Williams ; two names of which the presence of either sufficiently refutes the slander contained in Chalmers,[2] and copied by later writers, attributing the interpolated restrictions upon religious freedom to the act of this Assembly. That these words [professing Christianity] and [Roman Catholics excepted] were the additions of later times, is as clear as any fact in history. That they were never placed there at all by the deliberate act of the Legislature of Rhode Island, but were occasioned by some contingency of English politics, we fully believe, and that the time will come when this unjust aspersion upon the freedom of the State will be explained, and its character be vindicated beyond a doubt—as recent developments have brought to light the conspiracy against

[1] At the May session the next year, Calverly failing to prove his charges, the Governor was declared by a vote of the Assembly to be innocent of the matters charged.

[2] Political Annals, Book i. chap. xi.

CHAP.
IX.

1664.
Oct.

26.

Nov.

the reputation of Clarke—we are firmly convinced.   This subject will be considered at length in a later volume when we come to the repeal of the interpolated phrases.

Agents were appointed to treat with Plymouth, two of whom were the deputy Governor and Roger Williams. They were commissioned to run the eastern line of the colony in connection with Plymouth agents.   A letter was sent to Plymouth, suggesting the time and place for a meeting to arrange differences between the colonies.   A similar course was adopted as to Connecticut.   John Clarke, John Greene, and Joseph Torrey were commissioned to run the western line, and to arrange all other disputes with the Connecticut agents ; but should these refuse to run the line, the Rhode Island men were to do it alone. A letter was also sent to Connecticut, regretting that the day fixed by the Hartford Assembly for this purpose was passed, and naming the twenty-ninth of November as the time for a meeting at Southertown, alias Pawcatuck.

Warrants were ordered for the arrest of William Hudson, of Boston, and Richard Smith, sen., of Narraganset, for unlawfully exercising the office of constable within the limits of the colony under a Connecticut commission ; but these warrants were not to issue till after the time appointed to treat with Connecticut.

A law was passed at this session which shows the wisdom and foresight of our ancestors, in obviating the difficulties that might arise from the existence of third parties at a general election ; " that whereas there may happen a division in the vote soe as the greater halfe may not pitch directly on one certaine person, yett the person which hath the most votes shall be deemed lawfully chosen."   It will thus be seen that a plurality choice was early adopted in this State.   It was also provided, that in case of refusal to accept office, the vacancy was to be filled by the General Assembly until the place was supplied.

The old law requiring each town to furnish itself with

a cage, or a pair of stocks, wherein to secure offenders, was reënacted.

An audit of the accounts of John Clarke showed a sum of three hundred and forty-three pounds to be due to him by the colony for his expenses while obtaining the charter, one hundred and one of which were to be paid in England, and one hundred pounds had been voted as a gratuity the previous year. To meet this debt, and the expenses of the several boundary commissions recently appointed, a tax of six hundred pounds, current money, was laid. Of this Providence and Portsmouth were taxed one hundred pounds each, Warwick eighty pounds, Petacomscot twenty pounds, Conanicut thirty-six pounds, Block Island fifteen pounds, and Newport the balance, being two hundred and forty-nine pounds. In the collection of this tax wheat was valued, in colony currency, at four and sixpence per bushel, peas at three and sixpence, and pork at three pounds ten shillings per barrel. It was a heavy burden for the impoverished towns, and years elapsed before it was paid. Warwick sent a formal protest against the large proportion assessed to her.[1] More than a year elapsed before Portsmouth levied her proportion, and then she sent a deputation to treat with Dr. Clarke on the subject.[2] Providence was equally backward in meeting the demand. The northern towns complained that they had been at heavy charges for the two missions of Roger Williams, and therefore should not bear so large a proportion of those for that of Dr. Clarke. The rate remained uncollected until enforced by a subsequent Assembly. That it should be so, and that Mr. Williams also was never fully paid even his expenses, attests the poverty of the colonists at this time.

The arrival of Sir Robert Carr at Newport, where he was detained some days by a storm, gave great satisfaction to the people of Rhode Island. Whatever fears were felt

[1] Printed in R. I. Col. Rec. ii. 78.
[2] See Portsmouth Records, March 1665-

by the rest of New England at the coming of these men, their presence was no source of regret in this jurisdiction. The protection that a royal commission invariably afforded to the oppressed and hated colony, while it embittered the animosity of her neighbors, increased the feeling of loyalty that a sense of gratitude had inspired, and which was displayed in something more than fulsome or hollow profes-

27. sions.   Leaving Newport Sir Robert spent some days with Mr. Willet, at his residence on Narraganset bay, and persuaded him to go to New York, where, it will be remembered, he became the first Mayor of that city.   The letter
Feb.
2.
that Carr wrote at this time to Col. Nichols is full of interest.[1]   He had brought to Rhode Island the royal letter, and one from Lord Clarendon to the colony, which had been given them on their departure from England to be delivered in person to this Government.   A grateful ac-
3. knowledgment was made by the Governor to Col. Nichols, wherein the conduct of the Narraganset company was adverted to and protection sought against their proceedings.[2]

Complaints were made to Connecticut by the Pawcatuck Indians of the conduct of James Babcock and other inhabitants of Westerly in demanding rent, and threatening to drive them from their lands.   The Council at Hartford warned the Rhode Island men to forbear from urging
10. their claims while the question of jurisdiction remained open.   A special council was called to appoint a committee to attend Gov. Winthrop to Narraganset, there to meet the
20. royal commissioners and urge the claim of Connecticut to that country under her charter.

15. Upon the return of the three commissioners from New York, leaving Col. Nichols there in command, they prepared at once to visit the several colonies, and to investigate the conflicting claims for the soil of Rhode Island. Plymouth received their first attention.   The General As-

[1] Original in S. P. O. New England, Vol. i. p. 218.
[2] R. I. Col. Rec. ii. 86-9.

sembly held a special session to prepare for their reception at Newport, and appointed a committee[1] to meet with the commissioners at Seaconck to adjust the boundary with Plymouth. All the expenses of the royal commissioners were to be borne by the colony. The commissioners could not make a definite settlement of the line between Plymouth and Rhode Island. In their report to Lord Arlington they say that the two colonies could not agree, for that Rhode Island claimed a strip three miles in breadth east of the bay, which Plymouth could not concede without great prejudice to her interests, and therefore they had, for the present, established the bay as the boundary until his Majesty's will could be known. Thence the commissioners came to Rhode Island. In their instructions they were furnished with a series of propositions to present to each of the colonies, a copy of which was forthwith given to the Governor.[2] Soon afterwards the commissioners went over to Pettaquamscot to settle the affairs of Narraganset. There the submission of the Narraganset sachems was confirmed. The Indians agreed to pay an annual tribute of two wolf skins, and not to make war or to sell land without consent of the authorities appointed over them by the crown.[3] The whole country from the bay to Pawcatuck river was named Kings Province, and all persons were forbidden to exercise jurisdiction therein without authority from the commissioners. The governor and council of Rhode Island, fourteen in number, were appointed Magistrates of Kings Province, to hold office until the annual election in May. The mortgaged lands held by the Atherton company, were ordered to be released upon payment of seven hundred and thirty-five fathoms of peage by Pes-

CHAP.
IX.

1654-5.
Feb.
27.

March
3.

4.

20.

---

[1] John Clarke, John Sandford, John Cranston, Roger Williams and Randall Holden.

[2] These are printed in R. I. Col. Rec., ii. 110, with the action of the Assembly thereon.

[3] S. P. O. New England papers, Vol. i. p. 231.

sicus or Ninecraft to any of the claimants. The purchase of the two tracts, actually bought by this company, was declared void for lack of consideration in the deed, and because the country had previously been surrendered to the crown, and the purchasers were ordered to vacate the premises within six months, provided the Indians should refund the sum of three hundred fathoms of peage, which was all they had ever received for the land.[1] At the expiration of the time the order to vacate was revoked, and the settlers were permitted to remain till his Majesty's will was further known. From Pettaquamscot the commissioners proceeded to Warwick. There the controversy about the lands of Westerly was decided in unequivocal terms, by a decree that no lands conquered from the natives should be disposed of by any colony unless both the cause of the conquest was just and the soil was included in the charter of the colony ; and further that no colony should attempt to exercise jurisdiction beyond its chartered limits. The grants made by Massachusetts " or by that usurped authority called the United Colonies," were declared void, the settlers upon such grants were ordered to vacate before the twenty-ninth of September, and not to prevent the Pequots from planting during the summer nor to interfere with the improvements of the lawful purchasers.[2] Pumham, the subject of Massachusetts, who still refused to leave Warwick Neck, although the land had been fairly purchased from his superior sachem many years before, was ordered by the commissioners to remove within a year to some place to be provided for him either by Massachusetts or by Pessicus. For this he was to receive twenty pounds from Warwick, and if he subjected himself to Pessicus, the latter was to receive ten pounds, upon furnishing him and his men with a place. The money was paid by Warwick, but Pumham refused to ful-

April
4.

7.

---

[1] This important decree is in Potter's Narraganset R. I. H. C., iii. 179.
[2] R. I. Col. Rec., ii. 9 3.

fil his former contract or to obey the order of the commissioners, relying, as it appears, upon the continued protection of Massachusetts.[1] A further decree was issued making
the governor, deputy, and twelve assistants, who might
hold these offices, from time to time, by election in Rhode
Island, to be likewise magistrates of Kings Province, having the entire control of that territory, and any seven of
them might constitute a court therein.

At the May election a great change was made in the
list of Assistants, but three of the old set being returned.
Two additional deputies, elected from Block Island, took
their seats. A new form of engagement to be taken by
the officers, and of reciprocal engagement to be given to
them, by the administering officer, in the name of the State,
was adopted. The royal commissioners had not only to
adjust the disputes of a public nature in the colonies, but
a great number of private matters were submitted to their
decision upon petition of the parties. Such were, for the
most part, referred by them to the local authorities to determine, and much of the time of the Assembly at this
session was occupied in those affairs. Some of them had a
bearing upon the public interests, involving charges against
the Assembly itself, as did the cases of Calverley and of
William Harris, which, for this reason, were referred back
to the commissioners. William Dyre, the newly chosen
Solicitor for the colony, having been guilty of a similar im-
propriety, in a petition to the commissioners, admitted his
fault, in writing, to the Assembly, and received pardon.

The five propositions presented by the commissioners
on their first coming to Rhode Island were placed before
the Assembly. They are as follows : " It is his Majesty's
will and pleasure ;

" 1. That all householders inhabiting this colony take
the oath of allegiance, and that the administration of
justice be in his Majesty's name.

[1] R. I. Col. Rec., ii. 132.

"2. That all men of competent estates and of civil conversation, who acknowledge and are obedient to the civil magistrate, though of different judgments, may be admitted to be freemen, and have liberty to choose, and to be chosen, officers both military and civil.

"3. That all men and women of orthodox opinion, competent knowledge, and civil lives, who acknowledge and are obedient to the civil magistrate, and are not scandalous, may be admitted to the Sacrament of the Lord's Supper, and their children to Baptisme, if they desire it, either by admitting them into the congregations already gathered, or permitting them to gather themselves into such congregations where they may enjoy the benefit of the Sacraments, and that difference in opinion may not break the bond of peace and charity.

"4. That all laws and expressions in laws derogatory to his Majesty, if any such have been made in these late and troublesome times, may be repealed, altered and taken off the files.

"5. That the colony be put into such a posture of defence that if there should be any invasion upon this island, or elsewhere in this colony (which God forbid) you might in some measure be in readiness to defend yourselves, or if need be, to relieve your neighbors according to the power given you by the King in your charter, and to us in the King's commission and instructions."

Upon these proposals the Assembly took immediate action. For the oath required in the first, they plead the scruples of many in the colony against that particular form, but prepared "an engagement" of similar purport, and which, so far as concerned its binding force, was to the same effect. This was to be administered to all the freemen at their next town meetings, whoever refused to take it was to be disfranchised, and no one could be admitted a freeman without first taking it. The second proposal was accepted, and the mode of application for those who

desired to be made freemen was prescribed.   The third   CHAP.
met with the cordial concurrence of the Assembly.   It was   IX.
in unison with the spirit of the colony, and with the terms   1 6 6 5.
of the charter.   In embodying it in the instructions of the   May.
commissioners, for the good of all the American colonies,
Charles II. exhausted the force of his famous promise contained in the Declaration of Breda.   The toleration thus
extended to the remote dependencies was denied to those
to whom it had first been pledged.   The hearty acceptance by the Assembly of this recommendation contrasts
with the qualified assent given to it by Plymouth, the
most liberal of the other colonies, where payment for the
support of the settled ministers was insisted upon, in their
reply, to be made by all " until they have one of their own."
The essence of an established church, the compulsory support of its clergy, was thus maintained even in the liberal
colony of the Pilgrims.   Connecticut assented to the same
proposition on condition that the maintenance of the
public minister was not hindered.[1]   Upon the fourth proposal the Assembly declared that all acts of the nature referred to were repealed when the King was proclaimed,
and a further revision of the laws was ordered for that specific purpose.   It was probably owing to this step that
the leaf of the Warwick records was afterwards torn out by
order of the town.[2]

In obedience to the last command, to place the colony
in a posture of defence, the Assembly passed a militia law
requiring six trainings a year, under a heavy penalty, and
allowing nine shillings a year for the pay of each enlisted

[1] S. P. O. New England, v. i. p. 248–58.

[2] The inscription records the contents and is as follows : " This leafe was
torn out by order of yᵉ towne the 29th of June, 1667, it being yᵉ submition
to yᵉ Stat of England without yᵉ King Majesty, it being yᵉ 13th page."   Yet
a former entry to the same effect as the one here destroyed seems to have escaped the observation of the clerk, and remains to this day on the ancient
records of the town as passed March 8th, 1652–3.   The Providence records
were not mutilated, and the entry remains in the same words as that of Warwick.

soldier. Every man was required to keep on hand two pounds of powder, and four of lead. Each town was obliged to maintain a public magazine for its own defence, for which Newport was taxed fifty pounds and the other three towns each twenty pounds.

Coddington, who with Easton and others had become Quakers, had sent a paper to the commissioners in March, of what nature we are unable to say, to which an answer was made immediately and communicated to the governor, to be presented to the Quakers in presence of the Assembly. This was done, and at the same time a copy of the five propositions was served upon them to consider and obey.

The action of the General Assembly, in private cases, was not limited in these early times, to legislative measures. Indeed the Court of trials was made up from its members, and the whole body often exercised strictly judicial powers upon petition of individuals. Not only were divorces granted and a separate maintenance awarded to the wife, but the whole property of the husband was attached and held by the Assembly, until the provisions of the decree had been satisfied. In the case of John Porter, at this session, they went even further, and annulled all transfers of property, that had been made by him since the separation from his wife, which had not already been recorded. Upon his settling a satisfactory estate upon the wife these disabilities were removed.

Criminal causes were likewise tried, upon petition, by the Assembly. Peter Tollman applied for a divorce from his wife on the ground of adultery. The woman, being brought before the Assembly, admitted the charge. The petition was granted at once, and then the criminal, upon her own confession, was arraigned for sentence. The penalty was a fine and whipping, and she was accordingly sentenced, by the terms of the law, to pay the fine of ten pounds, and to receive fifteen stripes at Portsmouth on the ensuing Monday, and on the following week another fifteen stripes at Newport, and to be imprisoned until the sentence was fulfilled. Upon her petition for mercy the Court again examined her as to whether she intended to return to her husband. This she refused to do upon any terms. Her petition was denied, and she was remanded for punishment. [1]

The wide distinction recognized in our day between the three branches of government was not so early understood. Under the first patent the President and Assistants were executive officers, and had no share in legislation in virtue of their position. By the royal charter the governor and council became ex-officio legislators in common with the deputies, and all alike exercised judicial powers. At this time they sat together as one House of Assembly, and although a movement was made the next year to alter this system, it was still thirty years before the two bodies were fully recognized as separate and co-ordinate branches of the legislature, and more than eighty years before judicial powers ceased to be exercised by them, upon the establishment of a supreme court of judicature.

The necessity of a harbor at Block Island was so apparent to the first settlers, that they took the earliest occasion afforded by the presence of their deputies in the General Assembly, to petition for a committee of inquiry upon the subject ; and so important was it, in the opinion of the Assembly, that the governor, deputy governor, and John Clarke, were appointed to visit the island to see if a harbor could be made there, and what encouragement could thus be given to the fisheries. This was the first movement in a matter that has ever since occupied, at

---

[1] She escaped from prison and was gone two years. Upon her return to the colony in May 1667, she was arrested and petitioned the Court for mitigation of sentence. The fine and one-half of the corporal punishment was remitted, and the remainder, fifteen stripes to be inflicted at Newport, was executed.

various times, the public attention, and which has recently assumed its proper form as a national measure,
more important to American commerce than to the hardy
islanders themselves.

The Warwick men had presented to the commissioners,
upon their first coming to Rhode Island, a petition setting forth the grievances they had suffered from Massachusetts, and asking redress. They had in vain sought justice from their oppressors, by letters and remonstrance,
before appealing to the king,[1] and had once voluntarily
informed the United Colonies of their intention to appeal,
so that they might prepare their answer to the crown.[2]
Attention to their case was within the scope of the royal
commission. It was presented in proper season, and laid
before the authorities of Massachusetts for them to answer.
This they did at the session of the General Court, in a
30. very lengthy, abusive, and rambling document, made up
of theological discussion, personal invective, and positive
misstatements, wherein they profess " to compare the
petition, first, with its authors, second, with their principles, and third, with the whole transaction," and which
they style " an apological reply."[3]

The commission itself was very distasteful to Massachusetts. They regarded it, justly, as an interference
by the crown with their self-assumed prerogative to control New England, and they dreaded that any such power
should come among them. The proceedings of the commissioners were bitterly denounced by the General Court.
Among the alleged wrongs committed by them, " the
great countenance given to the Rhode Islanders," and
their " calling, in their public declarations, the United
Colonies ' that usurped authority,' " occupy a conspicuous

[1] One of these letters dated August 22d, 1661, is printed in R. I. H. C.,
ii. 224–31.

[2] Sept. 1, 1651. R. I. H. C., ii. 217–19.

[3] The petition and answer are given in full in M. C. R., vol. iv. Part ii.
p. 253–65, and in R. I. H. C., ii. 231–45.

place. The temper of the Court may be gathered from a
letter to the author of the petition, by one of the commissioners, while the subject was under discussion in that
body.[1] The controversy was again transferred to England. The General Court, fearing the effect of such a
report as the commissioners must necessarily make,
adopted an address to the King, sufficiently humble in its
terms, but peevish in its spirit, complaining that the
commissioners had violated the royal instructions by frus-
trating the objects for which they were sent. Deprecating the misrepresentations that these commissioners
would probably make with regard to Massachusetts, the
address vaunts the superiority of its authors by denouncing most of those who complain against them, " as Indians, Quakers, libertines and malefactors." It concludes
with a display of piety and loyalty as repulsive, in this
connection, as it was unfounded.[2]

Most of the towns being still in arrears for the debt
due to John Clarke, the General Assembly renewed the
order to collect the tax, and notified the delinquent towns
to that effect.

The commissioners, having completed their examination of all the New England colonies, seven in number, sent
home a long report, giving a sketch of the history and actual condition of each one. That concerning Massachusetts is the longest and expresses the most dissatisfaction.
It was the last colony visited, as the commissioners vainly
hoped that the condescension of the other colonies might

[1] " Mr. Gorton. These gentlemen of Boston would make us believe that
they verily think that the King has given them so much power in their charter to do unjustly, that he reserved none for himself, to call them to an account for doing so. In short they refuse to let us hear complaints against
them, so that, at present, we can do nothing in your behalf. But I hope
shortly to go for England, where, if God bless me thither, I shall truly represent your sufferings and your loyalty. Your assured friend, George Cartwright. Boston, 26th May, 1665." R. I. H. C., ii. 246. The government
copy is in British S. P. O. New England papers, vol. iii. p..3.

[2] M. C. R., vol. iv. Part ii. p. 274–5.

CHAP.
IX.

1665.
Dec.

tend to diminish the refractory spirit there shown ; but they could not obtain a hearing even upon some cases specified in the royal letter, to be determined by them.[1] The substance of the report on Rhode Island may be gathered from what has before been written. Of the Narraganset Bay, it says, " it is the largest and safest port in New England, nearest the sea, and fittest for trade." A very remarkable point in this report is the allusion to what is probably the earliest known temperance petition, that of Pessicus, Sachem of the Narragansets, desiring " the commissioners to pray King Charles that no strong liquors might be brought into that country, for he had thirty-two men that dyed by drinking of it." This and all the other original papers referred to, were unfortunately lost, the ship in which Col. Cartwright sailed for England having been captured by the Dutch.

Although the labors of the commissioners were now apparently ended, some of their decrees remained unnoticed, and required further attention. Pumham still lingered in the sylvan retreat of Warwick Neck. Sir Robert Carr held a conference with Cheesechamut, son of the old Sachem, at Smith's trading house, that resulted in an agreement to remove at once beyond the bounds of Kings Province, upon receiving the ten pounds that Pessicus was to have, and ten pounds more from the people of Warwick. He acknowledged receipt of thirty pounds, being ten pounds more than was formerly promised, and six days later the additional ten pounds was paid into the hands of Pumham. John Eliot, the Indian apostle, immediately wrote to Sir Robert Carr, interceding in behalf of Pumham, but without effect. Sir Robert, after waiting nearly a month, sent a peremptory order for the Indians to move within one week, and also replied to Eliot, rather sharply, for what he justly considered an ill-timed although

28.

1665-6.
Jan.
3.

9.

Feb.
24.

28.

---

[1] The entire report is in S. P. O. New England, vol. i. p. 248–58. The Report on Rhode Island is in R. I. Col. Rec., ii. 127–9.

well intended, interference on the part of the missionary, CHAP.
for whose satisfaction he graciously forwarded copies of the IX.
transactions in regard to Pumham. Roger Williams also 1666.
wrote to Carr upon the same subject, giving the history March
of the dispute, and wisely advising him that force could 1.
effect nothing permanent against Pumham, until the
commissioners had first reduced Massachusetts to obedience to his majesty, because these Indians were sustained
by Massachusetts in their resistance. He concludes by
suggesting that they be allowed to remain until harvest,
that thus, through his mediation, a peaceable adjustment
may be reached. Sir Robert sent for Mr. Williams, and, 5.
satisfying him of the proceedings, obtained his active assistance in the immediate removal of Pumham. Thus
this "old ulcerous business" was finally concluded, to the
great relief of the people of the colony, who, for more than
twenty years, had been harassed by the intrigues of their
neighbors with these turbulent natives.[1]

The delay of the towns, in paying Dr. Clarke, called
forth a severe letter from Roger Williams, addressed to
Warwick, as the greatest delinquent, which gave deep offence. It was received on a training day, and was read at 26.
the head of the company ; not an unusual mode of publication in those times, for even the banns of marriage were
by law proclaimed in the same manner. The action of
the town is worthy of note. It was at once emphatic, and
under the circumstances, feeling as they did insulted by
the tenor of the missive, it was perhaps the most digni-
fied course they could adopt. They "voted that the said
letter is a pernicious letter, tending to stir up strife in the
town, and that the town clerk record this vote and send a
copy of it to Mr. Williams, as the town's answer to the

---

[1] The orders and letters here referred to, relating to Pumham, are printed
in R. I. Col. Rec., ii: 132-8. The diligence of Secretary Bartlett in collecting the documents that go to make up a continuous history of the State, and
inserting them between the bare records of the Assembly's proceedings, is
worthy of all commendation.

CHAP.
IX.

1 6 6 6.
March

27.

29.

said letter, no man dissenting." It should be remembered that Warwick had, at the time, protested against her proportion of the tax, giving some cogent reasons for her dissent ; and it is probable that Williams's letter was not so mild in its language as so delicate a subject required. But that the colony agreed with his view of the case appears from the action of the Assembly that met the next day. The Warwick protest was considered, and it was ordered " that a letter shall be sent to them from the Court to provocke and stirr them up to pay the rate spedilye," and a similar letter was prepared to be sent to Providence.

The form of the engagements to be taken by freemen and officers was a frequent matter of legislation. So great was the variety of opinion, and the latitude given to tender consciences in the colony, that it was a work of time to devise some form of words that should not be objectionable to any. Verbal alterations and slight modifications were made at different sessions, some of which, in our less scrupulous times, appear puerile. At this session a committee consisting of the Governor and Nicolas Easton, the latter being a Quaker, reported upon the subject of the freemen's engagement, recommending either the form already prescribed by the Assembly, or the oath of allegiance as required in England, or if objections to either of these forms existed, the party might adopt any equivalent words satisfactory to the Court.[1]

An important subject brought to the notice of previous

---

[1] The officers' engagement was adopted May 1664, altered May 1665, amended May 1667. See R. I. Col. Rec., ii. 57, 97, 187. That for the freemen was adopted May 1665, modified March 1666, pp. 112, 141-2, and gave rise to the slander circulated by Brinley in 1 M. H. C., v. 219, and transmitted by Holmes, Annals, 1, 341, that the Quakers were outlawed by Rhode Island in 1665. This has been sufficiently refuted by Judge Eddy in 2 M. H. C., vii. 97 ; by Knowles' Memoir of Roger Williams, 324, and cursorily by Bancroft U. S., ii. 67. In fact at that time there were two Quakers, if not more, members of the Assembly, and one of them was the next year, 1666, chosen Deputy Governor.

Assemblies by petition from Warwick and Portsmouth,[1]
was now acted upon. This was that the deputies might
sit apart from the magistrates as a separate House, thus
creating two Houses of Assembly, with equal powers, acting
as a check upon each other. The rule was adopted, to
take effect in May, when the details of the change were to
be settled. This act was soon afterwards repealed, and the
measure was not adopted till thirty years later. The
King having received from the commissioners an account
of their proceedings in New England, wrote to the colony,
expressing his approbation of its conduct, and promising
his continued favor and protection.[2]

At the general election Governor Arnold retired from
office. He had served for three years, since the adoption
of the new charter, and had been for four years president
of the colony under the first patent. William Brenton,
who had been deputy governor for the past three years,
was chosen governor, and Nicolas Easton was elected to
fill that place. The same general officers were re-elected
except Torrey, general recorder, who gave place to John
Sandford, but there was a great change in the list of Assistants, only three of the former ones being retained. It
was the practice to admit as freemen those whose names
were sent in for that purpose by the clerks of the respective towns, as well as those who personally appeared before
the Assembly, being duly qualified. A large number were
thus admitted from all the towns at the opening of this
session. It was also allowed to the former Assistants, by
law, to sit as deputies in the General Assembly, in the absence of a full delegation, a contingency which now actually
occurred, so that several of the old Assistants were sent for
to aid the Court. William Blackstone petitioned for relief from molestation by Plymouth in regard to his lands.

[1] See Warwick Records, Oct. 8, 1664, and Portsmouth Records Feb. 21,
1664–5.
[2] The letter is in R. I. Col. Rec., ii. 149.

CHAP.
IX.

1666.
May

4.

Sept.
4.

The petition was recorded, and answer returned that, if his land proved to be within this jurisdiction, justice should be secured to him. The Assembly, or Court as it was commonly termed, could not proceed to legislation owing to the absence of deputies, and after waiting two days for their appearance, adjourned till June, but for some cause no session was held till September. At that time, the capture of Col. Cartwright by the Dutch, with the loss of all his papers, having been known, a new address to the King, and letters to Lord Clarendon were ordered. Maps of Plymouth, Connecticut and Rhode Island were prepared to accompany this address, in order to show their respective boundaries, which it was prayed might be confirmed according to the charter. The letter to Lord Clarendon expresses regret that no adequate return can be made by the colony for the many favors he has conferred upon it, but states that the colony had designed to set apart a tract of one thousand acres, suitable for a farm, and to beg his acceptance thereof. The present wants of the colony, for which they petition, are, that Narraganset bay should be fortified, that such commercial privileges be extended as may develope the resources of the place, and that a portion of the fund for propagating the gospel among the Indians may be applied to establish a school for the Narragansets. Enclosed in this letter was a paper setting forth seven reasons why the Kings Province should remain a part of Rhode Island, and another paper presenting also seven arguments why the eastern line of the colony should be made to conform to the terms of the charter.

The difficulty experienced of late, owing to the non-attendance of deputies, who hitherto had served without pay, caused the passage of an act to pay all the members of Assembly, and of the Courts, three shillings a day, while employed on these duties. The per diem of the Assemblymen was not paid in cash, but their accounts, certified by the Moderator, were to be allowed in offset of taxes levied in their respective towns. The Court fees were paid in cash, upon orders, signed by the governor, to the public treasurer. In case of absence a fine of six shillings a day was imposed. If the general sergeant, or any town, failed to give due attention to the summons of the governor calling an Assembly or a Court of Trials, a fine of five pounds was imposed upon the delinquent party. To hold a colony court of trial, the presence of the governor, or his deputy, and of four Assistants was required, and should that number not be present, every absentee was subjected to a similar fine of five pounds. Whoever should attempt to vote at any election, not being a freeman of the colony, was to pay a fine of five pounds, or to be otherwise punished as the General Assembly might see fit ; and no one was to be admitted a freeman upon election day.

The delay in paying the debt due to Dr. Clarke was likely to involve him in serious trouble. His house was mortgaged to Richard Dean for one hundred and forty pounds, advanced some years before in London, on account of the colony. The time for payment had long passed, and a foreclosure was threatened. The Assembly now assumed the debt. A special committee of eleven men was appointed, with extraordinary powers, to collect the arrears of the six hundred pound tax levied for this object two years before. The town sergeant and constables of every town and village were placed at the disposal of the committee, at whose order they were to assemble the people, and to levy by distraint, if required to do so. William Harris was placed at the head of this committee, who, with any other four of the number, were to act at their discretion and to report, the ensuing month, to the Assembly. They were unable fully to accomplish the object in so short a time, and were continued at the next session ; and, because of the difficulty of obtaining exchange on England, they were empowered to send an adventure to Barbadoes, or elsewhere, at the risk of the delinquent parties. Power was also given them to collect arrears due upon other rates laid by the colony, prior to the one for Dr. Clarke.

1666. John Clarke was appointed to make a digest of the laws, " leaving out what may be superfluous, and adding what may appear unto him necessary," and a committee of three was named, to examine the work when done, and to report at a future Assembly.

1667.
May
1
The next year there were very few changes made at the general election. Charges were brought against William Harris, one of the Assistants from Providence, for exceeding his powers as an officer. The specific allegations are not given. The engagement was administered to him notwithstanding a motion for delay. This caused a protest to be entered upon the records by those who thought that the charges should be examined before he was qualified as a magistrate.

England was now at war with France and Holland. Symptoms of disaffection on the part of the Indians were manifested. Invasion on one hand and treachery on the other threatened the feeble colony. Prompt measures were taken for defence. In each town a council of war was organized, consisting of the town council with the captain and lieutenant of the train band. These were required to provide ammunition to the value of fifty pounds for Newport and of twenty pounds for every other town. Commissions were issued by the Assembly to the military officers, who were required to be freemen of the colony. Cannon were mounted at Newport, and cavalry corps were formed in all the towns. The governor and council held frequent meetings between the sessions of Assembly. Their acts were equally binding with those of the latter body. The council empowered any magistrate to require assistance in case of need, and to impress men or appropriate property to the public service, being responsible only to the General Council. The Indians upon the island were disarmed, and the mainland towns were advised to adopt the same measure. A few days later all male Indians, CHAP.
IX. over sixteen years of age, were sent off the island, and no Englishman, above that age, was permitted to leave without a passport, or to go on board of any vessel that might approach the island, until her captain had reported himself to the chief magistrate of the town. All ammunition in private hands was required to be given up for the public use. A committee was appointed to examine and repair all arms belonging to the citizens. A special tax of one hundred and fifty pounds was levied in Newport for defence. Letters having been received from Plymouth concerning a suspected conspiracy by King Philip, a committee was appointed to treat with the Narraganset Sachems on the subject, and a letter was sent to them requiring their presence on a certain day at Warwick. The Assembly confirmed the acts of the council, and established a series of beacons, where signal fires should be lighted in case of attack, to spread the alarm without delay over all the colony. The principal beacon was on Wonemytonomi hill, whence the alarm could be spread along the whole coast by bale-fires on the rocks at Sachuest, at Pettaquamscot, and on Watch hill, and northward on Windmill hill, the highest point of the island, and thence to Mooshausuck, now Prospect hill, in Providence ; and a general system of defence was adopted for all the islands and exposed settlements in the colony and in Kings Province. These were the preliminary steps taken in view of a crisis which proved to be still quite remote.

Internal dissensions supplied the excitement that hostile demonstrations failed to bring. At the annual town meeting in Providence two sets of town officers were elected, and two sets of delegates chosen to the Assembly, at two separate meetings called by the Assistants resident in the town, at the same time and place ; one by Arthur Fenner, the other by William Harris in concert with William Carpenter, another Assistant. It was the duty of one of the

1667.
May
10.

14.

18.

21.

June
3.

Assistants to call town meetings, but of which one, in this
case, does not appear, nor is it known why two calls were
issued ; but it is supposed to be owing to a sharp controversy then existing upon local questions relating to the
town limits. The result was unfortunate in creating a
bitter feeling that it required many years to assuage. A
narrative of the affair, entitled " The Firebrand Discovered " was drawn up, by vote of the town, and sent to the
other three towns. This presents the view of the Fenner
faction. The other side entered a complaint to the Governor against Fenner, which led to a special session of the
July
2. Assembly at which both sets of deputies appeared. The
seats were awarded to the Fenner party. The complaint
of Harris against Fenner, charging the latter with " acting
in a route " upon town meeting day, was then examined,
and Fenner with his deputies were acquitted. The town
officers elected by the Fenner meeting were pronounced
to be the legally chosen officers for the year. A letter
was sent to Providence stating the action of the Assembly
with the reasons thereof. Harris having upon insufficient
grounds caused this session to be held, expressly for the
trial of Fenner, was fined fifty pounds, and for other more
serious reasons was expelled from the office of Assistant,
two of his colleagues· protesting, and another was chosen
in his place. The fine was remitted the next year by
advice of Col. Nichols, governor of New York, to whom
Harris had complained. To prevent similar vexatious
suits in future, an act was passed that no Assistant should
indict any person, for matters pertaining to another's interest, without the sworn evidence of two witnesses under
the hand of another Assistant, whose names should be endorsed on the bill of indictment.

Aug.
10.
The first troop of horse organized in Rhode Island reported for duty at Newport in August, and was commissioned by the governor and council. It numbered twenty-

one men well mounted and equipped.[1]   The Assembly continued to the towns, till further notice, the full military
powers before conferred on them.   The strife about the
Narraganset country still continued.   The mode in which
Rhode Island had run her western line, beyond the Pawcatuck river, caused great dissatisfaction, and many depositions on that subject were given by the people of Southertown, or Stonington as it was now called.[2]   Hermon Garret, the English name of Wequashcooke, who had been
made chief of the Pequots by the United Colonies, renewed
the complaints formerly made by the Indians against the
Westerly settlers, who had driven them across the river,
and sought relief from Connecticut.   The deputies from
Stonington also complained of intrusions on the west side
of the river, committed by John Crandall, who had laid
out a mile square of land for his son within the limits of
their town.[3]   These acts on the part of Rhode Island were
unjustifiable.   They proceeded no doubt from a spirit of
retaliation in the minds of those who had formerly suffered
so much from the men of Southertown.   The Assembly at
Hartford ordered notice of these encroachments to be given   10.
to Rhode Island with a request that they be discontinued,
and should this not suffice then the constable was required
to arrest the intruders.   A letter to this effect was sent to   17.
Governor Brenton.

Massachusetts, although her claims had been superseded by those of Connecticut, and her right to interfere,
even with the Indians had been denied by the royal commissioners, embraced an opportunity presented by the

[1] Their names, from the Council records, are given in R. I. Col. Rec., ii.
218.

[2] Southertown was incorporated by Massachusetts Oct. 19th, 1658.   The
name was changed to Mistick by the Connecticut Assembly Oct. 12th, 1665,
and then to Stonington, and bounded by the Pawcatuck river, May 10th,
1666.   Conn. Col. Rec., ii. 26, 36.

[3] Garret's petition was dated May 6th, that of the deputies was presented
Oct. 10th.   Conn. Col. Rec., ii. 80.

CHAP.
IX.
1667.
Oct.
31.

Nipmucks, who acknowledged her supremacy, to impose terms on the Narragansets. The Nipmucks petitioned for redress for spoliations committed by the Narragansets. The General Court took up the matter, as of right, and settled the difficulty. It was a measure of peace and therefore commendable, but it does not admit of rigid scrutiny into the claim of jurisdiction over the Nipmuck country upon which the interference was based.[1] A correspondence was carried on between various parties in Rhode Island, and Col. Nichols, Governor of New York, as the head of the late royal commission. His replies were made in a private capacity, his power as a commissioner having, in his opinion, ceased.

Nov.

1668.
May
4.

An urgent petition was presented by the town of Stonington to the Assembly at Hartford for protection against Rhode Island,[2] and on the same day the people of Wickford also petitioned to be again received under the jurisdiction of Connecticut.

6.

The general election made but little change in the officers, and is only remarkable for the triumph of the Harris party; William Harris, notwithstanding his expulsion, being again chosen an Assistant, and the other two Assistants from Providence being of his faction, while Fenner himself was dropped. This is the more singular as there is evidence that Harris at this time had, or was about to, become the agent of Connecticut in prosecuting her claim against Rhode Island. A very long document from his pen is preserved in the archives of Connecticut, arguing against the Assembly's apportionment of the taxes for the payment of Dr. Clarke, on the supposed ground of the rightful jurisdiction of Connecticut in the Narraganset country.[3] But the governor refused to administer the engagement until Harris should clear himself from an in-

[1] M. C. R., vol. iv. Part ii. p. 357–9.

[2] Conn. Col. Rec., ii. 530.

[3] This was filed Oct. 1666. A copy is in R. I. Hist. Soc., MSS. vol. of Conn. papers, p. 49–67.

dictment brought against him for charging the Court of
Trials with injustice. The deputy Governor was less
scrupulous ; by him Harris was duly qualified, and a certificate sent as usual to the towns. The town of Warwick
protested against this act as being irregular, and refused
to acknowledge him as a legal officer.[1] The town of Providence sent a bitter remonstrance to the Governor and
council against the election of Harris and his colleagues,
but no notice was taken of it.[2]

Connecticut appointed agents to treat with Rhode
Island upon the foregoing complaints, who were instructed to require the withdrawal of intruders, to assert the
jurisdiction of Connecticut according to her charter, and
to demand a written reply. These propositions were submitted to the council at Newport, who replied to Governor Winthrop, referring to the decision of the Royal
Commissioners, and to the Pawcatuck River clause in
the charter, but saying that if any violations of those
terms had been committed, justice would be rendered
upon due course of law.

Massachusetts again interfered in the affairs of Narraganset, by sending messengers to request the sachems to
appear at the General Court to answer complaints made
against them by the Narraganset purchasers. The Wickford men renewed their petition of May, to have the government of Connecticut extended over them. The Hartford
assembly desired advice from Col. Nichols on this matter.
They also notified Rhode Island to send commissioners to
meet a committee appointed by them to adjust differences at New London.[3] This notice was not received till
after the Assembly had adjourned, and hence could not be
acted upon before the next spring. The Wickford peti-

CHAP.
IX.

1668.
May
13.

June
1.

3.

Aug.
20.

Sept.
4.

Oct.
8.

---

[1] See Warwick records, June 1, 1668.

[2] It is dated 31st August, 1668, and is found in Staples' Annals, 147–50.

[3] Conn. Col. Rec., ii. 102, 103, 532—also R. I. Col. Rec., ii. 225–30,
where most of the foregoing papers are printed.

CHAP.
IX.

1668.
Oct.

tion was referred to England, and Mr. Willys, and Robert Thompson of London, were appointed to present the subject for the decision of his Majesty, but nothing decisive was effected.

29.

The General Assembly remitted the fine of fifty pounds imposed upon William Harris the previous year. Upon William Blackstone's petition, John Clarke was requested to write to Plymouth, warning that colony not to molest him in the quiet possession of his lands. A large number of freemen were admitted. The Assembly adjourned until March, to give place to the Court of Trials.

1668-9.
March
11.

Up to this time, it was usual for any party who was indicted to plead his own cause before the courts, but as this required more wisdom, or knowledge of the law, than every man possessed, the Assembly now enacted that any person who was indicted might employ an attorney to plead in his behalf, and further, that a pending indictment should not prevent any general officer, fairly elected, from holding his office ; but that he should nevertheless be subject to trial. This statute seems to be intended to meet the objections brought against William Harris by the town of Warwick. A sharp controversy existed between that town and the Assistants of Newport, who sustained Harris in the vigorous measures he had adopted, as chief of the committee for collecting the famous tax of

25.

six hundred pounds, levied in 1664. At a town meeting, held to hear a letter from the Newport Assistants on this subject, action was taken that deserves a place among the curiosities of legislation.[1]

---

[1] "Voted: Upon the reading of a letter directed to 'Mr. Edmund Calverley and Mr. John Greene and the rest of that faction,' &c., desiring to be communicated to the honest inhabitants of Warwick town, subscribed John Cranston, to the end of the chapter, dated the 20th January, 1668, and finding the same doth not answer the town's letter to that part of the committee, &c., who reside at Newport, touching the rate; but is full of uncivil language, as if it had been indicted in hell; Therefore the town unanimously do condemn the same, and think it not fit to be put amongst the records of the

The General Assembly met on Tuesday, a recent law requiring them to meet the day before election, that a full attendance might prevent delay in the choice of officers. Benedict Arnold was again made governor, and John Clarke was chosen deputy governor. There was but little change among the other general officers. The Harris party again prevailed in the choice of the three Assistants from Providence ; William Harris himself being, as before, one of the number. On Saturday they adjourned for the Court of Trials, and met again the following Friday, when the letter from Connecticut of the previous October, was read, and a reply was sent, apologizing for the delay, and accepting the proposal to send commissioners to New London. The letter was forwarded by a special messenger, whose expenses, as also were those of the committee named in the letter, were paid by voluntary contribution on the spot. The sums thus raised were to be deducted from the amount of the next tax. Misquamicut, as it had heretofore been called, was now incorporated as the fifth town in the colony, and named Westerly. Two deputies were allowed to it, and the

---

town, but do order that the clarke put it on a file where impertinent papers shall be kept for the future ; to the end that those persons who have not learned in the school of good manners how to speak to men in the language of sobriety (if they be sought for) may be there found." Warwick records, March 25th, 1669, (New Year's day, O. S.) We doubt if the idea of an "impertinent file" ever entered the minds of any other people, or if anywhere else in the arrangement of State Papers, so expressive, yet so convenient, a classification was ever employed. We have already referred to one document, "the pernitious letter" of Roger Williams, which probably served as the foundation stone for this remarkable structure. The notion of keeping a separate file for disagreeable communications was not started till this second letter, "indicted in hell," was received. This was not the last of the kind, as we shall presently see, and the character of the documents consigned to this significant receptacle, seems to have grown worse and worse as the collection increased. It is much to be regretted that the "impertinent file," or as it was afterwards termed more energetically, the "damned file," has disappeared, with many other of the records of this ancient town, for it would no doubt furnish materials that would amply justify the votes of the townsmen.

CHAP.
IX.

1 6 6 9.
May
14.

21.

July
5.

8.

usual courts for the trial of small causes, were there organized.   John Clarke was desired to write to Providence to persuade the people to settle the quarrels there existing.   At the same time a measure was adopted that produced a contrary effect in Warwick.   Execution was granted to William Harris against Edmund Calverly, and John Harrod of Warwick, unless the litigants should at once come to a mutual agreement, in the case of a land dispute of long standing between them, upon which Harris had recovered judgment in the courts.   Against this act, John Greene, Assistant, and the deputies from Warwick, of whom Calverley himself was one, protested, and desired to have their protest entered, but were refused, although the fee was tendered for that purpose to the recorder.   The town took up the matter in public meeting, refused to assist in serving the execution, and entered the protest upon their records in full, with the grounds of their action.[1]

The council appointed six additional justices of the peace in Kings Province, one of whom was Richard Smith, the earliest settler in Narraganset, and who had formerly given so much trouble in connection with the Atherton Company.   In the commissions issued to these justices, the bounds of Kings Province are accurately defined.   They embraced all of the present State west of the bay, south of the latitude of Warwick, being the south half of Kent and the whole of Washington counties.   Monthly meetings of the council were established, but the posture of affairs caused them to be held much oftener at this time.   Governor Lovelace, who had succeeded Col. Nichols at New York, wrote to Rhode Island concerning a plot against the English, supposed to be forming between the Long Island Indians and Ninecraft, sachem of the Narragansets.   The governor and council of Connecticut also wrote on the same subject.   The coun-

[1] See Warwick records, June 7th, 1669.

cil met at once, and sent some discreet persons to Narraganset to inquire into these complaints. They found
some emissaries from Philip of Mount Hope at the camp
of the sachem, which confirmed their suspicions.   On
their return the Council issued a warrant to apprehend
Ninecraft and bring him before them. A violent storm,
that lasted two days, preventing the immediate service of
the writ, it was renewed, and a letter was at the same
time written to Plymouth, advising that colony to question King Philip on the subject. Ninecraft appeared before the Council and sustained a long examination. He
declared his innocence of the charge of conspiracy, and
explained many suspicious circumstances that were
brought against him, but his answers not being in all respects satisfactory, he was dismissed upon his promise to
appear again if sent for. Letters were sent to Connecticut and to New York, giving details of the examination,
and desiring that any evidence in their possession against
Ninecraft might be forwarded in season for his next appearance before the Council. A broil between some
English and Indians soon occasioned another meeting of
the Council. Summons were sent to Ninecraft and Maw-
sup, another sachem, to appear before them. The Council recommended the five towns to take speedy measures
for defence, and also required the justices to assemble all
the people of the villages for consultation on the same
subject. The two sachems appeared, with the ringleader
in the recent broil, who was bound over for trial. Four
Long Island Indians accompanied Ninecraft. They were
examined at length, and so clearly explained what had
caused the rumors of a plot, that the whole were discharged, and the excitement soon passed away.

The Commissioners of the United Colonies took up
the complaints of the people of Stonington, denounced
Rhode Island, and advised that the General Court of Connecticut should demand satisfaction, and if refused, that

CHAP.
IX.

1 6 6 9.
July
20.

22.

28.

29.

18.

19.

26.

27.

28.

Sept.
13.

CHAP.
IX.

1669.

Oct.

4.

18.

27.

notice should be given to the several colonies, and their advice asked upon the mode of seeking redress. The New England league exercised less influence than formerly. It had become essentially weak, and a proposal to revise the terms of union was submitted at this time, but although it was approved and acted upon, nothing decisive resulted.[1] In a few years the confederacy expired by default, and Rhode Island was thus relieved from what had often been to her a source of oppression, and had always given her great annoyance.

So far from an amicable settlement with Harrod, as desired by the Assembly, Harris, the repeated verdicts in whose favor entitled him to the final process of the law, wrote to him a letter, wherein he so abused the people of Warwick that it was made the occasion for a town meeting. An address was prepared to be presented to the Assembly, condemning the conduct of Harris as dangerous to the existence of the colony. The address was read at the next town meeting; and the feeling of the town was expressed in a vote too plainly to be mistaken.[2] The letter was read in the General Assembly, and the parties to the lawsuit were earnestly entreated to settle their differences by arbitration, but in vain.

The quarrel at Providence was renewed with fresh virulence. Certificates from two town clerks, claiming to be legally chosen, were presented, one of which declared that there had been no election of deputies, and the other cer-

[1] Hazard's State papers, ii.

[2] " Voted, That the letter prepared by the town council touching William Harris shall be read, which was done accordingly, and ordered to be signed by the town clerk in the name of the town, and by the deputies to be delivered to the next General Assembly, by a unanimous consent; and that the town clerk do put the paper of William Harris, that occasioned the letter, *upon the dam—file* amongst those papers of that nature." Warwick records, 18th Oct., 1669. It will be seen by this that the remarkable file, referred to in the note a few pages back, was rapidly increasing in size, and becoming more intense in its character.

tifying to the election of the four deputies who claimed
their seats under it. They were rejected, so that Providence was unrepresented at this session. This deplorable
feud caused the Assembly to appoint a special committee
of five to go to Providence, and call a meeting of the
townsmen, to endeavor to persuade them to refer the subjects of dispute to the decision of disinterested parties.
If this was agreed to, they were then to call a town meeting to elect officers and deputies; meanwhile all actions
at law growing out of this quarrel were to be suspended
till another meeting of the Assembly. The six hundred
pound tax, the real cause of much of the disaffection now
existing in the impoverished colony, was not yet all collected. The powers of the committee were renewed, and
the sergeant was ordered to distrain at their bidding.
Warwick prepared to resist this act, and warned Harris
not to enter the town without leave.

The Council of Connecticut wrote to the men of Westerly to require them to give satisfaction for injuries inflicted, not only upon those of Stonington, but also upon
the heirs of the Atherton company, saying that time
would be allowed them till the next March to arrange
these matters. No notice was taken of this missive till
the time had expired, when an answer was returned, referring to the injuries formerly received by them from the
Stonington men, and stating that if Connecticut had any
complaints to make, the Courts of Rhode Island would do
justice to the litigants.

An extra session of the Assembly was called in consequence of internal, as well as of external troubles. Four
men [1] were appointed to go to Providence, two of whom
were empowered to make a list of the freemen, and to call
a meeting of all such to elect officers and deputies, and
to forbid any others from voting under peril of arrest as

---

[1] John Easton and Joshua Coggeshall, with Lott Strange and Joseph Torrey added for counsel.

CHAP.
IX.

1670.
March

25.

April
2.

11.

28.

May
4.

10.

12.

rioters. All names, titles and passages in the laws derogatory to the King, which under the various governments prior to the restoration had been used, were formally repealed ; but the laws in which they occurred were to be retained in full force. This was simply carrying out, more fully than had yet been done, the recommendation of the royal Commissioners on that point. A special commission was issued to the justices of Kings Province to arrest any person pretending authority from Connecticut, or elsewhere, who should presume to exercise jurisdiction in that province.

The Providence committee performed their duties by calling a town meeting, at which officers, selected from both the contending parties, were legally chosen. Affairs at Warwick proceeded less quietly. Writs were served upon the town clerk and upon Samuel Gorton, sen., and John Wickes, sen., two of the town Council, at the suit of the Attorney General, for debts due to the colony by the town on account of the old tax of 1664, and they were imprisoned. The town protested against this act as repugnant to the laws of England, and agreed to stand by their officers and each other in resisting it, in a paper entered upon their records and signed by nearly all the freemen. This difficulty was soon after settled.

At the general election the same officers were chosen, but John Clarke declining to serve again as Deputy Governor, Nicolas Easton was chosen in his place. In the choice of second Assistant from Providence, there being some doubt which of the rival candidates, William Harris or Arthur Fenner was elected, and neither being willing to serve under these circumstances, Roger Williams was chosen to that office. A committee was appointed, upon petition from Block Island, to obtain contributions for making a harbor there.

The Connecticut Assembly appointed a committee to meet such as Rhode Island might authorize, to treat on

the question of boundary at New London, with full powers to settle all disputes, and also in case Rhode Island
refused to treat, to reduce the people of Westerly and
Narraganset to submission. A letter to that effect was
sent to Gov. Arnold. The people of Stonington renewed
their former petition for redress. Gov. Winthrop now
took that manly stand, against the popular clamor, which
his own high sense of personal honor and of public right
dictated. In a formal message to his Legislature he dissented from the extreme course they had decided to adopt,
and refused, upon the ground of his agreement with Dr.
Clarke, to exercise jurisdiction east of the Pawcatuck
river until his Majesty's pleasure was further known, or
till the question should be settled by treaty. The Governor and Council of Rhode Island replied to the Connecticut letter, deprecating the threats it contained, expressing a desire for peace, and agreeing to the proposal
to send Commissioners to New London. A special session of the Assembly was called to appoint them. John
Greene, Assistant, Joseph Torrey, Recorder, and Richard
Bailey, Clerk of the Council, were empowered to treat on
the part of Rhode Island. Their instructions gave them
full powers, within the terms of the charter, and of the
decree of the royal Commissioners. The two committees
met at New London. The negotiations were conducted
entirely in writing, at the suggestion of the Rhode Island
men. They occupied three days, and embrace seventeen
letters. Connecticut claimed jurisdiction over Kings
Province by her charter. Rhode Island replied that that
only could mean Narraganset river, in the charter, which
was therein expressly described to be such. This was the
substance of the whole correspondence, which closed by
an assurance on the part of Rhode Island, that if Connecticut should attempt to usurp the government of
Kings Province she would appeal to the King. Thus
ended this fruitless effort at conciliation. The Connecti-

cut men, the same evening, read a declaration of their intention to establish a government at Westerly, and Wickford, in his Majesty's name. The next day they went to Stonington and formally proclaimed the authority of Connecticut over the people of Westerly, and summoned them, as being a part of the township of Stonington, to submit thereunto. They also issued a warrant to John Frincke to warn the inhabitants east of Pawcatuck river to appear the same day at Captain Gookin's house, in Stonington, to hear the proclamation, but they failing to obey the summons the paper was publicly read on Gookin's land. That night Frincke and two of his aids were arrested and sent to Newport jail, by James Babcock, sen., a Rhode Island officer, under a warrant issued by Tobias Saunders of Westerly. Saunders and Babcock were in turn arrested and brought before the Commissioners, to answer for the seizure of Frincke. They admitted the charge, defending it by virtue of their commissions as Rhode Island officers, and were discharged on bail. The next day news of these occurrences reaching Newport the Council was called together. A commission was issued to certain officers to proceed to Narraganset, there to forbid any one usurping government under authority from Connecticut, and to bring any such as prisoners to Newport, or in case of resistance, to read publicly the prohibition, and then to deliver it to the offending parties. The Connecticut Commissioners, with a force of fifty mounted men, went to Wickford on that day, proclaimed their government and read their charter. They then sent messengers to Petaquamscut, who were seized on the road, but were afterward delivered up on requisition. At this juncture the four men [1] sent by the Council at Newport reached Wickford, bringing the prisoner Frincke with them, and delivered their letter to the Connecticut officers. It was immediately answered in a

---

[1] Joseph Torrey, Richard Bailey, James Barker and Caleb Carr.

tone corresponding to the policy that Connecticut was now engaged, with a high hand, in carrying out. Harvard college had received a grant of five hundred acres of land in Southertown, at the time of the annexation by Massachusetts, and now petitioned Connecticut for relief against the people of Westerly. A similar proclamation to that at Stonington was set up at Wickford, nailed on the door of Captain Hudson's house, and local officers were appointed to administer the government in behalf of Connecticut. The like declaration was also made at Petaquamscut. The next day they went to Stonington and issued another proclamation, warning the Rhode Island officers not to exercise authority in Westerly, and enjoining upon the people of that town obedience to the magistrates, named in the paper, appointed by Connecticut. They also gave them liberty to use the County Court at New London for justice when required. Upon these bold proceedings being known, the Council of Rhode Island called a special session of the General Assembly to meet at Warwick on the following Wednesday. This was the first session under the new charter that had been held at any other place than Newport. The proximity of Warwick to the scene of disturbance doubtless occasioned this deviation from what had now become a settled usage. The charter named Newport as the place for the Assembly, but permitted it to be held " elsewhere, if urgent occasion doe require." The Assembly appointed Governor Arnold, as the agent of the colony, to proceed to England, there to defend the charter against the invasions of Connecticut ; or if he could not go, then Dr. John Clarke, who had obtained the charter, was appointed, with Capt. John Greene, Assistant, of Warwick, as joint agents for this object. The Governor was requested to write to Connecticut and the other colonies, as also to New York, on the same subject.

A debt of eighty pounds still due to Richard Dean

CHAP.
IX.

1670.
June.

21.

22.

23.

24.

29.

CHAP.
IX.
1 6 7 0.

July
2.

11.

12.

13.

14.

for services in obtaining the charter, was paid by a loan from private individuals to the colony, and a tax of three hundred pounds was levied to meet the expenses of the new agency. Of this tax Newport was assessed one hundred and twenty-three pounds, Providence and Portsmouth fifty-one each, Warwick thirty-two, Petaquamscot sixteen, Block Island fifteen, and Conanicut twelve pounds. The most favorable result of this Assembly was that it quieted the feeling of discontent, so rife in Warwick for six years past, if we may judge from the readiness with which the town now voted their portion of the new tax and of the arrears still due on the old one.

Gov. Arnold wrote a long and friendly letter to Gov. Winthrop, informing him of the preparations of the Assembly to appeal to the King in the autumn, attributing the conduct of Connecticut to the influence of men actuated by private interests, and also asking the surrender of a fugitive from Rhode Island, who had twice broken jail and was now harbored at Stonington.[1] The murder of Walter House by Thomas Flounders at Wickford, an act of private revenge, now served still further to complicate the difficulties between the two colonies. The Connecticut coroner held an inquest on the body. When the Rhode Island coroner came for that purpose he was denied access to the corpse. He forbade the burial, which however was performed. The Council at Newport ordered the body to be disinterred, that a legal inquest might be held, and sent a constable, with sufficient force, to arrest the murderer, and also those who had obstructed .the coroner, as well as any who might attempt to prevent the execution of this order. Thomas Stanton, one of the newly appointed magistrates at Stonington, wrote to Connecticut what had been done in the premises. The mur-

[1] This letter of July 11th, with all the papers relating to the acts of Connecticut, and of the joint commission from May 12th, are printed in R. I. Col. Rec., ii. 309–328, presenting a complete documentary history of this important period.

derer was arrested on the Rhode Island warrant and taken CHAP. IX. to Newport. Samuel Eldredge and John Cole, two of the Connecticut officers at Wickford, who had obstructed 1 6 7 0. July 15. those of Rhode Island, were also taken prisoners. Flounders was indicted for murder, and afterwards, in October, was tried and executed. The two officers were committed to the custody of the Sergeant till they should give bail to appear at the October Court. The Council of Connecticut appointed another constable at Wickford in 21 place of Eldredge, and issued warrants to arrest Samuel Wilson and Thomas Mumford, the Rhode Island officers who had torn down the declaration of authority that had been set up by the Commissioners at Hudson's house. They also wrote a letter to Rhode Island, complaining of the zeal with which she strove to maintain her rights over the Kings Province.

That the people of Connecticut were not unanimous in their approval of the conduct of their authorities in such high-handed proceedings, but that these were instigated, as Gov. Arnold intimates in his letter to Gov. Winthrop, by parties having private interests to subserve, appears, not only by the refusal of Winthrop to exercise jurisdiction, as Governor, east of Pawcatuck river, but also in a letter from Major John Mason of Norwich, to Aug. 31. the Connecticut Commissioners, enclosing that celebrated letter, recently received by him from Roger Williams, which contains so lucid a sketch of the early history of Rhode Island.[1] Mason, in this communication, deprecates the action of the Commissioners in Narraganset as unwise, and describes the territory to be gained as of doubtful value compared with the cost of contesting it, and significantly suggests that "the toll may prove to be more than the grist."

The General Assemblies of Connecticut and of Rhode Oct. 13.

[1] This important letter is printed at length in 1 M. H. C. i. 275–283, and in part in R. I. H. C., iii. 159–163.

Island met on the same day, one at Hartford, the other at Newport. The Connecticut Commissioners reported their proceedings at Narraganset, which were approved, and the officers named by them in Kings Province were confirmed. The former bounds of Southertown, as incorporated by Massachusetts, were granted to Stonington, which included the whole of Westerly. A new set of Commissioners, including one of the former body, were appointed to treat once more with Rhode Island on the questions at issue, and were invested with the same powers that their predecessors had received. Governor Winthrop sent in his resignation to this Court, but it was not accepted. The posture of affairs in Rhode Island is supposed to have influenced him in this step, as he had previously refused to violate his agreement with Clarke, and to trample on the rights of Rhode Island.

The Assembly at Newport issued new summons to the witnesses at Wickford to attend at the trial of Flounders, the former ones having been seized by a Connecticut officer before they could be served. A conciliatory letter was sent by two messengers to Connecticut, desiring that an easier mode of settling the differences than by appeal to England might be devised, and relying upon the temperate spirit of Gov. Winthrop's letter, it suggests a new commission, and that Connecticut meanwhile should forbear to exercise jurisdiction in the King's Province. To this overture Connecticut replied, approving the acts of her Commissioners in June, dissenting from the points of Gov. Arnold's letter of July, and accepting the proposal of a new treaty, but declining the proviso upon which the offer was made, that Connecticut should in the interval suspend the exercise of authority in Narraganset. This of course put an end to further negotiation, and Rhode Island resumed her preparations for a final appeal to the King. A special session of the Assembly was held, at which it was ordered that such persons as were qualified for public service in holding offices, should be made free-men by their respective towns, whether they desired it or not. This was a compulsory act, akin to that which im-posed a fine on any one elected to office who should refuse to serve, and presents a striking contrast to the spirit of later years on this subject. Summary means were adopted to collect the taxes levied for the purpose of sending agents to England. If not paid within two months the process of distraint was to be employed. The details of the act acquaint us with the market values of the chief articles of produce at that time. Pork was three pence, or two-and-a-quarter cents a pound ; butter, six pence ; wool, one shilling ; peas, three shillings and six pence a bushel ; wheat, five shillings ; Indian corn, three shil-lings ; oats, two shillings and three pence. A penny at that time was equal to a fraction less than three-quarters of a cent at the present day, and one shilling was about eight and one-quarter of our cents. Forty shillings of New England currency was then equal to thirty shillings sterling. For those who paid in silver coin of New Eng-land, one shilling was taken for two shillings in produce at the above rates.

By English statute the estate of a felon was forfeited. The murderer, Flounders, having been executed, the As-sembly restored to his widow the residue of his property, after deducting the expenses of his trial, as an act of mercy. Continued acts of violence on the part of Con-necticut again led to an extra session of the General As-sembly, the sole purpose of which was to pass an act con-fiscating the estates of those who presumed to exercise authority in Kings Province without a commission from Rhode Island, and also of those inhabitants of Westerly who should place their lands under the control of Con-necticut ; while the faith of the colony was pledged to make good any loss sustained by those who remained faithful.

CHAP.   The alarm of Indian war again aroused the colonies.
  IX.
         Gov. Prince wrote to Rhode Island concerning the suspi-
1671.   cious attitude of Philip of Pokanoket.   A council was
April
 11.   called to reply to the letter, and a conference, to be held
         at Taunton, was proposed, but for the present was post-
         poned.

May   The regular session of Assembly was held the day be-
  2.
         fore the election, for the admission of freemen.   At the
  3.   election John Clarke, who had been Deputy Governor the
         previous year but had declined office the past year, was
         again chosen to that place.   Another outrage occurred at
         Westerly.   Two of the Connecticut constables, while lay-
         ing out lands east of Pawcatuck river, were driven off by
         the Rhode Island officers, one of whom, John Crandall,
         was afterwards seized and taken to New London for trial.
         He applied to this Assembly for advice whether to give
         bonds or to go to prison.   They advised him to give no
         bond in any matter pertaining to his acts performed in
         maintaining his Majesty's authority in the colony, and as-
         sured him of protection.   This violence drew forth another
         letter to Connecticut, again tendering an appeal to the
         King as the only remaining solution of the difficulty.
 11.   The Hartford Assembly replied, reiterating their claim,
         but taking no notice of the proposed appeal ; to avoid
         which, if possible, they appointed another set of Com-
         missioners to open a new treaty with Rhode Island.   The
         General Assembly appointed meetings of the Court of
         Justices, that had been clothed by the royal Commission-
         ers with the exclusive jurisdiction of Kings Province, to
         be held at Westerly and other places, to examine the af-
         fairs of the province, and to restore quiet to its inhabit-
 16.   ants.   They accordingly met at Westerly, the Deputy
         Governor, John Clarke, presiding, and directed the Con-
         stable, James Babcock, to summon the people to attend
         on the morrow.   Babcock refused to obey, and was ar-
 17.   rested by order of the Court.   Another officer warned the

people to assemble, when the charter, the royal commission of the Justices, the agreement between Clarke and
Winthrop and other pertinent papers were read. The
meeting was disturbed by the intrusion of a mounted
force from Stonington, who asserted the authority of Connecticut, and ordered the Court to desist, but no collision
ensued. A written protest was delivered to the intruders,
maintaining the authority of Rhode Island. The freemen were then examined as to their fidelity, and nearly
all agreed to stand by the King and this colony. A dec-   18.
laration was issued by the Court, wherein John Crandall
and Tobias Sanders were confirmed as Justices, and the
reciprocal engagement of the colony to protect the people
of Westerly was affirmed. The Court then proceeded to
Petaquamscot, where, the inhabitants being assembled,   19.
similar proceedings were held without interruption, and
the Court adjourned to meet at Acquidneset. The proprietors there inquired if the Court claimed ownership of   20.
their lands in behalf of the colony, and upon being assured of the contrary, they readily gave their engagement
to Rhode Island, and elected officers, who were confirmed
by the Court.

All legal and peaceable means having thus been taken   June
to secure the loyalty of Kings Province, the General Assembly met at Newport. One Uselton, having been sen-   7.
tenced at the last Court of Trials to leave the island, but
still remaining, was brought before the Assembly, where
his conduct was so insulting that he was sentenced to be
whipped with fifteen stripes, and to be sent away forthwith, and if again found within the colony he was again
to be punished in the same manner. A burglar, under
sentence of death by the Court of Trials, petitioned for
reprieve, but was refused, and his execution was ordered
to take place without delay. The sum of three pence
per day was allowed for the support of each prisoner con-   9.
fined upon criminal process. Commissioners were again

CHAP.
IX.

1671.
June
14.

July
8.

21.

29.
appointed to treat with Connecticut, and a letter was sent to that colony reaffirming the authority of Rhode Island over Kings Province, until the King's will could be known, accepting the proposals for a new treaty, the Commissioners to meet at some place not within either colony, and proposing that the two agents, Dr. Clarke and Gov. Winthrop, should be present at such meeting. An active correspondence relating to Indian affairs was carried on with Plymouth. A letter from Gov. Prince, suggesting a conference at Taunton, was considered so important that the Council ordered copies of it to be sent to the other towns. The Connecticut Council replied to the last letter from Rhode Island, that they could not alter the place of meeting except by act of their General Court, to whom the proposal should be submitted at the next session.

Rumors of Indian hostilities again summoned the council at Newport, who wrote to Governor Prince, and the next day called a council of war to be held the following week, and ordered a troop of horse to attend as a guard. A special session of the Assembly was called at Newport. The vote of the previous year, appointing Dr. Clarke and John Greene as joint agents to conduct the appeal in England, was revised, and Clarke was named as sole agent for that purpose. His commission was directed to be made out by the Governor, and a new tax of two hundred and fifty pounds in silver was assessed. The accumulation of large tracts of land, upon the main, in the hands of a few persons incapable of improving so much, attracted the attention of the Assembly. While the tax necessary to the defence of these lands was onerous, the effect was to discourage many upon whom the burden rested without a hope of their sharing in the advantages of a freehold. The Assembly recommended that some of these wild lands be purchased on public account, that those in immediate want of land, or who might hereafter be received into the colony, could be supplied.

Upon a petition of the people of Westerly, the General Assembly of Connecticut promised them protection, and also a temporary cessation from all suits upon land titles, or for trespass, provided they peaceably submitted to her authority. The proposal in the Rhode Island letter of June was so far accepted that commissioners were authorized to settle all disputes, either by agreement with those of Rhode Island, or by a mutual reference of the subject to gentlemen selected from the other colonies, to meet at Rehoboth or in Boston, either in November or in April, and a letter to this effect was sent to Rhode Island. The General Assembly met at the usual time, and after hearing the correspondence read, adjourned one week to secure a further attendance of deputies. The alarm of war had subsided, as appears by a letter from the Assembly to Plymouth; but not so the troubles on their western borders. A reply was sent to Connecticut, selecting Seeconck, called also Rehoboth, as the place, and April as the time, to renew the attempt at a treaty; but further stating that the Rhode Island men would only be empowered to decide disputed questions of land title, and not the matter of jurisdiction, upon which they could concede nothing. To this end a committee was again appointed. When the letter reached Hartford, Governor Winthrop was absent, so that no definite answer could be returned.

Most of the towns were, as usual, in arrears for the last assessment, so that the act was renewed. Warwick refused to furnish her portion of it while the negotiation with Connecticut was yet in progress. At length a formal notice was sent by Connecticut, declining the meeting at Rehoboth, as a useless labor, unless the question of jurisdiction could be entertained. Thus ended, for the present, the attempt at negotiation.

Internal dissensions again occupied the attention of

CHAP.
IX.

1671-2.
Feb.

24.

March
5.

15.

1672.
March
25.

April
2.

the council. William Harris was now openly employed, on the side of Connecticut, against the chartered rights of Rhode Island, with a zeal and ability that could not be suffered to pass unnoticed. For this act of treason, whether real or constructive, a warrant was issued for his arrest, and he was committed to prison without bail, to await his trial at the May term.

An extra session of the Assembly was convened, at which John Clarke, for the third time within two years, was selected as the agent to appear for the colony before the King. The repeated renewal of this appointment, and the frequent revision of laws, especially in relation to taxes, arose from a feeling prevalent in those times, that the acts of one Assembly were not binding beyond the next session, unless then ratified ; each Assembly being in itself a sovereign body wielding the entire power of the colony. The absence of deputies from the mainland towns obliged the Assembly to dissolve, and a new one to be called, to meet speedily. At a town meeting in Providence deputies were elected for the next Assembly, which was to meet in April ; but as it was ascertained that these men would be unable to attend at that time, another town meeting was held,[1] to select such as could attend, and who were declared by the Assembly to be legally chosen.

A paper from William Harris was read, but not received, as it was not directed in a proper manner to the General Assembly. This being a full Assembly, the act of the previous one, appointing Clarke as the agent to England, and providing for his support, was renewed. It was also enacted, that no tax, raised for a specific purpose, should on any account be diverted to other uses, much harm having been sustained in this way by the colony. A very important bill was passed at this session, which deservedly caused great commotion among the people, and cost a large portion of the members their election. This

[1] New Year's day, old style, was 25th March.

was the famous sedition act, the origin of which appears, CHAP.
in the preamble, to have been the opposition made in the   IX.
several towns whenever a new tax was assessed.   The bill 1672.
declared that whoever opposed, by word or deed, in town   April
2.
meeting or elsewhere, any rate laid, or any other of the
acts and orders of the General Assembly, should be bound
over to the Court of Trials, or imprisoned till it met, at the
discretion of the justice, for " high contempt and sedition ;"
and if found guilty, should either be fined, imprisoned, or
whipped, as the Court might adjudge.   A bolder assertion
of the omnipotence of a Legislature could not be made,
and it speedily received the rebuke that it merited.   But
the act, severe as it appears, was not passed without reason.
The grasping spirit of Connecticut on one hand, the fearful symptoms of savage hostility on the other, and now
the evidence of treachery within, requiring prompt and
vigorous measures in the Government to provide means
of defence against these threatening calamities, dismember-
ment of territory and Indian war, would seem to justify the
assumption, for a time, of the almost dictatorial power herein usurped.   It was not intended to abridge the liberties of
the people, although represented to be so by George Fox,
the founder of the Friends, who was then in Rhode Island.
An Assembly that was subject to two, and often to three,
or four ordeals of popular election every year, could not do
that, or even attempt to do it.   But the framers of the bill
seem not to have reflected, amid the difficulties that surrounded them, upon the abuses to which such an act might
be perverted.   The people saw this directly, and within one
month, applied the remedy.

More violent proceedings, by the inhabitants of Stonington, than any that had yet occurred, demanded the attention of the Assembly.   They had crossed the river,
and by force and arms had carried away several persons in
Westerly to prison.   Redress was refused by Connecticut.
An act was now passed to confiscate the estates of the as-

sailants, being on the east of Pawcatuck river, and also those of such Westerly men who might be intimidated by these outrages into submission to Connecticut, while any damage sustained by those who remained faithful, was to be made good from the estates thus forfeited.

A committee was appointed to examine the waste lands in Narraganset, and to notify the owners, Indian or English, to appear at the May session to contract for a sale of the same to the colony. The schedule of salaries was revised, to ensure fuller attendance on the Assembly, and at the Court of Trials. The Governor was allowed six shillings, the deputy Governor, five shillings, the magistrates, four shillings, and the deputies, the same as by a former law, three shillings, for each day's attendance, with double fines in case of absence. A dinner was also to be provided each day, at public expense, for the whole Assembly, and also, during the Court of Trials, for the magistrates.

A further source of peril, and occasion of expense, was about to come upon the too heavily burdened colony. War was declared by England against the States General of the United Provinces, and letters warning the colonists to prepare for defence were forthwith despatched to America.

3.

30.
May
1.
The Assembly met as usual the day before election, and admitted many freemen. This election was the most remarkable one that had occurred for twenty years. The changes were almost complete, while repeated refusals to accept office threatened to leave some places unfilled. William Brenton was elected Governor, but refused to serve. He was absent in Taunton at the time, and as his answer could not be received for some days, the Court of election, after choosing the other officers, adjourned for two weeks, when Nicolas Easton was elected. His two sons were likewise chosen as general officers, John as Attorney, and Peter as Treasurer. John Cranston was made deputy Governor. Of the ten former Assistants. but four were

retained, while the change in the twenty deputies was entire, not a single one in the former Assembly being returned
from any town.

The charter and other important papers were always
kept in the custody of the Governor, who, on a new election, delivered them to his successor, taking a formal
receipt therefor from the committee appointed to receive
them. This was deemed so important that the receipt,
specifying the separate papers delivered, was usually entered upon the records. It was also the custom to open
every session of the Assembly by reading the charter,
thereby preserving fresh in the memory of the legislators,
the provisions of that fundamental instrument.

The Assembly adjourned for two weeks, after writing
a letter to Connecticut, requesting that Government not to
molest the people at Westerly, as it was intended soon to
propose a method of adjusting all difficulties. The Connecticut Assembly, as soon as it met, appointed new commissioners to treat with Rhode Island, and empowered
them, in case of failure, to establish their government in
Narraganset. They also wrote a conciliatory letter to
Rhode Island acceding to her request, and another to the
Westerly men, less mild in its import, requiring their submission until the treaty with Rhode Island was concluded.

The General Assembly met by adjournment, and having received Governor Brenton's refusal to return to office
elected Nicolas Easton Governor. Mr. Easton had been
for two years, President of the colony, just prior to the
usurpation of Coddington, and was more recently deputy
Governor for four years. The charter being then read, as
usual, the Connecticut question was at once debated.
Commissioners were appointed with full powers to treat,
and to conclude all differences, and a letter announcing
this fact, was sent by a special messenger. The subsequent correspondence upon this subject, for the next four
years, has not been preserved ; a loss of no great impor-

tance, as nothing more definite resulted from these writings than came from this renewed attempt to settle, by treaty, what could only be adjusted by the power that conferred the charters whose terms formed the basis of the dispute.

This done, the Assembly proceeded to undo the acts of their predecessors. This was performed as thoroughly as was the change effected by the recent elections. Not a single public act of the previous session remained unrepealed at the close of their labors, nor was there any new act passed by them. The mutability of legislation was never so perfectly exemplified. A preamble recites that " several acts and orders were made in the General Assembly in April last, some whereof seeminge to the infringeinge of the libertyes of the people of this colony, and settinge up an arbitrary power, which is contrary to the laws of England, and the fundamentall laws of this colony from the very first settling thereof, others seeminge much to the prejudice of the collony, and impoverishinge the people thereof, to the great disturbance and distraction of the good and well minded people thereof, who have many of them been sufferers in a great measure already, and like more to undergoe, if not timely prevented."

This strikes first at the sedition act, and then at the tax law, including the purposes for which the rate was laid. Accordingly, the sedition act was first repealed, the appointment of Clarke as agent to England, and the taxes for that object, were cancelled, the schedule of salaries was then rescinded, leaving them as fixed by the old law, the commission upon waste lands in Narraganset was revoked, as if it contemplated a forced sale by the owners to the colony, the confiscation of estates in Westerly was declared void, and finally, upon a complaint made by Arthur Fenner, a censure was passed upon the April Assembly, for having sanctioned the second election of deputies in Providence, after it was found that those first elected

could not attend.   The bitterness of party spirit could go
no farther, and the Assembly adjourned.

But the conduct of the Assembly was severely con- 1672.
demned in some portions of the colony.   The Assistants
and deputies of Warwick dissented, in behalf of their
town, from the action in reference to Connecticut.   To
them it appeared like a concession of rights that was not
to be tolerated.   The town sustained the views of its rep- 3.
resentatives, and at a full meeting, called for the purpose,
agreed " to oppose to the uttermost the intrusions of Con- 15
necticut," and engaged, at their own expense, with the aid
of those freemen in the other towns, who might be willing
to unite therein, to maintain the appeal to the King, and
to send an agent to England for that purpose.   This noble
and spirited pledge, signed by all of the town council, and
of the freemen present at the meeting, is still preserved in
the records of that ancient town.

The declaration of war with Holland caused meetings
of the council, at which measures were taken to proclaim 16.
it in all the towns, and afterward to place the colony in a
posture of defence.   Richard Smith was intrusted with 25.
these duties in Kings Province.   Letters to the other New
England colonies were also prepared, proposing a conference on these matters, as suggested in the King's letter.

A new subject of agitation now arose.   Rhode Island
had long been taunted by her Puritan neighbors, as the
refuge of every kind of religious or political vagary.   In
the fierce persecution to which the Quakers had been subjected, she offered a free asylum to the oppressed, and resisted alike the threats and the entreaties by which it was
sought to force her from her fidelity to the cause of religious freedom.   The security which this firmness afforded
to the preachers of the new sect, led Rhode Island to become a favorite resort of many of the followers of Fox, who
came hither from England and Barbadoes, to disseminate July.
their doctrines, as from a central point whence they might

easily make excursions in all directions through the American colonies. Their great leader himself spent two years in America, and was at this time in Rhode Island, together with Edmundson, Burnyeat, Stubbs, and Cartwright, all active and eloquent missionaries of the new faith. Everywhere, except in Rhode Island, toleration of doctrine implied, in the main, concurrence of sentiment. Hence it was asserted that the public feeling of this colony was friendly to the theology of Fox, and the assertion carried greater weight because, at this time, some of the magistrates were of that sect. Roger Williams, as the peculiar champion of intellectual freedom, wished to give evidence at the same time, of the devotion of his colony to the cause of " soul liberty," and of their dissent from the teachings of George Fox. " I had in my eye the vindicating of this colony for receiving of such persons, whom others would not. We suffer for their sakes, and are accounted their abettors." How could he better effect this object than by showing that the new doctrine was not generally accepted in Rhode Island, although its followers were not only protected here, but were admitted to the highest places of government? For this purpose, Williams drew up a paper containing fourteen propositions, denouncing in strongest terms, the tenets of Quakerism, and challenged Fox and his adherents to a public discussion of seven of these points at Newport, and of the remainder at Providence. For this he has been charged with inconsistency, and accused of persecuting the Quakers! In our day there appears indeed to be more of zeal than of wisdom in the conduct of this controversy. Yet, although he strenuously condemned the teachings of the Friends, and performed a marvellous feat of physical and mental labor to oppose them, he would have laid down his life sooner than have a hair of their heads injured on account of their doctrinal views. The qualities that enabled him to accomplish the one would have sustained him equally in the

15.

other. It should be remembered also that these public
disputes, upon points of dogmatic theology, were as common in Europe and America, in those times, as political
discussions are in our own day. In Germany especially,
for more than a century, they had furnished the arena for
those brilliant displays of intellectual gladiatorship which,
in the progress of civilization, had succeeded the martial
strifes of the feudal ages.

The challenge was sent, through some friends of Fox,
to Deputy Governor Cranston, to be delivered by him to
the Quaker apostle. Several days elapsed before Cranston received it, and meanwhile Fox had left the island.
Just before his departure he wrote a singular paper to
Thomas Olney, jr., and John Whipple, jr., at Providence,
known as " George Fox's instructions to his friends,"
which was answered with unseemly severity, the following year, by Olney, in a lengthy article entitled " Ambition anatomised." Fox's departure excited a suspicion
that the challenge was purposely retained until he had
gone away, which gave rise to an unbecoming pun by
Williams about " George Fox's *slily* departing."

The most remarkable incident connected with this
controversy was that Mr. Williams, then seventy-three
years of age, rowed himself in a boat from Providence to
Newport to engage in it. The effort occupied an entire
day. He reached his destination near midnight before
the appointed morning. The discussion was held in the
Quaker meeting-house and lasted three days. His opponents were three of the disciples of Fox, before named.
Burnyeat and Stubbs were able and learned men, and all
of them were well trained in the school of polemic divinity. Williams' brother Robert, then a teacher in Newport, offered to aid him in the discussion, but was prevented by his opponents. The first seven propositions
being concluded, the debate was resumed at Providence
by Edmundson and Stubbs, but continued only one day.

CHAP.
IX.

1 6 7 2.
July.

26.

25.

Aug.
8.

9
to
12.

17.

CHAP. That no immediate good resulted from the discussion, or
IX.   that there was more of human frailty than of Christian
1672. meekness displayed in the mode of conducting it, is not
Aug.   surprising. But the object of Williams was attained in
opposing what he held to be error, while defending the
principles upon which that error was tolerated, as being
a matter beyond the pale of human legislation.[1]

July.   A most unexpected invasion of the rights of Rhode
Island occurred at this time. Among the many worthless grants with which the Council of Plymouth overlaid
their boundless dominion, was one to the Earl of Stirling,
that embraced a large part of Maine, and included also
Nantucket, Martha's Vineyard and Long Island, with the
adjacent islands. This right he afterwards sold to James,
Duke of York, brother and successor of Charles II., on
whom the King, in his reckless bestowal of empire in the
new world, likewise conferred a large portion of the recent conquests from the Dutch, including the present
State called after his title. Prudence Island, originally
purchased by Roger Williams and Gov. Winthrop, sen.,
had long since passed out of their hands, and was now
the property of John Paine, a merchant of Boston. He
had contributed liberally to rebuild fort James, at New
25.   York, and now received from Gov. Lovelace, as attorney
of the Duke of York, a grant of Prudence island, to be
held as a free manor, by the name of Sophy Manor, for
an annual quit-rent of two barrels of cider and six pairs
Aug.   of capons. The following week the grant was confirmed,
1.

---

[1] We have before had occasion to refer the reader to dull treatises upon
doctrinal theology, where he may verify, if he chooses, the statements of the
text. There are many authorities whence the above account is derived,
which the theological student or the devout antiquary can consult for the details of this famous dispute. Williams' own account is in a book of over 300
pages, entitled "George Fox digged out of his Burrowes." The opposite
side is given in "A New England Firebrand Quenched," written by Fox and
Burnyeat in reply to the foregoing. See also "A Journal of the Life, &c., of
William Edmundson," London, 1713; "The Truth Exalted;" Burnyeat's
Memoirs, London, 1691 · and Knowles' Roger Williams, pp. 336–40.

and Paine was made Governor for life, with a Council to
be chosen from the inhabitants of the island, of whom
there were now a considerable number, and Courts for the
trial of small causes were established, larger ones to be
tried at the New York assizes. The seventh article of
the constitution of government contained in this grant
asserted the principle of religious freedom, as then understood abroad, limiting it to Christians, and requiring dissenters to aid in support of the church established by the
authorities of the place. On account of further pay-
ments made by Paine towards fort James he was relieved
from quit-rent, and the island was released from all taxes.
The estate was held by him in fee simple, and was now
an absolutely independent government, the smallest in
America. A few days later Paine's commission as Governor for life of Sophy Manor was confirmed. It will be
seen that this act of Lovelace was a great stretch of the
Stirling grant, and might with equal justice have included Acquednick, as the Plymouth Council patents
were long anterior to the first charter of Providence Plantations. Prudence island had pertained to Portsmouth
since the first settlement of Acquednick.

This act of intrusion aroused the spirit of the colony.
Paine was at once arrested and thrown into prison, as appears from the acts of the Council of New York, but was
discharged on bail. He wrote a long letter to Lovelace,
giving an account of the conflict of patents in Rhode Island, and of his own difficulties from that source. At
the Court of Trials he was indicted, under the law of
1658, for attempting to bring in a foreign jurisdiction,
and found guilty. The pleadings are preserved among
the records of New York. The matter was finally settled,
as many other difficulties were in those times, by tacit
consent, without any formal act of adjustment, and Prudence island quietly relapsed from the condition of inde-

CHAP.
IX.

1672.
Aug.

7.

Sept.
6.

9.

Oct.
23.

CHAP. IX.

pendent sovereignty to its early dependence on the town of Portsmouth.

1672. Oct.

Certain men in Westerly petitioned the Assembly at Hartford to be incorporated as a distinct plantation, and to be released from fines incurred and from taxes for one year. To this it was answered, that, being a part of Stonington, the first request could not be granted, but that the fines should be remitted, and also the colony tax, but not the town rate or the minister's dues.

16.

Nov. 6.

The General Assembly incorporated Block Island, and at the request of the inhabitants named it New Shoreham, "as signs of our unity and likeness to many parts of our native country." The freemen were authorized to choose two Wardens, who should have the power of Justices of the Peace, and to add three other good men to compose the town Council, who were to hold quarterly meetings, to see that a registry of births, marriages and deaths was kept by the Clerk, and to conduct the trial of causes under five pounds. The town was to send two Deputies to the Assembly, which had not been done since the year the island was annexed to the colony, and was not done for some years after this time. New Shoreham thus became the sixth town received into the colony, and was in reality at this time the fifth, since the controversy with Connecticut had practically withdrawn Westerly from all participation in colonial affairs.

The care of our ancestors to prevent any important act from becoming a law, without a fair expression of the will of the people, has been often illustrated in the course of this work. The neglect of deputies to attend the General Assembly led to further legislation on this subject. As the charter vested the full powers of the Assembly in the Governor and Council in cases of invasion, it was enacted, that in sudden emergencies of this sort the acts of the Assembly should be binding although but few deputies were present; but as the bill of rights of

third Charles I., protected the subject from any tax not
levied by consent of Parliament, it was declared that no
rate should be assessed upon the colony without a full
representation from all the towns ; neither could any act
affecting the King's honor, or the people's liberties, be
valid unless a majority of the deputies were present. The
pay of the deputies was reduced to two shillings a day,
and the fine for absence from any Assembly was laid at
twenty shillings, or double that amount if a quorum was
not present. The deputies were also, for the first time,
required to take an engagement, to be administered by
the Governor, upon entering on the duties of their office.
This was an innovation that met with strenuous opposition from the mainland towns. The owners of the Atherton purchase petitioned for relief from the law by which
their land was forfeited. Their prayer was granted, by a
repeal of the act so far as it applied to their direct purchase. Their title was confirmed, with a proviso that no
lawful complainant should be debarred from his right of
action by any thing contained in the said act of confirmation.

It would seem that the separate powers of the magistrates were not distinctly defined or well understood, for
a censure was passed upon John Greene, Assistant of
Warwick, for having granted, by his own authority, a bill
of divorce. This proceeding was sharply reproved by the
Assembly, as being a usurpation of judicial power in su-
perseding the action of the Court of Trials. The town
of Warwick declared the divorce to be legal, and protested against this censure upon their leader, and also
against the acts in favor of the Atherton company, and
that requiring the engagement to be taken by the deputies, as being repugnant to the accepted law of the colony. A remonstrance prepared by the clerk was adopted
at a special town meeting, and copies were ordered to be
sent to the other towns and to the General Assembly.

CHAP.
IX.

1672.
Nov.
6.

1672-3.
Jan.
23.

25.

CHAP.
IX.   When this body met, the Warwick deputies refused to
1673.   take the engagement, although all the others conformed
May   to the new law.   Governor Easton was re-elected.   For the
7.   office of deputy Governor, four persons were successively
chosen and declined, until William Coddington accepted.
This was the first public office he had held since the usurpation, except that once he had been a deputy, and then
an Assistant from Newport.[1]   Richard Smith was again
chosen an Assistant, but declined, having then in view the
acceptance of an appointment from Connecticut.   The
change in the list of Assistants was as great as it had been
at the former election, but three of the old set remaining.
William Harris having cleared himself of the charges
against him, and given satisfaction to the Court, was again
elected an Assistant.   Of the old deputies less than one-
half were returned.   The general officers remained nearly
as before.   The only act, worthy of notice, was the appointment of a committee to consult with all the chief sachems
upon some means for preventing the excess of drunkenness,
to which the Indians were addicted.

15.   The Connecticut Assembly again appointed resident
magistrates in Kings Province, and made Richard Smith
president of the court thus erected.

July   The capture of New York by a Dutch fleet, caused a
30.   special session of the General Assembly, to provide against
an expected assault upon this colony.   A pension act was
Aug.   passed for the relief of those who might be wounded in the
13.   war, or of the families of the slain, who were to apply to
the general Treasurer for necessary support, and if they
failed to obtain it from him, they were to have an action
of debt against him, to be prosecuted in their behalf, by
the proper officers, free of charge.   An exemption act was
likewise passed in favor of those whose consciences were
opposed to war.   A very long and curious preamble recites
the scriptural and other arguments against war, by reason

---

[1] In 1666 he was deputy, and in 1667 an assistant.

of which the Quakers were excused, with a proviso requiring them to do civil duty, in removing the sick and aged,
and valuable property, out of harm's way, in keeping watch,
although without arms, and in performing any other duty
of a civil nature that might be required by the magistrates.   At the next session, these acts were confirmed, and
a lengthy statute against selling liquor to the Indians, was
passed.   The committee on this subject had consulted
with the sachems, at whose request heavy penalties were
imposed upon Indians found drunk, as well as on the dealers who made them so.   A Sunday law was enacted to restrain gaming and tippling on that day, but with careful
reservations, for the liberty of conscience, that the act
should not be construed as enforcing attendance upon, or
absence from religious services.   The quaintness of many of
these early statutes is not more remarkable than the earnestness with which they insist that nothing therein contained shall be construed as permitting any violation of the
fundamental principles of the colony.   The preambles to
the exemption act, and to the Sunday law, are striking examples of this watchfulness.

The last two had been extra meetings of the Assembly.
These, although of frequent occurrence, never superseded
the regular sessions prescribed in the charter, although but
a few weeks, or even days, sometimes intervened.   An Indian being about to be tried for the murder of another, the
Assembly ordered that one-half the jury should be composed of Indians, and that Indian testimony might be received in such cases, which was not allowed when Englishmen were the sole parties.   The accounts of John Clarke
had not yet been settled.   Four hundred and fifty pounds
was claimed by him, as still due from the colony.   William Harris was empowered to negotiate with Dr. Clarke,
in writing, upon this matter, to examine the items of the
claim, and to report to a future Assembly.

At the next general election, William Coddington was

CHAP.
IX.

1674.
May
6.

chosen Governor and John Easton deputy Governor.   The offices of Treasurer and Attorney General were united in Peter Easton, the late Treasurer, his brother, the late Attorney, being now deputy Governor.   The Assistants remained nearly the same.   The deputies were always changing more or less.   The office was esteemed a burden, which but few would assume for more than one or two sessions as required by law.

The people of Narraganset felt the want of certainty in their condition of Government, and desired the Assembly to settle this point, for which purpose a committee was appointed.   It was quite common for the Assembly to take a recess of several days, in which the Court of Trials was held. This was now done, and at the remeeting, the difficulties which the conflict of jurisdiction caused in the business of the Courts, led to the passage of an act, by which any person summoned as a witness was freed from liability to arrest, during his attendance on the court.

18.

The events of this year were few and unimportant. The news of peace between England and Holland removed the chief source of solicitude to the colonists.   The Connecticut Assembly confirmed the Massachusetts grants of land in Westerly to Harvard college, and to divers individuals, and also, upon petition of Wickford men, established a Court there, and soon proclaimed the same in due form at that place, and afterwards appointed a Court to meet at Stonington, in behalf of the people of Narraganset, which was never held.[1]   These demonstrations were lightly regarded, and were effectually met by the Governor and council, who proceeded to Narraganset, and established the township of Kingston ; which act was approved by the Assembly, and Kingston was incorporated as the seventh town of the colony, upon the same terms with New Shoreham.   The excise of liquors which, by an old law, pertained to each town, was now ordered to go into the general treas-

20.

22.

June
12.
Oct.
8.

28.

---

[1] Conn. Col. Rec, ii. 227, 231, 246.

ury, and was to be farmed out to an officer engaged for CHAP.
IX.
the purpose, who might regulate the quantity to be used.
The probate of wills, which heretofore had been in the head 1674.
officer of the town, was at this session vested in the town
councils.

At the next general election, the same officers were 1675.
continued with uncommon unanimity. The only subject May
5.
of interest that was acted upon, was that of weights and
measures. These were ordered to be procured of the English standard, and one man in each town was to inspect
and to seal with an anchor, all that were in use, in conformity therewith.

The quiet that, for the past few months, had every
where prevailed, was not unlike that ominous calm which,
in the natural world, so often precedes some fearful convulsion of the elements. Slowly, but surely, for many
years, the storm of Indian war had been gathering. At
times the clouds had loomed above the horizon, and the
mutterings of discontent had warned the colonists, as the
rumbling of distant thunder foretells the approaching
tempest. We have seen how active preparations were
made at such times to avert the danger, and with apparent
success. But the clouds were only broken, not dispersed.
An unusual period of peace had lulled to fancied security
the unsuspecting English ; but this time had been employed by the great leader of the native tribes in perfect-
ing his secret plans. The moment had now arrived when June.
the terrible truth should be revealed. The massacre at
Swanzey startled all New England with the fearful vengeance that for years had been brooding in the dark mind
of Philip of Pokanoket.

Three men, remarkable in the history of Rhode Island
as pioneers of the infant settlements, passed away as the
clouds of war arose to threaten the destruction of their life
labors. William Blackstone deceased [1] but a few days be-

---

[1] May 26th, 1675, ante, chap. iv.

fore his dwelling, on the banks of the Seekonk, was destroyed by the savages. John Weeks, one of the founders
of Warwick, was butchered by the Indians at the commencement of hostilities, and Governor Nicolas Easton
died soon after at Newport. He was indeed a pioneer.
In the spring of 1634 [1] he landed in New England with
his two sons, Peter and John, and the following spring
they commenced the settlement of Agawam, or Newberry.
Three years later, they built the first English house in
Hampton, whence they removed to Pocasset, in consequence
of the Antinomian controversy, the same year. The next
spring they went to Newport, and there again erected the
first European dwelling, and in 1663, they built the first
windmill on the island.[2] Governor Easton was several
times chosen an Assistant, and was for two years, prior to
the usurpation of Coddington, President of the colony under the first patent, and again for the two years previous
to his death, he was elected Governor under the second
charter. His sons became equally distinguished, and to
one of them, John, now deputy Governor of the colony, we
are indebted for an authentic history of the war which we
are about to narrate.

------- ••• -------

APPENDIX C.

ERRORS OF GRAHAME AND CHALMERS.

Grahame in his History of North America, vol. i. p.
373, edition 1833, says :—

"The colony of Rhode Island had received the tidings of the restoration with much real or apparent satisfaction. It was hoped that

[1] May 14th, 1634.
[2] These facts are chiefly taken from marginal notes in the handwriting of
Peter Easton, in an old copy of Morton's Memorial, now owned by his de-
scendant, J. Alfred Hazard, Esq., of Newport.

the suspension of its charter by the Long Parliament would more than compensate the demerit of having accepted a charter from such authority; and that its exclusion from the confederacy of which Massachusetts was the head, would operate as a recommendation to royal favor. The King was early proclaimed; and one Clarke was soon after sent as deputy from the colony to England, in order to carry the dutiful respects of the inhabitants to the foot of the throne, and to solicit a new charter in their favor. Clarke conducted his negotiation with a baseness that rendered the success of it dearly bought. He not only vaunted the loyalty of the inhabitants of Rhode Island, while the only proof he could give of it was, that they had bestowed the name of *Kings Province* on a territory which they had acquired from the Indians; but meeting this year the deputies of Massachusetts at the Court, he publicly challenged them to mention any one act of duty or loyalty shown by their constituents to the present King or his father, from their first establishment in New England. Yet the inhabitants of Rhode Island had taken a patent from the Long Parliament in the commencement of its struggle with Charles II., while Massachusetts had declined to do so when the Parliament was at the height of its power and success."

In the London edition, 1836, p. 315, some slight verbal alterations appear in the above passages, which do not affect their purport. In the revised American edition the word "baseness" is changed to the expression "suppleness of adroit servility," which is equally inaccurate and unjust. The harsh charge here laid upon Dr. Clarke was rebutted by Mr. Bancroft in a note to chap. xi. vol. ii. p. 64, edit. 1837, of his History of the United States, wherein he says: "the charge of baseness is Grahame's own invention," an expression, perhaps, in itself too severe to apply to the learned and friendly Briton, whom Mr. Bancroft in the same note says, "is usually very candid in his judgments," since the accusation of "baseness" was not invented by Grahame, but was evidently the result of his misapprehension of the authority he cites—the partisan historian Chalmers. After the emendation appeared in the revised edition, Mr. Bancroft, in 1841, softened the charge of invention to that of "unwarranted misapprehension," in which he is fully sustained by the facts.

This note occasioned a prolonged controversy between Mr. Bancroft and Mr. Quincy, the American editor of Grahame's history, upon the merits of which we do not propose to touch, only so far as injustice has been done therein to Rhode Island, in the attempt to display the superior honesty and candor of the Massachusetts agents at the expense of Clarke. The passages in Chalmers' Political Annals, Book I. chap. xi. p. 273, 274–6, cited by Grahame, as his authority for the above quoted remarks on Rhode Island, read as follows. After referring to the exclusion of Rhode Island from the New England league, owing to the dislike felt in Massachusetts for her liberal principles, he says :—

"Necessity therefore obliged them to provide for their security by other means. They cultivated the friendship of the neighboring sachems with the greatest success; whereby they acquired considerable influence over their minds, which was of considerable importance. And that ascendancy they employed, during the year 1644, to procure from the chiefs of the Narragansets a formal surrender of their country, which was afterwards called the Kings Province, to Charles I., in right of his crown, in consideration of that protection which the unhappy monarch then wanted for himself. Yet no measure could be more offensive to Massachusetts, or could provoke more her resentment; because it was equally inconsistent with her usual practice and present views of acquiring the subjection of the same territory to herself. The deputies of these plantations boasted to Charles II. of the merits of this transaction, and at the same time ' challenged the agents of Boston to display any one act of duty or loyalty shown by their constituents to Charles I. or to the present King, from their first establishment in New England.' The challenge thus confidently given was not accepted." p. 273. " That event [the Restoration] gave great satisfaction to these plantations, because they hoped to be relieved from that constant dread of Massachusetts which had so long afflicted them. And they immediately proclaimed Charles II., because they wished for protection, and intended soon to beg for favors. They not long after sent Clarke as their agent to the Court of that monarch, to solicit for a patent, which was deemed in New England so essential to real jurisdiction. And in September, 1662, he obtained the object of his prayers. Yet, owing to the opposition of Connecticut, the present charter was not finally passed till July, 1663."

The remainder of the reference contains an abstract of the charter, and some erroneous statements of the action had under it, to which we shall hereafter refer.

Now, admitting, for the moment, that Chalmers is good authority, which we shall presently disprove, so far at least as regards this portion of his annals, an examination of the foregoing quotations from the two authors will show that Mr. Grahame has drawn two erroneous inferences, not warranted by his citations, and has stated them as facts. First, that the name of Kings Province was a proof, and, as he states, "the only proof" that Clarke could give of the "vaunted loyalty of the inhabitants of Rhode Island." Chalmers, it will be seen, says parenthetically, that the surrendered country "was *afterwards* called the Kings Province," which is correct, but is very different from the statement of Grahame. The fact is, that the name of Kings Province first appears in the instructions to the commissioners, at the head of whom was Col. Nicholls, who were sent by the King to visit New England, and were furnished with three sets of instructions regulating their conduct, one as to Massachusetts, one as to Connecticut, and the other secret, all dated 23d April, 1664, and also a commission to determine appeals, boundary disputes, &c., dated two days later. They are in New England Papers, bundle 1, pp. 182–194, in the British State Paper Office. Article 3 of the set of instructions for Connecticut relates to the Rhode Island boundary, and in article 4, referring to the submission of the Narraganset sachems, it orders that if it prove true, the commissioners should take rent from the occupants, and shall call the country Kings Province. This order took effect on 20th March following, by formal proclamation of the commissioners, as appears in New England Papers, vol. iii. p. 4, British State Paper Office, printed in 3 R. I. H. Col., 179–81. This is the earliest mention of the name of Kings Province, which was given by royal decree, nearly two years after the Rhode Island charter was issued, and in relation to the time of the submission by the sachems just twenty years " afterwards." Upon this point then Chalmers is correct and Grahame wrong.

The second false statement in which Grahame is not borne out by his authority is that Clarke " *meeting this year* (1662) the deputies of Massachusetts, challenged them to mention any one act of duty or loyalty shown by their constituents." A due attention to the above extract will show that Chalmers says no such thing. The faulty connection of the passage would perhaps give to a cursory reader the idea received by Grahame, and very distinctly and injuriously perpetuated by him. Chalmers' words are obscure, it is true, relating to another and later affair, as will directly be shown ; but certainly Mr. Grahame, before thus cruelly assailing Clarke, should have examined the authority to which Chalmers refers. He would have there found that Chalmers' citation was not to Clarke's conduct, but to a very different point, and he would thus have been led either to suspect the accuracy of the Annalist, or to discover his own misapplication of his language. Upon these two points, therefore, Mr. Grahame has erred in drawing inferences that are not sustained by his authorities, and as he has thus done a great wrong—all the greater from the acknowledged excellence of his character and general accuracy of his work—we have felt compelled to furnish what we consider as the proof of unpardonable carelessness in a historian. The only other reference which he gives, Hazard ii. 612, is to a copy of the charter.

It really seems as if Mr. Bancroft's charge of " invention," or rather of " unwarranted misapprehension," was not so unfounded as has been represented, or so unjustifiable, when we consider the pains that a writer of history is morally bound to bestow upon his work before assailing the private character or the public acts of any man whom he has occasion to mention ; and also when we see, as in these two points, how Mr. Grahame has distorted the authority upon which he relies. The note and reference attached to this passage of Chalmers, the first one before quoted, reads thus : " There is a copy of the Indian Surrender in New England Papers, bundle 3 ; and see the same, p. 25," the latter clause referring plainly enough to the document whence his extract is made. That document could be found in five minutes by the clerks in the State Paper Office, and placed before any applicant authorized by government to have access to its archives. The British Government are very liberal in granting permission, even to foreign students of history, who apply for this privilege, only limiting their range of research, in the case of Americans at least, with the commencement of the revolution. A British subject would, of course, as easily obtain entrance, and without such limitation. That Mr. Grahame did not use the privilege to verify his authority in this case is evident. The paper referred to is a " Petition of the Warwick deputies (Randall Holden and John Greene) to the Board of Trade, together with their reply to the Massachusetts agents," who on the 30th July, 1678, had answered a complaint made by the Warwick men, wherein was exposed the former conduct of Massachusetts toward Gorton and his company. The document embraces four pages, 24–27 of the volume, or bundle, and on page 25, the precise reference of Chalmers, occur the words, or nearly those, quoted by him. The aggravated circumstances of that case justified the challenge of the Warwick deputies, and the silence of those of Massachusetts, was a discreet reserve for which they could hardly be expected to receive the praises of any man conversant with the facts. Chalmers' obscurity and Grahame's oversight have furnished Mr. Quincy with an occasion for undue elation in contrasting the conduct of the two colonies at this time. We only regret that he should lend the sanction of his revered and distinguished name to the slander against Clarke, and to the defamation of Rhode Island. (See 3 Mass. Hist. Colls., vol. ix. p. 28, note, and " The Memory of the late James Grahame Vindicated," 8vo. 59 pp. Boston, 1846, *passim*.)

If, as he says, "The agents of Massachusetts would not condescend, for the sake even of saving their charter, to feign a sentiment which they were sensible had no existence," it is more than can be said of the general Court that deputed them, the first article of whose instructions to them is to "present us to his Majesty as his *loyal* and *obedient* subjects." (Hutchinson's Collections, 355.) Whatever else we may render to our sister colony as her just due, it is not in the qualities of honesty or of candor that Rhode Island or John Clarke should yield the palm to Massachusetts or her agents.

We have now to examine the reliability of Chalmers himself, with particular reference to chapter xi. on Rhode Island. No one can read the "Political Annals" without being impressed with the partisan spirit of that work. If the reader were ignorant of the circumstances of the author's life, he could scarcely fail to discover the principal points of it from a perusal of his pages. The bitterness of the loyalist refugee appears in the title-page, and is conspicuous to the last passage of his book. He writes in 1780, when the Declaration of Independence had been four years in operation, and but a faint hope remained that the prerogative of the crown could ever be re-established in America, and yet he styles the country "the present United Colonies," and he closes the volume with a formal denial of the "immutable truths" upon which that Declaration is based. Whenever an opportunity occurs to flout the principles of freedom by maligning the motives of its friends, he does so with an evident satisfaction which he takes no pains to conceal. An honest regard to the truth of history is everywhere secondary to his hatred of civil and religious liberty. With such sentiments for a groundwork it is only remarkable that his statements should be received without suspicion, and his ample references taken without verification by writers who, like Grahame, are imbued with opposite opinions. The position he held as a Secretary of the Board of Trade, to whose custody the colonial archives were intrusted, and the fulness of his references to original papers, have so long given currency to his work as the highest authority, that it seems bold at this day to question its correctness upon any point of colonial history. Nor would the writer venture to do so now except upon the clearest evidence, and because in the chapter that most concerns us the spirit of the author is more than usually apparent, and his erroneous statements have done more than those of all others to misrepresent the motives and the conduct of our ancestors.

Chalmers was born in Scotland, studied law in Edinburg, emigrated to America, and practised at the bar of Maryland for ten years. As a stanch loyalist, he returned home at the time of the revolution. There he devoted himself to historical pursuits. His situation with the Board of Trade was not obtained till six years after the publication of the Annals, when it was bestowed as a reward of his loyalty, and as a compensation for the sufferings he had endured. It is evident, however, that he had free access to the colonial papers before his appointment in that office. His ability is unquestionable ; but the facts we have stated require that discretion should be exercised in perusing the Annals, and demand the application of the severest canons of historical criticism, before receiving as truth the statements and deductions therein presented. As a general rule, in this case it may be said that whatever Chalmers states favorably for the colonists may be relied upon. The evidence must be very clear to his mind when he does so. Whatever he

states as fact unfavorable to them requires that his references should be verified, and if no reference is given, the
statement would more safely be thrown aside.   Whatever
he offers as a deduction from stated facts, as philosophy,
or as " remarks," should for the most part be discarded,
as being only the reflections of a mind opposed at every
point to the principles of the colonists, and hence unable
to appreciate their motives.   And finally, those statements that are susceptible of confirmation by the archives
of the plantations, kept by the Board of Trade, are in
the main reliable, while those which could only be verified
by the records of the colonies themselves, as being chiefly
matters of local concern, should not be credited without
examination of the original evidence in this country.
There is not an American colony that has not suffered
injustice in some way by this work, through those who
have blindly relied upon its accuracy ; and none more so
than Rhode Island.   To specify the errors of fact and of
inference contained in the single chapter upon this State,
would be tedious and superfluous.   Suffice it to say, that
the comments upon the charter near the close of the chapter begin with an error of date, and are so interwoven
with misstated facts and partial truths, and so colored by
party biases, as to destroy the value of the whole.

APPENDIX D.

CORRESPONDENCE BETWEEN THE ATHERTON COMPANY AND
JOHN WINTHROP, Jr., AGENT FOR CONNECTICUT, IN LONDON.

FROM MSS. TRUMBULL PAPERS, VOL. XXII., NOS. 38, 47 AND 45, IN THE AR-
CHIVES OF THE MASS. HIST. SOCIETY.

I.

BOSTON, 29th Sept., 1661.

Hon'rd Sr.—After our services presented to yo'selfe we make
boulde to request this favor to be added to al yo'r former, considering
it may be for our further comforte to have the Lands wee have at

Narragansett in some pattent and yo^rselfe being now in England and
having an interest with ourselves therein, we conceave that if you
could procure them into Connecticut pattent it would be best, and
therefore if you could procure the line to runne alonge from Conecticot by the Bays pattent til it meete with Plimoth pattent, and then
by plimoth pattent tile it come into Naraganset Bay and soe into the
sea, and bounded by the sea til it meete with the further parte of Conecticot jurisdiction with all the islands adjoyncing it would reach y^e
whole.   But notwithstanding this our advice wee desire to have our
particular Interest from the Indians to be reserved to us and onely y^e
jurisdiction or government to be within Conecticot, onely we leave it
to yo^rselfe ·which way you finde most feaseable whether in Conecticot
pattent or Plimoth provided whichever it be our particular Interest
be reserved to ourselves.   If you cannot attain these boundes yet wee
desire if it may be that our particular lands, the propriety alwaies reserved to ourselves, may be got into Conecticot pattent, however freed
from Roade Island.   Thus craving excuse for our bouldness we take
leave, onely subscribing ourselves yor real servants apointed to subscribe our names in the behalf of the rest.

Edward Hutchinson   Richd Lord

Willm Hudson   Am Richison.

The former is what we formerly writ by Mr. Lord and not haveing
anything to add send the same again, onely the Lord hath maide a sad
breach amongst us by taking to himselfe Maj^r General Atharton who
was slaine by a fall from his horse.

ffor the Right Worshipful

John Winthrope, Esqr

these present.

II.

FROM MR WINTHROP TO CAPT. ED. HUTCHINSON.

Honrd S^r.

According to yor desires in those Letters from yo^rself and Mr
Richardson, and the others of yor Company (of) ye Plantation of Narragansett was included within Connecticott Charter, yet so as it was
according to the very words of their old charter which was to Narragansett River, I had onely those words put in for Explication and
avoiding controversie about the meaning of Narragansett River ; these
words are added [commonly called Narragansett Bay where the said
River falleth into the Sea] and by what I saw of ye coppy of Providence charter the words are these, that the Whole Extent of ye Tract
was about 25 miles, which by calculation from ye further part of Providence would reach but to the Narragansett countrey.

After the Charter was under the Greate Seale and finished Mr Clarke then appeared wth great opposition, as Agent for Road Island Collony, he never before made it known to me that he was agent for them, nor could I imagine it for a good while after my arriveale heere. Mr Alderman Peake told me hee had Received Letters from Road Island, with an Address Inclosed, and was desired by those Letters to Deliver ye Address, and afterwards told mee he had procured Mr Mandrick to Deliver it. I could not by this conceive they had any other Agent, but was resolved in my Businesse to keep to ye words of the old Pattent, as neere as might be. I am sorry there should be any Controversye between friends. If they had Desired to have Joyned wth our Collony I doubt not but they might have had all Equall Liberties with them. Mr Clarke might have done their Business before my arriveall or all ye time since; I should not have opposed anything therein, and whether he had done any thing, or were about it, I did not enquire, but that he hath done nothing in it (if it be so) is not through the least act from myselfe; who only minded our Businesse according to a former Grant: And when y^t was finished then Mr Clarke began to stirr and oppose what he could, wch was a great wrong to ye hindrance of my voyage. Why he did not Rather act about their Businesse before when hee would have none to oppose, or all this time when he should have no opposition from myself or any other, but so act onely by making a Controversye after our Businesse was finished I know not ye Reason. I desire y^u to present my Remembrances to Mr Brenton and Mr Arnold and Mr Williams and our friends of those parts, and let them know that this is the whole truth of the Businesse, however Mr. Clarke may Represent itt to them; they are friends that I alwaye did and doe Respect and Love and had not the least Intent of wronging them, Intending onely that service to the Collony to their old charter wch they had purchased At a great price, and according to the Desires of yo^rselves the Purchasers of that in Narragansett.

I shall not add at present by (but?) my love and respects to yo^rselfe and Mr Smith and the rest of yor Company, and Rest

Your Loveing friend

John Winthrop.

Ln^o September 2, 1662.

For Capt. Edw. Hutchinson
at Narragansett.

III.

FROM CAPT. HUTCHINSON TO MR. WINTHROP IN LONDON.

BOSTON, 18, 9 m. 1662.

Honn^rd S^r.—Wee have Received yo^rs from London. We thought good to send you a copy of what wee sent to Connecticot to consider of, onely wee think good to add, y^t wee are bold to presume you doe not consider y^t what you have procured in ye Charter Reaches the Whole of y^e Narragansett Countrey, and Whereas you speake of 25 miles wee understand not yor meaning, for yor Pattent and Plimouth Joyns Reaching both y^e Narragansett River, and whereas Mr Clarke pretends a Pattent, Wee have sent a Coppy of one to the Massachusetts of the same Land dated before theirs w$_{ch}$ answers theirs, and wee conceive may give satisfaction.   But, however, It is necessary for avoyding Contention to yield no way to Road Island for they are not Rationall.   It seems Mr Clarke hath much abused you, but I wonder not at it, for their Principles leads them to no better.   But for any Tract of Land of 25 miles there is not any such Tract, for theire Pattent is bounded by the Countrey inhabited by the Indians (though after there be an expression reaching to Pequod River) yet the whole Countrey of ye Narragansett lyes betwixt Pequod River and Providence wch is Inhabited by Indians, and therefore that Expression is no better than a Cheate, for from the outside of Providence bounds to Pequod River is at least 60 miles taking in all the Indian Countrey wch they are not to do by their Pattent, therefore if Providence Township and Road Island should be granted a Pattent yett ye Countrey Inhabited by Indians is Excepted, which is that wee have purchased, therefore wee are bold to crave of you to consider w^t you yeild to before you yeild, and w'ever you doe to Reserve our particular Interest. But if y^t Providence, Warwick and Road Island should procure a Pattent for the Bounds of those 4 Towns to come as far as Warwick rails where they now stand, and so goe along by the River pawtucket not by the Bay but to Warwick pointe wch will be about 20 or 25 miles to Reach to Boston Line wee should not oppose wch is indeed more than anything they can pretend claime to.   Thus not further to trouble you wee take our leave and rest

Yo^r servants to our powers

Ed. Hutchinson by appointment

of the Company.

These letters are now for the first time printed.   The first is given to show the earnestness of the Atherton company to " be freed from Rhode Island," whatever else might be their lot, long before the charters were obtained.   It breathes the true spirit of Massachusetts at that day, and proposes a series of boundary lines that would annihilate the existence of Rhode Island.   It refers to Mr. Winthrop's ownership in the purchase, and closes with the news of the fatal accident that terminated the life of their gallant but unscrupulous leader. From this time the name by which the company was first commonly called in his honor was changed, in general use, to that of the Narraganset company.

The second letter recites the difficulties which Winthrop encountered, chiefly at the hands of Clarke, after he had obtained the Connecticut charter. That he should feel restive under the delay that Clarke's opposition occasioned was natural, but we see no reason why Clarke should have made known his intentions in regard to Rhode Island before he was obliged to do so by the course of events. He was surrounded by the agents of adverse interests, who, he had good reason to fear, if they faithfully represented their principals, would leave no means untried that bitter hostility could suggest, to accomplish the overthrow of Rhode Island. That influences to this end were brought to bear upon Winthrop the first letter shows, and it is due to his purity alone, and not to the justice or honesty of his principals and advisers, that the worst fears of Clarke were not realized. Under such circumstances sound judgment dictated the conduct of the Rhode Island agent in keeping his own councils. Winthrop's friendly feeling towards Rhode Island is seen at the close of his letter in his message to some of her leading men, to whom he says he intended no wrong, but thought he was doing a service to their old charter, as well as to the Narraganset company, in what he had secured for Connecticut. There is no reference in this letter to his agreement with Clarke, which in fact was not signed till seven months later, but an allusion in the next letter, which is the reply of Hutchinson to this one, would indicate that some compromise between them was already in view, and had come to the knowledge of the writer, probably through Winthrop's official correspondence with Connecticut.

The third letter displays the usual animosity of its authors against Rhode Island. It is chiefly valuable as showing, in connection with that portion of the preceding one to which it specially replies, the inaccurate notions of both the corresponding parties concerning the courses and distances of the territory in question. It will be seen that there is an irreconcilable difference between them on this point, and hence if either party were correct in his statements the other was entirely wrong. Winthrop is pretty nearly accurate in his distance of twenty-five miles " from the further part of Providence to the Narraganset country," if he means from Narraganset Bay to Pawcatuck river in an east and west course, which is probably what he does mean, as it is upon that basis the agreement was made and the charter of Rhode Island was granted. Hutchinson, on the contrary, is as nearly correct in his widely different estimate of distance, taking a north and south, or rather a northeast and southwest course from Providence to Pawcatuck. So that it is probable the misunderstanding between the writers was in regard to the courses rather than the distances. The reading of each letter would seem to convey the idea that a north and south course was meant in both cases. But if this were so, Winthrop was very wide of the mark and Hutchinson pretty nearly correct.

Another remarkable point in this letter is the allusion to the old
Narraganset patent held by Massachusetts, of which a copy appears
to have been sent by the Atherton company to Mr. Winthrop. The
references to this ancient patent are very few, and are almost always
merely incidental, as in this case, as if no great weight was attached
to it. Why this should be so we cannot tell, but so it is. Every allusion to the patent of Dec. 10th, 1643, is worthy of notice from this
peculiarity. In its proper place, chapter iv., this subject is more
fully considered.

APPENDIX E.

LETTER FROM JOHN SCOT, IN LONDON, TO CAPT. HUTCHINSON.

(FROM TRUMBULL PAPERS, VOL. XXII. NO. 35, MSS. IN MASS. HIST. SOC.)

April 29, 1663.

Mr. Hutchinson, and my honoured friend.—   E.
    Mr. Winthrop was very averse to my prosecuting yor affaires, he
having had much trouble with Mr. Clarke, whiles he remained in
England; but as soone as I received intelligence of his departure from
ye Downes, I took into the Societye a Potent Gentleman, and preferred a Petition against Clarke, &c., as enimyes to the peace and well
being of his Majestyes good subjects, and doubt not of effecting the
premises in convenient tyme; and in order to accomplish y^r businesse,
I have bought of Mr. Edwards a parcel of curiosityes to ye value of
60: to gratifye persons that are powerfull, that there may be a Letter
filled with Authorizing Expressions to the Collonyes of the Massachusetts and Connecticut, that the proprietors of the Naraganset coun-
trye, shall not onlye live peaceablye, but have satisfaction for Injuryes
already received, by some of the saide Proprietors, and the power
y^t shall be soe invested (viz.,) the Masachusets and Coneticott by ver-
tue of the saide letter, will joyntlye or severallye have full power to
doe us Justice to all intents as to our Naraganset concernes. S^r. Mr.
Sam^{ll} Sedgwick disburst y^r monye, the obligation I doubt not of satisfaction of accordinge to tyme which is by March next and by y^t time,
or long before, I doubt not of satisfyinge yor desires, or elce I will
satisfye y^r saide Bill to Sedgwick myself. I cannot deeme those termes
Mr. Winthrop made with Clarke any waye to answere yor desires,
were there a certaintye in what Clarke hath granted.

Yo^r friend and servantt
uncerimoniouslye
John Scott.

The foregoing letter is the most important evidence that has yet been brought to light upon this subject. Nothing could more clearly explain the whole conspiracy against Clarke, its authors, their plans, and the means adopted to accomplish their purpose. Their motive is shown in previous letters, the desire "to be freed from Rhode Island" in whatever way, and "the way" is here explained after the lapse of two hundred years. Parties who could adopt such means, "uncerimoniouslye," indeed, would hesitate at no other degree of baseness to shield their crime. Why the character of Clarke was traduced in every mode that unscrupulous corruption could devise, can no longer remain a mystery. That the slanders originated by these violators of both moral and statute law, and eagerly perpetuated by their sympathizing brethren in the adjoining colonies, by some, no doubt, through ignorance, but by all with a zeal that does no honor to their hearts, should now be traced to their source after so long an interval, must be gratifying to those who have steadily defended the purity of Clarke in this matter of the charter, reasoning from his exalted character in all the other relations of life. It furnishes one more proof of the fact, that the general character of a man is no unsafe criterion of his conduct in particular circumstances, and that the reputation which he holds in his own community is a tolerably safe standard of his real character. It thus affords a triumphant vindication of what Mr. Quincy (pamphlet on Grahame, p. 36) is pleased to term "a studied eulogy *on the general character of Clarke*," in Mr. Bancroft's 2d vol. p. 64, which must be grateful to that eminent historian who, in the face of so much printed evidence on the other side, has examined our records for himself, and in this, as in other disputed points, has dared to do Rhode Island justice.

The letter opens with a striking acknowledgment of Winthrop's purity, for although Winthrop had had difficulty with Clarke, he was so averse to the writer's scheme, that Scot dared not pursue them until Winthrop had embarked for America. He then gave an interest in the company to "a potent gentleman," preferred charges against Clarke and his principals as enemies to the crown, with what purpose is evident, and, these two points secured, he doubted not of speedy success. But to render assurance doubly sure, he adopts another form of bribery to apply to other powerful personages, whose taste for curiosities he supposed to be greater than their sense of right or their pride of character, and invests the sum of sixty pounds for that purpose. The object of all this nice calculation was twofold ; to hide his own infamy under the ruin of Clarke, and to obtain a letter from the King placing the Narraganset country under the jurisdiction of the United Colonies. No description could be more accurate in every item than is here given on the 29th April, of the royal letter of the 21st June following.

Corruption moved apace to further the plans of Scot. In seven weeks the character of Clarke was branded with infamy to remote posterity, and the Atherton company had accomplished their selfish purposes by a baseness that cannot easily be surpassed. We have no clue to the meaning of the paragraph about Mr. Sedgwick. Possibly it relates to some private matter, but not unlikely it refers to some other disbursement in connection with this nefarious scheme. A letter of this stamp might well be confined to the one subject of its infamy. It concludes with a doubt as to Winthrop's agreement being satisfactory, even if Clarke were authorized to make it ; and the last word it contains implies the confidential nature of the topic and the free and easy character of the writer. "Unceremoniously" indeed ! A cooler stab at all that an honest and honorable man holds most dear, or a clearer exposition of successful bribery was never made ; and but for the sometimes dangerous habit of preserving private papers, which Capt. Hutchinson possessed, we might never have known, in this world, the secret and real history of this transaction.

The agreement between the two agents was signed on the 7th April. That Winthrop had implicit confidence in Clarke's honor is evident from his embarking for home immediately afterwards, leaving Clarke, unfortunately for the latter as it proved, still in England. The above letter was written on the 29th April. The King's letter to the United Colonies, so accurately predicted and described in that of Scot was issued on the 21st of June, and the charter of Rhode Island passed the seals on the 8th of July.

CHAPTER X.

1675—1677.

FROM THE COMMENCEMENT OF PHILIP'S WAR, JUNE 1675, TO THE
TRIAL OF THE HARRIS CAUSES, NOVEMBER 1677.

To trace the causes of the most disastrous conflict that
ever devastated New England, it will be necessary to take
a rapid review of the intercourse between the English and
the Indians from the time of the landing of the Pilgrims.
Shortly before this event, a pestilence had wasted the
strength of the natives of this region, and caused them to
become an easy prey to the martial spirit of the Narragansets.   Soon after their landing, Massasoit, Sachem of the
Wampanoags, a powerful tribe who had formerly ruled the
whole country east of Narraganset bay, and extending
north to the territory of the Massachusetts, but who were
now, with their dependent tribes, subject to the conquerors, made a treaty with the Pilgrims, which he kept inviolate for forty years till the time of his death.[1]   He left
two sons, Wamsutta, by the English called Alexander, and

April
7.

CHAP.
X.
1620.

1621.
March
22.

---

[1] In the winter of 1661-2, Drake's Indians, B. 3, ch. ii. Various dates
from 1656 to 1660 are assigned by different authors as the period of the
death of Massasoit, but the diligence of Drake entitles his opinion to the
greatest weight, and the reasons given for it in Book 2, ch. ii., p. 28, are conclusive that the death of Massasoit did not occur till later than Sept., 1661.

CHAP. Pometacom or Metacomet, whose English name was Philip.[1]
X.   The faith with which Massasoit or Ousamequin, as he was
1621. also called, maintained the treaty on his side, was not so
well kept on the other.   He quietly submitted to repeated
aggressions upon his land and liberties, and besides having
sold large tracts of territory at various times to the English, he witnessed the gradual withdrawal of his subject
tribes to a condition of independence.   The fatal alliance
which had released him from his recent subjection to the
Narragansets, was destined to place a severer yoke upon
his own neck, to weaken, instead of strengthening, his influence over the subordinate tribes, and finally to effect the
extermination of his race.   He had several residences, the
principal of which, in the town of Bristol, was called Sowams by the Wampanoags, and Pokanoket by the Narragansets, and by the English Mount Hope.   The decay of
the nation, and the proportionate increase of the English,
made a deep impression upon the minds of the two sons
of Massasoit.   Wamsutta, the elder, succeeded his father,
1662. but survived him only a few months.   The manner of his
death added to the sting which the accumulated wrongs
of forty years had planted in the hearts of Philip and his
councillors.

    We have seen that Massasoit claimed portions of the
land of Providence, west of Seeconk river, and that Williams and others had satisfied his claims, although the
Narraganset supremacy was undoubted, and their Sachems

---

[1] The Indians often changed their names. Wamsutta was first called
Mooanam, and later Wamsutta or Sepauquet, both of which latter names are
signed, together with his English name, to the deed of March, 1661–2, to
Providence men. Any great event in life seems to have given occasion to
these changes; as Massasoit, upon commencing his war against the Narragansets in 1632, took the name of Ousamequin, by which he was afterwards
more generally known. This custom complicates the difficulties of Indian
history very much. The English names of Alexander and Philip were bestowed on the two young sachems at Plymouth Court about 1656, although
Mather says it was not till 1662 when the two sachems came to Plymouth.
Morton's Memorial, 286–7, and Drake, Book 3, p. 6.

had conveyed a clear title to the original purchasers.[1]
There is reason for more than suspicion that these claims
were instigated by our neighbors, in their desire to possess
themselves of an outlet to Narraganset bay, and that they
were not well pleased with their faithful ally that he should
consent to release his pretended right to those who already
held it from his superiors.   Wamsutta was associated
with his father in the government for some years before the
death of Massasoit, and joined with him in conveying lands
to Plymouth.[2]   Upon the death of his father he became
the chief Sachem, and conveyed to the town of Providence
some land on the west of Seeconck river, which had been
claimed by Massasoit as belonging to the Wampanoags.[3]
This act was never specifically charged against him as the
cause of the harsh treatment which he received under pretence of his plotting against the English, and which resulted in his death ; but in the absence of any proof of the
truth of those charges, and in view of the murder of Miantinomi, a few years before, whose greatest crime was his
kindness to Gorton, and his having sold Shawomet to the
" arch-heretic," we are inclined to think that this deed of
sale was one cause of the prejudice against him.   He had
strengthened his position by marriage with Weetamo,
squaw sachem of the Pocassets, who inhabited what is now
Tiverton.   This was a step towards restoring the ancient
unity of the tribes, which was still further effected at a
later day, by the marriage of Metacomet with the sister
of Weetamo.

It was soon after the sale to Providence that "some
of Boston, having been occasionally at Narraganset, wrote
to Mr. Prince, who was then Governor of Plymouth, that
Alexander was contriving mischief against the English,

[1] This satisfaction occurred Sept. 10th, 1646.   See ch. iv. ante.
[2] March 9th, 1653, these two sachems joined in the sale of a large tract
including Papasquash neck.   Drake, Book 2, p. 27–8.
[3] The deed is dated 12th March, 1661–2, and is given in Staple's Annals,
p. 574.

CHAP. and that he had solicited the Narragansets to engage with
  X.   him in his designed rebellion." [1]   We know that " some
1662. of Boston " were at this time. anxious to gain possession
of Narraganset, and also that the Wampanoags claimed
a portion of that country, and had long had a feud with
Pumham about the lands of Shawomet. [2]   These rumors
furnished sufficient grounds for the arrest of Wamsutta
upon the charge of conspiracy.   Capt. Willet, who resided
near Mount Hope, was sent to require his presence at the
next Court at Plymouth.   He did not appear, but, it was
said, continued his intercourse with the Narragansets.
Upon this, Governor Prince despatched Major Josiah
Winslow, afterwards governor, with a small force, to seize
Alexander and bring him to Plymouth.   Winslow found
him at one of his hunting stations, a few miles distant, and
captured him without resistance, although the anger of the
Sachem at this interference obliged the Major to adopt the
same resolute means resorted to by Atherton in his visit
to Pessicus twelve years before, and to present a pistol at
his breast.   The Sachem yielded, and with his whole train
of warriors and women, some eighty in number, who were
allowed to accompany him, was carried a prisoner towards
Plymouth, and stopped at Winslow's house in Marshfield.
Here the haughty chieftain, under the combined effects of
rage, fatigue and heat, was taken ill.   The day was very
hot, and although Winslow offered his horse to the Sachem,
it was gallantly declined, because there were none for his
squaw or the other women to ride.   On account of his
sickness, his attendants entreated that he might be sent
home.   This was granted upon his promise to appear at
the next Court, and meanwhile to send his son as a hostage.   But his death ensued almost immediately.   Hubbard says he " died before he got half way home." [3]

---

[1] Increase Mather's Relation, p. 70.

[2] President R. Williams' letter to Mass., May, 1656.   Knowles, 290.

[3] Hubbard's Narrative, London, 1677, p. 10.   Mather's Relation, p. 70-1
See also Davis's Morton, 287-9, note, and Drake's Indians, Book 3, p. 6-9,

Thus ended the brief and bitter reign of Wamsutta, CHAP.
the eldest son and successor of the earliest and firmest X.
friend of the Pilgrims.   Dr. Mather, in the passage before 1662.
cited, accuses Alexander of not being "so faithful and
friendly to the English as his father had been."   Forty
years had changed the condition of the tribe.   They were
no longer in fear of the Narragansets, from whose power
old Massasoit had sought refuge in a friendly alliance with
the white man.   Yet during his own life, he had more than
once been called on to explain his conduct.   Their jealousy
of the natives was natural in view of the immense disparity of numbers between them ; but had their care in preserving the terms of treaties been as great as was that of
their savage allies ; had there been less of the old theo-
cratic spirit of dominion, " the saints shall judge the world "
—' we are the saints,' and more of the religion they professed, in their dealings with the red man ; had there been
the same strict regard to the letter and spirit of their
agreements that was shown upon the other side ; or had
the temper of the founders of Rhode Island, in their intercourse with the aborigines, been displayed by the other colonies, there would have been less occasion, perhaps none at
all, for the alarms that so often distracted New England,
and the hope of the old Canonicus would have been realized, " that the English and my posterity shall live in love
and peace together."   The jealousy with which the Puritan colonies regarded the powerful Sachems around them,
was signally displayed towards those who showed kindness
to any whom they had placed under the ban of proscrip-
tion.   The style of their negotiations with Canonicus, the
clerico-judicial murder of Miantinomi, the savage treatment
of Pessicus, and now the unfeeling harshness that hastened
the death of Wamsutta, are examples of this, which it is
in vain that the Puritan writers attempt to justify or explain.   That Major Winslow conducted himself with courtesy towards his royal captive, or that the best medical at-

tendance and careful nursing was obtained for him in his illness, does not palliate the manner of his arrest, or mitigate the insult offered to a sovereign prince upon his native soil. Nor did the peculiar allies of the Puritans escape the frequent evidence of their displeasure. Uncas, their willing tool, Pumham, their abject slave, and even old Massasoit their most faithful friend, were often called before their severe tribunals, to answer for suspected treason or alleged misconduct. One cardinal error prevailed in all their treatment of the Indians. They regarded the submission of the tribes to the British crown, always cheerfully and often voluntarily made, as being an act of subjection to themselves. Nothing could be farther from the intention of these haughty Sachems. Repeatedly they asserted that they were the allies, not the subjects, of the colonists ; but the latter, taking the servility of Pumham, himself a renegade, as the type of the conduct they desired from all, insisted upon a like submission from his superiors, and when this was denied, they construed the attitude of equality into an act of hostility, and busied themselves in conjecturing plots where none existed. This was a certain method of producing the result they so much dreaded. What was only suspected in regard to Wamsutta was clearly proved, a dozen years later, in the case of Metacomet.

The treatment of Alexander was openly condemned, even among the Puritans, for its harshness and impolicy, although their own conduct towards Miantinomi had been if possible, yet more unjustifiable. Upon the savages, it produced a deep and lasting influence. They did not hesitate to charge the English with having poisoned their victim. False as this accusation was, it was less unjust than the act upon which it was grounded. Weetamo, the widow, although she subsequently soothed her sorrows by a second marriage with an Indian of lower rank, never forgave the death of her royal husband, but secretly nursed

her feelings of revenge, and gave currency among the
tribes to the story of English perfidy.

Metacomet, or King Philip as he was now called, succeeded his brother as chief Sachem of the Wampanoags.
Being sent for by the Court at Plymouth, he appeared and
renewed the treaty of amity with the English. He was a
prince as politic in counsel, as he was undaunted in war,
and he was a man too high-spirited tamely to submit to
private injuries or public wrongs, without seeking the
means of redress. His designs required concealment until
they could ripen into a general union of all the tribes
against the English. There were local jealousies to appease, and ancient rivalries to adjust, for which time and
diplomacy were requisite. Meanwhile he preserved, in a
measure, the same friendly aspect to the colonists that his
father had done ; and even after the demonstrations that
had led to the first disarming of the Indians, and to the
subsequent alarms in Plymouth, he freely made a treaty,
confessing his fault, and agreeing to surrender all his guns,
to be kept by the English so long as they saw fit. But
seventy of them were given up. Strange Indians continued to resort to Mount Hope. The Court of Plymouth
again sent for Philip to require his presence. He, with
his counsellors, chanced to be in Boston when news of this
order was received there, and so favorably did he state his
case that the government of Massachusetts suggested to
Plymouth, that instead of commencing hostilities as threatened, that colony should refer the dispute to the arbitration of the other colonies. When the mediators met at
Plymouth, Philip signed an agreement to pay one hundred
pounds within three years, and five wolves' heads annually
to that colony, to refer to them all disputes between his
tribe and the English, and neither to sell lands nor to make
war without their consent. This was a forced arrangement on the part of the Sachem, made under the alter-
native of war for which he was not yet prepared. That he

so considered it, is evident from his remarkable reply to Mr. John Borden of Rhode Island, an intimate friend of Philip, who, when the war was about to commence, attempted to dissuade him from it by urging the reciprocal benefits that would result from peace. " The English who came first to this country were but an handful of people, forlorn, poor, and distressed. My father was then Sachem. He relieved their distresses in the most kind and hospitable manner. He gave them land to build and plant upon. He did all in his power to serve them. Others of their own countrymen came and joined them. Their numbers rapidly increased. My father's counsellors became uneasy and alarmed lest, as they were possessed of firearms, which was not the case with the Indians, they should finally undertake to give law to the Indians, and take from them their country. They therefore advised him to destroy them before they should become too strong, and it should be too late. My father was also the father of the English. He represented to his counsellors and warriors that the English knew many sciences which the Indians did not ; that they improved and cultivated the earth, and raised cattle and fruits, and that there was sufficient room in the country for both the English and the Indians. His advice prevailed. It was concluded to give victuals to the English. They flourished and increased. Experience taught that the advice of my father's counsellors was right. By various means they got possessed of a great part of his territory. But he still remained their friend till he died. My elder brother became Sachem. They pretended to suspect him of evil designs against them. He was seized and confined, and thereby thrown into sickness and died. Soon after I became Sachem they disarmed all my people. They tried my people by their own laws, and assessed damages against them which they could not pay. Their land was taken. At length a line of division was agreed upon between the English and my people, and I myself was to

be responsible.   Sometimes the cattle of the English
would come into the cornfields of my people, for they did
not make fences like the English.   I must then be seized
and confined till I sold another tract of my country for
satisfaction of all damages and costs.   Thus tract after
tract is gone.   But a small part of the dominion of my
ancestors remains.   I am determined not to live till I have
no country." [1]   This is the preamble to a declaration of
war, more striking from its origin, and more true in its
statements, than any with which we are acquainted.   It is
the mournful summary of accumulated wrongs that cry
aloud for battle, not for revenge alone, but for the very existence of the oppressed.   It is the sad note of preparation,
sounded by a royal leader, that summons to their last conflict the aboriginal lords of New England.   It is the death
song of Metacomet, chanted on the site of his ancestral
home, before plunging into the fatal strife that was to end
only with his life, and to seal for ever the fortunes of his
race.

The fact that the war broke out before the conspiracy
was complete, has caused some historians to doubt whether
there was really any concerted design among the Indians ;
but the evidence of Col. Church, in his interviews with
Awashonks and Weetamo, queens of Seaconnet and Pocasset, appears conclusive of Philip's intrigues in that
direction, while other cotemporary writers adduce the testimony of captives, taken at Hadley and elsewhere, to show
that the plot embraced the remoter Indians of the Connecticut River, as well as the powerful tribe of the Narragansets.   An event that precipitated the war probably
averted the utter destruction of the English, by distracting
the yet incomplete alliance of the Indians.   Sausaman,
one of Mr. Elliot's "praying Indians," a man of unstable
mind, after being educated at the college, and employed
as a teacher at Natick, returned to savage life, and re-

[1] Foster papers, MSS., vol. ix. last page.

CHAP.   mained for many years with Philip as his secretary and
X.   chief counsellor. The persuasions of Elliot induced him
1674.   to abandon Philip, and resuming civilized habits, he became a preacher. Being thrown in company with some
1675.   of his old companions, he discovered the plot that was
June.   forming against the English. This he made known to
Governor Leveret. He was soon afterwards murdered, as
a betrayer of his tribe. Three Indians who committed
the deed were seized and executed at Plymouth. Philip
expected his own arrest as the instigator of the crime.
Enraged at his subjects being thus tried by English laws
for fulfilling his commands, in executing the vengeance
denounced by Indian custom against all traitors—that
they should suffer death, and determined not to submit
to the indignity of personal violence, Philip mustered his
warriors and commenced to scour the country in all directions. His forces rapidly increased by accessions from the
neighboring tribes, and at length the border town of Swan-
20.   zey received the first blow in this sanguinary war. Houses
were robbed and cattle killed. Four days later the mas-
24.   sacre commenced. Nine of the inhabitants were slain and
seven wounded. The troops of Plymouth marched at once
28.   to the defence of Swanzey. Forces were also despatched
from Boston, who attacked the Indians and drove them to
29.   a swamp. The next day other troops arrived, the whole
were placed under the command of Major Savage, and
marched into the Indian country to break up the head
quarters of Philip at Mount Hope. The savages fled before them leaving the traces of their retreat in burning
buildings, and the heads and hands of slaughtered English
stuck upon poles by the wayside, but not an Indian could
be seen. The wigwams were found deserted, with evident
marks of haste. A few prowling dogs were the only ves-
tiges of life that remained. A fort was thrown up at
Mount Hope, much against the advice of Church, and a
small garrison left to guard it. The enemy had crossed

over to Pocasset where it was now proposed by Mr., after- CHAP.
wards Colonel, Church to follow them.[1] With a small   X.
band of volunteers, he readily attempted the daring exploit. 1675.
Having, previous to the war, negotiated with the squaw   July
sachems of the two tribes in that vicinity, he hoped, on
this account, to withdraw their men from the alliance with
Philip. Crossing over to Rhode Island, he there found
boats to transport him the next night to Pocasset, where
the party laid in ambush for the Indians, but in vain.
The next day they followed the trail south, to a point near   7.
Fogland ferry, where they were attacked by a greatly su-
perior force. The skirmish continued for six hours till the
English ammunition was nearly spent, when a sloop from
Rhode Island came down and relieved them from their per-
ilous condition. They returned to the garrison at Mount
Hope.

It was of vital importance to prevent an offensive alliance between Philip and the Narragansets, for it was said
that the latter had promised to join him in the spring with
four thousand warriors. Commissioners were sent to treat

[1] There were many men who distinguished themselves by their courage
and address in the course of this war, but none more so than Col. Benjamin
Church. He was the first English settler at Seaconnet, now Little Compton,
then filled with Indians, and was just commencing his plantation when the
war broke out. He thoroughly understood the Indian character, and their
partisan mode of warfare, which latter he adopted with great success in the
subsequent struggle. His conquests were conducted with more humanity
than was displayed by many of his colleagues, while his courage and military
skill were conspicuous. He was to Rhode Island what Miles Standish had
been to the first generation of Plymouth colonists—a buckler and shield in
the hour of danger; but he had far more experience in military affairs than
fell to the lot of the Pilgrim captain. It was destined for him to strike the
first and the last decisive blows in Philip's war, by which he is now best
known to fame. So great was the reputation he gained, that he was afterwards constantly called to the field to repel the French and Indians at the
north and east. He served in no less than five expeditions against Canada
and Maine, as commander-in-chief of the colonial forces sent out by the royal
Governors of New England. The first time was at the request of Sir Edmund Andros, in 1689; again in 1690 by Hinckley; then in 1692 he was

CHAP.
X.

1675.
July.

15.

with them, and the Massachusetts troops marched into their country to enforce the terms that might be dictated. They found the villages in Pumham's district deserted. He had shaken off his English shackles, and joined with his countrymen against the common foe. Some days were spent in negotiating with the sachems before the articles of agreement were concluded. These required the surrender of any of Philip's subjects who might come in their power, stipulated rewards for such surrender, declared war against him, agreed that stolen goods should be restored, confirmed all former grants of land and agreements made with the United Colonies, pledged perpetual peace, and granted hostages for the full performance of all the articles. It was a forced affair throughout, calculated to irritate rather than to appease the Narragansets, and justly regarded by them as no longer binding when the restraint that compelled it was removed.

Meanwhile the war raged with great fury. In all directions the mangled corpses and burning towns of the English bespoke the relentless wrath and ceaseless ac-

commissioned by Sir William Phipps; next in 1696, by Staughton, and finally in the sixty-fifth year of his age he was urged by Gov. Dudley in 1704, to command the forces for the fifth time sent out against the French, and accepted. That no brilliant acts were performed in these expeditions, either by the English fleet or the New England forces is to be ascribed to the nature of the country. Operations were mostly conducted on the coast of Maine and Nova Scotia, a vast wilderness, where security to the enemy was certain and pursuit was vain. Col. Church died January 17th, 1717–18, in his seventy-eighth year. The history of his wars was written by his son Thomas before his father's death, and a Latin ode by his grandson, at the close of the memoir, attests the scholarship of his descendants. Some branches of the family have settled in different parts of the State, or moved elsewhere, but many of the direct descendants of the old hero still reside in Little Compton, where they preserve the position and the patrimonial estates inherited from their illustrious ancestor. Gov. Winslow in his letter to the King, June 26th, 1677, accompanying presents of the spoils of Philip, "being his Crowne, his Gorge and two Belts of their own making of their goulde and silver taken from him by Capt. Benjamin Church," speaks of Church as "a person of great loyalty, and the most successful of our commanders." The original letter is in the British State Paper Office. New England papers, vol. iii. p. 16.

tivity of the omnipresent foe.   We cannot follow these bloody chronicles in all their details of destruction, but must pass rapidly over the field, touching only upon the prominent points of the war, or on those which had a special reference to this colony.   Rhode Island was not a member of the New England confederacy, and therefore not bound to take part in hostilities provoked by the other colonies.   She disapproved of the war, which, from her exposed situation, threatened her very existence.   The government too was in the hands of the Quakers, yet she did what she could, in an unofficial way, to aid the English with provisions and volunteers, and to protect herself. Her inaction was perhaps the reason why she suffered less than her neighbors at the beginning, but the case was changed when her own territory became the battle-ground.[1] Upon the return of the troops to Taunton, they found   17 that Philip had fortified himself in a swamp at Pocasset. Joining with the Plymouth forces, the army marched to the attack, and were repulsed with some loss.   It was an   18. unfortunate affair, for it strengthened the firm and confirmed the wavering natives, and thus completed a general rising in behalf of Philip.   He withdrew from the swamp, effected a skilful manœuvre in the passage of Taunton river, accompanied by Weetamo who was ever at his side, and hastened to join the Nipmucks, who had already taken arms against the English.   Plymouth was thus for awhile relieved, and the burden of the war transferred to Massachusetts.   Brookfield was burnt, and Captain   Aug. Hutchinson with twenty mounted men was defeated with   2. the loss of half his troop, and himself mortally wounded. The Connecticut river Indians were fully enlisted in the

---

[1] Hubbard, in the table of assaults at the end of his narrative, says that eighteen houses were burnt at Providence, June 28th, 1675, and that on 29th March following, fifty-four houses were there destroyed.   The latter statement is correct, but we can find no verification of the former, which is probably an error.

CHAP.
  X.
~~~~
1675.
Sept.

war, and committed fearful ravages upon the defenceless towns. Hatfield, Hadley, Deerfield, and Northfield were successively attacked, many of the inhabitants slain, and the houses destroyed. These devoted villages were destined to feel still further the horrors of savage warfare. The commissioners of the United Colonies, whose union, at one time almost abandoned, had of late been revived,

9.

reviewed the causes of the war, gave it their official approval, and adopted the expenses of conducting it as a just charge to be paid proportionably by the confederates.

12.

The slaughter of Capt. Beers, with a troop of twenty men near Northfield, was followed by the defeat of Capt. Lathrop with a corps of young men, "the flower of the county of Essex," who were attacked by a force of seven or eight hundred Indians, near Hadley, and almost the whole party, including their leader, were cut off. This

18.

was the greatest loss the country had yet sustained. Nearly one hundred of the best troops of Massachusetts fell in this unequal fight. The English had not yet become accustomed to the Indian mode of warfare. Their small detachments could stand no chance against the lurking savage, in the deep forests and dense swamps of the country. The commissioners now ordered an army of one thousand men to be raised, one-half to be heavy dragoons. Springfield was the next object of attack.

Oct.

Near this town the Indians had a fort, into which some three hundred of Philip's warriors were received the night before the assault was made. The town was partly

5.

burned, when the arrival of Major Treat with a body of Connecticut troops saved the inhabitants from a general massacre by dispersing the assailants. For his gallantry on this and other occasions, Major Treat was offered the

14.

command of all the Connecticut troops, by the Assembly of that colony. A second attack was made upon Hatfield, where there was now a garrison, by a body of eight

19.

hundred Indians, who surrounded the town. It was a fu-

rious but unsuccessful assault. Major Treat with his CHAP.
field force, and the neighboring garrisons, coming to the X.
relief of the besieged, the Indians were repulsed with 1675.
great loss, and became so discouraged that the greater Oct.
part retired to Narraganset, and Massachusetts, in her
turn, was for a time relieved from peril, except only from
the small marauding bands that lingered within her borders.

    The General Assembly of Rhode Island, acting upon 27.
the petition of Capt. Cranston, referred the defence of the
colony to the councils of war established in the several
towns, whose decisions were to be absolute. The Narra- Nov.
gansets gave a cordial reception to the hostile Indians,
in violation of the compulsory treaty of July, and were
more than suspected of having taken an active part in
the recent battles, for some of their young men had returned home wounded. The United Colonies resolved to 12.
send an army of a thousand men to attack them in their
winter-quarters, and thus to prevent their openly joining
with Philip in the spring, an event that must have been
most disastrous to the English. The haughty reply of
Canonchet, son and successor of Miantinomi, and chief
sachem of the Narragansets, made to the English when
they sent to demand the surrender of Philip's Indians,
who had placed their women and children under his protection, displayed the spirit of the royal savage, and cut
off all hopes of peace. "Not a Wampanoag, nor the
paring of a Wampanoag's nail, shall be delivered up,"
was the answer of the indignant sachem. All attempts
at reconciliation were henceforth abandoned, and the colonies prepared for their last appeal to the stern arbitrament of arms. Massachusetts was to raise five hundred
and twenty-seven men, Plymouth one hundred and fifty-
eight, and Connecticut three hundred and fifteen. The
latter colony exceeded her quota, and sent three hundred
English and one hundred and fifty friendly Indians, Mo-

CHAP.
X.
1675.
Dec.
2.

hegans and Pequots, so that the whole force numbered eleven hundred and thirty-five, besides volunteers from Rhode Island, many of whom joined the army as it marched through Providence and Warwick to the scene of action. When all was ready a solemn fast was held, before setting out on the expedition.

Strange to say, this enterprise was undertaken by the United Colonies without consulting the government of Rhode Island, although the express command of the King, embodied in the royal charter, was in these words : " It shall not be lawful for the rest of the Collonies to invade or molest the native Indians, or any other inhabitants, inhabiting within the bounds and lymitts hereafter mentioned (they having subjected themselves unto us, and being by us taken into our speciall protection), without the knowledge and consent of the Governour and Company of our Collony of Rhode Island and Providence Plantations." The Narragansets had always been friendly to Rhode Island, and although portions of the tribe might engage in the war, the greater part were still subject to her restraint ; and whether they were so or not, the attack now made upon them, contrary to the advice and without the consent of Rhode Island, was a direct violation of the royal order, an unscrupulous disregard of the rights, and a wanton act of indifference to the welfare of a sister colony, which no exigency of State could excuse, since the remedy was easy, involving only a simple act of courtesy or friendship. But these feelings were strangers to the confederated Puritans, by whom heathens and heretics were classed together as beneath the regard of Christian fellowship.[1] The invasion of the Narragansets was kindred in spirit with the desertion of Rhode Island after the battle, leaving Providence a prey to the fury of savages, without a garrison to protect her from enemies whom they had roused against her.

[1] Easton's Narrative, pp. 27–31. Albany, 1858.

The Massachusetts troops left Boston under command CHAP.
of Major Appleton ; those of Plymouth were led by Ma- X.
jor Bradford, and the Connecticut troops by Major Treat. 1675.
The whole army was divided into thirteen companies of   Dec.
infantry and one of cavalry, and placed under the com-   8.
mand of Gov. Winslow of Plymouth. Captain Church
rode in the General's guard as a volunteer. We have no
means of ascertaining the number of recruits that joined
the expedition from this colony. It must have been considerable, for the people were roused to a full sense of the
mortal struggle at hand by the massacres which had already commenced, and although the government took no
direct part, yet they had placed the full power in the
hands of the councils of war. Bull's garrison house in
South Kingston was attacked, fifteen persons were slain
and but two escaped. This was the first overt act of war
within the limits of Rhode Island. The precise day is   15
not stated in the chronicles of the time, but is probably
that which we affix. The Connecticut troops expected
to find shelter at Pettaquamscot, but on their arrival   17.
found the buildings destroyed and the inhabitants butchered. The next day they joined the other forces, and the 18.
whole army encamped that night in the open air. The
weather was cold and stormy. At the dawn of the Sab-   19.
bath morning they took up their line of march towards
the strong fort of the Narragansets, fifteen miles distant.
This fort occupied a rising ground, some three or four
acres in extent, in the centre of a dense swamp, about
seven miles west from Narraganset south ferry. It was
just one o'clock when they reached the scene of action,
wearied by a long march through the snow. A renegade
Indian whom they found at the edge of the swamp served
as a guide to the fort. The position was a very strong
one, well fortified with palisades and breastworks, and enclosed by an impenetrable hedge. The single narrow entrance was flanked by a block house, whence a murderous

CHAP. fire was poured upon the advancing English. No less
  X.   than six of the captains, with a large number of men, fell
1675. in the first assault. The entrance was choked with the
 Dec. bodies of the slain. Over the mangled corpses of their
  19. comrades the desperate assailants climbed the logs and
breastwork to effect an entrance. The struggle on either
side was one for life. Whichever party triumphed there
was no hope of quarter to the vanquished. Christian and
savage fought alike with the fury of fiends, and the sanctity of a New England Sabbath was broken by the yells
of conflict, the roar of musketry, the clash of steel, and
all the demoniac passions which make a battle-ground an
earthly hell. It was the great conflict of New England.
A century was to roll by before the sons of the Puritans
were again to witness upon their own soil so fierce a struggle. The carnage was immense. The acts of personal
daring performed upon both sides were worthy of a wider
field of fame. The English were at one time repulsed.
For three hours the battle raged and the result was yet
doubtful, until an entrance was in some way effected in
the rear of the fort by a reserve guard of the Connecticut
troops. The Indians, who were all engaged at the first
point of attack, were surprised and confused by a heavy
fire in their rear. Their powder was nearly consumed,
still their arrows rained a deadly shower upon the charging
foe. The wigwams within the fort were set on fire, contrary to the earnest entreaty of Church, whose military
forecast discerned the importance of shelter to the exhausted conquerors. The tragedy of the Pequots was
thus re-enacted upon their ancient enemies. Humanity
and policy alike sustained the advice of the gallant Church,
but it was too late. The infuriated troops had already
commenced the work of destruction. In a few minutes
the frail material of five hundred Indian dwellings furnished the funeral pyre of sick and wounded, infant and

aged. The blazing homes of the Narragansets lighted their path to death.

The victory was dearly bought. Accounts of the losses on both sides differ widely. The entire loss of the Indians, in killed, wounded, and prisoners, was not less than one thousand, of whom at least three hundred perished in the flames and as many more in the fight. The English loss is variously estimated from two to four hundred, including a majority of the superior officers who fell leading the assault. More than one-half of this number might have been saved had the advice of Church been adopted. He was himself severely wounded, and with his suffering comrades was the next day carried over to Rhode Island, and there carefully attended until recovery. But the period of most intense suffering to the combatants was yet to come. When the night closed over the field of blood there was no shelter for victors or vanquished. The fort was a smouldering ruin. The Indians escaped to an open cedar swamp near by, where many perished without food or covering on that fearful night. Still worse was the fate of the English. They had taken a weary march of some fifteen miles, through deep snow, since daybreak, without halting for food, and had spent the remainder of the day in desperate conflict. They had now to retrace their steps in the dark, through a dense forest, with a deep snow beneath their feet and a December storm howling around them. By the glare of burning wigwams they formed their line of march, and bearing away their dead and wounded, their retreat was soon covered by the darkness of the forest. It was two o'clock at night before they reached their camping ground. The cold was severe. Many died on the march. The limbs of the wounded were stiffened, fatigue had disabled the rest, there was no shelter or provisions of any sort, and when the morning dawned death had done a melancholy work. A heavy snow storm during the night had

CHAP. wrapped many a brave soldier in his winding-sheet. The
X.   survivors could hardly move from the depth of the new
1675. fallen snow. The providential arrival of a vessel with
Dec.   provisions, in the course of the night, at Smith's landing,
20.   alone saved the remnant of that gallant army from destruction. The Connecticut troops were so disabled that
Major Treat led them home to recruit. The other forces
scoured the country during the winter, cutting off the
Indian supplies or straggling parties, and burning their
wigwams, but did nothing decisive. The Narragansets
returned to their ruined fort but no attempt was made to
dislodge them.

By some it is supposed that Philip was himself in the
fort during the battle, while others state that he was not.
It is, however, certain that his winter-quarters were with
the Narragansets, and that soon after the fight the In-
1675-6. dians sued for peace, but their overtures were rejected
through distrust. The remnant of the English army gar-
risoned at Wickford. A reinforcement of one thousand
Jan.   men was soon sent from Boston. So intense was the cold
at this time that eleven of their number were frozen to
death on the march, and many others were disabled by
sickness.

Philip removed his camp some twenty miles north to
a rocky swamp in the Nipmuck country. The distress of
the Narragansets for the want of provisions, all their winter stores having been destroyed in the battle, was extreme. A protracted and unusual thaw at midwinter, by
enabling them to obtain roots,[1] relieved their wants. The
army, now sixteen hundred strong, the Connecticut troops
having returned, proceeded to dislodge Philip from his
new position. The people of Warwick made arrange-
26.   ments to entertain the army as they should march through
that place. It was the last town meeting held there for

[1] " Ground nuts," as they are called by the old writers, meaning the wild
artichoke, a staple article of food with the Indians.

fifteen months. The place, left defenceless by the retiring army, was abandoned, and the inhabitants took refuge on the island, where their town meetings were regularly held, as if at home, for the choice of deputies and jurors. The town was annihilated for the time, but the corporation survived, and continued to discharge its legitimate functions. The Indians fled at the approach of the English, and retreated northward, driving off the live stock from Warwick. The army pursued them but a few miles, and soon after returned home and was disbanded. By this memorable campaign the power of the Narragansets was broken for ever. But the war was not ended, nor scarcely checked. It could not be, so long as the master-spirit of Philip survived. He went on an expedition to the Mohawks to obtain ammunition, and to secure if possible their alliance against the common enemy. The war was again transferred mainly to Massachusetts, but became more general than before. Everywhere the burning towns and mangled bodies of the English gave token of the relentless foe. Lancaster was burnt, and about forty persons killed and captured. Medfield next suffered to nearly the same extent. The boldness of the savages led them within about fifteen miles of Boston, where, at Weymouth, they burned several houses. The exposed condition of Providence led to an urgent call upon the governor for help. The reply of the deputy governor shows the exhausted condition of the colony, and their utter inability to support the force asked for, while at the same time it tenders to the distressed inhabitants the hospitalities of the island as a refuge—an offer of which they had speedy occasion to avail themselves. The letters addressed to Providence and Warwick by the General Assembly, especially convened on account of the war, were to the same effect.

The Indians on the island, above twelve years of age, were placed in custody of the whites, and were required

CHAP.
X.

1675-6.
Jan.

27.

Feb.
5.

10.

20.

25.

March
13.

CHAP.
X.

1675-6.
March
16.

1676.

26.

28.
to be guarded by day, and to be securely locked up at night. A further order was passed, "that no Indian in this colony be a slave"—a statute to which we shall again refer at the close of the war. An attack was now made upon Warwick. The town was entirely destroyed except one house, built of stone that could not be burnt. Only one of the inhabitants was slain. At the north and east the Indian ravages were still greater. Six towns in Massachusetts [1] were sacked, and more or less wasted by fire, and many persons slaughtered during this month. Disasters in the field were fearful and frequent. Captain Wadsworth, with fifty men, marching to the relief of Sudbury, was overwhelmed by a large body of Indians, and every man slain. The like fate attended Captain Peirse with the same number of English and some friendly Indians, a few days afterward, near Pawtucket Falls, and two days later Rehoboth, near which hostilities first began, was assaulted, and forty dwellings were burned This was the darkest period of the war. Success attended the savages on every side. The army had been too soon disbanded. The Narragansets, although broken, were not beaten in the great swamp fight, and terrible was the vengeance they executed far and wide over the land. Providence was nearly deserted, leaving it an easy prey to the enemy. Less than thirty men remained, as appears by a list, preserved on the records, of those "that stayed and went not away." Two places in the town had been fortified mainly through the efforts of Roger Williams, who, although seventy-seven years of age, accepted the commission of captain. A tradition is preserved, that when the enemy approached the town the venerable captain went out alone to meet and remonstrate with them. "Massachusetts," said he, "can raise thousands of men at this moment, and if you kill them, the

[1] Northampton, Springfield, Chelmsford, Groton, Sudbury, and Marlborough.

King of England will supply their place as fast as they fall." " Well, let them come," was the reply, " we are ready for them. But as for you, brother Williams, you are a good man ; you have been kind to us many years ; not a hair of your head shall be touched."[1] The savages were true to their ancient friend. He was not harmed, but the town was nearly destroyed. Fifty-four houses were burned.[2] The records were saved by throwing them from the burning house of John Smith, the miller, then town clerk, into his mill-pond. It was the north part of the town that was consumed. Within the memory of aged persons but recently deceased, the cellar walls of some of these houses were still standing, on the east side of the road just south of Harrington's lane, or North street, the northern limit of the city."[3]

At an adjourned meeting of the Assembly, a flotilla of gun-boats was ordered for the defence of the island. There were to be four boats manned by five or six men each, the force to be increased if necessary. These were employed in constantly sailing round the island to prevent invasion from the mainland. Of the size of these boats we have no certain knowledge, except that some of them were sloops.[4] This is the first instance, in the history of the

[1] Knowles, 346, and references in the note.

[2] Accounts vary as to the number. Some say twenty-nine, others thirty, and fifty-four. The largest number is probably nearest the fact. The discrepancy may arise from a distinction made but not stated, between dwellings and buildings. There is a difference of one day also in the date of this assault. The 29th and 30th of March are both assigned by different writers.

[3] The venerable John Howland, late President of the Rhode Island Historical Society, who died Nov. 5th, 1854, aged ninety-seven years, has often pointed out this spot to the writer, and told him that when he was a boy the foundation walls of several of these buildings were visible.

[4] A petition from Wm. Clarke in 1679, recites that he was " commander of *one of the sloops* in 1676," which was taken from him by the government, and for which he now asks indemnity. By a letter of Roger Williams in the archives of Connecticut, dated 27th June, 1675, it would appear that this naval force was composed of sloops, and that it was sent out nearly a year before it appears upon our records. Conn. MSS. vol. i. p. 200, in R. I. Hist.

CHAP. colonies, where a naval armament was relied upon for de-
X. fence.   It was the germ of a future Rhode Island squad-
1676. ron, one century later, and of an ultimate American navy.
April
4.   A classified census of all the people on the island was
ordered, English, negroes, and Indians, with those also who
had taken refuge there, and the amount of corn and arms
possessed by each, to be reported in detail to the Assembly.   The record of these interesting statistics cannot be
found.   Two heavy cannon were mounted at Portsmouth.
Sixteen " of the most juditious inhabitants" of the colony
were desired to attend the sittings of the Assembly, to ad-
vise with that body "in these troublesome times."

On the very day these proceedings were had, an event
took place that contributed more than anything which had
yet occurred to put an end to the war.   The capture of
Canonchet, the leader of the Narragansets, next to that of
Philip himself, was the most decisive blow.   It was he
who had defeated Capt. Peirse, nine days before, and had
cut off his entire command.   This terrible defeat roused
the United Colonies to more vigorous action.   Four companies of Connecticut volunteers, with three of friendly
Indians, immediately marched to attack Canonchet.   Capt.
George Denison of Stonington, who led one of the companies, was conspicuous for his zeal and bravery.   This force
surprised Canonchet near the scene of Peirse's massacre at
Pawtucket, and a rout ensued.   The Sachem fled, but
having slipped in wading the river, was overtaken on the
opposite bank by a Pequot and surrendered without resistance.   The first Englishman who came up to him was
a young man named Robert Stanton, who put some questions to the royal captive.   " *You much child!   No understand matters of war!   Let your brother or chief come.*

Soc. The same appears from Holden and Greene's petition in reply to the
Massachusetts agents. "The colony of Rhode Island and Providence, did, at
the request of the other colonies, assist them with several sloops well manned,
when the war was begun in Plymouth colony, to the utmost they could do,
and to the great damage of the enemy." Br. S. P. O. N. Eng., vol. iii. p. 26.

Him I will answer!" was the contemptuous reply after regarding the youth for a moment in silence. His life was offered him on condition of the submission of his tribe. He treated the offer with calm disdain, and when it was urged upon him, desired " to hear no more about it." He was sent in charge of Capt. Denison to Stonington, where a council of war condemned him to be shot. When informed that he must die, he made this memorable answer, which may challenge the loftiest sentiment recorded in classic or modern history. *" I like it well ; I shall die before my heart is soft, or I have said any thing unworthy of myself."* His conduct on this occasion has been justly compared with that of Regulus before the Roman Senate, than which the chronicles of time present but one sublimer scene. A higher type of manly character, more loftiness of spirit, or dignity of action, the qualities that make heroes of men, and once made demigods of heroes, than are found in this western savage, may be sought in vain among the records of pagan heroism or of Christian fortitude. To ensure the fidelity of the friendly tribes, by committing them to a deed that would for ever deter the Narragansets from seeking their alliance, it was arranged that each of them should take a part in the execution. Accordingly the Pequots shot him, the Mohegans cut off his head and quartered him, and the Niantics, who under Ninigret had joined the English, burned his body, and sent his head as " a token of love " and loyalty to the commissioners at Hartford. Thus perished the foremost of Philip's captains, and the last great Sachem of the Narragansets !

The death of Governor Winthrop of Connecticut was a severe loss to New England. Rhode Island had good reason to mourn his decease, for his inflexible justice would not assent to the spurious claims set up by his own colony in the Narraganset country, even while he was their chief magistrate. His personal qualities had endeared him in his youth to the people of Rhode Island, so that he was urged to move hither and become the governor. The conduct of his later years had served to confirm the esteem in which he was held, and now his death left Rhode Island without an influential friend in the councils of her ambitious neighbor.

Within a few days a still heavier loss befell Rhode Island. The two men who had been so long rivals in their public life, as agents of their respective colonies, but who had always maintained a mutual friendship, passed from the world almost together. Dr. John Clarke expired two weeks after Governor Winthrop, in the sixty-seventh year of his age. To him Rhode Island was chiefly indebted for the extension of her territory on each side of the bay, as well as for the royal charter. He was a ripe scholar, learned in the practice of two professions, besides having had large experience in diplomatic and political life. He was always in public life under the old patent, as commissioner and as general treasurer, from the first election of commissioners held under it, until sent to England, where he was employed as agent of the colony for twelve years. On his return, he served as a deputy in the Assembly from the first election under the charter till he was made deputy governor, to which position he was three times elected, and served twice, closing his public life with that office, five years before his death. With all these public pursuits, he continued the practice of his original profession as a physician, and also retained the pastoral charge of his church, as its records show. His life was devoted to the good of others. He was a patriot, a scholar, and a Christian. The purity of his character is conspicuous in many trying scenes, and his blameless, self-sacrificing life disarmed detraction and left him without an enemy. He was three times married but left no children. The colony was largely indebted to him for advances made in securing the charter, and this debt was not extinguished till many years after his decease.[1]

[1] He had mortgaged his Newport estate in July, 1663, to Capt. Richard

The General Assembly having provided for the naval defence of the island, adjourned one week and then created the office of Major-General. They elected Captain John Cranston, with the title of Major, to command all the militia of the colony. The commission is signed by Gov. Coddington, whose religious tenets were compelled, in this case, to succumb to the popular will under the stimulus of pressing danger. Providence was in ruins ; but as the time for planting was near, the handful of men who remained there again applied to the governor for aid in maintaining a garrison. Deputy governor Clarke replied, agreeing to sustain ten men at the colony's expense, until the next session of Assembly, when a committee was sent to Providence upon that business, and further action was postponed for another month.

At the general election, deputy governor Walter Clarke was chosen governor, and Major John Cranston deputy governor. Ten barrels of powder and a ton of lead were ordered to be bought.

For two months after the capture of Canonchet, there were no events of importance in the war. The Indians had gone north, and thither the Connecticut troops under Major Talcot pursued them. Their march to Brookfield and Northampton was a long and weary one, known, to this day, as "the hungry march," from the sufferings of the soldiers for want of food. They came in good time, for only four days after their arrival at the latter place, a force of seven hundred Indians made a furious assault upon Hadley, now for the third time attacked. It was then that the sudden appearance of Goffe,[1] the regicide, who

CHAP.
X.
1 6 7 6.
April
11.

12.

May
3.

June.
5.

12.

Dean, of London. The last payment was not made till Sept. 5th, 1699, when £115 was paid to the heirs of Capt. Dean, and the mortgage was lifted. Backus's Hist. of the Baptists.

[1] The tradition that Goffe and Whaley were at one time concealed in Narraganset, is strengthened by the suspicions of the royal Commissioners to that effect. In a letter from Fort James, New York, 31st Oct., 1666, to Mr. Richards, a constable in Kings Province, they, at his request, authorize him to

CHAP.
X.

1676.
June
12.

14.

19.

30.

unkown to the people was concealed near the town, served to rally the terrified inhabitants to battle until the troops from Northampton came to the rescue. His venerable aspect, mysterious appearance, and as sudden departure, so bewildered the population of Hadley, that they ascribed their deliverance to the interposition of an angel, so supernatural, in their minds, was the whole transaction. At this time, Col. Church concluded a treaty with Awashonks, queen of Seaconnet, by which her tribe was detached from the cause of Philip, and soon after united in the expedition under Church, that terminated the war. The daring displayed by Church in this negotiation, was equal to his skill in effecting the result.[1] Awashonks sent a messenger to Rhode Island, whose safe conduct was provided for by the Assembly. The Providence petition was granted by establishing a garrison of eight men, with two more, to be found by the owner of the garrison house at his own cost. Roger Williams, Arthur Fenner, William Harris, and George Lawton were appointed to select, from the garrisons already existing in Providence, the one best suited for the purpose, which was to be called the king's garrison. Captain Arthur Fenner was placed in command and duly commissioned. The Assembly had a series of adjournments all through this year, sitting every few weeks, as the exigencies of the time required. The army in passing through Providence, after the great swamp fight, had left there certain hostages or prisoners in charge of Roger Williams, who sent them for safe keeping to Newport. The Assembly ordered them to be returned to Providence, "judging they properly belong to Plymouth colony." It should be noted that the army left no garrison at Provi-

retain the cattle in his custody, giving security in the sum of £100 to the Governor of Rhode Island, for the surrender of said cattle when required, " as it appears to us by several testimonies and circumstances that the cattle are truly belonging to them," Goffe and Whaley. Br. S. P. O., New Eng. vol. i. p. 357.

[1] Church's History, 35–44.

dence, although, by the act of the confederates, the defenceless towns of Rhode Island were exposed to the merciless savages, who could not be expected, after the destruction of their fort by the English, to distinguish friend from foe among the whites. In fact every house between Providence and Stonington, except the stone one at Warwick, was burned, and every fertile field laid waste. The Assembly repealed the law exempting Quakers from bearing arms or paying military fines, and now required every citizen to do his part in personally defending the State. The exemption act was restored when the war was ended.

After the repulse at Hadley the Indians deserted that part of the country, and resumed their ravages to some extent in Plymouth. The English army marched to the south, and surprised them in a cedar swamp near Warwick. A great slaughter ensued. Magnus, the old queen of Narraganset, a sister of Ninigret, was taken, and with ninety other captives put to the sword. One hundred and seventy-one Indians fell in this massacre without the loss of a single man of the English. Thence they scoured the country between Providence and Warwick, killing many more. The effect of these repeated reverses was soon visible. The Indians were divided in their councils, and many sued for peace. Many came to Conanicut island, and submitted to the government of Rhode Island, and large numbers surrendered at discretion to the English forces. Others fled westward, and were chased from swamp to swamp. The main body of these were overtaken near the Housatonic river, by Major Talcot, and cut to pieces. Still Philip maintained his ground with a band of trusty followers. He had said that he would not live till he had no country, and the time was drawing nigh when his word would be redeemed.

Capt. Church was commissioned by Gov. Winslow to proceed with a volunteer force of two hundred men, chiefly Indians, to attack Philip in his retreats near Mount Hope.

CHAP.
X.

1676.
Aug.
1.

7.

12.

For several days they pursued the Indians from place to place, killing many and taking a large number prisoners, among whom were Philip's wife and only son. The sachem himself narrowly escaped being shot. Still his indomitable spirit sustained him. Two Rhode Island companies under Lieut. Richmond and Capt. Edmonds, brought in forty-two captives. These and all other prisoners were ordered to be sold into service in the colony for the term of nine years, one-half the proceeds to go to the captors and the rest to the treasury. No Indians were permitted to be brought into the island, or to be sent out of it without permission of the magistrates, under a penalty of five pounds.

Church closely followed up his successes, and in three days had captured over one hundred and seventy of Philip's followers. The sachem was driven to a swamp near Mount Hope, where one of his followers, advising him to sue for peace, was slain on the spot by the indignant chief. This indiscreet act hastened his own death. Alderman, a brother of the murdered man, deserted to Church, and guided the enemy to the place where Philip was concealed. The thicket was surrounded. Capt. Roger Goulding of Rhode Island went into the swamp to drive out the Indians. Philip in attempting to escape was shot through the heart by Alderman himself, thus singularly fulfilling the prophecy of the powaws at the beginning of the war, that Metacomet should never fall by English hands. The body was dragged out of the swamp, beheaded and quartered by an Indian. The head was sent to Plymouth, where it was set up on a gibbet for twenty years; one hand was sent to Boston as a trophy, and the other, which had a well-known scar, was given to Alderman, who made money by exhibiting it. The mangled body was hung upon four trees, a monument of the barbarity of the age. The great chieftain of the

aborigines fell by a traitor's arm, and was denied the rite CHAP. X.
of Christian burial by his vindictive foes !

Among those who fell in this attack was the Indian 1 6 7 6. Aug.
who had fired the first gun in the war. An idea was current in those days that whichever side began the war would be defeated, which may account for the report that Philip wept when he heard of the massacre at Swanzey. When we consider these two events, the manner of Philip's death, and the fall, at the same moment, of the Indian who commenced the war, and recall the two prophecies or traditions which contemporary writers record, the whole tragedy of the war assumes the air of an acted drama. The coincidences certainly could not be more remarkable in a written tragedy.

Most of the Indians escaped from the swamp guided by old Annawon, a noted warrior under Massasoit, and the chief counsellor of Metacomet. He was a wary savage, and none but a master of the art of Indian warfare, like Church, could have taken him alive. This was accomplished by Church a few nights after the death of Philip. Church wished to spare his life, but, in his absence, the Plymouth authorities ordered him to be shot. The most renowned captives met a similar fate. Quinapin, a cousin of Canonchet, and next to him in command 24.
at the great swamp fight, was sentenced to death by a council of war at Newport, and he with his brother were shot the next day. Pumham had already effaced the 25.
stain of a servile life by a manly death.[1] The friends of Philip were all executed, or met a fate worse than death in being sold away into perpetual slavery. Such was the fate of the young Metacomet, the only son of Philip, and hundreds of other captives were shipped to Spain and the West Indies.

One thing should be said to the lasting honor of the red

---

[1] He fell on the 25th July at the head of his warriors, in a battle near Dedham. Drake, Book iii. p. 75.

CHAP.
  X.   man.   The treatment of their prisoners was generally hu-
        mane, more so than was that of their Christian conquerors.
1676.   Some of the soldiers, it is true, were tortured, but only a
 Aug.   few, while the captives taken by the English were mostly
        butchered in cold blood, or sent into Spanish slavery.
        The English women were uniformly treated with respect.
        In not a single instance was violence offered to their per-
        sons during their captivity.   The chivalric honor of the
        savage was the inviolable protection of his female captive.
        This is the unvarying testimony of many women, of all
        ages and conditions, who were carried away in the sacking
        of the towns.[1]

        The war was ended.   Desolation reigned over New
        England, and destiny had placed the seal of annihilation
        upon the Indian race.   Victors and vanquished were alike
        exhausted.   Thirteen English towns were in utter ruin,
        and except in Connecticut, which altogether escaped,
        scarcely one remained unscathed.   The rural districts
        were everywhere laid waste.   One-eleventh of the avail-
        able militia of the country had fallen in battle, and a still
        larger proportion of buildings were destroyed.[2]   A heavy
        debt weighed upon the United Colonies,[3] while Rhode
        Island, excluded from the league and always opposed to
        the war, had suffered most severely of all.   Her mainland
        had become a desert, her islands fortresses for defence and
        cities of refuge.   We have already adverted to the sad
        fate of the captive Indians.   A few of the foremost in
        the war were condemned to death, but the greater part,

        [1] See Mrs. Rowlandson's narrative of her captivity.

        [2] Trumbull's Connecticut, 350, note.

        [3] Edward Randolph in his report to the Board of Trade, Oct. 12th, 1676,
        states the cost of the war at £150,000, that about twelve hundred houses
        were burnt, over eight thousand head of cattle destroyed, besides thousands
        of bushels of grain.   The English loss he puts at six hundred, with twelve
        captains, and the Indians at more than three thousand.   The original report
        is in the British S. P. O. N. England papers, vol. ii. p. 93–100.   See also
        Davis's Morton's Memorial, p. 458, Appendix, and Thatcher's Indian Biogra-
        phy, vol. i. p. 162.

in the other colonies, were sent abroad and sold into hopeless slavery. The conduct of Rhode Island was more humane, and her legislation on this subject, when we consider the spirit of the age and the example of her neighbors, was more enlightened. The act of March, to which we before referred, declared " that no Indian in this colony be a slave, but only to pay their debts, or for their bringing up, or custody they have received, or to perform covenant as if they had been countrymen and not taken in war." This was in fact a true apprenticeship system, whose terms were strictly carried out, such as generally existed until a recent day among the white population everywhere, differing only in the fact that one was voluntary while the other was not. It was not slavery either as it is recognized now or as it existed then ; and writers who have wasted regrets over the part that Roger Williams had in the final disposition of the Rhode Island captives, might have spared their words had they more carefully examined the nature of the transaction, or taken into account the spirit of the age and the conduct of the other colonies. At a town-meeting held in Providence upon this subject, a committee of five, of whom Williams was chairman, reported a scale by which the proceeds of the sale of Indians was to be divided among the towns- 14. men. The inhabitants were to be supplied at the rate current on the island. All captives under five years of age were " to serve till thirty ; above five and under ten, till twenty-eight ; above ten to fifteen, till twenty-seven ; above fifteen to twenty, till twenty-six ; from twenty to thirty shall serve eight years ; all above thirty, seven years." [1] An Indian named Chuff, who had been a ringleader in the assaults on Providence, was condemned by the council of war and shot. Still it was necessary to 25. preserve a strict watch over the natives. A warrant was

[1] An extract from an account of sales at this time, and showing the value of Indian service, is given in Judge Staple's Annals, 171.

CHAP.
X.
1676.

Aug.

29.

issued to stop all the canoes on Prudence Island, and not to permit any Indian to leave the island till further orders. Care was also taken to prevent their obtaining any arms or ammunition.[1] The refugees began now to return from Newport. Mrs. Williams was brought up in a sloop belonging to her son Providence, who on the same day carried away all the Indian prisoners to be sold at Newport. The eastern Indians, instigated by the French, continued for some years longer to harass the frontiers, and Col. Church was repeatedly sent against them. But the death of Metacomet closed the war in the settled portions of New England.

This war was the last struggle of an expiring nation. Before taking leave of the subject we may be allowed to present a few reflections suggested by the results. The Wampanoags and the Narragansets suffered the fate of the Pequots, and successive tribes, however powerful or warlike, have in their turn followed the same path to death. All history points to an inevitable law controlling the occupancy of the earth. Three races, and probably four, perhaps even more, have occupied this continent, but two of which remain, and one of these is fast retiring before the onward progress of the other. A century hence there will scarcely be a vestige of the Indian race upon this continent. They will have utterly disappeared, and, unlike their predecessors whose western tumuli and Aztec monuments survive the knowledge of their builders, and attest the existence of two successive races anterior to the Indians, they will not leave a proof upon the earth that they ever have existed. What is the law by which race after race of humanity succeed each other, each one continuing for untold ages, and then giving place to another utterly dissimilar to its predecessor? The question involves the very mystery of creation, and can never

[1] A copy of this warrant is in "Letters and Papers, 1632–1678," No. iii. p. 161, in the Mass. Hist. Soc.

be determined by finite minds. What we see daily occurring in our own and in other lands, where a higher
type of civilization is steadily and rapidly supplanting a
grosser and weaker barbarism, may serve to show the operation of a law that seems to have existed since the
formation of man. Wherever the arts, the customs, or
the religion of a superior race is brought in contact with
an inferior, the latter perishes. As geological science
teaches that successive eras in the material history of our
globe have produced steadily progressive forms of animal
life, adapted to each new change, so the law of progress
in the human family seems to be that a race which has
expanded to its utmost, filling the position that nature
assigned it, when brought in contact with a superior type
of humanity, must gradually but certainly disappear.
The Caucasian is the highest type of mankind, and
wherever it has appeared the inferior races have been
subdued or annihilated. The degree of resistance which
the inferior race opposes to this positive law is propor-
tioned to its approach to, or its remoteness from, the intellectual scope of the Caucasian. The changes that history presents in the different nations of the white race,
by conquest or assimilation, prove nothing against the
general law. Like modifies but cannot destroy like. The
different nations of the same type are improved by the
mixture of their elements. The history of Europe establishes this fact. It matters not whether the Anglo-Nor-
man or Saxon race is superior to all others of the Caucasian type, as some have claimed, or not. The question
is higher and deeper than that ; it is one of races, not of
nations.

It is a singular fact that the Indians, who before the
coming of the English were very prolific, soon ceased to
be so. Sterility became the rule and not the exception.
As the natural proclivity of mankind is to evil rather
than to good, the inferior race rapidly adopted the vices,

CHAP. while it rejected the religion, and but slowly apprehended
X. the arts and sciences of the white man. The Indians
1676. had attained their culminating point in mental and physical progress. Their intellectual powers admitted of no
higher development, and hence they were doomed, by this
inevitable law of Nature, to annihilation. They had fulfilled their destiny, and this continent was to be given up
to a higher type of humanity. Thus has it been in every
portion of the world where the white race has extended.

We do not present this as an excuse for the wrongs
inflicted upon the aborigines by our ancestors, and continued upon their feeble remnants at this day by ourselves ; but we do say, that this extinction of races is
something in the Providence of God which we cannot
avert if we would, and that everywhere the introduction
of the arts, religion, and commerce of Caucasian civilization has been attended with the same results. Centuries
may be required to accomplish the end, according as the
field of operation is extensive or limited, and as the influence exerted by the new race is concentrated or scattered ;
but the result is the same. From one cause and another,
some apparent and others not, the inferior race will gradually die out. So has it been on the Atlantic coast, and
thus is it progressing to the Pacific. War does not do it ;
the prevalence of new vices cannot fully account for it ;
famine and pestilence contribute but little in the aggre-
gate towards it, for all of these evils exist as actively, or
more so, among the dominant race. The law that gov-
erns it appears to be that which we have stated, and
which a recent writer thus announces, " that the organization God has created for one species of development is
radically unfitted to receive another." [1] That " other "

[1] Confessions of an Inquirer, by J. J. Jarves, Part I., p. 192. The writer
regrets that his limits do not permit him to expand this subject, but only to
throw out thus briefly a view which is the result of some reflection upon the
most interesting problem of human history. The curious reader will find a

has now been for two centuries at work upon this continent, and before its resistless advance the Indian——disappears. It is the fiat of the Almighty.

The General Assembly discharged Capt. Fenner and the King's garrison at Providence from further service. They also provided that all Indians who should come upon any islands in the bay, must have written authority therefor from the committee appointed to dispose of Indians, without which they would be liable to be sold into service as captives. The law of May, compelling every man to bear arms, was repealed, and that of 1673, exempting those who were conscientiously opposed to war from so doing, was re-enacted. Scarcely had the Indian war closed before the Connecticut colony renewed their claims to the Narraganset country. The council at Hartford, in addition to the words of their charter, now assumed to hold the Kings Province by right of conquest. The vigor with which they had prosecuted the war contrasted with the comparative inaction of Rhode Island, and to those who overlook the difference in their respective positions during this struggle, the claim appears reasonable. Connecticut had suffered nothing upon her own soil by hostile tribes. The Indians within her borders were friendly to the English, as the Narragansets had always been to Rhode Island, until exasperated by the wanton destruction of their stronghold by the United Colonies. She was thus enabled to send her troops abroad, and to render invaluable services to her more distressed neighbors, while Rhode Island, the most exposed of the

CHAP.
X.

1676.
Oct.
26.

27.

Aug.
23.

similar train of thought elaborated in chapter xxi. of the work above cited, which will richly repay the perusal. The observations of what is termed the American school of ethnologists, so far as they incidentally touch upon this branch of the subject, go to confirm the view here laid down, and that, too, altogether independent of the question mainly involved in their works, whether the Mosaic account of the creation is to be received in its literal signification. See Types of Mankind, Philadelphia, 1854. Indigenous Races of the Earth, Philadelphia, 1857.

CHAP.
X.

1676.

colonies, doing what she could to protect herself, and rendering efficient and acknowledged aid to the others, in supplies and men, according to her means, was now required to pay the penalty of her weakness, by surrendering the fairest portion of her domain. The council ordered that all persons, English or Indian, who had any rights in Narraganset, should apply to them for leave to occupy the same, and whoever should do otherwise would be dealt with severely. The Assembly took this matter in hand as the first business of the session, and sent a letter to Connecticut remonstrating in strong terms

Oct.
25.

against the act of her council, and protesting also against the policy and conduct of the late war, as well as the injustice of depriving her citizens of their property because they had been compelled to abandon it temporarily.

27.

They also set up a prohibition in Narraganset, forbidding any one to exercise jurisdiction there, or to dispose of lands except by authority of Rhode Island.

A fatal epidemic prevailed on the island at this time, so sudden in its effect, that two or three days sufficed to destroy the victim, and so general, that but few families escaped without the loss of some of their number.[1] Among the deaths that occasioned business for the Assembly was that of James Rogers, who had been longer and more steadily in public office than any other man in the colony, having been elected for twenty successive years, the first three as general solicitor, and the last eighteen as general sergeant—for one year he filled both offices. Thomas Fry was chosen as his successor.

[1] See A Journal of the Life, &c., of William Edmundson. London, 1713. After his first visit to Rhode Island, before referred to, in 1672, he returned to Ireland. In 1675 he made another missionary tour to the West Indies, and thence came to Rhode Island, made a journey to the eastward, and returned to Rhode Island at the close of the war, where he remained some time. He describes this pestilence, and was himself taken sick with it at Walter Newberry's house in Newport, but does not give the name of the disease.

A curious original document exists, showing the results of the sale of the first company of Indians on account of the townsmen of Providence. It is a receipt to the committee of sale, appointed by the August town-meeting, signed by those who were entitled to the proceeds, and showing the share of each man, thus far received, to be sixteen shillings and four pence half penny.[1] The Indians caused trouble by erecting their wigwams and mat sheds on the commons of the island and on private lands, where they became disorderly and drunken. Armed Indians also passed on and off the island without the required certificate. The governor and council ordered these wigwams to be removed, all liquors found therein to be seized and the bottles broken, and any armed Indian found without a proper passport to be brought before the magistrates. That the natives were not yet entirely peaceable, appears from the proceedings of a town-meeting at Providence, where a constant watch and ward was maintained, and armed bands or scouting parties, were ordered to scour the woods, and provision was made in favor of those who might be wounded on these expeditions. This precaution was often taken in later times whenever any alarm existed, and was required by the exposed situation of the town.

Peace being restored and planting time at hand, the people of Warwick and Narraganset returned to their now desolate plantations. But the latter were not permitted to rest in quietness. Three of their number were seized by Capt. Denison and carried prisoners to Hartford.[2] They immediately informed Gov. Clarke of the

CHAP.
X.

1676-7.
Jan.
1.

22.

March
4.

April
1677.

---

[1] The committee of sale were Arthur Fenner, William Hopkins, and John Whipple, jr. Foster Papers, vol. i. MSS.

[2] Thomas Gould, James Reynolds, and Henry Tibbitts. Gould afterwards compounded with Connecticut, and on 14th May petitioned for himself and others for leave to replant in Narraganset, acknowledging the authority of Connecticut. Conn. Col. Rec., ii. 540, note.

outrage, soliciting protection. The council promised relief, and also wrote to Connecticut, the same day, demanding their release, and threatening to make reprisals in case it was refused. This was the first business that occupied the new General Assembly.

At the election Benedict Arnold was chosen governor, in place of Walter Clarke, and Major John Cranston was continued as deputy governor. The Assembly confirmed the positions taken by the council in their letters to the Narraganset men and to Connecticut, and took measures for the re-settlement of Kings Province. A court of Justices was appointed to be held in Narraganset, with full powers to protect the settlers from the acts of the Connecticut officers. Ten thousand acres of land, to be equally divided among one hundred men, were appropriated for new settlers who should be approved by the Assembly, and all persons were forbidden to enter within the province except by authority of the Court. They also addressed another letter to Connecticut, reiterating their right to Narraganset, and declaring their intention to appeal to the King if these molestations were continued.

The election of Gov. Arnold was a triumph of the war party in Rhode Island. The militia law was now thoroughly revised ; but lest it should be considered as intrenching upon the rights of the Quakers, the preamble and the concluding proviso recited the necessity of military defence, and carefully proclaimed, in the words of the charter, the freedom of conscience. It was ordered to be published by beat of drum in all the towns of the colony. The King's garrison, as it was called, in Providence, which had been discharged in October, was re-established in the very words of the act by which it was first organized. The forms of engagement of officers, and of reciprocal engagement of the colony were redrafted, to be employed the next year, and an engagement to be at once administered to constables, who heretofore had never been formally qualified, was adopted. That Sabbatarian views were already maintained in the colony is shown by a petition presented at this time to change the market day, which heretofore had been Saturday only. The Assembly saw no sufficient reason to alter the day, but ordered that a market should likewise be kept in Newport on Thursday of each week. This and all other acts of the Assembly were "published in the town of Newport by beat of drum, under the seal of the colony, by the clerk of the Assembly." An adjournment was taken to allow time for a reply to be received from Connecticut, upon the most important business of the session.

The Assembly at Hartford, acting upon a petition of John Saffin in behalf of the Atherton claimants, appointed a committee to meet at Narraganset in June to lay out lands, and also encouraged the Wickford planters to return under their auspices. They replied to the two letters from Rhode Island, asserting their claims to jurisdiction, and acquiescing in the appeal to the King, but proposing, in a postscript, by way of compromise, that Cowesett, now East Greenwich, should be the boundary between the two colonies. This reply not being satisfactory, the General Assembly appointed Peleg Sandford and Richard Baily as agents of the colony, to proceed to England, and voted the sum of two hundred and fifty pounds for their outfit. A letter was sent, notifying Connecticut that Rhode Island would proceed at once to settle and govern Narraganset, and also offering to that colony one-half of all the unpurchased lands in the disputed territory, to be at their disposal, provided the settlers thereupon should submit to the government of Rhode Island. This was a futile attempt at compromise, suggested no doubt by the proposal made "for peace sake" by Connecticut. The Assembly then adjourned to the time appointed by Connecticut for the meeting of her committee in Narraganset. Upon reassembling, steps were taken to raise

CHAP. X.

1677
May 2.

10.

24.

June 11.

CHAP.
X.
1677.
June
11.

16.

15.

20.

27.

Oct.
31.

money in Newport and Portsmouth for the expenses of the agents to be sent to England. The sums raised were to be credited to account of the appropriation of ten thousand acres in Narraganset, at the rate of one shilling an acre. The Connecticut committee met on the same day in Narraganset, examined the country, and reported to their government concerning the quality and ownership of the lands. The proceedings of the Court of Justices held by Rhode Island are not preserved, although, upon its rising, the Assembly was again convened by warrant of the Governor, and ordered that the transactions of that Court should be a part of the public records. The council of Connecticut replied, rejecting the offer of land, and renewing their proposal to make Cowesett the boundary between the two charters.

At the fall session of the Assembly the law requiring deputies to take an engagement on entering upon the duties of their office, was repealed. It had been just five years in operation, was stoutly opposed, especially by the mainland towns, at the time of its passage, and had caused much hard feeling ever since. There seems to us no valid reason for all this, but the cause assigned for the repeal was that, as every freeman had already engaged true allegiance to the King and colony upon his admission, it was unnecessary to repeat the ceremony upon his taking office. This shows a degree of respect for the nature of an oath or engagement, more creditable to the morals of our ancestors, than is the constant and frivolous administration of oaths, in judicial and commercial affairs at this day, to ourselves. A tract of five thousand acres of land in Narraganset was laid out in two parts, one of five hundred acres on the bay, for house lots, and the remainder in farms of ninety acres each, and distributed among fifty men, who were now incorporated as the town of East Greenwich. The parties were to build upon their lots within one year or lose the land, and no one was to sell

his land within twenty-one years, unless by consent of the CHAP.
X.
Assembly, on pain of forfeiture. They were also to lay
out convenient roads from the bay up into the country.   1677.

The death of Samuel Gorton, the founder of Warwick, which occurred at this time, should not be passed
over in silence. He was one of the most remarkable men
that ever lived. His career furnishes an apt illustration
of the radicalism in action, which may spring from ultra
conservatism in theory. The turbulence of his earlier
history was the result of a disregard for existing law, because it was not based upon what he held to be the only
legitimate source of power—the assent of the supreme
authority in England. He denied the right of a people
to self-government, and contended for his views with the
vigor of an unrivalled intellect, and the strength of an
ungoverned passion. But when this point was conceded,
by the securing of a patent, no man was more submissive
to delegated law. His astuteness of mind and his Biblical learning made him a formidable opponent of the Puritan hierarchy, while his ardent love of liberty, when it
was once guaranteed, caused him to embrace with fervor
the principles that gave origin to Rhode Island. He lived
to "a great age." The time of his birth is not certainly
known, and the precise day of his death is equally obscure. "The exact spot," says his biographer, "where
his ashes repose, is marked by no pious stone or monu-
mental marble. Yet, if without other honors, may it at
least ever be their privilege to sleep beneath the green
sward of a free State!"[1]

A combination of local disputes, relating in the first
instance to proprietary rights, then involving questions
of boundary between Providence and Pawtuxet, and
finally extending beyond the present county of Providence, had commenced almost with the first settlement of

---

[1] He died between 27th Nov. and 10th Dec., 1677. Mackie's Life of Gorton, chap. viii. in Sparks' Am. Biog., vol. xv. pp. 378, 380.

the town, and now assumed a magnitude and importance that bring them within the legitimate province of State history. The details of these disputes are prolix and uninteresting. A survey of their chief points is all that we propose in this place.[1] They originated in a difference of construction put upon the deeds of Canonicus and Miantinomi to Roger Williams, and which was further complicated by a memorandum, added the following year, confirming the same. The last clause in the deed contained the words of disputed interpretation, " we do freely give unto him all that land from those rivers,[2] reaching to Pawtuxet river, as also the grass and meadows upon the said Pawtuxet river," which the confirmation made still more inexact by the words, " up the streams of Pawtucket and Pawtuxet without limits, we might have for our use of cattle." Hence arose a question, in after years, whether the tract whose limits, in the confirmation clause, were thus general and undefined, formed a part of the purchase, or whether it was merely a grant of the right of pasturage to the head waters of the two last-named rivers, with the fee still reserved in the grantors. It was a question of no importance at first, but when the town increased it gave rise to bitter dissensions, one party maintaining the former view, at the head of whom was William Harris, while the other, with Roger Williams as its leader, sustained the rights of the Indians. Williams had made the original purchase for himself, before the settlement of the town, and two years later drew this deed or memorandum, which does no credit to his legal acquirements. He however must have known better than any one else what it did mean ; but a party already existed against him who pressed their views with unnecessary asperity. When the Legislature, or " Court of Com-

[1] The reader will find a more full account of these divisions and disputes than is here given, in Judge Staples' Annals of Providence, chap. x.

[2] Mooshausick and Wanasquatucket.

missioners," as it was styled under the old patent, authorized the town to buy off the Indians, and to add three thousand acres to their territory by purchase from the sachems,[1] the town negotiated with the natives to obtain their removal, and in that year took three deeds, from the successors of Canonicus and Miantinomi, more clearly defining the disputed western boundary of the colony.[2] The two parties viewed these conveyances in different lights ; one considered them as simple confirmations of the original grant, the other as a new purchase. If they were only confirmations the whole tract belonged to the original proprietors of Providence, who were the owners of what was called, in the division of lands into two parts,[3] " the Pawtuxet purchase." But if these were in fact new purchases, the fee vested equally in those members of the corporation who had been admitted since the first grand division of lands. It is readily seen how important it was to each party that the settlement of this question should be in its favor. Again, whichever way this dispute of title might be settled, the deeds were so vague, and the rights exercised under them were so varied and unlimited, that nothing definite could be agreed upon as to the limits of the first grand division—where " the grand purchase of Providence" ended and " the Pawtuxet purchase" began. An attempt had been early made to determine this boundary,[4] but the line had never been run out, nor could it be, owing to the vagueness of the deed,

[1] May, 1659, ante, chap. viii.

[2] The first of these was given by Cawjaniquante, brother of Miantinomi, May 29th. 1659. It confirmed the old grant and defined it as extending from Fox's hill, twenty miles in a straight line up between Pawtucket and Pawtuxet rivers. His son acknowledged the deed 28th April following. The other two deeds, from resident sachems of the same family, were given 13th August and 1st December, confirming the first one, and granting the lands in fee simple, but with less exactness of boundary. All three deeds are printed in Staples' Annals, p. 567–70.

[3] Made Oct. 8th, 1638, ante ch. iv.

[4] July 27th, 1640, ante ch. iv.

both as to the nature and the limits of the rights conveyed in the concluding clause.   To restore peace among
the distracted townsmen Roger Williams made a proposition [1] for a new purchase from the Indians, and a separate
settlement in the disputed territory.   This was rejected
by Thomas Olney, William Harris, and Arthur Fenner,
in behalf of the town.[2]   A majority of the town having
decided [3] that the later deeds were simply confirmatory,
the Pawtuxet purchasers paid one-quarter of the cost,[4]
and the town limits were agreed to be at a point twenty
miles west of Fox hill.   A committee of three from each
place was named to run the line [5] between Providence and
Pawtuxet, and seven years afterward they made a partial
report covering less ground than was claimed by the Pawtuxet men, having ceased their surveys westward at a
point afterwards known as " the seven mile line."   Meanwhile William Harris made a voyage to England, to obtain justice from the King, but with no definite results.[6]

The disputes between Providence and Pawtuxet related solely to title, the whole tract being within the
township of Providence ; but soon after the purchase of
Warwick questions involving both title and jurisdiction
arose, the former between the purchasers of Warwick and
of Pawtuxet, the latter between the towns of Providence
and Warwick.   The Pawtuxet men were thus placed, as
it were, between two fires.   Legal measures were early
resorted to by the conflicting claimants for title.   Nu-

---

[1] 27th Oct., 1660.   [2] 29th Oct., 1660.   [3] March, 1660.

[4] The one-quarter paid to the Indians by the Pawtuxet purchasers for
these confirmation deeds amounted to twelve pounds one shilling and eight
pence, as appears by an agreement of a joint committee of the two parties,
composed of Roger Williams, Richard Waterman, Z. Rhodes, John Brown,
James Allen, and William Harris, in August, 1663. See MSS. papers of
William Harris, in possession of W. J. Harris, Esq.

[5] April, 1661.

[6] In 1663, the evidence of which is in a bill of costs presented by him
against the town of Warwick to the Court of Commissioners, 17th Nov., 1677,
preserved in the Harris MSS.

merous suits for trespass were brought in various Courts, without regard to jurisdiction.[1] Cross suits were instituted and counter writs of ejectment were issued, with no possibility of an unbiassed decision, owing to the mode in which the tribunals were constituted, the whole community being parties in interest, either directly or contingently, in every case, nor with any power to enforce a judgment, for the same reason. The progress of these various suits may be traced with great minuteness in the voluminous files of the Harris manuscripts. William Harris was generally successful in obtaining verdicts, but could rarely obtain execution, or have process served, under them. The officers were sometimes resisted by the contesting claimants, at others the awards of arbitrators or the decrees of Court failed to be carried out. He spent half his life in this fruitless litigation, the details of which, covering more than thirty years, would be tedious to the reader, and unimportant to the purpose of this work. So inextricable was the confusion, and so pressing the difficulties arising from these complicated sources, that William Harris, as agent for the Pawtuxet proprietors, at length resolved to go a second time to England, to petition the King for a special commission to decide upon them. The petition was referred to the Board of Trade.[2] It set forth the rival claimants to portions of the Pawtuxet lands, and prayed that the governors of the four New England colonies, or such men as they might appoint, with a jury chosen in part from each colony, should settle all differences in the premises.[3] The mission was successful. A royal order was issued to the

---

[1] The Pawtuxet subjects of Massachusetts in 1650 sued W. Harris for trespass, and judgment was rendered for the defendant July 31. Harris was himself one of the Pawtuxet proprietors.

[2] On June 11th, 1675.

[3] The petition of 1675, with the order upon it issued 4th August, and the royal letter to the four governors, dated August, 1675, is entered in the British State Paper Office, New England papers, vol. xxxii. pp. 38–47.

CHAP. four governors who, after some delay, appointed commis-
X. sioners to hear the disputes.[1] They met at Providence,
1677. and empanelled a jury of four from Massachusetts, two
Oct.
3. from Plymouth, and three each from Rhode Island and
Nov. Connecticut. The Court then adjourned to meet at Prov-
17. idence, where five cases were tried, three against private
parties for trespass, the other two against the towns of
Warwick and Providence, to compel them to run the
boundary lines before agreed on, and to decide the title of
lands on either side of these lines. William Harris,
Thomas Field, and Nathaniel Waterman were the plaintiffs, and Harris was the attorney for Pawtuxet, in all
these cases. Randall Holden and John Greene were appointed [2] by the town of Warwick to defend her cause.
Roger Williams, Gregory Dexter, and Arthur Fenner appeared in behalf of Providence. The trials occupied four
days, and resulted in a verdict for the plaintiffs on every
case.[3] The town of Warwick, being cast in the suit, at
once appointed [4] their two attorneys, as agents, to proceed
to England to represent their case before the throne, and
21. to protest against the second verdict of the jury. Warrants were issued to compel execution of the verdicts, but
the question of costs was reserved for advisement with the
respective governors, the Court doubting its powers to issue execution for them.

In order to present these controversies, so far as they
have a public interest, in a compact form, we shall be
obliged to pass somewhat beyond the period to which this
chapter is limited, condensing as much as possible the pro-

[1] These were Simon Lynde and Daniel Henchman of Mass., Thomas
Hinckley, Esq., and James Cudworth, Esq., of Plymouth, Capt. George Denison and Daniel Witherell of Conn., Peleg Sandford, Esq., and John Coggeshall, of R. I.

[2] Oct. 1, 1677. See Warwick records.

[3] The pleadings in full are preserved among the Harris MSS.

[4] 29th Nov., 1677. See Warwick records, and their commissions were
read and approved in town meeting, 18th January.

ceedings of the next two or three years upon these cases, and then leave the subject for ever.

To decide the question of costs, the Court met at Boston, but the Connecticut members being absent, it was adjourned to meet at Providence. The eight commissioners assembled there, but found that nothing had been done about running the line between Providence and Pawtuxet in accordance with the verdict, which required it to be run by the defendants "equally between Pawtuxet river and Wanasquatucket river, till they meet a thwart line from the head of Wanasquatucket river, directly running to Pawtuxet river." An imperfect line, contrary to the intent of the Court's order, had been surveyed between the two rivers, a map of which was presented by Mr. Fenner, but rejected by the Court, as being unfair towards the plaintiffs ; as the thwart line was drawn to intersect it at an acute instead of a right angle. The Court summoned the jury to appear in October, and explain their verdict in this case, the third in the order of trial. At this meeting, one of the commissioners being absent, the two from Rhode Island withdrew, deeming the Court disqualified to act unless every member was present. The others, considering a quorum to be sufficient, proceeded to act. The jurors were all present, but the three from Rhode Island refused to explain the verdict. The other nine explained the meaning of their third verdict, that the two lines were to intersect at right angles. Still, as some of the Court were absent, and others doubted their power, under these circumstances, to issue warrants to enforce its execution, as now explained, the whole matter was referred back to the king, and a full statement of the case was prepared and sent to England by Governor Leverett.[1]

CHAP.
X.

1678.
May
23.

June
18.

Oct.
2.

[1] This long statement details the manner in which the Court and jury were constructed, the five verdicts rendered, and all subsequent proceedings of the commissioners. It is entered in New England papers, vol. xxxii. p. 296. Br. S. P. O.

CHAP.
X.

1678-9.
Jan.
2.

1679.
June
19.

July
2.
9.

Sept.
30.

Nov.
24.

Holden and Greene went to England to protest against the second verdict, which required the town of Warwick and certain individuals in it, as tenants by force, to restore the land, with one hundred pounds damages, to the plaintiffs. They obtained an arrest of judgment by royal decree, till Harris should prove title before the king in council. Scarcely had they left London to return home, when Harris appeared, for the third time in England, to urge the cause which law and justice had so often decided in his favor. Exceptions had been taken by the Warwick agents against having referees from Massachusetts or Connecticut, by reason of their former difficulties with Warwick men, and a valid objection was now made by Harris against any Rhode Island referees, as being interested parties. The council therefore recommended that the Magistrates of Plymouth colony should decide the questions between Warwick and Pawtuxet, and that Rhode Island be required to put Harris in possession of his lands under the other four verdicts, within three months from the time of receiving the order, or otherwise that Plymouth should see it done. An order to this effect passed the council, and letters were prepared in accordance therewith.[1] Thus Harris was again triumphant before the highest tribunal in the realm, but justice was still withheld. Governor Winslow gave the parties a hearing and decided in favor of Harris, confirming the verdict against Warwick.[2] The governor and council of Rhode Island received the royal order brought over by Harris, and placed a warrant in the hands of the marshal, to execute judgment in accordance with the verdicts. This he attempted to do, but it would

---

[1] The report in full is entered in New England papers, vol. xxxii. p. 346, S. P. O. R. I. Col. Rec., iii. 66.

[2] Oct. 28th Gov. Winslow summoned the parties interested in the second verdict, and after a full hearing confirmed the action of the Court of Commissioners in favor of Harris. On 2d Nov. he sent a report of the case to the King, now preserved among the Harris MSS., giving a clear statement of the questions involved in that case, and the reasons of his decision.

seem that the plaintiffs themselves refused to receive possession except in the terms of the verdict, which required
the defendants to run the lines. This they had not done,
and the marshal properly refused to do it, although urged
to do so by the plaintiffs. At any rate, the plaintiffs failed
to point out the lands, and the marshal made his return
in accordance with these facts. The truth of this return
was denied by the plaintiffs who collected evidence to im-
peach it. Harris, resolute amid all these obstacles, immediately sailed for England for the fourth time. On this
occasion, besides his Pawtuxet business, he was the accred-
ited agent of Connecticut in her claim against Rhode
Island for the Narraganset country. The ship was captured by a Barbary corsair, and he, and other prisoners,
were taken to Algiers, and sold in public market as slaves.
For more than a year he remained in this sad situation,
when his ransom was effected at a cost of twelve hundred
dollars. The colony of Connecticut became responsible
for the whole amount and contributed handsomely towards
it. The money was afterwards refunded by his family.
Landing at Marseilles in the summer he travelled through
France, and broken down by the trials of Turkish bondage,
died in three days after reaching London.

Thus perished one of the strong men of Rhode Island.
He filled a large space in the early history of the colony,
as an active, determined man, resolute in mind and vigorous in body, delighting in conflict, bold in his views on
the political dogmas of his time, fearless in his mode of expressing them, striking always firmly, and often rashly, for
what he believed to be the right, and denouncing with the
energy of a concentrated intellect all men or measures
that did not conform to his ideas of truth or of justice.
His controversy with Roger Williams, we have before referred to. It was never forgotten, and scarcely forgiven,
by either of these great men, and presents the darkest blot
that rests upon their characters. The public career of

CHAP.
X.

1681.

Harris was almost uninterrupted, except by his frequent voyages, and these were always upon official business.   As an assistant or a deputy, his name constantly occurs in connection with important trusts, and no man, unless it be his great opponent, has left a deeper mark upon the records of his State.

1682.

The year following his death, another attempt was made to settle the controversy between Providence and Pawtuxet by mutual agreement.   The line agreed upon narrowed the limits of the Pawtuxet purchase more than any previous attempt at adjustment had done.   The same committee were to settle the Warwick dispute.   Both attempts failed, and the line between Providence and Warwick was finally settled by the legislature in 1696, as it now exists, making the Pawtuxet river the boundary. This gave to Providence jurisdiction over the litigated tract, which was on the north side of the stream included in a bend of the river.   The other controversy was maintained at great cost, agents being employed in England, and hearings had before the royal council as late as 1706, all to no practical result.   It was finally settled by compromise in May, 1712, when the line was run and bounds set up, reducing still further the limits of the Pawtuxet purchase.   The moral conveyed in the result of this protracted and costly litigation is apparent.

CHAPTER XI.

1678—1686.

FROM THE RENEWAL OF THE STRUGGLE FOR THE SOIL OF RHODE ISLAND, 1677-8, TO THE SUSPENSION OF THE CHARTER, JUNE, 1686.

THERE are many periods of Rhode Island history, some of which we have already passed, that could not be truly written without a free access to the archives of the British government. To no period does this remark apply more fully than to that upon which we entered at the close of the preceding chapter. The Harris controversy is scarcely referred to in the State records, the council minutes having been sent to England as evidence. The struggle for jurisdiction that was now to be resumed on every side against Rhode Island, was soon transferred to the English Court, in whose archives alone its progress can be correctly traced. The disasters suffered by Rhode Island during Philip's war, furnished the occasion for a renewal of the disputes that, with one exception, had been definitely settled by the royal commissioners of 1664. Even Connecticut, as we have seen, had acquiesced for a time in the decision of Sir Robert Carr, but soon took exceptions to that settlement based upon the absence of Col. Nichols, governor of New York, who was induced, upon no valid grounds, to dissent from the unanimous decree of his colleagues in favor of Rhode Island. The war had for a time suspended the dispute in regard to the jurisdiction of Narraganset, but now her claims were put forward with increased energy, on the new ground that it belonged to her by right of conquest—the same reason that had formerly been put forth by Massachusetts after the Pequot war. Massachusetts also entered the field again as a claimant, in behalf of the heirs of the Atherton company ; and Plymouth, not satisfied with the decision that bounded her upon Narraganset bay, until the King's pleasure should be further known, injudiciously sought to re-open the question, assigning reasons for so doing that may well excite surprise. Thus the ancient controversies with all her neighbors were re-opened, and Rhode Island, weakened by pestilence and wasted by war, was again involved in the struggle for existence.

It is not enough to say that, after nearly seventy years of further contest, she came out more than victorious over all her opponents, not only retaining the territory which they sought to wrest from her, but adding something to it from two of them at least ; but we must trace the progress of the struggle, if we would have even a faint idea of the difficulties that beset her. At one time it will appear as if all was lost, and that the colony must be absorbed by her ambitious sisters, and again the recuperative energy of the sturdy "heretics" will seem to have already won the battle. The plan of having resident agents in London soon came from necessity to be adopted by each of the New England colonies, the record of whose acts, in many cases, can only be found among the archives of the home government.

1678.
While the era upon which we now enter is memorable for the above-named causes, the present year is not less remarkable for the changes wrought by death in the chief magistrates of the colony. No less than three different

governors filled that place within five months, two of CHAP.
whom died in office.   The lapse of forty years was telling XI.
the tale of mortality upon the founders of the State. 1678.
The first generation of Rhode Islanders was fast passing
away.

The force of the colony at this time was from one May
thousand to twelve hundred freemen able to bear arms.[1] 1.
At the election Benedict Arnold was again chosen governor, and Major John Cranston deputy governor.   Gov.
Arnold was then too ill to attend the Assembly, so that
the engagement was administered to him by a committee
at his own house.   The tax law was further modified at
this session, and as taxation without representation was
one of the prime grievances which, a century later, roused
the American colonies to arms, it is important to notice
how early and deeply-rooted was this idea in the Rhode
Island mind, and how frequently it appears upon the statute book of the State.   By an existing law [2] no tax could
be assessed without a full representation of deputies from
all the towns.   This was now amended so as to require
legal notice to be given, by warrant from the governor, to
every town, that a tax was to be assessed, without which
notice no levy could be made.[3]   Since the creation of the
office of major, during Philip's war, the choice of that
officer had devolved upon the militia, but this was now
changed, and all freemen were admitted to vote upon the

[1] Report of Sir Edmund Andros to Board of Trade received 9th April,
1678, in reply to queries on the state of the New England colonies, addressed
to him the day previous.   A rough draft of the seventeen queries is filed in
Br. S. P. O.   New England, vol. ii. p. 140, and the original answer on pp.
149, 150.   By this the relative strength of the colonies may be ascertained.
Sir E. A. had lately returned from America, where he had been governor of
New York.   He estimates Connecticut force at 3000, Rhode Island 1000 to
1200, Plymouth 1000 to 1500, and Massachusetts 8 to 10,000.

[2] Passed Nov. 6th, 1672.

[3] It was soon found necessary to repeal this act.   The struggle to maintain the rights of the colony in England often required money to be raised to
meet emergencies, which could not be done promptly under this statute.   It
was therefore repealed in July, 1679.

question, provided they personally appeared to do so, upon election day. A permanent court-martial for the trial of delinquent soldiers was instituted, to consist of the major and a majority of the commissioned officers of the several military companies in the colony. A bankrupt law was also passed, based upon the statutes of Elizabeth and James. Five men were chosen as commissioners of bankrupts, who were sworn to make a just and proportionate distribution of insolvent estates among the creditors. They were to notify parties interested to present their claims, and had full power to do all acts necessary to the fulfilment of their commissions.[1] This law, for some reason not apparent, could not stand the test of the first case that was brought up for action under it, and was repealed within six weeks, at the beginning of the adjourned session of the Assembly. The conflict of land titles in Narraganset, among private owners as well as townships, led the Assembly to order a survey and plats to be made of the several tracts. They also required all purchasers, who held by Indian titles, to present their deeds to be passed upon by the Assembly, in order that the vacant lands might be known and should not be settled upon except by their order. Fast riding within the compact parts of Newport was forbidden under a penalty of five shillings, on account of an accident from that cause which had lately occurred. Constables were re-appointed for the towns in Kings Province.

A greater accuracy in the terms employed in framing statutes is observable at this time. The additional words, " and by the authority thereof be it ordained, enacted, and declared," appended to the enacting clause of a law, which surplusage, with slight modifications, continued in use till a very recent date, appear for the first time at

---

[1] The commissioners of bankrupts were the deputy governor, Major John Cranston, the general treasurer, Peleg Sandford, John Coggeshall, the general recorder, John Sandford, and the attorney-general, Edward Richmond.

this session. Again, the law of 1647 which empowered the town councils to appoint an " executor " upon the estate of a deceased intestate, was amended by substituting for that term " the word administrator ; it being in that case the more proper and usual term in the law." Among the curiosities of legislation may here be cited the concluding clause of an act making a final settlement of the accounts of the late general sergeant, which it seems were so involved as to be beyond the power of the auditing committee to strike a balance. It was therefore voted to call the accounts square, " and that by this act there is a full and fynall issue of all differences relating to the said accounts from the beginninge of the world unto this present Assembly ! " A more comprehensive statute cannot well be imagined. The military power, which during the war had been placed in the hands of the town councils, was now taken from them, and vested more completely in the major-general, who could call out all the troops for exercise at his pleasure, and was subject only to the orders of the Assembly, the governor, deputy-governor, or their council.

20.

Scarcely had the Assembly adjourned when Gov. Arnold died. He had been a resident of Newport for twenty-five years, having removed from Providence during the division that continued in the colony for more than a year after the revocation of Coddington's commission, and was very instrumental in effecting the subsequent reconciliation and union of the towns. From that time he was almost constantly in public office, first as a commissioner from Newport and then as assistant. For five years he was President of the colony under the old patent, and was named in the second charter as governor, which office he filled at seven different times by popular election.[1] His liberal views and thorough appreciation of the Rhode

[1] He was elected a commissioner in 1654, 1656—assistant in 1655, 1660–61—president in 1678-9, 1662–63—governor in 1663-4-5-9, 1670-1-77 and 78, and died in his sixty-fourth year.

CHAP. Island idea of intellectual freedom, appear in the letters
XI.
~~~~   that, as president of the colony, he wrote in reply to the
1678. arrogant demands of the United Colonies, when they urged
June
20.   the forcible expulsion of the Quakers.[1] That he was no
friend of the doctrines, or advocate of the conduct, of the
followers of Fox, is evident from his writings ; but that,
like Williams, he recognized the distinction between persecution and opposition, between legal force and moral
suasion, as applied to matters of opinion, is equally apparent. In politics and theology he was alike the opponent of Coddington and the friend of John Clarke, and
throughout his long and useful life he displayed talents
of a brilliant order, which were ever employed for the welfare of his fellow-men.

July   Active demonstrations were soon made both here and
in England by the several claimants for the soil of Rhode
Island. The first of these proceeded from Plymouth in
a letter to the King, recounting the disasters sustained
by that colony during the war. It goes on to say, " our
neighbors of Rhode Island were once so ungrateful, after
we had freely given them the said island,[2] to accommodate
them in their distress when banished by the Massachusetts, that by misinformation they obtained from your
Majesty a good quantity of the best of our land on the
maine, the same that we now call conquest lands, but
better informed by your commands, you were pleased to

[1] These two letters are printed in R. I. Col. Rec., i. pp. 376–80.

[2] The claim here set up that Aquidneck was "freely given," is somewhat
remarkable in view of the fact that when Williams and Clarke, with the Antinomian committee, went to Plymouth early in March, 1637–8, to inquire
about their contemplated settlement at Sowams, that spot was claimed " as
the garden of Plymouth patent," and the applicants were advised to select the
other location, which they had also in view, Aquidneck, because it was beyond the limits of Plymouth patent. See Clarke's Narrative, or Ill News
from New England, p. 24–5, and ante chap. ii. Now, forty years later,
they claim, to the King, that the island was " freely given," and charge Rhode
Island with being "ungrateful" for the signal favor of having received at
their hands what they admitted at the beginning did not belong to them.

return it again to us. We have reason to fear they are
coveting it, or part of it, again, and it may bee some of
them will pretende to have a right of purchase of the Indians, &c." It next assails the conduct of Rhode Island
during the war, in these words: " The truth is the authority of Rhode Island being all the time of the warr in
the hands of Quakers, they scarcely showed an English
spirit, either in assisting us, their distressed neighbors, or
relieving their own plantations upon the Mayne,[1] but
when, by God's blessing upon our forces, the enemy was
routed and almost subdued, they tooke in many of our
enemyes that were flying before us, thereby making profit
by our expence of blood and treasure," &c.[2]

These extracts indicate the spirit of the opponents of
Rhode Island, and the new line of policy they had adopted
to obtain their ends.

The proceedings of Massachusetts and of her agents
in England were equally decisive. A printed advertisement was struck off in Boston, and soon afterward posted
in the town of Newport, signed by a committee of the
Narraganset proprietors, in right of the Atherton purchasers, offering for sale, upon advantageous terms to actual settlers, tracts of land in that country, and describing
it as being within the jurisdiction of Connecticut.[3]

---

[1] There is more truth than poetry in this clause of the sentence, and indeed it is the only truth contained in the whole paragraph. But if the mainland towns, appreciating the reasons of the neglect they certainly experienced
from the island, failed to complain very much about it, we see no cause why
Plymouth should vex herself in their behalf; and it comes with an ill grace
from one of the United Colonies when they had wantonly made Rhode Island
their battle ground, and then failed to leave a garrison within her borders after the great swamp fight.

[2] This letter, dated 13th July, 1677, and signed "Nath. Morton, Secy., by
order of the Great Court," is entered in Br. S. P. O. New England papers,
vol. xxxiii. p. 5.

[3] This handbill is signed by Simon Bradstreet, John Saffin and Elisha
Hutchinson, and is preserved in New England papers, vol. iii. p. 46. Br. S.
P. O., and printed in R. I. Col. Rec., vol. iii. p. 18, from a copy in Mr.
Brown's MSS.

CHAP.
XI.

1678.

Aug.

10.

The course pursued by Holden and Greene, as the agents of Warwick in the Harris case, opened the whole discussion of the past conduct of Massachusetts. They had protested against having any Massachusetts referees in a matter where their town was concerned. This drew an answer from the agents of that colony,[1] wherein they incautiously ventured upon a sketch of the early history of Warwick, defending the acts of Massachusetts, assailing the character of the petitioners, and charging Rhode Island with disloyalty upon sundry occasions. This was an unfortunate train of argument for the respondents to adopt. The Warwick men at once retorted with great severity in a petition, relating the facts of the case, exposing the fallacies of their opponents, repelling their attacks upon the loyalty of Rhode Island, adducing record proofs of the disloyalty of Massachusetts, and concluding with a series of requests; first, that a Supreme Court of judicature over all the colonies may be erected in New England, whereby equal justice may be rendered, boundary disputes be adjusted, and civil war, which must otherwise result from "the oppressions of an insulting and tyrannical government," may be averted; second, that the royal letter of 1666, confirming the acts of the commissioners in behalf of Rhode Island, may be renewed; third, that Connecticut may be compelled to restore the town of Westerly, lately taken from Rhode Island by force; and lastly, that the decisions of Massachusetts against Warwick men, especially the decree of banishment against Randall Holden, now of thirty-five years standing, may be annulled.[2] The petition was accompanied by a number of documents going back to the pur-

---

[1] William Stoughton and Peter Bulkely. Their answer is of the same date in London as the handbill in Boston, July 30th, 1678. The original paper is in Br. S. P. O., vol. iii. p. 47, of New England papers.

[2] The original of this masterly state paper, as conclusive as it is severe, is filed in the Br. S. P. O. New England papers, vol. iii. p.24–7.

chase of Warwick, and corroborating the positions advanced by its authors.[1]

The General Assembly at the adjourned session proceeded at once to fill the vacancy in the office of governor, and William Coddington was chosen.   A committee
waited upon Mrs. Arnold, widow of the deceased governor, to obtain the charter and other public papers, late in
the official custody of her husband.   Attention was called
to the Atherton handbill, which had been set up in Narraganset by John Saffin, one of the signers, " whoe forthwith fled off the island from the hands of justice."[2]   A
declaration of ownership by Rhode Island, and prohibition to all persons against settling upon the lands without
leave of the Assembly, was immediately passed ; copies
of it were sent to every town in the colony, to be posted

---

[1] These documents are not filed with the petition, but are found scattered
among the papers in the same and other volumes, with other evidence presented at different times by Holden and Greene, upon these and other points
connected with their mission.   Seven of these documents are contained in
pages 2 to 6 of the same vol. iii. of New England papers, viz., Submission of
Narragansets, 19th April, 1644.   Reception thereof by the commissioners,
20th March, 1664.   Warning sent by Warwick to Massachusetts men,
28th Sept., 1643.   Sentence of Massachusetts Court against Gorton, 3d
Nov., 1643.   Naming and bounding of Kings Province, 20th March, 1664.
Appointment of Rhode Island officers as justices there, 8th April, 1665.
Cartwright's letter to Gorton, 26th May, 1665.   The facts of which these
and many other papers deposited at this period are confirmatory evidence we
have stated in their proper place, but have not before mentioned where the
official copies, if sought for, may be found.   Although sent originally by
Warwick upon the Harris land case, the general business of the colony soon fell
into their hands.   The colony agents, Sandford and Bailey, appointed 24th
May, 1677, did not go to England.   The Warwick men showed themselves
fully competent for the most difficult labors of negotiation or of defence, and
upon their return the Assembly, in July, 1679, voted them the sum of sixty
pounds, of which forty-five pounds had been disbursed by them on the colony's account in England, and the balance was for their passage home.

[2] He was afterwards arrested and imprisoned under a warrant issued by
Gov. Cranston, 14th April, 1679.   MS. files of Mass. Hist. Soc., and a letter was sent by Massachusetts to Rhode Island, 3d June, demanding his release—Trumbull papers, vol. xxii. No. 95—but no notice was taken of it by
the Rhode Island Assembly.   He was tried, fined, and his estate forfeited.

CHAP.
XI.
1678.

in conspicuous places, and the act was published by beat of drum in the town of Newport.

A case involving the question of the revising power of the Assembly over the proceedings of the General Court of Trials, which has since been often agitated in this State, was presented ; the action upon which shows that the importance of an independent judiciary was felt at that early day, and that the Assembly clearly understood their legitimate powers, and had no desire to exceed them. The case of Sandford against Forster had been twice legally tried by the Court, when one Colson petitioned the legislature, in behalf of the defendant, for a reversal of judgment. We quote the language of the vote upon this petition : " This Assembly conceive that it doth not properly belong to them, or anywise within their recognizance, to judge or to reverse any sentence or judgment passed by the Generall Court of Tryalls, according to law, except capitall or criminall cases, or mulct or fines."

Oct.
30.

When the next regular session of the Assembly was held, Governor Coddington was on his death-bed. " He died November 1st, in the seventy-eighth year of his age, a good man, full of days." [1] He was a man of vigorous intellect, of strong passions, earnest in whatever he undertook, and self-reliant in all his actions. Such a man could not fail to occupy a prominent place in any community. He was one of the Assistants of the Massachusetts Company in England, came over with it to America, and was a leading merchant in Boston, where he built the first brick house. With the larger number of the more liberal and educated people of that town, he espoused the Antinomian views, and upon the overthrow of that cause, emigrated to Aquedneck, which island he purchased in his own name for himself and associates. He was made the first judge or chief magistrate of the new colony, and continued to be its governor till the union of the towns under the first

[1] Callender's Dedication, p. 52, R. I. H. C., iv.

patent.   In Newport he was the first person who ever engaged in commerce.   The distraction that prevailed in the
colony was no doubt the motive of his voyage to England
to obtain a commission as governor of the island for life.
This was a direct, and as the event proved, an unwarranted
usurpation, in which he was opposed by Clarke, Arnold, and
nearly all the freemen of the island, and for which we can
best account in the words of one who thoroughly appreciated the principles and the men of early Rhode Island.
" He had in him a little too much of the future for Massachusetts, and a little too much of the past for Rhode
Island, as she then was." [1]   After the revocation of his
power he led a retired life for many years.   During this
interval, he embraced the views of the Friends, and was
distinguished for his zeal in their cause, and the vigor with
which he combated those who differed from his opinions.
Latterly he had engaged to some extent in public affairs.
He was once elected deputy governor and three times governor, in which office he died.[2]

The Assembly adjourned till the following Monday, 4.
when Conanicut island was incorporated as a township,
and called Jamestown in honor of the King.   Another adjournment then took place, probably for the funeral of Gov.
Coddington, after which the chief business of the session
was transacted.   The deputy governor, John Cranston, was 8
then elected Governor, and the first Assistant from New- to
port, James Barker, was chosen deputy governor.   Each 15.
took the engagement to his new office and was formally ab-
solved from his previous official engagements.   The two
Assistants next to Barker were each raised one step without taking a new engagement, and a third Assistant, Caleb
Carr, was elected and engaged.   The charter and other

[1] Chief Justice Durfee's Historical Discourse, p. 16.
[2] He was a deputy from Newport in March, 1666, and an assistant in October of that year. In 1673 he was chosen deputy governor, and the two
following years governor, and again in August, 1678, by the Assembly.

papers, as usual, were obtained from Mrs. Coddington and placed in custody of the new governor. The duplicate copy of the charter, which had hitherto been kept by John Clarke, was also obtained from his executors, and has ever since been preserved, first in the custody of the deputy governor, and then by the General Assembly in the Secretary's office.[1]

15.   A rate of three hundred pounds was laid. As this was the first tax assessed since the war, the great disproportion observed in its allotments, indicates the relative degree in which the towns had suffered. A comparison of this with previous taxes will show how recent events had affected the prosperity of different portions of the colony. Newport was assessed one hundred and thirty-six pounds, Portsmouth sixty-eight, New Shoreham and Jamestown each twenty-nine, Providence ten, Warwick eight, Kingston sixteen, one-half of which was afterwards remitted, East Greenwich and Westerly two pounds each. Thus it will be seen that while every town bore its share, the two towns on Aquedneck paid more than two-thirds of the whole levy, the three islands together paid seven-eighths of the tax, and the five mainland towns less than one-eighth. So great a disproportion has never been observed before or since. The prices placed upon articles of food and raiment, in commutation of this tax, give us valuable information as to the cost of living at this time. Fresh pork was valued at two pence a pound, salted and well packed pork, fifty shillings a barrel, fresh beef twelve shillings a hundred weight, packed beef, in barrels, thirty shillings a

[1] At the January session of the present year, 1858, it was " Resolved, That the Secretary cause the original charter, granted to this State when a colony, by King Charles II., and the copy thereof, to be framed and protected, in such manner as to ensure their preservation ; and that he deposit the duplicate of said charter in the cabinet of the Rhode Island Historical Society, for safe keeping ; and that the cost of such frames be allowed and paid out of the State Treasury, upon the order of the State auditor." This has accordingly been done.

hundred, pease, and barley malt, two and sixpence a bushel, corn and barley, two shillings, washed wool, sixpence a pound, and good firkin butter, five pence.[1] Most of this tax was paid in wool, and the price reduced to five pence. A report of the proceedings of the Court of Commissioners at Providence upon the Harris land cases, presented by the two Rhode Island members of that tribunal, was ordered to be forwarded to his Majesty, which was done, with a letter from the governor.[2]

The Warwick agents were fully employed at this time, not only with their immediate business, but in a defence of the rights of the colony, incidentally forced upon them by her opponents. Richard Smith, in behalf of the Narraganset proprietors, had sent a petition to the King, setting forth the Connecticut claim, and the defenceless condition of Rhode Island during the war, and praying that their country with the adjacent islands, Conanicut, Dutch, Patience, and Hope, might be restored to Connecticut. The matter was referred to the Board of Trade, and Holden and Greene were called upon for information on the subject, and to answer the averments of the petitioners.[3] This they did, in behalf of the colony, with signal ability, defending the claim of Rhode Island under the charter, and vindicating her conduct in the war.[4] The printed advertisement of the Narraganset lands, having been sent out

---

[1] A comparison of this tax with that levied for the same amount in June, 1670, forcibly illustrates the changes wrought by the war. A like comparison of prices with those current in Oct., 1670, shows a large decline in all the staple articles of life, while the relative values of English and colonial currency, as there stated, remained about the same, and hence the reduction of sterling to federal money, there given, will answer for this period.

[2] The letter is filed in Br. S. P. O., New England, vol. xxxii. p. 344.

[3] The original petition and order in council thereupon, July 3d, 1678, are in New England papers, vol. iii. p. 38–40, Br. S. P. O., and are printed in R. I. Col. Rec., iii. 50–1.

[4] The original paper is in Br. S. P. O., New England, vol. iii. p. 42— printed in R. I. Col. Rec., iii. 60–2.

CHAP.
XI.
1678.
Dec.
4.

13.

20.

1678-9.
Jan.

24.

to Holden and Greene, was presented by them to the royal council, and an order was at once issued for the Massachusetts agents to appear and show upon what title the lands were claimed.[1] Staughton and Bulkeley informed the council that it was a private claim. This admission, together with the representations of Holden and Greene in answer to Smith's petition, were embodied in an order of council,[2] issued the same day, requiring that notice should be sent to New England to leave Kings Province in its present condition, and that those who claimed ownership or jurisdiction there, should forthwith send agents to prove their rights before the King. The following week, upon petition of Randal Holden, a peremptory order was issued annulling the sentence of banishment passed by the Massachusetts Court against Holden and his associates, the men of Warwick, thirty-five years before, and commanding the said Court to repeal the same and to allow these persons, at all times, free access within their jurisdiction. The terms of this order were unusually decided, and indicate a strong feeling of condemnation, in the royal council, at the arbitrary conduct of Massachusetts towards the adherents of Gorton.[3]

The Warwick men having concluded their mission in England were about to return home, when another matter occurred to cause their delay for a few weeks. John Crowne petitioned for the grant of Mount Hope, lately conquered from the Indians, as an offset to losses sustained by his family in the King's service in Acadia.[4] A note was addressed by the council to the agents of Massachusetts and of Warwick, inquiring about the extent,

---

[1] This order is entered in vol. xxxii. p. 295, New England papers, Br. S. P. O. See R. I. Col. Rec., iii. 62.

[2] New England papers, vol. xxxii. p. 308, Br. S. P. O. R. I. Col. Rec., iii. 63.

[3] The original petition is in Br. S. P. O., New England papers, vol. iii. p. 49, and the order upon it is in vol. xxxii. p. 312.

[4] Br. S. P. O., New England, vol. iii. p. 52.

value, and proprietorship of Mount Hope.[1] To this Holden and Greene replied that the tract contained about four thousand acres, was worth as many pounds, and that the propriety was in the King. Staughton and Bulkeley estimated it at about six thousand acres, could not judge of the value, and claimed that it was included in Plymouth patent.[2] The diversity of these replies led the council to order that inquiries on the same points be made to the four colonies in the same letter that was preparing to be sent to them concerning Narraganset.[3] This letter, drafted in accordance with the order in council of two months before, recapitulated the points in dispute about Narraganset, and required claimants to send agents to England to prove their rights. It also made inquiries about Mount Hope,[4] and became, as we shall see, a fruitful source of contention in a few months.[5]

CHAP.
XI.

1 6 7 9.
Feb.
3.

6.

12.

At the next General Assembly all the towns except Westerly and Kingstown were represented by deputies. As we have before stated, it was the custom to organize on the day previous to the election in order to admit freemen. Those who had been received as freemen of the towns were, on these occasions, made freemen of the colony. Although in fact but one session, the two Assemblies, one meeting the day before and the other upon election day, were technically considered as distinct bodies, as indeed they were, and the towns chose their deputies for the spring sessions to attend both Assemblies. The changes

May.
6.

---

[1] Br. S. P. O., New England, vol. xxxii. p. 18. R. I. Col. Rec., iii. 38.

[2] The originals of these two replies are in Br. S. P. O., New England, vol. iii. pp. 50, 53. R. I. Col. Rec., iii. 37–8.

[3] Br. S. P. O., New England, vol. xxxii. p. 336. R. I. Col. Rec., iii. 38.

[4] The Mount Hope matter was settled in favor of Plymouth, by Report of the Board of Trade, 4th Dec., 1679, approved by the Council 21st Dec. Br. S. P. O., New England, vol. iii. p. 34–7, and confirmed by royal letter, 12th Jan., 1679–80, vol. xxxii. p. 315—granting their petition of 1st July, 1679, vol. xxxiii. p. 15, R. I. Col. Rec., iii. 64–6.

[5] Br. S. P. O., New England, vol. xxxii. p. 338. R. I. Col. Rec., iii. 40. 1 M. H. C., v. 221.

CHAP.
XI.

1679.
May

7.

made on election day were among the general officers and Assistants, who were chosen by popular vote. The meetings of the Assembly were held at hotels or in private houses. The vote of those present was by ballot, collected in a hat. Proxy votes were opened by a committee, and the Recorder made a list of the names of all those who voted. At this election, the choice of John Cranston as governor, made by the Assembly upon the death of Coddington, was confirmed by the people, and Walter Clarke was elected deputy governor.

A custom had grown up "among sundry persons, being evill-minded," of overworking their own servants, and of hiring other men's servants and under-letting them, to labor on Sunday. A law was passed to prevent this inhumanity, and also to forbid gaming, sporting, and tippling on the first day of the week, under penalty of the stocks, or a fine. The frauds practised by sailor landlords upon seamen, caused a law to be passed that no such person, who should trust a sailor, that had been shipped, for a sum greater than five shillings, without an order from his captain, could recover the debt ; and should he attempt to do so he rendered himself liable for damages at the suit of the master. The master of every vessel of over twenty tons burthen was required to report himself to the head officer of the town upon arrival and departure, and if over ten days in port then to set up notice in two public places in the town three days before sailing.[1] This act was passed in view of the English acts of trade and navigation which afterwards became so fruitful a source of contention between the mother country and her American colonies.

The colony now adopted the rule of paying the necessary expenses of the members of the Assembly, and also of the Court of Trials, for board and lodging during their at-

---

[1] This latter regulation still exists in some countries and is applied to all travellers, who, as in Russia at this day, must advertise their intention to leave, that creditors may have full notice.

tendance. The sums collected by fines and forfeitures
were appropriated to this purpose. The law of 1658 to
prevent innovation in the government of the colony was
revised, pronouncing forfeiture of the entire estates of all
persons who should subject their lands, lying within the
jurisdiction of this colony, to that of any other government.
There was ample occasion for severe legislation upon this
point. The settlement of Narraganset by Rhode Island
men had attracted the attention of Connecticut, and drawn
from that colony a letter demanding the recall of those
settlers ; to which Rhode Island replied, regretting a renewal of the strife, but asserting her claim, and looking
for justice to God and the King.[1] The General Assembly
of Connecticut appointed officers in Narraganset, and empowered the governor and council to punish intruders, to
treat with Rhode Island, and to settle the country.

Upon the return of the Warwick agents bearing the
royal letter of inquiry concerning Narraganset and Mount
Hope, the governor, by warrant, convened the Assembly.
A prohibition was sent to Westerly and Kingstown forbidding any persons from there exercising authority under
any other government, and requiring all the residents of
Kings Province to render obedience to this.[2] The magistrates were required to hold courts in Kings Province as
often as the governor should see cause, the better to enforce the King's commands. The arrival of Sir Edmund
Andros, governor of New York, being daily expected, provision was made for his reception at the public expense.
He was then on his way home, and was making the tour
of New England under orders to report upon the condition
of these colonies. It happened fortunately for Rhode
Island, when a few years later she, with the rest of New

CHAP.
XI.

1 6 7 9.
May

8.

July
9.

_____

[1] The two letters, dated April 7th and 21st, 1679, are in vol. i. p. 240–4
of MS. copies of Conn. records in the cabinet of the R. I. Hist. Soc.

[2] The prohibition is entered upon the records, and is in R. I. Col. Rec., iii.
40–2.

England, was placed under his government, that this timely civility had been shown to the royal governor ; but at this time no such calamity could have been anticipated.

19.　　　A warrant was issued for the arrest of Richard Smith on account of his petition to the King on behalf of Connecticut. He was to be examined preparatory to drafting the letter that was to be sent to England in reply to the royal missive brought by Holden and Greene. A survey of Mount Hope was ordered to be made for the same purpose, and other examinations, in respect to Narraganset, were
21.　　　made on each side of the question. The testimonies of John Greene and of Roger Williams were taken upon the
29.　　　facts of the first settlement of Narraganset by Richard Smith, and a lengthy petition was signed by a large number of the people of Narraganset praying that they may be erected into a distinct government.[1] The letter of Rhode
Aug.
1.　　　Island to the King was accompanied by a plan of Mount Hope, which tract was supposed to contain about seven thousand acres and was valued at three thousand pounds, and it asked that Kings Province may be preserved to Rhode Island as accorded in the charter.[2] The United
25.　　　Colonies in their reply to the royal letter claimed Mount Hope for Plymouth and Narraganset for Connecticut, and indulged in the usual vituperation of Rhode Island.[3]
Sept.
17.　　　A court was held at Westerly, in his Majesty's name, by the magistrates of Rhode Island, at which an oath of allegiance to the King and fidelity to the colony was administered, and signed by thirty-three freemen. The Connecticut Court for that county was then sitting at New London. A protest was sent by Governor Leete upon this subject. A prompt reply was returned by Governor Cran-

---

[1] These papers are all filed in Br. S. P. O., New England, vol. iii. pp. 44, 68, 69, 66. R. I. Col. Rec., iii. 52, 56–60.

[2] Original of this letter is in New England papers, vol. iii. p. 59, in Br. S. P. O., R. I. Col. Rec., iii. 43–6, 1 M. H. C., v. 223.

[3] 1 M. H. C., v. 226. Not found in Br. S. P. O.

ston, justifying the proceedings of the Rhode Island Court. The same energetic course was pursued by the Court of Trials. John Saffin, one of the signers of the obnoxious handbill, before described, and who had posted the same in Newport, having been arrested, was imprisoned, tried, and sentenced to pay a fine and to forfeit his estates in Narraganset. Richard Smith was arraigned at the same term but discharged, owing to a flaw in the indictment.[1]

The Connecticut Assembly, in compliance with the King's command, empowered the council to send an agent to England to defend the claim of that colony to Narraganset, and designated William Harris of Pawtuxet as a suitable person. They also disavowed the late Court held by Governor Cranston at Westerly, forbidding the inhabitants of Stonington in any way to recognize the same, and protested against any other act of jurisdiction heretofore, or hereafter to be, exercised by Rhode Island in the Narraganset country. Massachusetts also resented the grievances of her people, and upon the suit of John Saffin arrested Capt. John Albro, an Assistant of Rhode Island, then in Boston. He was discharged at once, and the slight expense incurred by this annoyance was met by the Assembly. This body met at the usual time and continued in session, with several adjournments, more than two months. Their first action was upon a petition from the town of Westerly that the western line of the colony should be run. It was voted to do so, surveyors were appointed, and notice was sent to Connecticut requesting the concurrence of that colony in the survey. This was a cool rejoinder to the recent fulminations from that quarter, but was perhaps the best notice that could be taken of them.

The same subject was at this time occupying the royal council. A brief historical sketch of Narraganset, drawn

CHAP.
XI.
1679.
Sept.

Oct.
9.

28.

30.

Nov.
10.

Dec.
4.

---

[1] This was at the May term of the Court. Letters from Saffin and Smith, dated May 23d and 26th, to Sec. Allen of Connecticut, giving an account of their trial are in MS. records of Conn., vol. i. p. 250-2, in R. I. Hist. Soc.

CHAP.
XI.

1679.
Dec.

up by Holden and Greene, was read,[1] and a full report was made by the Board of Trade soon after, upon the government and propriety of Kings Province, reciting the progress of the dispute to this period, and recommending that a commission be sent out to examine the subject, as it was too complicated for the Board to decide.[2]

11.

1679-80.
Jan.
6.

Connecticut replied to the last proposition of Rhode Island, refusing to run the line, and giving notice of the appointment of an agent to adjust the dispute in England that Rhode Island might also send one if she chose.[3] At an adjourned meeting of the General Assembly, a letter was addressed to the King, advising his Majesty of the appointment of an agent by Connecticut, and asking that time may be allowed to Rhode Island to make her reply before final judgment in the case.[1]

12.

Feb.
4.

March
8.

The grant of Mount Hope to Plymouth by royal letter[5] decided the petition of John Crowne, so long pending before the council. He then made a new application, petitioning the King for the grant of Boston neck in Narraganset.[6] This, like its predecessor, was referred to the Board of Trade, and met the same fate. The lands of Potawomet, about which there had been frequent contention between Warwick and her neighbors, both Indian and English, were finally disposed of in town meeting, by division into fifty equal parts or rights, and the names of the proprietors were inserted on the records.[7]

10.

A letter containing twenty-seven queries from the Board of Trade, relating to the condition of Rhode Island,

[1] Br. S. P. O., New Eng. vol. iii. p. 45.

[2] This report is without date, in Br. S. P. O., New England, vol. iii. p. 12–13.

[3] Conn. MSS., vol. i. p. 264 in R. I. Hist. Soc. A copy of the Connecticut instructions to W. Harris is in Br. S. P. O., New England, vol. iii. p. 107.

[4] Original filed in Br. S. P. O., New Eng. vol. iii. p. 93, R. I. Col. Rec., iii. 76.

[5] N. E., vol. xxxii. p. 315, Br. S. P. O.

[6] N. E., vol. iii. p. 55, Br. S. P. O.

[7] Warwick records, March 8th, 1680.

having been received, was probably the cause of a special
meeting of the Assembly. A committee of seventeen persons was appointed to collect the necessary information in
reply. The severe illness of the governor compelled an adjournment. He expired the next day, being the third governor who had died in office within two years.

CHAP.
XI.

1 6 8 0.
March
11.

12.

Governor John Cranston had borne a distinguished
part in the history of the colony, and filled the highest
military and civil positions in its gift. He was the first
who ever held the place of Major-general, having been selected to command all the militia of the colony during
Philip's war, and he was the father of a future governor
who became still more distinguished for his protracted
public service. Major Peleg Sandford was elected by the
Assembly to fill the vacancy. This was confirmed by the
people at the general election, and Walter Clarke was
again chosen deputy governor. A bell was now provided
for calling together the Assembly, the Courts, and the
Council, and ordered to be set up in some convenient place.
A committee was appointed to make a digest of the laws
"that they may be putt in print." [1] The prudent limitation of the power to be exercised over the Courts, prescribed
by a previous Assembly,[2] was swept away at this session
by a vote "that in all actionall cases brought to the
Generall Courts of Tryalls, if either plaintiff or defendant
be aggrieved after judgment entered in Court, they may
and have liberty to make their appeale to the next Generall Assembly for reliefe, provided such appeale be made
in the Recorder's office tenn days' time after judgment entered as aforesaid ; as also such person or persons soe ap-
pealinge, shall first pay cost of Court, and give in bond as

[1] We infer that they did not discharge the whole of their duties, as the
earliest printed copy of the laws now known is dated 1719, and repeated attempts were vainly made by the home government to procure from Rhode Isl-
and a copy of the laws, as we shall presently see ; and this could not have
been the case had a digest been provided.

[2] August, 1678

in case of review, and thereupon execution shall be stopped till the determination of the Assembly be knowne." It should be remembered that the General Court of Trials was composed of the General Council, being the governor and assistants, or what afterwards became the upper house of Assembly, who, at this time, formed a part of the General Assembly sitting as one body ; and it was not till nearly seventy years later that a reorganization of the Courts effected a complete separation of the legislative from the judicial branches of the Government.   An alteration in the time of holding the Courts of Trials was made, as they often interfered with the sessions of the Assembly. They were hereafter to be held on the last Tuesday in March and the first Tuesday in September, instead of in May and October as heretofore.   The pay of members of both bodies was fixed at seven shillings a week.   The statistical account of Rhode Island, in reply to the inquiries of the Board of Trade, having been completed, it was sent, with a letter from the governor, to England.[1]

8.

The dispute with Connecticut continued with unabated violence.   That colony attempted to set up Catopeci, a Pequot, as joint Sachem of the Niantics with Weeounkhass, daughter of the deceased Ninigret, and hereditary queen of the tribe.   The same policy that had placed the usurper Uncas at the head of the Mohegans, now sought to distract the remnant of the once powerful Narragansets who remained faithful to Rhode Island.   The injured queen petitioned the King against this violation of her rights, setting forth the conduct of Connecticut, and of the Atherton purchasers, as alike prejudicial to his Majesty, to herself, and to Rhode Island, and praying that

---

[1] The original replies and letter are filed in Br. S. P. O., New England, vol. iii. pp. 115-121.   As this is the earliest official information upon these points, and gives some interesting facts, we insert the substance in Appendix F.   The queries may be gathered from the replies.   They were addressed to all the colonies, and are printed in Antiquities of Connecticut, p. 130.   Hartford, 1836.

CHAP.
XI.

1680.
July.

6.

9.

15.

21.

23.

29.

the jurisdiction of the country might be left, as it ever had been, in the hands of the latter.[1] A constable of Stonington was seized by warrant of Governor Sandford, for exercising authority in Westerly, by arresting one Wells upon a warrant from Connecticut, and carried to Newport. A sharp letter from the Connecticut council followed, demanding his release, and for peace' sake agreeing " not to meddle on the east side of Pawcatuck river " till the matter was decided in England. The governor replied, giving the reason for the arrest, but retaining the prisoner for trial. The council issued a formal protest against the conduct of Rhode Island, to be published by the marshal of Stonington on both sides of the river, prohibiting the recognition of any authority not derived from them. They also wrote a letter to the Board of Trade containing seven pleas for their claim to the jurisdiction and soil of Narraganset.[2] Further than this they proceeded to make reprisals. The marshal and his posse broke open the house of Joseph Clarke in Westerly, before sunrise, and carried him off as a prisoner. The governor and council of Rhode Island and Kings Province demanded his release, in a letter setting forth their right of jurisdiction, both by charter and commission, over the invaded district. Clarke was released upon recognizance in the sum of two hundred pounds sterling for his appearance at the October term. Connecticut replied, placing the seizure of Clarke on the ground of retaliation, denying the allegations of the Rhode Island letter, and asserting her claims to Kings Province. Mr. Blathwayt, secretary of the royal council, wrote to Randal Holden and John Greene concerning the boundary dispute, and also the Warwick case with Harris. In their

---

[1] The original petition, translated by Job Babcock, interpreter, dated 4th April, 1680, and signed " Weeounkhass, the Queen in the Nihantick Cuntrey in the Kings Province in New England—with the consent of her Counsell," is in Br. S. P. O., New England, vol. iii. p. 77.

[2] Antiquities of Connecticut, p. 128.

CHAP.
XI.

1680.
Aug.

23.

30.

25.

reply, a minute account of the history of Narraganset and the grounds of the Rhode Island claim is given.[1] The secretary's letter shows a leaning on the part of the council in favor of Rhode Island. Connecticut continued to exert authority over the people of Westerly, summoning them to the Stonington town meeting to elect deputies, and to perform military duty ; while Rhode Island exercised her rights in bringing suits for eviction, in cases of land title under grants from Connecticut, in that town— a proceeding that brought out a strong remonstrance from Hartford,[2] closing with a proposal to negotiate.

Private no less than public concerns, in the colonies, were often the subjects of petition to the throne. Thomas Savage, one of the eighteen original proprietors of Aquedneck, who had returned to Massachusetts, now wrote to the Government of Rhode Island, claiming his right in the undivided portions of the island to which he was entitled, as well as to the eight acre lot that he received at Pocasset, by the original agreement of the purchasers. Copies of the necessary papers were given to his son, and also a letter to the town of Portsmouth, to the same effect, which was presented at town meeting, but refused record or hearing by the freemen. Major Savage then petitioned the King, stating the facts and asking that a commission from the adjacent colonies be appointed to try the case ; but no notice appears to have been taken of it.[3] The claim of one-eighteenth part of the island was a large one, and although technically well founded, would have worked practical injustice if allowed, since the settlers who re-

---

[1] Br. S. P. O., New England, vol. iii. p. 81. This account differs somewhat from the received opinion of the settlement of Narraganset. See note ante ch. vi. p. 195.

[2] Conn. MSS., vol. ii. p. 8–10, to which Rhode Island replied, 13th Sept., that she was ready to treat, as proposed by Connecticut, at any time. Do. p. 11.

[3] The original petition of Mr. Savage is in Br. S. P. O., New England, v. iii. p. 128.

mained had given up their equal rights for the benefit of
new comers as fast as such were admitted freemen of the
colony.

At the same time the proprietors of Narraganset sent
a long petition to the King, reciting the history of their
country, praying to be separated from Rhode Island, and
annexed to Plymouth or Connecticut, or to be erected into
a distinct government.   The acts of the royal commissioners are particularly dwelt upon, and much stress is laid on
the dissent of Col. Nicholls, and subsequent revocation of
the order for the Atherton company to quit the settlements.   They had sent by William Harris all the papers
relating to their case, but these were carried to Algiers,[1]
and being too poor to send another agent to England, they
ask that John Lewin and Thomas Dean, to whose care the
petition is sent, may be received as their attorneys before
the council, and also that a court of claims, made up from
the other colonies, may be constituted to examine land
titles and report to the King.[2]   The Government of Rhode
Island sent a remonstrance against this petition, recapitu-
lating the history of the colony, the agreement of Winthrop
and Clarke, and the terms of the Connecticut charter,
which so explicitly assigned Narraganset to Rhode Island.
The date of every settlement in the colony is given, and
the assertion of Richard Smith that he was the pioneer in
Narraganset is directly denied, a Mr. Wilcocks and Roger
Williams having preceded him by some years, and before
the purchase of Warwick.   The violent conduct of Connecticut is described, and an issue of the differences, by a
confirmation of the charter of Rhode Island, is earnestly re-

---

[1] While the writer was examining the archives in London, all these documents, and many more relating to the capture of Mr. Harris, were found in
the bundles marked " Algiers," where they had been filed for one hundred
and seventy years. They are now restored to their proper place among the
New England papers.

[2] Original in Br. S. P. O., New England, vol. iii. p. 84.   Received Oct.
11th, 1680

CHAP.
XI.
1680.
Oct.
5.

quested.   Papers in proof of the averments of the petition
accompanied it, with a letter [1] of the same date from Gov.
Sandford.   John Saffin also wrote to Lord Culpeper rehearsing the points of the Narraganset petition, and requesting him to represent their case, and to favor their
agent, Harris, and the attorneys. [2]

7.

27.

The trial of Clarke took place at Hartford.   He was
sentenced to pay a fine of ten pounds and costs.   The
General Assembly assumed the case and granted relief,
which was the only business of public interest transacted
at the session.

Nov.
12.

1681.
March
28.

A measure was now adopted in England of the most
vital character in its results upon the colonies.   A determination to enforce the famous navigation acts [3] and their
corollary, the acts regulating the plantation trade, was signified to all the colonies by royal edict.   Upon the reception of this decree, the governor and council ordained, in
pursuance of its mandates, that a naval office, or custom-

[1] Original letter and petition in New England, vol. iii. pp. 85–87, Br. S.
P. O.

[2] Br. S. P. O., New England, v. iii. p. 113.

[3] The author of the first of these acts was George Downing of Salem, a
nephew of the famous Hugh Peter, the father of New England commerce and
the founder of her fisheries.   Its object was to give to British shipping the
monopoly of the home trade.   Its motive was to weaken the overwhelming
commercial and naval power of Holland, then the carrier of the world and
mistress of the seas.   It was introduced into Parliament on the 5th August,
1651, by Whitelock, the republican leader, and passed 9th October.   It has
been well styled the Charta Maritima, and so beneficial was its effect that
Adam Smith is compelled to pronounce it "the wisest of all the commercial
regulations of England," although it is diametrically opposed at every point
to his favorite theory of free trade.   Immediately after the restoration it was
remodelled and passed by the King's Parliament in 1660, and its author received the honors of knighthood at the hands of Charles II.   The glory of
England in this as in many other important points, was the result of measures initiated by the republican Parliament.   "The navigation act, "says
Upham, "was not only the wisest, it was the boldest, it might almost be
said, the most high-handed legislative proceeding ever passed."   It built up
the maritime power of England, but it was one of the earliest sources of oppression to her American colonies, in connection with the kindred acts for the
control of the plantation trade.

house, should be established at Newport for the proper entry of all vessels arriving in this jurisdiction. The bonds
required by the act were to cost six shillings for every vessel above forty tons burden, and two and sixpence for those
of less tonnage. The act was published by beat of drum
in the town of Newport. The time was to come when the
same drum-beat should call the people to resist these acts
as being among the most oppressive impositions of a despotic government!

No changes were made in the general officers at the
next election. Benjamin Hernden, Jr., or Herendeen, of
Providence, having without provocation fired upon an Indian, the Assembly passed an act to prevent such outrages
in future, and caused it to be published, " with all expedition " at Providence. This man was a desperate character, as was his father before him. A romantic legend
of the latter is preserved, which, as it serves to illustrate
one phase of border life, when this was a frontier settlement
of the English, may be here related. In the earliest list
of " twenty-five acre men" received as inhabitants of
Providence [1] are found the names of John ⋈ Clawson
and Benjamin ⋈ Herendeen. Their families were very
intimate, and it is probable were connected by marriage.
Clawson was a hired servant of Roger Williams. One
night [2] he was attacked from behind a thicket of barberry
bushes, near the north burial ground, by an Indian named
Waumaion, whom Clawson supposed to be instigated
thereto by Herendeen. At the first assault Clawson's
chin was split open by a blow with a broad axe, from the
effects of which wound he soon afterwards died, but not
before he had pronounced the strange curse upon his murderer, which the legend records as having been so singularly fulfilled, " that he and his posterity might be marked
with split chins and haunted with barberry bushes."
More than a century later, testimony was collected in proof

[1] January 19th, 1645-6. [2] 4th January, 1660-1.

CHAP.
XI.

1681.
June

23.

July.

Sept.
12.

Oct.
26.

of the fulfilment of this dying malediction.   By this it
appears that the descendants of the murderer were remarkable for the excavated or furrowed chin, which caused the
curse of Clawson to be kept in remembrance, and many a
quarrel was excited among them at huskings and frolics
by mention of the word " barberry bushes." [1]

At an adjourned session, the towns were empowered to
choose one or more additional constables at regular town
meetings, the same as on election day.   A slight difficulty
arose between the Mohegan and Narraganset Indians,
owing to a murder committed by the latter, which led to
a friendly correspondence between Rhode Island and Connecticut, by which trouble was prevented, the dispute being settled by arbitration.   This was the only intercourse
of an official nature that took place between the two colonies for more than a year.

The Narraganset proprietors sent through Lord Culpeper another statement of their claims, contradicting the
positions taken by Holden and Greene.   This statement
was received while a commission for settling these disputes
was being discussed by the council. [2]

The next regular session of the Assembly was held at
Providence, being the first Assembly ever held there under
the new charter, and only the second that had met at any
other place than Newport.   This was perhaps owing to a
disagreement then existing in the town as to the number
of which the town council should consist ; one party desiring that two or three members should be added to make
the council equal in number to those of the other towns,

---

[1] The curse of Clawson, with the singular and undoubted evidence of its
fulfilment, collected from the most respectable sources by the Hon. Theodore
Foster, and also the account of the murder and trial, with a copy of a letter
from Roger Williams to the town of Providence, dated May 11th, 1661, concerning the estate of the murdered man, are preserved in the Foster MS.
papers.

[2] Br. S. P. O., New England, vol. iii. p. 109.   Potter's Narr. R. I. H. C.,
iii. 226.   1 M. H. C. v. 229.

the other party opposing any alteration. Every town
council consisted of six persons, including the resident assistants, who were chosen by all the freemen of the colony.
Three of these being from Providence, left but three members to be elected by the town, the rest being chosen by
the colony. This was a regulation prescribed when the
charter was adopted, and for which it is difficult to see
the reason. It certainly worked injustice to the townsmen
in this case. The Assembly authorized the assistants to
call a town meeting to elect a council of six persons in addition to the assistants. This was to be done annually,
and was carried into effect at the next town meeting.
Fast riding within the compact parts of Providence was
also prohibited by the Assembly.

Attention to the acts of trade and navigation, the
stumbling-block of New England, began now to be urged
upon the colonies. The dictatorial bearing of Randolph,
the special commissioner appointed from England to enforce these acts, as surveyor general of customs, maddened
the people of Massachusetts almost to open resistance, but
as yet no trouble from this source was felt in Rhode Island.
The reciprocal engagement of the colony to the governor
was amended by adding thereto a pledge to stand by him
in his performance of the said acts as required by the oath
therein imposed. The ordinance of the governor and council establishing a custom house, upon receipt of the royal
decree the year before, was confirmed by the Assembly.
The decree, or " charter concerning trade and navigation,"
as it was termed, was presented to the Assembly by Francis Brinley, and placed by them in custody of the governor.
Sandford and Clarke were again chosen to their respective
offices. The quarrel between Warwick and Kingstown
for the possession of Potowomet had proceeded so far that
the Assembly now interfered, to preserve peace, and forbade any persons whatever from entering thereupon until
further orders. They also warned certain intruders upon

CHAP.
XI.

1682.
June.

28.

the said lands to depart forthwith, but permitted the Warwick proprietors to mow and improve the meadows there
as heretofore.   The town officers of Kingstown, distracted
by the rival claims to the jurisdiction of Narraganset, had
avoided taking their engagement to this colony.   Two
" conservators of the peace " [1] were therefore elected for
that town, and the governor was desired to hold a Court
there and to call a meeting of the town to elect officers ;
or in case the town should refuse so to do the Court was
requested to elect all of them, to continue until further
orders or till new ones be chosen.

Oct.
25.

The autumn session was held at Warwick for the
second time in twenty years.   The question of the power
of town councils to reject persons coming into any town
was settled upon application of the deputies from Providence.   It was decided that any one might be rejected
who should fail to give bonds satisfactory to a majority of
the council ; and if any one, being warned by the council
to leave the town, should fail to do so, a warrant for his
removal might be issued to the constable, and in case of his
return to the town he should be subject to fine or whipping. [2]

The first company of cavalry in the mainland towns
was chartered at this session, to consist of thirty-six men
besides officers, with the same privileges given to the infantry, and the like obligation to exercise six days in the
year.   It was composed of residents of Providence, Warwick, and adjacent places, upon whose petition it was or-

[1] John Cole and Capt. John Foanes.

[2] A curious paper is preserved among the Foster MSS., which shows the
mode of applying for permission to reside in any town.   " To yᵉ Towne mett
this : 15th of Decemᵇʳ 1680.   My request to yᵉ towne is ; that they woold
grant the liberty to reside in yᵉ Towne during the Townes Approbation, behaving myselfe as a civell man ought to doe, Desireing not to putt yᵉ Towne
to any charge by my resideing here ; and for what yᵉ Towne shall see cause
farther to enquire of me, I shall see I hope to give them a true and sober
Answer thereunto.   Yᵒʳ friend and servant Tho. Waters."

ganized. Two majors were hereafter to be chosen annu- CHAP.
ally, one for the island and one for the mainland, at the   XI.
spring election. A crew of privateers had recently been 1682.
taken and brought into Newport as prisoners, whence they   Oct.
were sent to Virginia for trial. A portion of them having
broken jail, laid a plot to assassinate Governor Sandford,
which was disclosed by one of their number, who, in fear
for his life, petitioned that he might not be sent away with
the rest. The prayer was granted, and the informer sub-   25.
sequently released. Hog Island, which thirty years before
had been a matter of dispute with Plymouth, was again
claimed by that colony, which led to a correspondence between it and Rhode Island, and to a very long letter from
Governor Hinckley of Plymouth to the secretary of the
royal council, claiming the island as within their limits.   Nov.
Richard Smith, the original purchaser, had recently peti-   18.
tioned the General Court of Plymouth to protect him from
some Rhode Island intruders. This caused the appeal to
the council, which was accompanied by a present of fifty
guineas to the secretary for past services, and the promise
of more in case the Hog Island claim should be allowed.[1]

A royal commission at length issued to Edward Cran-   1683.
field, governor of New Hampshire, and eight others,[2] or to   April
any three of them, whereof Cranfield, or Randolph, the de-   7.
tested agent for the acts of trade in Massachusetts, should
always be of the quorum, to examine and report upon the
claims to the soil and jurisdiction of Kings Province.
Two more odious names could not be found in New England than those of the two prominent members of this

[1] Gov. Hinckley's MSS. in three folio vols., 1676—1699 in Mass. Hist.
Soc., vol. i. No. 40.

[2] Ed. Cranfield, Wm. Staughton, Joseph Dudley, Ed. Randolph, Samuel
Shrimpton, John Fitz-Winthrop, Ed. Palmes, Nathaniel Salstonstall and John
Pynchon, Jr., Esquires. Antiq. of Conn., p. 153. 1 M. H. C., v. 232. R.
I. Col. Rec., iii. 174. Printed copies of the commission date it April 17th,
but the original report in Br. S. P. O., New England, vol. iii. p. 332, gives
the date as on the margin.

CHAP.
XI.
1683.
May

commission. Cranfield had succeeded Mason as governor of New Hampshire [1] with the single purpose of making money, and ruled that ill-fated province with an arbitrary power exerted solely for gain. He had but recently arrived in the country,[2] and had commenced his despotic career with an act of tyranny that placed the province completely beneath his feet. Such was the character of the head of a commission that was now to decide upon questions vital to the interests of Rhode Island.[3]

2.

At the general election, the same officers were again chosen, but Governor Sandford declining to serve, William Coddington, son of the late governor of that name, was chosen in his place, and besides the usual engagement "also took the oath for trade and navigation." The power of the Assembly to expel its members was rarely ex-

June
26.

ercised, but at the adjourned session, a deputy from Warwick, against whom complaints were brought and a divorce granted on petition of his wife at this session, was deemed unfit to hold his seat, and was therefore expelled.[4] A movement was made for holding the October Courts annually at Providence and Warwick, which towns were required to furnish a cage and stocks preparatory thereto.

A complication of affairs at home and abroad, distinct in their characters, yet all of importance to Rhode Island, ensued at this time. Privateers began to infest the seas, and often resorted to the American coast, where the laxity in regard to the acts of trade favored their unlawful operations. This, as we shall hereafter see, in a few years degenerated into actual piracy. The first appearance of these naval freebooters in this vicinity we have al-

[1] 9th May, 1682.
[2] Oct. 4th, 1682.
[3] New Hampshire was at this period a provincial government, differing from the others in New England, which were all charter governments. A graphic sketch of the tyranny of Cranfield's administration is found in Belknap's New Hampshire, chap. viii.
[4] See Appendix B., ante chap. viii.

ready noticed.   The claim of the Hamilton family to the CHAP.
county of New Cambridge, which included all Kings Prov- XI.
ince, was again revived.   The Duke appointed Edward 1683.
Randolph, one of the commissioners, as his attorney to July
prosecute the claim.   The arrival of a privateer ship com- 30.
manded by Capt. Thomas Paine, of whom we shall have
further occasion to speak, caused Thatcher, the deputy
collector of Boston, to make a journey to Newport to seize Aug.
the vessel.   Governor Coddington refused to lend his aid 15.
in taking the prize.   The ship showed Jamaica papers 16.
that satisfied the governor, but were pronounced a forgery
by the officer, who a second time demanded assistance to 17.
capture her, and was refused on the ground that her papers 18.
were regular, and that if the collector did not think so, the
law courts were open for him to try the question.   Thatcher
returned to Boston, and sent to Coddington a pass from 19.
the governor of Jamaica to show that Paine's clearance
was a forged document.   The matter rested thus for
awhile, but subsequently caused much trouble to Rhode
Island.[1]

The second royal commission appointed to decide the
Narraganset dispute, now met upon that business.   The
General Assembly convened at Warwick, and refused to 20.
publish the summons[2] issued by Cranfield, alleging as reasons for their conduct that the summons were not granted
in his Majesty's name, that the commissioners had not
shown to the government their authority to act, and that
the King had not mentioned their appointment in any of
his letters.   The printed briefs that the commissioners
required to be published were both dateless and placeless.
Here were serious informalities, it is true, but it might have
been more politic to have waived these and to have ac-

---

[1] Thatcher's account of this affair is in Br. S. P. O., New England, iii.
301.
[2] R. I. Col. Rec., iii. 139. Br. S. P. O., New England, vol. iii. p. 225, printed
sheet.

CHAP.
XI.
1683.
Aug.

21.

22.

23.

24.

quiesced in the desires of the commissioners. The effect of the course adopted was to prejudice the parties who were to decide these vital questions, against the just claims of Rhode Island, while a more courteous treatment, such as had been shown to the previous commissioners, would have compromised no principle, and might have prevented any adverse bias in the court. A letter was addressed to the commissioners, calling upon them to produce their authority from the King before proceeding further. They were in session at the house of Richard Smith. The Assembly adjourned to meet the next day at the house of Capt. John Foanes, also in Narraganset, where the messengers made return that, upon delivering the letter, Governor Cranfield denied any knowledge of a governor in Kings Province. No answer was sent to the letter nor any commission shown. The Assembly unanimously ordered that the governor and council should issue a prohibition forbidding the commissioners from holding a court, and requiring them peaceably to depart. This was immediately done under the hands and seals of the governor and council. The prohibition recited the aforesaid reasons and order, and was posted by the general sergeant at Smith's house. The next day the commissioners notified the Assembly of the object of their meeting, and that they had waited two days in vain for Rhode Island to comply with the King's commands, and should now adjourn to Boston. To this the Assembly replied, defending their course, and stating that they had been four days in session expecting that the commissioners would show their commission. A great deal of testimony, some relevant, and more not so, was collected by the Court from the various claimants to the soil and jurisdiction of Narraganset, which was forwarded to England.[1]

[1] Some of this is in the archives of Connecticut, and more in Br. S. P. O. New England, vol. iii. p. 330, among which is a curious old map of Rhode Island, sent over the next year, dated 4 July, 1684.

The Assembly then elected and engaged conservators of the peace and other town officers for Kingstown, and adjourned for two weeks. Committees were then appointed to draft letters to the royal council, and Arthur Fenner and Ex-Gov. Sandford where chosen by ballot as agents to proceed to England. A tax of four hundred pounds was voted for this purpose. The letter complained of Cranfield and his colleagues for not showing their commissions, and explained the conduct of the Assembly consequent thereon, contrasting these with the acts of the former commissioners and the treatment they had received. It requested that notice should be given them in case any complaints were made by Cranfield on this subject, that they might reply thereto. The town of Warwick also sent an address [1] to the King, written by Randal Holden and John Greene, rehearsing the foregoing facts and referring to the statements they had given when in London. This paper substantiated the positions taken in the Assembly's letter. Rhode Island had nothing to hope from the royal commissioners whose haughty bearing she had so indignantly resented. They were the avowed enemies of all the colonies, as their private letters and official papers equally prove. Cranfield's correspondence is full of the spite of personal enmity engendered by the treatment that his insolent and unprincipled conduct caused him everywhere to receive. Connecticut approached him with that cautious courtesy which his place, if not his character, demanded, and for which she received in return his approbation of her claims. His letter to the Board of Trade, accompanying the Report, abounds in abuse of Rhode Island, in which it is difficult to separate the misstatements of fact from the expressions of invective. And lest he might seem, in using language which had too often before been applied to Rhode Island by her sister

CHAP.
XI.

1683.
Sept.
10.

15.

17.

Oct.
19.

---

[1] The originals of both these letters are in Br. S. P. O., New Eng., vol. iii. pp. 230, 234. R. I. Col. Rec., iii. 135, 137.

CHAP.
XI.

1683.
Oct.
19.

colonies, to be tacitly approving their course, he charged the same disloyalty upon them, and concludes by saying that "it never will be otherwise till their charters are broke, [1] and the college at Cambridge utterly extirpated, for from thence those half-witted Philosophers turn either Atheists or seditious Preachers." [2] On the same day Gov. Coddington, by order of the General Assembly, sent an address to the King to the same effect as the September letter, relating to the conduct of Cranfield. [3] The

20.

Report of the royal commissioners was a lengthy document reciting the parties' claimants, the disrespectful treatment of the commissioners by Rhode Island, the points of disputed jurisdiction, hanging upon the interpretation of the words "Narraganset river" in the two charters, which was declared in favor of Connecticut, and then the claims to propriety of the soil, which was decided fully in favor of the Atherton company. The agent of the Duke of Hamilton arrived too late to present that claim in season. It was therefore referred to the King, and the adverse

Dec.
13.

parties were notified thereof. [4] Connecticut sent her answer to the claim, alleging seven valid reasons against it, to which the Duchess of Hamilton afterwards replied, rebutting the positions taken by Connecticut, but in vain, [5] and the Narraganset proprietors also petitioned that the decision of the commissioners in their behalf be confirmed. [6]

Among the important events of this year there was one that had already occurred, more memorable than any

[1] This was the first direct intimation of the calamity that was soon to come upon New England.

[2] Br. S. P. O., vol. iii. p. 227. R. I. Col. Rec., iii. 146.

[3] Br. S. P. O., vol. iii. p. 232 of New Eng papers. R. I. Col. Rec., iii. 147.

[4] Br. S. P. O., New Eng., vol. iii., p. 332-7. R. I. Col. Rec., iii. 140-5. R. I. H. C., iii. 229-38.

[5] Both papers are in Br. S. P. O., New Eng., vol. viii., and the former is printed in Antiq. of Conn. p. 159.

[6] Br. S. P. O., N. Eng., vol. iii. p. 319.

we have recorded—the death of Roger Williams.   More   CHAP.
than half a century had elapsed since this ardent friend   XI.
of freedom landed on the shores of Massachusetts, and 1683.
forty-seven years had passed away since, twice exiled for
opinion's sake, he erected in this wilderness the altar of
free worship. He had seen the powerful tribes, that first
welcomed their "white brother" to the hospitalities of
the forest, melt away beneath the advance of a civilization which he had heralded ; and he had lived to see his
little band of six associates grown into a prosperous colony amid persecution, pestilence, and war.   With devout
thanksgiving he recognized the Supreme Power who had
preserved his infant colony through so many dangers, to
perpetuate and disseminate the eternal principles of civil
and religious freedom which he had sought to establish.
Of all the pioneers who settled the first four towns he was
nearly the last survivor ; but two, Randal Holden and
John Greene, outlived their leader.   He died in his
eighty-fourth year, but how or precisely when is not certainly known, [1] and "was buried with all the solemnity the
colony was able to show." [2]

The remarkable traits of his character may be gathered from what has heretofore been recorded in these pages.
His life has been written by able pens, and well repays
perusal by those who would learn the trials and appreciate the triumphs of this Christian statesman. [3] He suffered more than most men from the slanders of those who
should have been his friends, as well as from the oppression of his enemies. The bitterness of theological strife
spared no weapons which envy or malice could supply.
Coddington even accused him " as a hireling, who for the

[1] He died between January 16th and May 10th, 1683.   Knowles, 354.
[2] Callender, R. I. H. C., iv. 147, note.
[3] By Prof. J. D. Knowles, Boston, 1834, 12mo. pp. 437; by Prof. W. Gammell, in Sparke's Am. Biog. New Series, vol. iv. Boston, 1845 ; and by Dr.
Romeo Elton, Providence, 1853. 16mo. pp. 173.

sake of money went to England for the charter ! " Harris, in the long and angry controversy between them, left no means untried to undermine his influence with those for whom he had supplied a home when the gates of Massachusetts were closed against them. Scot earliest displayed those feelings of envy which successful merit is certain to excite in jealous or feeble minds, when the whole population turned out to receive Mr. Williams upon his return from England with the first charter. " The man," he says, " being hemmed in, in the middle of the canoes, was so elevated and transported out of himself, that I was condemned in myself, that amongst the rest, I had been an instrument to set him up in his pride and folly." [1] But posterity has rendered justice to his memory, and the founder of Rhode Island, the great champion of intellectual liberty, has outlived the efforts of his detractors. The leading peculiarities of his mind may be briefly sketched. A firmness, amounting in some cases perhaps to obstinacy, enabled him to suffer hardships, rarely if ever surpassed by those of any exile for opinion's sake. His generosity amounted to prodigality ; for after having purchased of the Indians all the lands around his new plantations, with his own money, he divided them equally among those who followed him. His charity was an active principle, that led him to brave all peril to effect good to the natives, or to reconcile feuds among his fellow-citizens. Of his forgiving spirit his conduct toward the neighboring colonies furnishes ample evidence. He harbored no feelings of revenge for injuries received, but pitied the weakness, or lamented the delusion whence they arose. His consistency and love of truth are alike apparent in his controversy with the Quakers at Newport, which has been so much misrepresented ; yet he would

---

[1] The Quaker controversy of 1672 was the fruitful occasion of these manifestations of malevolence, all of which, and many more, may be found in New England's Firebrand Quenched, a work before referred to.

have laid down his life rather than have a hair of their
heads injured on account of their doctrinal views.   His industry was unwearied ; he valued time and he well improved it.   "One grain of its inestimable sand," said he,
"is worth a golden mountain."   His faults were those of
an ardent mind, sometimes hasty, ever slow to yield ; but
these were few beside his exalted virtues.   He was a
varied scholar, a profound philosopher, a practical Christian, a true philanthropist—one whose deep knowledge of
men, and whose acute perception of principles as displayed
in the foundation of an American State, entitle him to
the rank, which posterity has bestowed, among the most
far-sighted statesmen of his age—one who, were it his
only praise to have been the first of modern legislators to
embody the principles of universal toleration in the constitution of a State, would, by this act alone, secure a
niche in the temple of fame, and cause his name to be
handed down through all future time as the great Apostle
of Religious Freedom.

The appearance of privateers upon the high seas engaged the attention of the home government.   Jamaica
was at first the head-quarters of these illegal proceedings,
and orders were sent to that island, and afterward to the
New England colonies, to pass laws against privateering
and piracy.   The claims of Plymouth to the soil of Rhode
Island were now extended to an absurd point, including
the island of Aquedneck, as well as the long disputed
islet at the mouth of Mt. Hope bay, known as Hog Island.
A letter from Gov. Hinckley to Secretary Blathwayt sets
forth this new claim, resting it upon the western boundary
of Plymouth patent, described as the middle of Narraganset bay, the mouth of which is between Seaconnet and
Point Judith, and the main channel westward of Aquedneck, and hence including that island.[1]   These two sub-

CHAP.
XI.

1683.

1083-4.

March
8.

16.

---

[1] Hinckley MSS. vol. i. No. 63. Mass. Hist. Soc.

CHAP.   jects presented the chief topics of legislation at the Gen-
XI.
        eral Assembly.

1684.   The same executive officers were again chosen, and
May   for the first time, two majors, John Coggeshall for the
7.
        island and John Greene for the main, were also elected by
        the people. The governor being ill, the Assembly met at
        his house, where the oath according to the act of Trade
8.   and Navigation was administered with the regular en-
        gagement. A difference between the towns of Portsmouth
        and Newport, which had existed ever since their separa-
10.   tion, was now settled by the Assembly, the line between
        them was established, and the tenure of lands upon the
June   island definitely fixed. The proclamation concerning
24.   privateers and pirates was received at an adjourned session,
        and published in Newport by beat of drum. The act re-
        quired thereby was at once passed, making it felony to
        serve under any foreign Prince against any power at peace
        with England, without special license, and making all
        persons liable as accessories who should give aid or coun-
        tenance in any way to those who might be adjudged as
        privateers or pirates. Time was allowed for those already
        employed under foreign flags to return and give security
        to the governor for their future behavior. The act was
        transmitted to England with letters from the colony.
        Similar acts were passed by the other colonies. The in-
        trusions of Plymouth, based upon her recent extravagant
        claims, were discussed, and a letter was sent to Gov. Hinck-
        ley, remonstrating in friendly terms against two acts of
        violence committed at Hog Island by N. Byfield of Bris-
        tol, and others, but making no allusion to any further claim
        of that colony.[1]

            The Jews, who afterwards contributed so much to the
        commercial prosperity of Newport, appeared for the first
        time, by petition, at this Assembly, and received the as-
        surance that they might expect as good protection here

                        [1] Hinckley MSS. vol. No. 64. Mass. Hist. Soc.

as any other resident foreigners, being obedient to the CHAP.
laws.[1] The autumn sessions of the Assembly were ap- XI.
pointed to be held hereafter alternately at Warwick and 1684.
Providence, and accordingly met this year at Warwick, Oct.
and assessed a tax of one hundred and sixty pounds, no- 29.
tice of which had been given at the spring session.

The death of Charles II. and the proclamation of his 1684-5.
brother James II., occurred soon after in England. What- Feb.
ever may be said of the public and private character of 6.
the deceased monarch, Rhode Island is bound to speak
well of his civil administration so far as it concerned herself, for to him she owed the confirmation of her glorious
privileges in the second charter, and was uniformly protected by him against the assumptions of her arrogant
neighbors. The broad principles of universal toleration,
which a distracted nation hailed in the famous Declaration of Breda, and which Clarke incorporated in its very
terms in his draft of the charter of Rhode Island, were
secured to her, although they were denied to his other
subjects. The new king was soon to inaugurate a new
policy subversive of all liberty, and to prostrate New
England beneath his feet by means of a royal governor.

While this storm was gathering, other claimants presented themselves for the contested soil of Narraganset.
One sixteenth of all the lands held by the Atherton company had been bestowed upon Lord Culpeper, governor March
of Virginia, who now petitioned the crown, in behalf of 24.
his associates, to confirm their possession, offering to pay
an annual quit-rent of two and sixpence for every hundred 1685.
acres. The Earl of Arran, son of the Duke of Hamilton, April
again urged the old claim of his grandfather the Marquis. 3.
These petitions took the usual course of reference to the

---

[1] This is worthy of note as evidence that the famous phrases, "professing
Christianity," &c., were not embodied in the law of 1663, as the enemies of
Rhode Island have charged, but were interpolated at a later date, and, as would
appear by this act, subsequent certainly to 1684.

CHAP.
XI.

1685.
Apri

18.

Board of Trade, where they slumbered for some years before any Report was made upon them.[1] The rival claims among the actual settlers in Narraganset was giving rise to disturbance, threatening serious results. To prevent this the governor and council of Rhode Island issued an order requiring that no man should molest any one in the quiet possession of his lands, until the King's pleasure could be known.

May
5.

6.

The first direct step was now taken in England by Edward Randolph against the liberty of the colonies. He complained to the Board of Trade of irregularities in Connecticut and Rhode Island, and urged that writs of *quo warranto* should be granted against them, for the purpose of revoking their charters. An order was at once issued for him to prepare articles of misdemeanor against these colonies, that might serve as a basis for the writs.[2] That some intimation of impending peril had reached Rhode Island, we infer from the proceedings at the general election. Gov. Coddington was absent when the Assembly met. He was re-elected, and an earnest letter informing him of the fact, and requesting his presence, was carried to him by a committee of the members. He appeared, but declined to serve. Henry Bull, a man who afterwards proved himself to be as fearless as he was honest, was then chosen governor ; and the deputy governor, Walter Clarke, was re-elected. The attorney general and several of the Assembly also refused to take their engagements, and others were chosen in their places. An address, in the usual style, was prepared, congratulating King James upon his accession, and asking a continuance of the favors bestowed by his predecessor. The proprietors of Narraganset sent a similar address.[3]

[1] Br. S. P. O., New Eng., vol. iii. pp. 322-3, 326-7.

[2] See original letter prefacing the articles. Br. S. P. O., New England, vol. iv. p. 245. R. I. Col. Rec., iii. 175.

[3] Originals of both in Br. S. P. O., New England, vol. iii. pp. 294, 348.

A royal letter announcing an impost upon sugar and
tobacco, to be paid by the retailers and consumers, and
mentioning also the defeat of Argyle and Monmouth in
Scotland, was sent as the first greeting from the new King
after his accession.[1] The General Assembly at an adjourned session filled the vacancies in the list of Assistants, two from Warwick having declined to serve.

As soon as Randolph had prepared the articles of misdemeanor, according to the order of council, they were
presented with the request that writs of *quo warranto* be
forthwith issued. The articles were referred to the Attorney General, with an order to issue the writs against
Rhode Island and Connecticut, and advising the same
process upon the proprietors of East and West Jersey
and Delaware.[2] The articles, as may be supposed, were
malicious in spirit and false in fact ; but they accomplished the purpose of their artful designer, who followed up
his scheme with untiring zeal. The Attorney General
placed the whole five writs in the hands of Randolph, who
urged the Board of Trade to send them to America by a
vessel about to sail. His anxiety was the greater on account of the failure of a similar writ issued nine months
before, against Massachusetts, which had lapsed owing
to the length of the voyage, the term at which it was
made returnable having passed. He therefore proposed
to the Board to take them himself to America, and asked
also for power to erect a temporary government in
Massachusetts until a royal governor could be sent out
for all New England.[3] This request was in the main
granted, and copies of the *quo warranto* were sent out
soon after from the sheriff's office, with letters explaining

CHAP.
XI.

1685.
June
26.

30.

July
15.

17.

Aug.
3.

18.

Oct.
6.

---

[1] Antiq. of Conn. 167.

[2] Br. S. P. O., New England, vol. iv. p. 247.   New York Docs. vol. iii. p.
362.   R. I. Col. Rec. iii. 175–7.

[3] Br. S. P. O., New England, vol. iii. pp. 349–366.   R. I. Col. Rec. iii.
177–8.

CHAP.
XI.
1685.
Oct.
8.

20.

28.

the contents.[1] Two days later a President and Council
were appointed to govern Massachusetts, New Hampshire,
Maine and Kings Province. This commission consisted
of seventeen persons, residents of New England, and
many of them proprietors in Narraganset. Joseph Dudley was named as President, and Edward Randolph was
made Secretary.[2] Judgment against Massachusetts was
entered up a few days after.

The General Assembly met at Providence. A petition from certain inhabitants of Rhode Island was presented, asking for a grant of vacant lands in Kings Province, sufficient to support a hundred and fifty families,
that they might commence a new plantation. The Assembly authorized the governor and council of Rhode
Island to locate this new settlement in the Narraganset
and Niantic countries, and to divide Kingstown into more
than one town, or adopt any other course in regard to the
difficulties there that they might deem best. A copy of

---

[1] The quo warranto cannot be found, but the original letter in which it was
enclosed is preserved among the Foster MSS. vol. iv. in R. I. Hist. Soc., and
is as follows : "London, October 6, 1685. Gentlemen. This day was delivered
to my hand (as I am secondary to the sheriff of London), a writt of Cowarranto
ishewing out of the Crowne ofice of the Court of King's bench at Westminster,
against you the Govnr and Company of the English colony of the Rhoade Island
and the providence plantations in New Ingland in America, Requiring your
appearance before his Magesty wheresoever he shall then be in Ingland, from
the daye of Easter in fifteen days to answer unto our Lord the King by what
warrant you claim to have and youse divers libertyes and franchieses wᵗʰin the
sᵈ Colony—vizt., in the parish of Saint Michæll Bassieshaw, London, of which
you are impeached, and that you may not be Ignorant of any part of the contents of the sᵈ writt, I have in Closed unto you a true Coppia of the sᵈ writt
(in his Magesty's name requiring your appearance to it), and aquainting you
that in defalte thereof you will be proseeded against to the outlawry, whereby
the libertys and franchises you claime and now Injoye will be forfited to the
King, and your Charter annulled. Of this Gents plese to take notiss, from
your humble servant (unknown) Rɪ. Nᴏʀᴍᴀɴsᴇʟʟ." A similar letter to Connecticut, dated a year later, in the print, and varying somewhat in terms, is
found in Antiq. of Conn. p. 171.

[2] 1 M. H. C., vol. v. 244. R. I. Col. Rec. iii. 197, 200. Randolph's commission as secretary of the council is dated 21 Sept. 1685.

this act, and also of the petition, was sent to England.[1] A divorce law, making five years' neglect or absence of either party a ground of separation, was passed at this time. The Narraganset proprietors published a protest against this settlement act of the Rhode Island Assembly, signed by the three agents of the company, the authors of the famous handbill, of eight years before, prohibiting any persons from entering upon the land without their consent, or that of Richard Smith and Francis Brinley, who resided on the spot.[2] A revival of the prosecutions upon the several writs of *quo warranto* was moved in the royal council.

At the general election the late deputy governor, Walter Clarke, was chosen governor, and Major John Coggeshall, deputy governor. The laws relating to excise on liquors, keeping taverns, and selling arms to the Indians, were repealed, and a committee was appointed to codify the laws, the former committee for that purpose never having reported. The speedy suspension of the charter rendered this committee equally inefficient. As soon as news of the arrival of Randolph, at Boston, reached Rhode Island, Gov. Clarke wrote him a friendly letter, offering his services in behalf of the King. Dudley, the new governor, or President of the Council, showed a copy of the royal commission to the General Court of Massachusetts, who took exception to its contents, and unanimously adopted a letter to him, stating their objections, which were as valid as they were impolitic. The Court also removed all papers, relating to their charter, from the custody of their secretary, and deposited them with a special committee for safe keeping.[3] The first proclamation of the new government confirmed all the existing officers of justice in the several provinces. A second proclamation

CHAP.
XI.

1685-6.

March
22.

1686.
April
21.

May
5.

13.

15.

17.

20.

25

28

---

[1] Br. S. P. O., New England, vol. iii. pp. 355 and 379. R. I. Col. Rec., iii. 183.

[2] A broadside in Br. S. P. O., New England, vol. iii. p. 381.

[3] M. C. R., vol. v. p. 516. 2 M. H. C., viii. 179. R. I. C. R., iii. 203.

CHAP.
XI.
1686.
June

3.

17.

22.

followed, establishing the royal government in Narraganset, erecting a Court of Record there, appointing civil
and military officers for the time being, and prohibiting
Connecticut or Rhode Island from further exercise of
jurisdiction in that country.[1]   But this government was
simply provisional, to continue only till the plan of con-
solidating all New England under one royal governor
could be perfected.   This was done by the appointment
of Sir Edmund Andros, formerly governor of New York,
to the supreme authority, by royal commission.[2]   Until
his arrival Dudley and his council had full sway within
the limits of their government.   They examined the proceedings of the Cranfield commission in regard to Narraganset, confirmed the records, and adopted the same book
for all subsequent entries of the acts of the proprietors.
They also rebuked. the other authorities for the injustice
that had so long been practised against all dissenters from
the Puritan Church.   The best act of the Dudley administration, and the only one for which the secretary,
Randolph, deserves commendation from Rhode Island,
was a letter that he wrote to Gov. Hinckley on account
of a tax laid at Scituate, upon a Quaker, for the support
of the ministry.   Randolph arrived in Rhode Island, with
the fatal order of council upon the *quo warranto*, and
there heard the complaint of this act of injustice committed about three weeks before in Plymouth.   The
liberality of the Pilgrim colony had long since yielded to
the overwhelming influence of Massachusetts, and there
was now but little difference between them, either on points
of doctrine or of ecclesiastical polity.   Although Plymouth
was not included in Dudley's government, the secretary

---

[1] R. I. C. R., iii. 197.   Richard Smith, James Pendleton, and John Foanes,
were named as Justices, Richard Smith as Sergeant Major of militia, and four
constables were also designated.   Both proclamations are on printed broadsides in Br. S. P. O., New England, vol. iii. pp. 375, 377.

[2] His commission is printed in full in R. I. C. R., iii. 212–18.

at once wrote to the governor, expressing regret that, while
liberty of conscience had been granted in the royal commission to the colonies therein included, it should be restrained in that colony without special license from the
King. The letter further stated that it would be as
reasonable to levy a tax on Plymouth for the support of
the Church of England minister, now preaching at Boston, as to make the Quakers pay to maintain the Puritan
clergy. This was a home thrust that admitted of no parry
except by adopting the principles of Rhode Island ; and
not a little of the impotent rage displayed against Dudley and his successor, may be fairly ascribed to the spirit
of religious intolerance.

Randolph having delivered the order of council upon
the writ, and at the same time soothed, in a measure,
the irritated feelings of the people by his unexpected defence of their favorite principle, the next day passed over
to Narraganset, where Dudley and his council held a
court. The commission was read, the oaths of office and
of allegiance therein prescribed were administered to the
justices and people, and John Foanes was made permanent clerk of the Court of Records. The militia were
duly commissioned, and the names of the three towns in
the Province were changed. Kingston, the chief town,
was called Rochester, Westerly, the second in size, was
named Haversham, and Greenwich, the smallest, Dedford.
Their boundaries were established, the western limits of
Haversham to be the Pawcatuck river, and the northern
bound of Dedford to be the town of Warwick, and to include within it the disputed neck of Potowomet, long
claimed by the latter.[1] Preëmption rights were allowed

---

[1] This gave rise to a dispute. In order to an amicable settlement, the town
of Warwick on 9 July, 1686, appointed three men to meet a deputation, probably the three agents of the Atherton company, at a place half way between
Warwick and Boston, to discuss the matter, but instructed them to yield nothing over which they had a just claim by purchase from the Indians. The re-

CHAP.
XI.
1686.
June

24.

29.

to those who, without leave of the proprietors, had settled upon the old "mortgaged lands," and time was given for them to arrange with the owners, by rent or purchase, with right of appeal to the government at Boston in the case of dissatisfaction. Two annual courts of Pleas were established, to be held at Rochester in May and October. Thirty wild, or unmarked horses were ordered to be caught and sold, the proceeds to be employed in building a prison and erecting stocks, and Daniel Vernon was appointed marshal of the Province and keeper of the prison.[1] The government of Kings Province was thus organized on what was believed to be a permanent basis. The western boundary was established in accordance with the early claim of Rhode Island, with which the Province was soon again to be incorporated never more to be divided.

The usual June adjournment of the May session happened to fall at the precise time when the summons of Randolph to assemble the freemen would have required it to meet. It was the last General Assembly that for nearly four years was to convene upon the free soil of Rhode Island. Notice had been given by Gov. Clarke for the freemen generally to attend and give their opinion upon the course to be pursued. A large number were present, and, after consultation, left the matter to the judgment of the Assembly, who wisely determined not to stand suit with the King, but to proceed by humble address to his Majesty, asking a continuance of their charter privileges. A committee was appointed for this purpose, and to procure a messenger to go to England.

But, although the freemen in General Assembly thus quietly and prudently surrendered their common charter at the dictation of a despot whose will was law, they had no idea of parting with their ancient liberties beyond a

sult of this conference, which was to be held on the 13th July, cannot be ascertained. The Warwick records of this period are lost.

[1] Potter's Narraganset. R. I. H. C., iii. 239. R. I. Col. Rec., iii. 200-3.

certain and inevitable point. Their distinct existence as a
colony was soon to be merged in a great central government.
The purpose for which they had first sought a patent, to
consolidate the towns so as to compel the neighboring colonies to respect their rights, was no longer essential under
an administration that was to reduce the whole of New
England to the same level in point of power. The new
government would not tolerate such acts on the part of
her neighbors as had led the four original towns of Rhode
Island to combine under the first charter. Before that
period each town was in itself sovereign, and enjoyed a
full measure of civil and religious freedom. They had
now only to fall back upon their primitive system of
town governments to be as free under the new regime as
they had been prior to the union of 1647 ; while a royal
government would secure to them the same protection
from their neighbors that the charters had done. For
these reasons the policy of James II. was less disastrous
to Rhode Island than to any other of its victims. It
caused her to fall back upon a system in which she had
already had experience, and which had proved chiefly defective in the single point that the new policy would ob-
viate. The American system of town governments,
which necessity had compelled Rhode Island to initiate,
fifty years before, now became the means of preserving
the liberty of the individual citizen when that of the
State, or colony, was crushed. To provide for this was
the last act of the expiring legislature. For this purpose
it was declared "lawful, for the freemen of each town in
this colony to meet together and appoint five, or more or
fewer, days in the year for their assembling together, as
the freemen of each town shall conclude to be convenient,
for the managing the affairs of their respective towns ; "
and that yearly, upon one of those days, town officers should
be chosen as heretofore, taxes levied, and other business
transacted at such meetings, as the majority should de-

CHAP.
XI.

1686.
June
29.

termine ; and that to prevent question of the legality of the meetings the townsmen should order their clerk, or other officer, to warn the freemen to attend at a certain day and hour. The Assembly then dissolved. The closing scene in the first period of Rhode Island history, under the Royal charter, was at hand. Although the arrival of Andros did not occur for some months, his commission had already issued, and as there was no change in his policy, so far as regards Rhode Island and Kings Province, from that which was adopted by Dudley in respect to Narraganset, his administration virtually commenced in Rhode Island with the suspension of the charter.

APPENDIX F.

ANSWER OF RHODE ISLAND TO THE INQUIRIES OF THE BOARD OF TRADE.

FROM THE ORIGINAL IN THE BRITISH STATE PAPER OFFICE, NEW ENGLAND PAPERS. B. T. VOL. III. P. 121.

Whereas wee the Governor and Councill of his Majesties Colloney of Rhoade Island and Providence Plantations receaved from your Lordships the Right Honorable, the Lords of his Majesties most Honorable Privy Councill, appointed a committee for Trade and Forreign Plantations certain heads of inquiery, subscribed by the honorable secretary William Blathwayt, in obedience to your Lordships commands requiring an answer thereunto ; wee the Governor and Councill aforesaid according to the best of our understandinge make answer as followeth, viz\`.

To the first wee humbly answer that the Councells and Assemblies are stated accordinge to his Majesties appointment in his gratious letters Pattents, and our Courts of judicature are two in the yeare certain appointed accordinge to Charter, and are carried on by Judges and Jurors, accordinge to Law and Charter.

To the second, concerninge the court of Admiralty wee answer that wee have made provision to act accordinge to the Lawes of England as neare as the constitution of our place will beare havinge but little occasion thereofe.

To the third wee answer that accordinge to our Charter the Legislative power is seated in our Generall Assemblies, and the executive power of the government is in our Courts of Trialls settled accordinge to Charter.

To the fourth wee answer that our Lawes are made accordinge to the Charter not repugnant but agreable to the Lawes of England.

To the fifth we answer, that as for Horse wee have but few, but the chief of our Militia consists of ten companys of foote, being Trayned Bands under one Generall Commander, and their arms are firelockes.

To the sixth, wee answer that in the late Indian warres wee fortified ourselves against the Indians as necessity required, but as for fortification against a Forreign enemie, as yet wee have had no occasion but have made as good provision as at present wee are capacitated to doe.

To the seventh wee answer, that our coast is little frequented and not at all at this time with privateers or pirates.

To the cighth wee answer, as with respect to other Nations, that the French being seated at Canada and up the Bay of Funde are a very considerable number, as wee judgé about two thousand, but as for the Indians, they are generally cut off by the late warr, that were inhabitinge our Colloney.

To the 9th wee answer, that as for Forreighners and Indians, we have no commerce with, but as for our neighbouringe English, wee have and shall endeavour to keepe a good correspondency with them.

To the 10th wee answer as to the Boundaryes of our Land within our Patent that our Charter doth declare the same viz—(extracts the bounds from the charter, and adds, " the greatest part of it uncultivated, and is about a degree as we conceave.")

To the 11th wee answer that the principal town for trade in our Colloney is the Towne of Newport, that the generality of our buildinge is of timber and generally small.

To the 12th, That wee have nine towns or divisions within our Colloney.

To the 13th, That wee have several good Harbors in the Colloney of very good depth and soundinge, navigable for any shippinge.

To the 14th, That the principall matters that are exported amongst us, is Horses and provisions, and the goods chiefly imported is a small quantity of Barbadoes goods for supply of our familyes.

To the 15th, That as for Salt Peter we know of none in this Colloney.

To the 16th, Wee answer that wee have severall men that deale in buyinge and sellinge although they cannot properly be called Merchants, and for Planters wee conceave there are about five hundred and about five hundred men besides.

To the 17th, that we have had few or none either of English, Scots, Irish or Forreighners, onely a few blakes imported.

To the 18th, That there may be of Whites and Blakes about two hundred borne in a yeare.

To the 19th, That for marriages we have about fifty in a yeare.

To the 20th, That for burrials this seaven yeares last past accordinge to computation amounts to foure hundred fifty and five.

To the 21st, That as for Merchants wee have none, but the most of our Colloney live comfortably by improvinge the wildernesse.

To the 22d, That wee have no shippinge belonginge to our Colloney but only a few sloopes.

To the 23d, that the great obstruction concerninge trade is the want of Merchants and Men of considerable Estates amongst us.

To the 24th, wee answer that a fishinge trade might prove very beneficiall provided accordinge to the former artickle there were men of considerable Estates amongst us and willing to propagate it.

To the 25th, That as for goodes exported and imported, which is very little, there is no Custome imposed.

To the 26th, wee answer that those people that goe under the denomination of Baptists and Quakers are the most that publiquely congregate together, but there are others of divers persuasions and principles all which together with them injoy their liberties accordinge to his Majesties gratious Charter to them granted, wherein all people in our Colloney are to enjoy their liberty of conscience provided their liberty extend not to licentiousnesse, but as for Papists, wee know of none amongst us.

To the 27th, That we leave every Man to walke as God shall persuade their hartes, and doe actively and passively yield obedience to the Civill Magistrate and doe not actively disturb the Civill peace and live peaceably in the Corporation as our Charter requires, and have liberty to frequent any meetings of worship for their better Instruction and information, but as for beggars and vagabonds wee have none amongst us ; and as for lame and impotent persons there is a due course taken. This may further humbly informe your Lordships that our predecessors about forty years since left their native countrey and comfortable settlements there because they could not in their private opinions conform to the Lithurge, formes and ceremonies of the Church of England, and transported themselves and familyes over the Ocean seas to dwell in this remote wildernesse, that they might injoy their liberty in their opinions, which upon application to his gratious Majesty after his happy restouration did of his bountifull goodnesse graunt us a Charter full of liberty of conscience, provided that the pretence of

liberty extend not to licentiousnesse, in which said Charter there is
liberty for any persons that will at their charges build Churches and
maintaine such as are called Ministers without the least molestation
as well as others.

CHAP.
XI.

APP.
F.

In the behalf and with the consent of the Councill, signed

PELEG SANDFORD, Governor.

Dated Newport on Road Island
the eighth of May 1680.

CHAPTER XII.

1686—1700.

FROM THE COMMENCEMENT OF THE ANDROS GOVERNMENT TO THE CLOSE OF THE SEVENTEENTH CENTURY.

CHAP.
XII.

1686.
July
3.

THE address of Rhode Island to the King acknowledged the receipt of the *quo warrantos* at the hand of Randolph, and declared that although the period had already passed at which the writ was returnable, they would not stand suit with his Majesty. The policy of this course was obvious. Resistance could only have incensed the monarch, and prove futile in the end. The Bermudas Islands and the city of London had both stood a trial and lost their charters. A large number of corporations in England had shared the same fate. The infamous Jefferies was then Lord Chancellor, to whom the will of the King was the only law. New England was doomed, and every consideration of principle or of policy that could actuate Rhode Island moved her to this course; the more so as James II. had proclaimed her favorite idea of freedom of conscience. The address asked for a continuance of her privileges in this respect, and that no persons should be placed over her "that suit not the nature and constitution of your Majesty's subjects here," and further,

that Newport might be made a free port.[1] Another address from certain freemen of Rhode Island was sent, to the
same effect, but injudiciously taking exception to the act of
the Assembly, and praying that they, the signers, may be
exempt from the tax for an agent to be sent to England.
This attempt at action independent from that of the Assembly in the premises, was, to say the least, in bad taste,
and its motive is sufficiently apparent at the close. It
indicates the preversity of party spirit at a time when all
parties should have united in view of a common danger.
It is signed by fourteen persons, representing various interests, several of whom were among the Atherton purchasers.[2] The two writs against Connecticut were not
served by Randolph till a month later than those against
Rhode Island. A special Assembly was thereupon convened at Hartford, who appointed an agent to carry
a petition to the King. A third writ was afterward
brought against them, and it was not till Sir Edmund
Andros had arrived and personally appeared with an
armed force before the Connecticut assembly, that the
colony finally submitted ; but they concealed their charter in a hollow of the famous tree since known as the
" Charter Oak."[3]

Randolph sent an account to the Board of Trade of
his proceedings, and of the state of government in the
colonies, urging that a general governor should be sent
without delay.[4] Major John Greene of Warwick was
commissioned by the governor to carry the letters and address to England and to act as agent for the Colony.[5]
His former colleague in the agency, Randal Holden, also
sent an address concerning Kings Province, rehearsing its

CHAP.
XII.

1 6 8 6.
July
16.

21.

28.

Aug.
6.

21.

---

[1] Br. S. P. O., New Eng., v. 3. p. 396. R. I. Col. Rec., iii. 193.
[2] Br. S. P. O., New Eng., vol. iv. p. 412. R. I. Col. Rec., iii. 194.
[3] Oct. 31, 1687. Trumbull B. 1. ch. xv. p. 368–72, edit. 1818.
[4] Br. S. P. O., New Eng., vol. iv. p. 315. R. I. Col. Rec., iii. 203.
[5] Br. S. P. O., New Eng., vol. iv. p. 435.

history since the submission of the Sachems, down to the government of Dudley, and advising that persons not interested in the lands should have the disposal of them, as his Majesty's interests were disregarded by the present rulers.[1] The justices of Narraganset, who were among its proprietors, sent an address assailing the character of Greene, the Rhode Island agent, as the author of their troubles, in order to counteract his influence at the Court,[2] and asking that their affairs might be referred to Dudley and his council. A similar petition against Greene was sent by the Pawtuxet proprietors, asking for a like reference of their dispute with Warwick on the famous second verdict, obtained by Harris in their behalf nine years before.[3] In a long communication from President Dudley, sent at this time to the Board of Trade, he dwells upon the violations of the acts of trade all along the coast from Nova Scotia to New York, and mentions the aggressions of the French upon the fishing vessels of New England. He states that, to prevent illegal commerce, the number of free ports had been much reduced, and gives also a full account of the proceedings of the council in organizing Kings Province.[4] The secretary, Randolph, in a letter denouncing the conduct of Massachusetts for resisting an impost of duties, which he estimates would yield a revenue of four thousand pounds sterling a year, when Connecticut and Rhode Island were added to the New England government, also mentions the appearance of piratical vessels upon the coast, to the great hinderance of trade.[5] In a private letter of the same date to the Lord Treasurer, Randolph complains bitterly of his colleagues in the government, especially of President Dudley, who he says refuses to aid him in the

23.

---

[1] Br. S. P. O., New Eng., vol. iv. p. 440.
[2] Br. S. P. O., New Eng., vol. iv. p. 411.   R. I. Col. Rec., iii. 208.
[3] Br. S. P. O., New Eng., vol. iv. p. 407.   R. I. Col. Rec., iii. 209.
[4] Br. S. P. O., New Eng., vol. iv. p. 311.
[5] Br. S. P. O., New Eng., vol. iv. p. 195.   R. I. Col. Rec., iii. 205.

schemes of enthralment which he proposes for New England, and he urges again the sending of a general governor. This letter presents a curious picture of the divided councils that prevailed in the colonies, even among the despotic ministers of King James.[1] The Quakers also prepared an address to send by Robert Hodgson, one of their members, in which they ask that their religious privileges may be preserved to them, and their peculiar views in regard to oaths and military service may be respected.[2]

Upon receipt of the address of the General Assembly, additional instructions were given to Sir Edmund Andros to demand the surrender of the charter, upon his arrival, and to take Rhode Island under his government, assuring the colony of the royal protection, and to do the same with Connecticut in case her people should likewise decide to surrender their charter.[3] A few days later the last acts necessary to the departure of Andros to enter upon the government of New England, were concluded by giving him the seal and flag prepared for the consolidated provinces. The seal employed by the president and council represented an Indian with a bow in his left hand and an arrow in his right, and the inscription, " SIGILUM PRÆSID. CONCIL. DOM. REG. IN NOV. ANGLIA," within the border.[4] The new seal was more elaborate, and is thus described in the receipt given for it by Andros—" engraven on the one side with his Majesty's effigies standing under a canopy, robed in his royal vestments and crown-

CHAP.
XII.

1686.
Aug.

25.

Sept.
13.

29.

---

[1] 3. M. H. C., vii. 154. R. I. Col. Rec , iii. 206.

[2] Br. S. P. O., New Eng., vol. iv. p. 419.

[3] 3. M. H. C , vii. 162. R. I. Col. Rec., iii. 218.

[4] THE SEAL OF THE PRESIDING COUNCIL OF OUR LORD THE KING IN NEW ENGLAND. Copies of this are attached to the proclamations of Dudley before mentioned, in the British State Paper Office, London. No copies of the Andros seal appear in the British archives. The proceedings of his council were transmitted to England but have not been found among the government records. It is to be hoped that they may some day be discovered.

CHAP.
XII.

1686.

ed, with a sceptre in the left hand, the right hand being extended towards an Englishman and an Indian, both kneeling; the one presenting the fruits of the country, and the other a scroll, and over their heads a Cherubin holding another scroll with this motto : Nunquam libertas gratior extat, with his Majesty's titles around the circumference ; there being on the other side the King's arms, with the garter, crown, supporters and motto, and this inscription round the circumference : Sigillum Novæ Angliæ in America." [1] A plate representing the New England colors, under the administration of Sir Edmund Andros, from the original design in the British archives, is here offered as a rare historical curiosity.[2]

Oct.
11.

It would seem as if every separate interest in Rhode Island determined to be heard on its own account by the King. The people of Providence sent an address resigning their charter, asking to be annexed to the general New England government, and disowning the Assembly's address. This was the seventh memorial that was sent from this colony within about three months.[3]

The revocation of the edict of Nantes, that glorious decree by which Henry of Navarre secured toleration to the Protestants of France, was the crowning act of Jesuit intrigue which only the genius of Colbert had hitherto foiled. Upon his death the last obstacle to the extirpation of Calvinism in France was removed. The edict of Henry IV. was revoked by Louis XIV., liberty of conscience was abolished, and a fierce persecution of the Huguenots ensued. More than half a million of the most skilful, industrious and loyal subjects of the Bourbon fled from their

---

[1] Br. S. P. O., New England, vol. iv. p. 267.

[2] Br. S. P. O., New England, vol. iv. p. 223.

[3] The 1st, from the Assembly, July 3. 2d. Divers freemen, July 16. 3d. Randal Holden's. 4th. Justices of Narraganset. 5th. Pawtuxet. 6th. Quakers, all in August. 7th. Providence, Oct. 11. Only the first of these is found upon our State records. The originals of them all are filed in the British State Paper Office, London, as referred to in the notes.

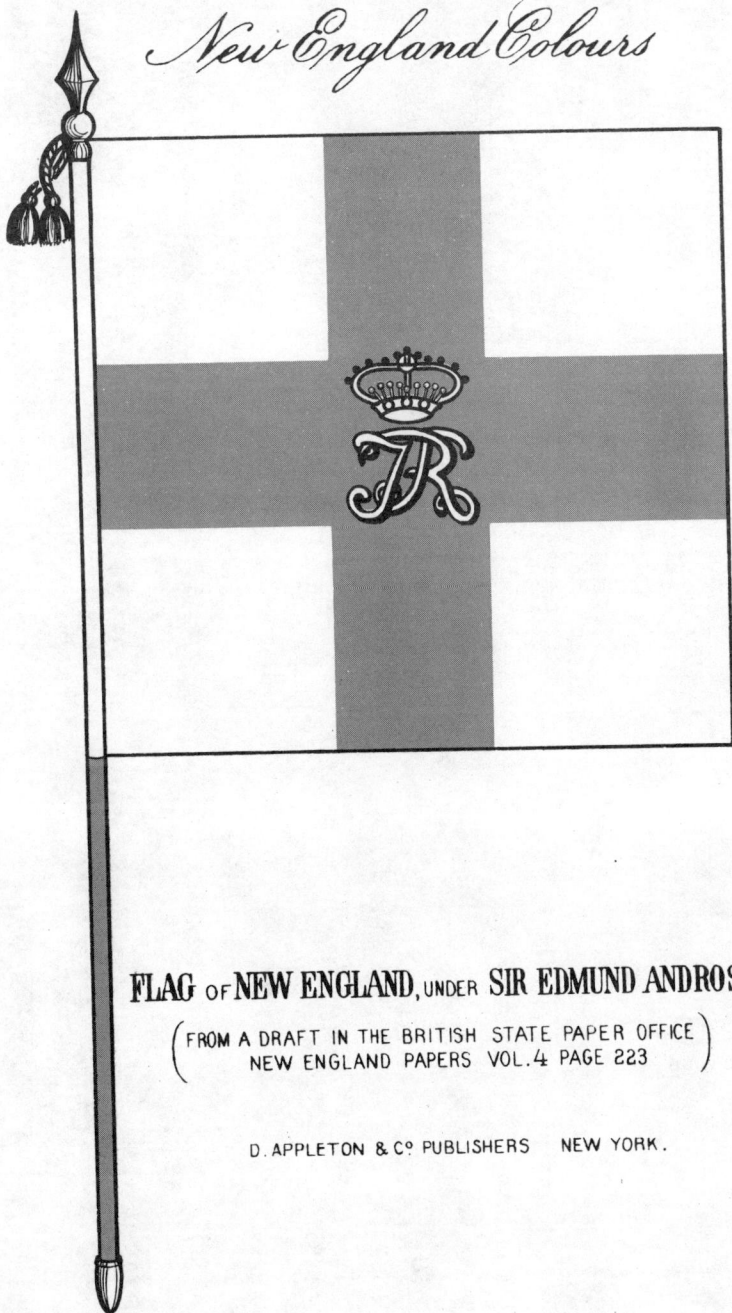

New England Colours

FLAG of NEW ENGLAND, UNDER SIR EDMUND ANDROS.

(FROM A DRAFT IN THE BRITISH STATE PAPER OFFICE
NEW ENGLAND PAPERS VOL.4 PAGE 223)

D. APPLETON & Cº PUBLISHERS   NEW YORK.

native land, and introduced into other countries the arts and commerce of which they were masters.[1] The effect upon France for a time was scarcely less disastrous than that which followed the expulsion of the Jews in Spain, two centuries before, by Ferdinand and Isabella. The banished Huguenots carried with them over the world the blessings of a vital faith, of frugal habits, and the knowledge of new sources of useful and elegant industry. Wherever they settled their descendants remain, to this day, living witnesses of the loss entailed by Jesuit craft upon the country of their origin. Numbers of them emigrated to America ; some of these found their way to New England, and settled in Rhode Island, where they could enjoy the freedom that was denied them at home. An agreement was made between the Narraganset proprietors and the Rev. Ezekiel Carre and P. Berton, in behalf of the French refugees, for the settlement of a place called Newberry Plantation, but this being too far from the sea, another spot was selected, near John Foanes' house in Rochester (Kingston), and a new agreement made between the parties. The price fixed was four shillings an acre, cash, or twenty-five pounds for every one hundred acres, being five shillings an acre, payable in three years, with interest at six per cent. thereafter. Each family was to have one hundred acres of upland, if they desired so much, and a proportionate part of meadow. M. Carre, the minister, was to have one hundred and fifty acres gratis ; one hundred acres were assigned as glebe land, and fifty acres to support a Protestant schoolmaster. Forty-five families commenced the

CHAP.
XII.

1686.
Oct.

12.

Nov.
4.

---

[1] This celebrated edict was issued by Henry IV. in 1598, and revoked by Louis XIV., Oct. 24. 1685. 800,000 Protestants fled from France during the persecution that ensued. England gained immensely by this fatal policy of her inveterate foe. 50,000 artisans sought refuge in London, and introduced the manufacture of silk, crystal glasses, jewelry, and other fine works, many of them before unknown, but ever since successfully prosecuted in England. Anderson's History of Commerce.

CHAP.
XII.

1686.
Dec.
20.

1686.
Dec.to
April
1689.

settlement, built a church and twenty-five houses, and prospered for some years until dispersed by the lawless conduct of their neighbors, as will hereafter be shown.[1]

At length the Rose frigate, bearing Sir Edmund Andros, with two companies of royal troops, the first ever stationed in New England, and, except those sent for the conquest of New Netherlands, the first ever seen here, arrived at Boston. The Dudley government was superseded, and the president made chief justice. Andros, by his commission, was in effect absolute, having power to appoint and remove members of his council. With their consent he could enact laws, levy taxes, and control the militia of the country. He proceeded at once to organize a system of despotism which has made his memory detested wherever freedom has a name. During the two years and four months that his administration existed, the people of New England were at the mercy of a tyrant. Massachusetts suffered most, as she was the wealthiest and most powerful of the colonies, and she felt most keenly the first blow inflicted by her persecutor—wherein Rhode Island could have no sympathy with her griefs—the overthrow of the Puritan theocracy, and the introduction of the services of the Episcopal Church. But in the greater part of his acts, all the colonies suffered alike in proportion to their strength. Taxes were levied without consent of the people. Public fees were enormously increased, that of probate some twenty-fold. Town governments were almost annihilated, colonies were made simple counties, and the whole country reduced to one vast province. Writs of intrusion involved landed proprietors in expensive suits to defend or confirm their titles. Marriages by

[1] The agreement, and the remonstrance of Dr. Pierre Ayrault in 1705, from which the above facts are taken, are filed in Br. S. P. O., New England, vol. 13, together with a plot of Frenchtown containing the names of all the families on their separate lots. A copy of the former is in Trumbull's papers, vol. 22, No. 114, in Mass. Hist. Soc.

civil magistrates were at first tolerated from necessity, and afterwards interdicted, and the performance of this rite was confined to the Episcopal clergy, of whom there was but one in Massachusetts. The odious system of passports was established. The form of administering oaths was changed from the Puritan mode of holding up the right hand, to that of laying the hand on the Bible—a dangerous approach, some thought, to the Papal custom of kissing the cross. By this innovation the Puritan might learn to regret his own disregard of the conscientious Quaker. And what was perhaps the bitterest infliction of all, in connection with the introduction of the Episcopal forms, the Baptists, Quakers, and other dissenters from the established Puritan church, were encouraged in their refusal to pay the tax for the support of the settled clergy. But in Rhode Island, where no established church ever existed, this latter grievance, and those springing from kindred sources, were not felt; but, on the contrary, a sympathy upon these points with the new government, that had the strength and the will to enforce one of her cardinal principles upon her early persecutors, was cordially entertained. The bearing of Andros, in his official communications with Rhode Island, was always in friendly contrast to his intercourse with the other colonies. The courtesy extended to him, as governor of New York, some years before, was not forgotten. The tyrant was at least a gentleman, and showed as much gratitude for former civilities as was consistent with the nature of his commission. He addressed a letter to Rhode Island, in mild terms, demanding the surrender of the charter, and designating seven persons as members of his council for this government, who were to meet at Boston at the first general council.[1] He also wrote friendly letters to Gov. Clarke, concerning the submission of the Assembly and

---

[1] These were Walter Clarke, Jo. Sandford, John Coggeshall, Walter Newbury, John Greene, Richard Arnold, and John Alborough, Esqs.

CHAP.
XII.

1686.
Dec.

surrender of the charter.[1] His arrival was the signal for sending petitions upon disputed land claims. Richard Smith, of Narraganset, lost no time in petitioning for relief from the molestations of the Rhode Islanders at Hog Island. This little islet had already occasioned the waste of almost as much paper since its purchase, forty years before, as would suffice to cover it.

30.

The first council of Gov. Andros, which met at Boston, consisted of nineteen members, of whom five were from Rhode Island.[2] The royal commission was read, and also the instructions to receive the charter of Rhode Island. The oaths of office and allegiance were then taken by all but the two Quaker members from Rhode Island, Clarke and Newbury, whose affirmation was received instead. A proclamation continuing all officers, civil and military, and all laws not repugnant to those of England, during his Excellency's pleasure, was agreed upon.[3] As this was the first, so was it the last full meeting of the Andros council. The distant members returned home, and those only who lived at or near Boston regularly attended. They had but little influence. Four or five, whose interests were chiefly in England, controlled the action of the whole. Opposition was silenced by the minions of Andros, some of whose advisers were not of the council. It does not appear that the Rhode Island members attended another general council. This was a gloomy period in New England history. Inaction prevailed among the freemen of the towns. The calm of despotism settled over the colonies.

1686-7.
Jan.
12.

Soon after this first council meeting, Andros' commission, as governor of this colony with the rest of New England, Connecticut excepted, was published in Rhode

---

[1] 2. M. H. C., vol. 8, pp. 180–181. R. I. Col. Rec., iii. 219.

[2] Those named in Andros' letter except Sandford and Greene, the latter of whom was in England as agent of the colony.

[3] 3. M. H. C., viii. 181. R. I. Col. Rec., iii. 220.

Island, and the colony was declared to be one county.[1] John Greene was then in England as agent. The policy of the crown was by this time too obvious to render it expedient to seek a continuance of the charter. He therefore confined his efforts to minor objects, and petitioned in behalf of the towns for relief from the interruptions given by the Narraganset proprietors, and others, to the quiet possession of their lands; and also to his Majesty's interests in Kings Province, and prayed that these matters might be referred to Gov. Andros.[2] The town of Bristol, which had been settled not quite six years, petitioned Andros for relief from a tax of one penny per pound, levied throughout the province for the support of government. It was the custom to relieve new settlements from taxation for seven years. This had been guaranteed to the purchasers of Bristol by the Plymouth committee, who made the sale. A representation of these facts was made by the selectmen of the town,[3] but with what effect there is no record to show.

The Narraganset proprietors applied to Sir Edmund for a confirmation of their titles. They furnished him a copy of the proceedings of the Cranfield commission, with the evidence there presented, and requested an opportunity to defend their claim against all opponents.[4] The event proved that this was an unfortunate step for the proprietors. The late Gov. Hinckley incautiously complained to Andros of the letter of Randolph, who retained the same position he had held under Dudley, as secretary of the council, in which he had reproved the Plymouth magistrate for taxing dissenters for the support of the ministry. Sir Edmund replied sharply, forbidding the

Margin notes:
CHAP. XII.

1686-7. Jan. 19.

Feb. 18.

24.

March 5.

---

[1] Callender in R. I. H. C., iv. 102. Chalmers' Political Annals, 278–9.

[2] Br. S. P. O., New Eng., vol. iv. p. 429. R. I. Col. Rec., iii. 221.

[3] Benjamin Church, John Rogers, Thomas Walker. R. I. Col. Rec., ii. 222.

[4] Trumbull papers, vol. 22, Nos. 127–8. Mass. Hist. Soc.

CHAP.
XII.

1686-7.
March
11.

1687.
March
25.

30.

May
21.

constable to execute the warrant against the Quaker, and warning Hinckley to be faithful to the King.[1]

In reply to the Rhode Island address, further instructions were sent to Andros, granting the freedom of conscience asked by the Assembly. This was consistent with the policy of James, who sought, by promulgating the doctrine of religious liberty, to undermine the Episcopal church, and thus, in time, to restore the Papal power in England. With this object he soon after issued the Declaration of Indulgence, nominally, at least, leaving his subjects to obey their own consciences in spiritual matters.[2]

The members of the Andros government were constantly changing. A new list of twelve names, to fill vacancies already existing in the council, was sent to London. Three of these were from Rhode Island and Kings Province.[3] In the letters accompanying this list, Andros gives an account of the condition of his province, and states that Connecticut has not yet submitted, and that it is important to unite her to the rest of New England, as wheat and provisions are chiefly supplied by her.[4] The difficulties that environed Andros, formed the subject of frequent letters from Randolph and himself to the home government. In one of these to the Board of Trade, the former says, "His Excellency has to do with a perverse people," and complains that but few members of the council manifest any interest for his Majesty.

The duties of the General Assembly and of the Court of Trials, both of which were superseded by the new government, now devolved upon a Court that met quarterly,

[1] Hutchinson's Mass., i. 357, note.
[2] Hume, chap. 70. The declaration was issued April 4, 1687. A copy of it, apparently the official one sent to this colony, is preserved among the Foster MSS., vol. i. in R. I. Hist. Soc.
[3] Richard Smith, Francis Brinley, and Peleg Sandford.
[4] Br. S. P. O., New Eng., vol. iv. pp. 287, 291, 297. R. I. Col. Rec., iii. 223-4.

and was called " The General Quarter Sessions and In- CHAP.
ferior Court of Common Pleas." The first meeting of XII.
this new tribunal was held at Newport, for Rhode Island, 1687.
Kings Province, and Providence. It was composed of June
nine justices, of whom Francis Brinley was chairman and 14–16.
judge. Its proceedings were unimportant. Jurymen and
constables were sworn. Private petitions were referred
to justices of the peace in the different towns. Overseers of the poor were appointed for every town. Licenses
for Newport were granted, but the sale of liquors in Kings
Province was forbidden.

The questions of ownership in Narraganset having been
referred to Gov. Andros, he ordered a careful survey of the 22.
country, and a plat to be made marking the several
claims.[1] Several parcels of land were granted by him to
Richard Wharton, at an annual quit-rent of ten shillings 29.
an acre.[2] This is the first case, except that of Prudence
Island, of the introduction of this species of tenure in
Rhode Island. The revenue duties under Andros were
farmed out by the treasurer of the Province, John Usher.
Nathaniel Byfield of Bristol was by him appointed farmer
of excise in this district, as appears by an original warrant July
in his name to John Whipple " to receive the whole excise 8.
of all sortes of drinke, that shall be sould within the town-
shipp of Providence by retaile," for one year.[3]

The intrusions that ultimately broke up the French
settlement were commenced by their neighbors on the first
summer of their planting. The meadows belonging to
them, or set apart for their use, were unlawfully mowed
and the hay carried off, leaving them without fodder for
their cattle. Complaints were made to Gov. Andros, who
ordered an examination of the matter. The hay was se- Aug.
cured and stacked, and a further order was issued dividing 5.

---

[1] Potter's Narr., R. I. H. C., iii. 220. R. I. Col. Rec., iii. 225.
[2] Br. S. P. O., New Eng., vol. iv. p. 795. R. I. Col. Rec., iii. 225.
[3] Foster papers, vol. i.

CHAP.
XII.

1687.
Sept.
14.

Oct.
25.

26.

31.

4.

8.

it, one half to certain needy persons in Rochester and Deptford, and the other half to the French families, until the rights of the parties could be determined.[1]

The next quarter court was held at Rochester, or Kingston, at which the overseers of the poor were empowered to assess taxes for the relief of paupers in their respective towns. A petty sessions, for probate business only, at which but three justices were present, was afterwards held at Newport.

Sir Edmund Andros, with over sixty regular troops, now proceeded to Hartford, where the Assembly was sitting, to overawe the government of Connecticut and compel a surrender of the charter. It was at this time that the sacred instrument was hidden in the ancient oak to preserve it from his grasp. This object was accomplished, but it did not prevent him from seizing the government. Taking the records of the colony, he wrote beneath them, with his own hand, the transfer of the government to himself, and closed the volume with the significant word, inscribed in glaring capitals—FINIS.[2]

Connecticut had more reason than any other colony to dread the despotic spirit of Andros ; for just at the commencement of Philip's war, when he was governor of New York, he appeared with a naval force before Saybrook, and was only deterred by the resolute conduct of Capt. Bull, commander of the fort, from making an attack in prosecuting the claim of the Duke of York, under an old patent that comprehended Connecticut in his dominions.[3] The memory of this repulse added to his rancor, while the Prince in whose behalf he was then acting was now the monarch of England. Well might the gallant colonists refuse to admit his authority, and resort to every

---

[1] S. M. H. C., vii. 182.   R. I. Col. Rec., iii. 228.

[2] Trumbull, Hist. of Conn., ch. xv. vol. i. p. 372.

[3] July 8 to 12, 1675.   Trumbull, ch. xiv. vol. i. p. 328.

means of throwing a taint of illegality over his proceed- CHAP.
ings.[1]

A full report was at this time made by Gov. Andros 1687.
upon the various claims to the Narraganset country. The Oct.
great claim of the Atherton company was thrown out, as
having been based upon grants extorted through terror
from the Indians by the illegal acts of the United Colonies. The submission of the Sachems, in 1644, vested the
propriety in Charles I., since which no grant of jurisdiction had been made in that region except to Connecticut
and Rhode Island. The Connecticut claim was repudiated
for the reasons expressed in the Rhode Island charter, which
latter had been confirmed by the commissioners of 1664,
who had disavowed both the other claims. Several titles
from the Indians, and from Rhode Island, to individuals
are mentioned. The rights of Rhode Island over the
Kings Province were thus again, for the third time, secured to her, as against Connecticut in point of jurisdiction, and against the so-called proprietors in point of
ownership.[2]

From Hartford Andros visited Fairfield, and returning Nov,
by the sea-side, completed the annexation of Connecticut
by appointing the principal persons in the various towns
as justices.[3] Stopping at Newport with his troops, he pro-

---

[1] An anecdote that illustrates alike the wit of the great Puritan divine,
Dr. Hooker, and the hatred felt in Connecticut for Andros, is preserved by
Hon. Theodore Foster, among his MS. collections. Foster Papers, vol. ix.
"While Sir Edmund Andros was at Hartford, he met Dr. Hooker one morning,
and said, 'I suppose all the good people of Connecticut are fasting and praying on my account.' The Doctor replied, 'Yes, we read, This kind goeth not
out but by fasting and prayer.'"

[2] Br. S. P. O., New Eng., vol. iv. p. 762. No date is affixed to this copy
of the Report, but a reference to it in a later document upon the same question in 1697 dates this paper, Oct. 1687. A marginal memorandum mentions that, prior to the submission of 1644, the Council of Plymouth had conveyed the tract to the Hamilton family, in 1635, in whom the title still vested,
if that conveyance was legal.

[3] Letter to Board of Trade from Boston, Nov. 28, 1687. Br. S. P. O., N.
E. v. 4, p. 579.

CHAP. posed to take possession of the charter of Rhode Island.
XII. But in this attempt he was foiled by the foresight of the
1687. cautious Clarke, who, on hearing of his arrival, sent the
Nov. precious parchment to his brother, with orders to have it
concealed in some place unknown to himself, but within
the knowledge of the secretary. He then waited upon Sir
Edmund, and invited him to his house. A great search
was made for the coveted document, but it could nowhere
be found while Andros remained in Newport. After he
left it was returned to Gov. Clarke, who kept it until the
fall of Andros permitted a resumption of the government
under it.[1] The seal of the colony was however produced
and broken by Andros. A new one was made as soon as
28. it was needed.[2] In his letter to the Board of Trade, concerning the annexation of Connecticut, written directly
after this affair, Andros makes no allusion to the successful ruse of the governor of Rhode Island, nor does he even
refer to the mysterious disappearance of the Connecticut
charter.

Dec. The third quarter sessions was held at Newport, with
13. but five justices present. An order was passed to prevent
danger from fire in the compact portions of the town.
Should any chimney take fire, the person using it was to
forfeit two and sixpence, and each householder was to place
a ladder, reaching to the ridge pole, against every dwelling
house that he owned. Andros, following an established
custom, had appointed the first of December as a day of
thanksgiving. The proclamation was generally disregarded, and parties were brought before the Courts for con-
14. tempt. One of these answered to the charge of keeping
open his shop on that day " that he was above the observation of days and times." Another said that his boy
opened the shop, and worked upon his own account, but
that if he had not been lame he did not know but he

---

[1] Foster MSS., Bound vol. ii. p. 337.
[2] Br. S. P. O., New Eng., vol. v. p. 74.

should have worked himself! Thus general was the spirit of discontent at the loss of their liberties felt even in Rhode Island, where the yoke of tyranny rested comparatively lightly. A tax of one hundred and sixty pounds was ordered for building a court house in Newport and one in Rochester. The committee appointed to do the work wrote to Gov. Andros on the subject, and nominated John Woodman of Newport to be treasurer of the Province or County of Rhode Island if his Excellency should approve.[1]

Soon after the report of Andros upon Narraganset reached England, Lord Culpeper again petitioned, in behalf of the Atherton company, for a number of grants, amounting in all to sixty thousand acres in Kings Province, to be selected by themselves, in lieu of the whole country, heretofore claimed. They asked that the land sold by them to the French refugees should be included in the grant, and that the bass ponds might be reserved to them, as also the use of the waste lands adjoining their settlements.[2] There were sufficient reasons why this request should be granted, although the terms in which it was expressed—"your petitioners for their parts being willing to consent, in lieu of the whole which is of great extent, to accept of part thereof under such quit-rent as your Majesty shall think fit"—were not very modest or appropriate for parties whose entire claim had just been set aside. The royal council accordingly instructed Andros that, as these petitioners had an equitable pretence to receive favor, he should assign to them such lands as were not already occupied, they paying a quit-rent of two and sixpence for every one hundred acres.[3]

The spring term of the Common Pleas was held at Kingston, or Rochester as it was then called. An order encouraging the fishery in Pettaquamscot pond was pass-

CHAP. XII.

1687. Dec.

15.

1687-8.

Jan. 13.

1688. April 10.

March 6.

[1] Potter's Narr. 221. R. I. Col. Rec., iii. 228.
[2] Br. S. P. O., New Eng., vol. iv. p. 762.
[3] Br. S. P. O., New Eng., vol. xxxiv. p. 8.

ed, and a tax of over fifty-three pounds was laid upon the whole Province, or County, to pay for the killing of wolves therein. These animals were still very numerous and troublesome. The records of Warwick show that some had been killed in that town within a recent period.[1]

7.
The commission under which Sir Edmund Andros had hitherto acted did not include Rhode Island and Connecticut, although he was empowered by it to receive their charters. A new commission was sent out, confirming his government over all New England, and annexing thereto the Provinces of New York and the Jerseys, under the general name of New England, with a council of forty-two persons named therein, seven of whom were from Rhode Island.[2] Five members were to constitute a quorum in emergencies, and seven in any case. The seal of New York was to be broken, and that of New England, before described, used in its place. Liberty of conscience, in accordance with the declaration of indulgence, was to be permitted ; but the freedom of the press was made subject to

16.
the will of Andros. The instructions accompanying the commission were very full, and are chiefly exceptionable from the discretionary power vested in certain cases in the governor.[3]

18.
The news of the prospect of a direct heir to the throne, caused great rejoicing among the Papal party in England, and was received with consternation by the Protestants. A proclamation for a day of public thanksgiving and prayer was issued by Andros, and sent to every county or province in his wide dominion. The appointed day was

29.
not observed with a zeal commensurate to the occasion, in

June
10.
the opinion of the Viceroy. The birth of the Prince of

---

[1] On 20 April, 1674, old Pumham killed a wolf in Warwick, and on 29 Jan. 1680, a bounty of twenty shillings a head was offered for their destruction.

[2] Walter Clarke, John Coggeshall, Walter Newberry, John Greene, Richard Arnold, John Alborough, and Richard Smith.

[3] R. I. Col. Rec. iii. 248–54.

Wales, afterward known as the Pretender, caused much discussion in England. Suspicions were rife against the legitimacy of this heir to the throne ; and when, upon news of the event reaching America, Andros issued another proclamation of thanksgiving for the Queen's happy delivery, it was less favorably received than the former had been. The people generally credited the injurious reports circulated in England.

CHAP. XII.

1688.
Aug. 24.

The June session of the Court was held at Newport. Nine justices were present. New constables were sworn for every town in the county. Providence having disregarded the orders relative to the last two taxes, the constables were required to levy by distraint for their collection. Some persons in the vicinity of Newport having escaped taxation, the assessors were ordered to perfect the rate list by including them.

June 12.

13.

Upon receipt of his new commission, Sir Edmund Andros moved his head-quarters to New York, supplanted Col. Dongan, the late governor, and settled the government. French intrigues with the hostile Indians led the government to take some measures to protect the friendly tribes, which were afterwards brought up against Andros as evidence of favor towards them, to the prejudice of the colonists. Depositions to this effect were taken in Rhode Island and elsewhere, tending to excite the people against him.[1]

July 5.

At the autumn Court, held in Rochester, granting licenses and the trial of criminal causes was the only business. The succeeding session at Newport was the last at which any legislation was had. The fire ordinance

Sept. 4.

Dec. 11.

[1] These were published in " The Revolution in New England Justified," p. 26. Boston, 1691. This book was called forth by one entitled, " An Answer to the Declaration of the Inhabitants of Boston and the country adjacent, on the day when they secured their oppressor," by John Palmer of New York, one of Sir Edmund Andros's Council. The declaration referred to was issued on the seizure of Andros, April 18, 1689—a printed copy of which is in Br. S. P. O., New England, vol. v. pp. 9, 10.

CHAP.
XII.
1688-9.
Jan.

2.

March
5.

18. in Newport, having been neglected, was re-enacted, and the fines resulting therefrom were appropriated for the poor of the town. A tax of one hundred and twenty pounds was levied, but never collected, for before the day appointed in the act for the assessors to meet, the revolution broke out. The justices often met for probate business, in the interval of the quarter Courts. One meeting is recorded during this winter. Once more the Court of Common Pleas assembled at Rochester, between which place and Newport the Courts for this county alternated. It was the last meeting of the Andros government in Rhode Island. The only thing done was to fine a man two and fourpence for planting a peach tree on Sunday. Some of the justices met a few days later for probate business, and this closes the records of the "usurpation," as it is often called, in Rhode Island.

Meanwhile a great change had taken place in English politics. The long struggle between privilege and prerogative had closed in violence, if not in blood. William, Prince of Orange, whose wife was the eldest daughter of James, had invaded England with a fleet of five hundred vessels, and an army of fourteen thousand men. The King had fled to France, and a Protestant dynasty was secured to England in the persons of William and Mary. The news of this revolution was the signal for the fall of Andros. The messenger who brought it was imprisoned at Boston, but the great intelligence could not be concealed. The minds of the people were ripe for revolt. The detested usurper was doomed. The principal citizens, including some members of his own council, assembled at the town house, and signed a summons to Sir Edmund Andros to surrender the government. This they urged for his own welfare, assuring him of safety in case of compliance, but otherwise threatening that the fortifications should be taken by storm.[1] A lengthy declaration

1689.
April
4.

18.

---

[1] A broadside in Br. S. P. O., New Eng., vol. v. p. 11.   R. I. Col. Rec., iii. 256.

of the inhabitants of Boston, set forth in thirteen sections the grievances of the people as the ground of their action, the burden of which instrument was, that "New England beheld the wicked walking on every side, and the vilest men exalted.'" Capt. George, of the Rose frigate, was seized as he came on shore in the morning, and carried to prison. The Governor and his attendants, attempting to appease the council assembled at the town house, were treated in the same manner. Andros refused to send orders to surrender the fort. Thereupon his secretary, Randolph, was seized, and a pistol presented at his breast, threatening him with instant death if he did not accompany his captors to the fort, and there represent to the commandant that the Governor required him to surrender it at once to the people. This ruse succeeded. Five thousand men were by this time under arms. The venerable Gov. Bradstreet, now eighty-seven years old, who had been supplanted by Dudley, was reinstated by acclamation. The castle, situated a league below the town, was summoned in the same manner, but with a different result. The commander, suspecting the violence offered to Randolph, refused to obey. The courage displayed by Andros at this crisis, was worthy of a better cause. Threats of violence were vainly employed to extort from him an order for the surrender of the castle. Although told that he and his adherents should be put to the sword unless instant compliance was made, he firmly refused to yield the point. The next day a committee of gentlemen prevailed on the garrison to surrender, with the promise of their liberty, but on reaching the town they were all thrown into prison. The fort, the jail, and the castle, were all used as prisons for the civil and military officers of the late government, twenty-five of whom were closely confined with their leader.[2]

19.

---

[1] See note ante p. 509. Br. S. P, O., New England, vol. v. pp. 9–10.
[2] Riggs' narrative of the Boston Revolution. Br. S. P. O., New England,

CHAP.
XII.   When news of this affair reached Rhode Island, Dud-
          ley, the chief justice, who had gone to Narraganset to
1689.   hold a Court, was seized by a party of Providence men,
April   taken to Roxbury, and afterwards committed to prison.
23.   A letter was circulated among the people, from Newport,
          in cautious terms, recommending them to assemble there,
          "before the day of usual election by charter," to consult
          upon what course should be adopted.[1] In accordance with
          this call, the freemen of Rhode Island, Providence, and
May   Kings Province, assembled at Newport, and put forth a
1.   declaration of their reasons for resuming the charter gov-
          ernment.[2] At the same time they adopted an address
          "to the present supreme power of England," stating that
          the fall of Andros obliged them to resume their old form
          of government, which they prayed might be confirmed to
          them; and that as they were "not only ignorant of what
          titles should be given in this overture, but also not so
          rhetorical as becomes such personages," they hoped their
          deficiencies on this point might be overlooked. Thus
          easily and quietly did Rhode Island revert to her former
          freedom; and not knowing yet who might be victorious in
          England, adopted this cautious and politic form of ad-
          dress. But the wary Clarke hesitated to accept his former
          post, and for ten months Rhode Island was without an
          acknowledged governor. The deputy governor, John Cog-
          geshall, with several of the old assistants, boldly resumed
9.   their functions. Connecticut followed immediately and
          more thoroughly, restoring all her former officers, conven-
          ing her assembly, and resuming at once the government

vol. v. p. 7. Capt. George's account, p. 34, and list of prisoners, p. 48. R. I.
Col. Rec., iii. 257.

[1] This letter is signed W. C., J. C. What appears to be the original is
preserved in the Foster papers, vol. iv. The handwriting, the cautious language, and the first initial signature, all attest the authorship of Gov. Walter
Clarke. It is printed in Staple's Annals, 176, and R. I. Col. Rec., iii. 257.

[2] R. I. Col. Rec., iii. 268, where by error of type the declaration is dated
1690.

under her long hidden charter.   Plymouth took the same
course under Hinckley.   In Massachusetts a convention of
representatives of the several towns was held, who unanimously voted to re-organize the government with the
same officers who had been superseded three years before.
These officers accepted the trust provisionally, declaring
that in so doing they did " not intend an assumption of
charter government." [1]   Two days later a ship arrived at
Boston with the joyful news that William and Mary had
ascended the throne.   The acting governor and council of
Rhode Island immediately proclaimed the new monarchs
in every town of the colony; and the same was done, with
the greatest demonstrations of loyalty and delight, throughout New England.

Dr. Increase Mather had secretly escaped from Boston, before the revolution, and gone to England to represent the cause of the colonists.   Upon the accession of
William III., he had an audience with the King, who
promised that Andros should be recalled.[2]   The order was
issued in due time, requiring the authorities of Massachusetts to send home Sir Edmund Andros and his fellow
prisoners, by the first vessel, to answer for their conduct
to the king.[3]   Andros, by the aid of his servant, who persuaded the sentinel to drink, and then to suffer him to
stand guard in his stead, escaped from the castle and fled
to Rhode Island.   At Newport he was captured by Major
Sandford, and sent back to Boston,[4] where a lingering imprisonment of half a year still awaited him.

The deputy governor and council of Rhode Island peti-

CHAP.
XII.

1689.
May
22.

24.

26.

July
30.

Aug.
3.

[1] Two broadsides in Br. S. P. O., New England, vol. v. pp. 12–14. The Br.
archives abound in documents pertaining to the revolution in New England.
Volume v. of New England papers is full of pamphlets, broadsides, and MS.
letters from both parties upon this subject.

[2] March 14, 1688–9. A curious account of this audience, from Cotton
Mather's Life of his Father, is in 1 M. H. C., ix. 245–53.

[3] Hutchinson, i. 391, note. 3 M. H. C., vii. 191. R. I. Col. Rec., iii. 256.

[4] Hutch. i. 392. Randolph to Board of Trade from Boston gaol, Sept. 5,
1689. Br. S. P. O., New England, vol. v. p. 94.

CHAP.
XII.

1689-90.
Jan.
30.

Feb.

tioned the throne for a confirmation of their charter, rehearsing the circumstances of its resumption, of the proclamation of their majesties, and of the late seizure of Andros.[1] The long confinement of Andros and his associates was about to terminate. For nearly ten months they had expiated their acts of tyranny in a Puritan prison. The order for their return to England for trial had arrived, and the vessel was now ready to sail. The haughty royalist, who had too faithfully executed the mandates of a despotic master, returned as a prisoner from the country which, sixteen years before, he had first visited as a ruler, and to which he was again to return, within two years, as governor of Virginia.

In reviewing the administration of Andros in New England, an impartial judge cannot fail to discover, among the principal causes which have made his memory odious, that he inflicted a mortal wound upon the Puritan theocracy. The hierarchy, of which Hooker, and Cotton and the Mathers were the heads, never fully recovered its prestige. To this, in a great measure, is due the detestation that attaches to his name. Cotemporary denunciation has been echoed in later times by those who have no sympathy with the religious intolerance that evoked it, but who, either through carelessness or timidity, have neglected to analyze the conduct of Andros, or have feared to present it in what we believe to be the just light. He conscientiously and fearlessly obeyed the commands of his sovereign, and in entering upon his difficult mission he displayed a nice sense of the delicate position he was called to fill, utterly at variance with the character of brutality assigned to him by his Puritan critics. The opinions of men who maligned the purity of Williams, of Clarke, and of Gorton, who "bore false witness" to the character and the acts of some of the wisest and best men who ever lived in New England, who strove to blast the

[1] Original in Br. S. P. O., New England, vol. v. p. 219. R. I. Col. Rec., iii. 258.

reputation of people whose liberal views they could not comprehend, who collected evidence to crush the good name of their more virtuous opponents, by casting upon them the odium of acts wherein they were themselves the guilty parties, who committed outrages, in the name of God, far more barbarous than the worst with which they ever charged " the usurper,"—the opinions of such men, we say, are not to be received without a challenge, and the conclusions to which a candid examination brings us are not to be withheld, because differing in some points from the wholesale denunciation hitherto employed against Andros. For the tyrannical points of his administration his master is to blame ; for the petty oppressions that often rendered its execution vexatious we believe that his tools were more culpable than himself. Their object was to enrich themselves at the expense of the people, and their practice was to charge upon their leader the extortions that rendered his administration grievous. The wide dominion over which Andros held control could only be organized, under the system of James, by delegating power, and this was too often placed in irresponsible hands. Randolph, the secretary, was the author of many of the acts for which Andros, as the governor, is held responsible. The mutual hatred between him and the colonists was undisguised, but posterity has shielded the infamy of the legislator beneath the mantle of the executive. William III. was looked upon as a mild and liberal monarch, yet upon the arrival of Andros in England the charges [1] against him were dismissed by the royal order on the ground of insufficiency—that he had done nothing which was not fully justified by his instructions ; and in compensation for his imprisonment in New England, he was soon after appointed to succeed Effingham, as governor of Virginia.

[1] These charges were prepared by Sir Henry Ashurst, Increase Mather and others, 14 April, 1690, and were answered by Andros and his associates, at great length, and with the result stated in the text. A draft of the charges, and the original reply are in Br. S. P. O., New England, vol. v. pp. 164, 166.

The republican spirit of New England could not quietly submit to such a form of government as was prescribed by James II., however well it might be administered. The prejudice against this form has been unjustly directed upon the instrument employed to establish it, and Andros has consequently been portrayed as a monster of tyranny. Yet it should be remembered, that for three years he ruled without interruption, which could scarcely have occurred had a tithe of these misrepresentations been true ; nor, till the news of the revolution in England reached Boston, was there a single attempt made to resist the government of this "incarnate despot."

Although the government of Andros has been held up as one of absolute tyranny, and necessarily so for the reasons here given, the other New England colonies complained most bitterly of those acts which Rhode Island could not but approve, and some of which, as seeming to be favors shown to her, were construed into acts of hostility to them. So general is the predjudice against him to this day, that it may sound strange to say that in any respect Sir Edmund Andros was a benefactor to Rhode Island. "The evil that men do lives after them, the good is often interred with their bones." So has it been with Andros. His will was arbitrary. His rule, even in Rhode Island, where it was mildest, was oppressive ; but his acts, where they were good, should not be forgotten, even though the evil predominates. He sought to establish universal toleration in religion. This was abhorrent to the Puritans. In their estimation it was rampant *Rhode Islandism.* His object, to be sure, was to secure a foothold for the church of England, not to favor the principle. But Rhode Island could not object to see her free ideas adopted by a despot, although what was a principle with her was merely policy with him. Again, the long disputed boundary with Connecticut was established by Andros, in accordance with the claims of Rhode Island. This added a new cause of complaint in which this State could not unite. And so long as he ruled, Rhode Island CHAP. was secure from the insults of her neighbors, and protected XII. against them in her rights. The courteous treatment 1689-90. which he here received, compared with the rudeness elsewhere shown him, led him to represent Rhode Island, in his despatches, in favorable contrast with the other colonies. It is not improbable that the assurances of her loyalty, repeatedly given by Andros, had some effect in securing the tacit confirmation of her chartered rights under the succeeding reign.

Two parties, royalist and republican, divided the colony. Prominent among the former was Francis Brinley, a distinguished merchant of Newport, whose letters display the bitterness of faction in these troublous times. He denounced the action of the republicans in resuming the Feb. charter, and called for a settled government, to be established by the king, over all New England.[1] The bold attitude of the republican party secured the freedom of the colony. In May they had reinstated all the old officers, and re-established all the laws superseded in 1686. The charter had been produced in open Assembly, and then returned to the custody of Gov. Clarke. The records of the colony were not forthcoming at that time, the former recorder being dead, and the present custodian having refused to deliver them except upon distraint. This act of resumption was afterward sanctioned by the king, upon receiving the written opinion of the law officers of the crown, that the charters of Rhode Island and Connecticut, never having been revoked, but only suspended, still remained in full force and effect.[2] Had the royalists, who doubted

---

[1] Abstracts of his private letters are in Br. S. P. O., New Eng., vol. v. p. 413. R. I. Col. Rec., iii. 259.

[2] The opinions of Ward, and of the then Attorney and Solicitor General, in the case of Connecticut, were rendered 2d August, 1690, and apply equally to R. I. Hutchinson, i. 406 note. The opinion of Attorney General Ward specially upon the R. I. charter, was given three years later, Dec. 7, 1693, confirming the acts of the people under it on every point. It is in Br. S. P. O., New Eng., vol. vii. and R. I. Col. Rec., iii. 493.

CHAP.
XII.
~~~~
1689-90.
Feb.

the legality of these acts, prevailed, and a renewal of the charter been applied for, it could not have been obtained with so liberal provisions as the old one, if at all ; and most probably Rhode Island would have met the fate of Plymouth, and been absorbed by Massachusetts under a general governor.

The defective government of the last ten months called for legislative action. The General Assembly was as yet unorganized, and the chief magistrate was doubtful of his powers, or shrank from the duties of his post. A meeting of the assembly had been called by Gov. Clarke, in October, the regular time appointed by charter; but a storm prevented the mainland towns from being represented, and the governor himself had failed to attend. At length the Assembly convened for the first time for

26.   nearly four years. The deputy governor, six assistants, the new recorder, chosen by the freemen in May, the general sergeant, and seventeen deputies, were present. The Assembly proceeded to fill the vacancies in their number. Absentees were sent for. The governor obeyed the summons, but declined to retain his office. Christopher Almy was elected in his place, but he also declined. It was

27.   then that "all eyes turned to one of the old Antinomian exiles, the more than octogenarian, Henry Bull; and the fearless Quaker, true to the light within, employed the last glimmerings of life to restore the democratic charter of Rhode Island." [1]   Benedict Arnold, son of the late governor, was elected an assistant ; and Almy, who declined to be governor, consented to fill another vacancy in that body. Gov. Clarke refused to deliver the charter, and other official papers, to a committee of the Assembly appointed to receive them. He gave them leave to take it, but refused himself to open the chest in which it was kept. It is said that his extreme caution was only overcome by an order for the sheriff to arrest and confine him

[1] Bancroft, chap. 17, vol. 2, p. 350.

in prison, upon which the required documents were handed over, and placed in charge of Gov. Bull ; but it appears from the records that he retained the charter till the annual election—two months later, and then gave it up, on a second demand, to the assembly.[1] There was a policy in all this which was so apparent that Clarke never lost the confidence of the people. The funds of the colony were in the hands of Roger Holden, to be appropriated to building a colony house. He paid them over without demur. A new seal "being the anchor, with the motto, Hope," was procured by the Assembly, in place of the one broken by Andros. The declaration of war between France and England was proclaimed. Col. Church was at this time fighting the French and Indians, at the eastward; and very soon the war was to be brought nearer home by the presence of a French fleet on our coast. The towns were put in a state of defence, and the French refugees in Narraganset were required to present themselves to John Greene, at Warwick, and take the oath of allegiance to the British crown, required by the king, in consideration of which they were to remain undisturbed, behaving peaceably.

At the next regular session of the Assembly, the day previous to the annual election, all the members were present. The charter was publicly read, as in former days, and the election proceeded with in usual form. Declining years compelled Gov. Bull to refuse a re-election. The deputy governor was then chosen, but refused, perhaps from the same cause. John Easton was then elected governor, and Major John Greene, deputy governor. The list of assistants was completed to ten, and the other general officers, and two majors, were chosen as heretofore.

The first grand period of Rhode Island history, the formation period, was ended. The era of domestic strife and outward conflict for existence, of change and inter-

[1] Foster papers, Bound vol. i. p. 337.

CHAP.
XII.

1689-90.
March

1.

3.

1690.
May
6.

7.

CHAP.
XII.

1 6 9 0.
May
7.

13.

ruption, of doubt and gloom, anxiety and distress, had almost passed. The problem of self-government was solved, and a new era of independent action commenced, which was to continue unbroken for an entire century, until her separate sovereignty should be merged in the American Union, by the adoption of the federal constitution ; and her royal charter, the noble work of her republican founders, was never again to be interrupted, not even by the storm of revolution, until the lapse of more than a century and a half had made its provisions obsolete.

The colony house, projected during the government of Andros, was now nearly completed, and received the name of the Town House. The governor, deputy governor, and assistants, on account of the expense attending their official duties, and their receiving no salary, were excused for the future from paying any colony tax. The war with the French and Indians raged all along the northern frontier. Leisler, governor of New York, demanded assistance from all the colonies. Rhode Island could not spare men, but voted a tax of three hundred pounds solely for this purpose. The effective force of New England at this time, as shown in a tabular statement of the enrolled militia, furnished by Sir Edmund Andros to the royal council, was over thirteen thousand men. Of these, eight hundred were in Rhode Island, exclusive of the eastern shore, which was included in Plymouth.[1] A fleet of seven sail of French privateers made a descent upon the coast,

---

[1]   *Rhode Island, &c.*   *Kings Province and Providence Plantations.*

Capt. Pelham, Newport, 1st Co.	104	Major Richard Smith.	
Capt. Rogers, do 2d do	85	Major Gen. Winthrop, Providence,	175
Capt. Arnold, Portsmouth,	105	Capt. Fones, Rochester, (Kingston,)	136
Capt. Joseph Arnold, Jamestown,	34	Capt. Gorton, Warwick,	60
	——	Capt. Davoll, Feversham, (Westerly,)	56
	328	Capt. Weaver, Deptford, (Greenwich)	37

These were under Major John Walley, with the County of Bristol troops, numbering 780.

464

It would seem by this that the Providence troops were attached to a Connecticut division.

Br. S. P. O., New Eng., vol. v. p. 202.

captured Nantucket, Martha's Vineyard, and Block Island, where they committed horrible excesses. Bonfires were lighted at Pawcatuck, and thence all along the shore, to arouse the country. A sloop with thirty-four men was at once sent out from Newport to reconnoitre. A portion of the enemy entered the harbor of Newport by night, to surprise the town ; but failing in this, they proceeded to attack New London, and were beaten off. Thence they landed at Fisher's Island, and burnt the only house upon it. There a small body of seventeen men, from Stonington, surprised a party of them, and killed one Trimming, an English renegade, who had served as their decoy at the taking of Block Island. An expedition, consisting of two sloops with about ninety men, under command of Capt. Thomas Paine, was sent out from Newport to attack the enemy. Capt. John Godfrey was Paine's second. The next day they fell in with five French sail near Block Island. Paine sent a few men on shore to prevent the enemy from landing, and ran his vessels into shallow water to avoid being surrounded. The French force numbered two hundred men, under one Pekar, a Frenchman who had sailed as a lieutenant with Capt. Paine, in privateering expeditions, some years before. At five o'clock in the afternoon the enemy came up with the intention of boarding, but was repulsed. A bloody action ensued for two hours and a half, till night separated the combatants. Pekar withdrew with the loss of nearly one-half his men, in killed and wounded. Paine's loss was only one man killed, and six wounded. The next day the French put to sea. Paine gave chase, and compelled them to sink a prize, loaded with wines and brandy, which they had taken. The alarm caused by this bold assault, induced many persons to remove their property from Newport, to places of greater security. To Block Island this was but the commencement of a series of sufferings to which that exposed spot was subjected from foreign foes, as it had often

CHAP.
XII.

1690.
July
12.

14.

20.

21.

22.

already been at the hands of the Indians. The dangers of the sea, and the sterner perils of war, united to produce a race of men whose courage and hardihood cannot be surpassed. The brilliant exploit of Paine at once inspired the people of this colony with a naval spirit. It was the first victory of Rhode Island on the open ocean, and the worthy harbinger of many daring deeds.[1] Three subsequent attempts upon Block Island were made by the French, during this war, as related by Niles. The second was a night attack :[2] the people were maltreated, and their cattle carried off, but no one was killed. The next time the privateers were captured by the Nonsuch man-of-war ;[3] and on the fourth, and last attack, the islanders themselves repulsed the marauders "in an open, pitched battle," after which they were no longer molested by the French.

9.

A great expedition consisting of thirty-two vessels and about two thousand men, under Sir William Phipps, sailed from Boston for the conquest of Canada, but were repulsed by Count Frontenac, before Quebec, and returned in disgrace. To pay off the men, bills of credit were issued, the first paper money ever seen in New England, but unfortunately not the last. French privateers covered the seas, plundering the commerce of the colonists and harassing the seaboard. In consequence of these troubles, a special session of the Assembly was called, to meet at Portsmouth, to adopt stringent measures for raising the tax levied in the spring, and not yet collected. A tonnage duty of one shilling, or of one pound of powder, per ton, was laid upon all vessels of more than ten tons, belonging to other colonies, that should break bulk in the harbor of Newport ; the

Sept.
16.

---

[1] Br. S. P. O., New England, vol. v. pp. 356, 365. Niles' Hist. of Fr. and Ind. Wars in 3 M. H. C., vi. 263–74, where many instances of the brutality of the French are given, to which Niles, a native of Block Island, was an eyewitness.

[2] May 20, 1691.   [3] In the summer of 1693.

receipts to be applied to maintaining a powder magazine CHAP.
for the use of the Island.   The regular session was held at $\underbrace{\text{XII.}}$
Providence at the house of John Whipple.   The smallpox 1690.
had broken out with great violence upon the Island.   The Oct. 29.
recorder and his family were ill with it, so that the reading of the charter, an indispensable prerequisite to legislation, was omitted, no attested copy of it being at hand, and
an entry was made of the reason for the omission.   The
whole affairs of the colony were deranged by the prevailing
sickness, and no business of general interest was transacted
by the Assembly.   So virulent was this formidable plague,
for which no remedy or preventive was then known,[1] that 1690-1.
a letter from Boston, written during this winter, says, Jan. 8.
"Rhode Island is almost destroyed by the smallpox."[2]
Newport was abandoned by the legislature for nearly a
year.   The general election was held at Portsmouth, "it
being removed from Newport by reason of the distemper." 1691
No changes were made in the principal officers, and no im- May 6.
portant business was done.   The French again attacked
Block Island in the night, but seem to have left before
any force could be sent against them.[3]   The adjourned 20.
session was opened at Portsmouth, and removed next day
to Newport, whence we infer that the pestilence, which June 23.
had ravaged that town for about ten months, had abated.
An address to their Majesties was adopted, but seems
never to have reached its destination.   The military system of the colony was revised, and the power placed in the
hands of the two majors.   The militia was divided into
two regiments, one under each major, and courts mar-

---

[1] The Christian world owes to the Turks one of the greatest discoveries in
medical science. Inoculation was introduced into England by Lady Mary
Wortley Montague, in 1721, who had learned it at Adrianople three years before. Vaccination was discovered by Dr. Jenner in 1796, and made public in
England in 1799, whence it was brought to the United States by Dr. Waterhouse,
the following year.

[2] Mr. Lloyd's letter. Br. S. P. O., New England, vol. v. p. 362.

[3] Prince's collection. Letters and Papers, p. 60, No. 3 in Mass. Hist. Soc.

CHAP.
XII.

1691.
June
27.

tial were established, to consist of a majority of the commissioned officers of each regiment. An addition to the court-house at Newport, and also a turret, where the bell might be hung, were ordered.

The records of the General Assembly from October 1690 to July 1695, except the fragment of a special session in August 1692, have disappeared from the files. A portion only has been found among the British archives, whither the whole were probably sent by Lord Bellemont. The history of the intervening period is derived chiefly from other records in the State Paper office at London, and from contemporaneous authorities at home.

Oct.
7.

Massachusetts and Plymouth were united under one charter, and the selection of their officers was left to their own agents, by whose recommendation Sir William Phipps, a native of Massachusetts, and then an Assistant of that colony, was named as governor. By his commission he

Dec.
12.

was made commander-in-chief of all the land and naval forces of New England, each colony being separately named therein. This was an infringement upon the chartered rights of Connecticut and Rhode Island which at once occasioned trouble. Connecticut was placed in a still worse position, by a similar power over her militia being also conferred afterward upon Col. Fletcher, governor of New York. The charters of both these colonies were so different from any others, that constant blunders of this sort were made by the Home Government, and many of the complaints, particularly against the conduct of Rhode Island, are attributable to this source. The firmness with which she clung to the Magna Charta of her freedom, through trials of every kind, is surprising ; and that she was legally as well as morally right in the ever varying positions that she was compelled to assume, as the attacks made upon her changed in their character and objects, is obvious from the almost uniform decisions in her favor, whenever she was called to plead in her own defence.

1692.

Upon the arrival of Sir William Phipps at Boston, the venerable Governor Bradstreet resigned his office. This was the era of witchcraft in Massachusetts, but as the infatuation never extended to the less gloomy people of Rhode Island, we do not propose to discuss it. The offence appears on the statute book, but no prosecutions were ever had under it. The people of this colony had suffered too much from the superstitions and the priestcraft of the Puritans, readily to adopt their delusions, and there was no State clergy to stimulate the whimsies of their parishioners. More important matters to them than the bedevilment of their neighbors engrossed their whole attention.

A revival of difficulties between Rhode Island and Connecticut was threatened. The latter colony wrote to Gov. Easton that some persons at Pawcatuck had appealed to them for the protection of their laws, and suggested that, for peace' sake, Rhode Island would consent, under these circumstances, that the request of the petitioners should be granted, until further orders were received from England. It was an amicable letter, far different in tone from the correspondence in former years on the same subject. Gov. Easton replied in a similar spirit, but maintained the claim of Rhode Island to the bank of the river, and that a submission to another government, by the people in question, could not convey the right of jurisdiction.

Meanwhile Governor Phipps wrote to Rhode Island requiring the militia of the colony to be placed under him, by the terms of his commission, and that an account of their numbers and condition should be sent to him. The deputy governor, Major Greene, and one assistant went to Boston upon this busines., and also to secure the establishment of a post-office in the colony. They were detained five days before they could obtain a hearing, and then received no satisfactory reply ; nor was any letter sent by Phipps to Gov. Easton, as was promised, but soon after-

CHAP.
XII.

1692.
May.
14.

20.

June
18.

2.

wards several commissions were sent to Major Sandford, to be distributed among the militia officers, displacing most of those already in commission. The Assembly was convened, and ordered that the present officers should retain their posts, and hold their companies ready for defence. In the towns that had neglected to choose military officers at the spring election, the former officers were reappointed. An address to their Majesties was adopted, stating the .facts of the case, suggesting that the conduct of Phipps was stimulated by private interests—some of his counsellors, by whose acts the settlement of Narraganset was thereby impeded, being members of the Atherton company—and praying that the charter limits of the colony might be confirmed to them, in accordance with former decisions. An attempt to run the lines of the colony was forbidden by Governor Phipps, whereupon the Assembly again met, and commissioned Christopher Almy to take another letter to their Majesties, enforcing the prayer of the address, with a plat of the colony, and the reasons for the petition.

Governor Phipps was equally foiled in his attempt upon the militia of Connecticut, and being a very passionate man he nearly involved himself in a quarrel with Col. Fletcher of New York, who also endeavored, by virtue of his commission, to control the troops of Connecticut ; but both were alike thwarted by the firmness of Gov. Treat. During the winter, Sir William, for the first time, came to Rhode Island, and read his commission to Gov. Easton in the presence of witnesses. The governor replied, that when the Assembly met, if they had any thing farther to say, he would write. There was little satisfaction in this cavalier reception, which offset Phipps' treatment of Rhode Island, and still less in the ultimate result ; but with such as it was Sir William declared himself contented, and went home.

The war between England and France continued

with great violence. Louis XIV. invaded England, in behalf of James the Pretender, and maintained a strong force in Canada, which threatened the conquest of British America. Orders were issued from Whitehall for all the colonies to send aid, in men or money, to the governor of New York, for the relief of Albany, then a frontier fort of the English.

The first postal arrangements in the United States were now adopted in the council of Massachusetts. The right to establish post routes in America had been granted for a term of twenty-one years, by royal patent, to Thomas Neale,[1] who deputed Andrew Hamelton to carry out the design. By him the plan was presented to the government of Massachusetts to establish a weekly mail from Boston to Virginia. The rate of postage for all foreign letters was fixed at twopence a letter. Inland letters paid, from Boston to Rhode Island, sixpence for each single letter, and proportionately for a package, which could not count less than three letters, ninepence to Connecticut, a shilling to New York, fifteen pence to Pennsylvania, and two shillings to Maryland and Virginia, with one penny for delivery at the house after any letter had lain two days in the post-office uncalled for. The act was passed by the representatives, and concurred in by the council.

Almy, the Rhode Island agent, became impatient at the delays that detained him in London, and petitioned that the address which he had brought might be read by the royal council. This was done and the subject referred, as usual, to the Board of Trade, who in turn submitted the address to the attorney general for his opinion upon the validity of the charter, and the right to control the militia against the demand of Phipps, and to have their eastern boundary explained. The decision was rendered in favor of Rhode Island upon every point. "I see nothing in point of law but that their Majesties may gratify the pe-

CHAP.
XII.

1692-3.
March
3.

1693.

March
30.

June
9.

Aug.
24.

Sept.
15.

[1] Feb. 17, 1691-2.

CHAP.
XII.

1693.
Oct.

25.

1693-4.
Jan.
2.

1694.
April
2.

21.

Aug.
2.

21.

titioners, and confirm their charter, and explain the eastern boundaries as is desired," is the conclusion of this important paper, which virtually crushed the hopes of the royalist faction in Rhode Island, and cooled the ardor of her ambitious neighbors. Meanwhile the General Assembly sent another address to their Majesties, assigning the exposed situation of the colony, as shown by the late attacks upon Block Island, as the reason for their not sending aid to Albany.[1]

The Board of Trade submitted further questions to the attorney general upon the charters of Connecticut and Rhode Island, and the Jersey grants, how the strength of the whole might be united under one Commander-in-chief to operate against the French. His opinion sustained the position which he had before taken, that these colonies had the exclusive control over their militia in times of peace, but added, that in case of war, if necessary for the common defence, a chief commander might order out a requisite number of troops, with the aid and assistance of the governor, leaving enough at home to secure the safety of each colony. The Board of Trade having reported this opinion to the royal council, an order was issued fixing the quota of troops to be furnished by Rhode Island, for service under the governor of New York, at forty-eight men, and also referring the boundary dispute to the members of the council of New York. The Queen forthwith sent her commands to Gov. Phipps, limiting his control over the militia of Rhode Island, in accordance with the report, and requiring him to furnish three hundred and

[1] All the foregoing documents referred to are in Br. S. P. O., New England, vol. vii., and are mostly inserted in R. I. Col. Rec., iii. 288-295. The admirable mode in which these Records are compiled, by supplying deficiencies in the existing files, and inserting explanatory documents obtained from other sources, in order to present a documentary history of the State as complete as possible, places the Rhode Island Colonial Records before any other State collection we have seen, and reflects great credit upon the industry and ability of the Hon. John R. Bartlett, Secretary of State, by whom they were prepared.

fifty men from Massachusetts for the defence of Albany. CHAP.
Similar orders were sent to Rhode Island and Connecti- XII.
cut. The quota of the latter was fixed at one hundred 1694.
and twenty men.[1]   May

The boundary question had been much discussed pre-
vious to this order of council. The new charter of New
England, by absorbing Plymouth, had bounded Rhode
Island on the east as well as the north by Massachusetts.
The old conflict for the eastern shore was therefore to be
continued with a new and more formidable opponent.
Almy wrote to the Duke of Leeds, President of the Privy   15.
Council, asking his special attention to the eastern boundary of the colony, and supplying the evidence to sustain
the claim of Rhode Island. The Massachusetts agents
petitioned the Board of Trade [2] for a hearing upon this
point before the question should be decided. The point
was referred to the attorney general, whose action was
hastened by a notice from the Board that they were wait- June
ing his report. While he was preparing it, the Earl of   18.
Arran presented the great claim of the Hamilton family   28.
to the attorney general, as including a part of Rhode Island,
but it was for the present thrown out. The opinion re-   July
cited in detail the charter bounds of Rhode Island, the   11.
Plymouth grant, and the decision of Sir Robert Carr, and
suggested a reference to disinterested parties near the spot
as the only mode of determining the dispute. Upon receipt of this report, the agents were summoned to attend a
meeting of the Board to consider this boundary question.   16.
Mr. Almy petitioned that no Connecticut man should be
placed upon the commission, as the dispute with that col-

[1] Br. S. P. O, New England, vol. xxxv., pp. 152, 165, 170. R. I. Col.
Rec., iii. 295-9.

[2] The official title of this body was " the Right Honorable the Lords of the
Committee of Trade and Plantations." A little later than this time they were
known as the "Board of Trade," by which name we style them in the text,
for brevity. All the colonial documents in the British archives are marked
B. T., as plantation affairs were their peculiar province.

CHAP.
XII.
1694.
Aug.
2.

ony in regard to the western line still existed. The at-· torney general prepared the draft of a commission to the arbitrators, which was approved by the Board, and the next day, when the order upon the militia was issued, as before stated, this draft was attached to it to be filled by the names of the New York council.

Sept.
6.

The acts of trade were so generally disregarded in the colonies as to form the subject of frequent remonstrance by the home government. Rhode Island came in for her share of rebuke, although at first she was more loyal upon this point than either New England or New York. In reply to a circular from the Board of Trade, issued a year before, Governor Easton wrote that the collector, Jahleel Brenton, would shortly be in England, and would represent the fact that for want of proper forts in the bay it was difficult to enforce the navigation laws.

June
21.

The friendly feeling between Rhode Island and Connecticut at this time was satisfactory to both parties, and could not easily be disturbed, although occasions were not wanting to renew the strife. There was a border conflict between Westerly and Stonington. Some persons in the latter town attempted to assess a tax upon the former, which was resisted, and a complaint was made by the governor of Rhode Island to the authorities of Connecticut on the subject, to which the latter replied, disowning the act of the intruders, and expressing a hope that no disturbance would be created by any act of Rhode Island west of the Pawcatuck river. So far as it went, this was a virtual concession of the points in dispute, in favor of Rhode Island. But the Narraganset proprietors, as they still styled themselves, were not satisfied with this tacit agreement which subjected them to Rhode Island, and petitioned to have the question settled. It was referred to the attorney general, with whom it rested for more than a year.

Oct.
19.

1695.
May.
22.

May.

At the general election Caleb Carr was chosen governor, and John Greene was re-elected deputy governor

The great break in the records does not cease till the adjourned session of the Assembly at Newport, when they again appear complete. The old tax of three hundred pounds was still uncollected. An additional rate of two pence on the pound was laid, and a more exact mode of assessment than had heretofore been used was adopted, by appointing three men in each town to examine the property of every citizen, and estimate his income. Formerly the rates were laid by guess work, both by the Assembly in apportioning a tax among the towns, and by the councils in assessing the inhabitants.

Complaint having been made that the Colony House was used for other purposes than that for which it was built, it was ordered that it should be occupied only for legislative or military affairs, and for no religious objects whatever. Committees were appointed to run the eastern and northern lines of the colony.

Governor Fletcher had written to demand the quota of troops assigned to Rhode Island for the defence of New York, to which Governor Carr replied that either the forty-eight men required, or some commutation should be sent, according as Fletcher himself might elect.[1]

From the death of Sir William Phipps to the appointment of the Earl of Bellemont several months elapsed, during which Lieut. Governor Stoughton was at the head of affairs in Massachusetts. A proposal was made by the Lords Justices to recall Fletcher, and to unite, under Bellemont, the governments of New England and New York, as in the time of Andros, when all of the American colonies north of Pennsylvania were known by the name of New England. But more than three years elapsed before the plan was perfected by the arrival of Bellemont at New York; meanwhile the two governments continued under their present rulers.

Stoughton refused to have the lines run between Mas-

CHAP. XII.

1695.
July

2.

5.

16.

[1] N. Y. Col. Mss. xl. 39.   R. I. Col. Rec., iii. 303.

CHAP.
XII.

1695.
Sept.
4.

sachusetts and Rhode Island, without which the quota of troops for New York could not be drafted fairly. Fletcher refused commutation and demanded the men ; whereupon the Rhode Island council wrote to him, assigning reasons why they could not send the men. Some further correspondence ensued, when the subject dropped. The Assembly met at Warwick. The boundary between Kingston and Westerly was settled. A prison was ordered to be built at Providence. A tax of a penny on a pound was laid, to raise the sum of one hundred pounds for the agent in England. Salaries had occasionally been paid to the civil officers, but most of the time public service had been performed gratuitously. It was now enacted that the governor should have ten pounds a year, the deputy governor six pounds, the assistants four pounds each, and the deputies three shillings a day while in session, or to pay a double forfeit when absent.

Oct.
30.

Nov.
2.

Dec.
17.

1695-6.
Jan.

Governor Carr died in December, being the third governor of the colony who died while in office ; and Walter Clarke, who was governor when the charter was suspended, was again chosen to that office, probably at an extra session of the Assembly in January, of which no record remains. Nearly seven years had elapsed since the resumption of the charter ; the government had acquired the confidence of all classes, so that Clarke and Newberry, the assistant, who had refused office after the fall of Andros, now cheerfully accepted their former places.

Feb.
15.

March
10.

1696.
April
20.

The Popish plot to assassinate William III. having been revealed by some of the conspirators, stringent measures were taken against the Roman Catholics. All ships bound to America were embargoed, and letters were sent to the colonies informing them of the circumstances. The activity of the French, in their operations against America, alarmed England, so that further orders were issued, and aid promised, to prepare for invasion. Associations were formed throughout England binding the subscribers to support the King, and to revenge any violence offered to his person. Notice of this was also sent to the colonies, with a form " proper to be entered into" as a mark of loyalty to his Majesty.[1]

Governor Fletcher wrote to Governor Clarke for the Rhode Island quota which had been refused by his predecessor. He rebuked the neglect of the colony, adding that her letters of excuse had been sent to England as witnesses against her. This letter was laid before the Assembly, and a reply returned that the exposed condition of the colony, with forty miles of coast line, having three inlets from the sea, undefended by forts, required all its strength for self-protection ; that the letters of excuse referred to by Fletcher, had already been sent by Rhode Island to the home government ; and that she did not fear the result, as his Majesty would not require impossibilities.[2]

A very important movement, proposed by the deputies from Warwick thirty years before,[3] was now adopted. The house of deputies was constituted a distinct body, a lower house of assembly, with power to choose their own Speaker and Clerk. It thus became a coördinate branch of the legislature, with the assistants, each house having a veto upon the proceedings of the other ; and thus has it ever since remained. The first instance of the deputies resolving themselves into a committee of the whole for the preparation of business occurred at this session. The practice was introduced three years later into the council board of Massachusetts by Lord Bellemont, and was of English origin, but has never been much used in this State.

Upon receipt of the royal orders relative to the Popish plot they were published in solemn manner, with great parade and joy, throughout the colony. A letter of congrat-

CHAP.
XII.

1 6 9 6.
April
24.

May
6

June
8.

---

[1] Smollet, B. i. chap. v. § 30. Antiq. of Conn., 233.
[2] N. Y. Docs., iv. 155–6. R. I. Col. Rec., iii. 315–16.
[3] Ante, chap. ix. p. 327.

CHAP.
XII.
1696.
July.

ulation was prepared by the council, promising vigilance in securing the conspirators should they appear in Rhode Island.

There was always great difficulty in collecting taxes in the colony. The people were poor, and their situation the most exposed of any in New England, while the vexatious proceedings of their neighbors not only kept them at great expense, from the very beginning, to maintain agents in London, but also furnished a constant pretext for refusal to pay by those who denied their jurisdiction. Not unfrequently many years would elapse after a tax was voted before it could be collected, and in view of the perplexities arising from these sources it is often a matter of surprise that a tax could be collected at all. Special sessions of assembly were repeatedly called on this account.

1.

One was now convened for this purpose ; and to increase the revenue, a duty was laid upon all foreign wines, liquors, and molasses imported into the colony. The latter article was to pay a half penny a gallon. Privateers fitted out from here had been engaged in illegal acts, to prevent which it was ordered that no new commission should be granted without a bond of one thousand pounds not to exceed the powers therein conferred. Wolves continued to trouble the plantations to such an extent that a bounty of ten shillings was offered for each old one that should be killed.

Sept.
2.

Oct.
28.

The governor and council of Connecticut entered into an association, in the form adopted in England, for the defence of the King against all conspirators, but we find no trace of any such act in this colony. The attorney general of England, after more than a year's delay, reported upon the Narraganset proprietors' petition, that the jurisdiction belonged to Connecticut by reason of the priority of her charter. This was the first opinion adverse to the claims of Rhode Island, if we except the *ex parte* report of the Cranfield commission, and seems to have been hastily drawn.   About the same time the proprietors, probably CHAP.
XII. weary of the delay, sent another petition asking to be joined to Massachusetts.   To this Major General Winthrop 1696.
Oct.
28. sent a counter petition, in behalf of Connecticut, to " insist on and claim the government of the said country." [1] Meanwhile Almy returned home, and on the same day that the attorney general's opinion was rendered against the colony, in England, he received from the Assembly, sitting at Providence, something over a hundred and thirty-five pounds for his expenses as agent.

The unsettled state of the eastern shore produced similar annoyances with those that had occurred in Westerly. The Massachusetts officers, having distrained for taxes in Tiverton, were seized and placed under bonds at Newport. Nov.
16. Complaints of these seizures were made to Stoughton from Bristol and Little Compton, and a vote was passed by the 23. representatives for the lieutenant-governor to protect the officers from the violence of Rhode Island.

An important step was now prepared in England to restrain the irregularities existing in America, with respect to privateering and to the acts of Trade, by establishing courts of admiralty in all the colonies.   The legality of 21. the measure was submitted to the attorney general, who, Dec.
4. on examining all the old charters and grants in America, gave as his opinion that they contained nothing which could restrain the King in his design.[2]

There were two parties in the colonies upon the question of uniting all the governments under a viceroy. 1696-7.
Jan.
2. Many in Massachusetts urged it in frequent letters to influential persons in England.   They complained of the small independencies, New Hampshire and Rhode Island, and denounced the latter as a great resort for privateers, which its commodious bay facilitated.   The New York in-

---

[1] Originals of the three papers last referred to are in Br. S. P. O., New Eng., vol. viii., as are most of the foregoing authorities not cited in the notes.

[2] Br. S. P. O. Proprieties, vol. i. p. 65.

CHAP.
XII.

1696-7.
Feb.

9.

25.

March
16.

23.

1697.

terest opposed the union, unless limited to strictly military purposes, on the grounds that the people were too dissimilar, and that the rivalry in trade between New York, the less, and Boston, the greater, would ruin the former. A circular was sent to all the colonies by the Board of Trade concerning their irregularities in not furnishing the required quotas against the French, in harboring each other's fugitives, and especially in giving countenance to piracy, which had naturally grown out of the system of privateering, so long maintained during the war with France.[1] The independent positions of Connecticut and Rhode Island made them a hindrance to the establishment of any general system of government in New England, or to the enforcement of acts intended to apply equally to all the colonies. Hence another attempt was to be made to restrain them, and the attorney general was directed to examine their charters with special reference to this design. The long-pending appointment of the Earl of Bellemont as governor of New York, Massachusetts, and New Hampshire, and as captain-general of the forces of Rhode Island, Connecticut, and the Jerseys, was at last announced. His coming was to open a new struggle in Rhode Island.

At an adjourned session of the Assembly, held at Newport, Pawtuxet river was established as the southern limit of Providence. Deputy governor Greene and the Warwick deputies protested, but to no effect, against this act, which terminated a struggle that had lasted for half a century between Warwick and Pawtuxet, and had formed one of the great points of dispute in the Harris trials twenty years before.

The entire records for the following year are missing, but the British archives supply the more important events. Although the long war with France was drawing to a close, there was as yet no cessation of hostilities in Amer-

[1] Br. S. P. O. Proprieties, vol. xxv. p. 42. Antiq. of Conn., 245. R. I. Col. Rec., iii. 321.

ica. Massachusetts applied to Connecticut and Rhode
Island for aid in men, money, and provisions, against the
common enemy, and appointed Capt. Byfield of Bristol to
obtain the same.

Town records throw very little light upon the general
history of the State after the government became settled
under the second charter, but occasionally they afford curious hints of the condition of society, or of matters affecting the prosperity of the people. An agricultural population will feel most sensibly those things that affect their
stock or their crops ; hence the frequent notice of wolves
and the lesser vermin, which became so troublesome as to
require State legislation. A new torment was added to
these, for we find that in Portsmouth, every householder
was required to kill twelve blackbirds before the tenth of
May ensuing, and to bring in their heads, or pay a fine of
two shillings, and for all above-twelve that were killed he
should receive one shilling each.[1]

Again the Hamilton claim came up, on petition of
the daughter of the late duke, to be confirmed in her
right to Narraganset, and to receive quit-rent from the
occupants. The case was fully stated, from the time of
the original grant by James I., down through all its subsequent stages, to the report of Andros upon it. Jahleel
Brenton was asked by the Board of Trade, what arguments Rhode Island had to urge against its validity. The
Board were resolved to have a careful examination of this
matter, which should be final. Rhode Island did not suppose the claim would ever be revived, and hence had
given Brenton no instructions upon it. He so stated in
his memorial, and asked that a copy of the duchess' petition might be sent to Rhode Island. The Connecticut
agent, Winthrop, was equally unprepared upon this question, and made a similar request in behalf of the proprietors,
of whom he was one. Somewhat later, Sir Henry Ash-

---

[1] Portsmouth records, end of vol. i., April 16, 1697.

CHAP.
XII.

1697.
Aug.
10.

April
22.

24.

urst replied to the same effect, on the part of Massachusetts.   But the Earl of Arran insisted on a report ; and
although *ex parte*, as the opposing claimants could not be
heard, it was so adverse to the petitioners as to be, in effect, final.   This document was of formidable length,
and chiefly historical.   It recited a decision of the Lords
and Justices upon a parallel case, that " the parties have
recourse to the Courts upon the place," and recommended
that the petition should not be granted, as it would establish a precedent fraught with disturbance to every land
title in America.   The report was equivalent to a legal
decision, so that Rhode Island was forever relieved from
this source of vexation.[1]

The acts of trade were not so easily disposed of.   A
royal letter called attention to their abuses in the several
colonies, and threatened a withdrawal of charters if these
were continued.[2]

The alarm in which the colonists were kept by the
sudden and frequent incursions of the Indians, can scarcely be imagined in our day.   The councils of war, composed of the local magistrates, were as active at this time
as they had ever been since the settlement of the State.
An original warrant, of this date, with the council seals
attached, is still extant, directed to twenty-one of the
principal inhabitants of Providence, as commanders of
scouting parties, composed of ten men each, who were to
range the country in pursuit of " the cruel and barbarous
Indians," beyond the limits of the plantations, for two
days at a time ; and each leader, on his return, was to
hand the commission to the one whose name was next in
order upon it.   This was continued long after the treaty
of Ryswick had restored peace to Europe.

The hasty opinion of the attorney general in favor of

[1] Br. S. P. O., New England, vol. xxxvi. p. 222.   The other papers above
referred to are in vol. viii.

[2] Br. S. P. O., New England, vol. xxxvi. p. 159.   R. I. Col. Rec., iii. 226.

the Connecticut claim to Narraganset, given in October, did not escape the keen eye of Brenton, who presented a memorial to the Board of Trade, pointing out the errors therein, that they might be advised of the facts before acting upon it. Letters were sent to both colonies, advising an adjustment by mutual agreement, or by reference to Lord Bellemont, or otherwise to send agents to England early in the Spring.[1]

The treaty of Ryswick restored peace to all Europe. A printed proclamation was issued in England, and sent out to America, with orders to suspend all privateering against the French. It reached New England in December, where it was published in due form. Mr. Brenton returned to Rhode Island, with all the letters and papers from the British government, above referred to, and delivered them to the General Assembly, at a special session held in Newport. He was empowered to administer to the governor the oath required by the acts of trade, which Clarke, being a Quaker, steadily refused to take. The creation of a Court of Admiralty in Rhode Island, was a further source of discontent to the governor. Brenton brought over a commission to Peleg Sandford, as Judge of Admiralty, and to Nathaniel Coddington, as Register, which Sandford presented to Gov. Clarke, who endeavored to persuade the Assembly to oppose it, but without success. He then kept the commission from Sandford, who complained to the Board of Trade of his conduct. A similar complaint was also addressed to the King. Brenton forwarded these letters to the Board, and advised the impeachment of Clarke, as a warning to others. He also urged that the government of Rhode Island should be required to print their laws, which as yet had never been done.[2] These perplexities, no doubt,

CHAP.
XII.

1697.
May
15.

Aug.
26.

Sept.
20.

Oct.
18.

Dec.
24.

1697-8.
Jan.
11.

17–21.

31.

March
8.

---

[1] Br. S. P. O., New England, vol. xxv. p. 109. Antiq. of Conn., 259. R. I. Col. Rec., iii. 328.

[2] Br. S. P. O. Proprieties, vol ii. pp. 445–7–9. R. I. Col. Rec., iii. 329–31.

caused the resignation of Gov. Clarke, at this time, in favor of his nephew, Samuel Cranston, who, it appears, presided as governor at the spring term of the Court of Trials.

The administration of Gov. Cranston is remarkable for many reasons. He held his position probably longer than any other man who has ever been subjected to the test of an annual popular election. He was thirty times successively chosen governor, holding office till his death, in 1726. His great firmness in seasons of unexampled trial, that occurred in the early part of his public life, is, perhaps, the key to his wonderful popularity, of which we shall find some signal proofs later in his career. The choice of the Assembly was confirmed by the people at the election ; and he was also retained in his military office of major, for the islands. John Greene was re-elected deputy governor. A majority of the civil officers chosen at this time, held military commissions. The Quaker regime expired with Gov. Clarke. The government passed into the hands of men whose scruples would not imperil the existence of the State, at a time when firmness was as much required as caution, in resisting the aggressions attempted by the royal governors of Massachusetts.

4.

The subject of weights and measures, which twenty-four years previously had received the attention of the Assembly, was again discussed. Want of uniformity in these particulars, injured trade. To remedy this, a sealer for the colony was appointed, with orders to procure standard weights and measures in Boston, whose duty it should be to seal, with an anchor, all such articles used in Newport ; and to furnish the other sealers, one of which was to be chosen in each town, with accurate models. Any town failing to appoint a sealer, was to be indicted at the Court of Trials.

8

Piracy now prevailed to an alarming extent. Privateers, clearing for Madagascar and the Red Sea on trading voyages, with roving commissions against the French, had become open pirates after the peace. All New England and New York, as well as the West India Islands, were deeply involved in these unlawful enterprises. The home government sent orders to repress them. The Rhode Island Assembly accordingly passed a law, requiring their officers to seize any suspected person, who should bring foreign coin or merchandise into the colony, and that he should be held for trial, unless he could produce satisfactory evidence to the magistrates how he came by the treasure. A proclamation was also issued, in obedience to the royal order, and published by drum beat in every town, requiring the officers to arrest any suspected pirates, and warning the people not to harbor any such, or to receive their goods, on pain of punishment as abettors. An address to the King was prepared, in which the remissness of the colony in respect to the acts of trade, is confessed, and their statute on the subject of piracy is mentioned. Their assumption of admiralty jurisdiction during the late war, is also admitted, and defended on the ground of expediency—there being a necessity for annoying French commerce, and no admiralty Court then established in the colony—and finally, a continuation of the royal favor, in the language of the charter, is earnestly sought. These papers were all enclosed in a letter from Gov. Cranston to the Board of Trade, apologizing for the irregularities of the colony in refusing the quota of troops for New York, and explaining the charges against it in regard to piracy. He also stated that two men suspected of piracy had just been examined, and would be brought to trial.[1] A bitter letter against the government of the colony was soon after written by that old enemy of New England, Randolph, the surveyor general of customs, who had just been to New York to welcome the arrival of Lord Bellemont.

CHAP.
XII.

1698.
May
4.

8.

30.

---

[1] The originals of these four papers are in Br. S. P. O., Proprieties, vol. ii. pp. 543-5-7. America and West Indies, vol. 379. R. I. Col. Rec., iii. 336-8.

CHAP.
XII.
1698.
June

4.

30.

Aug.
2.

The charges made against the rulers were most serious, as that they were in league with the pirates, by whom they were enriched ; and equally false was the statement that many of the people desired a royal governor, and would pay five hundred pounds a year towards the support of one.[1] Depositions against the deputy governor, for having issued privateer commissions, four years before, when Gov. Easton had refused to grant them, were obtained, and forwarded in confirmation of these charges ; and Mr. Brenton advised the Board of Trade to call for copies of all such commissions and bonds as had been granted during the late war, some of them being, in his view, illegal.[2]

In compliance with the orders of the home government, commissioners were appointed by Rhode Island and Connecticut to adjust the boundary between these colonies. They met at Stonington, but to no purpose. Each claimed all Narraganset, as heretofore. The negotiation was held in writing, as it had formerly been, and with the same result. The Rhode Island Assembly met, for the first time, at Kingstown, and voted a tax of eight hundred pounds, currency, of which Newport was to pay two hundred and twenty-five pounds; Portsmouth, one hundred and forty; Providence, one hundred and twenty-eight ; Kingstown, one hundred and twenty-five ; Warwick and Westerly, forty-six pounds each; Jamestown, thirty-eight; Greenwich, thirty, and New Shoreham twenty-two pounds. A tax law in twelve sections, the most complete that had yet been framed, was passed for its collection, providing for the first time for a poll tax upon all males between sixteen and sixty years of age, of whom a census was to be taken, as well as an account of their estates; and each man, except slaves and the like, was to pay one shilling a head. Provision was made for the reception of Lord Bellemont, who was expected soon from New York, on his

---

[1] Br. S. P. O., Plantations General, vol. v. c. 17.   R. I. Col. Rec., iii. 339.
[2] Br. S. P. O., Proprieties, vol. ii. pp. 581-3.

way to Boston. The governor's salary was increased to thirty pounds. A committee was named to prepare a digest of the laws, to send to England, as required, and another to present the case of the western boundary to Lord Bellemont.[1]

The next regular session was held at Providence. Want of uniformity in the size of casks and barrels, in which provisions were packed, led to the adoption of a standard gauge for the various sizes, and the appointment of gaugers in each town, with penalties for any violation of such standard.

Further letters were sent by the Board of Trade to the colonies, at this time, on the subject of piracy. The one to this colony, following the suggestion of Mr. Brenton, required copies of all privateering papers to be sent home, with an account of the trials of Munday and Cutler, who had been arrested for exceeding the powers granted in their commissions. The letters to the other colonies were equally specific on the same subject,[2] and were followed by instructions to the custom house officers how to conduct their business ; and soon after by an order from the British Cabinet to the governors of all the colonies, to apprehend the notorious Capt. Kidd, should he appear in their waters.[3]

CHAP.
XII.

1698.
Oct.

26.

25.

Nov.
10.

23.

[1] A letter from the R. I. commissioners to those of Conn., dated Kingstown, Dec. 8, 1698, proposing a reference of the dispute to the Earl of Bellemont, as their negotiations had proved fruitless, is in Trumbull papers, vol. xxii. No. 152.

[2] Br. S. P. O., Proprieties, vol. xxv. p. 253. Antiq. of Conn., 266. R. I. Col. Rec., iii. 341.

[3] Antiq. of Conn. 268–71. Kidd was of English birth, and a bold privateer during the war with France. The governor of Barbadoes induced William III. to give Kidd a commission to act against the pirates who then infested every sea. He received the title of Admiral, Dec. 11, 1695, and soon after sailed with 80 men in a government ship of 30 guns, to New York, where he doubled his crew, and went to the Red Sea. There he commenced his acts of piracy, and became the terror of his countrymen. A fleet was sent to the East Indies to take him, but he escaped, and came to the American coast. At length, grown reckless by success, he appeared in Rhode Island, and was soon after arrested in Boston, sent to England, and there gibbeted in 1700.

CHAP.
XII.

1698.
Dec.
21.

1698-9.
Jan.
5.

Feb.
3.

22.

March
9.

Feb.
14.

A formidable representation was made to the King by the Board of Trade, concerning the many irregularities in Rhode Island, as to their refusal to take the oaths, their encouragement of illegal traffic, their assuming admiralty jurisdiction to themselves, and resisting it from the crown, with other flagrant acts of disloyalty, and recommending that a commission of inquiry be sent to Lord Bellemont to examine into these matters, with a view to the issuing a *quo warranto* against the charter.[1] The inquiry was ordered at once—the instructions to Lord Bellemont were prepared, not only for this, but for all the colonies, and a copy thereof forwarded to each. But Rhode Island was the special object aimed at. The Board made inquiries of Mr. Brenton, then in London, about the extraordinary militia power of the colony, and were informed that it was conferred by the charter ; but that recently the Assembly had given to the military the power of selecting their own officers. His former communication upon the subject of privateering papers, with the queries to be put to the government of Rhode Island, were embodied in the instructions. They passed the council, and were presented on the same day for the royal signature.[2]

The differences between Connecticut and Rhode Island, and various difficulties arising from that cause, were the subject of much legislation at a special session of the Assembly. The former colony had spread a report that the people of Narraganset were not to be taxed while the dispute upon jurisdiction was pending. This was seized upon by the disaffected as an occasion of disturbance, by refusing to pay the late levy. Other parties, without leave, had intruded in that country. These were required to depart, or to arrange with the lawful owners without delay. The commission to treat with Connecticut was con-

---

[1] Br. S. P. O., Proprieties, vol. xxv., p. 275.   R. I. Col. Rec., iii. 351-3.
[2] Br. S. P. O., Proprieties, vol. ii. pp. 663, 767, and vol. xxv. pp. 305, 357.
R. I. Col. Rec., iii. 363-7.

tinued, and the legal rights of all persons, whether claiming ownership by Connecticut titles, or otherwise, were secured. A law against peddling was adopted, with a copious preamble, reciting the injuries to regular trade resulting therefrom. Warwick was again forbidden to exercise jurisdiction north of Pawtuxet river, as had been of late attempted in the collection of taxes. The registration act was reaffirmed, and marriages were legalized which had been performed in disregard of the previous registry act. The magistrate's fee for performing the ceremony was fixed at three shillings, with sixpence to the town clerk for recording the same.

The colony were informed by Jahleel Brenton of the movements of Connecticut in regard to the boundary question. She now claimed a great part of Warwick and of Providence as well as all of Kings Province. At the May session Mr. Brenton was appointed sole agent to London, in behalf of Rhode Island, and funds were remitted to him for this purpose. The three Narraganset towns, Kingstown, Westerly, and Greenwich, were not yet agreed as to their respective boundaries. A committee was fully empowered to adjust all differences between them. They at once entered upon their duties, and within a month were prepared to report to the Assembly definite limits for each of the towns, which were accepted with but little variation.[1] Gov. Cranston wrote a long letter to the Board of Trade deprecating the many false reports against the colony, circulated chiefly by Randolph, and announcing the appointment of Brenton as the agent.

At this time Lord Bellemont, who for the first year of his residence in America remained in New York, removed to Boston. He was afflicted with the gout, a circumstance which, if we may credit his own words, interfered not a little with the discharge of the pressing duties of his government, and seems to have affected his temper likewise,

---

[1] Potter's Narraganset. R. I. H. C., iii. 108.

to the serious detriment of Rhode Island interests.   His
present purpose was to break up the piracy that had
grown out of privateering, a work in which he found great
difficulty, many of the leading families, especially of Leisler's party, in New York, as well as a large part of New
England being concerned in it.   By stratagem he succeeded in enticing the notorious Capt. William Kidd to
come to Boston where he had him seized and thrown into
prison.   He had many friends in Rhode Island and Massachusetts, and influential persons came even from Albany and New York, upon Kidd's affairs, all of whom
Bellemont so far blinded as to induce Kidd through
their influence to come to Boston.   Bradish, and other
well-known pirates confined in the gaol, had recently
been permitted to escape.   The connivance was very
general in the plans of these lawless freebooters, which
much resembled the schemes of a later fillibusterism.
Bellemont's letter to the Board of Trade sets forth the
secret history of these transactions, and presents a lamentable picture of the state of society in America at
this period.   With the many letters that he sent home
this year, chiefly upon this subject, were inclosed a great
mass of documents, nearly a hundred in number, accumulated for the most part as evidence in support of the
charges against Rhode Island.   We shall refer only to
some of the most important, or interesting of these, extending throughout the year.   Among them is an order
from Sarah, wife of Capt. William Kidd, who was imprisoned with him, upon Capt. Paine who lived on Conanicut, to pay the bearer twenty-four ounces of gold, for
the support of herself and husband in gaol.   In a later
letter, Bellemont describes minutely the whole affair of
Kidd's arrest and examination.

    To further his designs upon Rhode Island, and to aid in
securing other pirates known to resort there, Lord Bellemont commissioned the members of the Admiralty Court,

Brinley, Sandford and Coddington, to collect evidence and to use their efforts in capturing Gillam, Palmer, and other confederates of Kidd. They accepted the trust, but deplored the difficulties attending it by reason of the sympathy everywhere felt for the freebooters. The feeling of the home government may be gathered from a letter written by the Board of Trade in reply to Gov. Cranston's letter of May. Its language was very severe, blaming the colony for sending only an abstract of the laws instead of a copy of them as required, and that too an incorrect and imperfect one, and sharply rebuking them for the encouragement given to piracy by the commissions granted in 1694 by the deputy governor, whose ignorance, if that were the real and not simply the ostensible cause, as the Board intimate, of his conduct, should have excluded him from public office.[1] The correspondence between the commissioners and Lord Bellemont is full of the names of the accomplices of Kidd, who at various times resorted to this bay, and of those who harbored them, many of whom were arrested. The urgency of these affairs led the governor to call a special session of the Assembly at Newport, of which the only record that remains is the speech made by Gov. Cranston at the opening, assigning his reasons for convening it, which is filed with the Bellemont papers in the British archives. The reasons were, the expected visit of Lord Bellemont to Rhode Island to inquire into the irregularities of the government and to settle the dispute with Connecticut, and the necessity of raising money to defray the expenses of this visit and of another agent to join Mr. Brenton in England, to defend the colony from the attacks of its enemies.[2] Just before going to Rhode Island, Lord Bellemont wrote to the Board upon the difficulty of enforcing the acts of trade in New York, " where the people have such an appetite for piracy

CHAP.
XII.

1699.
Aug.
10.

11.

21.

Sept.
8.

---

[1] The colony took the hint at the next election, as we shall presently see.
[2] Br. S. P. O., Proprieties, vol. iv. p. 643.

CHAP.
XII.

1699.
Sept.

and unlawful trade that they are ready to rebel as often as the government puts the law in execution against them," and he is equally severe upon the lawyers of that Province.

18.

20.

21.

22.

Bellemont has left a diary of his visit at Rhode Island and his proceedings there. The journey to Newport occupied two days. At Bristol ferry the governor and council, with a troop of horse, received and escorted him to Newport, where a meeting of the council was immediately held and the royal commission was read. The next day his special instructions to inquire into the mal-administration of Rhode Island affairs were read to the council, and ex-governors Clarke and Easton, Gov. Cranston and Deputy Gov. Greene and Peleg Sandford, were examined upon the several points charged in the instructions. The troublesome subject of oaths was then minutely inquired into. The scruples of many in Rhode Island upon this subject could never be comprehended by the British officers. A somewhat similar idea of legality pertained to the exact form of an oath, as was attached to the possession of a seal in those days. It was an emblem of loyalty as the latter was of sovereignty, and the letter of the law on this point was more insisted upon than its spirit. The omission of it was one of the chief causes of complaint against Rhode Island. This, and the volunteer militia system, were two grand stumbling-blocks to an English comprehension of Rhode Island peculiarities.

23.

25.

While they were under consideration Gov. Winthrop, with the Connecticut commissioners upon the Narraganset dispute, arrived. The conflicting clauses in the two charters were read, and also the agreement between the two agents, Dr. Clarke and John Winthrop, thereupon. The case was then argued by the commissioners on each side, and they were advised to come to a mutual agreement. This was attempted in vain. Bellemont then ordered

them to prepare a statement of their claims. This was
done and presented the next day, affidavits were taken
upon the case, and the two colonies were warned to send
their agents to England to lay the matter before the
King. Further examinations in regard to piracy were
had. Caleb and Josias Arnold were added to the members
of the admiralty court as commissioners to collect evidence upon the charges, and the governor and council
were requested to aid them in the work.

The earliest movement in favor of an Episcopal
church in Rhode Island now assumed an organized form.
A number of the people who preferred that service, had
commenced in the early part of this year to hold public
worship, and now petitioned the Earl of Bellemont to intercede with the home government that aid might be extended to them in support of a settled minister. The
paper was signed by sixteen persons, headed by two of the
old Huguenot names, whose establishment in Narraganset
had been abandoned amid the distractions occasioned by
the contest for jurisdiction. Of the whole number of
forty-five families who had settled at Frenchtown, all but
two had left for New York, and those two had removed
to Boston. But two individuals remained in the colony.
These settled at Newport and appear as the first signers
of the petition. Although the Huguenots differed essentially from the church of England upon many points, being themselves the direct offshoots of the Geneva school
of theology, their simple but beautiful ritual approached
nearer to that of the English church than it did to the
yet simpler forms of the Baptist, or to the strictly spiritual communion of the Society of Friends. Hence they
sympathized with the new movement, and appear as its
leaders.[1]

Meeting-houses were this year built by the Friends at
Portsmouth and Newport, the latter in place of an old

See Appendix G. for this interesting document.

CHAP.
XII.

1699.
Sept.

27.

Oct.
2.

5.

12.

15.

16.

21.

23.

25.

one, shortly afterwards taken down, which had been erected in the early years of the colony.

Bellemont having finished his business, placed the governors of Rhode Island and Connecticut under bonds of three thousand pounds each to enforce the acts against pirates, and left Newport, escorted as before to the ferry. He reached Seekonk that night, and arrived at Boston the next afternoon. He then wrote to Gov. Cranston, thanking him for the hospitalities he had received at Newport, and directing the arrest of Bradish, a pirate who had escaped to Rhode Island. An accurate copy of the laws and of the acts of council of the colony was required, a task not easy to perform in the disordered state of the records. But Gov. Cranston, in his reply, promised it should be done.

One more effort was made in the Connecticut Assembly, by appointing a new committee, to settle the question with Rhode Island, without sending an agent to England ; but foreseeing the futility of further effort in that way, Gov. Winthrop sent a commission to Sir Henry Ashurst as agent of the colony, and advised the Board of Trade of his appointment. Bellemont wrote to Gov. Cranston not to distrain for taxes in Narraganset until the dispute was settled, and also reproved his tardiness in not having yet sent the laws and acts of council as required. Brinley wrote that no council records could be found, but that the laws would be sent after the Assembly, about to meet, had put them in proper shape. Gov. Cranston replied to Bellemont, that they could not comply with the order to send an agent to England unless they raised a tax, and this they could not do if they were forbidden to levy upon the portion of the colony claimed by Connecticut, being nearly all the mainland. Here was a difficulty which the General Assembly, convened at Warwick, had to meet. It was met, as such hindrances often were, by ignoring it. A tax of six hundred pounds had before been assessed, and copies of the law, under seal,

had already been sent to the several towns. This was
considered enough, and no notice was taken of the injunction, or command of Bellemont. His other orders were
better respected. A committee to transcribe the laws
was appointed, to report at the adjourned session. In
compliment to the action of the Connecticut Assembly, a
committee of conference upon the matters in dispute was
appointed to meet in two weeks at Wickford. An attempt was made to appoint an agent to go to England,
but none would accept it, and the subject was laid over to
the adjournment. Depositions in regard to Gillam and
other pirates were taken at this time, and forwarded to
England by Lord Bellemont, with a letter denouncing the
government of Rhode Island, as " the most irregular and
illegal in their administration that ever any English government was." His criticisms were amply sustained by
the complaints constantly sent to him by the admiralty
commissioners at Newport. Sandford says that any commission direct from his Majesty is considered as an infringement of the charter privileges, and those who take
them are looked upon as enemies to the State.

The joint commission of the two colonies met at Wickford. Their correspondence was brief, and, as was anticipated on each side, inconclusive. An appeal to the King
was now the last resort. Bellemont wrote to the Board of
Trade a full statement of the case, and enclosed all the
documents relating thereto. The adjourned session of the
Assembly was held at Newport, and vainly attempted to
select an agent. Six nominees declined. The matter
was referred to a committee to find an agent who would
go, and to order all things requisite to that object. The
committee to revise and transcribe the laws, made a full
report, which was received, and all laws not included in
their transcript were repealed.

At length Lord Bellemont, having collected a great
mass of evidence to support the charges against Rhode

CHAP.
XII.

1699.
Nov.

6.

8.

9.

18.

21.

CHAP. Island, made his report to the Privy Council. It was a
XII.   formidable paper, presenting under twenty-five distinct
1699. heads, an array of testimony against Rhode Island, which
Nov.   we can only wonder at this day that the friendless colony
27.
       was enabled to resist. That she was not utterly crushed
       beneath the cumulative evidence of every kind of irregu-
       larity that was hurled upon her by the indefatigable zeal
       and the consummate ability of Bellemont, can scarcely be
       accounted for by any human agency. It is the greatest
       marvel in the history of Rhode Island in the seventeenth
       century. She had had many narrow escapes, but this was
29.   the most wonderful of them all.[1] Immediately following
       this report he sent a letter to the Board of Trade on the
       subject of piracy, wherein he denounced Gov. Cranston
       for "conniving at pirates, and making Rhode Island their
       sanctuary."

22.   Some people of Westerly, acting upon the prohibition
       issued by Bellemont, refused at town meeting to elect as-
       sessors of the tax laid by the Assembly for sending an agent
       to England. Upon this Gov. Cranston issued a warrant
       for the arrest of several persons who had signed a protest
       against the said election, and appointed a special con-
Dec.   stable with a sufficient force to serve the warrant. The
2.   firmness of Cranston at this crisis, did more than any
       other one cause to save the colony from extinction.

           A fair copy of the laws and acts of the colony was at
       last sent to Bellemont, with a letter explaining the causes
22.   of delay, and deprecating the conduct of the commission-
       ers appointed by his Lordship, as being adverse to the in-
       terests of the colony. Capt. Joseph Sheffield, one of the
       assistants, carried the papers; and that he might serve as
       a special envoy to soothe the anger of the Earl, his cre-
       dentials were stated in the letter, requesting Bellemont to
       " discourse with the bearer" upon the state of the colony.

       [1] The Original Report and Journal of Lord Bellemont are in Br. S. P. O.,
       Proprieties, vol. iv. pp. 565, 573. See R. I. Col. Rec., iii. 385–93.

The commissioners followed the next day, with a letter declaring that the copy of the laws sent was neither complete nor correct, and condemning the arrests made at Westerly, the parties taken having been carried to Newport jail. This act roused the anger of Connecticut. The governor and council of that colony empowered Capt. Mason to seize any Rhode Island officer who should attempt to distrain for taxes in Westerly. Brinley also wrote to Lord Bellemont in regard to the sedition act, which the last Assembly had revived, and under which the Westerly prisoners were to be tried ; and a few days later he again wrote in the same strain, denouncing the whole code, and the manner of its adoption by the Assembly. The laws were sent over to the Board of Trade, with abundant annotations and denunciations by Bellemont, together with the letters of Brinley upon the state of the government.[1]

The threatening aspect of affairs caused frequent sessions of the General Assembly. A permanent agent in England was indispensable to the salvation of the colony. Mr. Brenton had acted in her behalf upon the Connecticut dispute, and had since been empowered to defend her charter; but he was the collector of Newport, and liable to be sent home to his post, a purpose that Bellemont was seeking to accomplish. A man was at last found both able and willing to take the responsible position. Capt. Joseph Sheffield, who had lately served as envoy to Bellemont, was selected as the agent to defend the char-

CHAP.
XII.

1699.
Dec.

25.

26.

31.

1699.
————
1700.
Jan.
5.

Feb.
16.

[1] The original authorities for the events of the year 1699, above related, are so numerous and varied in the British State Paper office, that the writer deemed it best to insert them all in a single note at the end. For the local reader these references can have no interest, but to the historian who may wish to verify facts or dates herein stated, by examining the archives in London, they will be found of great importance in the saving of time and trouble. They are in the bundles marked as follows: New England, vols. ix. and x. Proprieties, vols. iii. iv. v. and xxvi. America and West Indies, vol. 379, and New York, vol. ix.

tered rights of Rhode Island, at the Court of Saint
James.   If he should find, on reaching London, that
Brenton had already acted upon his late commission in
defence of the charter, the two were to be united in the
agency ; otherwise, Sheffield was to be the sole agent,
with an annual salary of eighty pounds, besides his necessary expenses.   The Assembly adjourned to New Year's
day, when the only business done was to establish, upon a
25.   permanent basis, a horse-ferry between the mainland and
Conanicut.

The Court of Trials, held the next day, conducted
26.   with a high hand against Pemberton and the other Westerly prisoners, under the sedition act.   The grand jury
ignored the bills.   The Court refused to receive the return, and adding three more to the jury, sent them out a
second time.   Again they failed to find indictments.   The
Court then added six more persons to the jury, and again
sent them out to deliberate, with positive orders to find
true bills.   After several hours' consultation, twelve of the
twenty-one made a return in accordance with the instructions of the Court.   This was an exercise of power more
dangerous to the liberties of the colony than any they
were likely to suffer, even from the will of Bellemont; and
it was followed up by a verdict of guilty, obtained by a
similar violence on the part of the Court towards the
petty jury, who, at first, were for acquitting the prisoners.[1]

There was need of haste in the matter of Sheffield's
commission, for the Board of Trade, upon receipt of Lord
April
8.   Bellemont's report, sent an abstract of it to his Majesty,
and recommended its reference to the law officers of the
crown, " to consider what method may be most proper for
bringing the colony under a better form of government,"
and that they proceed forthwith.[2]

The memorial of the foreman of the grand jury at

[1] Br. S. P. O., Proprieties, vol. v. pp. 417–421.
[2] Br. S. P. O., Proprieties, vol. xxvi. p. 184.

Newport, who was one of the nine dissenters from the act of the majority, in finding a bill against the Westerly prisoners, was presented to Bellemont. He wrote a sharp letter to Gov. Cranston, pronouncing the proceedings in the case of Pemberton, to be the "most arbitrary and irregular he had ever heard of, next to taking away a man's life against law;" and also rebuking them for sending an armed force to levy taxes in Narraganset. This latter procedure was retaliated by Connecticut. Mallett, the sheriff of Rhode Island, was seized, with several of his posse, by a Connecticut force, and taken to New London jail, where the others were released on bail, but the sheriff was detained for trial.[1] Riots attended upon these attempts to collect taxes, and the whole of Kings Province was in a state of disorganization. A Court of Inquiry was held at Kingstown, at which a large number of persons were fined for resisting the officers.

At the general election, John Greene, who for ten successive years had been elected deputy governor, was dropped, and ex-Gov. Walter Clarke was chosen in his place. The ferry from Newport to Jamestown was settled upon similar terms with that to the mainland. News having arrived that Brenton had accepted and acted upon his commission as general agent for the colony, the appointment of Sheffield was revoked. The recent riots in Kingstown occupied the Assembly. Many persons appeared and confessed their fault. Some had their fines remitted, and others were bound over for trial at the September term. The seizure of the high sheriff by the Connecticut government did not impede the collection of the tax. Another sheriff was appointed, and also special constables, with sufficient force to complete the gathering of the six hundred pound tax forthwith. A new form of engagement for the deputies was adopted, binding them to allegiance to the King, and fealty to the chartered au-

CHAP.
XII.

1700.
April
22.

May
1.

4.

---

[1] Br. S. P. O., Proprieties, vol. v. p. 633.

CHAP.
XII.

1700.
May

13.

June.
22.

July
23.

thorities of the colony.   A determined spirit prevaded the proceedings of this Assembly, such as had not always been shown in critical times, but which was essential in the final struggle for existence, upon which the colony had now fairly entered.   At the close of the session, Gov. Cranston, in behalf of the Assembly, addressed a petition to the King, imploring a continuance of the charter.[1] He also wrote to the Board of Trade,[2] informing them that the late deputy governor had been left out of all offices of trust, at the recent election, on account of his illegally granting privateer commissions : that a more perfect copy of the laws was to be made and sent under seal, and that a new form of engagement had just been adopted to meet the views of the home government.   It was a diplomatic letter, well drafted to aid the efforts of Brenton in averting another *quo warranto.*

But the Earl of Bellemont was ready with a rejoinder sustained by documentary proof.   He wrote to the Board that he had given up all attempt at reducing the disorders in Rhode Island, and forwarded the petition of Pemberton, with other papers relating to the seizure and arbitrary trial of the Westerly prisoners.[3]   Nor were these the only outrages committed in the name of the law, during this period of turmoil and excitement.   The French settlement had been broken up, but Dr. Ayrault remained as a practising physician.   Greenwich had extended its limits to embrace the whole of Frenchtown.   It was charged that Ayrault had fenced in certain highways laid out through the settlement.   A court of inquiry, composed of the officers of Greenwich and Warwick, was held there to decide upon the question; and, after delib-

[1] Original in Br. S. P. O.   America and West Indies, vol. 379.   R. I. Col. Rec., iii. 419.

[2] Original in Br. S. P. O., Proprieties, vol. v. p. 317.

[3] Originals in Br. S. P. O., New York papers, vol. x. p. 256, and Proprieties, vol. v. p. 413

erating a whole day, the jury rendered a verdict of guilty against the doctor. That night a mob attacked his house, carried off himself and his son Daniel by force, maltreated his aged wife who attempted to plead with them ; and having taken the two men to where the court was held, compelled them to give bonds to appear at the next Court of Trials. The affidavit of Dr. Ayrault, with the concurrent testimony of John Fones, and others who were present, given soon afterwards at Newport, and yet more the subsequent conduct of the assailants in laying waste the premises, prove the whole affair to have been one of lawless violence, for which no excuse can be offered. It was a phase of border life, where law imposes but a feeble restraint upon the cupidity or the passions of men.[1]

A special session of the General Assembly was held at Newport. Acts were passed to lay a tax upon pedlars ; to require any man who should marry an executrix, to give bonds to perform the will of the testator so far as the estate would permit; to provide for a constable's watch in every town; and "that where the laws of this collony, or custom, shall not reach or comprehend any matter, cause, or causes, that it shall be lawfull to put in execution the laws of England." This last act forms a fitting conclusion to the legislation of Rhode Island in the seventeenth century. It contains a covert assertion of sovereignty, amounting almost to an act of independence. It was an extreme application of the famous clause in the charter, which conveyed far more than its grantors imagined—that the laws should conform to those of England as nearly as possible, "considering the nature and constitution of the place and people there."

Sir Henry Ashurst, agent of Connecticut, presented to the Board of Trade a memorial setting forth the claim of that colony to the jurisdiction of Narraganset. Brenton replied to it with a counter memorial on the part of

CHAP.
XII.

1700.

Aug.

29.

30.

Dec.
13.

17.

[1] Br. S. P. O., New England, vol. xiii.

CHAP.
XII.

1700-1.
Feb.
6.

7.

March
5.

Rhode Island. Both papers state concisely the grounds of their respective claims. After some delay, Brenton again called the attention of the Board to the subject, and requested an early decision, as his business required him to return to America.[1] But this long disputed point was not destined to be so speedily arranged. Another quarter of a century was to elapse before the rights of Rhode Island should receive their final confirmation by the King in council.

An event of the greatest importance to the people of this colony now occurred. The death of the Earl of Bellemont, at New York, removed the most formidable opponent to the charter of Rhode Island, who had ever ruled in New England. Unlike Sir Edmund Andros, Bellemont could neither be moved by flattery nor softened by courtesy. He acknowledged in becoming terms the civilities extended to him on his visit to Newport, and in the same letter rebuked the free spirit of a people who virtually set at defiance the laws that he was appointed to execute. Had his life been spared, the ability with which he prepared the charges and evidence against this colony, and the energy that he displayed in pursuing his purposes to the bitter end, might have given another and a fatal termination to a contest that involved the colonial condition, and determined the future fortunes of Rhode Island.

[1] Originals in Br. S. P. O., Proprieties, vol. v. pp. 675, 497–631.

APPENDIX G.

FOUNDING OF TRINITY CHURCH, NEWPORT.

(FROM BRITISH STATE PAPER OFFICE, NEW ENGLAND, VOL. IX.)

To his Excellency Richard, Earle of Bellemont, Capt. Generall and Govr in
Chiefe in and over the provinces of the Massachusetts Bay, New York
and New Hampshire and the Territoryes thereon depending in America,
and Vice Admiral of the same,

The humble Petition of the People of the Church
of England now resident in Rhode Island,

SHEWETH,

That your Petitioners and others inhabiting within this Island having
agreed and concluded to erect a church for the Worship of God according to
the discipline of the Church of England and tho' we are disposed and ready
to give all the encouragement we possibly can to a Pious and learned Minister
to settle and abide amongst us, yet by reason we are not in a capacity to contribute to such an Honble Mentenance as may be requisite and expedient;

Your Petitioners therefore humbly pray that your Lordship will be pleased
so farr to favour our undertakings as to intercede with his Maj^ty for his gracious letters to this Government, on our behalfe to protect and encourage us and
that some assistance towards the present mentenance of a Minister among us
may be granted as your Excellency in your great wisdome shall think most
meet, and that your Excellency will also be pleased to write in our behalfe
and favour to the Lords of the Council of Trade and Plantations, or to such
Ministers of state as your Excellency shall judge convenient in and about the
premises.

And your Petitioners as in duty bound will ever pray &c^a.

Gabriel Bernon	W^m. Brinley
Piere Ayrould	Isaac Martindale
Thomas Fox	Robert Gardiner
George Cuttler	Thos. Paine
Willm. Pease	Thos. Mallett
Edwin Carter	Robt. Wrightington
Fra. Pope	Anthy. Blount
Richard Newland	Thomas Lillibridge

This petition was delivered at Newport, 26th Sept. 1699, and forwarded to the Board of Trade by Lord Bellemont on 24th October.
It was received and read on 5th January following. In his letter enclosing it to the Board, Bellemont says, "I send your Lordships the
petition of several persons in Rhode Island for a Church of England

CHAP.
XII.

APP.
G.

Minister and a yearly settled maintenance for one.   I hope your Lordships will please to patronize so good a design, and will obtain his
Majesty's allowance of a competent maintenance for such a Minister.
It will be a means I hope to reform the lives of the People in that
Island, and make good Christians of 'em who at present are all in
darknesse." The petition was sent by the Board of Trade to the
Bishop of London, who presented it to the King, by whom it was referred back to the Board, April 16, for their opinion upon what was
proper to be done in the matter. Other petitions for promoting the
Gospel among the Indians were pending at the same time. From these
movements originated the "Society for propagating the Gospel in
foreign parts," incorporated in 1702, by whom, two years later, the
Rev. James Honeyman was sent out as a missionary to this station,
upon petition of the wardens of Trinity church to the society for aid.
Meanwhile, Rev. Mr. Lockyer, who had gathered the church early in
1699, new style, served as its rector, and the building was completed
some time in 1702.

END OF VOLUME FIRST.

GENERAL INDEX TO VOLUME FIRST.